Democratic Multiplicity

This edited volume argues that democracy is broader and more diverse than the dominant state-centered, modern representative democracies to which other modes of democracy are either presumed subordinate or ignored. The contributors seek to overcome the standard opposition of democracy from below (participatory) and democracy from above (representative). Rather, they argue that through differently situated participatory and representative practices, citizens and governments can develop democratic ways of cooperating without hegemony and subordination, and that these relationships can be transformative. This work proposes a slow but sure, nonviolent, ecosocial and sustainable process of democratic generation and growth with the capacity to critique and transform unjust and ecologically destructive social systems. This volume integrates human-centric democracies into a more mutual, interdependent and sustainable system on earth whereby everyone gains. This title is also available as Open Access on Cambridge Core.

James Tully is Professor Emeritus of Political Science and Law at the University of Victoria.

Keith Cherry is Postdoctoral Fellow of Law at the University of Alberta.

Fonna Forman is Professor of Political Science and Founding Director of the Center on Global Justice at the University of California, San Diego.

Jeanne Morefield is Associate Professor of Political Theory at the University of Oxford, Fellow at New College, and Non-Residential Fellow at the Quincy Institute for Responsible Statecraft.

Joshua Nichols is Assistant Professor of Law at McGill University.

Pablo Ouziel is cofounder of the Cedar Trees Institute and Associate Fellow with the Centre for Global Studies at the University of Victoria.

David Owen is Professor of Social and Political Philosophy at the University of Southampton.

Oliver Schmidtke is Professor of Political Science and Director of the Centre for Global Studies at the University of Victoria.

T0381572

Democratic Multiplicity

Perceiving, Enacting, and Integrating Democratic Diversity

Edited by

JAMES TULLY
University of Victoria

KEITH CHERRY
University of Alberta

FONNA FORMAN
University of California

JEANNE MOREFIELD
University of Oxford

JOSHUA NICHOLS
McGill University

PABLO OUZIEL
University of Victoria

DAVID OWEN
University of Southampton

OLIVER SCHMIDTKE
University of Victoria

CAMBRIDGE
UNIVERSITY PRESS

University Printing House, Cambridge CB2 8BS, United Kingdom

One Liberty Plaza, 20th Floor, New York, NY 10006, USA

477 Williamstown Road, Port Melbourne, VIC 3207, Australia

314–321, 3rd Floor, Plot 3, Splendor Forum, Jasola District Centre,
New Delhi – 110025, India

103 Penang Road, #05–06/07, Visioncrest Commercial, Singapore 238467

Cambridge University Press is part of the University of Cambridge.

It furthers the University's mission by disseminating knowledge in the pursuit of
education, learning, and research at the highest international levels of excellence.

www.cambridge.org
Information on this title: www.cambridge.org/9781009178389
DOI: 10.1017/9781009178372

First published 2022

A catalogue record for this publication is available from the British Library.

Library of Congress Cataloging-in-Publication Data
NAMES: Tully, James, 1946– editor.
TITLE: Democratic multiplicity : perceiving, enacting and integrating democratic diversity / edited by James
Tully, Keith Cherry, Fonna Forman, Jeanne Morefield, Joshua Nichols, Pablo Ouziel, David Owen, Oliver
Schmidtke.
DESCRIPTION: Cambridge, United Kingdom ; New York, NY : Cambridge University Press, 2022. |
Includes bibliographical references and index.
IDENTIFIERS: LCCN 2021062473 (print) | LCCN 2021062474 (ebook) | ISBN 9781009178389 (hardback) |
ISBN 9781009178372 (ebook)
SUBJECTS: LCSH: Democracy. | Democracy and environmentalism. | Common good. | Nature – Effect of
human beings on – Political aspects.
CLASSIFICATION: LCC JC423 .D44177 2022 (print) | LCC JC423 (ebook) | DDC 321.8–dc23/eng/20220401
LC record available at https://lccn.loc.gov/2021062473
LC ebook record available at https://lccn.loc.gov/2021062474

ISBN 978-1-009-17838-9 Hardback
ISBN 978-1-009-17836-5 Paperback

Contents

Contents   vii

Figures

Tables

Contributors

John Borrows BA, MA, JD, LLM (Toronto), PhD (Osgoode Hall Law School), LLD (Hons, Dalhousie, York, SFU, Queen's & Law Society of Ontario), DHL (Toronto), FRSC, OC, is the Canada Research Chair in Indigenous Law at the University of Victoria Law School in British Columbia. His publications include *Recovering Canada: The Resurgence of Indigenous Law* (Donald Smiley Award best book in Canadian Political Science, 2002), *Canada's Indigenous Constitution* (Canadian Law and Society Best Book Award, 2011), *Drawing Out Law: A Spirit's Guide* (2010), *Freedom and Indigenous Constitutionalism* (Donald Smiley Award for Best Book in Canadian Political Science, 2016), *The Right Relationship* (with Michael Coyle, ed., 2017), *Resurgence and Reconciliation* (with Michael Asch and Jim Tully, eds., 2018), and *Law's Indigenous Ethics* (2020 Best Subsequent Book Award from Native American and Indigenous Studies Association, 2020 W. Wes Pue Best Book Award from the Canadian Law and Society Association). He is the 2017 Killam Prize Winner in Social Sciences, the 2019 Molson Prize Winner from the Canada Council for the Arts, the recipient of the 2020 Governor General's Innovation Award, and the 2021 Canadian Bar Association President's Award Winner. He was appointed as an Officer of the Order of Canada in 2020. John is a member of the Chippewa of the Nawash First Nation in Ontario, Canada.

Robin Celikates is Professor of Social Philosophy at Free University Berlin and codirector of the Center for Humanities and Social Change Berlin. His work mainly focuses on critical theory, civil disobedience, democracy, and migration. Among his publications are *Critique as Social Practice* (2018) and *Analyzing Ideology* (coedited with Sally Haslanger and Jason Stanley, forthcoming). He is an editor of the journal *Critical Times: Interventions in Global Critical Theory* and directs the interdisciplinary research project Transforming Solidarities.

Keith Cherry is an academic and activist living on unceded Lekwungen territories. Keith is currently a Killam postdoctoral fellow at the University of Alberta, a graduate fellow at the University of Victoria's Centre for Global Studies, a postdoctoral fellow at the University of Alberta's Center for Constitutional Studies, and a fellow at the Cedar Trees Institute. Keith's research focuses on legal pluralism, decolonization, and agonistic politics, and he is active in Indigenous sovereignty and climate justice advocacy.

Fonna Forman is Professor of Political Theory at the University of California, San Diego, and founding director of the UCSD Center on Global Justice. Her work focuses on climate justice, borders and migration, participatory urbanization, and community-based solutions to poverty. With UCSD architect Teddy Cruz, she leads a variety of civic initiatives in the US–Mexico border region and beyond. Their work has been exhibited widely in cultural venues across the world, including MoMA (New York), the Yerba Buena Center for the Arts (San Francisco), M+ (Hong Kong), and the Venice Architecture Biennale. Current work includes an NSF-funded investigation of climate risk and vulnerability in California's underserved communities; a new University of California-wide curriculum on climate justice, resilience, and adaptation; and two forthcoming books with Teddy Cruz: *Spatializing Justice* (2022), and *Socializing Architecture* (2022).

David Held (27 August 1951–2 March 2019) was a specialist in political theory and international relations. He held a joint appointment as Professor of Politics and International Relations and was Master of University College at Durham University until his death. Previously, he was the Graham Wallas Chair of Political Science and the codirector of the Centre for the Study of Global Governance at the London School of Economics. He was joint editor-in-chief of the journal *Global Policy* and cofounder of Polity Press. He published more than twenty-seven authored and coauthored books on critical theory, global governance, the history of democracy, and cosmopolitanism. His last major work, with Thomas Hale, was *Beyond Gridlock* (2017).

Phil Henderson is a settler and a PhD candidate in Political Science at the University of Victoria. His research focuses on Canadian settler imperialism, anti-imperialist grassroots struggle, and white backlash politics.

Anthony Simon Laden is Professor of Philosophy at the University of Illinois at Chicago and Associate Director of the Center for Ethics and Education. He is the author of *Reasonably Radical: Deliberative Liberalism and the Politics of Identity* (2001) and *Reasoning: A Social Picture* (2012). His current projects include a series of papers about education as the engineering of trust networks and a book on democracy tentatively titled *How Democracy Doesn'tEnd*.

Jeanne Morefield is Associate Professor of Political Theory and Fellow at New College, University of Oxford, and a Non-Residential Fellow at the Quincy

Institute for Responsible Statecraft in Washington, DC. Her scholarship sits at the intersection of political theory, international relations, and intellectual history, with a particular focus on the relationship between liberalism, imperialism, and internationalism in Britain and America. She is the author of *Covenants Without Swords: Idealist Liberalism and the Spirit of Empire* (2005), *Empires Without Imperialism: Anglo American Decline and the Politic of Deflection* (2014), and the forthcoming *Unsettling the World: Edward Said and Political Theory* (Spring, 2022). Her next book project, *A Contemporary History of Sex Trafficking*, examines the role of sex-trafficking narratives in the construction and contestation of global liberalism, from the League of Nations to QAnon. Morefield's popular work has appeared in *The Boston Review*, *Jacobin*, *Responsible Statecraft*, and *The New Statesman*.

Chantal Mouffe is Emeritus Professor of Political Theory at the Centre for the Study of Democracy at the University of Westminster in London. She has taught and researched in many universities in Europe, North America, and South America, and she is a corresponding member of the Collège International de Philosophie in Paris. She is the editor of *Gramsci and Marxist Theory* (1979), *Dimensions of Radical Democracy: Pluralism, Citizenship, Community* (1992), *Deconstruction and Pragmatism* (1996), and *The Challenge of Carl Schmitt* (1999); the coauthor with Ernesto Laclau of *Hegemony and Socialist Strategy: Towards a Radical Democratic Politics* (1985); and the author of *The Return of the Political* (1993), *The Democratic Paradox* (2000), *On the Political* (2005), *Agonistics: Thinking the World Politically* (2013), *Podemos: In the Name of the People* (with Inigo Errejon; 2016), and *For a Left Populism* (2019).

Val Napoleon is the Acting Dean of the Faculty of Law, UVIC, and the Law Foundation Chair of Indigenous Justice and Governance. She is the co-founder of JID/JD (dual degree program in Indigenous legal orders and Canadian common law), and the founding director of the Indigenous Law Research Unit. She is Cree from Saulteau First Nation and an adopted member of the Gitanyow [northern Gitxsan]. Her areas of research include Indigenous legal traditions and methodologies (e.g., land, water, governance and democracy, human rights, gender, dispute resolution, and intellectual property), Indigenous legal theories, Indigenous feminisms, legal pluralism, Indigenous democracy, and Indigenous intellectual property. She teaches common property law and Gitxsan land and property law transsystemically in the JID/JD.

Rebeccah Nelems is a Pierre Elliott Trudeau Scholar, cofounder of the Cedar Trees Institute, Associate Faculty at Royal Roads University, and a PhD Candidate in Sociology and Cultural, Social and Political Thought at the University of Victoria (UVic). She weaves together a diversity of Western, Indigenous, social, and political theoretical traditions to explore generative and relational pathways toward transformative social systems change. Her dissertation, *On Intra-Being: A Phenomenological and Decolonizing Exploration of Eco-Social Connection on Turtle Island* (unpublished), builds upon her research interests in decolonizing research methodologies, Southern epistemologies, sociological theory, the youth climate justice movement, and sympagogy. Most recently, she published a creative nonfiction chapter, "Short Walk Home" in *Rising Tides: Reflections for Climate Changing Times* (2019), and coedited an international, interdisciplinary volume on empathy, *Exploring Empathy: Its Propagations, Perimeters and Potentialities* (2018).

Joshua Nichols is an assistant professor in the Faculty of Law at McGill University. His work has been published in several leading journals, including the *University of Toronto Law Journal, Osgoode Hall Law Journal, UBC Law Review, Alberta Law Review*, and the *Journal of Historical Sociology*. His latest book is entitled *A Reconciliation without Recollection: An Investigation of the Foundations of Aboriginal Law* (2019). He is a research fellow at the Wahkohtowin Law and Governance Lodge at the University of Alberta, and a member of the Law Society of British Columbia.

Pablo Ouziel is cofounder of the Cedar Trees Institute. He is Associate Fellow with the Centre for Global Studies, University of Victoria, and Visiting Fellow, University of Southampton, UK. Pablo holds a PhD in Political Science from the University of Victoria, and his research interests include democratization practices, joining hands relationships, horizontality, nonviolence, and interdependent social change. By standing within the tradition of public philosophy, the core of his work is centered on excavating networks of individuals governing themselves in numerous ways that supersede our current structures of representative government. In his book *Democracy Here and Now* (2022), he presents an account of the new form of participatory democracy enacted by the 15-M movement in Spain. Presenting an original participatory mode of research, the book reveals six types of intersubjective, joining hands relationships that 15-M brings into being and works to carry on in creative ways.

David Owen is Professor of Social and Political Philosophy at the University of Southampton. He has also been visiting professor at IAS Princeton and Goethe University, Frankfurt. He is a Fellow of the Academy of Social Sciences (UK). His most recent book is *What Do We Owe to Refugees?* (2020). He has published widely on issues of democratic theory and migration ethics, as well on Nietzsche, Foucault, and the Frankfurt School, among other topics. He is currently working on book manuscripts on Nietzsche and on global migration governance.

Oliver Schmidtke is a Professor in Political Science and History at the University of Victoria, where he has also served as the director of the Centre for Global Studies in Victoria since 2011. He received his PhD from the European University Institute in Florence and has been a JF Kennedy Fellow at Harvard

University, a visiting scholar at Humboldt University Berlin, a F. Braudel Senior Fellow at the European University Institute, a Marie Curie Fellow at Hamburg University, and a research fellow at the Hamburg Institute for Advanced Studies. His research interests are in the fields of the politics and governance of migration, citizenship, nationalism, democracy, and populism.

Boaventura de Sousa Santos is Emeritus Professor of Sociology, University of Coimbra (Portugal), and Distinguished Legal Scholar at the University of Wisconsin–Madison. He earned an LLM and JSD from Yale University and holds the Degree of Doctor of Laws, Honoris Causa, by McGill University. He is Director Emeritus of the Center for Social Studies at the University of Coimbra. His most recent project, ALICE: Leading Europe to a New Way of Sharing the World Experiences, was funded by an Advanced Grant of the European Research Council. Recent books in English include *Decolonising the University: The Challenge of Deep Cognitive Justice* (2021), *The End of the Cognitive Empire: The Coming of Age of Epistemologies of the South* (2018), *Epistemologies of the South: Justice against Epistemicide* (2014), *Toward a New Legal Common Sense: Law, Globalization, and Emancipation* (3rd ed., 2020), *The Pluriverse of Human Rights: The Diversity of Struggles for Dignity* (edited with Bruno Sena Martins; 2021), and *Demodiversity: Toward Post-Abyssal Democracies* (edited with José Manuel Mendes; 2020).

Stacie Swain is a fourth-generation settler of Ukrainian–British descent and a PhD candidate in Political Science at the University of Victoria, with a graduate certificate in Indigenous Nationhood. Her research focuses on the politics of Indigenous ceremony in relation to public space, the category of religion, Canadian settler colonialism, and Indigenous legal orders. Previous work can be found in edited volumes such as *Fabricating Identities* (2017), *Method Today: Redescribing Approaches to the Study of Religion* (2018), and *The End of Religion: Feminist Reappraisals of the State* (2020). She has forthcoming work in *Fabricating Authenticity* (2022), *Indigenous Religious Traditions in Five Minutes* (2022), and *Opening and Closing Relations: Indigenous Spirituality in Canada* (n.d.). She is presently engaged in dissertation research.

Lasse Thomassen is Professor of Politics in the School of Politics and International Relations at Queen Mary University of London. He is the author of *Deconstructing Habermas* (2007) and *British Multiculturalism and the Politics of Representation* (2017). He is currently working on deconstruction, the category of representation, and new forms of radical politics.

James Tully is Emeritus Distinguished Professor of Political Science and Law at the University of Victoria. He is the author of *Public Philosophy in a New Key* (2009) and *On Global Citizenship* (2014); coeditor and contributor with Michael Asch and John Borrows, *Resurgence and Reconciliation* (2018);

editor and introduction, *Richard Gregg: Power of Nonviolence* (2019); and contributor with Monika Kirloskar-Steinbach, Charles Mills and others, *Dialogue and Decolonization* (2022).

Jeremy Webber is Professor of Law at the University of Victoria. He has written widely in legal theory, constitutional theory, Indigenous rights, federalism, cultural diversity, and constitutional law in Canada and in relation to other countries (especially Australia). He is the author of *Reimagining Canada: Language, Culture, Community and the Canadian Constitution* (1994), *The Constitution of Canada: A Contextual Analysis* (2nd ed., 2021), and *Las gramáticas de la ley: Derecho, pluralismo y justicia* (2017). Professor Webber was the University of Victoria's Dean of Law from 2013 to 2018. He held the Canada Research Chair in Law and Society at UVic from 2002 to 2014, when he surrendered the chair to serve as Dean of Law. Prior to joining UVic, he was Dean of Law at the University of Sydney, Australia (1998–2002) and Professor of Law at McGill University (1987–98). He was appointed a Fellow of the Trudeau Foundation in 2009 and a Fellow of the Royal Society of Canada in 2016.

Antje Wiener is Professor of Political Science, especially Global Governance, at the University of Hamburg, and a By-Fellow at Hughes Hall, Cambridge. Her research interest focuses on norms research in International Relations theory. Her current research addresses contested norms, global opportunity structures, and societal agency for climate change at the Excellence Cluster Climate, Climatic Change, and Society (CLICCS) at the University of Hamburg. She has been an editor of *Global Constitutionalism* since 2012. Her most recent books include *Contestation and Constitution of Norms in Global International Relations* (2018) and *A Theory of Contestation* (2014).

Foreword: Democratic Self-and-Other-Determination and the More-than-Human World

John Borrows

Democracies thrive on mutual participation of one and all here and now. They are marked by a commitment to coordination and cooperation across various fields. Despite their strengths, democracies could more effectively connect with our more-than-human relatives. A universal theory or view is not required to take such action. Nonviolence, pluralism, and agonistic engagement with the natural world could further expand democracies' futures.

Throughout this book, you will read that interdependence and mutual engagement with those who are different is a key to joint action. This contrasts with politics built on force, coercion, and noncooperation, where power is concentrated in competing "us and them" camps. This book explains how democracies thrive when they move beyond assessments of "what is good for me" and inquire into what is good for "all of us together." In this light, human concerns should not monopolize political judgment; democracies should also revolve around what is good for the entire biosphere.

We must learn politics from our ancestors. Plants, insects, birds, and animals have much to teach us. We are their descendants and they are our elders. We would not exist without them. They came first and they continue to sustain us. Our evolutionary lineage and biophysical dependence points to this fact.

I am *nigig indoodem*, from the Otter clan of the Anishinaabe. Our legal order flows from a creation story wherein animals counseled together to bring dirt from the depths of a flooded world. A giant otter participated in this council. They dove with other animals who sought substance for further growth. The muskrat, the smallest diver, brought a paw full of earth from deep below the surface. The animals celebrated his efforts by seeding this soil as they danced along a giant turtle's back. In the process, the animals combined elements necessary for life's subsequent generation. When the giant otter died, the first person of my clan emerged from their carcass. Long after the council's actions spread life across Turtle Island's back, other clans formed in similar ways. Humans are the earth's literal offspring. We have much to learn from our genesis.

Countless stories from many societies narrate similar themes: we are born from the earth. In Hebrew, the biblical name for the first human is *adamah*, which means "the ground" or "earth." The Quran says that "among His signs is that He created you from the dust" (ar-Rum 30:20). Scientific accounts of life's origins circulate this truth. Proof of natural selection drawn from the elements around us is vast, varied, and magnificent. Evolution conveys essential facts about the nature of our physical existence. Our relatedness to the earth holds great political salience. Our constitutional genealogies spring from the elements found in the natural world.

We sever ourselves from what sustains us if we separate politics from the air, water, rocks, plants, insects, birds, animals, and other such kin. Our political lives depend on respectfully nurturing that which nurtures us, which includes our natural environments. The living world provides the very conditions from which all other activities flow. We cannot be reconciled with others unless we first reconcile ourselves with the living earth.

Democracies must look backwards to life's sources to narrate any political momentum forward. Human words do not precede us; they arrived much later than the winds, waves, pulses, vibrations, drones, barks, whines, growls, calls, and songs of our first teachers. Human politics, including democratic politics, is not *the* precondition to healthy living. Something primordial, beyond words, precedes us.

The question is, how can we better incorporate lessons from the natural world into democracies' futures? How might we listen to those we do not conventionally hear? How can we incorporate these politics into our everyday lives?

Let me suggest that lessons course through waters and winds. Listening to the natural world requires a literacy that is hard to convey through language. The earth is an archive that we must learn to read: scientifically, socially, culturally, legally, spiritually, and politically. Anishinaabe people have long taught that we can hear and read beyond words if we regard the earth as our relative and teacher. For us, earth-bound politics must be experiential and phenomenological. This requires listening with our bodies (alongside other bodies and life forms) to those whose forms may be very different from our own. This is a key to civility.

Our teachers may have wings, fins, tails, and antennae. They might be fossilized, dressed in leaves, or fall from the sky in small drops. Anishinaabe elder Basil Johnston taught me that we learn governance in context, which includes these more-than-human frameworks. He said we must attune ourselves to frequencies that emanate from fields, forests, and seas to better regulate our affairs and resolve our disputes. We must understand how the world is different from us, even as we find ourselves within them. He said, "until you can look at a squirrel and see yourself as no more or less than her, you will not understand humility," which is a key to effective living.

Anishinaabe practitioners of these forms of democracy realize that their own views of the earth are partial. The natural world is simply too vast, beautiful, precarious, and mysterious to capture in human terms. Thus, they must find ways to concede, cooperate, conciliate, and negotiate with those in the natural world whom they cannot fully understand. They recognize that democracy must give at least some space to our more-than-human fellow citizens to follow their own patterns for growth and development. We must allow them to be themselves. An oak must be given space to grow with other species in spontaneous and interactive ways. An old-growth forest might not be as economically profitable as a tree plantation, but if old-growth forests cease to exist, humans will never gain an enlarged and even-handed view of how we might better live.

Indigenous self-and-other codetermination sees the natural world as a key participatory space for engagement. Humans can learn how to be better relatives in these spaces. We must "go outside" more frequently when we talk with one another and make decisions – and listen to other ways of being.

This is why some Anishinaabe elders take their grandchildren outdoors when asked for guidance. This is why some Indigenous law professors take their students to their traditional territories to learn. It is easier to hear "more than human" contributions to political life if we get outside our courts, legislatures, classrooms, labs, conference rooms, books, and computer-mediated conversations. When we leave familiar human structures and political fora, it is easier to listen to the water, plants, insects, birds, and animals, and their voices. Learning from the natural world in all democracies requires direct experience. Ultimately, effective listening requires immersion in settings where humans are not at the center of every thought and interaction.

As Jim Tully reminds us in this book, judgment is perspectival. I am suggesting that we must see our politics through our neighbors' eyes, like those of the butterflies, frogs, geese, and otters. Their habitats, habits, and health must be viewed in ways that respect their intrinsic worth. We must participate with them, within environments ordered differently from how humans construct them. Contrasting and comparing others' needs with our own allows us to see our own assumptions and preoccupations more clearly. This is why we must become students of the oaks, salamanders, owls, and sturgeon. We must do more to learn from those who know them. We must work to support this kind of resurgence and regeneration if we hope for an effective reconciliation with the earth.

A commitment to democratic reciprocity means that human political communities must be more than self-determining. Self-determination is not enough to sustain our political goals. Too much focus on self can lead to insular, closed, and selfish activities, which can cause us to build walls that contain, divide, confine, prevent, repel, and deter interactions that are necessary to healthy living. Placing too much attention on the "self" can cause us to ignore the vital place of air, water, and rocks as participants in our polities. Thus, in addition to advancing self-determination, democratic communities must also recognize and affirm other-determination as a genuine political reality. I am advocating for *Indigenous-other-determination*, alongside *self-determination*, as an important democratic goal.

Recognizing democratic other-determination does not mean we should determine other's choices. People should be free to take as much responsibility for their actions as they possibly can. Moreover, I am not advocating for colonialism, imperialism, authoritarianism, or other forms of governance where so-called governors determine other peoples' fate without their involvement, participation, or consent. I am merely suggesting that self-determination is a necessary yet insufficient condition for democracies' futures. Freedom, as taught to me by Basil Johnston, is a practice realized by being responsible for our own relationships.

Democratic other-determination (alongside self-determination) merely accepts that we never exist in isolation. What others determine has an impact on us, and what we determine influences them. Our thoughts, our actions, and their consequences are never fully a product of self-determination. We always find ourselves entangled with others. Determination is never contained in any version of a self. Forces we will never recognize influence our own governance, for good and ill, and accounting for this truth is a deep democratic insight.

Since governance is never fully within any society's control, we must learn to see how we are mutually determined, including by the more-than-human world. We must learn to appreciate biosphere-wide differences in classification and conjugation to have any hope of hearing and appropriately responding to others. Along with learning how different histories, cultures, economies, and peoples coordinate their affairs, and tracing these impacts on our own organizational forms, we must see how the natural world also determines how we live.

Democratic self-and-other-determination is evolutionary. It encourages apprenticeship. In addition to its other strengths, studying diverse kinds of democracies here and now urges us to learn how to better listen, compare, and contrast our needs with the natural world to develop better political judgment. These are our clan responsibilities as humans. Stronger civic engagement with the plants, insects, fish, birds, and animals can help us identify significant insights on how they (and, by extension, we) experience the natural world. In this light, *Democratic Multiplicity* can better help us develop governance relationships with other living societies who also share this world.

Our political choices have consequences for those who were here first. Our democracies will not have bright futures unless we understand and act on this insight. This is "being democratic" with all affected fellow citizens of the living earth here and now in self-and-other codetermining ways: *dabagewagendan wiidokodaadidiwin gidakiiminan omaa noongom*.

John Borrows, Canada Research Chair in Indigenous Law, University of Victoria Law School

Acknowledgments

We acknowledge with respect the Lekwungen peoples on whose traditional territory we live and work and the Songhees, Esquimalt, and W̱SÁNEĆ peoples whose historical relationships with the land continue to this day.

The chapters in this volume originally began as papers submitted to and commented on during a workshop hosted by the Cedar Trees Institute (CTI) and the Centre for Global Studies at the University of Victoria, British Columbia, Canada, on March 21–22, 2019. The workshop was organized as part of the Jean Monnet Project "Canada Europe Dialogue on Democracy (CEDoD)" and cofinanced by the Erasmus+ Programme of the European Union and the Centre for Global Studies at the University of Victoria. The workshop documentation can be found at www.eucanet.org. We are most grateful to the contributors for their outstanding chapters. They show us new ways of studying and enacting democracies here and now. We are also thankful for the assistance they have given us in creating and editing this volume at various stages.

We are grateful to all of the participants, administrative staff, and student volunteers who helped cocreate the workshop from which this volume was born. In particular, we acknowledge Jodie Walsh, Beate Schmidtke, Phil Cox, Karen Yen, Chris Chan, Kadi Diallo, Stephen Gnanasihamany, Stephanie Gruhlke, Chorong Kim, Mabel Martinez-Dusan, Sam Alexander Rodriguez, Jennifer Swift, and Elissa Wittington for their help organizing the workshop. We would also like to thank all the participants in the preparatory sessions who helped shape the workshop themes and structures, especially Christina Gray, Taiwo Afolabi, Ben Isitt, Michael Carpenter, Didier Zuniga, Astrid Perez Pinan, Sara Naderi, Corey Snelgrove, Joëlle Alice Michaud-Ouellet, Stacie Swain, Franziska Fischer, Phil Henderson, Eszter Bodnár, Ramesh Bairy, Lana Lowe, Benjamin Perrier, Mike Simpson, Rebeca Macias Gimenez, Ryan Beaton, and Rebeccah Nelems. Many thanks to Kate Langridge and the team at Stream of Consciousness, Dennis Pilon, Laurel Collins, and Tom Junes for their participation in the workshop's public events. We are especially thankful to the University of Victoria's First Peoples House for hosting us in their beautiful ceremonial space, and to Tsartlip Elder May Sam for welcoming us to her traditional territories in a good way.

We are also grateful to a large number of people who have helped us shape this publication along the way, in particular Vanessa Udy for her editorial work, Helen Cooper and Vidya Ashwin for editing and production, and Robert Dreesen, Erika Walsh, Claire Sissen, and their team at Cambridge University Press for taking on this project and helping us develop it.

We gratefully acknowledge the financial support for Open Access and research provided by the Centre on Global Studies, University of Victoria; the Center on Global Justice, University of California, San Diego; New College, Oxford University; Department of Politics and International Relations, Oxford University; Book and Creative Works Subvention Fund, University of Victoria; University of Illinois at Chicago; Social Sciences and Humanities Research Council of Canada; (Project: 'Populism and its Effects on Liberal Democracy'), and Deutsche Forschungsgemeinschaft (DFG, German Research Foundation) for funding under Germany's Excellence Strategy – EXC 2037 'CLICCS – Climate, Climatic Change, and Society' – Project Number: 390683824.

NOTE ON THE COVER

Karen Yen *Homecoming*

This image began with an exercise of listening – listening to the human and beyond human world. From the rustle of leaves in gentle breeze, fluttering sounds as birds are startled by intruders, hidden silence of a deer resting among hazelnut trees, to my body immersed in the rushing waters of the river; in this context, humans are merely one more resident in this broad and diverse world. A world that is vibrant, complex, layered, interactive, interconnected and expansive. Why should our understanding and practice of democracy be any less? Wouldn't this kind of democracy serve to create a virtuous "Home" for all? The painting visits the idea of "Home" as a safe and nurturing space for humans and our beyond human siblings. Inspired by Bill Reid's "Spirit of Haida Gwaii", can we contribute by paddling our canoe in a direction that weaves the organic and the unknown with human created structures and processes, in the abstract, material and spiritual sense? These are the questions this work addresses.

INTRODUCTION

The Pluriverse of Democracies

James Tully

This volume on the study of multiple democracies critically and constructively began in a workshop hosted by the Cedar Trees Institute (CTI) and the Centre for Global Studies at the University of Victoria on unceded Lekwungen territory, Victoria, British Columbia, on March 21–22, 2019. After the presentations and discussions at the workshop, the participants rewrote their presentations into chapters in the course of correspondence and conversation over the following year. The volume editors assembled and edited the chapters. To understand fully the chapters and their interconnections, it is helpful to begin with the preliminary sketch of the pluriverse of democracies that we distributed to participants prior to the workshop. We then revised and rearranged it as the dialogue and writing progressed.

A PRELIMINARY SKETCH OF FIVE MODES OF DEMOCRACY AND THEIR DIALOGICAL ELUCIDATION

The field of democracy and democratization is disclosed in a wide variety of ways in both practice and theory. Our approach, in the workshop and in this volume, is to disclose the field as consisting of at least five overlapping and crisscrossing modes or families of democracy and democratization. Accordingly, citizens and researchers disclose the field of democracy in diverse ways, depending on the family of democracy they foreground and the mode of engagement they practice.

Indigenous forms of community-based (and networked) democracies throughout the world of more than 600 million Indigenous people comprise the first mode of democracy. These are the oldest family of democracies on the planet. Indigenous people are regenerating them today through the exercise of their rights of self-determination in accord with their own understanding of this concept and their Indigenous legal orders, as well as in partnership with the

United Nations Declaration on the Rights of Indigenous Peoples. In addition, over many centuries, Indigenous peoples have attempted to develop transformative, decolonizing relationships of democratic treaty federalism with settler colonial states. The workshop was held at the University of Victoria because it is a leading center for the study of Indigenous democracies.

Representative democracies within modern states comprise a second mode of democracy. These representative governments in all their varieties comprise the major family of democracy on the planet. State-centered democracies and the crises they are undergoing are of course the major focus of research on democracies today. We are concerned to give them due attention. Yet, we also aim to explore other existing modes of democracy and, most importantly, study them from their distinct ways of knowing and acting, rather than from the limited perspective of state-centered representative democracy and its theories.

Democracy "beyond the state" is a third mode of democracy. We divide this part into two subsections: (1) the democratization or failure of democratization (both the "deficit" and "disconnect" problems) and their consequences for institutions of the European Union, global governance, global law, international relations, democratizing the United Nations, and so on; and (2) the diverse ways in which citizens engage in democratic practices of contestation and interaction with global institutions of various kinds.

The fourth family of democracies consists of the multiple forms of community-based, self-organizing and self-governing ("cooperative"), direct or participatory democracies and their global networks around the world. As in two classic cases of "assembly democracies" – Potlatch democracy and Athenian democracy – the members are both citizens and governors. The people themselves (*demos*) exercise political power (*kratos*). Today these community-based democracies also tend to provide the basis of democratic practices of nonviolent resistance to and transformation of unjust relationships and social systems: participatory democratic democratization. The Gandhian tradition of democratic self-government (*swaraj*) and democratic contestation and transformation (*Satyagraha)* and the African-American beloved community tradition associated with Martin Luther King Jr. are well-known examples of this diverse global family of democracies.[1]

---

[1] John Restakis, *Humanizing the Economy: Co-Operatives in the Age of Capital* (Gabriola Island: New Society, 2010) estimates that about 800 million people are involved to some extent in these direct democratic communities of practice. See, for example, Mark Engler and Paul Engler, *This Is an Uprising: How Nonviolent Revolt Is Shaping the Twenty-First Century* (New York: Nation Books, 2016); Isabelle Ferreras, Julie Battilana, Dominique Méda, and 3,000 others, "Democratizing Work," *Il Manifesto*, May 15, 2020, https://global.ilmanifesto.it/democratizing-work; Joe Parker, *Democracy Beyond the Nation State* (New York and London: Routledge, 2017); Boaventura de Sousa Santos and Cesar A. Rodriguez-Garavito, eds., *Law and Globalization from Below: Towards a Cosmopolitan Legality* (Cambridge: Cambridge University Press, 2005); James Tully, *On Global Citizenship: James Tully in Dialogue* (London: Bloomsbury, 2014).

These four general modes of democracy are located within, conditioned by, and reciprocally condition other powerful nondemocratic social, economic, and military systems. This assemblage of complex global systems – of democratic *and* nondemocratic social, economic, and military-industrial systems – generates horrendous inequalities in the individual and collective well-being of humans and their communities. These inequalities obstruct and undermine the conditions of democratic relationships within and across these modes of democracy. Moreover, the assemblage of global systems exploits, degrades, and destroys the ecosystems and earth systems on which all life on earth depends. We have known since the 1970s that this gives rise to complex, interdependent, and cascading crises of democratic, social, ecological, and earth systems. We call these the "Gaia crises" for shorthand.[2] The generic democratic crisis across all four democratic families is the incapacity or gridlock of democracies to cooperate in responding effectively to the Gaia crises.[3]

The Gaia crises bring to human awareness a fifth mode of democracy: Gaia or earth democracy. Homo sapiens and their systems are interdependent members of symbiotic ecological and earth systems that have sustained and complexified life for more than 3.8 billion years. These life systems are symbiotic and cyclical in the virtuous or cooperative sense that they reciprocally sustain themselves in ways that cosustain the interdependent life systems on which they codepend. They exercise the power or animacy of life-sustaining-life (*anima mundi*) themselves without a ruler (the Gaia hypothesis). These complex cooperative systems are often far from equilibrium and often tip over into unsustainable vicious systems. Yet, they also have the capacities to transform vicious systems into sustainable systems by means of cooperative ecological succession, either before or after collapse, as has happened many times in the past. This living Gaia democracy is primary in the sense that it is the ground of being and well-being of all other forms of democracy and their members. Homo sapiens are thus "plain members and citizens" of Gaia democracy with responsibilities to care for and sustain the biodiverse life systems that sustain them, as Aldo Leopold famously argued in 1949.[4] How do the members of the other four families of democracy respond to the Gaia crises and integrate in and with Gaia democracy?[5]

One central theme is the ways in which the five modes of democracy and their distinctive activities relate to one another, for better or worse. These relationships

[2] See Mark Lynas, *One Final Warning: Six Degrees of Climate Emergency* (London: 4th Estate, 2020).

[3] See David Held, Chapter 16, this volume.

[4] Aldo Leopold, "The Land Ethic," in *A Sand County Almanac: With Essays on Conservation from Round River* (Oxford: Oxford University Press, 1966), 239–40.

[5] For this way of approaching the Gaia crises, see Akeel Bilgrami, ed., *Nature and Value* (New York: Columbia University Press, 2020); James Tully, "Reconciliation Here on Earth," in *Resurgence and Reconciliation: Indigenous-Settler Relations and Earth Teachings*, eds. Michael Asch, John Borrows, and James Tully (Toronto: University of Toronto Press, 2018), 83–131.

are not well understood because our disciplinary and everyday ways of perceiving the field tend to treat the various forms of democracy in isolation from one another. When they are studied together, they are often pictured as in oppositional and/or hegemon–subaltern relationships. If the entangled, crisscrossing, and overlapping relationships enacted among them and the larger social systems are disclosed and discussed, we would be able to examine the challenges and possibilities of finding ways for these families of democracy to *coordinate and cooperate* as equals ('democratic integration') in addressing and transforming the local and global systemic causes of the Gaia crises and other crises. It may be that this kind of transformative democratic integration among democratic families ('joining hands') could overcome what is called in the literature the "dysfunctionality," "hollowing out," "gridlock," "antagonistic self-destruction," "authoritarian supersession," or "death of democracy."

INTRODUCTION TO THE SIX SECTIONS OF DEMOCRATIC MULTIPLICITY

All the topics set out in the preliminary sketch of the pluriverse of democracies were discussed at the workshop and the virtual dialogues during the writing of the chapters. We rearranged the five families of democracy so their crisscrossing and overlapping relationships are clearer and we added a first section on democratic ethos. The chapters focus critically on the strengths and weaknesses of the different modes of democracy, and on their relationships with each other. As a result, the chapters seek to expose the underlying causes of the democratic crises and the pathways to address and transform them, both within specific democracies and then with democratic relations of coordination and cooperation among them. This is how it should be. We cannot begin to think about genuinely democratic coordination of different modes of democracy until we have learned to listen to and understand how democracy and coordination are articulated, understood, and enacted by different demoi and those affected by them. This basic democratic norm of *audi alteram partem* (always listen to the other side) enables us to avoid and challenge the tendency to take one mode of democracy as the dominant mode of action-coordination under which all others are disclosed and subalternized. These comparative and critical democratic dialogues of all affected are the groundwork of and for the transformative kind of democratic coordination and cooperation we call "joining hands."[6] They enact democratization by democratic means.[7] In joining hands democratically, they

---

[6] For practices of joining hands, see Ouziel, Chapter 20. For an insightful historical Marxist study of how the global "precariat" could join hands democratically, see Mike Davis, *Old Gods New Enigmas: Marx's Lost Theory* (London: Verso, 2020).

[7] Compare Edward Said, "A Method for Thinking about Just Peace," in *What Is a Just Peace?*, eds. Pierre Allan and Alexis Keller (Oxford: Oxford Scholarship Online, 2006), 176–94, https://doi .org/10.1093/0199275351.001.0001.

connect with the animating democratic spirit or power of cooperating and contesting with and for one another that sustains democratic communities. Aristotle called this democratic spirit *philia* (friendship). In response to the ecological crisis in 1976, Eric Fromm renamed and extended it to *biophilia* (the animacy of Gaia democracy).[8]

The Foreword by John Borrows presents a perspicuous representation of the guiding spirit of the volume from his Anishinaabeg perspective. Mutually sustainable and ecosocially just democracies should be grounded in relationships of self and other codetermination with each other and the living earth.

The chapters are arranged in six parts. Part I consists of surveys of the democratic ethical capabilities, virtues, character formation, and ethos of being free and equal citizens and governors reasoning and exercising powers of cogovernance with each other in various families of democracy. This complex democratic ethos is derived from the basic Athenian definition of democracy as bringing a people (*demos*) into being and carrying it on by organizing and exercising the powers of governance and citizenship (*kratos*) by, with, and for each other. It is based on the Aristotelian, Arendtian, and Gandhian premise that healthy and sustainable pragmatic representative democracies are grounded in and grow out of healthy and sustainable everyday participatory democratic relationships in which citizens acquire the democratic ethical skills of interaction through trial-and-error practice and guidance by exemplary citizens. This ethical self-formation (*ethos*) consists in the cultivation of democratic relationships with oneself (inner freedom), other humans, and the living earth. These skills or virtues comprise the difficult nonviolent arts of persuasion by means of words and deeds that enable humans to control their anger and knee-jerk reactions and come to understand and trust one another through dialogue. They disagree and agree, contest and cooperate, resolve conflicts, reconcile, and begin again.[9] This way of being democratic contrasts with the recourse to force, the imposition of ruler/ruled relationships (*arche*) of other forms of government, the creation of us/them relationships, the escalating campaigns and competitions of and for power-over, and thus the undermining of democratic relationships of power with, by, and for one another.

These civic virtues of being democratic are the seeds of healthy participatory and representative democracies. They are thus of crucial importance to the growth and well-being of democracies because they bring to light by contrast

---

[8] See Eric Fromm, *The Anatomy of Human Destructiveness* (New York: Henry Holt and Company, 1973); James Tully, "Life Sustains Life 2," in *Nature and Value*, ed. Bilgrami, 181–204; Kara Rogers, "Biophilia Hypothesis," in *Encyclopaedia Britannica*, www.britannica.com/science/biophilia-hypothesis.

[9] For the importance of ethics in Indigenous law and governance, see John Borrows, *Law's Indigenous Ethics* (Toronto: University of Toronto Press, 2019).

the following three crises of contemporary representative democracies. The first is the marginalization of everyday participatory democratic relationships in modern societies and the dominance of unequal and undemocratic ruler/ruled relationships across the public and private spheres. As a result, most citizens do not acquire the basic democratic virtues and ethos. The second is the resulting disconnection or alienation of representative governments from ongoing, participatory democratic relationships of consultation and accountability with all affected – engaged democratic citizens – and thus the rise of increasingly nondemocratic relationships over, rather than with, the governed. Third, even within representative political parties, campaigns, and institutions, gaining a majority or plurality and imposing a solution is much more common than trying to "work across the aisle" to reach agreements among free and equal partners. As we know from contemporary history, this kind of political power over others becomes concentrated in the hands of elites, authoritarian movements capture democratic institutions, the iron law of competing oligarchies becomes the norm, and politics resembles war by other means.[10]

The democratic virtues explicated by Laden, Owen, and Thomassen also initiate the internal and circular relationship between means and ends in politics. Nondemocratic means bring about nondemocratic ends, whereas participatory democratic means bring about democratic ends. They are autotelic.[11] If this is correct, then the response to these democratic crises is to democratize representative democracy by democratizing our everyday relationships across public and private spheres, and, in so doing, generate transformative cycles of democratic succession and transformation. This is what we call "democratic democratization." This structure of argument explains why the cultivation of culturally diverse democratic ethics is primary. It appears to be the condition of overcoming the three crises of representative democracies and building networks of democratic coordination, cooperation, contestation, and conflict resolution in response to the gridlocked problems of

---

[10] See John Keane, *The New Despotism* (Cambridge, MA: Harvard University Press, 2020); Tarik Kochi, "The End of Global Constitutionalism and Rise of Antidemocratic Politics," *Global Society* 34, no. 4 (2020): 487–507, https://doi.org/10.1080/13600826.2020.1749037.

[11] Mahatma Gandhi and Martin Luther King Jr. tested the truth of the thesis that means configure ends in practice and in their writings. Dennis Dalton, Joan Bondurant, Hannah Arendt, and Richard Gregg presented the classic theoretical defenses of it and the challenge it presents to Western political theory and practice, based as it is on the thesis that violent and non-democratic means are necessary to establish order (the rabble hypothesis that humans are incapable of self-organization and governance without an armed master), and these violent means somehow lead to peace and democracy in some distant future to come. See Hannah Arendt, *On Violence* (New York: Harcourt, Brace, Jovanovich, 1970); Richard Bartlett Gregg, *The Power of Nonviolence*, ed. James Tully (Cambridge: Cambridge University Press, 2018); Joan V. Bondurant, *Conquest of Violence: The Gandhian Philosophy of Conflict*, rev. ed. (Princeton: Princeton University Press, 1988); Dennis Dalton, *Mahatma Gandhi: Nonviolent Power in Action* (New York: Columbia University Press, 2012).

pandemics, climate change, ecocide, inequality, racism, poverty, homelessness, and war.

Schematically, this participatory response to democratic crises appears to consist in two major phases articulated in different ways in the five families of democracies and in different subject positions within them. As noted, the first phase of "constructive programs" involves the cultivation of democratic ethics and relationships here and now, and thus a corresponding noncooperation with nondemocratic relationships – a stance illustrated, for example, in the "democratize work" movement. On this participatory democratic groundwork, the second phase engages with and seeks to transform nondemocratic and antidemocratic governance relationships and their members into democratic relationships by democratic means. These diverse practices of transformative democratization usually involve "two-handed" or dialectical approaches.

On the one hand, democratic citizens speak and assert truthfully to the powers-that-be of the specific injustice of the relationship in question, as they see it, by means of their nonviolent words and deeds. Simultaneously, on the other hand, they offer to listen reciprocally to their opponents and enter into democratic dialogues and negotiations oriented to reconciliation. That is, they treat their opponents and bystanders as free and equal citizens with the capacity to learn from others and come to see the superiority of democratic means of conflict resolution and eventual cooperation in a coauthored relationship. The specific pragmatic reconciliation they reach is always open to further contestation in the future by all affected. The crucial democratic feature is not the specific agreement, which is always provisional, but the intersubjective, trustworthy democratic skill-set and means of nonviolent conflict and conflict resolution they acquire through participation in the process.

This democratic mode of democratization from below is qualitatively different from the dominant top-down and coercive modes of global democratization and conflict resolution that are a major cause of the gridlock crisis we face today.[12] Yet, it is alive and well in the local and global traditions of participatory democracy. It is important to realize that these techniques exist in everyday disputes and dispute resolutions among friends and neighbors before they are extended to alternative dispute resolution practices and truth and reconciliation commissions. In the West, they came to prominence with the Athenian democratic practice of speaking truth to power (*parrhesia*) with the aim of initiating a transformative democratic dialogue with the powerful (*parrhesiastic* pact). In India, it is associated with the Gandhian practice of *Satyagraha* on the basis of local constructive programs (*swaraj*). In the United States, it is associated with Rosa Parks, Jo Ann Gibson Robinson, Martin

---

[12] See, for example, Morefield, Chapter 7, and Held, Chapter 16, this volume, and Vijayashri Sripati, *Constitution-Making under UN Auspices: Fostering Dependency in Sovereign Lands* (Oxford: Oxford University Press, 2020).

Luther King Jr., John Lewis, and the African-American beloved community tradition, as well as with César Chavez's tradition of common sense nonviolence. In Africa, it is associated with Kwame Nkrumah's positive action program, Nelson Mandela, and the Ubuntu tradition. Engaged Buddhist traditions of nonviolent protest and reconciliation are practiced worldwide. Europeans also have distinctive traditions. Indigenous peoples have their long-standing traditions of nonviolent conflict resolution by treaty negotiations and other methods.[13]

There are three reasons to take these traditions and practices of democratization by participatory democratic means seriously. The first is that they always take the other as an end in themselves to be treated as a free and equal democratic citizen, never as a means to be treated as a thing to be ruled by force. As Martin Luther King Jr. put it, it is the method appropriate for people "in this country [the United States] and throughout the world, who are seeking ways of achieving full social, personal and political freedom in a manner consistent with human dignity" because it enacts what it demands.[14] Second, if the constitutive relation between means and ends is correct, then nonviolent democracy is the *way* to local and global peace and democracy. The continuation of democratization by force and authoritarian rule will lead to more of the cycles of violence, counterviolence, and noncooperation that Held describes in Chapter 16. As King put it at the beginning of the age of nuclear weapons and conventional weapons of mass destruction: "Today the choice is no longer between violence and nonviolence. It is either nonviolence or nonexistence."[15] Third, the recourse to arms and relations of coercive power-over others to resolve disputes has boomerang effects on all social relationships throughout the "world house," as we see in the present. Again, as King argued in 1967, the choice is thus between violent domestic and international "chaos" or nonviolent "community."[16]

Part II turns to analyses of the crises of the dominant form of democracy: state-centered representative democracy. These include noncooperation, concentration of power in competing elites, the rise of authoritarian rule, right and left populism, and the deepening, class, race, education, rural versus urban, gender, and intersectional divisions within the people, as well as deepening inequalities among nation-states. Schmidtke presents a case study of the disconnection between representative and participatory

---

[13] For an introduction, see Engler and Engler, *This Is an Uprising*; Robert A. Williams Jr., *Linking Arms Together: American Indian Treaty Visions of Law and Peace 1600–1800* (New York: Oxford University Press, 1997); Gregg, *The Power of Nonviolence*; Kurt Schock, *Civil Resistance Today* (Cambridge: Polity Press, 2015); War Resister's International, *Handbook for Nonviolent Campaigns*, 2nd ed. (2014), http://wri-irg.org/pubs/NonviolenceHandbook.

[14] Martin Luther King Jr., "Foreword," in Gregg, *The Power of Nonviolence*, pp. 13–15.

[15] Martin Luther King Jr., *Stride Toward Freedom: The Montgomery Story*, rev. ed. (Boston: Beacon Press, 2010), 221.

[16] Martin Luther King Jr., *Where Do We Go from Here: Chaos or Community?* (Boston: Beacon Press, 2010).

democracy. Santos delineates the main features of the emergence of authoritarian rule from within representative democracy in the case of Brazil. Mouffe explains the rise and central features of right and left populism in response to the democratic crises. Morefield explicates the limitations of the main responses to the crises and lays down the path to the participatory responses of Part III. Notwithstanding their diversity, a common theme unites these chapters. Participatory democracy and representative democracy are not two independent and opposed ways of relating to one another, as is often presupposed. Rather, our complex and crises-ridden present is composed of the entanglement of these two modes of relationships in all areas of society. Most social relationships that govern our conduct exhibit elements of both. These chapters guide us through the tangled relationships and point toward ways of differently situated citizens joining hands and working together to transform them.

The engaged authors of Part III explore areas of the rapidly growing world of new and creative forms of participatory democracy. Forman takes us beyond the walls of representative democracies to cross-border communities of practices and to networks from the local to the global. Nelems moves beyond the human/nature divide to participation in Gaia-centered democracies and their systemic and cyclical features. Celikates investigates the creativity, indeterminacy, and self-reflexivity of participatory democracy that is often overlooked by the conventional ways of describing and studying these movements. These chapters shine critical light on the crises of democracies, borders, racism, poverty, social capital, climate change, and ecological destruction, on the one hand, and on the multiplicity of place- and earth-based responses to them, on the other.[17]

Part IV is an introduction to the vast world of Indigenous democracies today.[18] It begins with a concrete example of Indigenous (Gitxsan) democracy "on its own terms" by Napoleon, so it is not redescribed and subsumed in the terms of Western democracies. Nichols explains the crucial importance of critical histories of the relationships between settler colonial states and Indigenous peoples for the success of decolonization movements. The following chapters by Swain and Henderson investigate the difficulties and possibilities of engaged settler citizens entering into democratic allyship relations with Indigenous citizens and governments in confronting social and ecological crises on the ground and in representative institutions. In the final chapter in the part, Webber explicates important lessons that democrats can learn from Indigenous (Gitxsan) democracy today.

---

[17] For a complementary engaged study of the exemplary participatory democratic 15M movement in Spain, see Pablo Ouziel, *Democracy Here and Now: The Exemplary Case of Spain* (Toronto: University of Toronto Press, 2022).

[18] For an introduction to this field, see Asch, Borrows, and Tully, eds., *Resurgence and Reconciliation*.

Part V begins with a brief synopsis of Held's classic description of multiple crises of the global system of unequal representative democratic states in terms of systemic and self-reinforcing noncooperation or "gridlock" at the international level. The two following chapters take up the challenge of unlocking gridlock by practices of democracy beyond the state: in international law and international relations, multinational federations, and Indigenous–non-Indigenous federations. Wiener presents a general theory of cycles of contestation for international law and relations, whereas Cherry develops an analysis of democratic negotiation among a multiplicity of democracies.

Part VI contains two chapters on democratic integration among diverse democracies. In the first, Tully explores the family of Gaia or Earth democracy. He develops the theme first introduced by Borrows in the Foreword. For the integration of democratic multiplicity to be socially and ecologically just and cosustainable, democratic citizens and governors need to learn how to be plain members and responsible active citizens of the biodiverse relationships of the living earth that sustain all life ("eco-democratic integration"). In the final chapter, Ouziel shows how the diverse democratic citizens of each and every chapter can work together in context-specific, integrative relationships of democratic cooperation and contestation. These are relationships of democratic "joining hands" or integration. He illustrates that they are not only possible, but actual, here and now, in the local and global field of democratic diversity. The further growth of these action-coordination relationships has the potential to generate and integrate robust democracies with the capacity to respond to our ecosocial crises and cocreate a sustainable, democratic future.

OVERVIEW OF THE CHAPTERS

Part I: Democratic Ethos

Chapter 1:   How Democracy Doesn't End
In "How Democracy Doesn't End," Anthony Laden draws a contrast between two approaches to thinking about democracy – what he calls "pictures." The first, perhaps more familiar one, pictures democracy as an institutional form that allows a collective to rule itself legitimately. The second picture conceives of democracy as a social form in which people work out together the terms by which they live together. Despite their apparent similarities, so described, Laden argues that each picture makes salient a different set of issues and concerns and thus which picture we work within will shape how we think about democracy. In particular, the first, institutional picture, leads us to think about a series of boundary-setting questions, and a concern that the boundaries of the collective and its institutions are well-established. As Laden puts it, this picture treats democracy as "closed." In contrast, the second picture treats the mechanisms by

which people live together in a way that always remains open to challenge and criticism as fundamental to democracy; democracy is thus pictured here as "open." One attractive feature of the picture of democracy as open is that it makes democratic living together an open-ended and thus ongoing practice – one that doesn't come to an end, either with its successes or with its failures.

Chapter 2: Democracy, Boundaries, and Respect
This chapter focuses on the relationship between democracy, boundaries, and respect in terms of the distinction between civil and civic pictures of democracy – a distinction which can be initially glossed as that between democracy as a particular mode of civil order or constituted authority and democracy as a specific mode of civic agency or constituting power. David Owen argues that this focus can help to clarify some conceptual tensions in democratic theory concerning the boundary problem as it stands in relation to democratization. It can serve as a way of reminding us of the priority of citizenship as a political practice before citizenship as a legal status and the salience of that priority for reflecting on contemporary problems of democracy.

Chapter 3: Democracy in a Provisional Key
Drawing on the work of Jacques Derrida, this chapter argues that we should think about democracy in a provisional key. Democracy is provisional because it puts itself into question. It does so when we take the question "what is democracy?" to be part of democracy, which means that we must ask "what is the demos?" and "what is rule?" We end up with a conception of democracy whereby the people is at once prior to and a result of the rule of the people, and so we never arrive at a final answer to the questions "who is the demos?" and "what is rule?" Treating democracy as provisional does not necessarily solve major challenges such as the environmental crisis and inequality, but it allows us to approach these challenges from a new and more fruitful angle. Lasse Thomassen discusses this with particular attention to current debates about the climate crisis.

Part II: Representative Democracies

Chapter 4: Democracy and Community: Exploring a Contested Link in Light of the Populist Resurgence
A central force propelling contemporary right-wing populist parties is their ability to offer a strong and emotionally charged sense of community. The nationalist rhetoric and promise to represent the genuine 'voice of the people' are constitutive elements in the populist political mobilization. Yet, the nationalist plea to re-establish the sovereign rights of a national community is rarely based on a democratic, participatory empowerment of the people in whose interests populist leaders claim to speak. Against the background of the populist surge in Western democracies, this chapter has two objectives: First, it

explores the link between democracy and community from a theoretical perspective, arguing that democratic self-governance is indeed reliant on a substantial, functionally and procedurally pertinent sense of communal existence and shared collective identity. In this respect, the chapter focuses on how the growing emphasis on individual rights and entitlements has overshadowed the constitutive role of community for the viability of democratic praxis. Second, the chapter demonstrates empirically how locally based communities can produce a social infrastructure that is essential for modes of engaged citizenship and revitalized democratic practices.[19]

Chapter 5: Democracies Can Perish Democratically Too: Brazilian Democracy on Edge

Liberal democratic elites facilitated the rise of an unequal, multilateral neoliberal economic order, nationally and globally, over the last seventy years. Authoritarian and right populist parties then found ways to gain political power by democratic means in several states and to accelerate a more state-centered and competitive form of neoliberal globalization. Boaventura de Sousa Santos carefully analyzes the major components of the transition to authoritarian rule in the classic case of Brazil. He draws general lessons from this case study and suggests ways of democratic resistance to this trend in Brazil and other states.

Chapter 6: Agonistic Representative Democracy in Europe

This chapter takes the form of an interview with Chantal Mouffe by Pablo Ouziel. In the course of thirteen questions and answers, it ranges over the main substance and central features of Mouffe's complex democratic thought. After exploring the complex theoretical grounding of Mouffe's engagement with and contribution to democratic theory, it explores the implications of her approach for addressing the current conjuncture, which she calls a postdemocracy age. She presents her arguments for a left populist response to dominant forms of right-wing populism and neoliberalism in Europe and diagnoses the role of right populism though the example of Brexit.

Chapter 7: For a Politics of Exile: Criticism in an Era of Global Liberal Decline

The Brexit vote, the election of Donald Trump, and the rise of anti-immigrant, white nationalist political movements throughout Europe have led to considerable handwringing among both liberals and leftists about the future of liberal democracy. For supporters of "the liberal world order" like John Ikenberry, these developments suggest that now is the time for liberal societies to double-down on the core values that make us "who we are." For left Schmittians like Chantal Mouffe, the rightward shift demands a left populist

---

[19] Compare Kochi, "The End of Global Constitutionalism."

reassertion of "the people," sharply contrasted with a reactionary enemy. This chapter argues that both of these responses are deeply misguided insofar as they reinstate imperialist forms of liberal disavowal and deflection, and thus fail to address the core issues behind the resurgence of the right in our era.

Instead, Jeanne Morefield maintains that a truly democratic response to the crisis of liberal democracy requires citizens in the global North to embrace a radically reflective, deconstructive subjectivity that relentlessly calls into question the historical and contemporary shape of "the people" under consideration. To develop this subjective perspective, the paper draws upon Edward Said's notion of exilic criticism and compares it with contemporary liberal cosmopolitanism and left populism. Morefield explores the way this unhoused, unstable perspective enables contrapuntal engagement with those histories of imperialism, settler colonialism, and racialized logics of extraction and dispossession that went into the creation of modern liberal democratic states in the first place. Ultimately, she argues, it is only by reflecting on this constitutive history that citizens in the global North can create the kind of solidaristic, compassionate, and authentically democratic practices necessary to fight the rise of white nationalism and the decline of liberal democracy on a global scale.

Part III: Local/Global Participatory Democracies

Chapter 8: Unwalling Citizenship

How can political theory be more practical, responsive, and projective in its solidarity with people struggling against injustice? Drawing inspiration from Albert Hirschman's work on bottom-up development in mid-century Latin America, Fonna Forman explores the epistemic challenges and theoretical and emancipatory possibilities of "coproducing" knowledge and civic strategies with communities who are navigating unjust asylum and migration policies at the US–Mexico border. Blurring the line between research and activism, she describes a way of doing political theory that is "grounded" through horizontal practices of engagement, in which the theorist accompanies struggle, and seeks dialogue with people and groups who are receptive to collaborative thinking and civic action. She likens this work to a curatorial activity, through which the theorist weaves unique capacities and experiences into a richer account of struggle.

Her case study is the UCSD Community Stations, a network of civic spaces located in four neighborhoods on both sides of the border wall at Tijuana–San Diego that she and partner Teddy Cruz designed in partnership with grassroots agencies for long-term collaborative work. Here, university researchers and residents assemble as partners to share knowledges, and coproduce new narratives, strategies, alliances, and projects. A key activity is designing civic tools to expose the complex histories and mechanisms of political power and injustice, too often hidden within official accounts of the border region, and to render them more accessible.

Forman's critical work on borders and citizenship is grounded in these practices of engagement. Citizenship itself is a fluid, performative concept – an experience of belonging that emerges through shared practices of living, surviving, and transgressing together in a disrupted civic space. While her work prioritizes local civic identity and action, she and her partners also seek to develop broader solidarities by developing "elastic" cultural experiments and civic "stretching" imaginaries that "nest" local conflict in incrementally broader spheres of circulation and interdependence, enabling people to understand themselves as part of larger spatial systems that contain the injustices they face. Her chapter concludes by illustrating this nested scaffold, which expands from the border neighborhoods where she works to the border bioregion, where belonging is oriented around social and environmental ecologies shared by the United States and Mexico, and ultimately to a speculative global border she calls "the Political Equator," which links border zones across the world.

Chapter 9: *Other Wise Democracies: What the Tree Canopies Know*
Just as certain human lifeways are making life on earth unsustainable, intensifying social and political polarizations are rendering genuine democratic dialogue less and less tenable in the West. The growing polarizations point to an ontological rift between two distinct worldviews that are gaining momentum in the West: an individualist, anthropocentric, us/them worldview up/rooted in a logic of disconnect and separation; and an interconnected, ecocentric, relational worldview of Intrabeing with all, including the nonhuman. In this chapter, Rebeccah Nelems argues that the underlying morbidity facing democracy today can be located in the ways it reproduces an individualist ontology to undemocratizing effects. Viewed through this lens, the growing backlashes against democracy appear as a symptom, not a cause, of democracy's crisis – though both must be addressed. Notwithstanding, possible protective factors are also already in our midst. The boundaries and enactments of representative democracies have long been troubled, stretched and shaped by democratizing processes and movements that reference an ontology of intrabeing. The horizons and possibilities for other/wise democracies beyond the bounds of individualism are not only possible, they already are.

Nelems argues that how actors, institutions, and governments within representative democracies engage with these distinct worldviews urgently matters – not just in terms of significance, but also with respect to what kinds of democracy are materialistically enacted in the world. However, if "the means sow the seeds of the end," framing differences as antagonistic, competitive polarities re-enacts the same individualist us/them worldview that underpins the undemocratizing processes. She proposes the "ecocycle," as understood within the living ecosystems of tree canopies, as a relational model of Intrabeing through which we might re-examine and reimagine both democratizing and undemocratizing processes. The ecocycle's two "traps" of poverty and rigidity offer critical insights into the points of connect and disconnect between these processes, as well as the relationship between the lifeways they generate. In their porous, dynamic, entangled, and grounded relationality, tree canopies offer pathways by which the roots of a constellation of democracies might be deparochialized, with a view to leveraging the transformative potential of other/wise democracies.

Chapter 10: Democratizing Revolution: Self-Reflexivity and Self-Limitation Beyond Liberalism

In order to understand the revolutionary potential of democracy, Robin Celikates argues that we need to move beyond homogenizing and nationalist-populist understandings of both revolution and democracy, as well as the notions of popular sovereignty and constituent power that often underlie them. One way to avoid reproducing the exclusions and hierarchies that continue to haunt many attempts to reactivate radical politics today, especially in the register of hegemony, is to pluralize the idea and practice of democratic revolution itself and to look for ways to preserve its internal heterogeneity and ambivalence against the urge of homogenizing its subject, to keep its open-ended character open against the temptations of closure, and to defend the revolutionary and democratic potential of marginalized people against hierarchizing reinscriptions of what counts as properly political or revolutionary.

Preserving both the indeterminacy and the self-reflexivity of democratic practices will not only allow for a more adequate understanding of past revolutions and their ambiguities, but also for a fuller comprehension of the democratic potential and risks of revolutionary action in the present. A radical-democratic and revolutionary remaking of the demos needs to start from those political struggles – most importantly for Celikates' argument, struggles by migrants and Indigenous communities – that call for a radical revision, pluralization, and deterritorialization of the demos, of peoplehood, and of its internal and external borders, all in ways that deeply unsettle the existing terms of the struggle for hegemony rather than making a move within its narrowly nationalist-populist confines.

Part IV: Indigenous Democracies

Chapter 11: Gitxsan Democracy: On Its Own Terms

Democracy is generally understood and discussed as operating within a state and applying to those people within it. How might we conceive of democracy within nonstate societies, such as historic Indigenous societies? In this chapter, Val Napoleon first demonstrates how current negotiations between Gitxsan communities located in northwestern British Columbia and the Canadian government are, in effect, a form of abyssal thinking and, as such, operate to further undermine Gitxsan distributive democracy and governance. Secondly, she examines one exemplar of Indigenous democracy: that of the historic and the present-day Gitxsan society. Finally, Napoleon applies Lon Fuller's account of legalities and relationships to expand how we think about law and governances in Gitxsan society and, by extrapolation, in other Indigenous societies. These explorations work to create another method and an accompanying grammar to analyze contemporary forms of Indigenous governance and some of the arising issues.

Chapter 12:   *Democratic Futures and the Problem of Settler States: An Essay on the Conceptual Demands of Democracy and the Need for Political Histories of Membership*

All states are riven by political histories of the exclusion and oppression of so-called "minorities" and "aliens." Where the uniqueness of the settler states begins to show is in terms of degree. That is, while all states deal with conflicts arising from issues of membership (e.g. secession movements, overlapping claims to territory by neighboring states), within settler states the entirety of their claim to territory rests on the legal exclusion and/or diminishment of Indigenous peoples. This difference of degree is particularly important when we are trying to get a sense of what the future of democracy could be at this particular moment in history. This importance is due to the fact that settler states face a strongly amplified version of the problem of membership, and this puts the formal presumptions of the nation-state (as the modular combination of a singular "people" and a bounded territory) under immense pressure. As a result of this unique degree of pressure on the question of membership, settler states have developed extensive and complicated legal and political structures to meet this challenge.

This means that the political histories of membership in settler states offer us a unique opportunity to gain some insight into the future of democracy in nation-states. Or, put somewhat differently, the intense pressures on the question of membership in settler states have produced something like a core sample of the political climate of Western modernity. In this way, Nichols proposes that one of our best chances to find something meaningful to say about the future of democracy now is to begin the work of writing the political histories of membership in settler states. These histories cannot serve as prediction machines for the future of democracy (this can only ever be the territory of prophets, seers, and charlatans), but they can provide us with concrete examples of situations where the presuppositions of membership in nation-states are exposed and contradicted by the demands of factual situations. In this chapter Nichols elaborates on what he means by a "political history of membership" and uses it to interpret *R. v. Sparrow* and the *Reference re Secession of Quebec* as cases within a political history of membership in Canada.

Chapter 13:   Cracking the Settler Colonial Concrete: Theorizing Engagements with Indigenous Resurgence through the Politics from Below

Stacie Swain's chapter contends that the movement of wild salmon through waterways helps to make visible the web of relationships that connect Indigenous resurgence movements and those who support them within Kwakwaka'wakw, Secwépemc, and Coast Salish territories in the Pacific Northwest. Throughout these territories, migratory salmon return to their headwaters each year to spawn. Along their route, salmon face difficulties created by settler colonialism and the infrastructure of capitalism: open-net fish farms, increased tanker traffic, and pipeline construction. These difficulties, which also create conflicts within Canadian society, can be understood through a spatial conceptualization of settler colonialism in which logics of containment not only attempt to redefine the lands and waters but also subjectivate both Indigenous peoples and settlers within colonial and capitalist relations that foster disconnection.

Too often, she argues, these relations can seem permanent or inevitable. In contrast, Swain shows how we can think differently about relations by using a place-centered and bottom-up methodology inspired by John Borrows' physical philosophy and Heidi Stark and Gina Starblanket's thoughts on relationality. This account draws on personal narrative and critical reflection upon her own involvement, as a settler graduate student and activist working with Kwakwaka'wakw, Secwépemc, and Coast Salish resurgence movements. She describes how Indigenous movements such as the Swanson Occupation, the Matriarch Camp, and the Tiny House Warriors understand wild salmon as relatives within their respective nation-based kinship and governance systems. These movements not only defend salmon as such, but sometimes also invite others to act alongside them. In doing so, these movements open up the possibility for both settlers and Indigenous peoples from other territories to act in accordance with localized Indigenous legal and political orders. This chapter thus contributes a fluid yet grounded perspective to the literature on community-based and participatory democracies, particularly those concerned with how Indigenous and non-Indigenous people can enact mutually beneficial relations and responsibilities to each other and the places we inhabit.

Chapter 14:   Like a Brick Through the Overton Window: Reorienting Our Politics, from the House of Commons to the Tiny House

On June 18, 2019, Canadian Prime Minister Justin Trudeau reapproved the Trans Mountain pipeline expansion. If completed, this project promises to massively expand both the production and the distribution of diluted bitumen from Alberta's tar sands. Trudeau's commitment to this project comes in spite of his global reputation as a progressive legislator and climate warrior, and in stark contrast to his commitments toward "reconciliation" with the Indigenous nations of North America, many of whom have staunchly opposed this project. Indeed, on the same day as Trudeau reapproved the pipeline, a display of counterhegemonic-hegemonic solidarity occurred. Representatives from the Tsleil-Waututh, Squamish, and Musqueam nations, alongside elected officials from the City of Vancouver and the Grand Chief of the Union of BC Indian Chiefs, stood together to redouble their commitment to protecting a coastal ecosystem which they and their communities all share and on which they all depend for survival. Days later, on June 22nd, there was yet another display of resistance to Trudeau's policies, this time in the form of a nearly 20 kilometer march up the length of the Saanich Peninsula, at the head of which was towed a Tiny House. Destined for Secwépemcul'ecw, in the interior of British Columbia, this Tiny House was pulled along by a grassroots coalition of Indigenous leaders from throughout the region and headwaters of the Salish Sea and their settler allies. These displays of resistance represent not merely a redoubling of a fight in the courts or legislatures, but the drawing of a frontline of resistance and a commitment of solidarity that extends from Metulia/ Victoria all the way to the homelands of the Secwépemc nations.

Phil Henderson's chapter begins with this series of events as a vantage point from which to interrogate what Martin Lukas has named "the Trudeau Formula." In his recent book of the same name, Lukas argues that Prime Minister Trudeau mobilizes the language of social justice and, in particular, of "reconciliation," even as his policies evacuate that rhetoric of nearly all its substance. Positing this formula as a core imperative of liberal democratic institutions, Henderson considers at length the manner in which Trudeau's pantomiming of social justice rhetoric serves to close the so-called "Overton window" of political possibility in Canada today, while also suggesting that counterhegemonic and grassroots responses offer the potential of a renewed and reinvigorated radical imagination.

Chapter 15: *Governing Ourselves: Reflections on Reinvigorating Democracy Stimulated by Gitxsan Governance*

This chapter describes the nature and functioning of citizenship (or its equivalent) in nonstate societies, focusing specifically on the Gitxsan societies of northwestern British Columbia. It examines how their nonstate character is reflected in understandings of members' public roles and responsibilities in which lateral relationships count more than hierarchical relationships, kinship plays an essential structuring role, each member is a custodian of their legal culture, and governance and law are continually affirmed, sustained, interpreted, and applied through acts of mutual recognition and affirmation. This comparison leads one to ask whether comparable lateral relations exist in attenuated form in state-structured societies, to inquire into the value of building upon these remnants and extending them in democratic self-organization, and to reflect upon how practically they might be reinvented to revitalize democratic engagement. While the chapter takes seriously lessons from nonstate social organization and argues that we should look for and valorize the nonstate mechanisms that persist within state-structured societies, it does not contend that nonstate forms alone are sufficient for our current predicament. Our challenge, Jeremy Webber proposes, is how to reinstill the reality of citizens' responsibility, stewardship, and agency, while nevertheless enabling the possibility of large-scale democratic decision-making.

Part V: International/Global Democracies

Chapter 16: *The Overlapping Crises of Democracy, Globalization, and Global Governance*

David Held submitted this succinct synopsis of the paper he planned to discuss at the Workshop. He died before the Workshop took place. Held was a world authority on globalization and democratization. He made an unparalleled contribution to these two topics over the last forty years. His premature death is a huge loss to all of us who have learned so much from him and all those who will continue to learn from his scholarship for generations to come.[20]

Held's contribution is a precise summary of the crisis of democracy that he and his coauthors have described at length in *Gridlock: Why Global Cooperation Is Failing When We Need It Most* (2013) and *Beyond Gridlock* (2017). His argument is that the global system of representative democratic states is now locked in a vicious cycle ("gridlock"). While it was initially a virtuous system after World War II, it produced a set of processes that transformed democratic globalization into a vicious system. He gives four reasons for this. The system now undermines democratic cooperation and freezes problem-solving capacity. He describes this gridlocked system in terms of four self-reinforcing stages of noncooperation. This is a "crisis of democracy, as the politics of compromise and accommodation gives way to populism and authoritarianism." In the conclusion, he cautions that we are heading down a path that is similar in several respects to the 1930s. He does not discuss ways forward in this brief chapter, but he does so in *Beyond Gridlock*. It is a testament to the continuing importance of David's work that the chapters in this volume address gridlock and possible paths forward, albeit in their distinctive ways.

Chapter 17: *The Contested Freedom of the Moderns: Conceiving Norm Contestation as the "Glue" for Reordering the Globalized World*

Arguing from an International Relations (IR) theoretical standpoint, Antje Wiener engages cultural multiplicity as both a challenge and a resource for addressing democratic legitimacy in global society. The argument brings long-standing

---

[20] See in particular his classic account of the nine models of democracy within the Western tradition: David Held, *Models of Democracy*, 3rd ed. (Cambridge: Polity Press, 2006).

propositions about cultural diversity in the public philosophy literature to bear in IR theory. It centers on Tully's observation that "different practices of reasoning-with-others are grounded in *distinctive customary local knowledges*, repertoires of practical skills, genres of argumentation and tacit ways of relating to one another. These culturally and historically diverse genres of practical know-how or savoir-faire (*metis* in Greek) are the *intersubjective bases of culturally diverse practices of deliberation*."[21] To account for and evaluate practices of cultural diversity in global society, the chapter presents a "cycle-grid model" to study normative change with reference to the distinct practices of contestation and validation. The chapter elaborates this argument in more detail in three sections. The first section recalls Tully's argument about the "unfreedom of the moderns" and the lack of accounting for cultural diversity as a potential resource to enhance democratic legitimacy based on a practice-based approach to norm(ative) change. The second section turns to the practices of contestation and validation to illustrate how this practice-based approach may be applied to counter the unfreedom of the moderns in global society. The third section concludes with guiding research assumptions for a more pluralistic and diversity-aware IR theory in light of the turn toward "multiplicity."

Chapter 18:   *Conditional Authority and Democratic Legitimacy in Pluralist Space*
This chapter explores how different democratic traditions, each with its own institutions, interact with one another. Drawing on two very different examples – the relationship between the EU and its member states, and the relationship between Indigenous peoples and early settlers – Keith Cherry argues that surprisingly similar mechanisms can be observed in very different contexts. Focusing on one such similarity, he shows how actors in both cases have turned to forms of conditional authority wherein each actor recognizes the legitimacy and autonomy of the other subject to certain substantive conditions. As a result, each actor must satisfy multiple distinct, even strongly divergent, standards of legitimacy in order to maintain effective authority. This practice allows multiple different conceptions of democracy to shape public action without establishing a hierarchy between them or synthesizing their differences.

Part VI: Joining Hands: Eco-Democratic Integration

Chapter 19:   *On Gaia Democracies*
This chapter argues that to respond effectively to the climate and sustainability crises, humans have to think and act as plain members and citizens of democracies with other living beings and within the webs of life that sustain

---

[21] James Tully, "The Unfreedom of the Moderns," in *Public Philosophy in a New Key*, vol. 2, *Imperialism and Civic Freedom* (Cambridge: Cambridge University Press, 2008), 116. The word "metis" is italicized in the original text; other italics are Wiener's own emphasis.

all life on earth. James Tully calls these Gaia democracies. He examines two families or traditions of Gaia democracies. The first are Indigenous democracies akin to the ones John Borrows discusses in the Foreword. The second are recent participatory democracies that are oriented to learning from and modeling their democratic practices on the way in which life systems sustain themselves cyclically and regeneratively. He then examines the vicious and unsustainable global social systems that are the nonlinear causes of the cascading sustainability crises. He argues that the dominant model of representative democracy is subject to these unsustainable systems and unable to respond effectively to the crises. In the final section, he suggests how the growth and integration of Gaia democracies locally and globally can respond effectively to the ecological and social crises by means of democratic ecosocial succession.

Chapter 20: Democracies Joining Hands in the Here and Now
Pablo Ouziel offers his reflections on the workshop and the volume. He describes the development of some of the main themes. Next, he presents six distinct types of working relationships among democratic citizens that he first developed in his research with citizens involved in the 15 M movement in Spain. Then, he shows the presence of these six 'joining hands' relationships in the various chapters. This exercise enables us to see the connections and modes of democratic coordination that are both possible and actual among the diversity of ways of being democratic citizens explicated in the volume. These modes of action-coordination and networking are constitutive features of cogenerating socially and ecologically sustainable democracies.

PART I

DEMOCRATIC ETHOS

I

How Democracy Doesn't End

Anthony Simon Laden

Although worries about the fragility and death of democracy are probably as old as democracy itself, they have, once again, become pressing and fashionable.[1] While not wanting to downplay the dangers of the rise of authoritarianism at home and abroad, in this chapter I try to call into question the familiar story that locates the end of democracy in the breakdown of democratic institutions and their replacement by authoritarian ones. My goal is not to convince you that democracy is more robust than it currently appears, or that there is nothing to worry about, but to offer an alternative approach to thinking about democracy that shifts how we understand what makes democracy fragile and what that tells us about the end of democracy, as well as its futures.[2]

The bulk of the chapter contrasts two pictures of democracy: one that depicts democracy as closed, and one that depicts it as open.[3] The first picture focuses on democracy as an institutional form that enables collectives to legitimately rule themselves. The second picture starts from the idea of democracy as a social form in which people work out together the rules under which they live together. Shifting from the picture of democracy as closed to the picture of democracy as open changes how we think about the relationship of democracy

---

[1] Look no further than the best-selling status of Steven Levitsky and Daniel Ziblatt, *How Democracies Die* (New York: Crown, 2018).

[2] Although my focus here is on how democracies end, and thus assumes that there are (or can be) genuine democracies, and thus the pressing issue is how to sustain and preserve them, the analysis developed herein can also be helpful if we reject that assumption. If there are not (yet) any democracies to preserve, or we are not living in one of them, then the question is less about the end of democracy and more about the beginning. Understanding how democracies don't and do end will shed light on how they don't and do begin.

[3] This contrast has close affinities with and is much indebted to the distinction James Tully draws between modern and diverse forms of citizenship in James Tully, *On Global Citizenship: James Tully in Dialogue* (London: Bloomsbury, 2014).

to its possible end. Exploring that space generates three thoughts about democratic fragility, as suggested by my title. First, from the point of view afforded by the open, social picture, the closed, institutional picture is wrong about what constitutes the death of democracy. Even when democratic institutions are subverted or overthrown, these events need not constitute the death of a democracy. This is not *how* democracy ends. Second, democracies need not end this way because even when democratic institutions break down (or when they never get fully up and running in the first place), democracy does not end as long as people remain committed to continuing to work out together how to live together. So, the demise of institutions is not how democracy *ends*. Third, once we begin to think of democracy as a way of living together, we will also see that democratic politics is an activity that is in principle ongoing: it is not the sort of action that can be completed or finished. If we picture democracy as a way of living together, then our work as democratic citizens is never over and done with. Thus, democracy *doesn't* end.

Though the questions and circumstances driving this chapter are practical and political, the chapter itself is a work of philosophy. It thus deals primarily with ideas, and how they might be described, fit together, and be contrasted with one another. Nevertheless, my approach to philosophy is broadly pragmatist in the following sense: I do not take myself to be involved in a theoretical or metaphysical investigation into the true nature of democracy. I think of concepts as tools we use to make sense of the world around us. The value of a tool comes in what it allows us to do: here, how it allows us to think about some part of the world or our lives. The concepts with which we think are useful when they illuminate features or possibilities we might otherwise overlook, or when they show their connections to other, seemingly unrelated, ideas or phenomena. Altering the shape of those concepts can thus reveal features of our world that would otherwise remain obscure. My aim in laying out the two pictures and bringing out how they shape our thoughts about the end of democracy is to help us see both where our vision is blinkered if we insist on one picture and what possibilities for action emerge when we think differently. By seeing how familiar thoughts about the end of democracy draw strength and plausibility from the first picture, and seeing how a different picture refocuses our attention, we can begin to see the possibilities hinted at in my title that the first picture obscures.

DEMOCRACY AS CLOSED

Democracy, like any social, political, or governmental form, offers a solution to a problem. We can thus begin to describe each picture of democracy by laying out the problem it takes democracy to solve and the particular features that make its picture of democracy a solution to that problem. What I am calling the picture of democracy as closed takes democracy to be a solution to a problem about collective action and decision. In particular, it starts from the question of how a large group of people can make and enact truly collective decisions in ways that give those decisions authority and thus make the actions that follow from them legitimate. Among the many things that make the problem of collective decision-making hard is the problem of dissent. A genuinely collective decision should be one that even those members of the collective who disagree with it can nevertheless regard as legitimately theirs. The picture of democracy as closed offers a solution to this picture by, centrally, describing a set of procedures and rules protected and enacted by institutions that serve the function of legitimate decision-making. At the heart of this picture of democracy, then, are things such as free and fair elections, representative legislative and executive institutions, and the rule of law. Among the features of these institutions, rules, and procedures that make them democratic (apart from enabling collective self-government) is that they treat citizens as both free and equal. Citizens are equal because the procedures for collective decision-making give them (in principle) equal say in the decisions. Citizens are free because, by giving them the capacity to issue authoritative commands to themselves, democratic institutions allow them to be self-governing, which is a form of freedom. It offers a solution to the problem of dissent and disagreement insofar as citizens can accept the authority and legitimacy of the procedure, and thus its results, even if they otherwise disagree with those results.

Starting from this basic outline, a number of familiar features of democratic institutions follow naturally. First, for democratic institutions and procedures to be mechanisms of legitimate collective decision-making, they must be fixed and settled before the decision in question is made. Consider the design of elections in this regard: elections are able to bestow legitimacy on their winners only if, among other requirements, it is not open to officials or others to change, after the fact, how votes are counted or what decision follows from the votes cast. What renders the decisions and actions taken through these procedures democratic is precisely that they result from following these procedures and working within these institutions. This is why violations of election law, whether through voter fraud, ballot tampering, voter suppression, or post-election reinterpretations of what counts as a valid vote, are thought to strike at the heart of the democratic character of a society. But notice that it also lends force to judgments that are dismissive of protests, marches, and other extra-electoral activities in a well-functioning democracy that aim to change policy or demand that duly elected government officials step down. Although such actions can be understood as attempts to change the views of elected officials or the voting public, they are also always the action of a small minority of that public. Since it is only by following established rules and procedures for decision-making that the entire public can make legitimate decisions, acting to change such decisions by other means will appear to be democratically suspect.[4]

---

[4] My point here is not to deny that one could develop a democratic theory within this picture that gave a legitimate role to such action, but that the picture shapes a particular orientation toward such action to begin with.

Of course, the actual procedures and institutions adopted by a given society need not be perfect. So, this picture will accept that democratic procedures and their outcomes can be criticized at any time for being neither free nor fair. But such criticism, on this picture, will only be legitimate if it points out how the procedure and institutions fail to yield legitimate collective decisions and acts of self-governance, and its "proper" use will be to reform how the next election is run, not to "overturn" the results of the previous one.

This is, I hope, a familiar line of thought. It sketches out, for instance, the terrain on which a number of central debates in democratic theory take place: between aggregative and deliberative conceptions of democracy, among various theories of deliberative democracy, and among institutional approaches over the place of representation in democratic institutions. In fact, I suspect that for some readers this characterization of democracy appears not to be a particular picture of democracy at all, but merely a basic description of what democracy is.[5]

Note, however, how starting from this basic picture highlights some issues and obscures others. First, it leads us to focus, as we assess the democratic nature and health of a society, primarily on its procedures, laws, and institutions, rather than on the actions of its citizens. We need not take this point too starkly. A focus on institutions need not deny or ignore that the well-functioning of institutions depends on the proper behavior of those who run, maintain, interact with, and inhabit them, just as a focus on the behavior of citizens need not deny or ignore that citizens interact in large part via various institutions. The difference, rather, shows itself in two ways. The first is the order of priority we assign to the well-functioning of institutions in contrast to various good civic behaviors. On this picture, we see the value of good civic behavior as allowing for the properly democratic institutions to continue to function, rather than seeing the value of democratic institutions as enabling and easing certain forms of civic interaction. The second is whether we look to elites and office holders or ordinary citizens as the source of democratic health or fragility. On the picture of democracy as closed, the health of democracy lies primarily with elites and officeholders and, to the extent that the actions of the rest of us matter, insofar as we hold the office of citizen (primarily as voters).[6]

---

[5] See, for instance, Levitsky and Ziblatt, *How Democracies Die*, 17: "for the sake of clarity, we are defining democracy as a system of government with regular, free, and fair elections, in which all adult citizens have the right to vote and possess basic civil liberties such as freedom of speech and association"; and Rainer Bauböck, *Democratic Inclusion: Rainer Bauböck in Dialogue* (Manchester: Manchester University Press, 2018), 8: "Democracy is a system of political rule that provides legitimacy for collectively binding decisions and coercive government legitimacy under conditions of deep and persistent diversity."

[6] I hope to say more in future work about how each picture, in particular the open one, generates an approach to civic virtue. Note here that on the closed picture, the civic virtues will be those traits and abilities that support the well-functioning of democratic institutions, and they will be of particular importance for those whose positions give them influence over those institutions:

A perhaps less obvious but for my purposes more important feature of the picture of democracy as closed is that it supports an attitude of what I will call "gatekeeping." If the health of a democracy lies in the health of its institutions, rules, and procedures, then those merit protection from forces that might undermine them. On this picture, those forces interfere with proper democratic principles governing who is allowed to participate in collective decision-making and on what grounds. Protecting democracy then involves making sure that the various boundaries laid out by our democratic principles are respected and protected. This follows from the thought that our procedures, rules, and institutions must be fixed ahead of time in order to properly render and legitimately generate truly collective decisions. In addition, breaches of well-drawn boundaries compromise and corrupt the procedures that the boundaries safeguard by allowing those procedures to be hijacked or turned away from their basic purpose of generating legitimate collective decisions of those properly understood to constitute the demos.[7] Setting up those boundaries incorrectly or allowing them to be porous can allow undemocratic elements into or exclude certain legitimate voices from our politics. In either case, we risk threats to democracy. Thus, working within the picture of democracy as closed leads us to understand the work of protecting democracy, keeping it from coming to an end, in terms of defending those boundaries.

The focus on boundaries is not merely a question of geographical borders and immigration, although immigration is one terrain on which this gatekeeping orientation manifests itself. Nor is such a focus merely the position of those who want to keep others out or draw the boundaries narrowly. Many advocates of greater democratic inclusion are also arguing about where the gates and boundaries should go: they just want them further out. They are no less interested in and concerned with patrolling the boundaries once they are properly drawn. The orientation to gatekeeping shows itself not in the wish to draw the boundaries narrowly, but in the thought that the basic questions to be answered in working out a theory of democracy are where to erect those boundaries and how to protect them.

The first and most prominent set of boundaries separates the members of the demos from those outside of it: it determines who gets to participate in the collective decision-making. Debates about this boundary include debates about immigration, but also about the extent of the suffrage within a given territory. Historically, these have included arguments about expanding suffrage to the poor, women, and formerly conquered or enslaved peoples. In political theory these days, a more common debate concerns whether fair principles of inclusion

---

officeholders in their official functions, and citizens when they interact with the state and especially when they vote.

[7] For a recent example of this line of thinking, from a closed institutional picture of democracy concerned with the importance of gatekeeping, see Levitsky and Ziblatt, *How Democracies Die.*

should extend to various resident noncitizens as well as both citizen and noncitizen nonresidents. Thus, debates between advocates of an all-affected or an all-subjected principle for determining the demos are debates about this kind of boundary.[8] Although these recent debates appear to go beyond where and how to draw geographical or demographic boundaries, they nevertheless rely on the same picture. They assume that it is only once we have properly established the membership criteria for the demos, and thus properly drawn the boundaries between those who constitute the demos and those who are outside of it, that the procedures that allow the demos to make collective decisions can be properly legitimate and authoritative. They merely acknowledge that, in an age of mass migration and global interaction, the demos need not form a geographically cohesive set of individuals.

One of the more perverse effects of taking the question about the constitution of the demos as fundamental in these ways is how it shapes discussions in settler colonial states, such as the United States, Canada, Australia, and New Zealand, about how to secure justice for Indigenous peoples. Its model of treating others as free and equal involves their inclusion in the demos, and thus their subjection to the principles and institutions of a given democratic state as citizens. Treating colonized people who wish to maintain their own sovereignty as full members of the colonial demos does not, however, undo the injustice of colonialism. It finalizes it.[9]

The second boundary concerns the inputs to the democratic procedures: the types of speech or action that can contribute to the collective decision-making process. Many debates over the proper definition of "reasonable" or over the criteria of public reason aim to settle the proper place of this boundary. Thus, both those who draw those concepts narrowly and those who argue for a more capacious understanding of appropriate methods of civic discourse and action are oriented toward gatekeeping along this boundary.[10] In both cases, the underlying assumption is that, in order for democratic procedures and institutions to serve their purpose, we need to work out ahead of time a set of criteria to determine their acceptable inputs, and thus distinguish the inputs that

---

[8] For a recent discussion of this debate and a proposal that blends elements of each side while not abandoning the basic framework being outlined here, see Bauböck, *Democratic Inclusion*.

[9] For two versions of this diagnosis that offer different but perhaps complementary responses, see Glen Sean Coulthard, *Red Skin, White Masks: Rejecting the Colonial Politics of Recognition* (Minneapolis: University of Minnesota Press, 2014), and Dale A. Turner, *This Is Not a Peace Pipe: Towards a Critical Indigenous Philosophy* (Toronto: University of Toronto Press, 2006). For further discussion of Indigenous responses to Canadian settler colonialism, see Michael Asch, John Borrows, and James Tully, eds., *Resurgence and Reconciliation: Indigenous-Settler Relations and Earth Teachings* (Toronto: University of Toronto Press, 2018).

[10] See, for instance, Stanley Fish, "Boutique Multiculturalism, or Why Liberals Are Incapable of Thinking about Hate Speech," *Critical Inquiry* 23, no. 2 (1997): 378–95; Iris Marion Young, "Activist Challenges to Deliberative Democracy," *Political Theory* 29, no. 5 (2001): 670–90; and Iris Marion Young, *Inclusion and Democracy* (Oxford: Oxford University Press, 2002).

are necessary for the procedure to be democratic from those which would pose a threat.

Finally, there is the boundary that sets the legitimate scope of the outputs of democratic procedure: the scope and limits of democratic authority. Debates about where to locate the boundary between private and public, or the extent of certain basic, fundamental, and inalienable rights, often take this form. In each case, we are working out and trying to institutionally establish the terms under which our collective decision can be legitimate, and where the authority of that process runs out. From this perspective, we can see one role of the individual private rights often described as the liberties of the moderns as placing a gate beyond which democratic action cannot proceed.[11]

It is this orientation toward gatekeeping and boundary-drawing questions that leads me to call this a picture of democracy as "closed." It also supports the familiar picture about how democracies end: democracies die when they can no longer maintain their boundaries. Depending on which boundary is breached, we get a different form of concern about the fragility or end of democracy. Breaches of the membership boundary are the particular concern of nationalists, who worry that hitherto foreign people may enter the decision-making process and change its results ("undermining our way of life"). Breaches of the input barrier tend to concern institutionalists, who worry that democracies end when prominent agents within democratic institutions (again including citizens qua voters) fail to safeguard them against antidemocratic ideas or behaviors.[12] Finally, breaches of the output barrier tend to concern libertarians, who worry about state overreach: democracy ends when the state starts to meddle in the lives of individuals or the market.

A second broad feature of this picture of democracy is the sharp distinction it draws between the civic action of democratic citizens and the background structure of institutions and laws in which those activities take place, and thus also between what might be called constitutional and ordinary politics. The point of basic democratic institutions and laws is not only to identify the class of citizens, but also to enable them to engage in action that counts as legitimately political and thus democratic. My actions count as legitimately political and democratic as long as they are carried out within the established boundaries and via the various institutions and procedures that have been established for that action, since it is through such institutions that my individual action can contribute to legitimate collective decisions and actions. And while those procedures and institutions can be challenged and changed, this picture leads us to hold them fixed in our thoughts when we are thinking about what might be

---

[11] Tully, *On Global Citizenship*, especially 14–15. As Tully points out, on this picture of democracy, private individual rights set out bounds beyond which democratic institutions can't go, thus limiting the scope of public, political rights.

[12] This, in various ways, is the sort of threat that Levitsky and Ziblatt discuss in *How Democracies Die*.

called ordinary democratic politics. The model at work here is of a stable container that is sharply distinguished from what it contains. The actions we take and the speech we engage in within the boundaries of these institutions make a difference to what those institutions do but not to what those institutions are. We do not, on this picture, shape the institutions that contain our ordinary politics (electoral campaigns, legislative debates, regulatory hearings, etc.) through our ordinary politics. On this picture, it is, after all, precisely the ability of democratic institutions to contain our politics that renders our political actions democratic and thus capable of being legitimate.

This sharp distinction is what leads those working with this picture of democracy to think that the health or death of a democracy is to be read from its institutions, laws, and procedures – its constitutional structure – and not in the behavior of its citizens. On this picture, democracies die when their boundaries no longer hold and their institutions collapse or are corrupted and transformed into nondemocratic ones, not when their citizens stop acting like democratic citizens. Note, however, that this means that if we are trying to figure out whether a democracy is healthy or coming to or at an end, our attention will be drawn toward institutional and constitutional features, and not the manner in which we conduct our ordinary political lives.

This has two consequences that I note briefly here but return to when discussing the contrasting picture of democracy. The first is a reformulation of a point I made earlier: on this picture, the death of democracy is primarily an institutional and elite affair. It happens when elections are subverted or ignored by *officials*, when *leaders* put themselves above the law, find ways to change the law without following established democratic procedures, or use their authority beyond its established limits, and no one else *in authority* (including, of course, citizens in their office of voter) rises up to stop them. When these things happen, it is somewhat irrelevant what ordinary citizens do outside of the voting booth. Their main role is through their participation as gatekeepers in prescribed institutional procedures.[13] The second concerns what this picture obscures: it makes it hard to see how the manner in which we conduct ourselves politically as ordinary citizens can itself mark the end of democracy, as well as how it can work to preserve a democracy even as its institutional structure breaks down. As we turn to the picture of democracy as open, I hope to bring into our vision how such actions can change how we think about how democracies don't end.

DEMOCRACY AS OPEN

What I call the picture of democracy as open sees democracy as a solution to a different problem than the picture of democracy as closed. Here, we start with

---

[13] Citizens can, for instance, interrupt the antidemocratic attack on institutions by a given political party by rejecting it at the polls at the first sign of such tendencies, before the party has a chance to remake or merely ignore the electoral system.

the problem not of collective decision-making but of living together. Specifically, how can a group of people live together under conditions of pluralism in a manner that treats them all as free and equal? The rough democratic solution to this problem is that we can do this if we also work out together the terms on which we live together.

By focusing on several aspects of this formulation, we can see why it generates a different picture of democracy – as open. First, the emphasis is on living and doing things *together*. I mean to signal here a more robust form of interaction than mere coordination or a procedure to which each has an input. We can begin to see the force of the idea of "acting together" if we contrast it, as I have done elsewhere, with "acting side-by-side."[14] Acting and living side-by-side requires us to coordinate our actions to avoid running into each other or getting into irresolvable conflicts, and thus requires that each be aware of others and what they are doing. But that coordination can be achieved without there being anything that *we* see as *our* action by, for instance, a procedure for collective decision-making that pools our individual choices in a fair manner. In contrast, when we act and live *together*, we undertake a more robust form of sharing, where we not only coordinate our actions but understand those actions as *ours*, as what *we* are doing (together) that is not reducible to what each of us does. We act together when we act in a way that is governed by shared norms, rules, or goals that don't merely coordinate our behavior (lay out what each of us is to do) but make our action intelligible to us as our action (as what *we* are doing).

This feature of acting and living together generates a particular problem under conditions of pluralism, given that pluralism involves precisely not agreeing about particular values, norms, and meanings. If we are united by a single faith, worldview, or mission, acting together may be psychologically difficult, but it is more or less clear what it would entail. The problem that democracy aims to solve is how to act and live together, given that we are not so united. It does so by giving us a task to do together that turns out to be possible under conditions of pluralism: working out together the terms of our living together.

To genuinely work out together those terms, we need to treat one another as free and equal: we cannot impose those terms on others. And this, in turn, generates a surprising result. My continual acceptance of what we do as done in my name means that I need to always have a way of challenging and criticizing the terms on which we act together. If I am prohibited from raising concerns about or criticisms of what we do, or if these concerns and criticisms are not taken normatively seriously,[15] then I am no longer working out with others how

---

[14] Anthony Simon Laden, *Reasoning: A Social Picture* (Oxford: Oxford University Press, 2012), 20–23.
[15] I mean here to distinguish cases where citizens take a protest movement or its tactics seriously by straining to grasp its criticisms and appreciate their normative force from those where they take

we live together or what we do, and so I am no longer interacting democratically with them. But, of course, this also means that if I am not open to hearing and taking seriously the criticisms and concerns of others, then I am not engaging democratically with them. So, on this picture, the activity of working out together the terms on which we live together requires continual openness to criticism, challenge, and contestation. In fact, it is this constant remaining open to criticism, challenge, and contestation that comprises, in large part, the activity of working out together the terms on which we live together. Moreover, since among the things we need to keep open to challenge are the very institutional forms through which we engage in this activity, we cannot preserve or sustain this activity by locking it into a fixed institutional form. Instead, we preserve this openness by sustaining an ever-shifting pluricentric conversation, wherein we engage with different people in different situations and for different purposes, but in which from any of them we can raise challenges to and criticisms of those different people. This, then, is the basic outline of the picture of democracy as open. Rather than being built around a set of fixed, fair procedures, it is modeled on a set of ongoing conversations. And so, preserving the health of a democratic society will not be a matter of patrolling its boundaries, but of widening the scope and enlivening the quality of its various conversations.

In fact, on this picture, establishing and patrolling fixed boundaries will serve to undermine rather than protect the democratic character of our interactions insofar as it cuts off certain avenues of criticism and contestation from democratic legitimacy. Giving up on the gatekeeping function of boundaries also dramatically changes how we think of the demos. Rather than thinking of this as a group whose membership is determined ahead of time and then given a certain status within various institutions, we can think of it as one whose membership is always open: my being a citizen is a matter of whether I engage with others about how to live together in this open fashion.[16]

That a democracy is not marked by firm boundaries also gives us a way to rethink what democracy might look like in colonial societies. Challenges from Indigenous people to settler colonial societies' practices of occupation and colonization do not, generally, come in the form of demands to integrate more fully into the colonial society. They more often take the form of wanting the colonizer to withdraw and recognize the sovereignty and dignity of the colonized society to run its own affairs in its own ways and relate to its land

the movement seriously because it poses a threat to their comfort or security and so needs to be dealt with in either the positive or negative sense of that phrase even though they do not think of it as addressing its concerns in a legitimate way.

[16] For an approach to citizenship that works this way, see Tully's discussion of what he calls "civic citizenship" in Tully, *On Global Citizenship*. One consequence of this approach is that the category of "citizen" becomes broader than those with a certain legal status. Being a citizen is a matter of participating in the activities of democratic life: one becomes a civic citizen by acting like one. In what follows, this is how I will use the term.

in a manner it might not share with the colonial society. Such demands often include insisting on borders and erecting barriers to entry, and so seem to involve a rejection of democratic relationships between settler and Indigenous peoples. However, if we think of these demands and these borders from the perspective of the picture of democracy as open, we can make, hear, and respond to these demands differently. One way to think about how to do so is to use an image from early attempts to work out such relationships between Indigenous peoples in North America and European settlers: we can hear them as a demand that each side paddle its own canoe while acknowledging that we share the same river. That is, we can interact democratically without all sitting in the same canoe (sharing the same institutions) so long as we can continue talking with and listening to one another as we work out where we are vis-à-vis each other.[17] Because democracy on this picture need not be contained within and protected by fixed and solid boundaries, we can develop means of democratic interaction that take place across borders. A demand to establish or respect a border, then, need not involve a rejection of continued democratic relations across it.

Because this picture of democracy does not require a fixed set of institutions, rules, and procedures to contain the action of its citizens and render them democratic, it also need not insist on a sharp divide between constitutional and ordinary politics. Among the things we do in the course of democratic living together is working out the terms on which we live together (as well as, as we have seen, who *we* are). The terms of living together are not something that is, in principle, to be set up, worked out, and nailed down prior to our democratic interaction. These terms also require openness to challenge and contestation from within the activity of living together; the form of the container is shaped by the activity of what it contains. To turn that around, the mere fact that a group of people are challenging the very terms on which they live with others does not put it outside the boundaries of proper civic action. In fact, it is precisely that they are challenging those terms that makes it properly democratic civic action. This means that the democratic quality of our life together is in part a function of how we conduct that life and the ordinary politics that we undertake along the way. We can erode the democratic features of a society by erecting gates and failing to be open to other voices, criticisms, and contestations, and we can revive and bolster it by taking seriously those criticisms and contestations and taking each other normatively seriously.

This blurring of the line between ordinary life and politics and constitutional politics then changes the place of law and other democratic institutions on this

---

[17] The image of the two canoes comes from the two-row wampum that signified early treaty relations between the Haudenosaunee Confederacy and European settlers. See Turner, *Peace Pipe*, 45–55, 127–29; and Kayanesenh Paul Williams, *Kayanerenkó:wa: The Great Law of Peace* (Winnipeg: University of Manitoba Press, 2018), 48. On the general importance to Indigenous societies of different forms of recognition, see Coulthard, *Red Skin*.

picture. Although laws and institutions continue to provide a framework for our interaction, they are also the outcome of that interaction, and it is precisely their being vulnerable to the effects of that interaction that make them democratic, insofar as this vulnerability is what it means for them to be open to contestation and challenge. Because the role of laws and institutions is not only to enable legitimate collective decisions but to provide a framework for and an expression of our mode of living together, they cannot be thought of or justified by their gatekeeping function. Serving such a role would be a sign they were not fully democratic on this picture.

Adopting a picture of democracy as open has several implications for our thinking about democracy (for what we notice, see, and pay attention to) that are important for addressing the questions with which I began. First, the democratic character of society lies not merely in a set of fixed laws and institutions, but in how we live together or fail to, and thus in our ordinary interactions as well. A society with representative institutions in which citizens no longer engage with each other in the project of working out together how to live together, or are no longer invested in that project, is not merely a democratic society burdened with bad or apathetic behavior, but one whose democratic character has frayed. In contrast, a society in which people genuinely work together in an open fashion to determine the terms of how they live together but do so without the traditional institutions of representative democracy is one that displays signs of democratic health. A society in which we are concerned to delineate and enforce various boundaries, to ignore or silence certain voices, or to cease to interact in a way that counts as genuine engagement will, to that extent, be undemocratic, while one where we work to make ourselves intelligible to others and strive to understand them and their criticisms and concerns will be democratic, possibly independently of the form of the institutions in which we take these actions. This means that when we are assessing whether a society is democratic or whether its democratic character is imperiled or at an end, we need to look beyond the health of its formal institutions. Note that the focus of the open picture on civic practices does not deny the importance of institutions. Institutions play a central role in making it possible for groups of people to live together democratically, and some sorts of institutions do this better than others. Some institutions and other large-scale social dynamics obstruct or block attempts to work and live together. Adopting the open picture, then, does not entail an anti-institutional orientation or an exclusive focus on civic practices and virtues. Nevertheless, on the open picture, what constitutes a society as democratic is its civic practices, not its institutions, and so the institutions will be justified to the extent that they help to enable those practices and proper targets of criticisms if they erode or block those processes. So, for instance, it might be more important for state institutions to be trusted and trustworthy than for them to be formally democratic as defined by a set of fixed criteria.

Second, picturing democracy as open in this way shifts us from thinking of the ideal democratic citizen as one who faithfully patrols various boundaries toward one who displays attitudes and practices of hospitality, inclusion, and neighborliness. That is, it suggests that, as citizens, we should be less concerned with which people, behaviors, or topics are a threat to various democratic norms, institutions, or values and how to protect ourselves and our institutions from them. Rather, we should learn to see our democracy as supported and sustained when we strive to be open to everyone's contribution to how we live together: when we treat others not as outsiders and threats, but as neighbors and potential civic friends. The idea of hospitality I want to invoke here is not one that makes a sharp distinction between residents and guests and works out a special set of norms for the treatment of those who are mere guests, but one which welcomes those who cross various boundaries and treats them not as outsiders at all, but as welcome members of society. That is, it is an attitude which approaches those who might be taken for outsiders and accepts them as full members whose voices, concerns, and needs are taken as seriously as anyone else's, and which recognizes that each of us is also an outsider and guest to the extent that we are dependent on the hospitality of our neighbors and fellow citizens for our position within the demos. This contrasts with a view that delineates and protects boundaries by placing various burdens and conditions on those who find themselves on the other side of those boundaries before they can be admitted in good standing to democratic processes.

Third, the interactions that constitute our living together democratically on this picture are, in principle, ongoing. The actions that constitute democratic politics on this picture are not undertaken merely to achieve a fixed goal or end point, but are, in principle, such as can be continued indefinitely. Living together democratically, unlike passing this piece of legislation or electing that candidate or winning this argument, is not something we come to the end of even when we complete some particular action. There is thus no end point of democratic action: democracy does not, in this sense, end. However, actions that are in principle ongoing can only continue if the conditions for their continuation are met; these democratic actions are not eternal and their continuation is neither automatic nor guaranteed. Ongoing action must be sustained even as it is carried out. Furthermore, there is no guarantee that, in succeeding at our proximate aims in an ongoing activity, we thereby lay the conditions for continuing on beyond that point. It is thus part of the work of doing such actions well that we attend to and provide for the continued existence of those conditions. While in conversation with you, I can successfully tell a joke or argue a point in a way that nevertheless undermines the conditions which would allow us to keep conversing. Being good at conversing, and not merely telling jokes or making arguments, depends on my also attending to the conditions necessary for us to continue our conversation. Similarly, I can successfully work toward an institutional or legal reform that I regard as improving the justice of my society, but do so in a way that erodes the conditions under which we can continue living together democratically. Moreover, since the activity of working out together the terms of living together is pluricentric, both the mechanisms of sustenance and those of erosion may involve effects on other conversations and interactions. Making the ongoing nature of democratic action visible helps us see the value of acting in ways that are democratically sustaining, which support and sustain the conditions under which we can go on living together, and thus why it might be worth bearing their extra costs.

Finally, if democracy is to be thought of as open in this way, then it cannot have a fixed and settled institutional form. That is, we cannot set out ahead of time the essential institutional features of a democratic society and then ask of any given society or practice whether it conforms to that template. Since being democratic is being open to contestation, it must be that the shape of a democracy can change in response to criticism without it thereby becoming undemocratic. What will mark societies as democratic is not that they conform to a particular range of familiar shapes, but that they display a certain kind of self-preserving activity, a way of going on, and that the shapes they come to both arise out of and make possible the continuation of that form-preserving activity.

We can sum up the points noted here by saying that if we picture democracy as open, then we need to pay attention to the activities that might sustain or undermine the possibility of going on together.[18] We cannot assume, as we will if we approach the matter from within the closed picture, that the democratic character of our society inheres entirely in a set of fixed and stable institutions and laws that can persist indefinitely without any further upkeep even if they are also vulnerable to attack and subversion. Rather, on this picture, the lifeblood of democracies is how their citizens interact, and this is something to which they must both continually commit and whose conditions they must continually sustain going forward. This, then, gives us a way to understand how democracy doesn't end as well as how it does.

Democracy doesn't end as long as those living together continue to work out together the terms on which they live together, something they do by remaining open and responsive to the challenges and criticisms of the forms that living together takes, and do so in ways that preserve the conditions under which they can continue to do that. Since such activities and such conditions are not entirely dependent on particular institutional forms or policies, democracy need not end when democratic institutions break down or adopt antidemocratic policies and laws. Of course, acting this way can be made easier or harder by various institutions and material conditions, and so institutional break down can be a step on the way toward, and increase the likelihood of, a democracy coming to

---

[18] I borrow the phrase "going on together" and its connection to the task of democratic societies from Josiah Ober, *Athenian Legacies: Essays on the Politics of Going on Together* (Princeton, NJ: Princeton University Press, 2018).

an end. Nevertheless, from the point of view of this picture of democracy, the end of democracy is not something that can just happen to us; it is something we must do to ourselves. That means, however, that it is also always within our power to forestall the end of democracy or even renew and sustain it. Actions that are in principle ongoing can be restarted even after they have been cut off or wound down if the conditions for their continuation can be regenerated.

On the other hand, it means that democracies do end when citizens stop acting and living together as democratic citizens, when we replace democratic engagement with forms of interaction that lack the features described herein, or when we neglect the conditions that make it possible for us to continue doing so. Democracies can die in this way with all of their institutions, laws, and constitutional structures intact. When that happens, although we can revive our democracy by developing and deploying new democratic habits, there is no one else, and no institution, law, or procedure, that can do it for us. In other words, democracy ends, or doesn't, with us.

Democracy, Boundaries, and Respect

David Owen

In this chapter, I focus on the relationship between democracy, boundaries, and respect in terms of the distinction between civil and civic pictures of democracy, a distinction which can be initially glossed as that between democracy as a particular mode of civil order or constituted authority and democracy as a specific mode of civic agency or constituting power. The motivation for taking up this focus is not just that I think it can help to clarify some conceptual tensions in democratic theory concerning the boundary problem, but that it can serve as a way of reminding us of the priority of citizenship as a political practice to citizenship as a legal status and the salience of that priority for reflecting on contemporary problems of democracy.

The argument proceeds as follows. In the first section, I sketch out the conceptual distinction between the civil and civic pictures of democracy, while in the second section I consider their relationship. In the third section, I turn to address the implications of this picture for reflection on the democratic boundary problem before, in the final section, elucidating the importance of the civil–civic relationship for democratization and forms of democratic solidarity. I conclude by drawing out some wider lessons of this way of reflecting on democracy for its theory and practice.

THE CONTRAST BETWEEN CIVIL AND CIVIC MODES OF CITIZENSHIP AND PICTURES OF DEMOCRACY

Let me begin by introducing the distinction between "civil" and "civic" orientations by drawing on James Tully's contrast between the two modes of citizenship – civil citizenship and civic citizenship – which is sketched thus:

Whereas modern citizenship focuses on citizenship as a universalisable legal status underpinned by institutions and processes of rationalisation that enable and constrain the possibility of civil activity (an institutionalised/universal orientation), diverse citizenship focuses on the singular civic activities and diverse way that these are more or less institutionalised or blocked in different contexts (a civic activity/contextual orientation). Citizenship is not a status given by the institutions of the modern constitutional state and international law, but negotiated practices in which one becomes a citizen through participation.[1]

Two dimensions of this account need spelling out for our current purposes.

The first is the concept of "modes of citizenship," which refers to both "a distinctive language of citizenship and its traditions of interpretation" and "the corresponding practices and institutions to which it refers and in which it is used."[2] Modes of citizenship are thus to be conceived in terms of praxis, where this praxiological approach is one in which "the praxis of practice" is seen as "the medium of constitution of subjectivity."[3] Through the praxis of practice, we acquire the abilities that are, at once, the ability to perform actions that realize the goods of the practices in which we are engaged and the ability to direct our own activity as practitioners of and as participants in the practice: thus "subjectivity is the practical self-relation of self-direction that is located in being able to carry something out."[4] What distinguishes different modes of citizenship is the orientation or, more precisely, the *practical attitude* with which they engage in the activity – that is, their practical attitude as participants in a practice, where such attitudes cannot simply be adopted at will, but are acquired through practice.

The second is the contrast between the two modes of citizenship. In general terms, civil citizenship as a mode of citizenship stands toward citizenship "as a [legal] status within an institutional framework," whereas civic citizenship is oriented to citizenship "as *negotiated practices*, as praxis – as actors and activities in contexts."[5] On the former view, civil action necessarily presupposes an institutional structure of legal rules; on the latter view, primacy is accorded to "the concrete games of citizenship and the ways that they are played."[6] Thus, in relation to civic citizenship, Tully stresses: "Civic activities – what citizens do and the ways they do them – can be more or less institutionalized and rationalized (in countless forms), but this is secondary."[7] Notice that this general contrast already constructs a fundamental difference in the mode of self-relation of individuals to themselves as citizens. The mode of citizenship-formation characteristic of the civil stance is of the individual standing to themselves as occupant of an "office" specified by a range of rights and duties, whereas that of the civic stance is of the individual standing

---

[1] James Tully, *Public Philosophy in a New Key*, vol. 2, *Imperialism and Civic Freedom* (Cambridge: Cambridge University Press, 2008), 248.
[2] Tully, *Public Philosophy*, 246.
[3] Christoph Menke, "Two Kinds of Practice: On the Relation Between Social Discipline and the Aesthetics of Existence," *Constellations* 10 (2003): 200.
[4] Menke, "Two Kinds of Practice," 201.   [5] Tully, *Public Philosophy*, 269 (my emphasis).
[6] Tully, *Public Philosophy*, 269.   [7] Tully, *Public Philosophy*, 269.

to themselves as an agent whose agency is fundamentally relational, bound up in relations of acting in concert with other agents. Civil citizens stand toward themselves as persons who are *at liberty* (i.e. free from subjection to the will of another) in virtue of their enjoyment of the civil rights and duties that compose the office of citizenship under law to take up opportunities to participate as political equals in determining the law to which they are subject as subjects of a given political institution of governance. We can see a version of this stance in, for example, Rawls' characterization of citizens as bound by a duty of civility (with respect to matters of basic justice and constitutional essentials) that requires them to engage in public reasoning by standing to themselves as if they were lawmakers. By contrast, civic citizens "manifest the freedom *of* participation":

Civic freedom is not an opportunity [to participate] but a manifestation: neither freedom *from* nor freedom *to* … but freedoms *of* and *in* participation, and *with* fellow citizens. The civic citizen is not the citizen of an institution (a nation-state or an international law) but the free citizen of the "free city": that is, *any* kind of civic world or democratic "sphere" that comes into being and is reciprocally held aloft by the civic freedom of its citizens, from the smallest *deme* or commune to glocal federations.[8]

This contrast has significant implications for how we understand rights in citizenship contexts. On the modern view, civil rights[9] are necessary institutional preconditions of citizenship in that they comprise the entitlements, liberties, immunities, and powers which secure the liberty of the citizen, that compose the condition of being *at liberty*. On the civic view, rights are neither necessary nor sufficient conditions of civic freedom. Rather, Tully argues, rights are products of civic activity, are secured by such activity,[10] and

---

[8] Tully, *Public Philosophy*, 272.

[9] "Civil rights" here refers to what are more usually called civil, political, socio-economic, and cultural rights: see Tully, *Public Philosophy*, 250–56.

[10] Tully, *Public Philosophy*, 273. Tully's understanding of civic freedom is predicated on the basic claim that human beings in relationship are characterized by "field freedom":

The freedom of *Spielraum* (free play) in the field of any relationship is both the existential field – the room or space of manoeuvrability (the range of possible moves) – and the experiential ways in which partners can and do disclose and act on their possibilities – the games (*Spiel*) they play *in* the relationship or in the confrontation of its limits. … Humans are always unavoidably *homo ludens*, creative game players and prototypical civic citizens before and *as* they take on any other identities.

The fact that power can only be exercised over people insofar as they are free in this sense implies that the relationship of governor and citizen can never be one in which the citizen's subjectivity is *determined* by the governor. The governor "cannot eliminate completely the interactive and open-ended freedom *of* and *in* the relationship or the room to appear to conform to the public script while thinking and acting otherwise, without reducing the relationship to one of complete immobilisation." But while this point is fundamental for Tully in making clear that, for example, the freedom exhibited in the struggles of Indigenous peoples "in the sparsely, limited *Spielraum* open to them," he also effectively acknowledges through this example that

can serve as *enabling* conditions of civic freedom and, in particular, of the *effective* exercise of civic freedom. The point is simply that civic citizens have compelling reasons to struggle – as, of course, historically they have – for those rights, and conditions of exercise of rights, which are sufficient to make the exercise of civic freedom effective.

With this sketch of the distinction between the two modes of citizenship in place, let us turn to how civil and civic orientations picture democracy.

The civil picture can be formally stated thus:

> Democracy is a reflexive relation of political authority in which those ruled also co-rule as political equals, and rule that they so self-rule.

There are three elements to democracy so conceived. First, it is a form of collective self-government in which those who are subjects of rule are also coauthors of the rule to which they are subject in the sense that they command and obey, whether indirectly via representatives or directly. Second, the relationship of coauthorship is one of status equality expressed in the institution of citizenship. Each member counts as one and no more than one. Third, the citizenry authorize their self-ruling as this "self" rather than another one (for example, as two distinct political communities). As a civil condition, the democratic ideal refers to a constituted political order (a polity or civil association) in which status-citizens enjoy equal liberty to pursue their projects within a framework of rules that they coauthor as equals, that is free from alien rule, whether formal or informal, and where the polity is at liberty to pursue its projects subject to reasonable norms of conduct that it is an equal participant in codetermining. Importantly, the civil picture conceives of the foundation of a polity as the act that transforms a multitude into a people; it is being ruled that constitutes a people as such.

The contrasting civic picture can be put this way:

> Democracy is the practice of acting with other agents as equals to shape and contest the field of interaction between agents; those actions affect each other's conditions of agency in order to govern matters of common concern.

Here the focus is on agency: first, on democratic agency as a particular way of acting with others ("freedoms *of* and *in* participation"); second, to address a consequent of the fact that we are agents who, in acting, may alter the conditions of agency for others; third, to acknowledge that such interactions may give rise, directly or indirectly, to the need for common rules to regulate interactions and/or their effects. As a civic practice, the democratic ideal is a constituting political activity in which those affected by and through the (non)constitution or (non)exercise of public power exercise freedoms *of* and *in* participation in constructing, contesting, and transforming institutions and

---

the exercise of civic freedom by Indigenous peoples is quite compatible with their being subject to political domination.

practices of governance.[11] By contrast to the civil picture with its dichotomy of multitude and people, the civic picture sees peoples as self-organizing collectives who adopt particular institutional arrangements as expressions of their self-governing activity.

In sum, we may say that the civil picture of democracy is oriented around an image of democracy as a constitutional form of political authority in which, at least presumptively, all subjected to collectively binding rules are entitled to equal status in the codetermination of those rules, whereas the civil picture of democracy pivots around an image of democracy as a constituting exercise of power in which all actors whose conditions of agency interact are able to participate in shaping (or contesting) the norms regulating their relations to one another.

THE RELATIONSHIP OF CIVIL AND CIVIC MODES OF CITIZENSHIP AND PICTURES OF DEMOCRACY

Given the contrast between these two modes of citizenship and attendant pictures of democracy, how should we conceive of their relationship to one another? I want to highlight three key features of this relationship.

The first is that civic citizenship is prior to civil citizenship in the sense that it is through the civic practice of exercising freedoms *of* and *in* participation with others that civil orders and the distribution and practical expression of civil statuses are constituted, deconstituted, and reconstituted. Civic citizenship views the citizen/governor relationship as a scene of agonistic interaction in which governors seek to structure the field of possible action of citizens, to govern civic activity, not least through civil statuses – and civic citizens, as free agents, reciprocally seek to structure the field of possible actions of governors, to "civicize" governance. Both partners, ideally, "enter into and subject themselves to the give and take of negotiation in and over the relationship they share."[12] This takes the form of social, cultural, and political struggles within and over the terms of constitutional and nonconstitutional recognition that structure the social, cultural, and political fields of interaction. It is important to stress here the point that civic citizenship is not only a matter of contesting, for example, the distribution of civil statuses within a polity, but also of enacting a mode of relationship to others as civic equals, and the former is a by-product of the latter. The second and third key elements of the relationship between civic and civil citizenship help to further clarify this point.

The second key element for conceptualizing this relationship involves grasping that the scope of civil membership is not identical to the scope of civic membership with respect to a constituted polity. The scope of civil

[11] James Tully, *On Global Citizenship: James Tully in Dialogue* (London: Bloomsbury Academic, 2014), 3–100.
[12] Tully, *Public Philosophy*, 281.

membership concerns those persons subject to the *political authority* of the polity as civil association – that is, it includes *all those subject to rule*, to the (coercively enforceable) collectively binding decisions of the polity, whereas the scope of civic membership refers to *those affected by* the constitution (or nonconstitution) and exercise (or nonexercise) of governmental power. Thus, whereas the *civil demos* is composed of all (competent) persons who are subject to the (coercively enforceable) political authority of the polity, the *civic demos* is comprised of all persons whose autonomy or well-being is affected by the (non)constitution and (non)exercise of public power by the polity. As we will see, this *nonidentity* of the democratic people of constituted power and the democratic people of constituting power is central to the dynamics of democratization.

The priority of the civic to the civil registers the fact that those struggling for civil membership in the form of, say, equal voting rights are already, in virtue of that struggle, practicing civic membership. Think, for example, of the suffragettes or contemporary struggles by immigrants. But it also speaks to a wide diversity of other forms of civic action, many of which may be transnational in scope, such as the current Black Lives Matter protests; the rich history of worker internationalism, including workers in one state striking in support of workers in another state; or the relations of solidarity and communication between many anticolonial movements.

The third key element can be drawn out by borrowing from a recent discussion in the philosophy of law which proposes that a civil order is constituted by boundaries, limits, and fault lines.[13] Adapting Lindahl, we can say that a civil order orders behavior by setting spatial, temporal, material, and subjective boundaries. A civil order as a legal order constructs relations between places, between subjects, between times, and between act-contents – and "integrates these four kinds of relations as dimensions of a *single* order of behavior, such that certain acts by certain persons are allowed or disallowed at certain times and in certain places."[14] Civil boundaries can only join and separate ought-places, ought-times, ought-acts, and ought-subjects given the putative unity of a civil order as a species of joint action with a normative point – that is, as a form of political order that constitutively involves the first person plural standpoint as "we, together." In being bounded, a civil order is also necessarily limited, because limits (along each boundary) are conditions of collective civil identity (e.g. nationality). *Limits* open up a realm of practical possibilities and close down others, and this opening up and closing down is just the articulation of the collective identity – in both *idem* and *ipse* senses – of the "we" whose joint action with a normative point individuates a civil order as this/*our* civil order. Limits – which denote the distinction between civil (dis) order and the "unordered" (that which is seen as "irrelevant and unimportant"

---

[13] Hans Lindahl, *Fault-Lines of Globalization* (Oxford: Oxford University Press, 2013).
[14] Lindahl, *Fault-Lines of Globalization*, 16.

from the standpoint of this/*our* civil order) – are disclosed when *civic activity* interrupts civil (dis)order to bring to light the possibility of an-*other* civil order. Civic activity encompasses activity that makes the limits of a civil order appear by introducing the strange in relationship with the familiar. Civic activity can run from weak to strong poles where, at one end, a transformation of the civil order can be accomplished in such a way that the civil collective identifies itself in terms of continuity-in-transformation (e.g. amendments to a constitution), while, at the other end, sustaining continuity-in-transformation is not viable and civic activity discloses not simply a limit but a *fault-line* which marks out the conditions of (im)possibility of the civil collective as a continuing "we" across time.[15] One might note here a distinction between liberal and radical views of Indigenous self-governance. Liberals construe Indigenous self-governance as disclosing a limit of the civil order; radicals as disclosing a fault-line.

DEMOCRACY, BOUNDARIES, AND THE CIVIL–CIVIC DISTINCTION

It should already be apparent that these civil and civic pictures of democracy each align with one of the two principles that are widely proposed for addressing the constitution of the demos. The civil picture is aligned to the "all subjected" principle, according to which the demos should be composed of all who will be bound by the collectively determined rules of the polity. The civic picture is aligned to the "all affected" principle, which proposes that all affected by exercises of collective political agency should be included in the demos that determines how such agency is exercised. What is perhaps less immediately apparent is the way in which the distinction between these pictures helps to dissolve the democratic boundary problem itself. To elucidate this, it is worth recalling that the democratic boundary problem is framed – and draws its force from being framed – in purely civil terms. Consider Frederick G. Whelan's framing of the issue thus:

1) Democracy is proposed as the sole legitimate decision-making method;
2) Democratic norms entail that the demarcation of the demos should be democratically legitimate;
3) But that would require that the demos that demarcates the demos is itself democratically legitimate, which would entail that the demos that determines the demos that demarcates the demos is democratically legitimate, etc.[16]

The regress conjured here arises from the civil picture of democracy invoked – and the debates' captivity to the civil picture of democracy has shaped its

[15] David Owen, "Hans Lindahl's *Fault Lines of Globalization*: Identity, Individuation and Legal Order," *Contemporary Political Theory* 16 (2017): 254–58.
[16] Frederick G. Whelan, "Democratic Theory and the Boundary Problem," *Nomos* 25 (1983): 13–47.

development. A revealing illustration is provided by Robert Goodin's argument for the all-affected-interests principle in which he proposes that the logical response to the problem is a global demos for all decisions – the logic being that the only coherent version of the all-affected-interests principle is one according to which any person whose interests are affected by any possible decision on any possible agenda is included in the demos.[17] It is notable, however, that in motivating the all-affected-interests principle as the appropriate norm, Goodin considers that a reason why we may consider territorial, historical, or national groups as appropriate units for collective decision-making is that "typically if not invariably, the interests of individuals within those groups are affected by the actions and choices of others in that group."[18] The point here is that it is the fact (where and when it is one) that the interests of a range of persons are interlinked in virtue of the effects of their agency on each other's conditions of agency that underwrites the constitution of civil associations.

It is worth dwelling on Goodin's insight because this focus on "interlinked interests" suggests that all those whose choices affect each other's conditions of agency have *pro tanto* reasons to exercise their powers in constituting, reconstituting, or even deconstituting the formal or informal institutions and practices of governance through which they negotiate their relations to one another. Rather than specifying who is entitled to membership of the constituted demos of a polity, the all-affected principle in its suitably capacious form identifies all those having *pro tanto* reasons to exercise constituent power in relation to their current condition of governance in order to sustain, reform, or overthrow it. The civic picture of democracy is one that is oriented around the effective exercise of such constituent power by all affected agents through civic practices in which agents act in concert with one another as equals in shaping and contesting the normative character of their relations to one another, whether that may take the form of establishing, amending, or abandoning a specific practice limited to a particular type of relationship, an institution regulating a general domain of conduct, or a whole constitutional order of governance.

Why does this matter for the democratic boundary problem? It matters because, once we recognize the civic picture of democracy as part of the story, we don't get thrown into a regress argument caused by the separation of the constitution of the polity from the constitution of the demos. It is perfectly reasonable – as a general abstract rule – for all those who are subject to the collectively binding decisions of the polity to compose the demos of that polity as long as the constituted form of the polity is open to effective contestation or

---

[17] Robert Goodin, "Enfranchising All Affected Interests, and Its Alternatives," *Philosophy and Public Affairs* 35 (2007): 40–68. I have developed a range of specific criticisms of Goodin's argument elsewhere but these are not my focus here; see David Owen "Constituting the Demos, Constituting the Polity," *Ethics & Global Politics* 5 (2012): 129–52.

[18] Goodin, "Enfranchising All Affected Interests," 48.

renegotiation by all affected by its current constitution (that is, by the full range of actions available to it as an agent). Democratic legitimacy in its civil aspect requires the inclusion in the authorship of law and policy of all subject to the constituted authority of the polity; democratic legitimacy in its civic aspect requires the inclusion in the shaping and contestation of the form of governance that the constituted polity instantiates (and the practices of governance in which it engages) of all those affected by its constitution as agents having the potential to act in a wide variety of ways.

I noted in the previous section that rights are neither necessary nor sufficient conditions of civic agency but are, typically, enabling conditions for the effective exercise of such agency. What might that mean in the context of a constitutional democratic state? At the very least we might think that such enabling conditions would include, for example, publicity rights concerning state decision-making, border-crossing communicative rights, transnational mobility rights, and rights to contestatory processes that support the ability of all persons whose interests are affected, whether they are within or without the territory of the state, to engage in action in concert, to exercise freedoms in and of participation with respect to the negotiation of their relations to one another. But, importantly, the relevant enabling conditions extend beyond rights to encompass material circumstances and forms of collective organization.

These reflections on the democratic boundary problem raise the question of how we should understand processes of democratization in the context of the distinction and relationship between civil and civic orientations.

DEMOCRATIZATION IN ITS CIVIL AND CIVIC ASPECTS

Democratization denotes a relation between civil order and civic practice that:

(i) *under the civil aspect*, more fully realizes a democratic polity as a civil condition that is internally nondominating and externally nondominated and nondominating;
(ii) *under the civic aspect*, more fully enables all affected by the (non)constitution and (non)exercise of governmental power to engage as equals in the coexercise of civic freedom.

Struggles for democratization may focus on (or foreground) either the civil or civic aspects of democratization as forms of democratic solidarity. To draw out this difference, it is helpful to distinguish between two modes of respect: "respect as observance" and "respect as respectfulness."[19] The former denotes observing your status as a rights-bearer: I recognize the dignity *of* your person by not breaching your rights or undermining your ability to

[19] I draw this distinction from Michael Rosen, *Dignity: Its History and Meaning* (Cambridge, MA: Harvard University Press, 2018).

exercise them. The second refers to an attitude with which I interact with you: I acknowledge the dignity *in* your person by engaging respectfully with you.

Democratic solidarity in its civil aspect expresses "respect as observance" by, for example, holding states accountable to human rights standards and international conventions or developing and extending the rights of citizens and noncitizens through judicial, legislative, and diplomatic methods. Contemporary exemplars of civil democratic solidarity are all the local, national, and transnational advocacy groups who fight for the recognition and extension of groups subject to forms of civil discrimination, ranging from human rights organizations such as Amnesty International to groups such as No One is Illegal, as well as those organizations offering legal services and representation in defense of such groups.

Democratic solidarity in its civic aspect expresses "respect as respectfulness" by, for example, empowering the voices of those marginalized and excluded to be heard within civil contexts, or engaging in mutual civic relationships and building civic communities. Here is an example. Sana Mustafa, a cofounder of the international *Network for Refugee Voices* (and a Syrian refugee) recently noted that

There are some organizations that are doing refugee participation well. Oxfam International recently hosted an *International Refugee Congress* that engaged refugee-led groups and host countries as key actors. WeWork hired refugee consultants to advise on their World Refugee Day campaign on cultural sensitivity. The United Nations Refugee Agency (UNHCR) has formed a *Global Youth Advisory Council* of young refugees. Independent Diplomat provides diplomatic advice to refugee leaders to inform their participation in global policy discussions. Some nongovernmental organizations, like the Refugee Council of Australia, that have traditionally been responsible for representing refugee views in international policy discussions are instead funding refugees to travel to conferences to represent themselves. Perhaps most inspiring, however, is the initiative refugee-led groups are taking to redefine refugee participation and inclusion. Refugees are leading by example. Next week, a group of over 70 refugee leaders from around the world will descend upon Geneva to convene the *Global Summit of Refugees*. The summit will be the first ever strategic-level meeting of refugees, run by refugees, in the interests of refugees. Conceived by group of nine refugee leaders from Syria, Colombia, South Sudan, the Democratic Republic of Congo, Myanmar and Afghanistan, living on six different continents, Global Summit refugee participants represent 26 countries of origin and 34 hosting countries. If there is one message that echoes forth from the Global Summit it will be: "Nothing about us, without us."[20]

What is particularly significant about the example of the Global Summit of Refugees is that these practices pre-figure a world in which refugees have the

[20] Sana Mustafa, "Nothing About Us Without Us: Why Refugee Inclusion Is Long Overdue," *Refugees Deeply*, June 20, 2018, www.newsdeeply.com/refugees/community/2018/06/20/nothing-about-us-without-us-why-refugee-inclusion-is-long-overdue.

standing that is currently denied them – that is, as having the democratic right to have a "say and hand" in engaging in dialogues and negotiations that work out how they should be recognized and what counts as democratically or civilly legitimate forms of inclusion and accommodation in the community of all affected by the international order of governance.

It is important to note a point in relation to these two modes of democratic solidarity concerning the relationship between "respect as observance" and "respect as respectfulness." To see why, consider the general point that although breaches of your human or civil rights may be more immediately *serious* than dignitary wrongs, it can also be the case that the latter is more *fundamental* than the former in the specific sense that dignitary wrongs act to undermine the target's claim to dignity as equal status. As Michael Rosen puts it:

One of the features that have characterised many of the most violent and destructive acts of the twentieth century has been the humiliation and symbolic degradation of their victims. … It seems to be a fact about human nature that human beings are able more easily to engage in the most violent behaviour towards one another if at the same time they expressively deny the humanity of their victims.[21]

Dignitary wrongs work by introducing hierarchy into a category that marked equality, by differentiating the dignity due to different types of persons in ways that enable the phenomenon that Didier Fassin identifies when he remarked that "whereas many European states once regard asylum as a right, they now increasingly regard it as a favor," where this development required that "the image of refugees had to be transformed from victims of persecution entitled to international protection to undesirable persons suspected of taking advantage of a liberal system."[22] Fassin's point here is that the undermining of the civil right of asylum ("respect as observance"), its transformation into the register of charitable favor, involved undermining the civic acknowledgment of refugees ("respect as respectfulness") by shifting the perception of refugees in ways that undermine their equal claim to dignity in their person.

Democratic exemplarity in its civil mode enacts respect as observance, and that is vitally important, but democratic exemplarity in its civic mode performs respect as respectfulness, and that it is fundamental. The former instantiates commitment to showing that another world is possible and understands its activity as the vehicle through which such a possible world can be brought into being. The latter enacts another world as actual and understands itself as the medium in and through which this world is given expression.[23]

---

[21] Rosen, *Dignity*, 97.
[22] Didier Fassin, "From Right to Favor: The Refugee Question as Moral Crisis," *The Nation*, April 5, 2016, www.thenation.com/article/from-right-to-favor [link defunct as of March 2022].
[23] David Owen, "Exemplarity and Public Philosophy," in *Civic Freedom in an Age of Diversity: The Public Philosophy of James Tully*, eds. Dimitri Karmis and Jocelyn Maclure (Montreal: McGill-Queen's University Press, forthcoming).

CONCLUSION

What are the implications of this analysis for contemporary democratic struggles? Perhaps the central point is that such struggles need to be bifocal processes in which one focus is on defending, securing, and extending rights that both support relations of nondomination and enable civic practices across multiple levels of governance, and the other is on the prefigurative civic enactment of *an-other* civil order. However, civil struggles around rights also hang on creating or sustaining a civic ethos; the lesson of the mass killing fields of the twentieth century (and, indeed, of the prior history of imperialism) is that "respect as observance" is dependent on "respect as respectfulness." A good example of a practice directed to such a civic ethos is provided by *Refugee Tales*, in which writers and poets work with refugees and asylum seekers to tell their stories, lending their cultural capital and skills to forcibly displaced persons, enabling their testimony to reach public audiences and to support a condition of hermeneutic democracy in which the dignity in their persons is acknowledged in public culture. Such initiatives are, of course, swimming against the tide of nationalist/nativist populism, whose power depends critically on undermining the social bases of "respect as respectfulness" and cultivating an attitude of othering that denies commonality, but sustaining democracy as more than a kind of formal shell whose next stage is exhibited in the "authoritarian democracy" of states such as Turkey, Russia, and Hungary (in which executive power has hollowed out the democratic substance of the state) requires precisely such civic ethos-work. The civic is prior to the civil because, ultimately, the latter cannot sustain itself without the former. Democracy requires not just that we observe each other's rights but that we attune ourselves to each other as equals. In a recent lecture, Beverley McLachlin, the former Chief Justice of the Supreme Court of Canada, gave eloquent expression to this process of attunement in a remark which captures its spirit:

Over the centuries, the passengers in the Canadian ship of state – the indigenous peoples, the European settlers, the immigrants, and refugees – have all contributed to the conversation in their unique ways. They have squabbled, they have vied for recognition. But what distinguishes the Canadian experience is that these passengers have not only squabbled and vied for recognition – they have listened to each other. Sometimes belatedly, sometimes incompletely. But more than in many nations, they have shared their stories in a spirit of respect, and from that respect has come accommodation and agreement.[24]

Whether this is an accurate portrayal of Canada is a question that I will leave to others; for my purposes, its significance is its recognition of the centrality of the civic spirit of "respect as respectfulness" enacted in dialogues of mutual listening to the achievement of forms of civil accommodation that better support relations of nondomination between civil citizens and enable the further development of civic practices.

---

[24] Beverley McLachlin, "Canadian Constitutionalism and the Ethic of Inclusion and Accommodation," *Western Journal of Legal Studies* 6, no. 3 (2016): 12.

3

Democracy in a Provisional Key

Lasse Thomassen

INTRODUCTION

To start answering questions about the challenges facing democracy today and about its futures, one must first ask "what is democracy?" I want to argue that this means treating democracy in a provisional key. There are several keys here. There is, first, the fact that, because democracy is so crucial to our political imaginaries, it is crucial to understand the challenges we face also as challenges to democracy. Second, there is the fact that when we ask what democracy is – or, as I will argue, what it means to make the question "what is democracy?" part of the answer to the very same question – then we are taking a particular perspective, one that will open some doors and not others. And, third, while this perspective helps us think about how to act, I will also argue for a conception of democracy as aporetic, where aporia means nonpassage, but a nonpassage that must nonetheless be navigated and, therefore, negotiated.

With a taxonomy offered by Thomas J. Donahue and Paulina Ochoa Espejo, the key – the crucial task *and* the way forward – becomes to treat democracy as a question not to be solved, dissolved or resolved, but to be pressed. Democracy becomes a question, or a problem, not to be resolved by "offering an answer to the problem's question while providing reasons for thinking that the answer is correct."[1] Nor is it a problem to be resolved as if we could "reconcile ourselves to the problem's eternal presence" despite all solutions to it turning out to be unsatisfactory.[2] Nor is it a problem that can be dissolved by arguing that it "is not a genuine problem [but] rather a pseudo-problem, resting on a false

Research for this paper has received funding from the European Union's Horizon 2020 research and innovation program under the Marie Skłodowska-Curie grant agreement No 794037.
[1] Thomas J. Donahue and Paulina Ochoa Espejo, "The Analytical-Continental Divide: Styles of Dealing with Problems," *European Journal of Political Theory* 15, no. 2 (2016): 144.
[2] Donahue and Ochoa Espejo, "The Analytical-Continental Divide," 146.

presupposition."[3] Instead, democracy is a question to be pressed, which is to say "that it can never be solved [but] will press itself upon us and haunt us until the end of time."[4] Not only that, but the question of democracy is pressing: it is not one that we can postpone, given the importance of democracy for our political imaginaries. This aporetic character of democracy is what makes it both solution and experiment, in line with the etymological roots of "key" in the Old English *cǣǧ*.

While there is an urgency to the question of democracy, such that we cannot postpone an answer, I also argue that democracy should be treated as provisional. By provisional, I do not mean that we do not yet have the answer to the question "what is democracy?," as if it were a difficult question that we might one day, and with skill and luck, be able to answer. Rather, I mean provisional in the sense of Jacques Derrida's "to-come": democracy not as a horizon or critical ideal, but as a question that will "haunt us until the end of time," in Donahue and Ochoa Espejo's words.[5] And yet we must face the question. To say that democracy is provisional in this sense also means that we must speak of the futures of democracy in the plural: all we are left with are provisional answers to the question "what is democracy?," and because there is no ultimate answer to the question, all we have are a plurality of answers.

PROVISIONAL DEMOCRACY

Democracy is aporetic. The etymology of aporia is nonpassage, and this is also how it should be understood. It is a nonpassage that we are forced to navigate, but one where we cannot simply proceed on the basis of, for instance, an essential concept of democracy. We are forced to proceed without "some superordinate master language, absolute foundation, or final arbiter."[6] Aporia therefore requires negotiation and decision.[7] We navigate it without banisters,

---

[3] Donahue and Ochoa Espejo, "The Analytical-Continental Divide," 147.

[4] Donahue and Ochoa Espejo, "The Analytical-Continental Divide," 146. Donahue and Ochoa Espejo's example of a theorist who presses problems is Jacques Derrida, whom I will draw upon later in the chapter.

[5] Giovanna Borradori and Jacques Derrida, "Autoimmunity: Real and Symbolic Suicides," in *Philosophy in a Time of Terror: Dialogues with Jürgen Habermas and Jacques Derrida* (Chicago: University of Chicago Press, 2003), 120; Jacques Derrida, *Rogues: Two Essays on Reason* (Stanford: Stanford University Press, 2005), 8–9; Jacques Derrida, *Specters of Marx: The State of the Debt, the Work of Mourning and the New International* (New York: Routledge, 1993), 64–65; Alan Keenan, *Democracy in Question: Democratic Openness in a Time of Political Closure* (Stanford: Stanford University Press, 2003), 10, 13, 141–42; Lasse Thomassen, "Deliberative Democracy and Provisionality," *Contemporary Political Theory* 10, no. 4 (2011): 423–43, https://doi.org/10.1057 /cpt.2010.39; and Lasse Thomassen, "Political Theory in a Provisional Mode," *Critical Review of Social and Political Philosophy* 13, no. 4 (2010): 453–73.

[6] Dominick LaCapra, *Writing History, Writing Trauma*, 2nd ed. (Baltimore: Johns Hopkins University Press, 2014), 62.

[7] Jacques Derrida, *Aporias* (Stanford: Stanford University Press, 1993), 8, 12–17.

but we must be careful here. Any individual negotiation of the aporia of democracy happens by specific subjects in specific circumstances shaped by inherited conceptions of democracy. Our negotiation of democracy is rooted in these inheritances, but not in some firm root; nor is it rooted in the soil of a nation, a common image today when invoking democracy as the rule of a natural national people. Rather, the provisional democracy that emerges from the aporia of democracy is a radical democracy in the sense of the etymological root of radical: *radix*, meaning root. Navigating the aporia means going to the root of democracy, not in search of an ultimate foundation or to dissolve the aporia, but in the postfoundational sense that there is no ultimate foundation or root. Yet, our negotiations of democracy are always rooted in particular, partial and overlapping conceptions of democracy or political imaginaries.[8]

If we are dealing with a postfoundational conception of democracy, it is because it is a nonessentialist one. In Derrida's words: "What is lacking in democracy is proper meaning ... Democracy is defined, as is the very ideal of democracy, by this lack of the proper ... there is no absolute paradigm, whether constitutive or constitutional, no absolutely intelligible idea, no *eidos*, no *idea* of democracy."[9] The question "what is democracy?" – as in "what *is* democracy?" – therefore becomes part of democracy as a concept and as a practice. This opens up a discussion of democracy and what it involves: rights, social equality, the role of the people, who belongs to the demos and so forth. The yardstick ("democracy") against which we decide upon these questions is itself in question, and this extends to the discussion itself, because we can ask whether the discussion itself is democratic.

If we say that democracy means rule by the people, then democracy is defined by the two questions "what is the demos?" and "what is rule?," which is another way of saying that it is defined by the question "what is democracy?" Any democratic discourse would have to answer those two questions, and there would be a host of different answers to them. Democracy then consists of these questions and the answers given to them. Democracy opens an argument about those two questions, and this means that democracy is a peculiar practice that puts itself into question – that puts itself at stake – because there would be no way of deciding a priori what the people, what rule and what democracy are – in short, what democracy is.[10] And so a major problem facing democracy is how to negotiate this, especially how to negotiate limits to democracy while treating democracy as provisional.

Brexit is a good example that connects the two questions about democracy. If we think about the demos as a silo, so that sovereignty is siloed, then the rule of this demos must also be siloed, and something like the EU can only be seen as

---

[8] Oliver Marchart, *Post-Foundational Political Thought: Political Difference in Nancy, Lefort, Badiou and Laclau* (Edinburgh: Edinburgh University Press, 2007), chap. 1.
[9] Derrida, *Rogues*, 37.   [10] Keenan, *Democracy in Question*.

a betrayal of the British demos. But if we see the demos as internally fractured and as overlapping with other demoi (and so view sovereignty more in terms of a network), then it makes much more sense to pool sovereignty. This can be done in the name of a common demos (the European people, although this is itself a potentially problematic entity), but it can also be done by stressing interconnectedness. In neither case can we say that "*this* is democracy" because we cannot say that "this *is* democracy." Or, to be precise, there can be provisional answers that take democracy to be this or that, but no ultimate answer; there are *only* provisional answers *because* there is no ultimate answer.

Democracy is provisional because it is aporetic. Derrida makes the connection thus: "*aporia*: the difficult or the impracticable, here the impossible, passage, the refused, denied, or prohibited passage, indeed the nonpassage, which can in fact be something else, the event of a coming or of a future advent [*événement de venue ou d'avenir*]."[11] Here, provisional does not mean "not yet," as if we will, or could, someday arrive at a final answer to the question "what is democracy?" Rather, provisional means to-come in Derrida's sense of *à venir* (to come) and *avenir* (a future advent): "'Democracy to come' does not mean a future democracy that will one day be 'present.' Democracy will never exist in the present."[12] Democracy is not everything, while at the same time it is nothing. It cannot be just anything because it will always consist of particular articulations of democracy, differentiating it from what it is not (for example, populism, in some discourses on democracy). At the same time, it *is* nothing because it has no essence. Democracy is extended between these two: between the need to rearticulate it again and again and the ultimate lack of essence, foundation or root; and that tension is expressed by making the question "what is democracy?" part of democracy. Put differently, democracy is extended between conditional democracy (because it is always articulated in particular ways) and unconditional democracy (because any particular articulation of democracy can be put into question with reference to the democracy to-come, which always exceeds our particular articulations of democracy).[13]

DEMOCRACY AT RISK

If the question "what is democracy?" is part and parcel of democracy, then we have no yardstick independent of particular answers to that question. We have no independent yardstick with which to judge if a particular answer to the question is democratic or not; all we have are different answers. As a result, we do not have a bedrock definition of democracy that we can use in the defense of democracy

---

[11] Derrida, *Aporias*, 8.

[12] Borradori and Derrida, "Autoimmunity: Real and Symbolic Suicides," 120.

[13] I leave aside the question of the status of this provisional democracy: is it a general and inherent aspect of democracy as such, or is it a particular discourse of democracy? It seems to me that neither of these options is attractive.

against those who will use democracy for undemocratic ends. The distinction between democratic and undemocratic is itself at stake within democracy, and to the extent that we cannot say whether we are on one or the other side of the distinction when struggling over how to define it. Indeed, it is not clear that we can struggle democratically over the meaning of democracy when this struggle also pertains to what it means to be "democratic."[14] There is an inherent rogueness to democracy as what happens in its name cannot simply stay within a norm of democracy.

These are the aporias that Derrida tries to capture with the notion of autoimmunity.[15] By autoimmunity, Derrida means a situation where an organism destroys its own immune system, which was supposed to protect the organism against external threats: "an autoimmunitary process is that strange behavior where a living being, in a quasi-*suicidal* fashion, 'itself' works to destroy its own protection, to immunize itself *against* its 'own' immunity."[16] Democracy is autoimmunitary in that it is caught between a closure to protect democracy against the undemocratic and an openness to what is to-come and cannot be predicted (which could be any answer to the question of what democracy is, to the extent that it would no longer be recognizable as democratic). Whatever we do, democracy is at risk.

To illustrate this, consider contemporary debates about democracy and populism and the relationship between them. Some discourses on populism oppose democracy and populism and treat populism as an existential threat to democracy. Other discourses take populism as a correction to a form of liberal democracy that has become more liberal and less democratic. Yet other discourses take populism to be an essential part of democracy.

Jan-Werner Müller's work is an example of the first kind of discourse opposing populism to democracy.[17] According to Müller, populism is defined by its antipluralism. Populism is a discourse that imposes a particular image of the people on the pluralism of society, thus branding those who are different as illegitimate. It is a discourse of closure: "This is the core claim of populism: only some of the people are really the people."[18] Müller gives as an example Nigel Farage's claim that Brexit was a victory for the real British people;[19] his other examples include the governments of Viktor Orbán in Hungary, Recep Tayyip Erdoğan in Turkey and Hugo Chávez and Nicolás Maduro in Venezuela. However, when it comes to defending democracy against populism, things are murkier. On the one hand, Müller says that only populists who cease to be

[14] Derrida, *Rogues*, 71–73.
[15] Borradori and Derrida, "Autoimmunity: Real and Symbolic Suicides," 94–102; Derrida, *Rogues*, 33–35.
[16] Borradori and Derrida, "Autoimmunity: Real and Symbolic Suicides," 94.
[17] Jan-Werner Müller, *What Is Populism?* (London: Penguin, 2017).
[18] Müller, *What Is Populism?*, 21.   [19] Müller, *What Is Populism?*, 21–22.

populists can be included within liberal democracy because you cannot be both a democrat and a populist at the same time.[20] That makes sense if you see populism as an existential threat to pluralism and democracy. On the other hand, he does not want to ban populist parties, and he writes that "as long as populists stay within the law – and don't incite violence, for instance – other political actors (and members of the media) are under some obligation to engage them."[21] That makes sense if you associate democracy with pluralism. Müller seems to equivocate because he thinks of pluralism as a zero-sum game: if we exclude populists (because they want to limit pluralism), we limit pluralism.[22] If we accept the autoimmunitary character of democracy, however, the relationship between exclusion and pluralism is much more difficult and unpredictable.

Ernesto Laclau's and Chantal Mouffe's works on populism are examples of the kind of discourse that takes populism to be an essential part of democracy.[23] They link populism to popular sovereignty and argue that popular sovereignty is an essential part of democracy. There is no democracy – liberal or otherwise – without the construction of a people, or a demos. There is no natural people, only discourses that performatively bring peoples into being; in Mouffe's words, "the 'people' is not an empirical referent but a discursive political construction."[24] Populist discourses provide answers to the question "what is the demos?" Laclau argues that populist discourses can move in different directions, some more totalitarian and some more democratic. He suggests that Mouffe's conception of agonistic democracy is a fruitful way to think about democratic forms of the construction of a people.[25]

Mouffe thinks of agonistic democracy as providing a "conflictual consensus." Agonistic democratic adversaries all subscribe to the defining values of liberal democracy – liberty and equality for all – but they interpret them differently.[26] The consensus among adversaries makes it possible to draw a line and defend democracy: "A line should therefore be drawn between those who reject those values ['the ethico-political values of liberty and equality for all'] outright and those who, while accepting them, fight for conflicting interpretations."[27] At the same time, any consensus is the result of hegemonic struggles. Mouffe writes that "every consensus exists as a temporary result of

[20] Niels Boel, Carsten Jensen and André Sonnichsen, "Populism and the Claim to a Moral Monopoly: An Interview with Jan-Werner Müller," *Politik* 20, no. 4 (2017): 77.
[21] Müller, *What Is Populism?*, 84. See also Boel, Jensen, and Sonnichsen, "Populism and the Claim," 85.
[22] Müller, *What Is Populism?*, 83.
[23] Ernesto Laclau, *On Populist Reason* (London: Verso, 2005); Chantal Mouffe, *For a Left Populism* (London: Verso, 2018).
[24] Mouffe, *For a Left Populism*, 62.   [25] Laclau, *On Populist Reason*, 166–69.
[26] Chantal Mouffe, *The Democratic Paradox* (London: Verso, 2000).
[27] Chantal Mouffe, *On the Political* (London: Routledge, 2005), 121.

a provisional hegemony, as a stabilization of power, and that it always entails some form of exclusion." She adds that "any political order is the expression of a hegemony, of a specific pattern of power relations."[28]

With Mouffe's agonistic democracy, we are back to provisional democracy.[29] The conflictual consensus is conflictual all the way down. This is so despite the consensus around the values of liberty and equality for all. That consensus should be understood as a provisional placeholder for the hegemonic struggles over the interpretation of the values, where the interpretations performatively constitute the consensus. It is a "dimension of performative interpretation, that is, of an interpretation that transforms the very thing it interprets."[30] Put differently, the values of liberal democracy are values we have inherited – not in the passive sense that they have already been defined and we now just need to accept them and put them into practice, but in the active sense of appropriating them through a process of interpretation that should be understood as a process of performative articulation.[31] This appropriation of the values of liberal democracy is not the reappropriation of an original meaning of the values, whether understood as an essence or as a historical origin. Rather, since there is no proper meaning to the values of liberal democracy, the interpretation of them consists of tropological – or, more precisely, catachrestical – displacements that are constitutive of the values.[32]

If there is a totalitarian populist threat to democracy, Laclau and Mouffe provide us with no guarantees. In their terms, populism is an inherent part of democracy, and, as such, it may also be a threat to democracy. To paraphrase Mouffe, the question becomes how we can articulate forms of closure more compatible with democratic values.[33]

MAJOR CHALLENGES TO DEMOCRACY

What are the major challenges facing democracy today, especially if understood as provisional democracy? The first thing to note is that there are no objectively major challenges to democracy, above all because there is no objective essence to democracy. Challenges must be articulated as challenges, and major challenges must be articulated as major challenges, and the link to democracy must also be articulated (why are they challenges *for democracy*?). This is just what has happened to what we call "the environment" and, especially "the climate crisis." It is not that these challenges are new, but that they have entered mainstream political discussions as major challenges, including as challenges to

---

[28] Mouffe, *The Democratic Paradox*, 104, 99.
[29] Note that, in the case of Derrida, he identifies an aporia of democracy; in the case of Mouffe, she identifies a tension between the two parts of liberal democracy (individual liberty from the liberal tradition and equality/popular sovereignty from the democratic tradition).
[30] Derrida, *Specters of Marx*, 51.
[31] For this notion of inheritance, see Derrida, *Specters of Marx*, 16.   [32] Derrida, *Rogues*, 37.
[33] Mouffe, *The Democratic Paradox*, 100.

how we think about democracy. To take just one obvious example, we must ask ourselves how we take future generations into consideration while at the same time acting with urgency here and now. Indeed, there seems to be a general tension between the futures of democracy – futures that are not simply "ours," but also "theirs" – and the urgent need for "us" to make decisions in the present, and where it is difficult to say who "we" and "they" are.

What, then, are the major challenges facing democracy today, especially if understood as provisional democracy? I will venture two major challenges: the environment and inequality. The environmental crisis is a challenge for democracy because it raises questions about who "the people" of democracy is: how do you include those affected in the future and those affected elsewhere? Inequality – within states and on a global scale – is a challenge because, even if everyone is included in the people that rules, they will not be so equally; some will rule more than others, for instance because they have better access to representation in national and international institutions. The two challenges are linked because the effects of the environmental crisis are not evenly distributed across inequalities of class, geography, gender and so many other things. It thus matters not only *who* is included in the demos, but also *how* they are included. The latter is not only a matter of inequality, but of what it means to be part of a demos that rules – for instance, the relative role of popular participation and formal institutions. Here, too, the two challenges are linked: we need to ask what forms of politics best promote urgent and lasting solutions to the environmental crisis – for instance, popular participation in the form of climate strikes or intergovernmental negotiations in international institutions. And with regard to that question, inequality also matters, because inequalities are distributed differently across different forms of politics.

Both the environmental crisis and inequality are challenges for any regime, democratic or not. The question is whether there is anything specific about democracy – and democracy in a provisional key – in the face of these challenges. The twin challenges of the environmental crisis and inequality take on a particular importance and inflection in democracy in a provisional key. This is so because in provisional democracy, the people – or the demos, the "who" of democracy – is representational.[34] By that I mean that the people is brought into being by performative invocations of it – that is, by representative claims about the people. The people does not exist, and therefore it must be represented. There is no essential or natural people that is then represented in political institutions or in representative claims about the people. That is why it must be represented in order to be brought into existence. The people "is" what it is represented "as." While there is no natural nation, people or humankind waiting to be represented (or misrepresented), the performative conception of representation does not imply that, for instance, "the people" is created with

[34] Lasse Thomassen, "Representing the People: Laclau as a Theorist of Representation," *New Political Science* 41, no. 2 (2019): 331–34.

a single representative claim. Rather, representative claims draw on existing representations of the people for their authority, and they must be taken up by others – politicians, institutions, subjects – who are themselves shaped by existing representations of the people.

If the people – the demos of democracy – is representational, democracy is provisional. This is so because the people cannot simply be given as a fact prior *to* the rule of the people, because it is also at stake *in* the rule of the people. Yet, the rule of the people assumes the people: it assumes that once the people starts ruling itself, it is already constituted. This is the aporia that makes democracy provisional: the people is at once prior to and a result of the rule of the people, and so we never arrive at a final answer to the questions "what is the demos?" and "what is rule?"

The performative conception of representation sheds new light on current debates about the crisis of democracy and of representative institutions. This is so in particular when the climate crisis is articulated together with a crisis of representative democracy: Extinction Rebellion, protests against airport expansions, and so on all challenge the representativity of representative institutions. Likewise, school children striking against climate change challenge our preconceptions of what it means to have an equal voice in the making of political decisions, because children can claim a strong stake in the future of the polity, but do not have full political rights in the present.

Usually, when we talk about representation it goes something like this: someone (a representative) represents someone else (the represented). The represented may be a person, a group or an interest, but we start from the represented, and the question is then whether the representative really represents the represented. We would think that there is representation, and not misrepresentation, if the representative reflects the interests of the represented. In this model of representation, we move from the represented to the representative. If we think of representation in this way, we can imagine a crisis of democracy when elected representatives do not represent the interests of those who elected them, but instead represent the interests of big business. The crisis arises from a mismatch between the represented and the representatives.

There is another way of thinking about representation. We can think of representation as not simply reflecting a state of affairs, but performatively constituting that state of affairs. This is what is referred to as a constructivist conception of representation.[35] Take, for instance, the French Yellow Vests (*Gilets jaunes*) movement. The French political system and especially the established parties are embroiled in a crisis – a crisis we could call a crisis of representative institutions (parliament, media, police, etc.). We can think of the right-wing populism of the Front National and the left-wing populism of Jean-

[35] Derrida, *Specters of Marx*, 84; Lisa Disch, Mathijs van de Sande, and Nadia Urbinati, *The Constructivist Turn in Political Representation* (Edinburgh: Edinburgh University Press, 2019); and Mouffe, *For a Left Populism*, 61.

Luc Mélenchon as reactions to this crisis of representation: these parties claim to speak for – that is, represent – a people that is not otherwise represented by political parties. Then comes along the Yellow Vests movement, which rejects representative politics outright.

How can we understand this claim by the Yellow Vests that they are not represented by the political system, let alone the political parties? If we think of representation in the usual sense, the claim of the Yellow Vests makes immediate sense: there is no one in the political system who speaks for the Yellow Vests; or, if they do, they misrepresent them. However, what if we think of representation in a different way: as moving in the other direction, so that the interests of the represented are not given, but are constructed through the very act of representation? In that case, we have to think differently about the crisis of representative institutions. We cannot simply say that French democracy is in crisis because the political parties do not reflect the true interests of the French people and the diversity of interests and identities within French society. Put differently, if "the people" is an effect of representative claims about the people, then we cannot claim that, say, Emmanuel Macron does not represent the true or real interests of the people, because the latter do not exist independently of the claim to represent them. If we think of representation as not limited to formal representative institutions, we can then think of, for instance, the Yellow Vests as engaged in (democratic) representative politics even when they refuse to engage directly with representative institutions. What we have are representative claims about the people – some from elected politicians, some from activists in movements, some in popular culture, some from your colleagues, neighbors and friends. We end up with a struggle between different representative claims – without any way of adjudicating between them by pointing to the "true" or "real" interests of the people.

Returning to the question of the climate crisis and of how to respond to the problem of future generations in the context of the climate crisis, thinking of democracy as provisional and of the people as representational gives us a new angle on the question. One of the problems with future generations is that they are indeterminate; the same applies to the problem of how to include those affected by decisions but not included within the polity. We do not know who and how many generations to include, what their interests are, and so on. With the conception of the people as representational and democracy as provisional, we can now see that this is a *general* feature of democracy. Democracy should not be conceived as a transparent medium for the will or the interests of a people, but as one way of constructing the people.

This conception of democracy in a provisional key does not solve, resolve or dissolve the problem of future generations. It presses the problem because it forces us to see that, with democracy, we are (also) in the business of constructing answers to the questions "what is the demos?" and "what is rule?," here in the context of the environmental crisis. The same goes for inequality and how to think about that in a provisional key. For instance, what do "the demos" and "rule" mean in the context of a New International (Derrida) or a Green New Deal (Mouffe)?[36] What kind of subjects, sovereignty and representation can be articulated for a New International or a Green New Deal?

Gross and systematic inequalities exist across the world. They are a challenge and a threat to democracy (among other things) because they put into question the character of the demos, whether the demos of the nation-state or a global demos. From a postfoundational perspective, there is nothing essential about equality and no natural subject of equality. From this perspective, equality is an open question. It is this lack of essence which means that all we have are particular answers to the question "what is equality?" – that is, particular discourses of equality, or particular images of the subject of equality. Since there is nothing natural about equality, it must be represented and, thus, brought into being in a performative fashion. In the context of democracy, we therefore have to ask how the demos and those making up the demos are represented: what kind of (equal) subjects are they? What kind of image connects particular subjects to a demos? Historically, this image has often been that of a nation, with everything that comes with that in terms of religion, language, ethnicity, and so on. But there is no image of the demos and no image of the subject of equality without some exclusion, without a limit. An image of European democracy also carries exclusions, and even images of humankind rely on particular images of what it means to be a human being, and some are, if not excluded, at least marginalized vis-à-vis that image. There is no equality without subjects of equality, subjects that can be counted as equals. Equality is suspended between conditionality and unconditionality. The bottom line is that because equality is provisional like democracy – because there is no ultimate answer to the question "what is equality?" – there are no guarantees that equality will be articulated in a progressive direction.

CONCLUSION

There is nothing new about democracy being challenged. The challenges may be new, or at least relatively new in the case of the environmental crisis. What is new is that democracy is a universal language. Thinking of democracy in a provisional key – democracy as provisional democracy – invites us to press the problem of democracy: to take democracy not as a problem to be solved, resolved or dissolved, but as a question. To do so is also to proceed without guarantees that a better or more progressive result will follow.

[36] Derrida, *Specters of Marx*, 84; Mouffe, *For a Left Populism*, 61.

PART II

REPRESENTATIVE DEMOCRACIES

4

Democracy and Community: Exploring a Contested Link in Light of the Populist Resurgence

Oliver Schmidtke

INTRODUCTION

The appeal to a community unified by a strong collective identity and a menacing notion of the outside "other" has become a driving force in the resurgence of right-wing populism. While populism lacks a coherent ideological core, the reference to a community of a virtuous people pitted against the elite is a defining feature of its mobilizing efforts.[1] The mass rallies of right-wing populists provide a tangible sense of how the image of a homogenous community frames political grievances and fuels anger. The affective and immediate appeal to the community of ordinary people has been instrumental in challenging the procedural practice of liberal democracy.

The populist appropriation of community as a foundational element of this actor's political identity raises questions about the conceptual link between community and democracy. Is populism's reliance on mobilizing a communal identity simply a reiteration of the regressive nationalist ideology, or does it bring to the fore legitimate questions about the current state of democracy? Does the plea for renewing democratic practices in the public sphere need to develop a more robust understanding of how the infrastructure and resources of the community facilitate civic engagement? In other words, does the effective evocation of community by populists provide lessons when considering the future of democracy in an emancipatory key?

Against the background of the populist surge in Western democracies, this chapter has two objectives. First, it will explore the link between democracy and community from a theoretical perspective, arguing that a vibrant democratic

I would like to acknowledge that this chapter draws on research supported by the *Social Sciences and Humanities Research Council of Canada*. Furthermore, I would like to express my gratitude to the *Hamburg Institute for Advanced Study* where I had the privilege of being a fellow while completing this text.
[1] Benjamin Moffitt and Simon Tormey, "Rethinking Populism: Politics, Mediatisation and Political Style," *Political Studies* 62, no. 2 (2014): 381–97.

practice that is appropriate for the challenges of the twenty-first century is indeed reliant on a substantial, functionally and procedurally pertinent sense of communal existence and shared collective identity. In this respect, the chapter alludes to how the growing emphasis on individual rights and cosmopolitan values has overshadowed the constitutive role of the community in which citizens interact as a *zoon politikon* (political animal). Second, the chapter describes how the center-left has gradually abandoned its underlying sense of a collective identity rooted in community-based political ideas and social practices. In this regard, I interpret the resurgence of right-wing populism also as a reaction to the advancing disintegration of those community practices and resources that have provided an important dimension of the social infrastructure on which a thriving democracy rests.

First, I explore the strategic use that right-wing populists make of community as a vehicle for promising democratic empowerment understood in terms of a revitalized notion of popular sovereignty. In this context, I discuss how the center-left has largely neglected the pivotal role of community in promoting democratic processes, not least with a view to a common good beyond the neoliberal market model. Second, this chapter provides an inquiry into the link between democracy and community, drawing on the empirical example of a study on Neighbourhood Houses (NHs) in Metro Vancouver. The central hypothesis that I intend to advance based on these theoretically grounded and empirically illustrated arguments is that community-based practices and values could play an essential role in fostering (radical) democracy beyond its current anemic stage.

THE POWERFUL POPULIST REFERENCE TO COMMUNITY: THE PROMISE OF EMPOWERMENT

The invocation of a resilient and continuously reaffirmed sense of the "people" is constitutive for populism. At its core is the claim to represent the vox populi, the "voice of the people" defined by a dramatized contrast to the political elite or establishment.[2] Populism's ideological ambiguity[3] and popular appeal make this an intellectually fascinating – albeit theoretically challenging – subject of study. The conceptual uncertainty is rooted in the versatility of the claim to represent the interests of ordinary people in a direct and authentic manner. Cas Mudde and Ben Stanley call populism a "thin-centred ideology"[4] that is qualitatively different from other core political ideas.[5] Populism is a mode of

---

[2] Robert R. Barr, "Populists, Outsiders and Anti-Establishment Politics," *Party Politics* 15 (2009): 29–48.

[3] Daniele Albertazzi and Duncan McDonnell, "Conclusion: Populism and Twenty-First Century Western European Democracy," in *Twenty-First Century Populism*, ed. Daniele Albertazzi and Duncan McDonnell (Basingstoke: Palgrave Macmillan, 2008), 217–23.

[4] See, for example, Cas Mudde, *Populist Radical Right Parties in Europe* (Cambridge: Cambridge University Press, 2007), 33; and Ben Stanley, "The Thin Ideology of Populism," *Journal of Political Ideologies* 13, no. 1 (2008): 95–110.

[5] Similarly, see Jan-Werner Müller, *Contesting Democracy: Political Ideas in Twentieth Century Europe* (New Haven: Yale University Press, 2011).

engaging in politics that is not exclusive to a particular ideological position or type of political actor. The form of political engagement – its reliance on direct political action, a strong mobilizing collective identity, and charismatic leadership – is the constitutive mark of populism.[6]

If indeed populism can best be conceptualized as a mode of political mobilization, it is critical to shift the analytical focus on the claims constituting its popular appeal in the current political climate: At the core of right-wing populist political strategy is the reference to the "people" as a collective that is depicted as deprived by the elite with a view to its shared identity and socioeconomic interests.[7] The charismatic leader regularly claims to articulate the direct "voice of the people," untamed by procedural rules associated with liberal, rules-based democracy. Given the centrality of the "people" in justifying the populist cause and the mode of conducting politics, populism needs a tangible and emotionally charged sense of the community on which it claims to rely as its raison d'être. The rallies and manifestations of populist actors are no coincidental manifestation; they speak directly to the significance attributed to the dramatized depiction of the community of regular people. Populists draw on the sense of unity and cohesion staged at mass gatherings. It is here where the "imagined community" gains a fleeting manifestation; the demos takes on a theatrical existence sanctioning the people and, by virtue of the latter, its populist leader.

It is in this respect that the affinity between right-wing populism and nationalism becomes apparent. The discourses of both revolve around the notion of the sovereignty of "the people." In the scholarly discussion on comparing the discourses of both, populists are depicted as operating based on a vertical axis pitching ordinary citizens against unresponsive elites, while nationalists are portrayed as promoting a horizontal sense of the people as a politically or culturally bounded community.[8] Yet, as Brubaker has argued convincingly, these dimensions of invoking the "people" normally intersect in the practice of both political movements.[9] In populist political narratives, the

---

[6] See Moffitt and Tormey, "Rethinking Populism," 381–97; and Cas Mudde and Cristóbal Rovira Kaltwasser, "Populism: Corrective and Threat to Democracy," in *Populism in Europe and the Americas: Threat or Corrective for Democracy?*, ed. Cas Mudde and Cristóbal Rovira Kaltwasser (Cambridge: Cambridge University Press, 2012), 205–22.

[7] Margaret Canovan, "Taking Politics to the People: Populism as the Ideology of Democracy," in *Democracies and the Populist Challenge*, eds. Yves Mény and Yves Surel (London: Palgrave Macmillan, 2002), 25–44.

[8] See, for example, Bart Bonikowski et al., "Populism and Nationalism in a Comparative Perspective: A Scholarly Exchange," *Nations and Nationalism* 25, no. 1 (2019): 58–81; Benjamin De Cleen, "Populism and Nationalism," in *The Oxford Handbook of Populism*, ed. Cristóbal Rovira Kaltwasser et al. (Oxford: Oxford University Press, 2017), 342–62; and Benjamin De Cleen and Yannis Stavrakakis, "Distinctions and Articulations: A Discourse Theoretical Framework for the Study of Populism and Nationalism," *Javnost: The Public* 24, no. 4 (2017): 301–19.

[9] Rogers Brubaker, "Populism and Nationalism," *Nations and Nationalism* 26, no. 1 (2020): 44–66.

politically potent reference to the "people" points to people as those who have been deprived of their legitimate rights and people as a bounded community whose identity and interests need to be protected and nurtured.[10]

For instance, the strong anti-immigrant rhetoric and insistence on (national) borders as the ultimate defense of the sovereign rights of the people regularly shapes the political discourse of nationalists and populists. In this regard, I consider Brubaker's claim persuasive that "this strict conceptual separation cannot capture the productive ambiguity of populist appeals to 'the people', evoking at once plebs, sovereign demos and bounded community."[11] Populists employ the nationalist allure of portraying people united as equals by cultural traits and a shared collective decision-making process. Yet, in the discourse of right-wing populism, the issues of inequality and deprivation are regularly fused with an (often belligerent) notion of the community's identity and borders.[12]

This collective identity is instrumental in turning the perceived social and cultural marginalization into a vehicle of political protest. Borrowing from nationalist ideologies, yet being far more versatile in staging the defining characteristics of the "people," populists articulate a yearning for belonging and a romanticized past when this identity was supposed to be pure and untainted. In populist rhetoric, the invoked notion of the people as community is – far from being a territorially, linguistically, or ethnically defined nation – a *chiffre* to direct political anger and frustration. The "Make America Great Again" slogan allows ambiguity in defining a nation's interests and identity.[13] Its primary purpose is to fuel a form of agonistic politics whose driving force is the contestation of the status quo.[14]

It is worth noting that the versatility and multiplicity with which populists reify the community is instrumental for their political mobilization. What constitutes the community is deliberately left ambiguous, thus allowing the building of broad political coalitions. Using this extensive communal appeal, Donald Trump was able to unite evangelicals, farmers, union representatives, and white voters from the American suburbs. He created a support base wherein the extremely wealthy claim to guard the interests of those who feel disempowered by politics and threatened by socioeconomic change (the latter

[10] See, for example, Roger Eatwell and Matthew Goodwin, *National Populism: The Revolt Against Liberal Democracy* (London: Penguin, 2018).

[11] Brubaker, "Populism and Nationalism," 44.

[12] Christian Lamour and Renáta Varga, "The Border as a Resource in Right-Wing Populist Discourse: Viktor Orbán and the Diasporas in a Multi-Scalar Europe," *Journal of Borderlands Studies* 35, no. 3 (2020): 335–50.

[13] The Italian Lega provides a similar illustration for this argument. For further discussion see Daniele Albertazzi, Arianna Giovannini, and Antonella Seddone, "'No Regionalism Please, We are *Leghisti*!' The Transformation of the Italian Lega Nord under the Leadership of Matteo Salvini," *Regional & Federal Studies* 28, no. 5 (2018): 645–71.

[14] Ilan Kapoor, "Deliberative Democracy or Agonistic Pluralism? The Relevance of the Habermas-Mouffe Debate for Third World Politics," *Alternatives* 27, no. 4 (2002): 459–87.

process significantly driven by the very billionaires who assert to be the champions of the ordinary people's cause). To build this coalition, the staged community is deliberately left void of a clear notion of shared interests or political objectives. A general and unifying sense of deprivation and loss of control provides the rationale for claiming to transcend the traditional left–right divide. The notion of community staged by right-wing populists is at the same time horizontally defined by nationality or ethnicity and vertically defined by anti-elitist sentiments. The glue between these two dimensions is regularly provided by the representation of the threatening "other." This role can be assigned to the external "other" (the immigrant, the refugee) or the domestic "enemy," the socioeconomic or political elite (the "deep state," etc.). Both images of the "other" often merge in the anti-Semitic trope of the global Jewish elite as the menacing risk to the well-being of the people.

The German context and the rise of the so-called Alternative for Germany (AfD) party provides a vivid illustration of how nativist rhetorical elements are fused with the anti-elitist political trait: The collective identity based on a clear sense of "Us" (the locals, the Germans) and "Them" (the foreigners, the EU) is critical for the mobilizing efforts of the AfD. This strong collective identity promises to provide a remedy against the experience of social decline or marginalization: pride in the national community and the promise of solidarity based on a nativist identity. Salmela and von Scheve describe how, from a social-psychological perspective, right-wing populists offer a politically effectual strategy to address the fear of social decline and status inconsistency.[15] Their underlying collective identity provides an ideational avenue to transform uncertainty and fear into resentment and hatred toward the perceived enemy of the people.[16] Using the ethnic or cultural "other" as a scapegoat for social ills is as emotionally exhilarating as it is politically shrewd. This reliance on a strong, predominantly ethnocentric Us-versus-Them binary is at the core of many right-wing populist parties. With respect to the German AfD, Rensmann's diagnosis that the political radicalization of the party is not detrimental to its popular appeal points to how central discourses of othering and exclusionary nationalism are to the recent electoral successes of this party.[17]

The agonistic politics displayed in this latter sense promises a democratic empowerment of those depicted as deprived and disenfranchised. The

[15] Mikko Salmela and Christian von Scheve, "Emotional Roots of Right-Wing Political Populism," *Social Science Information* 56, no. 4 (2017): 567–95.

[16] Bart Bonikowski, "Ethno-Nationalist Populism and the Mobilization of Collective Resentment," *The British Journal of Sociology* 68 (2017): 181–213.

[17] Lars Rensmann, "Radical Right-Wing Populists in Parliament: Examining the Alternative for Germany in European Context," *German Politics and Society* 36, no. 3 (2018): 41–73. For further discussion, see Manuela Caiani and Patricia Kroll, "Nationalism and Populism in Radical Right Discourses in Italy and Germany," *Javnost: The Public* 24 (2017): 336–54; and Oliver Schmidtke, "Politicizing Social Inequality: Competing Narratives from the Alternative for Germany and Left-Wing Movement Stand Up," *Frontiers in Sociology* 5 (2020): 1–11.

rhetoric of winning back the sovereign rights of the people (in the Germany, the right-wing AfD has appropriated the slogan of the opposition against the GDR regime: "We are the people") links the plea for radical political change, an agonistic critique of consensus-focused liberalism, with the notion of a cohesive, homogenous community. This chapter does not intend to engage in a discussion about if and in what form this democratic promise of strengthening the sovereign rights of the people is actually kept or betrayed in practice. There have been compelling accounts of how right-wing populism mobilizes and strengthens authoritarian, antipluralistic impulses.[18] In the next section, I will examine why the evocation of a community has played such an important role also in the political mobilization of right-wing populism and how leftist, progressive forces have tended to underestimate this instrumental role of communal ties in promoting radical-democratic reforms.

THE CENTER-LEFT'S LOST SENSE OF COMMUNITY: ABANDONING A NOTION OF THE COMMON GOOD?

The left has a historically well-founded aversion to affective notions of community and its intrinsic reactionary, authoritarian political tendencies. As is evident in the current global resurgence of right-wing populism, the emphasis on the qualities and boundedness of the community tends to promote a form of identity politics wherein rules-based democracy and standards of universal rights are easily compromised or even systematically undermined by nativist ideas. With good reason, commentators have alluded to the "democratic pathology" of populist movements and how it challenges critical elements of liberal democracy.[19]

However, it is important to acknowledge how – under the auspices of the New Labour transformation of social democracy – the center-left has undervalued the power the reference to a community can have in terms of nurturing a sense of both the common good and a lived solidarity. Over recent decades the established left has shifted toward a form of politics that is firmly rooted in individual rights and entitlements. In his recent book *The Tyranny of Merit*,[20] Michael Sandel presents a scathing critique of what he frames as the meritocratic ideal. Further, it is this ideal that has become the dominant framework on which also the center-left has formulated its responses

---

[18] Tarik Kochi, "The End of Global Constitutionalism and Rise of Antidemocratic Politics," *Global Society* 34, no. 4 (2020): 487–506, https://doi.org/10.1080/13600826.2020.1749037.

[19] Most notably, the independence of political institutions such as the parliamentary or the judiciary system. For further examples, see Koen Abts and Stefan Rummens, "Populism versus Democracy," *Political Studies* 55, no. 2 (2007): 405–24; and Cas Mudde, "Populist Radical Right Parties in Europe Today," in *Transformations of Populism in Europe and the Americas: History and Recent Trends*, ed. John Abromeit et al. (London: Bloomsbury, 2016), 295–307.

[20] Michael J. Sandel, *The Tyranny of Merit: What's Become of the Common Good?* (New York: MacMillan, 2020).

to the challenges of globalization and rising levels of social inequality.[21] Sandel focuses on what he describes as a corrosive left-wing individualism:

The solution to problems of globalisation and inequality – and we heard this on both sides of the Atlantic – was that those who work hard and play by the rules should be able to rise as far as their effort and talents will take them. This is what I call in the book the "rhetoric of rising." It became an article of faith, a seemingly uncontroversial trope. We will make a truly level playing field, it was said by the centre-left, so that everyone has an equal chance. And if we do, and so far as we do, then those who rise by dint of effort, talent, hard work will deserve their place, will have earned it.[22]

At the core of Sandel's book is the claim that meritocracy is corrosive of the common good. Assigning the responsibility and blame for growing social inequality to individuals' virtues and resources deepens, in his interpretation, the political divide between "winners and losers." Those who lose out economically or culturally are subjected to a socially sanctioned humiliation as "not trying hard enough." These animosities in turn fuel the populist anger with established elites. Sandel underlines the significance of the dignity of work and our social understanding of success as ways to reanimate civic life.

One can also interpret his insights with a view to the role of community under consideration here. Under neoliberal guises, the reliance on individual merit has eroded a substantial notion of how citizens are social beings whose well-being is fundamentally shaped by the community of which they are a part. Our political approaches to address deepening forms of social inequality – arguably one of the pivotal drivers of the populist resurgence – are based on ideologies justifying or questioning the legitimacy of these inequalities and injustices. Yet, at the same time, it is a strong notion of community that provides the ideational and social basis for considering the common good and the way individuals should participate in it. The demand for social inclusion presupposes a form of social contract or a notion of the common good that would be difficult to achieve based on individual merit alone.

Patriotism has become tainted by the demand of the populist-nationalist right; its ideological affinity to nativist ideas has made the left shun any of the conceptions and emotions attached to them. Yet, without a substantiated form of fellowship and community, without the experience of practiced solidarity in communal settings, individuals are largely left with the logic of a competitive, market-based meritocracy. Under these circumstances, the value of social equality becomes reduced to a market competition in which individuals ultimately become responsible for their own social status. In contrast, the working-class movement had a strong mobilizing notion of community-based identity and solidarity. The values and practices attached to the common good

---

[21] Similarly, see Sheri Berman, "Populism is a Symptom Rather Than a Cause: Democratic Disconnect, the Decline of the Center-Left, and the Rise of Populism in Western Europe," *Polity* 51 (2019): 654–67; and Sheri Berman and Maria Snegovaya, "Populism and the Decline of Social Democracy," *Journal of Democracy* 30, no. 3 (2019): 5–19.

[22] Berman and Snegovaya, "Populism and the Decline of Social Democracy," 23.

represented in this community were instrumental in spurring its political fight and challenging the logic of capitalist socialization. Without this narrative and communal network, the social-democratic left has gradually lost the ability to provide a voice to those who feel threatened by the global economy and the social changes it has triggered.[23]

In a similar vein, Wendy Brown, in her book *Undoing the Demos*, has pointed to the political implications of the neoliberal age.[24] Brown demonstrates how the neoliberal logic of economic metrics has subjected all domains of social life to market-based standards, thereby eroding the basis for democratic citizenship. In her interpretation, organizing social life exclusively in a market-based logic corrodes the political imaginary and social-institutional framework that makes democracy work. She establishes the direct link between the dominance of neoliberalism, the erosion of democratic citizenship, and the strengthening of the toxic political debate on which right-wing populism thrives:

As neoliberalism wages war on public goods and the very idea of a public, including citizenship beyond membership, it dramatically thins public life without killing politics. Struggles remain over power, hegemonic values, resources, and future trajectories. This persistence of politics amid the destruction of public life and especially educated public life, combined with the marketization of the political sphere, is part of what makes contemporary politics peculiarly unappealing and toxic – full of ranting and posturing, emptied of intellectual seriousness, pandering to an uneducated and manipulable electorate and a celebrity-and-scandal-hungry corporate media.[25]

Without community-based standards of justice and entitlements, all that is left is the deepening animosity between social groups. Depriving people of the dignity of work and the recognition that they contribute to the common good paves, in Brown's and Sandel's interpretation, the road toward a society that is deeply divided, both socially and politically. It is worth considering how the impact of COVID-19 has drawn public awareness to the way in which individuals are integrated into and dependent on a net of social relations in the public sphere. For instance, frontline workers in the service industry and the healthcare system have recently been recognized as indispensable for the functioning of our social fabric (including a growing awareness of the vulnerability of this workforce that is constituted in large part by women, migrants, and racialized people[26]). Around the world, the effectiveness of the response to the global pandemic has been

[23] See Luke March and Cas Mudde, "What's Left of the Radical Left? The European Radical Left After 1989: Decline *and* Mutation," *Comparative European Politics* 3, no. 1 (2006): 23–49; and Michael McQuarrie, "The Revolt of the Rust Belt: Place and Politics in the Age of Anger," *The British Journal of Sociology* 68 (2017): 120–52.
[24] Wendy Brown, *Undoing the Demos: Neoliberalism's Stealth Revolution* (New York: Zone Books, 2015).
[25] Brown, *Undoing the Demos*: 39.
[26] See Michael Simpson, "For a Prefigurative Pandemic Politics: Disrupting the Racial Colonial Quarantine," *Political Geography* 84 (2021): 1–3.

critically shaped by how robust the communal response to the crisis was and how much trust there has been in the sense of mutual commitment in this community. In essence, the global pandemic underlines how strongly the vitality of a community and forms of civic engagement are coconstitutive.

THE ENABLING SOCIAL INFRASTRUCTURE OF LOCAL COMMUNITIES: CIVIC ENGAGEMENT

One of the central deficits of liberal democracy is the detachment between the collective decision-making process in the parliamentary system and the democratic engagement of individual citizens. Populists thrive on frustration with the established functioning of democratic institutions and challenge the status quo with the notion of a popular sovereignty that could be restored to the "people." Yet, at the same time, populists regularly fall short in providing avenues toward a meaningful and substantiated form of civic engagement.[27] One significant element in populists' attempt to promote what it means to reinstall genuine popular sovereignty is the reliance on mass rallies and the turn away from the practices of place-based communities. The appeal for a populist response to the crisis of democracy reflects the loss of trust that many citizens feel toward their ability to govern their communities in a democratic fashion.[28]

In this section, I focus on the features of social life – networks, norms, and trust – that enable participants to act together more effectively to pursue shared objectives. The sociology of (urban) public space and community organizations offers us multifaceted findings on the vital resources that such spaces provide for creating communities rooted in shared civic practices.[29] In his recent book *Palaces for the People*, Klinenberg underlines the centrality of a "social infrastructure" as a physical environment that enables the interactions of people in a community.[30] As Klinenberg suggests, a robust social infrastructure "fosters contact, mutual support, and collaboration among friends and neighbours."[31] The encounters in public spaces and webs of social interactions

---

[27] Nadia Urbinati, *Me the People: How Populism Transforms Democracy* (Cambridge, MA: Harvard University Press, 2019).

[28] Gregor Fitzi, Juergen Mackert, and Bryan S. Turner, eds., *Populism and the Crisis of Democracy*, vol. 3, *Migration, Gender and Religion* (New York: Routledge, 2018).

[29] For further examples, see Elijah Anderson, *The Cosmopolitan Canopy: Race and Civility in Everyday Life* (New York: W. W. Norton & Company, 2011); Adrian Little, "Community and Radical Democracy," *Journal of Political Ideologies* 7, no. 3 (2002): 369–82; Warren Magnusson, "The Symbiosis of the Urban and the Political," *International Journal of Urban and Regional Research* 38, no. 5 (2014): 1561–75; and Nicole P. Marwell and Michael McQuarrie, "People, Place, and System: Organizations and the Renewal of Urban Social Theory," *The ANNALS of the American Academy of Political and Social Science* 647, no. 1 (2013): 126–43.

[30] Eric Klinenberg, *Palaces for the People: How Social Infrastructure Can Help Fight Inequality, Polarization, and the Decline of Civic Life* (New York: Broadway Books, 2018).

[31] Ibid., 5.

that these create in the community are foundational resources also for cultivating civic engagement and democratic practices on the ground. These recurrent, institutionally sanctioned forms of social interaction play a formative role in creating trust, solidarity, and mutual commitment in the community. The community-rooted social infrastructure facilitates shared experiences and activities (from public squares to community gardens and child care facilities) based on which citizens develop common interests and the collective capacity in governing the commons.

A recent multi-year study that colleagues and I conducted on NHs[32] in Metro Vancouver provides a brief illustration of the central role this community-based social infrastructure is able to provide for democratic practice.[33] The services and programs that NHs offer often open the door to meaningful interaction and engagement. In the fundamental way that Putnam described social capital as providing the infrastructure for making democracy work, NHs are a key player in nurturing a sense of trust and reciprocity in community life. They are also advocates for their communities as they have a profound effect on the network of interactions and encounters that make up a community. They sustain the capacity to find a voice in the community, both individually and collectively.

Thus, the seemingly mundane practice of interacting at NHs and participating in community-based activities can enable the learning and practice of important civic and political skills. The effect on the skills and confidence of the respondents is particularly pronounced for those born outside Canada. The local community at a NH validates and recognizes a person's contributions. These civic skills learned through involvement and relating to others are a pivotal resource that contributes to overcoming social isolation and encouraging engagement in the wider community. Sean Lauer reports that more than 60 percent of respondents stated that they made at least one close friend through the NHs, and he finds a significant increase in civic and community engagement directly related to being involved in NHs. Similarly, qualitative interviews with this group underlined the fact that social isolation is a major concern, and one that can be addressed effectively by NHs.

One critical reason why immigrants and minorities in particular find themselves isolated and unable to contribute to public debates is the absence of low-threshold opportunities for engagement. NHs offer precisely this entry into communal engagement in a nonthreatening, service-based environment. The project conducted oral histories with participants about their personal

[32] Neighbourhood Houses are nonprofit, community-organized places that offer multiple services in particular for less privileged groups. In 2014, NHs in Metro Vancouver provided a total of 444 programs/activities (overall 208,664 participants).
[33] For the results of the project, see Your Neighbourhood House, www.yournh.ca; and Miu Chung Yan and Sean Lauer, eds., *Neighbourhood Houses: Building Community in Vancouver* (Vancouver: UBC Press, 2021).

experiences of NHs. One recurrent theme in these interviews is how the use of services gradually built trust and turned NHs into "safe places." Instrumental in this respect is the reliance of NHs on volunteers: in 2012–13, more than 3,670 people registered as volunteers in NHs in Metro Vancouver. In the same vein, NHs have become socializing agencies that regularly allow immigrants to become leaders in their community and take on prominent roles in public life. In 2013, more than 60 percent of staff members at NHs were either current or former resident service users. As an active part of the NGO community at the urban level, NHs pave the path of immigrants toward professional careers with third-sector organizations, community engagement, and leadership.

At the collective level, NHs facilitate residents working together to achieve collective goals. They provide a physical and social framework for social networks, dialogue, and collective-communal empowerment. The skills that community members acquire in taking part in or organizing events can easily be transferred to other forms of active engagement. Through low-cost, family-friendly services and social events, NHs offer tangible incentives to overcome alienation from communal life, particularly for those who have a more precarious social status (low-income people, seniors, immigrants, and minorities). These self-governing community associations can be interpreted as entry points and networks that facilitate democratic participation in a basic yet essential way. As Yan puts it, "motives of democratic participation, sharing, and reciprocity are actualized through services"[34] offered at NHs.[35]

Social capital researchers have suggested that bridging ties is important for political participation. Our research suggests that NHs play such a bridging role in connecting citizens to communal affairs and opening the door for modes of participation.[36] Building on the insight from social capital frameworks, one can argue that NHs bring people together, contribute to overcoming social isolation, convey information about issues in the community, and provide low-threshold forms of participation in grassroots initiatives (see the findings of the survey documented in Table 4.1).

Considering the nature of program activities at NHs in Metro Vancouver, it is evident that the most important type of program consists of direct services to

---

[34] Miu Chung Yan, "Bridging the Fragmented Community: Revitalizing Settlement Houses in the Global Era," *Journal of Community Practice* 12, nos. 1–2 (2004): 58.

[35] Based on their case study of neighbourhoods in Los Angeles, Juliet Musso and Christopher Weare similarly point to the significance of networked-based social capital in supporting the democratic functions of neighbourhood governance networks. For further discussion, see Juliet Musso and Christopher Weare, "Social Capital and Community Representation: How Multiform Networks Promote Local Democracy in Los Angeles," *Urban Studies* 54, no. 11 (2017): 2521–39.

[36] Caroline Patsias, Anne Latendresse, and Laurence Bherer, "Participatory Democracy, Decentralization and Local Governance: The Montreal Participatory Budget in the Light of 'Empowered Participatory Governance'," *International Journal of Urban and Regional Research* 37, no. 6 (2013): 2214–30.

TABLE 4.1 *Perceived changes in social skills through involvement at neighbourhood houses*

| | Total (%) | | Place of birth | | | |
| | | | Inside Canada | | Outside Canada | |
Change in social skills	Increased a little	Increased a lot	Increased a little	Increased a lot	Increased a little	Increased a lot
Has your ability to work with people from different backgrounds changed?	42	34	34	29	46	38
Have your decision-making abilities changed?	42	26	30	19	48	29
Have your skills in organizing or managing events and programs changed?	36	21	24	17	42	23
Have your skills in speaking in front of other people changed?	35	27	22	19	42	32

the community (e.g. daycare, services for families and seniors), which also cover a main part of the NHs' funding scheme. Yet, it is striking to see that a considerable number of those activities are also directly related to community- and advocacy-oriented initiatives. Some of these activities are explicitly designed to serve this purpose; others might start with a local issue and morph into a broader concern for the well-being of the community. Food-related activities are an example. As evidence from multiple NHs suggests, work on a local communal garden project can be a rewarding socializing experience, sensitizing NHs participants to and involving them in issues related to food security, urban planning, and healthy living.

The results of the survey provide us with an interpretative lens through which to view the broader sociopolitical functions that such civil society associations can take on in giving a voice to newcomers and minorities. By investigating the role that NHs play in municipal and provincial policy-making, our research found consistent evidence of how these self-governing associations in Metro Vancouver establish an institutional infrastructure for building and strengthening urban communities and nurturing their collective capacity. The case study of NHs emphasizes the importance of *bridging* social capital – establishing vertical social networks between socially diverse groups or organizations. The experience of these organizations in the urban context is that, when previously unrelated or dissimilar community organizations and groups connect with one another, the created ties strengthen the overall social fabric.[37]

The case of NHs sheds light on how the social infrastructure of the local-urban context can facilitate democratic processes in a fundamental sense: First, nongovernment actors such as NHs provide an institutional infrastructure for building and strengthening urban communities and nurturing their collective capacity. Second, they build social capital as a key component of democratic and socially sustainable civic communities, thus delivering a response to the growing social inequality and alienation in urban communities. Third, place-based organizations are a critical part of addressing the increasingly complex challenges of urban communities (joint government–civil society problem-solving) through horizontal and vertical coordination as key to effective policy-making.

MULTI-SCALAR COMMUNITIES: REIMAGINING POLITICAL COMMUNITY

The example of the NHs in Metro Vancouver speaks to our established understanding of communities as local associations. And indeed, my argument is that these place-based communities where people interact, debate, and become politically engaged will be a cornerstone of a revitalized democratic public sphere.[38] Contrasting the local context, with its rich opportunities of generating a sense of community shaped by a dense network of face-to-face social interactions on the one hand and the imagined, more abstract national community on the other, has been a long-standing issue in democratic theorizing.[39] However, it is doubtful whether a strengthening of governance practices in local communities by itself will be able to provide a sufficiently robust response to the declining trust in democratic institutions and practices more broadly. Indeed, cynics would argue that democratic

---

[37] See, for example, Yan and Lauer, *Neighbourhood Houses*.

[38] Along those same lines, for the case for local democracy in a global era see Thad Williamson, David Imbroscio, and Gar Alperovitz, *Making a Place for Community: Local Democracy in a Global Era* (New York: Routledge, 2003).

[39] Janet Newman and John Clarke, *Publics, Politics and Power: Remaking the Public in Public Services* (London: Sage, 2009).

engagement and participation in local communities could also be instrumental in sheltering power structures from democratic oversight.

The widespread frustration with democracy and the associated populist response are vitally rooted in the growing incongruity between sites of economic and political power, on the one hand, and the institutional reach of principles of democratic accountability and citizens' involvement in the political decision-making process, on the other. While causally attributing the rise of right-wing populism simply to the frustration of the "losers of globalization" is misleading, it points to an important enabling factor of this political actor: Politics in the age of globalization is characterized by a heightened sense of losing control – sentiments populists capitalize on ardently. In this respect, the populist challenge to liberal democracy is at its core also indicative of how our traditional sense of the democratic community is being transformed and challenged. Historically, democracy has been tied to the nation-state as the sole (territorially defined) mode of political community in which citizens are bestowed with rights and the democratic decision-making process unfolds. Yet, given the internationalizing realities of the twenty-first century, community-driven processes of democratic reform would need to be recalibrated in response to multiple, overlapping sites of power and governance structures.[40] In this regard, populism raises legitimate questions about fundamental challenges of contemporary liberal democracy: What defines a people as a bounded political community (*demos*), and how do we establish effective forms of self-government by providing citizens with the opportunity to participate in decisions that affect their lives?[41]

Europe provides a straightforward example of reconsidering the politics of scale when it comes to revitalizing community and citizenship practices: The internationalization of European societies in particular, both with respect to the integration of national economies into bigger supranational regional blocks and the transferral of political authority from the national to the European level, has caused a level of anxiety and uncertainty that has demonstrated to be exploitable by simplistic and populist forms of protest.[42] In relinquishing

---

[40] For further discussion, see Daniele Archibugi, David Held, and Martin Köhler, *Re-Imagining Political Community: Studies in Cosmopolitan Democracy* (Cambridge: Polity Press, 1998); David Held, "The Changing Contours of Political Community: Rethinking Democracy in the Context of Globalisation," *Theoria: A Journal of Social and Political Theory* 94 (1999): 30–47; Sandra Lavenex, "Globalization and the Vertical Challenge to Democracy," in *Democracy in the Age of Globalization and Mediatization*, ed. Hanspeter Kriesi et al. (London: Palgrave Macmillan, 2013), 105–34; and Jan Aart Scholte, "Reinventing Global Democracy," *European Journal of International Relations* 20, no. 1 (2014): 3–28.

[41] Kaltwasser frames these issues in terms of a response to Dahl's democratic dilemmas: Cristóbal Rovira Kaltwasser, "The Responses of Populism to Dahl's Democratic Dilemmas," *Political Studies* 62, no. 3 (2014): 470–87. For further discussion, see also Brendan McCaffrie and Sadiya Akram, "Crisis of Democracy?: Recognizing the Democratic Potential of Alternative Forms of Political Participation," *Democratic Theory* 1, no. 2 (2014): 47–55.

[42] For further examples, see Ben Crum and John Erik Fossum, "The Multilevel Parliamentary Field: A Framework for Theorizing Representative Democracy in the EU," *European Political Science*

considerable power to supranational institutions, vital questions are raised about the range and meaning of democratic rule.[43] At the core of these questions lies the conundrum of how we should define the demos as a bounded political community that provides the social framework for democratic deliberation and decision-making.

Considering multiple and overlapping levels of scale when it comes to the forces shaping our lives, the institutional arrangement of democratic intervention is of central importance. With a view to effective democratic practices, how can we match the nature of the sociopolitical, economic, and environmental challenges – also sites of power – to modes of engaged citizenship and democratic decision-making? Could a notion of the community and the common good still exclusively rely on the nation-state as the sole territorial marker of the political community? How can we adjust democratic practices to a changing social and economic reality in terms of cogenerating spaces and mechanisms for citizen engagement that allow us to address these challenges effectively?

Addressing these questions clearly is beyond the scope of this chapter, but it is worth pointing to how the potential of place-based, local communities for democratic reform could be a fruitful starting point in addressing the transformation of the political ordering of space.[44] Political practices of social movements have already adapted to the spatial reach of democratic actions. For instance, Della Porta has empirically and conceptually demonstrated how transnational social movements have developed effective modes of civic engagement that are commensurable with the nature and scope of their political claims (the environmental crisis, social inequality, racial exclusion, etc.).[45] Della Porta calls this practice a form of "local contention, global framing" articulated in transnational global activism.[46] New communication

---

Review 1, no. 2 (2009): 249–71; Thomas Risse, *A Community of Europeans?: Transnational Identities and Public Spheres* (Ithaca, NY: Cornell University Press, 2015); Fritz W. Scharpf, "After the Crash: A Perspective on Multilevel European Democracy," *European Law Journal* 21, no. 3 (2015): 384–405; Vivien Schmidt, "Democracy and Legitimacy in the European Union Revisited: Input, Output and Throughput," *Political Studies* 61, no. 1 (2013): 2–22.

[43] Richard Bellamy and Dario Castiglione, "Three Models of Democracy, Political Community and Representation in the EU," *Journal of European Public Policy* 20, no. 2 (2013): 206–23.

[44] See Quintin Bradley, "Bringing Democracy Back Home: Community Localism and the Domestication of Political Space," *Environment and Planning D: Society and Space* 32, no. 4 (2014): 642–57.

[45] Donatella della Porta, *Can Democracy Be Saved? Participation, Deliberation and Social Movements* (Malden, MA: Polity Press, 2013); Donatella della Porta and Gianni Piazza, "Local Contention, Global Framing: The Protest Campaigns Against the TAV in Val di Susa and the Bridge on the Messina Straits," *Environmental Politics* 16, no. 5 (2007): 864–82.

[46] Similarly, see Patrick Hayden, *Cosmopolitan Global Politics* (London: Routledge, 2017); and Sidney Tarrow and Doug McAdam, "Scale Shift in Transnational Contention," in *Transnational Protest and Global Activism*, eds. Donatella della Porta and Sidney Tarrow (Lanham, MD: Rowman & Littlefield, 2005), 121–50.

technologies combined with the political imagination of activists on the ground have opened up new avenues for redefining and expanding political communities.[47]

CONCLUSIONS

The relative strength of populist parties across Western democracy is centrally based on the claim of empowering the "people"; Koppetsch speaks in this context of the populist promise of being "collectively re-sovereignized."[48] The plea to represent ordinary people in their relationship to an unresponsive elite is discursively couched in strong images of community, a people joined by a shared collective identity. The emotionally charged sense of a community nourished and staged by nationalist populists has become one of the central political weapons to challenge what they perceive to be the technocratic modus operandi of liberal democracies. With their focus on national identity, populists have been able to offer a captivating and politically instrumental sense of community. In the case of right-wing populism, this invocation of a unified people in whose name their charismatic leaders claim to speak has had substantial undemocratic implications, both with respect to the contempt for procedural rules in the parliamentary system, if not openly authoritarian aspirations, and with a view to the exclusionary impetus with which the community is mobilized against alleged outsiders and "enemies of the people."

This chapter makes the argument that progressive forces considering the future of democracy should not simply dismiss the idea of community as integral to attempts to deepen democratic practices. Taking into account place-based communities and their modes of democratic empowerment is more than a nostalgic imagination of small-scale practices of self-governance. Exploring the conceptual link between community and democracy, I argue that the center-left has erroneously abandoned the reliance on a community defined by shared values and practices. Having bought into the neoliberal creed, the social-democratic left has not been able to find an effective counternarrative to the populist right's exclusionary nationalism.

While the promise of democratic empowerment of the "sovereign people" is regularly betrayed in the practice of right-wing populists, the affective reference to the community is powerful in its ability to challenge the political status quo in liberal democracy. Without such a mobilizing sense of community it will be difficult for those forces on the left, determined to deepen democratic practices and civic engagement, to respond to the populist resurgence from the right.

---

[47] On the idea of communicatively integrated communities, see Lewis A. Friedland, "Communication, Community, and Democracy: Toward a Theory of the Communicatively-Integrated Community," *Communication Research* 28, no. 4 (2001): 358–91.

[48] Cornelia Koppetsch, *Die Gesellschaft des Zorns: Rechtspopulismus im Globalen Zeitalter* (Bielefeld: Transcript Verlag, 2019), 217.

Historically, the working-class left could rely on a strong notion of community. Its strong collective identity, continuously reproduced through a network of civil society organizations, formed the cultural resources needed for the political fight. Without such a vibrant idea of what brings individuals together in a joined political cause, of what generates recognition, solidarity, and mutual commitment, the political identity of the left would remain pale and anemic compared to the dramatized narrative of the people and its elitist enemies on the right.

Similarly important for the future of democracy is the recognition that communities can produce a social infrastructure whose practices are essential for a revitalized engaged citizenship. Local communities can be powerful vectors of sustaining a social infrastructure that ties citizens into a collective decision-making process and provides them with the tools to become *citoyens* in the radical, Republican tradition. For the future of democracy it will be essential that citizens perceive modes of democratic engagement as meaningful and commensurable to the fundamental challenges that the current political and socio-environmental crisis poses. Transnational social movements are a promising approach to reimagining political communities and modes of civic engagement in multiple spatial contexts. Community and civic engagement sustain and nurture each other. If citizens are deprived of these avenues of exercising their democratic, participatory rights in a meaningful fashion, populism's simplistic political answers informed by narratives of exclusionary nationalism will continue to gain in appeal.

5

Democracies Can Perish Democratically Too: Brazilian Democracy on Edge

Boaventura de Sousa Santos

INTRODUCTION: FOUR ANTIDEMOCRATIC COMPONENTS
WITHIN DEMOCRACIES

We have long been accustomed to the idea that political regimes are divided into two major types: democracy and dictatorship. After the fall of the Berlin Wall in 1989, (liberal) democracy came to be almost universally regarded as the sole legitimate political system. Notwithstanding their internal diversity, the two types are basically contradictory in nature. They cannot coexist in the same society, and opting for one or the other always spells political struggle, which in turn entails some kind of rupture with the existing legal order. During the last century there was a growing belief that democracies could only collapse through an abrupt and almost invariably violent interruption of constitutional legality, carried out by a military or civilian coup aimed at imposing a dictatorship. This narrative used to be largely accurate, but not any more. Violent disruptions and coups d'état are still possible, but it has become increasingly obvious that the dangers that now beset democracy are of a different kind, and that they originate, paradoxically, in the normal functioning of democratic institutions. Antidemocratic political forces infiltrate the democratic system and then set about hijacking and decharacterizing it in a more or less stealthy and steady fashion, through legal means and no constitutional changes. Then there is a moment when the existing political system, without having formally ceased to be a democracy, appears as completely devoid of democratic content as regards the lives of both people and political organizations, until finally individuals and organizations alike begin to behave as if they were living

This chapter is adapted and revised from an earlier Portuguese version: Boaventura de Sousa Santos, "As democracias também morrem democraticamente," *Jornal de Letras, Artes e Ideias*, October 24, 2018, 29–30.

under a dictatorship. The following is a description of the four main components of that process.

Electing Autocrats

From the USA to the Philippines, to Turkey, Russia, Hungary, India, Poland and Brazil, we have witnessed the democratic election of authoritarian politicians who, while being the product of the political and economic establishment, present themselves as antisystem and antipolitics and insult their opponents, whom they view as corrupt and as enemies to be brought down. They reject the rules of democracy, make intimidating appeals for the violent resolution of social problems, flaunt their contempt for freedom of the press and pledge to repeal the laws that guarantee the social rights of workers and of those who are discriminated against on ethnoracial, sexual or religious grounds. In short, they stand for election on the basis of an antidemocratic ideology and still manage to secure a majority of votes. Autocratic politicians have always been around. What is new is how often they manage to rise to power these days, and apparently by democratic means.

The Plutocratic Virus

Money has decharacterized electoral processes and democratic deliberations at an alarming rate. One should even question whether, in many instances, elections are truly free and fair, and whether political decision-makers are ultimately driven by conviction or by the money paid to them. Liberal democracy rests on the notion that citizens have the means to access an informed public opinion and use it as a basis on which to freely elect their rulers and assess their rulers' performance. For this to be possible at all, the market of political ideas (i.e. of the values that are priceless, because they are deeply held beliefs) has to be totally separated from the market of economic goods (i.e. of the values that have a price and get to be bought and sold on that basis). In recent times, these two markets have been merging under the aegis of the economic market, so that nowadays everything is bought and sold in the realm of politics. Corruption has become endemic. In today's world, the financing of parties and candidates in election campaigns and the lobbying actions directed at parliaments and governments have gained central importance in the political life of many countries. In its 2010 decision *Citizens United* v. *The Federal Election Commission*, the US Supreme Court struck a fatal blow to US democracy when it allowed unlimited and private funding of elections and political decisions by large corporations and the super-wealthy. Hence the emergence of so-called "Dark Money," which is nothing other than legalized corruption. This "dark money" is what helps explain the preponderance of the bullet (firearms industry), bible (conservative

evangelism) and bovine (industrial agriculture and cattle raising) benches – that
cruel caricature of Brazilian society – in Brazil's Congress.

Fake News and Algorithms

For a time, both the internet and the social networks made possible by it were
seen as capable of enabling an unprecedented expansion of citizen
participation in democracy. After Brexit and in light of what is currently
happening in the USA and Brazil, we can say that unless they are properly
regulated, they will end up being the gravediggers of democracy. I allude here
to two specific tools. Fake news has always existed in societies marked by
deep divisions, especially in times of political rivalry. However, nowadays its
destructive potential through disinformation and the dissemination of lies is
alarming. This is particularly grave in countries such as India and Brazil,
where social networks, notably WhatsApp (whose content is the least
controllable of all, by reason of its being encrypted), are widely used, to the
point of being the major, if not the sole, source of citizen information (Brazil
has 120 million WhatsApp users). According to a denunciation by Brazilian
research groups published in *The New York Times* (October 17, 2018), of the
fifty most widely shared (viral) images generated by the 347 WhatsApp public
groups supporting presidential candidate Jair Bolsonaro, only four were
truthful.[1] One of those fake photos was that of Dilma Rousseff, the
impeached President in 2016 and at the time a candidate for the Senate,
seen with Fidel Castro in the Cuban Revolution. This was actually
a montage based on a 1959 piece by John Duprey for the *New York Daily
News*.[2] Dilma Rousseff was an 11-year-old child at the time. Supported by
large international corporations and national and foreign military
counterintelligence services, Bolsonaro's campaign, which led to his
election, was a monstrous montage of lies Brazilian democracy will find it
most difficult to survive.

The destructive effects are maximized by another tool: algorithms. This
word of Arab origin denotes the mathematical calculation for defining
priorities and making rapid decisions based on big data and a number of
variables, with a view to obtaining certain results (namely, success in
a corporation or in an election). Despite their neutral and objective
appearance, algorithms contain subjective opinions (What does being
successful mean? How do you define best candidate?) that lie hidden in
the calculations. When pressed to disclose their criteria, companies invoke
business secrecy. In the domain of politics, algorithms make it possible to

---

[1] Cristina Tardáguila, Fabrício Benevenuto and Pablo Ortellado, "Fake News Is Poisoning
Brazilian Politics. WhatsApp Can Stop It," *New York Times*, October 17, 2018, www
.nytimes.com/2018/10/17/opinion/brazil-election-fake-news-whatsapp.html.
[2] John Duprey, *New York Daily News*, April 22, 1959.

feedback on and amplify the topics that are widely disseminated via social networking and that are considered relevant by the algorithms for the very reason that they are popular. It thus happens that what is being widely disseminated may be the result of large-scale disinformation efforts performed by robot networks and automated accounts that send millions of people fake news and comments in favor of or against a given candidate, making the topic artificially popular and ultimately even more prominent thanks to the algorithm. An algorithm cannot tell true from false, and the effect of that is all the more destructive where people are especially vulnerable to lies. That is how, in recent times, electoral preferences have been manipulated in seventeen countries, including the United States (in favor of Donald Trump) and Brazil (in favor of Jair Bolsonaro), on a scale that could prove fatal to democracy. Will public opinion survive such levels of toxic information? Does real news stand a chance of resisting this avalanche of fake news? It is my contention that what people need most during flood situations is drinking water. Out of a similar concern regarding the rise of the computer-driven manipulation of our opinions, tastes and decisions, computer scientist Cathy O'Neil has termed big data and algorithms "weapons of math destruction."[3]

The Hijacking of Institutions

The impact that authoritarian and antidemocratic practices have on institutions tends to be gradual and steady. The presidents and parliaments elected by the new type of fraud I've just described (fraud 2.0) are given free rein to instrumentalize democratic institutions, and they are free to do so supposedly within the boundaries of the law, no matter how blatant the abuses or how skewed the interpretations of the law or the Constitution. In recent times, Brazil has turned into an immense laboratory for the authoritarian manipulation of legality or lawfare. This hijacking was what made it possible for a neofascist presidential candidate, such as Jair Bolsonaro, to make it to the second round of the elections and get elected on October 28, 2018. As has been the case with other countries, the first institution to be hijacked is the judicial system. The reason for this is twofold: because it is the institution whose political power is most removed from electoral politics, and because, in constitutional terms, this sovereign body is viewed as a "neutral arbiter." I shall analyze this hijacking process later in this chapter. What will Brazilian democracy be like if such hijacking comes to pass, followed by the hijackings it will render possible? Will it still be a democracy?

---

[3] Cathy O'Neil, *Weapons of Math Destruction: How Big Data Increases Inequality and Threatens Democracy* (New York: Penguin Random House, 2016).

DEMOCRACY AND JURIDICAL SYSTEMS

When, almost thirty years ago, I began studying the judicial system of various countries, the administration of justice had the least public visibility among the state's institutional dimensions.[4] The big exception was the United States, because of the central role played by the Supreme Court in defining the truly decisive public policies. Being part of the sole nonelected sovereign body and given their reactive nature (for as a rule they cannot be mobilized of their own initiative) as well as the fact that they depend on other state institutions (correctional services, public administration) to have their decisions enforced, the courts tended to play a relatively modest role within the organic life of the separation of powers introduced by modern political liberalism, so much so that the judicial function was credibly viewed by liberal political philosophy as apolitical. The reason for that had also to do with the fact that the courts dealt exclusively with individual rather than collective disputes and were designed not to interfere with the ruling classes and elites, which were protected by immunity and other privileges. Little was known about how the judicial system worked, the citizens who typically used it and their purpose in doing so.

Since then, everything has changed. This was caused by, among other things, the crisis of political representation that hit elected sovereign bodies, the citizens' growing awareness of their rights, and the fact that, when faced with political deadlocks in the midst of controversial issues, the political elites began to regard the selective use of the courts as a way of lifting the political weight off certain decisions. Equally important was the fact that the neoconstitutionalism that came out of the Second World War assigned a considerable weight to the control of constitutionality by constitutional courts. This novel development lent itself to two opposite readings. According to one reading, ordinary legislation had to be subjected to control in order to prevent it from being instrumentalized by political forces bent on scrapping all constitutional requirements – as had been the case, in the most extreme fashion, with the Nazi and fascist dictatorships. According to the other interpretation, the control of constitutionality was the tool used by the ruling political classes to defend themselves against potential threats to their interests as a result of the vicissitudes of democratic politics and of "majority tyranny." Be that as it may, these developments all led to a new kind of judicial activism that came to be known as the judicialization of politics and inevitably led to the politicization of justice.

The high public visibility of the courts over the last decades was largely caused by court cases involving members of the political and economic elites. The major watershed was the series of criminal proceedings known as

---

[4] See Boaventura de Sousa Santos, *Toward a New Legal Common Sense: Law, Globalization, and Emancipation*, 3rd ed. (Cambridge: Cambridge University Press, 2020); Boaventura de Sousa Santos, *Toward a New Common Sense: Law, Science and Politics in the Paradigmatic Transition* (New York: Routledge, 1995); and Boaventura de Sousa Santos et al., *Os Tribunais nas Sociedades Contemporâneas: O Caso Português* (Porto: Afrontamento, 1996).

Operation Clean Hands (Mani Pulite), which struck virtually all of Italy's political class and much of its economic elite. Starting in Milan in April 1992, the operation comprised the investigation and arrest of cabinet ministers, party leaders, members of parliament (with about one-third of all members being investigated at one point), businessmen, civil servants, journalists and members of the secret services, variously accused of such crimes as bribery, corruption, abuse of power, fraud, fraudulent bankruptcy, false accounting and illegal political funding. Two years later, 633 people had been arrested in Naples, 623 in Milan and 444 in Rome. As a result of its having hit the entire political class under whose leadership the country had been governed in the recent past, the Clean Hands investigation shook the foundations of the Italian political system and led to the emergence, years later, of the Berlusconi "phenomenon." Given these and other reasons, the courts of many countries have gained much public notoriety ever since. The most recent, and perhaps the most dramatic of all, to my knowledge, is Brazil's Operation Lava Jato ("Car Wash" – or rather, and literally, "speed laundering").

This anticorruption operation mounted by the judiciary and the police was first launched in March 2014. Targeting more than a hundred politicians, businessmen and managers, it gradually came to occupy center stage in Brazil's political life. In view of the criminal charges brought against former President Lula da Silva, and the way this was effected, it generated a political crisis similar to that which led to the 1964 coup whereby a vile military dictatorship was established that was to last until 1985. The judicial system – supposedly the ultimate guarantor of the legal order – has become a dangerous source of legal disorder. Blatantly illegal and unconstitutional judicial measures, a crassly selective persecutory zeal, an aberrant promiscuity in which media outlets were at the service of the conservative political elites and a seemingly anarchic judicial hyper-activism – resulting, for instance, in twenty-seven injunctions relating to a single political act (President Dilma Rousseff's invitation to Lula da Silva to join the government) – all these bespeak a situation of legal chaos that tended to foster uncertainty, deepen social and political polarization and push Brazilian democracy to the edge of chaos. With legal order thus turned into legal disorder and democracy being hijacked by the nonelected sovereign body, political and social life became a potential field of spoils at the mercy of political adventurers and vultures.

Mainly due this grotesque lawfare experiment, Jair Bolsonaro was elected President of Brazil in 2018. Proudly claiming that he knew nothing about economics, Bolsonaro chose Paulo Guedes to head the ministry of finance – an extreme neoliberal economist who trained at the Chicago School of Economics. Having collaborated with the Pinochet regime, Guedes proposed dismantling whatever remained of the (always weak) welfare state and to bring about a sweeping process of privatization. The newly elected president combined this war against the popular classes (those most dependent on public social policies) with an extreme-right ideological outlook that included praising the military dictatorship that ran the country between 1964 and 1985 and, more specifically, the torture practiced by the dictators against political dissidents (including the former president Dilma Rousseff); nominating generals for key ministerial positions (besides having chosen a general as his vice-president); assuming a racist and sexist disposition to eliminate antidiscrimination, affirmative action and women's reproductive rights; deregulating the acquisition of weapons by civilians as the best policy to fight rampant crime rates; refusing to grant new territories to Indigenous peoples that he considered to be an obstacle to development; expanding industrial agriculture even at the cost of the final destruction of the Amazonian rain forest; condoning and even promoting an extreme politicization of the judicial system by choosing Sérgio Moro, the truculent and procedurally reckless coordinator of the Car Wash operation, to head the ministry of justice (with new national security functions); threatening to send to prison or into exile all the main leaders of the different left parties; banning thousands of Cuban doctors that provided primary health care to the impoverished communities of the vast hinterland, a highly ideological gesture; assuming an anti-immigrant politics (in a country of immigrants and slavery); and defending a mindless and belligerent alignment with the most reactionary imperialist policies of US President Trump, be it possible military intervention against Venezuela, denial of global warming or moving the Brazilian embassy to Jerusalem, against all the UN resolutions.

The Covid-19 pandemic exposed and intensified most dramatically the necropolitics that has characterized Bolsonaro's presidency all along. At the time of writing (early September 2020) the total deaths are coming close to 131,000, second only to the USA. More than grossly neglecting to protect the lives of Brazilian citizens, the government seems to be engaged in a sinister contempt for life (negationism combined with measures that willfully endanger lives) – so much so that several criminal complaints have been filed against Bolsonaro in the International Criminal Court: he is accused of crimes against humanity and of genocide against the Indigenous peoples.

At this point, several questions have to be addressed. How did it come to this? Who benefits from the present situation? What should be done to save Brazilian democracy and the institutions on which it stands, including its courts? How is one to attack this many-headed hydra, so that new heads do not grow for each severed head? I suggest a few answers in the following sections.

HOW DID IT COME TO THIS?

Why has Operation Lava Jato gone well beyond the limits of the controversies that habitually arise in the wake of any prominent case of judicial activism? The similarity with Italy's Clean Hands probe was often invoked to justify the public display and the public unrest caused by this judicial activism. But the similarities were more apparent than real and there were indeed two very definite differences between the two investigations. On the one hand, the Italian magistrates always kept a scrupulous respect for the criminal proceedings and, at most, did nothing but apply rules that had been strategically ignored by a judicial system that was not only conformist but also complicit with the privileges of the ruling political elites in Italy's postwar politics. On the other hand, they sought to apply the same unvarying zeal in investigating the crimes committed by the leaders of the various governing political parties. They assumed a politically neutral position precisely to defend the judicial system from the attacks it would surely be subjected to by those targeted by their investigations and prosecutions. This is the very antithesis of the sad spectacle offered to the world by a sector of the Brazilian judicial system. The impact caused by the activism of Italy's magistrates came to be called the Republic of Judges. In the case of the activism displayed by the sector associated with Lava Jato, it would perhaps be more accurate to speak of a judicial Banana Republic.

Indeed, an external push clearly lay behind this particular instance of Brazilian judicial activism, one which was largely absent in the Italian case: the illegal interference of the FBI and the US Department of Justice under the umbrella of the so-called war against corruption. That push dictated the glaring selectivity of the investigative and accusatory zeal toward implicating the leaders of the progressive social-democratic party, PT (the Workers' Party), with the unmistakable purpose of bringing about the political assassination of former Presidents Dilma Rousseff and Lula da Silva, thus clearing the ground for the election of Bolsonaro. In view of the selective nature of the legal action it generated, Operation Lava Jato shared more similarities with another judicial investigation: that which took place in the Weimar Republic after the failure of the German revolution of 1918. Starting that year, and in a context of political violence originating both in the extreme left and the extreme right, Germany's courts showed a shocking display of double standards, punishing with severity the kind of violence committed by the far left and showing great leniency toward the violence of the far right – the same right that within only a few years was to bring Hitler to power. In Brazil, the US imperialistic interference came to the rescue of the national and global economic elites which, in the midst of the current global crisis of capital accumulation, felt seriously threatened by the prospect of another four years with no control over that government-dependent portion of the country's resources on which their power had always rested. The height of that threat was reached when Lula da Silva – viewed as the best Brazilian president since 1988, with an 80 percent approval rating at the end of his term – began being regarded as a potential presidential candidate for 2018.

At that moment Brazilian democracy ceased to be functional for this conservative political bloc, and political destabilization ensued. The most obvious sign of the antidemocratic drive was the movement to impeach President Dilma Rousseff within a few months of her inauguration – a fact that was, if not totally unheard of, at least highly unusual in the democratic history of the last three decades. Realizing that their struggle for power was blocked by democracy's majority rule ("majority tyranny"), they sought to make use of the sovereign organ, the judicial system, least dependent on the rules of democracy and specifically designed to protect minorities, namely the courts. Operation Lava Jato – in theory, a highly worthy investigation – was the tool to which they resorted. Backed by the conservative legal culture that is widely predominant in Brazil's judicial system, its law schools and the country at large, as well as by a full arsenal of high-powered, high-precision media weapons, the conservative bloc did everything it could to distort Operation Lava Jato. It thus diverted it from its judicial goals, which in themselves were crucial for the consolidation of democracy, and turned it into an operation of political extermination. The distortion consisted in keeping the institutional façade of Operation Lava Jato while profoundly changing its underlying functional structure, which was accomplished by ensuring that the political took precedence over the judicial. Whereas judicial logic is based on the fit between means and ends, as dictated by procedural rules and constitutional guarantees, political logic, if propelled by the antidemocratic drive, subordinates ends to means and defines its own efficacy according to the degree of that subordination.

In this process, the intentions of the conservative bloc had three major factors in their favor. The first was the dramatic change in character undergone by the PT as a democratic party of the left. Once in power, the PT decided to rule according to the "old (i.e. oligarchic) style" to attain its new, innovative goals. Ignorant of the Weimar lesson, it believed that any "irregularities" it might commit would be met with the same leniency traditionally reserved for irregularities committed by the elites and the conservative political classes that had ruled the country since its independence. Ignorant of the Marxist lesson it claimed to have absorbed, it failed to see that capital will allow no one to govern it but its own people and is never grateful to any outsiders who happen to do it favors. Taking advantage of an international context in which, as a consequence of China's development, the value of primary products saw an exceptional increase, the PT government encouraged the rich to get richer. This was seen as a precondition for raising the resources it needed to carry out the extraordinary measures of social redistribution that made Brazil a substantially less unjust country, thanks to which more than 45 million Brazilians were freed from the yoke of endemic poverty. When the international context was no longer favorable, nothing short of a "new style" of politics would do to ensure social redistribution. In other words, a new policy was required that, among other things, might use political reform to end the promiscuous relationship between political and economic power, tax reform to tax the rich as a way of financing social redistribution in the post-commodity boom period and, finally, media reform, not to impose censorship, but rather to ensure diversity in published opinion. As it turned out, however, it was too late for all those things, which should have been done in their own time and not in a context of crisis.

The second factor is linked to the first: It is the global economic crisis and the iron grip in which it is held by finance capital and its relentless self-destructiveness, which destroys wealth under the pretext of creating wealth and turns money from a medium of exchange into a prime commodity of financial speculation. The hypertrophy of financial markets calls for austerity policies under which the poor are invested with the duty of helping the rich to stay rich and, if possible, to get richer. Under these conditions, the frail middle classes created in the previous period found themselves on the brink of sudden poverty. With their minds poisoned by the conservative media and fake news, they were quick to hold responsible for what might befall them in the future the very governments that turned them into new middle classes. This was all the more likely to happen since people were promoted as consumers (access to consumer society) rather than as citizens (political activism). This was the fare they paid to travel from the slave quarters to the Manor's outside patios.

The third factor working in favor of the conservative bloc was the fact that, after its fatal adventures in the Middle East, US imperialism returned to the Latin American sub-continent. Fifty years ago, imperialism knew no means other than military dictatorship to submit the countries of the continent to its own interests. Today, imperialist interests have other means at their disposal, namely sectors of the judicial system and US-financed local development projects run by nongovernmental organizations whose gestures in defense of democracy are just a front for covert, aggressive attacks and provocations directed at progressive democratic governments ("down with communism," "down with Marxism," "down with Paulo Freire," "we are not Venezuela," etc.). In such times as these, when the establishment of dictatorships can be avoided by low-intensity democracy and when the military, still traumatized by past experiences, seems unwilling to embark on new authoritarian adventures, these forms of destabilization are viewed as more effective in that they allow replacing progressive governments with conservative governments while maintaining the democratic façade. All the financing currently abounding in Brazil comes from a wide variety of funds (the novel nature of a more pervasive imperialism), from the proverbial CIA-related organizations to the Koch brothers – who fund the most conservative policies in the USA, their money coming mainly from the oil sector – and North American evangelical organizations.

HOW CAN BRAZILIAN DEMOCRACY BE SAVED?

The first and most pressing task is to save the Brazilian judiciary from the abyss into which it is sinking. In order to achieve that, its wholesome sector – surely the majority of the judicial system – must take upon itself the task of re-establishing order, serenity and restraint among its members. The guiding principle is simple enough to state: the independence of the courts under the rule of law is intended to allow them to fulfill their share of responsibility in consolidating democratic order and democratic coexistence. For that to happen, they are barred from putting their own independence at the service of any corporate or sectorial political interests, no matter how powerful. Although easy to state, the principle is very difficult to enforce. The top responsibility for enforcing it, at this point, lies with two different bodies. The STF (Federal Supreme Court) must assume its role as the ultimate guarantor of the legal order and put an end to the spreading legal anarchy. The STF will be faced with many important decisions in the near future, which must be obeyed by all, irrespective of what it decides. At present, the Supreme Court is the only institution capable of halting the plunge toward the state of emergency. As to the CNJ (National Council of Justice), which has disciplinary power over the magistrates, it should initiate immediate disciplinary proceedings by reason of reiterated prevarication and procedural abuse, not only against judge Sérgio Moro, who directed the investigation in a blatantly biased manner, but against all those who conducted themselves in similar fashion. If no exemplary disciplinary action is taken, the Brazilian judiciary runs the risk of squandering the institutional sway it has earned in recent decades, which, as we know, has not been used to benefit left-wing forces or policies. It was earned simply by ensuring sustained consistency and the right balance between means and ends. There are some signs that the judicial system is trying to recover its credibility. The Lava Jato Operation is now being discredited and may be dismantled. Unfortunately, this may be the result of yet another spell of politicization of the judiciary, rather than of the renewed strength of the rule of law.

The second task is even more complex, because Brazilian democracy now has to be defended both in the country's institutions and in the streets (more difficult in conditions of pandemic crisis). And since policy-making is not conducted in the streets, institutions will be given due priority even in these times of authoritarian drive and antidemocratic emergency. Popular organizations and movements, as well as peaceful demonstrations, will be infiltrated by provocateurs. Constant watchfulness is in order, as this type of provocation is currently being used in many contexts to criminalize social protest, reinforce state repression and declare states of emergency, albeit behind a façade of democratic normalcy.

6

Agonistic Representative Democracy in Europe

Chantal Mouffe, as interviewed and translated by Pablo Ouziel

You have written extensively about how one can think about politics and the political. Could you say something about how to weave poststructuralist thought with the thinking of Antonio Gramsci?

Theoretical and political reflection on a given political conjuncture and how one can intervene within it has been an essential and recurrent aspect of my work since *Hegemony and Socialist Strategy* (1985).[1] I often refer to Louis Althusser's reading of Niccolò Machiavelli's work as thinking within the conjuncture and not about the conjuncture. This is something with which I identify. My point of departure is always a specific conjuncture and then I develop the theoretical elements that help me think through it. I find of paramount importance that we grasp the fact that there are certain ways of understanding politics that blind us from understanding particular conjunctures. Gilles Deleuze argues that certain images of thought prevent us from thinking. I would paraphrase him by saying that there are images of politics that prevent us from thinking politically. Unfortunately, I think that the left has an image of politics that prevents thinking politically. It also prevents an understanding of the specificity of problems being raised in a particular conjuncture.

Ernesto Laclau and I wrote *Hegemony and Socialist Strategy* at a time during which what was then referred to as new social movements began to mobilize boldly. This was after '68; the feminist, antiracist, gay rights and environmental movements were making demands. Yet, we were concerned about the fact that neither the Marxist nor the social-democratic left were capable of understanding the importance of these new demands. The book came out in 1985, but we began writing it at the end of the '70s. At the time, Marxist perspectives were still very important and those within the Marxist and social-democratic left continued to

---

[1] E. Laclau and C. Mouffe, *Hegemony and Socialist Strategy: Towards a Radical Democratic Politics* (London: Verso, 1985).

defend a socialist project centered on working-class interests. In doing so, they viewed these other demands as petit-bourgeois or subsidiary. We, on the other hand, were convinced of the importance of rethinking and re-formulating the socialist project to include these demands in order to weave them together with the demands of the working class. We began to think about the problem, and soon realized that it was a particular theory that we referred to as class essentialism that prevented these parties from seeing the importance of these new demands. This class essentialism consisted in thinking that the subjectivity of social agents was determined by their position in the relations of production. Therefore, demands that were not identified as working-class demands were not considered important.

In thinking about this problem, we reached the conclusion that there was a need for a theory that would break with this class essentialism and could conceive of society in a completely different manner. Two key theoretical sources were instrumental in the shaping of these ideas. First, we drew from what was referred to as poststructuralist thinking and its conception of society as a discursive space; within this strand, we found the work of Jacques Derrida, Michel Foucault and Jacques Lacan very important. Second, contributing to the specificity of our approach, we combined poststructuralist theories with the thinking of Antonio Gramsci. Since at the time I was in the feminist movement and was part of a magazine influenced by Foucault, I began to understand the specificity of different demands and the importance of the demands being made by feminists. What those within the movement insisted on was the fact that there existed many specific struggles and that all these fronts needed to be fought separately. Ernesto and I disagreed with this perspective because we thought that in order to act politically there was a need to create an 'us'.

This is where Gramsci's idea of hegemony was important for us. Articulating poststructuralist ideas with Gramsci's thought constituted the specificity of what we called an anti-essentialist approach. This was the principle theme in *Hegemony and Socialist Strategy*, and from this perspective we posited that in order to think about the political there are two central concepts: the concept of 'antagonism' and the concept of 'hegemony'. When speaking about the concept of antagonism we referenced a theoretical perspective that insisted on what one can refer to as 'radical negativity'. This perspective understands that there are certain forms of negativity that cannot be overcome through a dialectical process. Whereas in both Marx and Hegel antagonism can be overcome through a dialectical process, from poststructuralist thought, this radical negativity cannot be overcome. Lacan's thinking around this issue is particularly important, but so is Derrida's challenging of the idea of totalization. From a poststructuralist position totalization is challenged; there can never be a totality. This is one specificity of poststructuralism. Whereas the traditional structuralism of Lévi-Strauss and Ferdinand de Saussure presents a kind of totalization, poststructuralism challenges this idea. In this radical negativity that cannot be overcome poststructuralism presents what we really refer to as antagonism. There are conflicts in society in which, in some sense, society is always necessarily divided. This evidently implies a conception of the political that is very different from other conceptions. According to the *associative* conception, the political is the field of joint action, acting in common, freedom and consensus. This is the dominant conception in most liberal political philosophy. When I say liberal, I mean liberal in a philosophical sense, and both Rawls and Jürgen Habermas are part of this associative conception of the political. In addition, within this conception, one finds more heterodox people like Hannah Arendt. Within their conception of politics, the negation that exists cannot accept the presence of a radical negativity. Therefore, antagonism, the idea that there are conflicts that can never be rationally resolved, is always excluded.

A different conception of the political, one that is *dissociative*, accepts radical negativity and the fact that society is divided. This conception can be found in Thucydides, Machiavelli, Thomas Hobbes, Carl Schmitt and Max Weber. One of the theses that Ernesto and I have defended is that if there is politics it is because there are conflicts that cannot be overcome rationally because of the existence of antagonism.

CAN YOU ELABORATE ON YOUR UNDERSTANDING OF THE CONCEPTS
OF ANTAGONISM, CONTINGENCY AND HEGEMONY, AND CLARIFY WHAT
IT MEANS TO THINK OF POLITICS FROM A POSTFOUNDATIONALIST
AND ANTI-ESSENTIALIST PERSPECTIVE?

The concept of hegemony is important when thinking about politics from our perspective. This is tied to antagonism because if there is antagonism, it means that all existing order is an order that corresponds to a specific position that excludes another possibility. This is tied to two ideas that are also important in our conception of the political and are clearly drawn from poststructuralism. The *first* idea is what can be described as post-foundationalism; if there is antagonism there is no ultimate foundation. Every order is a contingent order that is precarious; there will never be an order that is absolutely rational. I think this is important as it means that all order is a result of hegemonic practices trying to establish order in a field traversed by antagonism. This is why orders are precarious, because all orders presuppose the existence of something that has been excluded and that could also be reactivated. That is hegemony: there is no ultimate foundation. This, however, does not imply a relativist position. There are orders and the objective of politics is always to establish an order. Nevertheless, this order is always precarious and contingent. Contingency is the *second* important idea in our conception of the political. From an anti-essentialist position, society is understood as a discursive space. What we refer to as discourse is an articulation of linguistic elements but also of material elements. It is similar to what Ludwig Wittgenstein describes as a language-game; speaking of language is part of an activity, or a form of life. It is something materialistic, and not idealistic, as many of our critics have suggested.

We make a clear distinction between the political and politics. We speak of the political at an ontological level, whereas politics is always ontic. Speaking of politics refers to the practices of organization of society. There is nothing too original about this, but what is important is seeing that these practices take place in an antagonistic space. This is why orders are always contingent and precarious. Hegemony implies that in every situation there has always been a path that has not been taken, therefore there is always an alternative. This is especially important when one is going to think about how we can think politics from this view point. If we think it from the perspective of hegemony, we are automatically in a position to critique the neoliberal thesis. We can challenge Thatcher's famous phrase: "there is no alternative." There is always an alternative from a hegemonic conception of politics. This seems very abstract, but it impacts politics directly.

Another element of our anti-essentialist approach is how we think about political subjects. From our perspective, political subjects are always collective subjects. This is an important thesis of ours, which evidently opposes liberal individualism. Of course, when you act politically you act as a person but as part of an 'us'. Here one can see the distinction between a political language game and a moral language game. Moral issues are dealt with from an individual perspective, yet politics is always carried out as a citizen, otherwise it is not a political position.

Another important element that I should have mentioned is the fact that from a dissociative conception, politics always has to do with the construction of an 'us' and this always requires a 'them'. Politics always has to do with collective subjects that are going to enter into partisan relations. This is why from a dissociative-perspective of politics 'us' and 'them' are understood as discursive constructs. This is an important point in order to understand populism. The anti-essentialist perspective helps us to grasp the fact that 'the people' is not simply the population but a discursive construction.

FOLLOWING FROM THIS, IF POLITICS REQUIRES
THE CONSTRUCTION OF AN US, HOW ARE COLLECTIVE SUBJECTS
CONSTRUCTED?

In relation to the construction of collective subjects, one should speak first of the subject before speaking of collective subjects. Here is where the influence of psychoanalysis is very important for our perspective. There are no predetermined identities. As Freud said, all identities are a form of identification. Using language that is not Freud's, identities are discursive constructions that are transformed through practices in which the subject is inscribed. This is important because it reveals the importance of political practice. What would politics be if identities were already a given? Politics would only represent identities and this leads us to the question of representation, which, from an anti-essentialist viewpoint, is articulated differently. From this perspective identities are not a given, they are always constructed discursively. This is heavily influenced by de Saussure's idea that all identities are relational; this is key in the anti-essentialist thesis. The creation of an identity implies the establishment of a difference. For example, de Saussure insists that the concept 'mother' has no meaning per se: it has meaning in relation to other concepts like 'father' or 'daughter'. Without these other positions, we could not understand the meaning of 'mother'. Therefore, all identities are relational. This means that in regards to political identities, which are collective identities, the construction of an 'us' implies that there is a 'them'. There can never be an 'us' without a corresponding 'them'. In addition, another important element is the fact that in the construction of subjects there is always an affective element that is important. This also comes from psychoanalysis; affects are always involved in forms of identification. Identification is not a rational issue; this is why I prefer to talk about affective-discursive constructions. Affects are important in discursive constructions and this is very important for politics.

Therefore, the question one can ask is as follows: If politics always has to do with an us/them relationship, how can we imagine the necessary conditions for a pluralist democracy? Here is where I often reference Carl Schmitt, and this needs some clarification. The importance that we give to antagonism in *Hegemony and Socialist Strategy* has led some people to say that our perspective is influenced by Schmitt. It is important to say that when we wrote the book neither Ernesto nor I had read Schmitt. It was following the publication of the book that a Greek friend asked me if I knew Schmitt's work. I responded that I did not and he told me that in Schmitt I was going to find a lot of affinity with my work regarding the political. At that point, I began to be interested in Schmitt. I found him helpful as I reflected on how to criticize liberalism.

WHAT HAS YOUR WORK OVER THE YEARS TAUGHT YOU REGARDING ALTERNATIVE MODELS OF DEMOCRACY AND HOW TO IMAGINE A PLURALIST DEMOCRACY?

First, I looked at existing models of democracy. On the one hand, there is an aggregative conception of democracy, which, for example, we find in Joseph Schumpeter. This is the dominant or most common conception one finds in political science departments today. Its argument is that democracy has to do with the aggregation of interests. On the other hand, there is a different conception of democracy, referred to as deliberative democracy, that has developed primarily from Rawls' critique of the aggregative conception. From this conception, the field of democracy has to do more with moral considerations or types of justice than simple interests.

Without a doubt, I am more sympathetic toward the deliberative conception of democracy. I agree with its critique of the aggregative model. I find the aggregative model very restrictive. Nevertheless, I also find many missing elements in the deliberative conception, as it fails to give space for thinking through antagonism. This is clear in Habermas' ideal speech situation. Although he is conceiving it as a regulative idea, the end goal is to reach a rational consensus. Ultimately, the deliberative model attempts to establish the procedures that can lead to a rational agreement. There are many deliberative models and they all propose different processes. Nevertheless, for all of them the ultimate aim is to figure out how to establish a rational consensus. This, in essence, means that there is a negation of antagonism. This I say because antagonism means to accept that there are conflicts that cannot be resolved rationally. In addition, the deliberative perspective does not allow for an imagining of hegemony in a postfoundationalist key. Ultimately, this model presumes that there is always a point at which everyone can come to an agreement on what it means to be rational: an inclusive consensus from which there is an 'us' without a 'them'.

COULD YOU SAY A LITTLE MORE ABOUT THE RELATIONSHIP BETWEEN YOUR WORK AND THAT OF SCHMITT?

It was in thinking about pluralist democracy from a dissociative and anti-essentialist conception that I found Schmitt's critique of liberalism interesting. In the 1920s, Schmitt argued that the problem of liberalism was that it needed to negate politics. Here he understood politics as the friend/enemy relationship. When Ernesto and I speak of antagonism, Schmitt speaks of the criteria of the political as friend/enemy. Nevertheless, we are ultimately speaking about the same thing. Of liberalism, Schmitt says that when it attempts to speak of politics it does so from a model either borrowed from the economy or from morality, but it cannot speak of antagonism, which is what is specific to politics. This moral model is what corresponds to the deliberative model. Schmitt was helpful at the time, as I was developing my own critique of a certain type of liberalism. What I was really critiquing was the rationalism and individualism of liberalism. Schmitt was evidently also critiquing political liberalism (pluralism) but I was not interested in following him along that path. In fact, my goal was to reformulate political liberalism in order for it to incorporate the dimensions of antagonism and hegemony. This, for Schmitt, was impossible. If one accepts that the us/them relationship is partisan and that there is antagonism, it is impossible to imagine a pluralist society in which there is the possibility of legitimate dissensus. This is why Schmitt ends up defending an authoritarian model of democracy.

Interestingly, it is worth noting that Schmitt and Habermas are in agreement on one point: that one cannot have pluralism and antagonism together. Schmitt asserts that antagonism is ineradicable and that the idea of a pluralist democracy is impossible, while Habermas holds the opposite position. Habermas wants to defend pluralist democracy; therefore, he has to negate antagonism. Nevertheless, both are in agreement about the fact that you cannot at the same time have an acknowledgment of antagonism and a pluralist democracy. Hence, my challenge to demonstrate through my agonistic conception that this was actually possible. This is how I developed what I call an agonistic model of democracy. It consisted in pointing out that Schmitt did not envisage that antagonism can manifest in different ways. Of course, from the Schmittean friend/enemy conception in which the enemy needs to be eradicated, the legitimacy of the demands of the enemy cannot be recognized and it is impossible to think pluralist democracy because that would lead to civil war. Nevertheless, one can understand that there is another form of 'antagonism' that I call 'agonism'. Opponents understand that the objective is not to find the procedures that will lead to consensus because there is an antagonism between the positions they defend, but they do not treat each other as enemies. Instead, they treat each other as adversaries.

That is, agonism involves recognizing opponents' rights to defend their own point of view; they abide by certain mutually accepted principles that shape the struggle. They do so according to procedures that they themselves have mutually recognized. This is why I speak of conflictual consensus, which requires a kind of consensus about what, following Montesquieu, I refer to as the ethico-political principles of the regime. In the case of a liberal pluralist democracy, the principles that are going to shape our coexistence are freedom and equality for all. We must be in agreement on those principles, but evidently there is going to be disagreement in the way they are interpreted: What is 'freedom'? What is 'equality'? Who are we referring to when we say 'all'? There is obviously no possibility for a rational consensus. The point is not to put people together to deliberate and argue until they reach consensus. There is always going to be disagreement.

Political theory speaks of concepts like freedom and equality as essentially contested concepts. There is no way of saying that a particular definition is the true definition of equality. The same happens with freedom. Therefore, I think that in a democracy it is important for an agonistic struggle to be able to exist between different interpretations of what it means to be democratic. This is the essence of a pluralist democracy, and from a perspective of dissociative democracy it is perfectly possible to understand its existence. Of course, this requires institutions that facilitate the articulation of the conflict in an agonistic and not antagonistic manner. In order to understand this, one has to situate oneself within an anti-essentialist perspective. It is not about positions that are already defined, but about something that is constructed in different ways.

Politics consists, in this sense, in seeing how one can transform antagonism into agonism; creating the conditions so that when a conflict arises it does not adopt an antagonist shape but an agonistic one.

Let me emphasize that in no way do I pretend to say that this conception of politics is the truth about politics. I will never say I have the true conception, and Habermas, for example, does not. In the conception of politics that I defend there is no conception of truth. Of course, I would attempt to defend my conception of politics with respect to Habermas'. Nevertheless, I would do so in a pragmatic manner. I would argue that starting off from such a conception helps us to understand many more political phenomena than beginning from the other. For example, one cannot understand the dissolution of Yugoslavia from a liberal perspective. It was very interesting to see how liberal thought responded to these events. Think of Francis Fukuyama who came out with his *The End of History and the Last Man*, in which liberal democracy was the only possible model.[2] Yet, this lasted very little time because the end of antagonism was followed by the dissolution of Yugoslavia. What was interesting about this event was seeing how liberal theorists attempted to justify the contradiction between what was happening and their theories. They spoke of remnants of communism or specifically of the Balkans; theorists were unable to comprehend that in politics the possibility of antagonism can never be eliminated.

COULD YOU SPEAK ABOUT THE DIFFERENT CONJUNCTURES ON WHICH YOUR WORK OVER THE YEARS HAS FOCUSED?

In *On the Political* (2005), I examine the Third Way of Tony Blair and Anthony Giddens.[3] The book is a critique of their idea that we are no longer in the first modernity but in a second one in which the adversarial model of the political has been overcome.

At that time, I had many arguments with people who celebrated this model as an advance for democracy. They claimed that we were living in a more mature democracy and I responded that this was an antipolitical, or postpolitical (as I called it at the time) position. For me this model was a danger to democracy. I argued that it would create the conditions for right-wing populism to grow. There was not much right-wing populism in Europe at the time. There was Jean-Marie LePen in France, there was a right-wing populist party in Austria with Jörg Haider, and there was the Vlaams Blok in Belgium. I considered it a mistake, pretending that there was no more antagonism and that the idea of left and right had been overcome. Conflicts were not going to disappear but would take on a different form. This would create the possibility for opposition to be formulated in ethnic terms, which is exactly the field of right populism.

[2] F. Fukuyama, *The End of History and the Last Man* (New York: Free Press, 1992).
[3] C. Mouffe, *On the Political* (Abingdon: Routledge, 2011).

Now we see that this is exactly what has happened as a consequence of the abandonment of leftist values by the social-democratic project. This has created the conditions for the growing success of right populism.

Agonistics: Thinking the World Politically (2013) was a reflection on the occupation of the squares movements.[4] It was a critique of the limits of movements like the Indignados and Occupy Wall Street. In essence, it was a critique of pure horizontalism. For example, I think that especially the Indignados avoided defining an adversary. They shouted *democracia real ya!* ("real democracy now!"), and there was a hope of creating a completely inclusive 'us'. What caught my attention was the fact that they were against voting in assemblies because they said that if they voted they would become divided. Granted, Occupy Wall Street was better than the Indignados and at least acknowledged that there was an adversary that was the 1 percent. Having said this, I think the Indignados and Occupy had commonalities in their rejection of institutions, political parties and trade unions. Theirs was a purely horizontalist perspective and I think it missed the fact that building hegemony must necessarily pass through the state. I am not defending in any way that politics is limited to the parliamentary sphere. The horizontal dimension is very important, but to have a real impact and transform things a vertical element needs to be articulated. Its objective being one of '*becoming* state' (Gramsci) rather than one of seizing state power.

Up to today, I am yet to see a purely horizontal movement that can transform our societies in a meaningful manner. In the case of the Indignados, Spain was lucky that Podemos did not allow the impulse of the 15M to disappear and worked toward structuring it. In the case of Occupy Wall Street this did not happen and therefore it disappeared. The same thing happened with Nuit Debout in France and I think this is the risk that the Gilets Jaunes are facing.

I think that at this point we have enough examples demonstrating that unless there is a vertical articulation aimed at reaching the power of state institutions, it is unlikely that true transformation can take place. The key is to build a new hegemony and this passes also through the apparatuses of the state.

In my latest book, *For a Left Populism* (2018), my particular interest is with the current conjuncture in Western Europe.[5] The conditions in Eastern Europe are completely different and the reasons for the emergence of right populism there are also different. This is why I always insist on reflecting on a specific conjuncture. Obviously, the studying of a particular state of affairs can provide insight for other cases but the reflection must be of a particular conjuncture. What is specific to the current conjuncture is that we are living through a crisis of neoliberalism. The failures of the model began to show with the crisis of 2008. Before this, the hegemony of neoliberalism was almost uncontested. Now

---

[4] C. Mouffe and E. Wagner, *Agonistics: Thinking the World Politically* (London: Verso, 2013).
[5] C. Mouffe, *For a Left Populism* (London: Verso, 2018).

things look different. We see a series of resistances against what I refer to as the postdemocracy that is the consequence of thirty years of neoliberal hegemony.

CAN YOU CLARIFY WHAT YOU MEAN BY POSTDEMOCRACY?

When I speak of a situation of postdemocracy I do so in reference to two primary phenomena happening at both the political and the economic levels. At the political level, I am thinking of what I have been studying as postpolitics: consensus to the center so that eventually there are no fundamental differences between left and right when citizens go to the polls. As the Indignados would say, "we have a vote but we have no voice." Ultimately, there is no possibility for citizens to choose between different political projects. The element of popular sovereignty, which I consider one of the central ideas of democracy, has been eliminated. I use this term in a very specific and simple manner. For me popular sovereignty refers to the fact that citizens have a voice. That they have a genuine capacity to choose. If they do not have such a capacity, this is what I call postpolitics.

The second element has to do with economic transformations. I speak of a process of oligarchization of our societies. We are living through the broadening of the gap between a shrinking group of ever richer people and the remaining population that is undergoing a process of impoverishment and precaritization. This is a consequence of financial capitalism. One of the main features of the neoliberal model is that it gives primacy to financial capitalism and this has led to a situation of oligarchization.

What we are seeing now is that many citizens have stopped accepting this postdemocratic situation and there is a growing rebellion. We are witnessing the birth of antisystem movements saying that they no longer want this model. This is what I call the populist moment. I use the term "populism" in the way that Ernesto Laclau defines it. In *On Populist Reason* he says that populism is a strategy of construction of political frontiers between those from below and those from above.[6] Evidently, in order to understand this one has to situate oneself in a dissociative conception of politics as it is this conception that describes politics as the drawing of a frontier between us and them. I think that the reason there is so much hostility toward populism coming from liberal thinkers, including the most progressive, is that they situate themselves within an associative conception of politics for which there are no frontiers. On the contrary, they argue that in democracy there is no us and them. When you begin from such a conception you are going to see populism as a pathology of democracy, as a perversion of democracy. Yet, what I think we are seeing with the rise of populism is a return of the political: a challenging of the consensual model and the re-establishment of what politics is. We begin to see again the re-establishment of the partisan character of politics. Obviously, the

---

[6] E. Laclau, *On Populist Reason* (London: Verso, 2005).

re-establishment of a frontier does not necessarily lead to more democratic or progressive decisions. This depends on the manner in which the us and them is constructed and this is where the difference between left and right populism lies.

In both cases a frontier is drawn but the way in which it is drawn differs. Generally, right populism constructs its frontier in an ethno-nationalist key. It limits the us to a certain category of citizen. It includes nationals and excludes immigrants. From this conception immigrants are constructed as the them. Left populism, on the other hand, constructs the us and them in a completely different manner. A left populist conception constructs a much more inclusive us. In my conception of left populism, the us being drawn includes numerous democratic demands that are not only socioeconomic; they have to do with other forms of domination and discrimination. When, for example, we incorporate LGBT demands, the us we are constructing is different, and the them becomes the forces maintaining the neoliberal order at the core of all forms of oppression.

As I explain in *For a Left Populism*, the political challenge that we face is both a great opportunity and a great danger. This is why at the beginning of the book I make clear that I write it as a political intervention. I feel a real urgency because we are in a key moment. We are facing the crisis of neoliberal hegemony and this can open the way for more authoritarian regimes or can lead to a process of radicalization of democracy. It can allow for the creation of a different hegemony, but what kind of hegemony is constructed will depend on which forces are going to win. This is why I insist on the importance for the left to understand the nature of the conjuncture. Realizing that this is an important moment for them to intervene in a manner that allows for a progressive exit out of the crisis.

Currently, we see a lot of references to the fact that we are returning to the 1930s. Many intellectuals see the return of fascism. We start hearing people talking about it rearing its ugly head. Personally, I think this is the worse way to react. Demonizing right populist parties as the expression of the return of that malignant force of fascism is a mistake. Doing this, we stop trying to figure out the reasons, the origins, of the rise of right populism. From this position, which treats it as a sort of meteorological phenomenon that returns, one is not going to understand how to struggle against it. In order to understand how to struggle against it in an efficient manner one has to grasp what exactly is going on. This is a new phenomenon and one cannot think about it through traditional concepts like fascism and extreme right. This is something very specific to the current conjuncture. In addition, as I keep emphasizing, I think social-democratic parties are in great measure responsible for the success of right populist parties, as they have converted to neoliberalism and to the idea that there is no other alternative. They have abandoned the popular classes.

In all countries, social-democratic parties have taken the side of the winning sectors of neoliberal globalization and have been unable to present a defense for its losers. Without such a defense, the field has been left completely open for right populist parties to speak to those that feel excluded. The origin of right populism is not immigration but the fact that social-democratic parties have forgotten to defend the losers of neoliberal globalization. Therefore, instead of demonizing the voters of these parties, as many on the left do, we must engage them. Most of these people are not fundamentally and intrinsically racist or homophobic. Of course, some are, but Didier Eribon's book *Retour a Reims* clearly reveals the point I am trying to make.[7] Eribon came from a poor working-class family that had always voted for the communist party. Due to the fact that he was gay and not accepted in his community he left Reims for thirty years. When he returned, he found that all his family was voting National Front (now known as National Rally). Eribon reflects on this and concludes that their community has been abandoned by the Left, that the only party that actually engages with them and claims to be there to give them a voice is the National Front.

IS THE RISE OF RIGHT POPULISM AND THE NEED TO RESPOND TO IT WITH LEFT POPULIST OPTIONS AN INDICATION OF THE CRISIS OF REPRESENTATIVE DEMOCRACY?

Evidently, we are living through a crisis of the representative model. Nevertheless, I think this has been wrongly interpreted by a certain part of the left. Some theorists say that the problem is with representative democracy per se. Following from this, they suggest that the solution to the current crisis is the elaboration of models of direct democracy. I see it differently, I think that the problem of our crisis of representation is that our societies are not representative enough; there are numerous sectors of society that do not have a voice. This is, I think, a consequence of our democracies no longer being agonistic. When people think there is no left and right anymore, then there are no alternatives. Therefore, what we need to do in this conjuncture is to re-establish partisanship. This is what the populist moment offers and, therefore, it is a return of the political. The key during this moment is not to accuse the others of being fascists, because by doing this you will not have an agonistic relationship with them. All constructs of politics on moralizing grounds should be avoided. If one sees their opponents as evil, then instead of their right to their own point of view being recognized they are seen as needing to be eradicated. Under such conditions there is no room for an agonistic relationship.

CAN YOU CLARIFY HOW AN ANTI-ESSENTIALIST CONCEPTION CAN HELP US UNDERSTAND THE RISKS AND OPPORTUNITIES OF THE POPULIST MOMENT AS YOU CONCEIVE IT?

The anti-essentialist conception is very important here. Many of the critiques coming from the left of people that vote for right populist parties is that they are

---

[7] D. Eribon and E. Louis, *Retour à Reims* (Paris: Flammarion, 2018).

intrinsically racist and/or homophobic. This is an essentialist conception; it assumes that this is the essence of these people and that they cannot be transformed. Following from this, the response to these people from many on the left is to stigmatize them. I think this is a mistake. If we want to understand how to fight against this phenomenon of right populism, what we need to do is to acknowledge that in the origin of many of the demands being made by these voters there is a genuinely democratic nucleus. These demands are resistances against what I call postdemocracy. There is a request for democracy; people are saying that they want a voice. Politics is about how one responds to these demands, how one is going to articulate them. I think on this front La France Insoumise has made great advances. In the elections of 2017, they managed to win in various parts of France that were strongholds of the Front National. This was the case because La France Insoumise took the time to speak with these people. It helped them understand that their problems were not caused by immigrants but by neoliberalism. It was interesting to see how a kind of very traditional extreme left was completely against this move and critiqued La France Insoumise for going to speak to 'fascists'. Refusing to speak to these people because they are seen as intrinsically fascists is the worse strategy possible. We must attempt to transform and give a progressive response to these demands. One can only understand this from an anti-essentialist conception of politics. Identities are not a given but are always constructed through political discourse. Hence, they can be constructed in the manner of left populism or in the way of right populism. This I see as a big challenge for the left in the current conjuncture.

YOU HAVE DESCRIBED YOUR WORK AS POST-MARXIST. COULD YOU CLARIFY WHAT YOU MEAN BY THIS?

In order to think about the work that Ernesto and I have done, post-Marxism is an important term. We did not present ourselves as post-Marxist. Nevertheless, right before the publication of *Hegemony and Socialist Strategy*, the traditional Marxist left was already labeling us in this manner because of a series of articles that we had published. In calling us post-Marxists they claimed that we had abandoned Marxism. Following from this, when we published the book we accepted the "post-Marxist" label with the condition that it was post but also Marxist. We were not rejecting Marxism. We acknowledged the important elements in Marx's work that help us understand capitalism, while refusing to read Marx like one would read the Koran. We do the same with Gramsci. We borrow from different people in order to develop our own theories. Otherwise, it would be like saying that physics is limited to Newton. Without a doubt, Marxism is an important element in our biography. But Marxism is just one of the elements in our thinking on the political.

There is an aspect of our book that has been misunderstood. I am afraid that Ernesto did not help with this because of certain statements that he made. As an example, he once said that the class struggle did not exist. What he was criticizing was the idea of class struggle as theorized by Marxism. Personally, I think that the idea of the class struggle understood as the motor force of history has to be completely abandoned. Having said this, we must not abandon the idea that there are what could be referred to as class antagonisms. In a metaphorical sense, this references certain antagonisms at the socioeconomic level. Ernesto and I do not reject the idea that there is antagonism at this level; what we are saying is that this is just one kind of antagonism amidst a multiplicity of different forms of antagonism and that it does not have an a priori privilege. Moreover, anticapitalist struggles are not limited to issues of class. For example, a lot of feminist struggles have an anticapitalist dimension. In some way or another, the impact of the neoliberal system and financial capitalism manifests itself in the lives of everyone. Traditional Marxism sees the proletariat as having an ontological privilege in the struggle against capitalism, and from that a metaphysics of the evolution of history is constructed. Yet, today it is not only the working class, the proletariat, the factory workers that are exploited and affected by the neoliberal regime. We are all affected by austerity politics. Therefore, many struggles have an anticapitalist dimension. The anticapitalist struggle is not the prerogative of the working class.

This is why in left populism we speak of a construction in terms of the 'people' versus the 'oligarchy'. Liberal thought negates the existence of frontiers, Marxism does not. Marxism constructs frontiers but it does so by creating a distinction between capital and labor, proletariat and bourgeoisie. According to left populism the frontier is between the people defined as an articulation of democratic demands against diverse forms of domination and a them, which includes all that are at the core of these forms of domination. We are not taking an anti-Marxist position. We do not reject Marxism but present instead a post-Marxist conception that broadens the struggle and shows that it cannot be limited to a mythical class struggle. We do show our disagreement with the Marxist conception of a law of history that will necessarily lead to the realization of socialism. From a post-foundationalist conception everything is contingent; there is no direction of history.

COULD YOU ELABORATE ON YOUR UNDERSTANDING OF REPRESENTATION AND REPRESENTATIVE DEMOCRACY?

In the traditional conception of representation there is something that is a given before representation. It is an essentialist conception; there are always interests that are first given and then are represented. From an anti-essentialist perspective, however, there are no identities or demands that are a given. There are no objective interests that need to be represented (or not). All interests are constructed and this construction is a form of representation. Therefore, there are no collective identities that are not the product of representation, because of the fact that they are not a given in an essentialist sense. Following from this, the idea that there can be a democracy that is not representative is impossible. This would imply a democracy without a subject of democracy. If democratic subjects are always the result of a discursive construction then representation is inscribed into the very construction of the identity. All ideas of direct democracy or the critique of representative democracy imply what Derrida calls a metaphysics of presence. Interests are not a given but are constructed; thus, representation is inscribed in the very heart of the construction of identity.

Another important aspect is the fact that to put into practice a pluralist democracy one needs representative institutions to give an institutional form to pluralism. This is why I think political parties are key if we want to have an agonistic democracy. One cannot think agonistic democracy without parties that represent different interests. This does not mean that existing parties are the best form of representation. Evidently not, since, lacking any fundamental difference, they do not allow for an agonistic struggle to materialize. Having said this, the point is not to say that all this has to be replaced with a kind of direct expression of the will of the people; this would not allow for pluralism to be represented. A pluralist conception of democracy implies the existence of institutions and parties that are going to permit the expression of this pluralism. Everyone that defends direct democracy does so, ultimately, from a consensualist position. They are ultimately defending the idea that there is one people and what is needed is the articulation of a sole voice for it. Contrary to this, if one departs from a position in which society is understood as divided, then this implies that there is a need to represent this division and this implies the existence of political parties or whatever one choses to call them.

AS A FINAL QUESTION AND THINKING ABOUT THE CURRENT CONJUNCTURE, COULD YOU SHARE YOUR THOUGHTS ON BREXIT?

I think that the anti-essentialist perspective helps us to understand better a phenomenon like Brexit and the strategy of right populists in the United Kingdom. The success of the "leave" vote in the referendum came from the capacity of those defending leaving the EU to articulate a whole series of demands that were in some sense heterogeneous. Tony Blair's politics has largely been responsible for Brexit. He implemented a program that benefited the middle classes of the south of England, while completely abandoning the more industrial northern regions. Neoliberal globalization has truly devastated these sectors and the leave camp in the Brexit referendum has managed to present the European Union as the origin of all the problems that these communities are experiencing. Brexit has become the hegemonic signifier that has crystalized a whole series of demands. Initially, these sectors were worried about the conditions they were facing but they did not identify the EU as the cause of their problems. The leave campaign crystalized this and discursively constructed all these demands around the signifier 'take back control'. In the construction of a people, heterogeneous demands are always articulated. This requires a hegemonic signifier that becomes the symbol that represents these demands; it is around this symbol that a people crystalizes. The people of the leave campaign crystalized around the signifier Brexit that symbolized all those heterogeneous struggles that were in fact resistances against the postdemocratic conditions created by neoliberal hegemony. Those running the Leave campaign managed to express these not as effects of neoliberal hegemony but of being a part of Europe. Following from this, the solution was to take back control and leave the EU. This has become the cement that has crystalized a collective will. This collective will is not the expression of existing demands; there were no such existing demands against Europe. These demands have been constructed discursively by the Leave campaign.

Many of the Remainers have said that the Leave campaign is the expression of racism and xenophobia. I do not think this is the case. The demands have been constructed in this manner, but one must acknowledge that at the origin of that vote there exists a series of democratic demands. If one is going to struggle against this construction of a people then one must articulate demands around a different signifier and construct a different people. I am convinced that a Green New Deal could be the hegemonic signifier that will allow for the crystallization of a whole series of demands. The Green New Deal is the articulation of ecological objectives with demands concerning different forms of inequality. Following from this, I think it has the necessary strength to appeal to many different sectors of the population. For example, many of the feminist demands and different democratic demands about equality and racial justice can find a space in a project like the Green New Deal.

What I think is key for a left populist project is to be able to offer a vision of a society with which people can identify, a vision which offers hope of something different. The way a left populist project can struggle against a populist right movement is by identifying what are the demands being articulated and how are they crystalizing. Once these have been identified, one can determine which of these demands could be articulated in a different and progressive manner and what type of society needs to be defended and/or proposed. This requires recognizing the affective element of the mobilization of passions. I say this because I remember that the week before the referendum in the United Kingdom everyone seemed convinced that there would be no problem and that the Remain vote would win. At the time, I remember thinking that they were completely wrong, that they were going to lose. I could see all the passion being mobilized around Brexit. On the Remain side, the arguments were mainly economic; the discussion was about what people were going to lose. There was no passion being mobilized. Whereas in the Leave side people really identified with a project and passions were being mobilized. In the Remain side people simply insisted on the negative effects of abandoning the EU. Brexit serves as an example of the importance of creating new forms of collective identity through the mobilization of affects. Critiquing rationally and saying what the opponent is saying is false is not enough for a progressive left option to succeed. The question for the left today is whether the key is to show the mistakes of the opponent or to propose something different that can give people hope.

7

For a Politics of Exile

Criticism in an Era of Global Liberal Decline

Jeanne Morefield

The election of Donald Trump in 2016 and the white nationalist movement it has engendered, the Brexit vote, the rise of anti-immigrant movements throughout Europe, and the collapse of so many social welfare institutions in the wake of the Covid-19 pandemic have led to considerable handwringing among some political theorists about the future of democracy. This has prompted a surge of interest in the politics of populism and identity. For liberals such as Rogers Smith and Michael Walzer, this means both puzzling through the "stories we tell ourselves" about "who we are" and recommitting "ourselves" to what liberalism means "for us" in the context of a country in which 40 percent of Americans clearly prefer the leadership of a racist autocrat.[1] For left Schmittians such as Chantal Mouffe, this rightward shift demands a left populist reimagination of "the people," sharply contrasted with a reactionary enemy.[2] And yet, both of these reactions to the rise of xenophobia and the decline of liberal democracy in the Global North fail to adequately grapple with the way the very construction of "the people" in the Global North – the demos upon whose shoulders settles the weight of the liberal state – has been linked historically to practices of imperialism, settler colonialism, and the antidemocratic processes of resource extraction, dispossession, slavery, and military expansionism.

To begin with the conceit that the liberal, state-bounded peoples of the Global North are coherent units, in and of themselves, is to deny the co–constitutive history of European imperialism and "Western" liberal

---

[1] See Keith E. Whittington, "Rogers M. Smith: The Stories We Tell Ourselves," PS: Political Science & Politics, 51 no.4 (2018): 895–99; Rogers M. Smith, That Is Not Who We Are! Populism and Peoplehood (New Haven, CT: Yale University Press, 2020); Michael Walzer, "What It Means to Be a Liberal," *Dissent*, Spring 2020 www.dissentmagazine.org/article/what-it-means-to-be-liberal.

[2] Chantal Mouffe, *For a Left Populism* (London: Verso, 2018).

democratic states. Such a move erases the structural relationship between practices of colonial resource extraction and land dispossession and the emergence of those liberal welfare states whose citizens are now explicitly rejecting both immigrants and democracy. Political responses that ignore these constitutive relationships and privilege notions of "the people" also inadvertently give succor to precisely the mode of rhetorical deflection that has sustained liberal imperialism for hundreds of years, a phenomenon embodied today in the ideological justifications of liberal internationalists like John Ikenberry who lean on "such Western values as openness, the rule of law, human rights, and liberal democracy" to justify American military and political hegemony.[3] Finally, the indwelling fixation with peoplehood makes it more difficult to identify potential sites of human coexistence and democratic futures that emanate from beyond the blessed circle of those Anglo-European, liberal democracies, now in crisis and yet as self-contained in memory as ever.

This chapter thus begins with a provocation: how would the kinds of questions scholars of politics ask about our political moment change if we thought in more historically capacious ways about the relationship between "the people" as a bounded site of political action and the history and ongoing politics of imperialism? What would happen if political theorists in the Global North who are interested in the future of democracy – both global and domestic – began their theorizing from an unsettled position of radical reflection and humility about what went into the creation of both modern, liberal democratic states and their own conceptions of "the political"? I first explore what such an orientation might look like by engaging Edward Said's approach to living, being, thinking, and writing in exile. I then compare this approach to the closed notions of "the political" that still dominate political theory as well as to that mode of political thought that has traditionally been most committed to the concerns of the world outside of the nation-state: cosmopolitan, global justice theory. I conclude with some thoughts about the conceptual reorientation toward politics and the democratic humanism that a reflective mode of exilic inquiry enables.

EDWARD SAID AND EXILIC CRITICISM

Edward Said, who died of leukemia in 2003, was one of the most productive scholars and influential public intellectuals of the late twentieth century. His groundbreaking 1978 book *Orientalism*, and the similarly powerful *Culture and Imperialism*, transformed the academic study of imperialism from historical engagement with a known historical object whose policies, theories, and cultural practices run solely in one direction – from Western metropoles to

[3] John Ikenberry, "The Next Liberal Order: The Age of Contagion Demands More Internationalism, Not Less," *Foreign Affairs* 99, no.4 (2020): 133–43.

Asian/African/Latin American sites of occupation – into engagement with the
"constantly expanding," "inexorably integrative" ideological formation that
buttressed domination in the past and rationalizes imperial politics in the
present.[4] Said's work explored the way active traces of the imperial past on
the present (including the grotesque inequality of resources between the
Global North and South) continue to appear sui generis, untethered from
a history of imperialism, slavery, settler colonialism, dispossession, and
resource extraction – the natural order of things. In addition, his work
stressed the increasing urgency with which he believed it necessary to pair
interrogations of imperial culture's constitutive, disciplinary power with
genealogical investigations of anticolonial resistance. Finally, the corpus of
Said's work stresses the need to cultivate a contrapuntal orientation toward
history, culture, and politics that "sees Western and non-Western
experiences as belonging together because they are connected by
imperialism."[5] Indeed, for Said, the "great imperial experience of the past
two hundred years is global and universal," implicating all of us, "the
colonizer and the colonized together."[6]

Throughout his work, Said repeatedly tied his orientation toward
imperialism to his own experience as a Palestinian living in exile and to the
more generally productive qualities of an "exilic" perspective that resists
domination and upends univocal accounts of identity and history.[7] As he put
it in a 1994 interview:

If you're an exile … you always bear within yourself a recollection of what you've left
behind and what you can remember, and you play it against the current experience. So
there's necessarily that sense of counterpoint. And by counterpoint, I mean things that
can't be reduced to homophony … And so, multiple identity, the polyphony of many
voices playing off against each other, without, as I say, the need to reconcile them, just to
hold them together, is what my work is all about. More than one culture, more than one
awareness, both in its negative and its positive modes.[8]

Exile, critique, and counterpoint thus sit at the very core of Said's
approach to politics, history, and text, generating a mode of analysis
which is itself always "out of place." Throughout his work, the friction
created by exile – by the strange juxtaposition of a home lost, a home
remembered, and a contemporary moment lived otherwise – gives rise to
an unreconciled, "unhoused and rootless" disposition toward text and the
world which is, by its nature, irresolvable, contradictory, and paradoxical.[9]

---

[4] Edward Said, *Culture and Imperialism* (New York: Vintage, 1994), 6, 8.
[5] Said, *Culture and Imperialism*, 279.   [6] Said, *Culture and Imperialism*, 259.
[7] Edward Said, *Out of Place* (New York: Random House, 1999), 293.
[8] Edward Said, "Criticism, Culture, and Performance," in *Power, Politics, and Culture: Interviews with Edward Said*, ed. Gauri Viswanathan (New York: Vintage, 2002), 99.
[9] Edward Said, "Narrative, Geography, and Interpretation," *New Left Review* 180, no. 1 (1990): 84–97.

The unfixedness of exile is precisely what makes it, in Said's words, "strangely compelling to think about but terrible to experience."[10] This tension between concept and experience is particularly true, he argued, in our era. Whereas the romantic idea of exile in western literature and philosophy often focuses on isolated intellectuals forced from home – Cicero's time in Thessalonica, James Joyce's years of alienation abroad – exile today is primarily a mass phenomenon. For this reason, Said argues, any analysis of exile must begin by "setting aside" exiles by choice (e.g. Joyce) and then purposefully turning our minds to "the uncountable masses for whom UN agencies have been created."[11] The disruptions created by settler colonialism, imperialism, violent nationalism, mass warfare, and covert intervention since the nineteenth century have led to waves of mass migration, floods of refugees, and a constantly expanding global population of displaced persons. Thus, contemporary exiles may sometimes look like Said himself – a Columbia professor living on the Upper West Side of Manhattan – but they are far more likely to look like traumatized Central American children trudging hundreds of miles with their parents through Mexico, Syrians caught in the no-mans-land of Greek refugee camps, Rohingyas trapped in temporary settlements in Bangladesh, or the third generation of Palestinians to grow up in the Shantila refugee camp in Beirut. The fact that, throughout his work, Said looked straight into the desperate and disparate faces of exiles, saw the experience for what it was, and still insisted that the perspective it provided offered the world a powerful, even necessary, way of seeing, is a testament to how strongly he believed in its illuminative power.

For Said, exiles bear within themselves recollections of what has been left behind, which they then play against the current experience. This ebbless loss, this constant friction between past and the present, home and displacement, becomes the exile's "permanent state." That state is characterized, above all, by contradictions within and between experiences; between state violence on a grand scale and the profundity of individual suffering, between mass migration and the longings of the lonely poetic soul, between political violence and political art. This "agonizing distance" remains unsutured for the exile, like an irritating open wound whose healing is relentlessly stymied by the reality of "terminal loss."[12] Loss, therefore, is the pebble in the exile's shoe that pains with every step and, in that pain, brings insight.

Said does not argue that the experience of exile *necessarily* leads to reflection and, in fact, notes that it is often "a jealous state." Exiles, he argues, often "look

[10] Edward Said, "Reflections on Exile," in *Reflections on Exile and Other Essays* (Cambridge, MA; Harvard University Press, 2000), 173.
[11] Said, "Reflections on Exile," 174.
[12] Said, "Reflections on Exile," 173; and Edward Said, "Secular Criticism," in *The World, the Text, and the Critic* (Cambridge, MA: Harvard University Press, 1984), 8.

at non exiles with resentment," which can lead to an "exaggerated sense of group solidarity" and a stubborn "hostility to outsiders, even those who may in fact be in the same predicament as you," a feeling that sometimes resembles the "bloody minded affirmations" of nationalism.[13] But what differentiates the experience of exile from nationalism, Said argues, is the permanence of loss.[14] Exile, he notes, "unlike nationalism, is fundamentally a *discontinuous* state of being" wherein subjects are constantly drawn up hard against the jagged edge of today's reality and forced to occupy an indeterminate space endlessly mediated not just by distance but also time and the fundamental uncertainties of memory. If the exile can resist the impulse to sit "on the sidelines nursing a wound," he argues, they can transform this unsettledness into a particularly revealing mode of subjective reflection.[15]

Thus, Said maintained, because their sense of natality – their supposedly natural connection to a place and a culture-in-place – has been severed, exiles are often in a position to observe the way all connections between culture and place are essentially unnatural. In other words, seeing the world through exile is to see the guts and sinews of culture itself revealed, to catch a glimpse of the braided relationship between what Said referred to as *filiative* and *affiliative* forms of cultural connections.[16] For Said, filiative understandings of culture are commonsensical, in Gramsci's sense of the term: they appear to reflect the "mere natural continuity between one generation and the next."[17] For instance, scholars who are interested in tracing the coherence of western civilization over time often present that coherence in filiative terms as an inheritance linked directly to particular populations through genealogical descent. *Affiliative* connections, by contrast, are both consciously made and compensatory, often replacing the perceived loss of filiative relations. Looking at the relationship between "the west" and its culture through affiliative lenses implies taking a denaturalizing attitude toward the relationship between culture and population, one which interprets these links ideologically as rhetorical lines of descent forged through the active and creative fusing of particular ideas with particular peoples rather than the simple gift of one generation to the next. It thus means interrogating the way culture is sustained and re-instantiated by the intellectual work of human beings who are themselves situated within a complex web of cultural/political/material connections they participate in weaving.

Exile, Said argued, wrenches the critic out of their situated perspective and compels reflection on the relationship between place and people, self and home, thus illuminating the constructed/affiliative realm of culture more generally.

---

[13] Said, "Reflections on Exile," 177–78. [14] Said, "Reflections on Exile," 177.
[15] Said, "Reflections on Exile," 184.
[16] Said, "Secular Criticism," 16. Said developed his notion of filiative and affiliative connections through an engagement with the work of Raymond Williams, Antonio Gramsci, and others.
[17] Said, "Secular Criticism," 16.

Fundamentally, this orientation toward culture, history, and politics entails, as Said noted in *Representation of the Intellectual*, seeing things "not simply as they are, but as they have come to be that way."[18] Such a denaturalizing orientation – one that disrupts filliative associations between "the people," place, and culture – is particularly useful for analyzing inherently global political phenomena such as imperialism. Thus, because it is always unstable, always balanced on the interstitial lip of identity and place, the exilic disposition illuminates how the ideology of imperialism works to disassociate Western culture from the "institutions, agencies, classes, and amorphous social forces" that constitute its relationship to (and dependence on) imperial rule.[19] As a discursive apparatus, Said argued, imperialism works to "make invisible and even 'impossible' the actual *affiliations* that exist between the world of ideas and scholarship, on the one hand, and the world of brute politics, corporate and state power, and military force on the other."[20] The distance between the exile and her natal culture opens the door on a vista of critical reflection that renders those ongoing affiliations – between ideas and power, culture and domination, history and contemporary practice – more visible. Moreover, Said argues, the very unsettledness of life in exile means that exiles tend to approach their lived attachments "*as if* they were about to disappear." This gives rise to a mode that constantly queries these experiences themselves: "What would you save of them," Said asks, "what would you give up, what would you recover?"[21]

Two further aspects of Said's approach to exile differentiate it from other approaches to critique similarly oriented toward exposing the multiple, overlapping, disciplinary modes of power at work in culture (e.g. Foucaultian genealogy and poststructuralist criticism). The first is that, beyond its critical, illuminative capacity, exile in a Saidian sense is also a deeply compassionate mode of seeing. Because living in exile is, in Said's words, "a median state, neither completely at one with the new setting nor fully disencumbered of the old," the exile's feelings are never entirely detached from home but are, rather, "predicated on the existence of, love for, and a real bond with, one's native place."[22] What is thus true of all exile, he insisted, "is not that home and love of home are lost, but that loss is inherent in the very existence of both."[23] Therefore, analyzing politics through the lens of exilic loss doesn't mean abandoning sympathy for critique, nor does it mean dismissing all notions of belonging – national, local, regional – as affiliative fictions. Rather, it means combining sympathy with a baseline discomfort for easy, commonsense

---

[18] Edward Said, *Representations of the Intellectual* (New York: Vintage Books, 1994), 60.

[19] Edward Said, "The American Left and Literary Criticism," in *The World, The Text, and the Critic* (Cambridge, MA: Harvard University Press, 1984), 174.

[20] Edward Said, "Opponents, Audiences, Constituencies, and Community," in *Reflections on Exile*, 19.

[21] Said, *Culture and Imperialism*, 336.   [22] Said, *Culture and Imperialism*, 336.

[23] Edward Said, *Representations of the Intellectual*, 185.

explanations about who belongs and who does not belong to a given community.

Second, and perhaps most controversially, Said sometimes wrote about exile as a tangible, clawing thing into which one is born or forced. But he also claimed that an exilic perspective can be voluntarily adopted by intellectuals willing to unsettle their view of the world. In his words, while exile "is an *actual* condition," it is also "for my purposes a *metaphorical* condition," an act of will that committed intellectuals can perform in order to stand outside the familiar, a disposition likely "to be a source not of acculturation and adjustment, but rather of volatility and instability."[24] But there is nothing flip or easy about adopting a metaphorical exilic position. Rather, for Said, being an exilic intellectual is a vocation, a way of being and seeing that is deeply transformative. Occupying the perspective of exilic loss is thus different from assuming, for instance, a Rawlsian "original position": that is, a methodological perspective one can move in and out of in order to clarify the basic foundations of justice for a given "people." Instead, the exilic critic is resigned to remaining permanently unsettled. "You cannot go back to some earlier and perhaps more stable condition of being at home," Said notes, and thus "you can never fully arrive, be at one with your new home or situation."

On a fundamental level, the exilic critic alters their relationship to their homeland in a way which makes them perennially uncomfortable with assumed, commonsense notions of peoplehood and closure, modes of inclusion and exclusion built into the very collective pronouns that structure politics. For instance, Said argues, an American reporter writing about the Vietnam War who uses "the words 'us' and 'our'" has "appropriated neutral pronouns and affiliated them consciously either with that criminal invasion of a distant Southeast Asian nation" or "with those lonely voices of dissent for whom the American war was both unwise and unjust."[25] The impulse of the exilic critic, by contrast, is to interrogate what makes the national "we" a "we" in the first place. Embracing the alienation of exile means remaining hyper-attentive to the way the subtleties of language mask some identities while constructing others, hide some histories while highlighting others. Ultimately, unsettling the "we" voice and reconnecting it to histories of conquest, resistance, and connection is perhaps the most productively *disruptive* quality of the exilic disposition, particularly for those of us doing critical work that links the history of imperialism to the present.

TURNING IN AND CLOSING DOWN

Surprisingly, given the number of major figures in political theory who were exiles and who theorized the experience, political theorists have remained astonishingly uninterested in Said's interpretive approach. While most fields

[24] Said, *Representations of the Intellectual*, 53.   [25] Said, *Representations of the Intellectual*, 33.

in the humanities – from history and comparative literature to anthropology and cultural studies – were fundamentally (if not completely) transformed by the publication of *Orientalism* and the postcolonial revolution to which it gave rise, political theory as a subdiscipline has remained resolutely unaffected by that work.[26] Aside from the work of James Tully, when political theorists do mention Said it is usually briefly and only in regard to orientalism as a concept or *Orientalism* as a totemic reminder of the postcolonial turn.[27] On those rare occasions when scholars of political theory have expressed interest in Said's other works, it is usually gestural or, worse, without attribution.[28] Stranger still, political theorists and scholars of politics who are part of the discipline's "turn to empire" since the late 1990s *still* largely fail to engage Said's work.[29]

Why has it been so hard for political theorists just to *see* Said – this man whose scholarship and politics sat at the fulcrum of a transformative intellectual movement elsewhere – for so long? There are a variety of responses to this question, but the most illuminative set of explanations cluster around that same phenomenon that helps explain why, in Jennifer Pitts' words, the discipline of political theory came so "slowly and late to the study of empire relative to other disciplines": our disciplinary attachment to Political Science and Political Science's attachment to state sovereignty.[30] Thus, following World War Two, Political Science in North America began to organize itself around its current four subdisciplines, an act of professional hiving off that led to the confinement of almost all scholarship concerned with politics on a global scale within the emerging field of International Relations (IR).[31] Moreover, during this early

---

[26] Gauri Viswanathan, "Introduction," in *Power, Politics, and Culture: Interviews with Edward Said*, ed. Gauri Viswanathan (New York: Vintage Books, 2002), xi. Note that critical IR theorists have been more engaged with Said than political theorists. See, for instance, Geeta Chowdhry, "Edward Said and Contrapuntal Reading: Implications for Critical Interventions in International Relations," *Millennium* 36, no. 1 (2007): 101–16; and Raymond Duvall and Latha Varadarajan, "Travelling in Paradox: Edward Said and Critical International Relations," *Millennium* 36, no. 1 (2007): 83–99.

[27] See Brown's use of the term "imaginative geography" in Wendy Brown, *Walled States, Waning Sovereignty* (Princeton, NJ: Princeton University Press, 2010), 73–74. Tully references Said's work explicitly and thoughtfully in James Tully, "Dialogue and Decolonization," in *Dialogue and Decolonization*, ed. Monika Kirloskar-Steinbach (Bloomington, IN: Indiana University Press & Bloomsbury, forthcoming); and James Tully, "Political Philosophy as a Critical Activity," *Political Theory* 30, no. 4 (2002): 533–55; James Tully, *Public Philosophy in a New Key*, vol. 2, *Imperialism and Civic Freedom* (Cambridge: Cambridge University Press, 2008).

[28] See Amy Allen, *The End of Progress: Decolonizing the Normative Foundations of Critical Theory* (New York: Columbia University Press, 2016) for an example of the former. For the latter, see Wendy Brown's discussion of a "contrapuntal strategy" that "agitates" along political theory's disciplinary parameters, in Wendy Brown, *Edgework* (Princeton, NJ: Princeton, 2005).

[29] See Pitts' brief discussion of Said in Jennifer Pitts, "Political Theory of Empire and Imperialism," *Annual Review of Political Science* 13 (2010): 211–35.

[30] Pitts, "Political Theory," 212.

[31] It was not until the late 1970s that theorists such as Beitz and Schue began challenging at least part of this distinction. Bell describes contemporary IR and political theory approaches as

postwar period, founding thinkers within IR began associating their work explicitly and exclusively with the relationships between sovereign states, an assumption that remains foundational to this day. As a field, IR continues to read the contested landscape of world history through the lenses of sovereign statehood, often by re-inserting the "security dilemma" into the writings of a selected canon of Western political philosophers such as Thucydides, Machiavelli, and Hobbes.[32]

Political theorists reflect the state-orientation of the discipline by containing their thinking about democracy and its possibilities to bounded notions of "the people" structured by a foundational notion of nation-statehood which usually functions as deep background for theorizing. Rawlsians, for instance, "work up" their theories about the basic structure of society, justice, distribution, etc., by assuming a historically grounded social grouping attached to a particular kind of (liberal democratic) state with a particular economic form.[33] Critical theorists such as Nancy Fraser may challenge some of the baseline assumptions of liberalism by critically analyzing the development of liberalism in the context of capitalism and the welfare state, but these analyses circle around Eurocentric conceptions that fail to account for the constitutive role played by extra-state practices of imperial extraction, slavery, settler violence, and land dispossession in the emergence of capitalism itself.[34] Likewise, critical acolytes of Carl Schmitt, like Mouffe, argue for democratic, pluralist, and populist responses to reactionary politics by consistently reasserting the necessity of a "people" bound by a "moment of closure."[35] Even when Mouffe is most strenuously insisting, as she does in *Left Populism*, that "the people" is itself the product of democratic contestation rather than state, nation, or ethnicity, she simply fails to account for the fact that "the people" just happens to cohere to the nation-state and fails to consider the limitations baked into that formative "closure."[36]

The obsession of political scientists and political theorists with *bounded* notions of political identity and community runs counter to the way political identity and community has actually been experienced historically. As David Armitage reminds us, the vast majority of human beings "for most of history

"parallel universes" with markedly different literatures and understandings of the very same terms (e.g. "liberalism" and "realism"). See Duncan Bell, "Political Realism and International Relations," *Philosophy Compass* 12 (2017): 12.

[32] See Morgenthau's discussion of Thucydides, in particular his insistence that the centrality of state interest "is indeed of the essence of politics and is unaffected by the circumstances of time and place." Hans Morgenthau, *Politics Among Nations*, 7th ed. (New York: McGraw Hill, 2005), 10.

[33] See John Rawls, *Justice as Fairness: A Restatement* (Cambridge, MA: Harvard University Press, 2001).

[34] Nancy Fraser, "A New Form of Capitalism? A Reply to Boltanski and Esquerre," *New Left Review* 106 (2017): 57–65.

[35] Chantal Mouffe, "Carl Schmitt and the Paradox of Liberal Democracy," *Canadian Journal of Law & Jurisprudence* 10, no. 1 (1999): 21–33.

[36] Chantal Mouffe, *For a Left Populism*.

lived not in nation-states but in empires," a reality that persisted well into the 1960s.[37] A fixation with sovereignty and boundaries as the only historically identifiable forms of political association not only fails to account for the contrapuntal richness of this history, it also fails to appreciate the extent to which today's liberal democratic states – often the background political communities assumed by political theorists – were themselves forged through imperialist practices: explosions of settler violence, prolonged resource extraction, predatory taxation. Perhaps not surprisingly, then, this mode of unseeing also fails to account for the "continuing colonial presence" of the USA and its European/Great Power allies throughout the world today.[38] As Gurminder Bhambra argues, today's European welfare states are the products of long-standing historical patterns of racialized immigration policies that were normalized within their imperial ambit, while today's white settler nations would not exist if not for the near genocide of first nation peoples. These same states developed labor markets grounded in racial forms of domination and exclusion. In postwar Britain, for instance, the "apparently domestically inclusive welfare state regime" depended upon a political economy "of Imperial and (subsequently) Commonwealth preferences which was designed to enrich the British state while restricting the rights extended to subjects throughout its territories."[39]

Given the tendency of political theorists to attach their thinking about "the people" to enclosed sovereign units untouched by imperialism, it is hardly surprising that Said's kaleidoscopic perspective on politics – his cross- and trans- and sub- and antinational way of reading culture and imperialism in history – make him almost indecipherable to so many. This also means that those few theorists who have looked at his work often emerge confused or unsatisfied. Both Frederick Dallmayr and Joan Cocks, for instance, are similarly attracted by much of what they see in Said's work but are, at the end of the day, deeply dissatisfied with his unfixed, exilic perspective. Cocks believes that his conception of exile fails to "map out and fight for clear political alternatives to the nation-state" while Dallmayr is critical of Said's unwillingness to abandon disruptive tensions for the hope of reconciliation provided by a Hegelian notion of *Sittlichkeit*.[40] And yet, I think it is fair to say that both of these critiques miss the point. Said's is not a theory of political/epistemological closure, nor does it provide theorists with an alternative *theory of* politics. Rather, Said's approach

[37] David Armitage, *Foundations of Modern International Thought* (Cambridge: Cambridge University Press, 2013), 13.
[38] Edward Said, "Representing the Colonized: Anthropology's Interlocutors," *Critical Inquiry* 15, no. 2 (1989): 205–25.
[39] Gurminder Bhambra and John Holmwood, "Colonialism, Postcolonialism and the Liberal Welfare State," *New Political Economy* 23, no. 5 (2018): 574–87.
[40] Joan Cocks, "A New Cosmopolitanism? V.S. Naipaul and Edward Said," *Constellations* 7, no. 1 (2000): 47; and Frederick Dallmayr, "The Politics of Nonidentity: Adorno, Postmodernism – And Edward Said," *Political Theory* 25, no. 1 (1997): 33–56.

to exile provides us with a critical disposition, a mode of humble reflection and opening up, that begins from an uncomfortable sense of being *out of place*, which then fundamentally disrupts the way "we" – as political theorists – approach questions of justice, democracy, power, and domination that are our bread and butter.

Imagine, for instance, how occupying such an unstable position might alter the way political theorists approach an issue as fundamentally transnational as global justice. As it stands, since the 1980s the debate about global justice engaged in by major figures in political theory, such as David Held, Thomas Pogge, David Miller, Martha Nussbaum, and Will Kymlicka, has circled around a clash between what Fraser calls "the right" and "the good."[41] Thus, cosmopolitan thinkers argue that, in Nussbaum's words, "reason rather than patriotism or group sentiment" ought to guide moral action when it comes to theorizing solutions to the vast inequality of resources between peoples in the first and third worlds.[42] Regardless of the particularities of their approaches, cosmopolitan theorists today generally agree that human beings within nation-states have obligations to human beings in other parts of the world and that a right understanding of these obligations can be determined through (some form) of Kantian or Stoic reason. Cosmopolitans thus ask questions such as: What obligations do citizens in the first world owe to citizens in the third? To what extent are first-world citizens responsible for rectifying poverty in these countries? What responsibilities do developed countries have to mitigating the effects of climate change? All of these questions boil down to some version of: What do "we" owe to the global poor?[43]

Over the years, debates between cosmopolitans and their critics have tended to focus on the role of local or national communities in the formation of moral obligations, and they almost always revolve around questions of *identification*. That is, whether citizens within nation-states can really sustain a robust sense of moral and political connection to others with whom they do not identify as fellow nationals. For cosmopolitans, cultural and political identification with "the other" isn't necessary since people are capable of understanding moral obligation through reason. But for a communitarian like Alasdair Macintyre, this faith in reason ignores the role that identification with one's community plays in the development of moral consciousness.[44] Conservative scholars such as Jack Goldsmith similarly argue that individuals first learn lessons of morality from "members of their community ... with whom they identify," and Will

---

[41] Nancy Fraser, "Recognition without Ethics?," *Theory, Culture & Society* 18, nos. 2–3 (2001): 22.

[42] Martha Nussbaum, "Kant and Stoic Cosmopolitanism," *The Journal of Political Philosophy* 5, no. 1 (1997): 3.

[43] Mathias Risse, "What We Owe to the Global Poor," *Journal of Ethics* 9, no. 1 (2005): 81–117.

[44] Alasdair MacIntyre, *After Virtue: A Study in Moral Theory* (Notre Dame, IN: University of Notre Dame Press, 2007).

Kymlicka frames his critique of David Held's "communities of fate" in terms of the "sorts of collectivities" with whom people also identify.[45]

From a Saidian-inspired, exilic perspective, cosmopolitan theorists *and* their critics share an untroubled surety about the fixedness of the position from which they validate or minimize identity. This argument is similar to, but distinct from, those posed by postcolonial critics of cosmopolitanism, many of whom have already exposed the Eurocentrism of Enlightenment universalism, in part by "provincializing it," by linking it to the "cultural discourses" that sustain imperialism.[46] My argument, by contrast, is meant to demonstrate the way both champions of universal reason (cosmopolitan global justice scholars) and critics of that universal reason (communitarians, etc.) actually share certain subjective assumptions which then impose epistemological limits on political thinking. Thus, cosmopolitans consistently ask questions about "our" ethical obligations toward "others": impoverished nonnationals, climate refugees, potential victims of genocide, etc. In response, communitarian and conservative critics then raise concerns about the extent to which human beings within communities can identify with that broader conception of humanity. But whether they take identification as key to morality or not, neither Nussbaum and Beitz on the one hand, nor Macintyre, Goldsmith, and Kymlicka on the other, question *their own* identity.

In other words, none of these scholars ever wonders whether the ground upon which *they* stand – as theorists writing about the promises or problems of cosmopolitanism – is solid. Nor do they consider what questioning the solidity of that ground might do for their theorizing. Whether they think of themselves as citizens of the world, assume themselves to be linked in a thin, liberal fashion to their natal communities or communities of choice, or personally experience the ethical impact of their "little platoons" as vitally important to their identity, they know that when and if they leave, they can come "home" again. By contrast, Said's exilic subject begins their analysis of the world from the perspective that return is impossible and from the position that the ground upon which they stand, from which they critique and theorize, is not the home with which they identify fully. Indeed, sometimes even that tenuous connection is uncertain. Because exilic critics begin from a place of instability rather than closure, Said maintains, they are less likely "to derive satisfaction" from assumed connections and foundations. They are thus more likely to ask questions about the world that differ significantly from the core question asked by cosmopolitans or their critics: "What do *we* owe to others and what

---

[45] Jack Goldsmith, "Liberal Democracy and Cosmopolitan Duty," *Stanford Law Review* 55, no. 5 (2003): 1677; and Will Kymlicka, "Citizenship in an Era of Globalization," in *The Cosmopolitan Reader*, eds. Garret Brown and David Held (Cambridge: Polity, 2010), 437.

[46] See the work of Gurminder Bhambra, "Whither Europe? Postcolonial versus Neocolonial Cosmopolitanism," *Interventions: International Journal of Postcolonial Studies* 18, no.2 (2016): 187–202; and Ines Valdez, *Transnational Cosmopolitanism: Kant, Du Bois, and Justice as a Political Craft* (Cambridge: Cambridge University Press, 2019).

enables or prohibits *us* from identifying with them?" Rather, the exilic intellectual who begins from the unstable ground of wondering "Do we exist? What proof do we have?" asks questions about the *filiative* appearance of the "we" itself and about the *affiliative* relations that naturalize the categories of "us" and "them."

When oriented, for instance, toward those same problems of global injustice that preoccupy cosmopolitans, an exilic perspective is more likely to query affiliative connections between culture, politics, domination, forgetting, and collusion that, when woven together, set the stage for the current international environment. Rather than "what do we owe others?," the exilic theorist asks "How, in a global historical context framed by movement, violence, dispossession, extraction, domination, and connection, did *we* come to be *us* in the first place?" That then leads to a whole series of other questions: What is the relationship of today's global resource distribution to the history of imperial extraction that has allowed "us" to maintain "our" welfare state which we now argue is in crisis? How might the relationships between entities we call "liberal states" and entities we call "non liberal states" reflect that complicated history of imperial governance and extraction? What theoretical (moral, ethical, critical) resources for theorizing might be available to "us" were we to take the contrapuntal, interconnected histories of "the west and the non-west" seriously?

An exilic orientation pushes the question of identification – and all the subsequent questions of distribution, justice, reparations, obligation, and intervention that flow from it – inward, backward, outward, toward an investigation of those affiliative connections that structure the current global order today. An exilic inclination reorients the object of theoretical concern away from the shivering, starving, bomb-throwing masses ("them") toward an interrogation of how they came to be "them" and we became "us" in the first place. It thus recasts the terrain of global justice as, in Said's words, "a series of reflections rather than a string of assertions and affirmations."[47]

UNCLOSING DEMOCRACY

Because liberal democracy has increasingly come under attack by forces on the right, many scholars of politics have correctly responded with a sense of urgency. Unfortunately, that urgency is often misplaced, reactionary, or even nostalgic. Jeffrey Isaacs warns darkly about the "danger" lurking behind this move away from liberal norms, while William Connolly has stressed the resemblance between our moment and the fascist aesthetic of the 1930s.[48]

---

[47] Edward Said, "A Method for Thinking about Just Peace," in *What Is a Just Peace?*, eds. Pierre Allan and Alexis Keller (Oxford; Oxford University Press, 2006), 176.

[48] William Connolly, *Aspirational Fascism: The Struggle for Multifaceted Democracy Under Trumpism* (Minneapolis, MN: University of Minnesota, 2017); Jeffrey Isaac, "It's Happening Here and Now: Thoughts on the Recent Immigration Detentions and William E. Connolly's

Supporters of "the American-led liberal world order," like Ikenberry, clutch their pearls in horror that the "hostile revisionist power" who now intends to destroy liberal democracy sits in the Oval Office scheming against "trade, alliances, international law, multilateralism, environmental protection, torture, and human rights."[49] Both responses seek to counteract the attenuation of democracy on the level of the nation-state by burrowing into narratives about the exceptionalism of Trump and his resemblance to fascists of old rather than to "us." They then combine these narratives with nostalgic accounts of "our" essential goodness as a liberal democratic people overcome by reactionary, "revisionist" forces.

By contrast, adopting an exilic orientation toward the affiliative relationships between imperialism, identity, and history has the potential to pry open political theory to new ways of theorizing the *demos* that ask questions about what is being occluded by the "we" that inhabits the shape of democracy. Rather than mourn the loss of liberal democracy, adopting Said's exilic disposition prompts us to look at the world and our own theoretical perspectives contrapuntally and to ask: "What would we save of them, what would we give up, what would we recover?" Such an approach is, by design, unsettling and can feel like a willful act of throwing the baby out with the bathwater precisely at a historical moment when the world appears to crave not deconstruction and problematization but solutions. What could feel worse in this moment of crisis than looking down and seeing your foundations of belonging shift beneath your feet? At the same time, Said's work presses us to consider whether the security of that foundation is worth sacrificing the clarity of insight that comes from exile, from an interrogation of the liberal democratic state's imbrications with the ongoing politics of imperialism. After all, according to Said, it is "only in the precarious exilic realm [that] can one first truly grasp the difficulty of what cannot be grasped and then go forth to try anyway."[50]

At the same time, a Saidian perspective that works to destabilize the assumed foundations of peoplehood lurking in the background of so much democratic theorizing also aims to open up our conceptual horizons to new forms of human comity and global solidarity. At the end of the day, for Said there is no escaping the fact that the long history of global imperialism was grounded in both the "enabling rift between black and white, between imperial authority and natives" *and* in the historical interdependence between the Global South and the Global North, connections and affiliations sewn over time which now assure that "No one today is purely *one* thing."[51] Drawing on the work of anticolonial

---

'Aspirational Fascism'," *Public Seminar*, June 25, 2018, www.publicseminar.org/2018/06/its-happening-here-and-now.
[49] John Ikenberry, "The Plot Against American Foreign Policy," *Foreign Affairs* 96, no. 3 (2017): 2.
[50] Edward Said, *Humanism and Democratic Criticism* (New York: Columbia University Press, 2003), 144.
[51] Said, *Humanism and Democratic Criticism*; Said, *Culture and Imperialism*, 336.

scholars Aimé Césaire, C. L. R. James, and Franz Fanon, Said argued that a critique of colonialism couched from within the disruptive register of exile ultimately encourages a rejection of both nationalism and imperialism and an acceptance of what Césaire called "true humanism – a humanism made to the measure of the world."[52] Said's contrapuntal reading provide us with a glimpse into, as he saw it, "a more integrative view of human community and human liberation" untethered from both the rigidity of states and the exploitation of empires.[53] This is a vision of democratic humanism framed not in terms of "some tiny, defensively constituted corner of the world" but rather – from the beginning and always – in light of "the large, many-windowed house of human culture as a whole."[54]

[52] Aimé Césaire, *Discourse on Colonialism* (New York; Monthly Review Press, 2000), 73.
[53] Said, *Culture and Imperialism*, 216.
[54] Edward Said, "The Politics of Knowledge," in *Reflections on Exile* (Cambridge, MA; Harvard University Press, 2000), 382.

PART III

LOCAL/GLOBAL PARTICIPATORY DEMOCRACIES

8

Unwalling Citizenship

Fonna Forman

For most of the twentieth century, the border between the United States and Mexico performed like a line in the sand, with obelisks and later low chain-link and corrugated metal fences that demarcated where one country began and the other ended. In many places along its continental trajectory people moved back and forth quite freely. Children hopped across in one direction, and back as easily in the other. Over the last decades, with the upsurge of protectionist politics and anti-immigrant fever in the United States, the border has become increasingly militarized, with concrete pylon walls, ranging from 18 to 27 feet tall, crowned by electrified coils and panoptic night-vision cameras. The border now performs more like a partition than a line, because its goal is less to demarcate than to obstruct the flows and ecologies that have always defined life in this binational territory.[1]

But borders are ultimately porous things; they cannot stop environmental, hydrological and viral flows, economic flows, normative and cultural flows, ethical and aspirational flows. These often informal and invisible circulations shape the transgressive, hybrid identities and practices of everyday life in this part of the world.

Racist political narratives in the United States portray our region as a site of criminality, of dangerous undercurrents of drugs and unwanted people who undermine the safety and prosperity of good, hard-working Americans. But in my work, I have been committed to telling very different stories about life in this border region, grounded in the experiences of those who inhabit it.

I am a principal in a research-based civic and architectural practice located at the San Diego–Tijuana border, an unconventional partnership between a political theorist (me) and an architect (Teddy Cruz). We investigate

---

[1] For further discussion, see Fonna Forman and Teddy Cruz, "Access All Areas: The Porosity of a Hostile Border," *Architectural Review*, May 27, 2019, 18–23; Fonna Forman and Teddy Cruz, "The Wall: The San Diego–Tijuana Border," *Artforum* 54, no. 10 (2016): 370–75.

informal practices in the city – social, moral, economic, civic and spatial. We focus particularly on the ingenuity and resilience of people who inhabit the periphery in conditions of scarcity: how they assemble housing and infrastructure, markets of exchange, democratic practices and general strategies of collective survival.

By "informal" we mean practices that emerge "extra-officially" from the bottom-up to address the urgent challenges of marginalized and displaced populations, almost always in the absence of formal support, and often subverting or circumventing "formal" power structures and policies. By "formal" we mean the top-down institutions of planning and governance that organize cities and regions from a macro perspective.[2]

Formal planning arranges space through a deliberate civic armature that is subsequently 'in-filled' with private interventions. In the absence of committed public leadership in recent decades, civic agendas in cities across the world have been hijacked by private interests and corporate agendas, shrinking accessible public space, accelerating gentrification, dispossession, dramatically uneven urban growth patterns, and explosive informal development at the periphery. These dynamics have intensified in recent years with the globalization of cities across the planet and rapid urbanization caused by political instability, climate change, food scarcity and the neoliberalization of the global economy. Periurban slums, the underbelly of global economic growth, are growing faster than the urban centers they surround.

While we condemn the economic forces that marginalize people into slums, we are nevertheless inspired continually by the ingenious self-built logics of spatial retrofit and adaptation, the vibrancy of informal market dynamics, and the solidarity of communities confronting scarcity and marginalization. While the informal border neighborhoods where we work are denigrated by formal planners and their corporate developer friends as ugly, criminal, neglected, to be avoided, to be cleared, to be cleaned up, we observe intensely active, creative urban agents who challenge the dominant paradigms of neoliberal growth that exclude them. Their counterhegemonic everyday practices demonstrate other more inclusive and collective ways of inhabiting the city.

In the San Diego–Tijuana border region, much of this informal activity also involves dense networks of cross-border cooperation, productive transgressive flows of people, money and materials that are largely discounted in formal accounts of our divided binational region. From this vantage, the jurisdictional line between the United States and Mexico is less a solid than

---

[2] Some have argued that polarizing formal and informal dynamics can undermine progressive consensus-agendas for the city. While we accept their hybridity in practice, we believe the formal–informal binary helps to convey power, disparities and resistance in the neoliberal city. For discussion, see Fonna Forman and Teddy Cruz, "Changing Practice: Engaging Informal Public Demands," in *Informal Markets Worlds – Reader: The Architecture of Economic Pressure*, ed. Helge Mooshammer, Peter Mörtenböck, Teddy Cruz, and Fonna Forman (Rotterdam: naio10 Publishers, 2015), 203–23.

a mesh, a sieve of regional ecologies that circulates what walls cannot contain. Citizenship itself, we argue, is a fluid, performative concept. It is not a formal identity corroborated by documents in one's pocket, but a practical experience of belonging that emerges through shared practices of living and surviving together, sometimes actively resisting and countering divisive narratives and practices together, in a disrupted civic space. We seek to inspire more inclusive imaginaries of coexistence and cross-border citizenship in contested territories like ours.[3]

Blurring the line between research and activism, we have committed to *grounding* our critical claims about borders through horizontal practices of engagement where university researchers and residents of border neighborhoods assemble as partners to share knowledges, learn from each other, and ultimately coproduce new narratives, new strategies, new alliances and new, more equitable projects in the city. These commitments are embodied in an initiative called the UCSD Community Stations, which I will explore in this chapter.

As a political theorist, I think about the ethical and epistemic challenges of doing research in places of marginalization and struggle. I am keenly attuned to dynamics of power when universities arrive in communities, and am critical of both extractive research methods and humanitarian problem-solving missions. In the next section I will explore some of the challenges we have encountered doing political theory in solidarity with border communities, as well as strategies we've devised to mitigate them. I believe these reflections are generalizable and can contribute to broader dialogues on doing more activist political theory. I will then illustrate the kind of solidaristic political theory I do through a set of projects focused on citizenship that we have coproduced at the border with community partners.

POLITICAL THEORIST AS CURATOR

At the workshop gathering of this group in Victoria in March 2019, we discovered a shared commitment to doing political theory that is relevant and topical, that generates better arguments not only for academic audiences but for citizens and policy-makers as well. This entails that the political theorist take a position on conflicts and injustices in the world. But what does it mean for a political theorist to take a position in solidarity with people struggling against injustice? How do we avoid overconfidence in our knowledge or our capacity to say something relevant and faithful to real experiences? In this section I want to reflect on the epistemic challenges of doing political theory in solidarity with people struggling against injustice.

---

[3] These themes are explored in Fonna Forman and Teddy Cruz, *Unwalling Citizenship: The Political Equator* (London: Verso, forthcoming).

I've always been inspired by Albert Hirschman's work on community-based development in mid-century Latin America. His commitment to traveling, observing and listening as a way of countering centralized World Bank planning practices has oriented the kind of theoretical work that I aspire to do.

In 1954, Hirschman was appointed by the IBRD as an economic advisor to Colombia's National Planning Council.[4] He was young, and it was his first time working on a team of economic experts designing policy for a country struggling to emerge from poverty. It didn't take long before he became exasperated with grand development planning and its stultifying obsession with probabilities and linear balanced-growth paradigms.

So he quit, and spent the next several years traveling across Colombia as a private consultant, determined to understand how real problems were solved collectively in context by real people. He believed there was no other way to understand but to go and see. By the light of an "empirical lantern,"[5] as he would later call it, Hirschman set out to observe the diverse, scrappy, incremental, bottom-up reform projects, animated by the sweat, ingenuity and creative collective adaptability of people navigating conditions of scarcity. Hirschman was drawn to the unintended, the spontaneous and the unplanned. He was inspired by unexpected genius and the "interaction effects" that were lost on the mid-century planner and his blueprints for development. Hirschman's subversion of balanced growth – perhaps his greatest heresy ever – was incubated during this period of fieldwork. It was on the ground, talking with real people solving real problems, that he discovered a phenomenon that would situate his work over the next decades: that it is actually tension and disequilibria, and not the pursuit of ends such as growth and happiness, that trigger collective capacities into motion.

Years later, in 1984, Hirschman published *Getting Ahead Collectively: Grassroots Experiences in Latin America*, a slim, richly illustrated essay written in the days immediately following a 14-week immersion in grassroots development projects funded by the Inter-American Foundation across Latin America.[6] The title, he explained, was a reformulation of Adam Smith's famous line about "bettering our condition," but given a distinctively collectivist bend. He saw the book as a journalistic rather than an academic exercise, but his case studies elucidate themes that had become dominant in his work since his IBRD days in Colombia: inverted sequences, the complex motivations for collective action and the intangible benefits of social cooperation, like a deepened sense of collective capacity and possibility that can remain latent in communities and be reawakened by new tensions.

[4] The International Bank for Reconstruction and Development (IBRD) is the lending arm of the World Bank Group.
[5] Albert Hirschman, *Crossing Boundaries: Selected Writings* (New York: Zone Books, 1998), 88
[6] Albert Hirschman, *Getting Ahead Collectively: Grassroots Experiences in Latin America* (Oxford: Pergamon, 1984).

Hirschman spent a good deal of time in *Getting Ahead Collectively* reflecting on "intermediary organizations" who take it upon themselves to do what he called, with some tempered cynicism, "social promotion" among the poor. Social promotion had exploded across the continent in the 1970s and 1980s among young professionals – restless, educated middle-class youth who wanted reform, were increasingly cognizant of human rights, increasingly intolerant of the inequality around them, and yet who resisted pathways conventionally available to them: either dismal professional careers that tended to bolster the status quo, or guerilla fighting. Young lawyers, economists, engineers, sociologists, social workers, architects, agronomists and priests packed their bags and took to the field, eager to steward a more equitable future.

Hirschman observed that grassroots activism tends to accelerate in periods of increasing privatization, filling a vacuum left by the retreat of public investment. In this sense, he believed social promotion could help to temper an era of selfishness and produce more caring social relations. He also saw these organizations as bridges to funding opportunities and to planning agencies for whom these sites and their practices were so often below the radar. Often they also introduced new technical skills and capacities to communities, and information for better local decision-making. But he didn't like the opportunist language of intermediary or broker or facilitator to describe this activity, and he was critical of the presumptions these organizations often carried with them into the field.

He described social promoters as naïve do-gooders, arriving essentially the same way development economists did: well-intentioned, and with blueprints for improving lives. Like the "visiting economists syndrome" he attributed to World Bank apparatchiks, social promoters would descend with a copy of Paulo Freire's *Pedagogy of the Oppressed* under their arm, ready to "spread literacy" without much regard to the particular people they hoped to save, their local perceptions, priorities and aspirations. Perhaps a desire for education would be a *consequence* of development, Hirschman speculated, rather than the instigator, as conventional development theories would have it. He did not hide his skepticism. His narrative is sprinkled with examples of intermediary organizations that suddenly appear, rarely through participatory processes, and succeed only in mucking things up, the pivot in his stories of development dysfunction: and *then* came the architects and the engineers …. and *then* came the sociologists and the anthropologists …

Long before academics began to worry in large numbers about development imperialism and epistemic justice, Hirschman reported brilliantly from the field that charitable impulses and planning schemes typically misfire when they bypass local knowledges and practices. He was critical of social promotion understood as a one-way, top-down enterprise of experts descending to fill empty vessels, and instead advocated horizontal processes of engagement and reciprocal learning. Through his own work in *Getting Ahead Collectively* and elsewhere, he demonstrated a way of doing theory that is grounded in the voices and collective practices of grassroots actors themselves.

Political theory can learn a lot from Hirschman's work in mid-century Latin America. If we aspire even implicitly to advance justice, fairness, equity, etc., on behalf of people who are already marginalized, excluded, dispossessed and exploited, we inflict double harm by assuming that our concepts hold meaning for them, that our wishes for them align with their own. Political theorists in general are motivated by real challenges and urgencies in the world. With some obvious exceptions, this is ultimately what distinguishes us from more analytical or historical modes of engaging political ideas. We explore justice, equality, freedom, rights and agency because we believe it matters to real people. Some of us might characterize our work as solidaristic in this sense, but fewer of us include the voices of marginalized and exploited people in our theoretical work, or consider narrative accounts of the injustices they experience. How, then, do we know that our ideas resonate with theirs? Poignant outrage at the state of world affairs can drift unwittingly into advocacy and well-intended claims on behalf of, in defense of, or in solidarity with real people struggling against injustice. But do these claims expose real harms, describe real struggle, or are they well-intended approximations of these things? Does it ultimately even matter if we are writing primarily for academic audiences?

We cannot all be anthropologists or do fieldwork, but a more ethnographic sensibility would help.[7] Drawing on the research of others is one possibility. But I propose that political theorists interested in doing solidaristic work can also cultivate skills of listening to the experiences of people struggling against justice. I have been inspired by Jim Tully's commitment to "always listening."

My approach begins with listening carefully to those suffering the lived experience of injustices in their own ways of knowing and articulating them. This application of the norm of always listening to the other side helps to free us from our own sedimented descriptions of the real and disclose new possibilities.[8]

Moreover, our ideas as political theorists can *do* more than appear in a book or journal read by a handful of academic colleagues. Too often we write and publish long after a provocation has passed, long after it can be of *use* to anyone. How can political theory be more practical, responsive and projective in its solidarity?[9] Here I will propose, and later through examples demonstrate,

[7] Lisa L. Herzog and Bernard Zacka, "Fieldwork in Political Theory: Five Arguments for an Ethnographic Sensibility," *British Journal of Political Science* 49(2) (2019): 763–84.
[8] James Tully, *On Global Citizenship: James Tully in Dialogue* (London: Bloomsbury, 2014), 282.
[9] A question explored in Brooke Ackerly, Luis Cabrera, Fonna Forman, Genevieve Fuji Johnson, Chris Tenove and Antje Wiener, "Unearthing Grounded Normative Theory: Practices and Commitments of Empirical Research in Political Theory," *Critical Review of International Social and Political Philosophy* (2021). See also Michael Goodhart, *Injustice: Political Theory for the Real World* (Oxford University Press, 2018).

a model of "coproduction" that entails *accompanying* struggles against injustice, seeking dialogue with people and groups who are receptive to collaborative thinking, and possibly also collaborative advocacy and intervention.

Reflecting on political theory in this more practical, or activist, solidaristic mode, I borrow a concept from the visual and performing arts, and suggest that political theorists can be "curators." I will use this concept often in the next section to describe the sort of work I do. My intuition here emerges from a conversation many years ago with Carlos Uribe, a community-based curator and director of the *Museo Casa de Memoria* in Medellín, Colombia. Uribe's goal is to support collective healing and foster intergenerational civic memory of Medellín's violent histories of injustice. His methods include visualizing and continually recontextualizing the experiences of real people, refracted through the artistic vision of local cultural producers and the experiences of the communities they work with. He describes his role as a curator as "accompanying the process" of cultural production and public display. For Uribe, the curator is not simply arranging objects on a wall, motivated by sterile aesthetics or conceptual considerations oriented by art history or genre. Instead of seeing curation as a revisionist enterprise, he engages solidaristically in the process of cultural production itself through intimate dialogue with the public artist and the communities the artist engages. Motivated by a commitment to collective memory and healing, Uribe brings his unique skills of spatial organization and public pedagogy into a shared agenda of performance and display. Political theorists, like curators, can "accompany" struggles against injustice. Instead of producing speculative work, like a revisionist object on a wall that is often irrelevant by the time it sees light, political theorists can partner with communities in real-time, weaving diverse skills, knowledges and experiences into a richer account of struggle, and more responsive strategies of resistance, advocacy and intervention. While helping to improve real conditions, coproduction also produces better theory, grounded in real experiences.

Recognizing communities as coproducers of knowledge entails a shift in academic norms. University research culture is filled with assumptions that *we* know more, that *we* are trained, that *we* have languages to communicate complexity and the tools needed to solve the world's problems (if only *they* would listen to us). Universities tend to think of community-based work in one of two ways: as "applied research" or as provision of "services." These vertical tropes place the university in an epistemically privileged position, and conceive of communities as a subject of investigation or a passive recipient of benefits without knowledge or agency.

I am not suggesting that universities and other wealthy institutions shouldn't share their resources, or ever do research *in* communities: they absolutely should! When done ethically, these can be legitimate and important activities. I am also not saying that communities have nothing to learn from academic researchers. But we need to distinguish vertical modes of engagement from horizontal and collaborative ones, in which university and community both contribute knowledges and resources, and everyone learns and coproduces something that could not have been produced by either partner alone. Coproducing knowledge with communities is not an *applied* activity. We do not figure everything out in our campus labs and then descend to test our solutions in the world.

It is important to emphasize too that coproduction is not about flipping conventional academic presumptions and reproducing verticality with the community on top and the researcher as a passive vessel. I am proposing a horizontal model wherein diverse experiences, knowledges and skills meet. Horizontality is inherently agonistic in this sense, or at least has great potential for agonistic moments. Sometimes even trusting partners find themselves at odds when diverse experiences and knowledges push and pull in different directions. We experience contestation in our work all the time. Learning how to listen and dialogue respectfully during moments of difference and disagreement, how to negotiate compromise, typically has made our partnerships stronger.

There is no formal category for coproduction in the academic merit trinity of "research, teaching and service." Because community work looks like charity to an uncurious bureaucrat, coproduction is typically relegated to "service" – that zone of activity in the research university reserved for the unproductive and the big-hearted. But coproduction is not charity. Teaching our students the ethics of community engagement, and cultivating skills of dialogue, respectful listening and collaborating, is not "service-learning." Tipping the model of community–university engagement from a vertical to a horizontal plane is an ethical move, motivated by considerations of epistemic justice and labor equity. Universities must never take for granted the rooted knowledges, resources, social capital and labor that community-based agencies and residents invest when they engage academic researchers, when they divert from the intense demands of everyday life to open their spaces, minds and hearts, and share sometimes agonizing experiences and stories of injustice.

Communities are justifiably skeptical of research universities, who often suddenly appear with requests, plant their flag and then disappear just as abruptly once they extract what they need. University projects come and go with the wind, "one offs" associated with a research project, an academic course, an internship or a grant that ends, leaving communities feeling instrumentalized and abandoned, with diagnoses left unaddressed, challenges left unmet, projects feeling half-done, critical consciousness stirred perhaps but with few outlets for meaningful action. Often times, it doesn't even dawn on researchers to share their research and publications with their community "subjects." Moreover, because research universities are big, fragmented institutions, sometimes multiple projects and requests land at once, without coordination or knowledge of each other, creating confusion about what's what and a sense of overload. Sometimes researchers are reckless with the delicate social ecologies of community-based work, unaware of alliances, but also rivalries and pecking-orders that often exist among nonprofits operating in conditions of scarcity. Bringing resources and opportunities to a community organization, researchers sometimes unwittingly take sides in local controversies and power dynamics, and stir up trouble.

We designed the UCSD Community Stations as a platform for community–university engagement in the San Diego–Tijuana border region, a model of horizontal partnership, long-term trust, and coproduction. In the next section, I say more about the UCSD Community Stations, how they perform as civic spaces for the exchange of knowledges, and how they orient the kind of solidaristic political theory that I do.

LOCALIZING THE GLOBAL: THE UCSD COMMUNITY STATIONS

San Diego–Tijuana is a zone of conflict and disparity, and presently a lightning rod for American nativism. ICE[10] continues its dehumanizing sweeps, while thousands of Central American migrants escaping violence and poverty wait at the wall for asylum that never comes, reviled by the Mexican public as a nuisance, an "infestation," a drain on scarce public resources. Or else they sit in US detention centers as tools of deterrence, exposed to a raging pandemic, and, until very recently, separated forcibly from their children. Global injustice is an intensely local experience here. When I founded UCSD's Center on Global Justice a decade ago, my intention was explicitly to *localize the global.*

Against these local atrocities, border communities and activists on both sides of the wall have devised compelling strategies to defy and circumvent unjust power, transgress boundaries and confront hateful political narratives, often at great personal risk. Some of this contestation is dedicated to sanctuary and protecting people targeted by, or rejected by, the state. Some of it is working through the courts and other institutions of power to advocate for people already ensnared in the net of political violence. Some of it is a more considered exercise of civic freedom, in Tully's sense, organized around exposing and countering unjust power and devising new strategies, including cultural strategies, for doing that.[11] Much of it arises informally through everyday collective practices of adaptation and resilience in conditions of scarcity and danger. Over the years we have accompanied some of these bottom-up emancipatory transgressions, and irruptions of democratic agency, in close partnership with community organizations rooted in the neighborhoods that flank the borderwall.

In the recent period, the borderwall has attracted artists and cultural producers from around the world to engage in acts of performative protest.

---

[10] ICE is the Immigration and Customs Enforcement wing of US Homeland Security.
[11] I will use this concept as James Tully does: to describe practices of dialogue and negotiation around power and contestation that produce solidarities from the bottom-up.

While these gestures by visitors are often creative and provocative, we have been mostly critical of this uptick in ephemeral acts of resistance that dip in and out of the conflict. They tend to be extractive in their processes, and their impacts on public consciousness are as fleeting as the Instagram posts they generate. What happens the day after the happening?

With our partners, we have been advocating for a longer view of resistance and more strategic thinking about cultural, institutional and spatial transformation in the border region. To enable this longer-term work, we developed the UCSD Community Stations, a network of civic spaces in four border neighborhoods, two on each side, where university researchers, community organizations and residents convene to share knowledges and generally "act otherwise" together through research, education and civic programming.[12] Each Community Station is designed, funded, built, programmed and managed collaboratively by the UCSD Center on Global Justice and a deeply rooted community organization. Inspired by the famous Library Parks project of Medellín, Colombia, which we've studied and written much about,[13] we have transformed urban remainders into civic spaces, richly programmed for dialogue, collaborative research, urban pedagogy, participatory design and cultural production. The Community Stations also present a new model of urban codevelopment between public universities and community organizations to fight the creeping gentrification of border neighborhoods. We've demonstrated that the university's economic power, social capital and programmatic capacity can become leverage for communities to build *their own* public spaces, as well as housing and green infrastructure.

The content of civic programming varies from station to station based on the priorities of all involved, but all the stations seek to increase public knowledge; challenge divisive political narratives; devise strategies to counter exploitation, dispossession, deportation and environmental calamity; foster solidarity and collective agency; and imagine possible futures. These agendas often invite agonistic encounters with formal institutions of power that govern the border

[12] "Acting otherwise" is James Tully's concept. See James Tully, *Public Philosophy in a New Key*, vol. 1, *Democracy and Civic Freedom* (Cambridge: Cambridge University Press, 2008), 4. For more on the central commitments of the Community Stations see Fonna Forman and Teddy Cruz, "Critical Proximities at the Border: Redistributing Knowledges Across Walls," in *Spatial Practices: Modes of Action and Engagement in the City*, ed. Melanie Dodd (London: Routledge, 2020), 189–201.

[13] For discussion, see Fonna Forman and Teddy Cruz, "Global Justice at the Municipal Scale: The Case of Medellín, Colombia," in *Institutional Cosmopolitanism*, ed. Luis Cabrera (New York: Oxford University Press, 2018), 189–215; and Fonna Forman and Teddy Cruz, "Latin America and a New Political Leadership: Experimental Acts of Co-Existence," in *Public Servants: Art and the Crisis of the Common Good*, ed. Johanna Burton, Shannon Jackson and Dominic Wilsdon (Boston: MIT Press, 2016), 71–90. *The Medellín Diagram* is a visualization project by Teddy Cruz, Fonna Forman, Alejandro Echeverri and Matthias Görlich, commissioned in 2014 by the Medellín Museum of Modern Art for the United Nations World Urban Forum.

zone. Sometimes contestation opens opportunities for mutual recognition and cooperation, and sometimes it does not. For us, the goal is less about resolving conflict than about understanding, recognizing and *civicizing* it. We see democracy in the border zone as a fundamentally agonistic process of exposing the complex histories and mechanisms of injustice that are too often hidden within official accounts of who "we" are. We believe that recuperating this information and generating counternarratives is foundational to the exercise of civic freedom. To accompany this process, an active area of our research (and teaching) is codeveloping civic tools with our partners – diagrams, radical cartographies and story-boards – that visualize conflict and render the complex histories and mechanisms of political power more accessible. We also exhibit these visual tools in cultural institutions, museums and biennials, to increase public knowledge and rouse broader public indignation and solidarity.

There are four UCSD Community Stations in operation: two in southeast San Diego, and two in Tijuana. Here, I will discuss two that participate in solidaristic work on citizenship, which I will explore in the second half of this chapter.

UCSD-CASA

The UCSD-CASA Community Station is located in the border neighborhood of San Ysidro, California, a few blocks from one of the busiest international land crossings on earth. With 100,000 crossings everyday, the neighborhood is under continual surveillance by US Homeland Security, and fragmented by freeway and surveillance infrastructure. San Ysidro is 90 percent Latinx, many of whom are DACA recipients; many are undocumented. There are regular reports of egregious human rights violations in San Ysidro, mass sweeps, entry and seizure without warrant, and the detention of minors in adult facilities. San Ysidro's proximity to the borderwall means that illicit deportation can take a matter of minutes. Families are terrorized by threats of the proverbial "knock at the door."

Our Community Station is a partnership with the community-based social service organization Casa Familiar. The Station is located inside a beloved historic church, purchased by the organization many years ago, but left essentially vacant and in a state of disrepair. Together we pursued grants from ArtPlace America and the PARC Foundation to renovate the church into a black box community theater, equipped with sound and recording studios for youth groups. The Station also includes social service pavilions and an open-air classroom for civic and educational programming. The funding we raised to codevelop these cultural and civic spaces became leverage for our partners to qualify for municipal subsidies to build ten units of housing around the Station. In conventional affordable housing projects, developers try to reduce non-revenue-generating collective spaces to the greatest extent possible. Our model was very different: to codevelop robustly programmed collective spaces *first*, as foundational to a community-based social housing project at the border; and *then* leverage that funding to facilitate a development package for housing. The project broke ground in December 2018, and was completed in February 2020 when the tenants moved in.

Programming at the UCSD-CASA Community Station focuses on cultural processes that expose injustice and increase capacity for collective political and environmental advocacy. UCSD researchers partner closely with community activists, *promotoras*, residents and youth to document experiences of injustice through dialogue, storytelling, and "transurbance," nomadic/walking workshops inspired by the Stalker/Osservatorio Nomade collective in Rome. These experiences then become evidentiary material for new cultural strategies to engage hearts and minds, including community theater, music, dance and visual arts. Against the backdrop of political repression, San Ysidro has a young, energetic community of cultural producers and border activists with deep roots on both sides of the border, for whom art and performance are tools for exposing injustice and communicating with wider publics and institutions of power. Much of this youth activity is homegrown at The Front, a gallery and cultural venue Casa Familiar launched more than a decade ago. To illustrate our "cultural process" take, for example, our work on air quality, a major challenge for border neighborhoods such as San Ysidro. Our undergraduate student Annika Ullah, a double-major in biology and visual arts, was invited to visit the backyard of San Ysidro resident Guillermo Cornejo, to see his lemon trees. Every lemon was coated with black silt, produced by tens of thousands of cars idling daily a few blocks away, as they wait for hours to cross the border. The lemons became powerful bottom-up evidence for a documentary film exploring the intersection of border policy, community health, storytelling and activism. *Border Lemons* was a cultural strategy for visualizing power, and for mobilizing community awareness and arts activism around air quality – that high rates of lung disease in San Ysidro are not "the way of the world" but an injustice. The lemons also became a tool for dialogue with agencies that govern air-quality policy and resources in the border region.

UCSD-ALACRÁN

Our two Community Stations in Tijuana are located a mile apart in the Laureles Canyon, an informal settlement of 92,000 people that literally crashes against the border wall in the western periphery of Tijuana. Laureles Canyon lacks water and waste management infrastructure and is highly susceptible to erosion, landslides and dramatic flooding when its channelized sewage canals get clogged with trash.

The UCSD-Alacrán Community Station sits in the most rugged and polluted sub-basin of the Laureles Canyon. It is a partnership with the faith-based organization Embajadores de Jesús, led by activist economist and *pastor*, Gustavo Banda-Aceves, and activist psychologist and *pastora*, Zaida Guillen.

With limited resources, in recent years they built a refugee camp at this site to provide shelter, food and basic services to hundreds of Haitian and Central American refugees navigating unjust asylum processes in the United States and Mexico.

The shelter began in 2016 when Banda-Aceves met a group of Haitian men whose wives and children were granted US asylum, leaving them waiting on the Mexican side of the wall. These men were skilled in construction; together, they built a warehouse structure at the Embajadores site in Alacrán to shelter dozens of tents. As migration accelerated over the next years, with the arrival of thousands of Central American migrants in Tijuana, Embajadores opened its doors, and occupancy began to swell. What began as a single structure evolved incrementally through necessity, ingenuity and self-built logics into a full-on sanctuary neighborhood of informal housing units and public spaces of varying sizes and configurations, threaded into what seems like impossible canyon topography. This was all well underway when we began working together. When we met, Embajadores was receiving no formal institutional support or public subsidy of any kind, but it was rich in social capital. A cohesive core of migrant men and women were already dedicated to the life and future of the sanctuary, and through their sweat equity over time asserted collective ownership of the spaces.

Our work together began with envisioning future scenarios, which focused on increasing housing capacity, but also more fundamentally on how the sanctuary could evolve into a more solidified home. With our partners we reimagined the idea of refugee camps, from charitable holding stations or ephemeral sites of shelter, into spaces of inclusion where staying becomes an option. Hospitality is an essential first gesture when the migrant arrives, when the needs of the body, for food and water, medicine and shelter, are most acute. A humanitarian response to migration at the point of arrival is the mark of an *ethical* society. But as needs become more complex over time, charity is not the appropriate model for building an *inclusive* society. Inclusion demands a transformation of the city and of ourselves, welcoming the migrant and their children into our collective civic identity, ensuring participation in public life, opportunities for education, financial stability, and health and well-being – physical, psychological and spiritual.

Together, we conceived of the UCSD-Alacrán Community Station as an *infrastructure of inclusion* to embed housing units in communal spaces dedicated to holistic well-being, small cooperative businesses, fabrication, a computer lab, a health clinic, an industrial kitchen, a laundry and a nursery – all codesigned and managed by Embajadores, residents and UCSD researchers and students. We also committed to a sustainable sanctuary that includes bio-filtration infrastructure, native planting, water and waste management and zero-net energy, with photovoltaic panels and battery storage.

The project broke ground in March 2020 and, at the time of this writing, the site has been graded and the foundations poured. The participatory process that got us to this point is a powerful story of cross-sector collaboration. It's a complex story, but as we began to design and assemble resources for the project, we approached one of the NAFTA factories that encircle Tijuana's slums, a Spanish *maquiladora* that produces lightweight metal shelving systems used in warehouses across the world. It was an agonistic impulse: Can we hold these factories accountable to the settlements that provide cheap labor for their global production chains? Can they become partners in social housing? We had worked with Angel de Arriba, CEO of the Mecalux factory, a couple years earlier. As part of a social housing exhibition in 2015 at the Haus der Kulturen der Welt (HKW) in Berlin, he partnered with us to adapt Mecalux systems into structural pilot applications, like small bus stops to shelter workers from the hot Baja sun while they wait for maquiladora vans to transport them to their shifts. The HKW project illustrated that institutions of power, public and private, can help to reorient a city's surplus value toward public priorities. Meeting us again, de Arriba remained receptive to what he called our "humanitarian" agenda, quite apart from the "virtue-signaling" that typically motivates corporations to engage in charitable activity. On the spot, he agreed to a materials subsidy for our housing project in Alacrán.

With philanthropic support (a long story which involves the selling of a rare Jean Prouvé armchair at Sotheby's[14]) we are now accelerating construction of a 16,000 sq. ft. housing project in Alacrán, anchored in Community Station spaces. We are designing a framework that hybridizes Mecalux frames with concrete post-and-beam frames, typical of local construction practices, and affordable plastic coverings and shadings. We are building the "bones" and "skins" of the buildings, so to speak; the interior systems will be in-filled by the residents who will inhabit them. Incremental building practices are conventional in informal conditions. Most houses evolve this way over years, as needs evolve and resources become available. To expedite this process, we have raised funds for a fabrication lab, with a tool library, a couple of trucks and tractors and a flow of recycled materials. This will enable rapid completion of the Station itself; it will also incubate a construction cooperative ready to take on other building projects across the Laureles Canyon. Owned and managed entirely by the residents, this cooperative will enable flows of income, with a portion dedicated to the longer-term collective needs of the sanctuary.

BUILDING TRUST, MANAGING COMPLEXITY

To conclude this discussion of the UCSD Community Stations, a brief comment on how an initiative so complex, with so many participants and so many moving parts, complicated by a militarized international border, can avoid

[14] Bob Rubin, "A Rare Prouvé Armchair Sold to Benefit Urgent Housing Initiatives in Tijuana," *Sotheby's 20th Century Design*, November 26, 2019, www.sothebys.com/en/articles/a-rare-prouve-armchair-sold-to-benefit-urgent-housing-initiatives-in-tijuana.

placing unreasonable burdens on already-stressed community organizations. We resolved long ago that the university must never become a weight on our community partners.

First and foremost, we don't disappear. Our capital investment in Community Stations infrastructure quite literally cements campus commitment to our community partners, and we have secured programmatic funding that will enable us to carry this work resolutely into the future. Additionally, we designed unconventional staff positions called *Bridge Staff*, who keep one foot on campus, and one foot in the community organizations, beholden to both, managing flows of money, people and materials, and coordinating our collaborative research and programming. Imagine the temperament and skill-set needed to authentically bridge and build trust in such vastly different worlds: knowing how to navigate university bureaucracy while possessing intimacy with the delicate social ecologies of community-based work.

We also recognize that that our community partners invest time, resources, social capital and knowledges when they collaborate with us. As a matter of epistemic justice and labor equity, we are committed to always validating and compensating these contributions. We designed a second unconventional role called Public Scholars: community leaders who codesign the content of our Community Stations programming, become bridges of trust to residents and youth, and coproduce research with us and our students. But we also ensure that they will never be saddled with managing our students in the field. UCSD students participate in Community Stations activities through fully supervised field internship programs, led by seasoned Field Coordinators who have built relationships of trust with our community partners over time, and who understand the complexities of navigating border dynamics accompanied by student teams.

Universities wishing to develop long-term collaborations with communities need to invest in positions like this, which build trust and manage complexity. In our case, enthusiastic support from the Andrew W. Mellon Foundation for these unconventional dimensions of our work made it easier to explain to university bureaucrats why we need salaried staff who spend half their time in community organizations, and why we fund "scholars" who don't have conventional academic credentials.

GLOBALIZING THE LOCAL: PRACTICES OF CIVIC ELASTICITY

We have always resisted the abstraction of global justice theories, as if justice is something that happens "out there" in the world somewhere. Our work engages struggles against injustice in the "here and now" of our border region, where the rubber hits the road, so to speak. Unlike the *critical distance* taken by scientists in their drive for objectivity, we pursue *critical proximity* to accompany the process of struggle.

Our work *localizes the global*. But we also recognize that "the local" can quickly devolve into myopia and protectionism. As part of our local activism with our Community Stations partners, we experiment with more expansive civic imaginaries that situate border neighborhoods within broader spheres of circulation, interaction and solidarity. To *globalize the local* in this sense, we create cartographical experiments that "nest" border neighborhoods within incrementally expanding spatial scales – from the greater San Diego–Tijuana border region, to the continental border that divides the United States and Mexico, to border zones across the world. Through this nesting strategy we seek to provoke more elastic civic thinking, through which local communities can visualize and situate themselves within broader ecologies – regional, continental and, ultimately, global. Nesting has both particularizing and universalizing effects: it reaffirms local uniqueness, that we experience and counter injustice in our own particular ways; but it can also provoke resonances and more expansive feelings of solidarity with others and possibilities for coalition-building.

Recognizing spatial alignment on a map is much easier than recognizing solidaristic affinities with people inhabiting these broader ecologies, which is necessarily a more speculative and provisional activity. Unlike a comparative approach, where one reflects conceptually on similarities and differences, a nested approach enables a person to understand herself incrementally as part of larger spatial systems that contain the challenges she faces. Her civic affiliations and identities can become more elastic in this sense. By elasticity we mean the ability to stretch and return: the ability to move between local and more expansive ways of thinking and connecting, to expand and contract, over and again. Elasticity is a civic skill. With our community partners we curate convenings and workshops, using visual tools to nurture more elastic civic thinking. A rubber-band that is rigid can snap if stretched too far, too fast. In this sense we see our cross-border civic dialogues in the Community Stations as stretching exercises, so to speak.

Some years ago I wrote a book called *Adam Smith and the Circles of Sympathy* that explored Smith's localist moral psychology in similar terms.[15] Smith believed cosmopolitan philosophy was anthropologically flawed since human behavior tends to bias spatially, affectively and culturally toward local places and people. He was not terribly troubled by this, since he believed humans produce better ends with better knowledge, access and motivation, which local proximities tended to provide. But he also suggested that our affinities and perspectives can grow, can be stretched to use the current metaphor of elasticity, to include broader spheres as we come to understand our interdependencies and shared interests with others.

[15] Fonna Forman, *Adam Smith and the Circles of Sympathy: Cosmopolitanism and Moral Theory* (Cambridge: Cambridge University Press, 2010).

In what follows, I will illustrate the kind of solidaristic political theory I do through this nested scaffold which expands incrementally across interdependent scales – from border neighborhoods, to the border region, to the continental border, and ultimately to a speculative global border we call *The Political Equator*. I will explore these scales through the visual tools we've designed for civic dialogue and have exhibited in cultural institutions across the world.

REGIONAL: CROSS-BORDER COMMONS

In this era of escalating tension and militarization at the border, where racist public rhetoric defines who people are and assigns them in a Foucauldian sense to their fixed geographical place, we offer counternarratives of interdependence and coexistence that reflect the cross-border circulations and transgressions of everyday life across our region. Our Community Stations themselves are a transgressive infrastructure. Distributed on both sides of the wall, they become observatories for documenting these flows through ethnography and scientific research, increasing public awareness of the social and ecological ties between San Diego and Tijuana, between the United States and Mexico.

Our aspiration is to foster what we call a "cross-border citizenship culture," where belonging is oriented not by the nation-state, but by the shared stories, challenges, everyday practices and aspirations among people who inhabit a violently disrupted civic space.[16] Those who benefit from narratives of separation and mistrust prefer that we remain a fragmented public, and that the idea of citizenship divides rather than unites. As a corridor of knowledge flows across the wall, the Community Stations become a platform for constructing a regional civic identity from the bottom-up, a cross-border *res publica*, as Jim Tully describes it: "Participation in dialogues and negotiations over how and by whom power is exercised over us constitutes our identities as citizens and generates bonds of solidarity and a sense of belonging to the *res publica*."[17]

With our partners we curate "convergences," "cultural performances" and "unwalling experiments" supported by visual tools like the ones I will discuss,

---

[16] See Antanas Mockus, "Building 'Citizenship Culture' in Bogotá," *Journal of International Affairs* 65, no. 2 (2012): 143–46. In partnership with Mockus, in 2013 we designed the Cross-Border Citizenship-Culture Survey that helped us identify latent opportunities for fostering a cross-border public in the San Diego–Tijuana border region. For more, see Fonna Forman, "Social Norms and the Cross-Border Citizen: From Adam Smith to Antanas Mockus," in *Cultural Agents Reloaded: The Legacy of Antanas Mockus*, ed. Carlo Tognato (Cambridge, MA: Harvard University Press, 2018), 333–56; Gregory Scruggs, "New San Diego-Tijuana Survey Holds Mirror Up to Border Cities," *Next City*, February 25, 2015, http://nextcity.org /daily/entry/binational-survey-san-diego-tijuana-border-antanas-mockus. The project was exhibited publicly in 2017 at the Yerba Buena Center for the Arts in *Visualizing Citizenship: Seeking a New Public Imagination*.

[17] Tully, *Public Philosophy*, vol. 1, 147.

to facilitate broader recognition of our cross-border citizenship: to expose it, name it and embrace it as uniquely ours.

The movement of water through shared canyon systems has been a powerful device to stimulate more elastic civic thinking in our region.[18] The neighborhoods where our two Tijuana-based Community Stations sit are nested inside the Tijuana River Watershed, shared by San Diego and Tijuana. Twenty-five percent of the watershed is in the United State; 75 percent is in Mexico. This San Diego–Tijuana *bioregion* is radically bisected by the international border. The two cities have never adequately recognized the watershed that unites them, or engaged in collaborative urban planning for the benefit of everyone across the region. Municipal planning maps in both cities literally stop cold at the line, as if there is nothing but blank white space on the other side. Intensification of borderwall infrastructure in recent years has interrupted sensitive environmental and hydrologic systems, deepening the environmental health impacts of this mutual neglect.

The collision of natural and jurisdictional systems, of environmental and political forces, is perhaps most profound and visible precisely where our two Community Stations sit. The Laureles Canyon is an important finger of the binational watershed that crosses the borderline and drains northbound into the Tijuana River Estuary, a precious, environmentally protected zone in southern San Diego county, before discharging into the Pacific Ocean. The estuary is considered the "lungs" of our bioregion, and a critical environmental asset to populations on both sides of the wall.

Because the informal settlements of Laureles Canyon lack public water and waste management infrastructure, waste is managed in one of two ways: through trash-burning, which spews black carbon particulates into the air and into lungs; and through wide-scale dumping into canyon creeks and drainage culverts that clog during rain events. Industrial toxic dumping is also a common practice among the *maquiladoras*: the multinational factories that dot the periphery of Tijuana, often located on the ridges of canyon slums to access cheap labor and circumvent feeble municipal attempts at environmental regulation and zoning. Waste in the canyon mixes with copious quantities of loose sediment, exacerbated by the informal building practices of squatters, as well as speculative developers who buy cheap land on craggy hillsides and flatten the topography with backhoes to subdivide into mini-pads. Informal development produces tons of loose sediment every year that become sludgy flows whenever it rains. Waste and erosion challenges in Tijuana's canyon slums are aggravated by "precipitation whiplash" in this part of the world: erratic and heavy rainfall patterns caused by climate change that produce dangerous mudslides and flooding across the Laureles Canyon. Because the canyon sits

[18] A strategy first proposed in the 1970s by Donald Appleyard and Kevin Lynch in *Temporary Paradise? A Look at the Special Landscape of the San Diego Region: A Report to the City of San Diego* (Cambridge, MA: Massachusetts Institute of Technology, 1974).

at a higher elevation than the estuary in San Diego, this waste flows northbound, carrying tons of trash, sediment and industrial waste that inundate and compromise the binational estuary. In recent years, US Homeland Security carved concrete dams and drains into newly built borderwall infrastructure, which serve to siphon and accelerate these calamitous northbound flows.

The borderwall is sold to the American public as the key to national security, but in our region it causes great environmental *insecurity*. Some have observed that the chickens have come home to roost.[19]

The *Cross-Border Commons* is a visualization project that illuminates these topographical and hydrological dynamics in accessible ways, to communicate to publics on both sides of the wall that regional wastewater flow is not a "Mexican problem" – the way Americans typically dismiss the challenges of our neighbors – but a shared bioregional challenge that Tijuana and San Diego need to tackle together. At the very local canyon–neighborhood scale, where we work, this means working closely with our community partners to cultivate a sense of *bioregional* well-being, of ownership and civic commitment toward an estuary that sits behind America's wall. To cultivate this more elastic sense of belonging and commitment, we have codesigned visualization tools and cartographies that nest local neighborhoods in this larger watershed ecology.

We often lead nomadic workshops and visit a promontory located high above the Laureles Canyon, called Mirador, where one can witness these dramatic environmental collisions from above. Imagine Mexican children standing on a narrow sliver of land along the eastern rim of the canyon, hundreds of feet above the borderwall. Imagine they plant their feet facing due west, with the vast blue expanse of the Pacific Ocean in front of them, Mexico to their left, the United States to their right. Below, to their immediate left, they see the dense informal settlement where they live; they can spot their houses, their schools and experience their proximity to the border and a country they and their families are not permitted to enter. Below, to their immediate right, almost directly beneath their feet, they see the borderwall which, from this vantage, looks like a flimsy and ridiculous strip inserted onto a vast and powerful natural system. Lifting their eyes further to the right, they see the green expanse of the Tijuana River Estuary, with its lush wetland habitats and sediment basins contrived to catch the northbound flows of waste from their community. From this vantage the characters of this cross-border environmental story about flows and interdependence come to life. We've witnessed this moment of recognition again and again over the years, among children, our students, policy-makers and even foundation presidents. I will

---

[19] In a similar vein, see our study of harmful water-flows from Gaza into Israel: Fonna Forman and Teddy Cruz, "Interdependence as a Political Tool: Three Building Blocks for Gaza," in *Open Gaza: Architectures of Hope*, ed. Michael Sorkin and Deen Sharp (New York: American University in Cairo Press, 2020), 302–25.

always remember the first time I witnessed it. There are places on the US side where one can grasp these dynamics, but it is most profound from Mirador. I suspect there are few places on earth where the dramatic collision of informality, militarization and environmental vulnerability can be so vividly experienced.

Patrick Geddes, the early-twentieth-century Scottish sociologist and early urban planner, designed the Camera Obscura in the center of Edinburgh, one of the first museums dedicated to urban research. A five-story building constructed as an observation tower, the ground floor was dedicated to global dynamics; the topics of each ascending floor contracted in geographic scale, culminating on the top floor, which was an open-air diorama dedicated to the local. It enabled people to look out across the territory, observe its geographic composition, and comprehend the environmental systems that organize the city. Geddes claimed that visual cognition of the territory, comprehending the city from a spatial vantage, an ability to name the rivers and valleys, plateaus and mountains, was essential to the construction of a civic identity and of collective political will. He coined the words "regionalism" and "conurbation," which are often used today to describe binational zones such as San Diego–Tijuana.[20] Our commitment in the Community Stations to cultivate an elastic civic identity through visual cognition, to experience the local as part of a region, a conurbation, is inspired by Geddes' Socratic impulse to ascend from the city.

Sometimes, however, nurturing civic elasticity entails descending below the familiar, going down with an empirical lantern, as Hirschman described it. Several years ago, we curated a cross-border public action through one of the sewerage drains Homeland Security carved into the wall, between Laureles Canyon and the estuary. We negotiated a permit with US Homeland Security to transform the drain into an official southbound port of entry for twenty-four hours. They agreed, disarmed by our self-description as "just artists," as long as Mexican immigration officials were waiting on the other side, in Mexican territory, to stamp our passports. Our convoy comprised 300 local community activists and residents, representatives from the municipalities of San Diego and Tijuana, and artists and border activists from around the world. We understood the event as an "agonistic" intervention because we summoned institutions and agencies who are often at odds with one another. In Chantal Mouffe's words, we created an itinerant "vibrant 'agonistic' public sphere of contestation where different hegemonic political projects can be confronted."[21] As we moved together southbound under the wall, we witnessed slum wastewater flowing northbound toward the estuary beneath our feet. This strange crossing from estuary to slum under a militarized culvert, and the stamping of passports inside this liminal space, amplified the most profound contradictions and interdependencies of our border region. The great insight

[20] Notably in Patrick Geddes, *Cities in Evolution: An Introduction to the Town Planning Movement and to the Study of Civics* (London: Williams, 1915).
[21] Chantal Mouffe, *On the Political* (London: Routledge, 2005), 3.

was that protecting the US Estuary demands investment in the informal settlements in Mexico, increasing bioregional awareness, and codeveloping neighborhood-scale participatory waste and sediment management initiatives.

Our border-drain crossing was more than an ephemeral happening; it helped to solidify a durable, cross-border, public commitment to action. We are now leading a binational land conservancy project, the *Cross-Border Commons*, which identifies unsquatted slivers of land in the Laureles Canyon, bundles them into an *archipelago of conservancy*, and connects them with the Estuary in a continuous political, social and ecological zone that transgresses the international line.[22] Our binational coalition is comprised of state and municipal agencies, environmental nonprofits, university researchers like us and community organizations such as Divina Providencia and Embajadores de Jesús. Every participant brings a unique set of knowledges and capacities to this bioregional effort: some do environmental research, some advance policy, some mobilize public knowledge and support and some advance sustainable practices in communities. With our Community Stations partners in Laureles we are codeveloping sustainable waste management and anti-erosion practices in the canyon, oriented around conservation, reuse and the separation, composting, collection and removal of trash, as well as native planting, reforestation and the development of bio-swales and pervious ground cover to keep precarious topsoil intact. With this 'green cross-border stitch', as we all call it, we are rethinking the border through the logics of natural and social ecologies, and reimagining citizenship through a shared commitment to the health of our bioregion.

CONTINENTAL – MEXUS: GEOGRAPHIES OF INTERDEPENDENCE

Our *Cross-Border Commons* project in San Diego–Tijuana has provoked curiosity about other sites of porosity and ecological interdependency along the continental border between the United States and Mexico. Over the years we have collected aerial photographs across this continental span that document precise moments when the jurisdictional line of the nation collides with natural systems. At some of these junctures, like ours, the borderwall cuts through and violates delicate natural ecologies. San Diego–Tijuana, El Paso–Juarez, Brownsville–Matamoros and many less populous locations powerfully illustrate what dumb sovereignty looks like when it "hits the ground" in a complex bioregion. But at other junctures, nature is too mighty to be bisected. Mountains, canyons and bodies of water frequently interrupt America's great wall and complicate its territorial dominion. Of course, these landscapes are generally impossible for human transgression as well, so the

---

22 For more, see Fonna Forman and Teddy Cruz, "Citizenship Culture and the Transnational Environmental Commons," in *Nature's Nation: American Art and Environment*, ed. Karl Kusserow and Alan Braddock (New Haven: Yale University Press, 2018), 416–27.

border-builder simply militarizes their edges and co-opts them in its strategies of spatial division and control.

In recent years we developed *MEXUS: Geographies of Interdependence*, a visual project that stretches our elastic civic aspirations to the continental scale. *MEXUS* visualizes the continental border between the United States and Mexico without the jurisdictional line.[23] Because the border is not a place where things end, *MEXUS* dissolves the border into a bioregion whose shape is defined by the eight binational watershed systems bisected by the international border. Our Tijuana River watershed in San Diego–Tijuana is nested at the westernmost corner of *MEXUS*, where the 3,145 kilometer borderwall descends absurdly into the Pacific Ocean. The Rio Grande Valley, and the cities of Brownsville–Matamoros, anchor the other end.

MEXUS also exposes other systems and flows across this bioregional territory that the wall cannot contain: 11 tribal nations, 110,000 square kilometers of protected lands, 16,000 square kilometers of croplands, 28 urban crossings, many more informal ones, 15 million people and more. By erasing the line, *MEXUS* exposes and unwalls this thick system of ecologies and interdependencies and challenges the legitimacy of the colonizer's rationalist nineteenth-century line imposed onto complex systems shared among nations. As one San Ysidro resident once put it: "if the border needs to be there, why does it need to be so stupid?" The borderwall proposed by the Trump administration threatened to close these spaces even further, compromising the common destiny of border communities. Only the most myopic or racist of nationalist politics could conclude that walling the other will solve our problems. While the borderwall satisfies protectionist urges for physical security, it simultaneously harms the nation by interrupting the environmental, economic and social flows essential to the health and sustainability of the larger region. By fortifying its violent line against the other, the United States violates its own people and its own natural resources.

Ultimately, our civic purpose for designing *MEXUS* was to counter America's wall-building fantasies with more expansive imaginaries of belonging and cooperation beyond the nation-state. Instead of seeing the border through the lens of division and control, *MEXUS* provokes more ecological thinking oriented by dynamic regional circulations. It provokes a more inclusive idea of citizenship oriented by coexistence, shared assets and cooperative opportunities between artificially divided communities. The ecologies of *MEXUS* become an organizing framework for dialogues about a bioregional civic identity among Mexicans, Americans and diverse Tribal Nations who inhabit this contested space.

[23] Fonna Forman and Teddy Cruz, *MEXUS: Geographies of Interdependence* was first presented in the 2018 Venice Architecture Biennale, commissioned by the United States pavilion for the exhibition *Dimensions of Citizenship*.

GLOBAL: THE POLITICAL EQUATOR

From our border at San Diego–Tijuana we have imagined an elastic civic identity, rooted in local experiences and affective ties, that is able to recognize resonances and solidarities with others at broader scales, as a strategy of resistance against injustice. Our "final stretch" in this cross-border civic imaginary (and in this chapter) is a visualization project called *The Political Equator*. Taking the Tijuana–San Diego border as a spatial point of departure, *The Political Equator* traces an imaginary line across a flattened map of the world, visualizing a corridor of global conflict between the thirtieth and thirty-eighth parallels north. Along this trajectory lie some of the world's most contested thresholds, including the US–Mexico border at San Diego/Tijuana, the most-trafficked international border checkpoint in the world and the main migration route from Latin America into the United States; the Strait of Gibraltar and the Mediterranean, the main route from North Africa into "Fortress Europe" thickened in recent years to contain flows of humanity from Lampedusa into Italy and from Lesbos into Greece; the Israeli–Palestinian border that divides the Middle East, emblematized by Israel's fifty-year military occupation of the West Bank and Gaza; India/Kashmir, a site of intense and enduring territorial conflict between Pakistan and India since the British partition of India in 1947; the border between North and South Korea, which represents decades of intractable Cold War conflict; and China's militarization of sovereign islands in the South China Sea, and colonizing ambitions toward Taiwan and Hong Kong.

While the *Political Equator* is represented lyrically as a flat line that bisects an astonishingly diverse assemblage of recognized violent border conflicts across the world, it operates ultimately as a *critical* threshold that conceptually bends, fragments and stretches to engage the forces of nationalism and border closure everywhere. Visualizing the *Political Equator*, again lyrically, alongside the climatic equator is revealing. This band, give or take a few degrees, contains our planet's most populous slums, its sites of greatest natural resource extraction and export and its zones of greatest political instability, climate vulnerability and human displacement. It also contains all of Trump's "shithole countries." The collision of nationalism, environmental catastrophe, forced migration and borders is the great crisis of our age, the global injustice trifecta of our time, and is perfectly recognizable to our community partners at the San Diego–Tijuana border.[24]

CROSS-BORDER CITIZENSHIP

In our work, we seek to reclaim the idea of citizenship for more inclusive, democratic and environmentally proactive cross-border agendas. In an

---

[24] On climate and migration specifically, see Fonna Forman and Veerabhadran Ramanathan, "Climate Change and Mass Migration: A Probabilistic Case for Urgent Action," in *Humanitarianism and Mass Migration: Confronting the World Crisis*, ed. Marcelo M. Suárez-Orozco (Berkeley: University of California Press, 2019), 239–50.

increasingly walled world, with reactionary nationalism surging everywhere, we challenge the claim that we are living in or somehow moving toward a postsovereign reality. Right now, the demand to protect national borders is ascending across the world, with citizenship tethered to territory and inherently closed to those beyond the gate. The cosmopolitan retort to these xenophobic urges across our planet is satisfying from a humanistic vantage, but thinking of ourselves as "citizens of the world" ultimately lacks visceral appeal and mechanisms for meaningful collective agency. Everything interesting about citizenship in political theory today happens somewhere between these two extremes, with attempts to ground citizenship in something real while remaining compassionate, nondiscriminatory and inclusive. Through our work in border communities, we have come to embrace an elastic idea of citizenship that is grounded in local experiences and affective ties but is nevertheless fluid and open, its boundaries continually renegotiating themselves around the confluences, shifting challenges, opportunities, interests and aspirations among diverse people who together inhabit contested space. Border regions are a natural laboratory for rethinking citizenship along these lines.

Now, it may seem naïve or even insulting to some that we propose discussing citizenship in a context like the US–Mexico border, where formal belonging is so rigidly fixed to nation and documentation and has been so dramatically denied through racialized political violence. But we advocate turning the concept back on itself, recuperating the idea of citizenship as a cultural concept that emerges more inclusively from the bottom-up through everyday practices of mutual recognition and more deliberate acts of civic freedom. Through civic programming in the UCSD Community Stations we are committed to identifying these confluences, overlapping sensibilities, crosscutting resonances, and aspirations among jurisdictionally ruptured publics, often hidden behind the shadows of walls.

By means of our partnerships we discover new and sometimes sudden opportunities to mobilize solidarities. For example, there is a pervasive mistrust of conventional progressive political leadership on both sides of the border, especially among young people who no longer connect with the dominant social justice narratives of earlier generations. How can researchers, cultural producers and agencies on the ground help to mobilize these convergences into productive forces? Outrage over US policies of gratuitous hate – like family separation at the US–Mexico border, like high rates of COVID-19 infection among migrants deported back to their home countries – are opportunities to unite cross-border publics in solidarity. This kind of solidarity can be fleeting, topical, but openings like these become powerful summoners for curating civic dialogue in contested places like ours.

Our local experiences in San Diego–Tijuana have oriented our aspirations for broader critical reflection on unjust migration policies and border conditions *everywhere*. Moving from local experiences to a global project is a necessarily speculative and provisional activity. But what we propose here should be distinguished from an abstract normative position. Ours is a *grounded critical theory* that has emerged through our participation over many years in civic processes along the US–Mexico border. The broader resonances we claim have also been validated over the years through partnerships with colleagues and activist networks who work in similarly solidaristic modalities in conflict zones across the world. In the words of Tijuana-based artist Marcos Ramirez ERRE, borderwalls exist only to be transgressed. For him, this is the ultimate aspiration of public art. In sites across the world characterized by rising nationalism, surveillance and control, and the criminalization of migrants, this is the ultimate aspiration of civic freedom as well.

9

Other Wise Democracies: What the Tree Canopies Know

Rebeccah Nelems

[P]erhaps it is time to touch the algorithms of our longings, to linger at the terrifying fault line where a different kind of politics might sprout. Perhaps it is time to name the electoral politics that hides its shrivelling body behind the spectacle of who won and who lost, and nurture its weirder cousin. A politics of the otherwise.

- Bayo Akomolafe[1]

INTRODUCTION

Brazilian sociologist Boaventura de Sousa Santos recently observed that "democracies are dying democratically"[2] through the election of antidemocrats around the world. The ballot-box wins of antidemocratic parties around the world are quick to hail public attention. However, Santos' words point to an even deeper source of morbidity troubling Western democracies, warranting a deeper interrogation into the societal conditions within which democracy might be dying by its own hands. Can the current precariousness of democracy be blamed on antidemocratic movements, leaders and/or supporters alone? Or might democracy not be as democratic as thought? In this chapter, I take up the call to critically examine the sources of democracy's morbidity from a social systems perspective.[3]

---

[1] Bayo Akomolafe, "Without prejudice to my American brothers and sisters, who have been, and are, fighting with every drop of their blood to topple the alarmingly pro-fascist villainy of Donald Trump," Facebook, August 30, 2020, www.facebook.com/permalink.php?story_fbid=635532823741994& id=130394687589146.

[2] Boaventura de Sousa Santos, "The Crises of Democracy: Boaventura de Sousa Santos and James Tully" (webinar, *Global Politics in Critical Perspectives – Transatlantic Dialogues*, University of Victoria, Victoria, BC, March 15, 2019), www.youtube.com/watch?v=-i9aFUsTipk.

[3] Babic calls for three entry points to be examined with respect to the interregnum he argues we find ourselves in. These entry points are drawn from his Gramsci-inspired tripartite framework, which includes "the global political economy level of analysis (the processuality of the crisis) . . . the state

This lends itself to considering that the ongoing swell of antidemocratic movements might be symptoms rather than causes of democracy's crises. From this vantage point, important new lines of inquiry come into view.

The chasm between democracy's rhetoric and people's lived experiences is vast. From racialized state violence and systematic discrimination, to the denial of Indigenous nations' sovereignty, to ecocide, it is clear the "emperor" has no clothes. Too many state-sanctioned injustices are happening on democracy's watch – brutalities that the rhetoric of equality, inclusion and representation cannot conceal. Transmuted through the nation-state's webbed relationships with systems of anthropocentrism, colonialism, cisheteropatriarchy, racism/whiteness and capitalism, some are more equal, included and represented than others.

In the rift between democratic rhetoric and lived experience, the "demos" takes matters into their own hands. On the one hand, these matters include guns and others' throats. On the other hand, they include care and cooperation across the usual lines of separation, and the resurgent deepening of ecocentric ways of being. The effect is a present surge in both "democratizing and undemocratizing processes"[4] across local and global stages alike. I distinguish between the "undemocratizing" vs. "democratizing" processes of which Santos speaks according to the worldview and ontological canopy that each enacts:[5] respectively, individualist ways of being that reference an us/them ontology of "disconnect";[6] and relational ways of Intrabeing that enact an interconnection with all that is, including the more-than-human.

As elaborated in this chapter, an individualist ontology of separation and nonrelationality erects the unfounded, *terra nullius* grounds upon which structures of hierarchy, dominance, violence and exploitation become both possible and justifiable. Such grounds become the basis of all "us/them" logics and binary structures, including anthropocentrism, colonialism, cisheteropatriarchy, racism/whiteness and capitalism. While the particular modalities, institutions, practices and processes of each of these structures differs across regions and contexts, their enactments depend on lifeways that generate a vicious ontology of disconnect and separation. It is this commonality of ontological structure to which I wish to draw attention. Understanding how democratic institutions operate in ways that can

---

(organicity) and . . . the societal level (morbidity)," as detailed in Milan Babic, "Let's Talk About the Interregnum: Gramsci and the Crisis of the Liberal International Order," *International Affairs* 96, no. 3 (2020): 767–86.

[4] Santos, "The Crises of Democracy."

[5] It is likely that some of the processes that are named by their constituents as democratizing may not adhere to the definition I offer. This is not to discount another's claim to a distinct brand of democracy as defined by them, but rather to present with clarity the framework from within which I interpret and define democracy.

[6] Aaron Mills, "Rooted Constitutionalism: Growing Political Community" in *Resurgence and Reconciliation*, ed. Michael Asch, John Borrows, and James Tully (Toronto: University of Toronto Press, 2018), 133–74.

(intentionally or unintentionally) uphold and reproduce this hegemonic ontology is critical to understanding what democratizing, counterhegemonic and decolonizing projects might entail. Operating through institutions, processes and ways of being, the lifeways that enact these structures generate the "abyssal,"[7] invisible lines of privilege and discrimination that invoke injustices and violence on human and more-than-human lives and bodies alike.

It is often argued that such structures threaten democracy by superseding or "rolling back" its powers. However, to the extent that democratic actors and institutions participate in and reproduce these structures of dominance, I concur with Gane that what we are witnessing is not the "roll back," but the "roll-out"[8] and emboldening of these structures *through* democratic institutions.

The Canadian government's "nation to nation" relationship with Indigenous nations offers one helpful example. Insofar as Canadian law is asserted as the universal, sovereign frame within which Indigenous nations must negotiate and Indigenous legal systems must be interpreted, there is no possibility of genuine dialogue between equal parties wherein each might be encountered on its own terms.[9] Canada's engagement in nation-to-nation relationships is thus enacted as a form of "false dialogue"[10] that drains dialogue of its democratic and transformative potential. This move within setter colonial states can be understood as an example of what Tully describes as the representative democracy's "pretense of inclusion and dialogue [which] is often simply the assimilating and subordinating ruse of the hegemonic partner."[11] Such assertions of sovereignty rely on the false and unfounded grounds of nonrelationality. In other words, by imposing an external colonial law and order, they uproot or disembed themselves from relational accountability[12] to Indigenous peoples and the lands, waters and more-than-human ecosystems over which they have claimed sovereignty. This disembedding claim to sovereignty is inherently violent, as claiming the universal requires not only an erasure of its own parochial roots,[13] but both legalizes and necessitates the moves to systematically and genocidally eradicate Indigenous democracies and lifeways, as in Canada.

---

[7] Boaventura de Sousa Santos, "Beyond Abyssal Thinking: From Global Lines to Ecologies of Knowledges," *Eurozine*, June 29, 2007, https://www.eurozine.com/beyond-abyssal-thinking/.

[8] Nicholas Gane, "The Governmentalities of Neoliberalism: Panopticism, Post-Panopticism, and Beyond," *The Sociological Review* 60 (2012): 613.

[9] For Tully, the deparochialization of one's system is a necessary condition for "genuine dialogue" to be possible, in which actors might encounter one another on "the terms of their own traditions without inclusion, assimilation or subordination." James Tully, "Deparochializing Political Theory and Beyond: A Dialogue Approach to Comparative Political Thought," *Journal of World Philosophies* 1, no. 5 (2016): 52.

[10] Ibid., 54.

[11] James Tully, "Reconciliation Here on Earth," in *Resurgence and Reconciliation*, eds. Asch, Borrows, and Tully, 58.

[12] Shawn Wilson, *Research Is Ceremony* (Black Point: Fernwood Publishing, 2008).

[13] Tully, "Deparochializing Political Theory."

In another example, US government trade negotiations with democratically elected governments in countries such as Kenya are brokering deals at the behest of the world's largest chemical makers and fossil fuel companies. Such agreements have resulted in the quadrupling of plastic waste exports from the USA to Africa. More than one billion pounds of plastic waste was exported from the USA to ninety-six countries in one year alone, with millions of pounds of hardest-to-recycle plastics landing in their rivers and oceans.[14] In the growing awareness of the interconnectedness of all of life, these democratically elected governments are privileging colonial, anthropocentric and capitalist logics at the cost of ecosystems, the human citizens who rely on these ecosystems and the more-than-human who become the "collateral damage" of such actions. Upstream are the practices that condone and enable the proliferation of plastic production and consumption.

While these examples differ in important ways, they are both cases in which democratic actors and institutions invoke a relationally disembedded, undemocratic logic of individualism that constitutes a lethal blow to the very premises and promises of democracy. In so doing, democratic actors create critical points of vulnerability for the system of representative democracy itself. The vulnerability lies in its inconsistency, as noted by Santos: "Democracy is incompatible with the kind of capitalism that rules the world today. So we either have democracy or we have capitalism."[15] These points of democracy's vulnerability become the conditions of its own morbidity, hollowing out the values it purports to uphold, effectively dumping them in the waterways alongside the unrecyclable plastics. So long as democratically elected representatives and governments reproduce the entangled and settled logics, hierarchies and structures of anthropocentrism, colonialism, cisheteropatriarchy,

---

[14] "According to documents reviewed by The New York Times, an industry group representing the world's largest chemical makers and fossil fuel companies is lobbying to influence United States trade negotiations with Kenya, one of Africa's biggest economies, to reverse its strict limits on plastics – including a tough plastic-bag ban. It is also pressing for Kenya to continue importing foreign plastic garbage, a practice it has pledged to limit. Plastics makers are looking well beyond Kenya's borders. 'We anticipate that Kenya could serve in the future as a hub for supplying US-made chemicals and plastics to other markets in Africa through this trade agreement,' Ed Brzytwa, the director of international trade for the American Chemistry Council, wrote in an April 28 letter to the Office of the United States Trade Representative … In 2019, American exporters shipped more than 1 billion pounds of plastic waste to 96 countries including Kenya, ostensibly to be recycled, according to trade statistics. But much of the waste, often containing the hardest-to-recycle plastics, instead ends up in rivers and oceans. And after China closed its ports to most plastic trash in 2018, exporters have been looking for new dumping grounds. Exports to Africa more than quadrupled in 2019 from a year earlier." Hiroki Tabuchi, Michael Corkery, and Carlos Mureithi, "Big Oil Is in Trouble. Its Plan: Flood Africa with Plastic," *New York Times*, August 30, 2020, www.nytimes.com/2020/08/30/climate/oil-kenya-africa-plastics-trade.html.
[15] Santos, "The Crises of Democracy."

racism/whiteness and/or capitalism, they themselves enact undemocratizing processes.

In this context, it is no surprise that representative democracies find themselves facing populist, undemocratizing "backlashes":[16] the latter are entirely ontologically consistent with the undemocratizing processes being democratically enacted, as outlined earlier. As any parent can tell you, such "do as I say, not as I do" behavior effectively extends an invitation for citizens to follow suit. In the democratic void between words and practice emerges a dystopian chasm within which disenchanted and/or alienated citizens decrease, withdraw and/or refuse their hegemonic consent to the democratic system on offer. In these ways, the crises of democracy lie in the ways representative democracies reproduce individualist ways of being.

If the cause of democracy's morbidity is in our midst, however, so too are the protective factors. The boundaries and enactments of representative democracies have long been troubled and shaped by democratizing processes and movements that stretch and are situated well beyond the individualist canopy of understanding. Enacting an ontology of Intrabeing, the horizons and possibilities for otherwise democracies beyond the bounds of individualism are not only possible, they already are. Drawing on the wisdoms of humans (Indigenous and non-Indigenous) and more-than-humans (in the ecosystems of tree canopies), this chapter presents a relational framework within which democracy might be resituated and reconceptualized. In their porous, dynamic, entangled and "grounded relationality,"[17] tree canopies embody a rooted relational framework within the context of which distinct and diverse democratic traditions might be considered. Additionally, tree canopies invite us to consider how the relational accountability of the ecosystem offers a model for democracy that is regenerative, porous, adaptive, diverse and resilient. In contrast, I propose an "*ego*-cycle" diagram, which depicts how hierarchical, us/them structures and lifeways enact an individualist logic of disconnect that thwarts and distorts each stage of the ecocycle in unsustainable, violent ways. Like the tree cut down to build the slave ship, individualist or egocentric ways of being violently uproot the individual from self, others and earth.

---

[16] Babic, "Let's Talk About the Interregnum," 767–86.

[17] My conceptualization of "grounded relationality" intersects with that presented in Jodi A. Byrd et al., "Predatory Value: Economies of Dispossession and Disturbed Relationalities," *Social Text* 36, no. 2 (2018): 1–18. Drawing on the work of Coulthard and Simpson (Glen Coulthard and Leanne Betasamosake Simpson, "Grounded Normativity / Place-Based Solidarity," *American Quarterly* 62, no. 2 (2016): 249–55, https://doi.org/10.1353/aq.2016.0038), Byrd et al. use the term "grounded relationalities" to refer to "a being grounded and living relationalities in which the nonhuman world and the materiality of land and other elements have agential significance in ways that exceed liberal conceptions of the human"; Byrd et al., "Predatory Value," 11. They ask: "What would it be, then, to think and work for a grounded relationality, at once addressed to Black placemaking, geographies, and other racialized diasporas, as well as to proprietary violences incommensurate to yet not altogether separate from Indigenous land and sovereignty?"; "Predatory Value," 14.

A TALE OF TWO WORLDVIEWS

As ontologies, worldviews can be understood through distinct types of creation stories or stories of origin.[18] Despite their coexistence, one can see that the individualist and relational worldviews introduced above represent two very different types of creation stories. Not only do they have different beginnings, plotlines and backdrops, they generate radically different endings: the first characterized by unsustainable lifeways that cogenerate ecocide, social, political and economic injustices (Tully's vicious cycle), the other characterized by gift–gratitude–reciprocity lifeways that regenerate reciprocal, sustainable and relationally accountable ways of living (Tully's virtuous cycle).[19]

I refer to the first of these worldviews as *individualist* (as opposed to liberal, Western, etc.) to reflect the fact that the central unit around which this ontological orientation is organized is that of the discrete, disembedded individual human. The "individual" in these stories stands in for the inherent dissociative logic of disconnect:[20] from self (as relational being), from others and from the more-than-human. It is critical to note that the structures and processes that generate this dissociative orientation constitute forms of epistemic violence[21] that also enact physical violence and embodied traumas on human and more-than-human alike.

While one may consider certain groupings such as the nation-state as social or collective instead of individualist, Tully shows how the very logic of such institutions rests on the conceptual disembedding of individuals from prior inherent relationships as the foundational prelude to installing modern conceptions of citizenship. This "first process" entails: "the ongoing dispossession and alienation of human communities from their participatory ways of being in the living earth as plain members and responsible citizens, and the discrediting of the participatory ways of knowing that go along with them."[22] Calling this the "great dis-embedding," Tully references Polanyi to document the processes by which modern civil citizenship then re-embeds humans "in abstract and competitive economic, political, and legal relationships that depend on yet destroy the underlying interdependent ecological and social

---

[18] This draws from Charles Eisenstein's framing of two distinct societal stories: the story of Separation and the story of Interbeing, as outlined in Charles Eisenstein, *The More Beautiful World Our Hearts Know Is Possible* (California: North Atlantic Books, 2013). Additions I offer to his discussion of stories include the pluralization of these stories, the reframing of Interbeing as intrabeing, and the framing these stories as distinct types of creation stories.

[19] Tully, "Reconciliation Here on Earth," 83–129.

[20] Mills notes that insofar as settler peoples found their political communities upon a logic of disconnect, it is founded on "violence, which slowly destroys it from within": Mills, "Rooted Constitutionalism," 135.

[21] Peyman Vahabzadeh, *Articulated Experiences* (Albany: State University of New York, 2003).

[22] Tully, "Reconciliation Here on Earth," 108.

relationships."[23] The new groupings are then structured as if they were individual units in binary relation to Others – whether nation, race, gender or other. Insofar as Western representative democracy is a system of governance based around the rights and representation of individual humans and collections of individual humans, it enacts a story in which the human individual is the unit through which life is encountered and apprehended. It is thus necessarily located not only upon an "us/them" foundation of anthropocentrism,[24] it is also built on the primacy of the individual human unit[25] over the relational. In this way, an individualist logic is core to the very structure of nation-state and nationalism. The latter's borders separate humans by geographies and citizenship while relegating and demarcating lands, waterways and the more-than-human within its borders to property or the "wild," denying it its own agency and representation. (As any river might tell you, the borders of nation-states do not make much sense to them, though their effects are sensed.)

In contrast, relational worldviews reflect interconnected, intra-active,[26] relational lifeways between all that is. While grounded in the distinctiveness of each, there are key points of shared relational ontology found in a range of traditions and cultures around the world. Drawn from the concept of Interbeing found in contemporary theorists ranging from Eisenstein[27] to Thich Nhat Hahn,[28] the relational premise of intrabeing has articulations across many distinct traditions. For example, the concept of "All Our Relations" within Indigenous traditions across Turtle Island, the Zulu phrase *Umuntu ngumuntu ngabantu* commonly known as *Ubuntu* ('I am because you are'), and the tenets of animistic, pantheistic East Asian nature religions such as *kami-no-michi* (Shintoism) all point not just to a communal nature of life but to an indivisible interdependence of being. Nuu-chah-nulth Hereditary Chief Umeek (E. Richard Atleo) explains the specific context within which a relational ontology of interconnectedness is specifically rooted and enacted in Nuu-chah-nulth traditions, through the concept of *heshook-ish tsawalk*:

In a view of reality described as *tsawalk* (one), relationships are *qua* (that which is). The ancient Nuu-chah-nulth assumed an interrelationship between all life forms – humans, plans, and animals. Accordingly, social, political, economic, constitutional,

[23] Ibid., 104

[24] An exception to this is Ecuador's extension of personhood to nature in its 2008 constitution. New Zealand has also made moves to recognize the rights of certain more-than-humans, including the Whanganui River, which is of particular significance to Maori peoples.

[25] Linda Tuhiwai Smith, *Decolonizing Methodologies: Research and Indigenous Peoples*, 2nd ed. (London: Zed Books, 2012).

[26] Karen Barad's concept of "intra-action" posits that while *inter*-action presumes separate actors, *intra*-action depicts an enmeshed relationship that more accurately depicts the assemblage and nonseparate nature of all life forms. From Karen Barad, *Meeting the Universe Halfway* (Durham: Duke University Press, 2007).

[27] Eisenstein, *The More Beautiful World.*   [28] Tully, "Deparochializing Political Theory," 62.

environmental, and philosophical issues can be addressed under the single theme of inter-relationships, across all dimensions of reality – the material and the non-material, the visible and the invisible.[29]

The concept of oneness within a relational frame of Intrabeing is notably distinct for its pluralistic dynamism versus the assimilative, binary and/or exclusionary orientations of individualism. As in an ecosystem, this oneness comes not as the result of assimilation or the erasure of difference, but through the inherent plurality, relationality and agency of all. Within the context of another Indigenous tradition, Kimmerer, a member of the Citizen Potawatomi Nation, depicts the dynamic process of weaving sweetgrass as an act of gift-reciprocity between weavers that reflects the reciprocal relationships of living between peoples with one another and the earth.[30] Wilson of the Opaskwayak Cree Nation reflects on this relationality by disrupting the notion of the individual unit that is often embedded in Western conceptions of relationship: "Rather than viewing ourselves as being *in* relationship with other people or things, we *are* the relationships that we hold and are part of."[31] This intersects with the self-proclaimed relational ontologist, feminist Karen Barad's concept of "intra-action"; while *inter*-action presumes separate actors, they note that *intra*-action depicts an enmeshed relationship that more accurately depicts the assemblage and nonseparate nature of all life forms.[32] Zen master Thich Nhat Hanh offers another take on this point, stating that we should not regard individual beings as having life, but of life being in them: "You shouldn't say, life *of* the leaf, but life *in* the leaf, and life *in* the tree. My life is just Life, and you can see it in me and in the tree."[33]

Within a relational ontology of Intrabeing, individualist stories are artificial[34] and without foundation. Extraction or expulsion from the relational world is simply not possible. Conceiving of the self as separate from other beings constitutes a bifurcated, dissociated conception of the self – what Einstein called a "delusion of consciousness."[35] However, it is this perception of disconnect that renders egocentric ways of thinking and being possible,

---

[29] Umeek E. Richard Atleo, *Principles of Tsawalk: An Indigenous Approach to Global Crisis* (Vancouver: UBC Press, 2011), ix.

[30] Robin Wall Kimmerer, *Braiding Sweetgrass: Indigenous Wisdom, Scientific Knowledge, and the Teachings of Plants* (Minneapolis: Milkweed Editions, 2013), ix.

[31] Wilson, *Research Is Ceremony*, 80.   [32] Karen Barad, *Meeting the Universe.*

[33] Thich Nhat Hanh, *The Heart of Understanding* (Berkeley: Parallax Press, 2009), 23.

[34] Mills writes: "Rooted constitutionalism would say disconnection doesn't exist except artificially, and I would add that it's the first step off of the path of growth, onto the path of progress": "Rooted Constitutionalism," 160.

[35] "A human being is a part of the whole called by us universe, a part limited in time and space. He experiences himself, his thoughts and feeling as something separated from the rest, a kind of optical delusion of his consciousness. This delusion is a kind of prison for us, restricting us to our personal desires and to affection for a few persons nearest to us. Our task must be to free ourselves from this prison by widening our circle of compassion to embrace all living creatures and the whole of nature in its beauty." Albert Einstein to Mr. Robert S. Marcus, February 12,

characterized by the "aggressive refusal of non-attachment, openness, empathetic dialogue, and so of deparochialization."[36]

Umeek[37] also sees the perception of differences as naturally antagonistically, competitively and hierarchically oriented as inherent to the individualist view– one that has led the world into its current intertwining sets of economic, political, social and ecological crises. In contrast, he and other Indigenous thinkers such as Kimmerer[38] reflect on the lessons learned from the more-than-human world wherein diversity and polarities are not inherently competitive, but rather viewed as essential for the co-generation of life. Umeek's *Tsawalk* shows that within stories of intrabeing, insofar as everything is connected, everything somehow belongs: "Nuu-chah-nulth perspective on the nature of reality is that all questions of existence, being and knowing, regardless of seeming contradictions are considered tsawalk – one and inseparable. They are all interrelated and interconnected."[39] Tully's work might be read as the tracing of individualist and relational ontologies within and across distinct histories and traditions of political thought. While Tully particularly highlights the relational ontologies and lifeways of Indigenous traditions, he also observes the presence of relational lifeways across a plurality of democratizing practices, movements and processes around the world, including the West.[40] These lifeways are characterized by Tully as enacting practices of ecological and Gaia democratic engagement across a diversity of ethno-cultural and spiritual traditions. These lifeways enact a relational ethos of interconnectedness that nurtures relationships with self, others and earth, are regenerative of virtuous cycles of life – resonant with conceptions of gift–gratitude–reciprocity within Indigenous governance and legal systems. In this way, Tully's work consistently points to what Indigenous traditions and communities have long showed – the ongoing proliferation of lifeways that, in their resilience and rootedness, even in the face of systematized structures of genocidal oppression, persevere. In the *Hermeneutics of the Subject*, Foucault also traces patterns of relationality across Western thought, which he traces back to Ancient Greece. A master trickster, he shows how even individualism has historical roots in a "relational mode of knowledge."[41] By troubling a contemporary[42] individualism's self image, Foucault's observation suggests that individualism's inclination to banish relationality in its midst is so strong it would even negate its own ancestry.

    1950, quoted in John Briggs, "Reembodying, Human Consciousness in the Earth," in *Consciousness: Ideas for the Twenty-First Century* 2, no. 2 (2016): 1–23.
[36] Tully, "Deparochializing Political Theory," 63.   [37] Umeek, *Principles of Tsawalk*.
[38] Kimmerer, *Braiding Sweetgrass*.   [39] Umeek, *Principles of Tsawalk*, ix.
[40] Tully, "Reconciliation Here on Earth," 83–129.
[41] Michel Foucault, *Hermeneutics of the Subject* (New York: Palgrave MacMillan, 2001), 235.
[42] As Benjamin noted, "History is the subject of a structure whose site is not homogenous, empty time, but time filled by the presence of the now." Walter Benjamin, *Illuminations* (New York: Shocken, 1969), 261.

WORLDVIEWS AS CANOPIES OF UNDERSTANDING

In the sociological literature, ontologies or worldviews are often conceptualized as "canopies" of understanding, drawing on the work of Berger and Luckmann.[43] As a metaphor for the structures by which a social group makes sense of the world and governs itself, the structure of the canopy is constituted by the institutions, laws, discourses, norms and lifeways that a social group enacts. Signifiers, concepts and institutions within this canopy of meaning are reified as "common sense" and naturalized, providing its constituents with what phenomenologists call a "natural attitude" toward the world, in which the constructed and parochial contexts of one's worldview is a settled fact that remains unseen, like the air one breathes. For Berger and Luckmann, the perceived objectivity of social institutions "'thickens'" and "hardens," generating a certain fixity to their structures and "firmness of consciousness."[44] Within the enclosing canopy, the institutions, laws, discourses, norms and lifeways that uphold the canopy are both structurally imposed upon its constituents and actively reproduced by them to the extent that they are internalized and socialized into them.

Berger and Luckmann's canopy is thus experienced as an integrated, comprehensive understanding of the world while the particular contours of it remain unseen. However, in its social constructedness, the canopy operates as a singular lens through which one might encounter the world, like a flashlight in a forest.[45] Although canopies offer the experience of having a comprehensive view on reality, they only light a narrow cone on the world, leaving "the totality of the world opaque ... [in] a background of darkness."[46] Phenomena that do not fit within the bounds of Berger and Luckmann's sense-making canopy thus appear as "non-sense,"[47] remaining unencountered, unintelligible, banished and forbidden. Hall refers to "common sense" or "the regime of the 'taken for granted'" as "a moment of extreme ideological closure."[48] In this way, Berger and Luckmann's canopy resembles that of a *tent* canopy and, like a tent, this canopy is constructed upon an uprooted, nonrelational foundation the underpinning "law-gic" of which shapes the tent's structure, contours and borders.

While presented as a universal theory for theorizing about worldviews, a reparochialization[49] of Berger and Luckmann's canopy shows it to have distinctly individualist features. The first clue of this is insofar as Berger and Luckmann's canopy refers only to the human world. In this theory of worldviews, the earth and the more-than-human are anthropocentrically relegated to incidental backdrops to human existence. The establishment of the canopy thus metaphorically relays the very process of re-embedding

---

[43] Peter Berger and Thomas Luckmann, *The Social Construction of Reality* (Random House: New York, 1967).
[44] Ibid., 59.   [45] Ibid., 45.   [46] Ibid., 44.   [47] Vahabzadeh, *Articulated Experiences.*
[48] Stuart Hall, "Signification, Representation, Ideology: Althusser and the Post-Structuralist Debates," *Critical Studies in Mass Communication* 2 (1985): 105.
[49] Tully, "Deparochializing Political Theory."

FIGURE 9.1 *Tent Canopy* by Karen Yen

disembedded individual humans in socially sanctioned institutions such as Tully describes.[50] Uprooted from relationships with the earth and the more-than-human, a key feature of the canopy is categories of membership, both within the walls of its particular institutions as well as those on the outside who are refused entry. More than being left in the metaphorical darkness, beings, experiences and aspects of beings that fall surplus to the cognitive bounds of the canopy manifest as other or are rendered into the abyss. Any acting outside the bounds of the canopy are encountered and treated as fugitives according to the settled colonial lawgic of the canopy.

   Further, in its concealment of what its inhabitants might otherwise encounter, the tent canopy is also a metaphor for hegemony. The tent canopy mirrors the hegemonic process Vahabzadeh describes by which actors are "resettled" within new "cognitive grounds and experiential terrains" with reconstituted selves.[51] Although the "hegemonic worldview" is presented as "objectively" true,[52] it will never be fully referential to one's experience that precedes and exceeds the frames of the tent. Insofar as it both enables and limits how one thinks of and apprehends the world – a phenomenon he calls "experiential hegemony"[53] – the erection of the tent canopy is a moment of epistemic violence for Vahabzadeh. In all of these ways, Berger and Luckmann's conception of the way worldviews function is a version of Otto Scharmer's egocentric system that can not see itself.[54]

[50] Tully, "Reconciliation Here on Earth," 109.   [51] Vahabzadeh, *Articulated Experiences*, 65.
[52] Ibid., 67.   [53] Ibid., 97.
[54] Otto Scharmer, "Impacting Climate Change by Operating from a Place of Awareness-Based Collective Action" (webinar, *TEDxGAIAjourney: Impacting Climate Change by Operating*

A DIFFERENT TYPE OF CANOPY

A relational worldview articulates a radically different structure than Berger and Luckmann's canopy. The latter's abstract and universal prototype is at fundamental odds with relational conceptions of the world that are rooted in particular contexts through ongoing intra-active relationships with others and the earth. To extend Berger and Luckmann's theoretical concept of worldviews as tent canopies to relational ways of thinking and being would be to engage in the same type of "discursive translation" that Coulthard notes is imposed on Indigenous nations within the settler colonial state, resulting in the "reorientation" of meanings of Indigenous self-determination.[55] Starblanket and Stark caution of the ongoing ways in which such mis-translations reinscribe Indigenous concepts and practices – such as relationality – through the settler colonial lens of states such as Canada, noting the tendency of colonial ways of thinking to absorb and co-opt.[56] In true hegemonic form, the individualist worldview moves quickly to repair any challenges that might compromise the integrity of its canopy of being, resulting in alterations and patchwork rather than transformation. Tully refers to this as a form of "hegemonic ventriloquism,"[57] in which one may use the same words as another but fail to encounter or understand them on their own terms – a practice core to genuine dialogue and the ethical engagement of another.[58] It thus becomes important to imagine a relational canopy on its own terms rather than "discursively translated"[59] through the lens of an individualist conception of worldviews.

As opposed to an enclosing and self-concealing structure, a relational ontology is characterized by its self-disclosure (or deparochialization) and an openness to encountering and engaging difference through "reciprocal elucidation."[60] By a relational logic, one can only understand and know themselves through their relationships with others. For this reason, thinkers from across a diversity of traditions (Borrows, Derrida, Lorde, Foucault, Scharmer and Tully, to name a few) note that such disclosure can only take

---

from a Place of Awareness-Based Collective Action, Presencing Institute, Cambridge, MA, October 15, 2020), www.presencing.org/programs/live-sessions/tedxgaiajourney.

[55] Glen Sean Coulthard, *Red Skin, White Masks: Rejecting the Colonial Politics of Recognition* (Minneapolis: University of Minnesota Press, 2014), 78.

[56] Gina Starblanket and Heidi Kiiwetinepinesiik Stark, "Towards a Relational Paradigm – Four Points for Consideration: Knowledge, Gender, Land, and Modernity," in *Resurgence and Reconciliation: Indigenous-Settler Relations and Earth Teachings*, ed. Michael Asch, John Borrows and James Tully (Toronto: University of Toronto Press, 2018), 175–208.

[57] Tully, "Deparochializing Political Theory," 64.

[58] The conditions for "genuine dialogue . . . include the ethical practices of openness and receptivity to the otherness of others that enable participants to understand one another in their own traditions (mutual understanding) and to appreciate the concerns of one another regarding globalization and the injustices and suffering it causes (mutual concern)": Tully, "Deparochializing Political Theory," 52.

[59] Coulthard, *Red Skin*. [60] Ibid., 60.

place through relationship with, and in the presence of, another. Tully writes: "Humans literally need dialogue with other limited traditions of political thought to see their own limitations and to see beyond them by means of the perspectives of others. Hence, it is dialogue itself that deparochializes."[61] Similarly, from the systems-thinking tradition, Scharmer states that a system cannot "see and sense itself" unless there is another who plays the role of mirror within "a learning structure" which supports awareness, listening, openness, curiosity, compassion and courage.[62]

Inspired by Mills' rooted constitutionalism,[63] tree canopies offer a radically different type of canopy that exist through their rootedness in relationships and specific contexts vs. the uprooted foundations of the tent. There are countless distinct tree canopies, and no two tree canopies are the same. Insofar as tree canopies are intra-active assemblages of beings and the lifeways that constitute them, they are defined by their specific and evolving constituents, pluralisms and relationships – not their borders. However, they share a porousness to the diversity of life forms in their midst, who cocreate the particularities of a given tree canopy's pathways, permacultures, landscape, lifeforms, enclosures, points of gestation, growth, maturity, destruction, rigidities and boundaries.

In these ways, tree canopies disclose themselves in ways similar to Tully's multiverse of "being-there (*Dasein*) and being-with (*Mitsein*)":

> Ways of life of humans are seen perspectivally, as one moves around; neither as independent, all the same, nor antagonistic; but, rather, interconnected and interdependent by infinitely complex webs of similarities and dissimilarities expressed in the languages of the world. This is the participatory experience of diversity awareness, of the lifeworld as a multiverse rather than universe, and of being-human *as* both being-there (*Dasein*) and being-with (*Mitsein*).[64]

It is from the wisdom of the tree canopies that I invite a reconceptualization of democracy.

WHAT THE TREE CANOPIES KNOW

> During Hurricane Katrina, you would have thought the live oaks ... would have died when actually only four out of over seven hundred trees died. Why is that? ... It turns out the whole thing is a blueprint for how to survive hurricanes. Their trunk is spiraled so they flex in the wind and their branches are spiraled so they flex and their leaves when the wind hits them, they curl ... which allows the wind to flow through with minimal friction. And even more importantly, under the ground its roots are entwined with the roots of the trees next to it. So when a hurricane hits a live oak in New Orleans, it's not hitting one tree, it's hitting a whole community. So perhaps in rebuilding New Orleans to be more hurricane resilient, instead of

---

[61] Tully, "Deparochializing Political Theory," 56.
[62] As presented in Scharmer, "Impacting Climate Change."
[63] Mills, "Rooted Constitutionalism," 133–74.   [64] Tully, "Reconciliation Here on Earth," 62.

our individual ... foundations, we may think about foundations that have horizontal components that twine together with the foundations of the buildings next door so that you've got the wind hitting an entire community of buildings and not just one ... think like a live oak tree.[65]

The logic of tree canopies is found in the trees' inseparable relationality with the countless beings that simultaneously enable and are enabled by their existence, those with whom their lives are entangled. Trees are but one entangled and inseparable form of life within a tree canopy amidst soils, minerals, mycelium, sunlight, air, bugs, creatures, waters, rocks and mosses with whom they transmutatively cocreate the life of their ecosystem – along with the countless others that migrate and porously traverse through. From within the knowing of the tree canopy, each "being" in the canopy might not be considered a single entity – though the uniqueness and diversity of each is required for the existence of all. Like all ecosystems on earth, tree canopies are dynamic, emergent, elaborate labyrinths of beings that engage in the collaborative regeneration of life distinctly in that ecosystem and – as citizens of the earth – also to that of the planet.

Turning to the contrasts between the trees and the tent canopies, one might consider that while the tent can block or distort the view of the tree canopy, the latter might be able to coexist with the former. Indeed, the image of a tent canopy situated within or encroaching upon a tree canopy lends itself well as a metaphor for the relationship between, respectively, a settler colonial state and the Indigenous governance systems in which this colonial state enacts itself. However, to restrict an analysis to this point is to stop at the us/them binary frame that individualism itself establishes. There is more to see in a forest. Tree canopies invite ways of thinking and being beyond a colonial sense of spatiality – ways that offer critical insights into conceptions of democracy.

Tree canopies' resilience and regenerative, democratizing capacities lie in their participation in ecocentric, relational modes of being, as articulated in the ecocycle model. While its roots hail from global governance theory, the ecocycle[66] is used in systems theory to explore the complexity of human systems in which apparently contradictory or incommensurate impulses are at play. Sharing the same shape of the Métis and the infinity symbols, the ecocycle depicts four distinct moments in an ecological system, with a directionality of moving from the lower left quadrant ("Birth: tending"), to the upper right quadrant ("Maturity: harvesting"), to the lower right quadrant ("Creative Destruction: plowing"), to the upper left quadrant ("Gestation: sowing"), then moving back to the lower left quadrant of Birth again.[67] These can be

[65] WIRED, "Using Live Oak Trees as a Blueprint for Surviving Hurricanes," August 26, 2015, YouTube video, 1:31, https://ed.ted.com/best_of_web/dKKIiKsz.

[66] Keith McCandless and Henri Lipmanowicz, "Ecocycle Planning," in *The Surprising Power of Liberating Structures* (Seattle: Liberating Structures Press, 2013), 294–99.

[67] Please note, there are different versions of the ecocycle or panarchy model. The language I am using is consistent with the ecocycle diagram presented by McCandless and Lipmanowicz:

conceived of as the distinct stages in a single entity's life cycle (or even as the four seasons of Spring, Summer, Fall and Winter). However, within systems thinking, it is recognized that in any natural ecosystem (including human systems), each stage is always at play somewhere in the system at any given moment – for example, the presence of new tree growth, mature trees, trees falling to the forest floor to make way for and support the incubation of new life.

When systems theorists apply the lens of this cycle to human organizations and systems, they note two "traps" that the latter tend to fall into: the "rigidity trap," which falls in between the stage of Maturity and Creative Destruction, and the "poverty trap," which falls in between the stages of Gestation and Birth. They are called "traps" within organizational theory because of the tendency in human systems for parts of those same systems to inhibit regenerative movement between the stages where they are located. The effect of these traps is to impede, destabilize or incapacitate the ecosystem's regenerative capacities. The "rigidity trap" lies between the stages of Maturity and Creative Destruction.[68] In human-dominated systems, indicators of this trap include the material structuring of the world according to individualist logics of ownership, hierarchy and capitalist-colonial accumulation, ownership, dispossession and legalized hierarchies. Relational structures, such as Indigenous governance and legal systems, are circumscribed, limited hegemonically absorbed or destroyed in the service of keeping the hegemonically dominant structures and processes of capitalist-colonialism intact.

The "poverty trap," on the other hand, is located between the stages of Gestation and Growth[69] In human systems, this trap is encountered when there is insufficient investment in the permaculture needed to cogenerate life (whether social, legal, economic, political or ecological), leading to the starvation or extinction of needed diversity and new growth that ultimately benefits the overall system. In a human system, this trap can entail the excessive depletion, exploitation and/or destruction of the resources needed by distinctive lifeways in order to regenerate, proliferate or thrive.

Building on the notion of these traps, Tully's vicious cycle might be understood as the disproportionate and distorted investment in the linear segment of the ecocycle between the stages of birth (tending) and maturity (harvesting). When the logic of relationality is replaced with that of "us/them" disconnect and separation, a linear logic of individualism becomes possible – a tending to, and the over-harvesting for the few, at the direct cost and expense of others. Humans' separation from self, others and earth thus serves as the paramount moment when the lifeways that enact

---

"Moving Online in Pandemic: Ecocycle to Attend to What Is Shifting," Full Circle Associates, Nancy White, https://fullcirc.com/2020/03/08/moving-online-in-pandemic-ecocycle-to-attend-to-what-is-shifting.

[68] McCandless and Lipmanowicz, "Ecocycle Planning."

[69] McCandless and Lipmanowicz, "Ecocycle Planning."

disconnect and inequality establish the "artificial"[70] grounds of individualism. This point of disconnect becomes the uprooted foundation of the tent canopy that leads to the thwarting and distortion of each of the stages of the cycle in distinct ways that threaten all of life as we know it in the world today. The egocycle diagram (Figure 9.2) outlines how each stage is reframed.

Mills writes, "Rooted constitutionalism would say disconnection doesn't exist except artificially, and I would add that it's the first step off of the path of growth, onto the path of progress."[71] The stage of "Maturity" of this linear progress sees the establishment of "Settled hierarchies" by which privileges are extracted and over-harvested for the few at the direct subjugation of others – human and more-than-human alike. The stage of "Creative destruction" is in turn directed into "Systemic violence" that organize and administer the costs and burdens onto these same bodies and lifeways. Finally, the "Incubation" stage becomes "Exploitative depletion," wherein instead of revitalizing the permaculture in which new seeds might be sown, further extraction and depletion occurs.

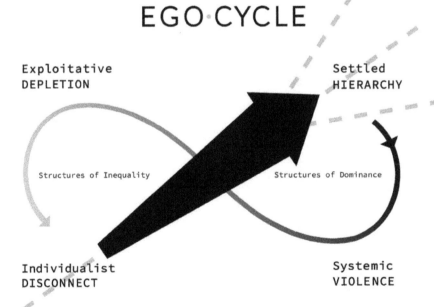

FIGURE 9.2 Egocycle by Rebeccah Nelems; graphic co-designed by Rebeccah Nelems and Amanda Pentland

---

[70] Mills, "Rooted Constitutionalism," 160.   [71] Mills, "Rooted Constitutionalism," 160.

As reflected in the diagram (Figure 9.2), while the linear logic of individualism rigidifies and generates structures of violence, inequality and exploitation, its own delusional narrative of nonrelationality and linearity simultaneously erases lines of relational accountability. Deluded, artificial and dissociated conceptions of self, other and earth thus become the uprooted and baseless grounds upon which individualist lifeways are settled. Experientially, these moments of dissociation are moments of trauma.[72] Having established "us/them" lifeways, the grounds for anthropocentrism, colonialism, cisheteropatriarchy, racism/whiteness and capitalism are paved with intersectional bodies and beings. By over-producing, over-exploiting, dominating and over-consuming rather than sympoetically regenerating through gift-reciprocity and relational accountability, these lifeways traumatize rather than revitalize and thwart the inherent abundance of diversity by wielding and generating scarcity.

If "the means sow the seeds of the end,"[73] democratizing processes need to operate in ecocentric ways. In this light, democratizing processes are the modes by which actors seek to transmute the egocentric modes into the ecocentric, and undemocratizing processes might be understood as egocentric ways of being that thwart the stages of the ecocycle, or those that uphold or reinforce the stages of the egocycle.

However, ecocentric modes of being must radically disrupt and thwart the egocycle while not reproducing its egoic modes of being. This is why Hall says we must "address ourselves 'violently' towards the present as it is, *if we are serious about transforming it*"[74] and not if we are serious about destroying it.[75] Akomolafe's use of the concept of *composting*[76] suggests pathways forward

---

[72] Peter A. Levine, *Waking the Tiger* (Berkeley: North Atlantic Books, 1997).

[73] Tully, "Reconciliation Here on Earth," 114.

[74] Stuart Hall, "The Great Moving Right Show," *Marxism Today*, January 1979, 14–20 (emphasis added).

[75] While hopeful, the popular argument that human society is in an interregnum, a transition between an era of individualism and an era of interdependence, is also unhelpful, ultimately relying upon an individualist narrative of progress that implicitly claims society is always epistemically and ethically improving over time. Charles Taylor describes "stadial consciousness" as the sense of superiority of "our present understanding over other earlier forms of understanding," noting that it is the "ratchet at the end of the anthropocentric shift, which makes it (near) impossible to go back on it": Charles Taylor, *A Secular Age* (Cambridge, MA: Harvard University Press, 2007), 289. This trope would well benefit from Santos' injection of fear – "Hope without fear is terrible but fear without hope is also terrible. Most people in the world today are fearful and have no hope and a few have only hope. We have to instil fear into the hopeful ones and instil hope in the fearful ones." Santos, "The Crises of Democracy" – as world events consistently attest that the move from undemocratic to democratic is not unidirectionally predetermined, especially in a context where Western representative democracies have only been at play for an infinitesimally short period of time. The narrative also invokes the notion that it is possible or desirable to eliminate or expel the "old" – another "tell" of an individualist, competitive logic of exclusion.

[76] "There is some urgency in the felt vocation to investigate the ways our bodies are being made and remade within the regime of whiteness. The point is not to defeat whiteness, to treat it as an evil,

here, referencing social change as a process of intra-active cotransformation through fugitive, relational and decolonizing practices. Inspiring visions of a pluralistically enriched "regenerative permaculture,"[77] the notion of composting invokes practices that transform through structurally disrupting that radically transforms egoic lifeways. Akomolafe points to a fugitive perspective that refuses to believe the hegemonic guards of individualism who say there is no escape from egoic individualism. Democracy in this light entails the radical transformation of political, social and economic structures – including representative democracies – through the tending, harvesting, plowing and sowing of relationships, systems and processes in ways that necessitate and demand accountability to the relationships that always already are.[78]

CONCLUSION

Representative democracy is ultimately a system that includes and represents some while excluding and failing to represents others, built within an anthropocentric story of disconnect that values the human over all other forms of life. With the exception of Ecuador and New Zealand, representation is denied to the more-than-human as well as to the countless categories of humans that the system itself produces, including the 82.4 million displaced peoples in the world, of which 20.7 million are refugees,[79] and the unknown "many millions" who are stateless.[80] Historical and current examples show countless Indigenous and other peoples and nations whom representative democracies fail to represent, whether through denying them the right to vote, acts of hegemonic ventriloquism or other. Transmuted through its webbed relationships with anthropocentrism, colonialism, racism/whiteness, cisheteropatriarchy and capitalism, it would be a gross understatement to say that within representative democracies, some are more equal than others.

The ways democratic actors and institutions intersect with ecocentric and egocentric lifeways matters, with the results leading to either the "abyssal lines"[81] that enact undemocratizing injustices on lives and bodies, or enacted

to transcend it, or to imagine it as a pathogen we can rid ourselves of in small doses of workshop attendances: the invitation is, I feel, to compost it, to trace all the ways it is still connected to the earth, to mistletoes everywhere, and then to inhabit those 'spots', and allow ourselves to be acted upon." Bayo Akomolafe, "Through the imprisoned archetypal figure of Baldur, I continue to find a useful way to think and talk about 'whiteness'," Facebook, August 6, 2020, www .facebook.com/permalink.php?story_fbid=6159591056993668&id=130394687589146.

[77] Tully, "Reconciliation Here on Earth," 109.   [78] Wilson, *Research Is Ceremony.*

[79] These figures are cited by the United Nations High Commissioner for Refugees for 2020: "Figures at a Glance," UNHCR, www.unhcr.org/figures-at-a-glance.html. It is recognized that many refugees are also stateless; however, the numbers are presented as such to specifically reference the categories of humans the state system generates.

[80] "Statelesness Around the World," UNHCR, www.unhcr.org/statelessness-around-the-world.html.

[81] Santos, "Beyond Abyssal Thinking."

democratizing ways of being that are relationally accountable. To the extent that representative democracies fail to invest in new permacultures of democratic Intrabeing always already in their midst, and the transformation of structures of dominance and violence, individualistic or egocentric lifeways are reproduced and reinforced – contributing to the very same us/them ontology that gives rise to antidemocratic movements. It is entirely consistent that within such a system, polarization and undemocratizing processes operating according to the same underpinning logic of disconnect emerge.

In this way, democracies have been generating their own morbidity, and, like the emperor in *The Emperor's New Clothes*, are exposed. However, in this moment, they need not double-down and recloak. The tailors in *The Emperor's New Clothes* are but fugitives seeking to democratically hold an empire to relational account. While egoic conceit may have inspired the Emperor to parade naked through the street, perhaps their unexpected exposure affords them the chance to see themselves from the standpoint of another.[82]

While representative democracies may have historically enacted individualist ontologies of disconnect, relational and democratizing processes have also long intra-actively shaped their becoming in critical ways. Just because many actors, institutions and processes within Western representative democracies have endorsed and invoked the egoic structures of individualism to undemocratizing effects, they have not uniformly done so, and their continued allegiance to these structures is up for relationally accountable, democratic debate and contestation. "Post-abyssal thinking"[83] demands of us that we think and act beyond the ontological bounds of individualism and in terms of relational accountability.[84]

Francisco Varela, the Chilean biologist and neuroscientist who cointroduced the concept of sympoiesis to biology, states: "When a living system is suffering from ill health, the remedy is found by connecting with more of itself."[85] For this to take place, critical practices of dialogue and engagement need to be carved out. As Tully notes, "Unless there is a critical practice within a tradition or within the course of the dialogue that brings this problem to self-awareness and addresses it by bringing aspects of one's background horizon of disclosure into the space of questions at the centre of the dialogue, genuine dialogue cannot begin."[86] Across history, processes, practices and precedents exist whereby undemocratizing processes at play have been addressed democratically. Given what is at stake, a revisiting of the question "what is

---

[82] For Derrida, "There is no nudity 'in nature'" and human animals are "[a]shamed of being naked as a beast": Jacques Derrida, *The Animal That Therefore I Am (More to Follow)* (New York: Fordham University Press, 2008), 4–5.

[83] Santos, "Beyond Abyssal Thinking."   [84] Wilson, *Research Is Ceremony*.

[85] Various versions of this quote are attributed to Francisco Varela, including sources such as Curtis Ogden, *Strengthening the Network Within* (Boston: Interaction Institute for Social Change, 2016).

[86] Tully, "Deparochializing Political Theory," 53.

democratic?' is warranted. The resilience and regenerative capacity of all social systems – including representative democracies – rests on the willingness and actions of those actors and institutions upholding them to connect, reconnect and enter into genuine dialogue with the countless democratizing traditions and movements alive and well beyond their borders.

Democratizing Revolution

Self-Reflexivity and Self-Limitation Beyond Liberalism

Robin Celikates

For almost two decades after 1989/90 it seemed to many in the West that "we" are living in a postrevolutionary era – and indeed, political thought was dominated by a reformist mindset for which radical ambitions betrayed a naïve, outdated, and excessive desire. However, since the "movements of the squares" – the "Arab Spring," Occupy in its different instantiations, Istanbul's Gezi park protest, Black Lives Matter, and the Ni una menos movement – radical social and political transformation is back on the agenda. This is not surprising given the "new normal" of manifold and interlocking crises and catastrophes – from structural racism via the neoliberal destruction of social infrastructures to environmental apocalypse. Against this bleak background, the desire for radical change appears as significantly more realistic than the standard defenses of the status quo that rest on phantasies of self-sufficiency and denials of relational entanglement.

Whether this shift amounts to a return of revolutionary politics, or whether these movements should rather be seen as decidedly postrevolutionary, is a question that will not be decided with reference to "the facts." Rather, the corresponding discussions can serve as a reminder that struggles around the concept of revolution are central to the trajectories of radical political thought after Marx – for whom "to be radical is to grasp things by the root"[1] – and to the contested self-understanding of contemporary societies. As a concept that is not only contested but plays an irreducible role in contestations, revolution is precisely

---

This is an extended and revised version of a chapter that previously appeared in German as "Die Negativität der Revolution: Selbstreflexivität und Selbstbegrenzung jenseits des Liberalismus," in *Negativität: Kunst, Recht, Politik*, eds. Thomas Khurana et al. (Berlin: Suhrkamp, 2018), 329–40. I would like to thank Pablo Ouziel, David Owen, Kiyomi Ren Mino, Yves Winter, the members of the "4 Columns" group, and especially Jim Tully and Josh Nichols for their immensely helpful comments on the English version.
[1] Karl Marx, "Contribution to the Critique of Hegel's Philosophy of Right: Introduction," in *The Marx-Engels Reader*, ed. Robert C. Tucker (New York: Norton, 1978), 60.

located at the intersection of radical political thought, societal self-understandings, and practices of resistance.[2] Like other contested concepts – what, in German, one would call 'Kampfbegriffe', or concepts deployed as weapons in a struggle[3] – the concept of revolution is bound up with a series of dichotomies that seem to require taking sides: voluntarism or determinism, spontaneity or organization, agency or structure, tendency or event, permanence or rupture, violence or nonviolence, etc. Confronting rather than denying the fundamental ambivalences and ambiguities of both the concept and the practice of revolution, however, requires us to understand these dichotomies as giving rise to tensions that are as irreducible as they are essential for both concept and practice.

In what follows, I argue that it is precisely in a constant oscillation between the above-mentioned poles – and in the impossibility of determination – that the specific negativity of revolutions and their potential for radical-democratic practice today can be located.[4] In order to retain this potential, evidenced in contemporary movements and struggles, we need to move beyond homogenizing and nationalist-populist understandings of both revolution and democracy and the notion of popular sovereignty or constituent power that often underlies them. The homogenizing logic inherent in the quest for determination risks denying the irreducible tensions, arresting the productive oscillation and thereby jeopardizing the radical-democratic potential of revolutionary politics. Against this background, one way to avoid reproducing the exclusions and hierarchies that continue to haunt many attempts to reactivate radical politics today, especially in the register of hegemony, is to pluralize the idea and practice of revolutions. Revolutionary practice is thus confronted with the need to look for ways to preserve its internal heterogeneity and ambivalence against the urge of homogenizing its subject. Its own processual character needs to be kept open against the temptations of closure. And we need to defend the revolutionary and democratic potential of the apparently marginal – as exemplified, amongst others, in the struggles of migrants and Indigenous people(s) today – against hierarchizing reinscriptions of what counts as properly political or revolutionary, or who counts as the proper political or revolutionary subject. This perspective allows us to see that revolutionary practices are essentially practices of enacting radical democracy "here and now."

---

[2] See, for example, Ariella Azoulay, "Revolution," *Political Concepts* 2 (2013): www.politicalconcepts.org/revolution-ariella-azoulay; Asef Bayat, *Revolution without Revolutionaries: Making Sense of the Arab Spring* (Palo Alto, CA: Stanford University Press, 2017); Rebecca L. Spang, "How Revolutions Happen," *The Atlantic*, July 4, 2020, www.theatlantic.com/ideas/archive/2020/07/revolution-doesnt-look-like-revolution/613801.

[3] For an influential perspective on this role of concepts, see Reinhart Koselleck, "Begriffsgeschichte und Sozialgeschichte," in *Vergangene Zukunft: Zur Semantik geschichtlicher Zeiten* (Frankfurt: Suhrkamp 1995), 111.

[4] See, for example, Etienne Balibar, "The Idea of Revolution: Yesterday, Today and Tomorrow," *ΑΡΙΑΔΝΗ* 22 (2015–16): 228–44.

Building on ideas experimentally developed in the long and troubled history of revolutionary practice and elaborated in the works of Hannah Arendt, Cornelius Castoriadis, and others, I argue that indeterminacy – or, rather, the constant process of dismantling determinacy and of preserving indeterminacy – and the self-reflexivity this process requires can be seen as two important features of revolutionary practice. They will not only allow for a more adequate understanding of past revolutions and their ambiguities, but also for a fuller comprehension of the democratic potential and risks of revolutionary action in the present. A radical-democratic and revolutionary remaking of the demos needs to start from those political struggles that call for a radical revision, pluralization, and deterritorialization of the demos, of peoplehood and of its internal and external borders. In the contemporary constellation, migrant and Indigenous struggles and movements in my view provide important lessons for the theory of revolution despite the differences between them and their internal heterogeneity. As I argue, these movements deeply unsettle the existing terms of the struggle for hegemony rather than making a move within its narrowly nationalist-populist confines (a similar argument could be made with reference to antiracist and anticolonial struggles). Attention to the ways in which they enact democracy will provide an important counterweight to the incapacitating co-optation of revolution into the realm of the "to come." My hope is that in the process the contours of a new – grounded and pluralist – understanding of revolution will emerge that does not subordinate the radical-democratic practices in the "here and now" to some future project, but, rather, grounds revolution precisely in this "here and now."

POLITICAL, NOT METAPHYSICAL

It is a long-standing topos of the conservative critique of revolution that the very idea of revolution as well as the practice it inspires is anachronistic, romantic, quixotic, politically dangerous, and deeply metaphysical. In this vein, Edmund Burke famously diagnosed the French revolutionaries as suffering from "much, but bad metaphysics."[5] As Albert Hirschman has demonstrated, the rhetoric of reaction that unfolds in the wake of revolutions and seeks to preempt their success and recurrence is structured around a threefold accusation: revolutionary ambitions are naïve and in vain, their consequences endanger reformist achievements we should hold on to, and they lead to a perverse reversal of the intentions that motivate them.[6] Against this background, there

---

[5] Edmund Burke, *Reflections on the Revolution in France* (New Haven: Yale University Press, 2003), 154; see also Christoph Menke, *Reflections of Equality* (Palo Alto, CA: Stanford University Press, 2006), ix.

[6] See Albert O. Hirschman, *The Rhetoric of Reaction: Perversity, Futility, Jeopardy* (Cambridge, MA: Harvard University Press, 1991).

are at least three types of reasons for retaining and foregrounding the concept of revolution and defending it against the suspicion that all these supposed deficiencies are due to a metaphysical and therefore genuinely antipolitical desire for total upheaval.

First, as noted, our time is characterized by multiple interlocking and mutually reinforcing systemic crises and an increasingly widespread realization of their (often historically deep) destructive effects. This realization encompasses a growing sense that even political and social achievements that have long been regarded as irreversible in parts of the Western world – achievements usually secured at the expense of exploited, dominated, and abandoned populations elsewhere and at home – are, as a matter of fact, fragile, reversible, and subject to an orchestrated roll-back that unites neoliberal and authoritarian agendas.[7] Against this background, there are obvious *political* reasons for a perspective of radical political transformation beyond the longue durée of social learning processes, the micropolitics of local initiatives, the organized but domesticated world of NGO activism, and the reformist remnants of formerly left-wing political parties. The current convergence between anticapitalist, promigrant, and climate and racial justice struggles and movements, despite continuing conflicts and misunderstandings, attests to the resilient and emerging potentialities of such a radical perspective.[8]

Second, there are *historical* reasons for inscribing current struggles in the fragmented continuum of past emancipation movements. The preserving and potentially redemptive commemoration of defeated and lost revolutions needs to be defended against the escalating counterrevolutionary politics of memory driven by the often cruel and vindictive attempts of modern states to erase all traces of previous attempts to challenge their authority.[9] Far from being merely symbolic, this seemingly irrational mnemonic violence seeks to silence the potentially revolutionary memory of revolutions as well as neutralize the hopes and mobilizing potential associated with it. Understanding their own practice as part of a revolutionary tradition can, in contrast, enable movements to overcome short-termism, broaden possibilities of solidarity, and develop more radical political horizons.

Third, on a *philosophical* level, one can argue that the idea and practice of revolution, far from being metaphysical, can develop a distinctly antimetaphysical potential, since they owe their own conditions of possibility to the contestedness, underdetermination, and contingency of the social and

---

[7] See, for example, Wendy Brown, *In the Ruins of Neoliberalism: The Rise of Antidemocratic Politics in the West* (New York: Columbia University Press, 2019).

[8] See, for example, Keeanga-Yamahtta Taylor, *From #BlackLivesMatter to Black Liberation* (Chicago: Haymarket Books, 2016); Amna A. Akbar, "The Left Is Remaking Politics," *The New York Times*, July 12, 2020, www.nytimes.com/2020/07/11/opinion/sunday/defund-police-cancel-rent.html.

[9] See Enzo Traverso, *Left-Wing Melancholia: Marxism, History, and Memory* (New York: Columbia University Press, 2017).

political order. At the same time, this contestedness, underdetermination, and contingency is revealed through revolutions as they interrupt and break open an order that seemed without alternative, unbreakable.

Following from this final point, at first glance the negativity of revolutions may seem to be primarily, or even exclusively, located in this negation of the existing order, in the rejection of its claim to obedience, and the liberation from its coercive embrace. Surely, revolutions are inconceivable without the determinate negation of the status quo – and of the suffering and injustice it produces structurally and not merely contingently. Taking a closer look at the practice and theory of revolution, however, reveals that revolutions are more than mere interruptions and go beyond breaking with the existing order. The revolutionary dynamic is generative and exceeds the logic of insurrection and revolt, although both are entangled in complex genealogies and trajectories of reversal and inflection. As Glen Coulthard puts it:

> Forms of Indigenous resistance, such as blockading and other explicitly disruptive oppositional practices, are indeed reactive in the ways that some have critiqued, but they are also very important. Through these actions we physically say "no" to the degradation of our communities and to exploitation of the lands upon which we depend. But they also have ingrained within them a resounding "yes": they are the affirmative enactment of another modality of being, a different way of relating to and with the world, … a way of life, another form of community.[10]

Cornelius Castoriadis makes a similar point when he insists that, beyond the break, transformative politics is revolutionary insofar as it is "animated by an overall will and an overall aim," namely "to modify the social institutions 'from top to bottom'."[11] It is this "enactment" or "institution" of an alternative political reality that distinguishes the very idea and practice of revolution from that of revolt. For Castoriadis, this project of self-institution is an open-ended and reflexive process that he sees as incompatible with the phantasy of a fully self-transparent and self-identical individual or collective subject ("self").[12] Accordingly, the negativity of revolutions goes beyond determinate negation and encompasses the process of transformation itself. Since the tensions built into the very concept of revolution make a positive and

[10] Glen Sean Coulthard, *Red Skin, White Masks: Rejecting the Colonial Politics of Recognition* (Minneapolis: University of Minnesota Press, 2014), 169.
[11] Cornelius Castoriadis, "The Revolutionary Exigency," in *Political and Social Writings*, vol. 3, *1961–1979*, ed. and trans. David Ames Curtis (Minneapolis: University of Minnesota Press, 1993), 239.
[12] For the corresponding notion of autonomy as tied to the open-ended process of self-questioning and the need for a self-reflexive form of self-institution, see Cornelius Castoriadis, "Power, Politics, Autonomy," in *Philosophy, Politics, Autonomy* (New York: Oxford University Press, 1991), 143–74. Indeed, Castoriadis identifies the "syllogism … : the revolution intends the transparency of society; a transparent society is impossible; therefore, the revolution is impossible (or is possible only as totalitarianism)" as the effect of an obsessive misrecognition of the very practice of revolution. Castoriadis, "The Revolutionary Exigency," 230.

unambiguous determination of revolutions – of their possibility, their beginning, their course, their end, their success and failure, their subject, their terrain – impossible, we can speak of a specific negativity of revolutions. This negativity constantly urges revolutionary politics to relate to itself – that is, to become self-reflexive – in practice, and to work to preserve rather than overcome its own heterogeneity.[13]

It is well known that Hannah Arendt linked the radically transformative potential of revolutionary political practice to the fact that revolutions can be seen as "the only political events which confront us directly and inevitably with the problem of beginning."[14] They exemplify political action, itself the privileged expression of the fundamental agential ability to make a new beginning. In order to counter the risk of hypostatizing the idea of a new beginning, it should be understood in a pluralist fashion (in part against Arendt's own intentions) as encompassing different ways of making a new beginning or of beginning again, of affirmatively enacting another modality of being (to return to Coulthard's formulation) that may, as in the case of many Indigenous struggles, have deep historical roots. Against this background, revolutions are beginnings primarily in the sense that they instantiate and enable new forms of acting together, aiming to establish an order that institutionalizes, or at least aims or claims to institutionalize, the "spirit of the revolution." As Christoph Menke puts it,

the revolution does not only transform individual conditions and institutions, it rather changes how there are conditions and institutions – because it converts them into our deeds, the revolution begins a new, different history. The revolution is not the solution to any kind of crisis. It is nothing but a new commencement of a history in which there are new commencements. The revolution begins beginning.[15]

On my understanding, this kind of beginning can and does often involve recovering, resurging, and renewing traditional ways of being and acting with others that have been sidelined, suppressed, and destroyed by the modern state.

The fundamentally antimetaphysical character of revolutions is expressed in the fact that as collective acts of beginning anew, of beginning again, they practically articulate a basic insight of political ontology: While it may become especially evident in revolutionary situations that power is lying in the streets waiting to be picked up,[16] ultimately all regimes depend on the

---

[13] See Christoph Menke, "The Possibility of Revolution," *Crisis and Critique* 4, no. 2 (2017): 312–22.

[14] Hannah Arendt, *On Revolution* (London: Penguin, 1990), 21; see also Oliver Marchart, *Neu Beginnen: Hannah Arendt, die Revolution und die Globalisierung* (Vienna: Turia + Kant, 2005).

[15] Menke, "The Possibility of Revolution," 320. Accordingly, in order to be adequate to the "postrevolutionary" situation, the very meaning of concepts such as "order" and "principle" would have to be revised.

[16] See Arendt, *On Revolution*, 48, 116.

recognition of those who are subject to them because they could not, in the long run, maintain themselves based on violence alone. This is the fundamental point articulated in the young Marx's claim that democracy is "the solved riddle of all constitutions," as it is the only form of politically organizing society that gives institutional expression to the fact that the state, the constitution, and the law find their "actual basis" in the social and political practices of the actual demos.[17]

In addition, during revolutions, those framing or background conditions of political action that usually remain unquestioned and are accepted as given suddenly become problematized and politicized: They are revealed as contingent and subject to transformative political practices.[18] The new beginning, or beginning again, the founding or refounding marked by revolutions is thus a form of joint action that makes new forms of joint political action possible, a form of "acting in concert" (as Arendt says, with a term borrowed from Burke[19]) that aims at self-determination. Before the revolution, insofar as it makes sense to conceive of politics as self-determination or self-institution at all, it is a severely constrained practice, one that is subject to conditions it cannot fully understand and therefore is not in a position to reflect upon or to recognize as changeable. Again, the point is not to overburden revolutions with the hubris of total self-institution, which is, after all, another metaphysical fantasy. Rather, it is to emphasize that in their process, and as a result of collective political agency, revolutions can dramatically transform what people regard and treat as changeable and unchangeable. When theorists try to capture this dynamic (rather than explain it away or ignore it), they often resort to relatively metaphorical language. Think of the empowering collective experience of overcoming fear and what Hannah Arendt called the joy of acting together, or Jean-Paul Sartre's theoretical narrative of the storming of the Bastille, which would later become the beginning of the French Revolution, in terms of the "groupe en fusion," or invocations of the spirit of the revolution (e.g. in its incarnation as the "spirit of Gezi").[20]

---

[17] Karl Marx, "Contribution to the Critique of Hegel's Philosophy of Right," in *The Marx-Engels Reader*, ed. Tucker, 21; see also Miguel Abensour, *Democracy Against the State* (Cambridge: Polity, 2011).

[18] See, for example, Bini Adamczak, *Beziehungsweise Revolution: 1917, 1968 und kommende* (Berlin: Suhrkamp, 2017), 100.

[19] Hannah Arendt, "Freiheit und Politik," in *Zwischen Vergangenheit und Zukunft: Übungen im politischen Denken I* (Munich: Piper, 2000), 224 (this passage is not included in the English version).

[20] See Arendt, *On Revolution*, 279; Jean-Paul Sartre, *Critique de la raison dialectique*, vol. 1, *Théorie des ensembles pratiques, précédé de Questions de méthode* (Paris: Gallimard, 1960), 391–94; and Serhat Karakayalı and Özge Yaka, "The Spirit of Gezi: The Recomposition of Political Subjectivities in Turkey," *New Formations* 83 (2014): 117–38.

In order to counteract the risk of self-subversion, of subjecting their potential to deeply unsettle the existing terms of the struggle for hegemony to the relative certainties of making a move within its narrowly state-centered confines, revolutions thus need to counter the temptation to install unquestionable commitments or determinations that are removed from further political contestation. In this, revolutions are radically democratic: the revolutionary process is one without metaphysical foundations – that is, it is a process that ultimately cannot be founded in or justified by reference to God, human nature, the course of history, science, or truth, even if in their beginnings revolutions often only get off the ground if they can tap into the ideological and motivational resources offered by such foundations and even if the invocation of foundational certainties continues to haunt them.

Both revolutionary and democratic practices articulate the same radical – and radically antimetaphysical – insight: Political orders and communities are never simply given and to be accepted, but both the result and the continuing terrain of political practices of contestation and transformation, of cooperation and self-organization. As they make the very form of politics and society changeable,[21] the negativity of both democracy and revolution is thus due to the absence of a stable foundation, of a univocal logic that would yield substantial orientations, and of clearly demarcated boundaries: Essentially conflictual and indeterminate, in order not to subvert their own logic and potential both require a permanent struggle to keep open the possibility of self-revision in the "here and now." Therefore, both lead to an essentially open-ended process of democratization and revolutionization that – despite its necessary directedness and contextuality – not only keeps the social and political order but also democracy and revolution themselves from ever achieving closure.

In addition to the ability of initiating a new beginning or of beginning anew, this also points to the second aspect in which revolutions resist their metaphysical (self-)misunderstanding: their processuality and plurality. No doubt, the metaphysical misunderstanding often appears in the guise of a self-misunderstanding. This can take the form of the mythological, fetishistic idea of the revolution as a total, all-encompassing break that can be organized and controlled in the name of a homogeneous revolutionary subject, and that leads to a completely new, rationally established, and self-transparent social order beyond all antagonisms and contestations.[22] Tendencies of fetishistic self-mythologization might be at work in all historical examples of revolution, but in many of them the problematic nature of these tendencies and the need to the struggle over and against this mythologization have also been recognized. In

---

[21] See Christoph Menke, *Critique of Rights* (Cambridge: Polity, 2019), 224; Cornelius Castoriadis, "Does the Idea of Revolution Still Make Sense?," *Thesis Eleven* 26 (1990): 123–38.

[22] See, for example, Ernesto Laclau, "Beyond Emancipation," in *Emancipation(s)* (London: Verso, 1996), 1–19.

counteracting these tendencies to (self-)mythologize, the pluralization of the idea and practice of revolution must operate on different levels. It needs to account for the plurality of political terrains and conflicts, of political actors and subjects, and of practices, strategies, and tactics at work in revolutions. These different levels stand in a complex and sometimes contradictory relationship to one another, opening up an internal heterogeneity that can be substantial, spatial, and temporal (and all at the same time), and that regularly gives rise to a powerful desire to ensure the unity and univocality of revolutions by means of one-sided determinations. Ultimately following a statist logic, such a "becoming-state" of revolutions goes hand in hand with suppressing their own internal heterogeneity and ambivalence. This heterogeneity and ambivalence is often tied to the multiple "revolutions within the revolution" that harbor alternative emancipatory pathways – such as, in the case of the French Revolution, the revolutions of women, the enslaved people of Haiti, and the poor, and their neglected legacies of insurgent universality.[23] Against the centralist urge of top-down unification and the risk of "becoming-state," revolutions must in practice experimentally invent and secure ways of preserving their polyvalence, indetermination, and openness.[24]

Because of their essential heterogeneity and indeterminacy, revolutions thus need to be understood as complex processes in which heterogeneous logics, dynamics, temporalities, and forms of practice are inextricably intertwined. As a result, processuality and plurality become essential characteristics of revolutionary acting-in-concert rather than temporary weaknesses that need to be straightened out or merely contingent aspects that are only of accidental importance.[25]

SELF-REFLEXIVITY, SELF-LIMITATION, AND THE LIMITS OF INSTITUTIONALIZATION

In their quest for certainty, for avoiding and suppressing misunderstandings, and for bringing the revolution to a "successful" end, revolutionary movements themselves risk reproducing structural features of the very power relations against which they turn. Revolutions therefore need to find ways to account for the counterrevolutionary risks emerging from within themselves. In order to counteract these self-undermining tendencies, revolutions need to and can develop – and in fact have developed – revolutionary practices and forms of organization that not only allow for internal plurality, processuality, and complexity, rather than suppressing them, but that politically reflect, sustain,

---

[23] See Massimiliano Tomba, *Insurgent Universality: An Alternative Legacy of Modernity* (Oxford: Oxford University Press, 2019), chp. 2.

[24] See, for example, Adamczak, *Beziehungsweise Revolution*, 67.

[25] See, for example, Daniel Loick, "21 Theses on the Politics of Forms of Life," *Theory & Event* 20, no. 3 (2017): 800–1.

and strengthen these characteristics. To do this, revolutions have to become self-reflexive without postulating a unitary self. For Arendt, this includes renouncing the phantasm of sovereignty and accepting that the "virtuosity" of acting together with others, which is essential for revolutions, is only possible under conditions of nonsovereignty.[26] It also includes, in Judith Butler's words, a form of "reflexive self-making," a recognition that "democratic politics has to be concerned with who counts as 'the people,' how the demarcation is enacted that brings to the fore who 'the people' are and that consigns to the background, to the margin, or to oblivion those people who do not count as 'the people'."[27] Insofar as it continues to make sense to speak of a subject, a self, here, it is one for which relationality and interdependency are constitutive and, as a result, the boundaries between self and other are blurred.

In addition, revolutionary processes have a logic of their own and their unpredictability and uncontrollability – in the strong sense that leads Arendt to speak of a "miracle"[28] – often impose themselves on their revolutionary subjects, transforming the nature of their collective agency. In this transformation, any claim to organize or "make" revolutions in a top-down fashion thus comes to appear as a historically momentous category mistake. The mistake lies in conceptualizing revolutionary action – a praxis, in the Aristotelian sense – according to the model of poiesis. If this happens, revolutionary practices are subjected to technological control, disciplined, and cut off from the "spirit of revolution."[29] Precisely as political practice, and insofar as they are practice, revolutions stand in contradiction to the myth of total controllability on the basis of privileged insight or scientifically founded certainty, which is often foisted upon them – admittedly not only by its opponents.

Against this background, it seems too simple to interpret Arendt's distinction of two stages of revolutions – liberation and foundation, or constitution – as a sequence of negative and positive forms of political practice. Just as liberation requires "positive" or constitutive forms of acting together and of collective organization, (re)foundation and (re)constitution must embrace and structurally incorporate elements of negativity: forms of self-reflexivity and self-limitation. The self-limitation in question does not coincide with the liberal call

---

[26] Arendt, *On Revolution*, 213; see also Hannah Arendt, "Freedom and Politics," *Chicago Review* 14, no. 1 (1960): 40–41.

[27] Judith Butler, *Notes Toward a Performative Theory of Assembly* (Cambridge, MA: Harvard University Press, 2015), 5, 171.

[28] Arendt, "Freedom and Politics," 44–45. Arendt's emphasis on the unpredictable character of revolutionary action contrasts starkly with Herbert Marcuse's quasi-utilitarian "historical calculus" embedded in the "inhuman arithmetic of history" that has justified sacrifice throughout history and is supposed to guide the revolutionaries in their cause. Herbert Marcuse, "Ethics and Revolution," in *Ethics and Society: Original Essays on Contemporary Moral Problems*, ed. R. T. de George (Garden City, NY: Anchor, 1966), 140, 145.

[29] Arendt, *On Revolution*, 224.

for unambiguous – clearly determinable – moral constraints on political action (such as catalogues of presumably extra-political human rights). Rather, and in contrast to liberalism, the self-reflexivity and self-limitation in question arise precisely from the internal logic of revolutionary acting-in-concert itself and connect to its – always politically precarious – indeterminacy, openness, and processuality.

In Arendt's view, acting-in-concert, if it is to achieve anything, remains dependent, even in its execution, on freedom being constantly reactivated, on beginnings, as it were, constantly flowing anew into sequences of action that have been begun in the past.[30] This holds for revolutions as well. As Castoriadis puts it: "The form of the revolution and of postrevolutionary society is not an institution or an organization given once and for all, but the *activity* of self-organization, or self-institution."[31] That its form is this activity means that institution and organization must take on another form – one determined, or rather, interrupted in its determinations, by negativity and self-reflexivity.

Within the horizon of modernity, one of the historically most significant examples of the attempt to institutionalize, in a self-reflexive and at the same time open way, the "spirit of the revolution" can be found in "the communes, the councils, the Räte, the soviets."[32] In Arendt's view, they are "the only form of government to develop directly out of the spirit of the revolution."[33] This "amazing formation of a new power structure which owed its existence to nothing but the organizational impulses of the people themselves" confronted the professional revolutionaries with "the rather uncomfortable alternative of either putting their own pre-revolutionary 'power', that is, the organization of the party apparatus, into the vacated power centre of the defunct government, or simply joining the new revolutionary power centres which had sprung up without their help."[34] According to Arendt, it is no coincidence that the radical-democratic power of the councils, communes, and soviets emerges in virtually all revolutions, before it is crushed, co-opted, or taken over by the party or the newly established state apparatus.[35] Even the Hungarian

---

[30] See Arendt, *On Revolution*, 224.   [31] Castoriadis, "The Revolutionary Exigency," 238.

[32] Arendt, *On Revolution*, 256. Here we can note a convergence with Jim Tully's nonsovereign view of civic citizenship; see, for example, Adam Dunn and David Owen, "Instituting Citizenship," in James Tully, *On Global Citizenship: James Tully in Dialogue* (London: Bloomsbury, 2014), 247–65.

[33] Hannah Arendt, *Über die Revolution* (Munich: Piper 1994), 327 (this passage is not included in the English version, translation author's own) – whether "form of government" is the right term here would have to be debated.

[34] Arendt, *On Revolution*, 257.

[35] On the communist party take-over of the soviets during the "October Revolution," see Pierre Dardot and Christian Laval, *L'ombre d'octobre: La révolution russe et le spectre des soviets* (Montreal: Lux, 2017); on its ambivalent legacy, see Michael Hardt and Sandro Mezzadra, eds., "October! The Soviet Centenary," special issue, *South Atlantic Quarterly* 116, no. 4 (2017).

Revolution of 1956, celebrated by Arendt as the first example of Rosa Luxemburg's "spontaneous revolution" – "this sudden uprising of an oppressed people for the sake of freedom and hardly anything else"[36] – is of interest to her primarily as a resurrection of the council system buried by the "October Revolution."

Many of the social and political struggles and movements of the last ten years may not be revolutions in Arendt's or Castoriadis' sense, and the assemblies in public squares and occupied buildings may not be classic councils. Nevertheless, the work of both suggests that the "spirit of the revolution" is often kept alive in political practices that may at first glance not necessarily seem revolutionary. These practices are part of a continuum that includes occupations, strikes and walk-outs, protest encampments, noncooperation, civil disobedience, and uprisings, all of which can be seen as attempts to enact radical democracy "here and now." For example, following Arendt, but turning against her own exclusion of racialized political subjects from the realm of civil disobedience, the radical-democratic potential of this political practice can be highlighted. It then appears as articulating the "power of the people," the "potestas in populo," in a way that actualizes the horizontal social contract by opening up a space of indeterminacy in which politics in the potentially revolutionary sense can emerge in the first place.[37] Similarly, assemblies, just as councils, can be seen as carrying the promise and prefiguring the reality of a "plurality of powers" that allows for "equal access" and keeps the democratic process open to its own "democratic excess."[38] As Verónica Gago argues with reference to the feminist strike and Ni una menos:

The feminist movement takes to the streets and constructs itself in assemblies; it weaves together its potencia in territories and elaborates a comprehensive analysis of the conjuncture; it produces a counterpower that is able to win new rights while retaining its focus on a more radical horizon. In short: our movement dismantles the binary between reform and revolution.[39]

[36] Hannah Arendt, "Totalitarian Imperialism: Reflections on the Hungarian Revolution," *The Journal of Politics* 20, no. 1 (1958): 8. For a similar assessment, see Cornelius Castoriadis, "The Hungarian Source," in *Political and Social Writings*, vol. 3, 250–72; and Cornelius Castoriadis, "The Proletarian Revolution Against the Bureaucracy," in *Political and Social Writings*, vol. 2, *1955–1960*, ed. and trans. David Ames Curtis (Minneapolis: University of Minnesota Press, 1988), 57–89.

[37] Hannah Arendt, "Civil Disobedience," in *Crises of the Republic* (New York: Harcourt Brace & Company, 1972), 86–87; see also Robin Celikates, "Radical Democratic Disobedience," in *Cambridge Companion to Civil Disobedience*, ed. William Scheuerman (Cambridge: Cambridge University Press, 2021), 128–52. On the deeply problematic politics of race that structures Arendt's account, see, for example, Ayça Çubukçu, "Of Rebels and Disobedients: Reflections on Arendt, Race, Lawbreaking," *Law and Critique* 32 (2021): 33–50.

[38] Tomba, *Insurgent Universality*, 67.

[39] Verónica Gago, *Feminist International: How to Change Everything* (London: Verso, 2020), 241–42.

Similarly aiming to establish a revolutionary continuum rather than an exceptionalism of the revolution, the notion of prefigurative politics not only turns away from privileging the aim of conquering power (or the struggle for hegemony), but also articulates a fundamental critique of the authoritarian and vanguardist traditions of the left from within. Far from abandoning its revolutionary ambitions, this is in fact an attempt to rescue them from statist capture, organizational ossification, and metaphysical hypostatization. As evidenced in the movements of the squares across the globe, political practices are prefigurative in attempting to realize what they strive for in the future in an anticipatory mode in the here and now – above all in horizontal and participatory, inclusive and solidary organizational structures and practices. In so doing, they come to regard ends and means, goals and processes, as standing in a relationship of mutual determination that is always in need of experimental revision and readjustment.[40] A similarly prefigurative logic seems to be at work in many Indigenous struggles for self-determination that do not primarily see it as an institutional goal to be demanded from and granted by the state or another authority, as part of an aspiration to become like a state. Rather, these struggles seem to aim at and enact an alternative, nonhegemonic, ethical-political practice of "self-determination from below," as part of a long-term and often subterranean struggle that seeks to transform power relations rather than appropriate predetermined positions within such relations.[41] In this transformation the very meaning of land rights, control over resources, and governance – all central elements of self-determination in Indigenous struggles – is at stake and reconfigured beyond its hegemonic configuration. It is therefore no surprise that in his reconstruction of the long history of Indigenous struggle Nick Estes prominently references Marx's figure of the revolution as the burrowing mole: "Hidden from view to outsiders, this constant tunneling, plotting, planning, harvesting, remembering, and conspiring for freedom – the collective faith that another world is possible – is the most important aspect of revolutionary work."[42] More precisely, it is in enacting another world that revolutionary political action demonstrates the possibility of another world.

Both the councils foregrounded by Arendt and the various politics of prefiguration from the recent past can be seen as attempts to enact and institutionalize negativity and self-reflexivity, which are at the same time

---

[40] See, for example, Paul Raekstad, "Revolutionary Practice and Prefigurative Politics: A Clarification and Defense," *Constellations* 25, no. 3 (2018): 359–72; and Mathijs van de Sande, "Fighting with Tools: Prefiguration and Radical Politics in the Twenty-First Century," *Rethinking Marxism* 27 (2015): 177–94.

[41] See Jakeet Singh, "Recognition and Self-Determination: Approaches from Above and Below," in *Recognition versus Self-Determination: Dilemmas of Emancipatory Politics*, ed. Avigail Eisenberg et al. (Vancouver: UBC Press, 2014), 62–7.

[42] Nick Estes, *Our History Is the Future: Standing Rock versus the Dakota Access Pipeline, and the Long Tradition of Indigenous Resistance* (London: Verso, 2019), 19.

aware of the limits of institutionalization. They therefore try to find forms of acting-in-concert that are not merely situational and that make it possible for "beginnings" to constantly flow anew into what has once been begun. Both also exemplify another – neither necessary nor arbitrary – implication of the negativity and self-reflexivity of revolution: a form of self-limitation of revolutionary action that is again not liberal (i.e. grounded in prior rights or referring to a status quo ante), but radical or radical-democratic. Far from mandating nonviolence in an absolutist sense, this form of self-limitation manifests itself in a troubled and ambivalent relationship to violence, which also sets itself apart from the instrumentalism of influential classical conceptions of revolution.

A striking example of such classical conceptions is provided by the polemic realism of Friedrich Engels's characterization of the revolution as "certainly the most authoritarian thing there is," as an "act whereby one part of the population imposes its will upon the other part by means of rifles, bayonets and cannons – authoritarian means, if such there be at all."[43] In stark contrast, an alternative tradition of self-limiting (but not necessarily for this reason nonviolent or postrevolutionary) revolution has emerged that stretches from the anarchist and feminist movements of the nineteenth and twentieth centuries via the South African ANC and the Polish Solidarność to, amongst others, the movements of the squares, BLM, and the feminist strike. This alternative tradition consciously positions itself against hegemonic friend–enemy logics – prominently exemplified in the antipopulist refusal of discourses of othering ("ötekileştirme") in Gezi Park.[44] It also rejects statist fantasies of sovereignty, and ultimately antipolitical and demobilizing attempts at a centralist reduction of the complexity or contingency of revolutionary practice.[45] Insofar as this reorientation does problematize violence as a means of achieving revolutionary goals – in contrast to a line that leads from Engels via Lukacs to Marcuse[46] – it is neither an external or top-down counterrevolutionary critique of subversive violence, nor a purely strategic recommendation, nor a principled – for instance, ethically justified – rejection of the use of violence under all circumstances (including, say, self-defense). Rather, this self-limitation is grounded in a certain understanding of political and revolutionary practice – in a thoroughly practical act of self-reflection – which builds on the

---

[43] Friedrich Engels, "On Authority," in *The Marx-Engels Reader*, ed. Tucker, 733.

[44] Karakayalı and Yaka, "The Spirit of Gezi," 128.

[45] See, for example, Jean L. Cohen and Andrew Arato, *Civil Society and Political Theory* (Cambridge, MA: MIT Press, 1992), 72–4. From this perspective, recent attempts to ascribe to the party once again a revolutionary role and to contrast it with a supposedly otherwise disoriented and dispersed nature of the crowd should be met with skepticism. See, for example, Jodi Dean, *Crowds and Party* (London: Verso, 2016).

[46] On the complex but ultimately one-sided theorization of violence in Marxism, see Etienne Balibar, "Reflections on Gewalt," *Historical Materialism: Research in Critical Marxist Theory* 17 (2009): 99–125.

antivoluntarist historical experience and sociological insight that violence can neither be easily overcome nor controlled and that it fundamentally threatens the collective enactment of democracy in the "here and now."[47] As a result, one can neither simply step away from violence nor embrace it in order to use it in a measured way. Rather, revolutionary practices and forms of organization need to find ways to counter the reality and dynamics of violence with a radical politics of civility, understood here as the collective capacity to act within conflicts and upon them, transforming them from excessively violent to less violent ones.[48]

Consequently, self-limitation, too, is not an external constraint, but owes its existence to the insight into the inescapable precariousness of revolutionary acting-in-concert – a precariousness that affects its possibility, its success or failure, its subjects, terrains, and temporalities, all of which must be regarded as "unsecured." Although it can of course be instrumentalized, such self-limitation is in itself neither reformist nor disciplining. Rather, it is essentially linked to the task of permanent self-reflection and self-transformation in and as part of revolutionary transformation – a task the struggles and movements discussed in this chapter have experimentally taken up in their manifold practices and discourses of enacting democracy in the "here and now." In this way, the self-reflection of revolutions proves not to be a foundation, but rather – negatively – an essential feature of a practice that is constantly refracted by its own consequences, and questions and limits itself in their light. As Marx said of proletarian revolutions, it is thus no accident that revolutions "criticise themselves constantly, interrupt themselves continually in their own course, come back to the apparently accomplished in order to begin it afresh, deride with unmerciful thoroughness the inadequacies, weaknesses and paltrinesses of their first attempts."[49]

RADICAL DEMOCRACY IN A NONHEGEMONIC KEY

Today, migrant and Indigenous struggles and movements might provide the most instructive examples of a transformative and potentially revolutionary force aimed at reconstituting the political order in a democratizing way. Via collective practices that link unburied pasts with different futures, they promise to break open the present and generate a force that keeps the unresolvable dialectic of constituent and constituted powers in play against those social and political forces that seek to

[47] See Hannah Arendt, *On Violence* (New York: Harcourt Brace Jovanovich, 1970).
[48] See, for example, Etienne Balibar, *Violence and Civility* (New York: Columbia University Press, 2015), chp. 1; Judith Butler, *The Force of Nonviolence* (London: Verso, 2020); Robin Celikates, "Learning from the Streets: Civil Disobedience in Theory and Practice," in *Global Activism: Art and Conflict in the 21st Century*, ed. Peter Weibel (Cambridge, MA: MIT Press, 2015), 65–72.
[49] Karl Marx, "The Eighteenth Brumaire of Louis Bonaparte," *The Marx-Engels Reader*, ed. Tucker, 597.

arrest and contain it (also under the name of 'left' populism).[50] Manifesting a specific kind of constituent power – namely, the power to initiate and enact a fundamental reconstitution of borders, political community, and membership by denaturalizing, politicizing, and democratizing them – migrant and Indigenous movements exemplify the kind of democratic and potentially revolutionary reflexivity set out here, insofar as they constitute "a force or a political movement [that] can only democratize society [because] it itself is fundamentally more democratic than the system it opposes, with respect both to its objectives and to its internal operation."[51]

From the *Sans papiers* in 1990s France to the recent Migrant Caravans from Latin America to the US–Mexican border and the so-called "march of hope" in which thousands of refugees marched from Budapest to the Austrian border, politicizing the question of borders and forcing an actual political break, breach, or opening in 2015,[52] migrants have entered the political stage and claimed political agency in ways that do not follow the official scripts of liberal or even radical democracy. Their struggles highlight the fact that it is often precisely those who do not count as citizens, or even as political agents (women, workers, colonized subjects, migrants, and refugees), who develop new – or rearticulate pre-existing – forms of citizenship and of democracy that promise to be more adequate for our current political constellation of disaggregated sovereignty, traversed as it is by transnational challenges, power relations, actors, and struggles. This constellation is characterized by complex processes of debordering and rebordering that undermine the idea of territorially bounded political spaces with borders that are clearly defined and unilaterally controlled by the state.[53] At least those futures of democracy that go beyond statist imaginaries and regressive nationalist-populist tendencies (and thus manage to qualify as futures at all) will only come into view once the challenge migration and migrant political agency pose to dominant ways of thinking and practicing citizenship and democracy is taken seriously.

[50] See Etienne Balibar, *Equaliberty: Political Essays* (Durham: Duke University Press, 2014), conclusion; Robin Celikates, "Constituent Power Beyond Exceptionalism: Irregular Migration, Disobedience, and (Re-)Constitution," *Journal of International Political Theory* 15, no. 1 (2019): 67–81.

[51] Etienne Balibar, *Citizenship* (Cambridge: Polity, 2015), 128–29. For a perspective on Indigenous struggles that emphasizes their revolutionary dynamic and potential, see Estes, *Our History Is the Future*.

[52] See Madjiguène Cissé, *Parole de sans-papiers* (Paris: La Dispute, 1999); "The Border Crossing Us," *Viewpoint Magazine*, November 7, 2018, www.viewpointmag.com/2018/11/07/from-what-shore-does-socialism-arrive; Bernd Kasparek and Marc Speer, "Of Hope: Hungary and the Long Summer of Migration," trans. Elena Buck, *bordermonitoring.eu*, September 9, 2015, http://bordermonitoring.eu/ungarn/2015/09/of-hope-en.

[53] See, for example, Anne McNevin, *Contesting Citizenship: Irregular Migrants and New Frontiers of the Political* (New York: Columbia University Press, 2011); Maurice Stierl, *Migrant Resistance in Contemporary Europe* (London: Routledge, 2019).

This challenge also requires rethinking the radical-democratic and revolutionary idea of democratization as the actualization of constituent power that is sometimes presented as the source from which any future of democracy would have to spring. It is no longer convincing, if it ever was, to portray this power as a quasi-mythical force that is wholly external to the existing order and erupts only in extraordinary founding moments in which the people as a unified agent enters the political scene (think of the iconic dates of 1776, 1789, 1917). Rather, constituent powers would have to be conceptualized as a plural dynamic situated within revolutionary movements that unsettle established orders and their porous boundaries, transgressing their logic and reconfiguring them from within and from their margins. This would also make it possible to reverse the ahistorical and asociological uncoupling of the event of the eruption of constituent power (in founding moments or great revolutions) from ongoing struggles and movements that seek to enact it in the "here and now."

In my view, this points to the antihegemonic and antipopulist logic of revolutionary democratic practice. The deep nationalist logic of populist appeals to the "real people" in an "us vs. them" register only "serves to recapture the insurgent energies of emancipatory struggles and entrap the 'common folk' within the borders of the Nation, reinscribing a democratic political enclosure whereby human life is subordinated to and subjected by the nationalist metaphysics of state power."[54] Against such capture, democracy requires us to acknowledge and institutionalize as far as possible "the open and contestable signification of democracy," to find ways to "release democracy from containment by any particular form while insisting on its value in connoting political self-rule by the people, whoever the people are."[55] What does this requirement imply for the forms of organization and self-understanding of revolutionary struggles and movements? What are its consequences for thinking about emancipatory politics in the register of hegemony, populism, and hegemonic populism?

As I argue, revolutionary struggles for emancipation and democratization in the "here and now" cannot have the same form and follow the same logic as struggles for hegemony "from the right" that are evidently not concerned with, and indeed embrace the task of, constructing an exclusionary and homogeneous collective subject that can serve as the firm ground of affective identification and mobilization. As I have attempted to show in the preceding sections, the revolutionary potential of enacting radical democracy "here and now" is tied to acknowledging its fundamental open-endedness, plurality, and self-reflexivity against the pressures of closure and homogenization that

---

[54] Nicholas de Genova, "Rebordering 'The People': Notes on Theorizing Populism," *South Atlantic Quarterly* 117, no. 2 (2018): 368.

[55] Wendy Brown, *Undoing the Demos: Neoliberalism's Stealth Revolution* (New York: Zone Books, 2015), 20.

necessarily come with the hegemonic logic of populism and its "us vs. them" logic.

Turning to Indigenous and migrant struggles – despite the differences between them and their internal heterogeneity – allows us to highlight alternative ways of undoing the *demos* and remaking *demoi* from forms of political struggle that question established notions of the people and its boundaries but might not end up embracing a positive vision of 'We the people' in the singular. Without being able to do justice to their complexity, let me briefly sketch in how far both Indigenous and migrant struggles question rather than instantiate the logic of hegemonic claim-making that is still so often associated with revolutionary and radically transformative political projects.

In a settler colonial context, struggles for self-determination by Indigenous and occupied people and peoples obviously clash with the state's claim to exclusive territorial sovereignty and the underlying imaginary of popular sovereignty.[56] The radically democratic potential of Indigenous struggles today can be seen precisely in the dual displacement of hegemony, which can no longer serve as the privileged logic of political articulation, and of the modern nation-state, which can no longer serve as the unquestioned terrain for democratic struggle.[57] As a result, Indigenous struggles for self-determination and against the colonial and imperial project of the modern nation-state to impose homogeneity and (territorial, cultural, political, legal) uniformity have the potential to escape both the framework of protest and that of dominant notions of civility, even if they might appear as "constituent powers" and "civic powers" in the plural.[58] At the same time, they can fundamentally transform the very meaning of "self-determination" beyond the bounded and sovereign model of the (individual or collective) self toward an acknowledgment of the interdependency and relationality of all (human and nonhuman) members of the community.

Similarly, and despite important differences, in a world in which nation-states claim a unilateral right to control their borders – both the borders of their territory and the borders of membership and belonging – migrant and refugee movements challenge a whole way of life and a political imaginary that entirely abstracts from its own structural implication in the production of the conditions that violate migrants' "right to stay" as well as their "right to escape."[59] These

[56] See, for example, Nick Estes and Jaskiran Dhillon, eds., *Standing with Standing Rock: Voices from the #NoDAPL Movement* (Minneapolis: University of Minnesota Press, 2019); and Audra Simpson, *Mohawk Interruptus: Political Life Across the Borders of Settler States* (Durham, NC: Duke University Press, 2014).
[57] See Janet Conway and Jakeet Singh, "Radical Democracy in Global Perspective: Notes from the Pluriverse," *Third World Quarterly* 32, no. 4 (2011): 689–706.
[58] See James Tully, *Public Philosophy in a New Key*, vol. 2, *Imperialism and Civic Freedom* (Cambridge: Cambridge University Press, 2008), 195–221, 243–309.
[59] See, for example, Celikates, "Constituent Power Beyond Exceptionalism"; Sandro Mezzadra, *Diritto di fuga* (Verona: Ombre Corte, 2006); for a response to the claim that Indigenous commitments to land and jurisdiction betray an antimigrant and anti-Black character, see

struggles are, of course, also struggles for and about politicization and the
boundaries of the political. They seem to be misidentified both in their
content and in their form when they are interpreted as contestatory responses
to the question of "who the people really are." The "We" in "We didn't cross
the border, the border crossed us" and "We are here because you were/are
there" is not, and does not necessarily aspire to be, the same as the "We" in
"We, the People."

Not all political and social struggles of our age can thus equally well, or at all,
be articulated in the language of popular sovereignty, of sovereignty and of the
people in the singular. Such nationalist-populist articulations would also miss
the prefigurative potential that resides in the ways in which these struggle
challenge and transcend the dominant logic of the nation-state and its border
regime by developing, resuscitating, and enacting alternative forms of political
agency, belonging, and solidarity in the here and now. The point is not to find
a new vanguard in Indigenous and migrant struggles onto which frustrated
revolutionary desires can be projected, but to see the collective enactment of
denied freedoms, the temporary realization of utopian possibilities in the here
and now, and the practical decentering of the state for what they are: openings
of political space that reveal a revolutionary potential.[60] Radical democracy in
a nonhegemonic key would thus start from the margins of the demos, from the
refugees, the migrants, the exiles and those who come after them, from "the
discounted, the ineligible," "the stateless, the occupied, and the disenfranchised,"
"confounding the distinction between inside and outside" and questioning
established notions of the people and its boundaries without ending up
embracing a positive vision of "We the people."[61]

Both Indigenous and migrant struggles can be seen as pointing beyond claims
to access existing legal statuses (such as citizen, refugee) to a different political
logic that questions the foundations of how political belonging is imagined in the
homogenizing terms of nation-states, borders, and citizenship. At the very
least, these struggles challenge unquestioned notions of belonging and as
a consequence call for a radical revision, pluralization, and deterritorialization
of the demos, of peoplehood and of its internal and external borders in ways that
unsettle the existing terms of the struggle for hegemony rather than making
a move that conforms to its nationalist-populist logic. They can thus be seen as
steps toward overcoming a politics of citizenship as membership in a bordered
and homogeneous community – a truly revolutionary horizon that goes against
the construction of their claims as inherently limited and marginal.[62]

Glen Sean Coulthard, "Response," *Historical Materialism: Research in Critical Marxist Theory*
24, no. 3 (2016): 96. As one slogan has it, indigenous sovereignty means no borders; its enemy is
settler colonialism, not migration.
[60] See Stierl, *Migrant Resistance*, chp. 7.   [61] Butler, *Notes Toward*, 51, 80, 78.
[62] See Sandro Mezzadra, "Abolitionist Vistas of the Human. Border Struggles, Migration and
Freedom of Movement," *Citizenship Studies* 24, no. 4 (2020): 424–40; and Anne McNevin,

These struggles potentially reconfigure what bell hooks calls "imposed marginality" as "a site of deprivation" into a "space of radical openness" and a "site of radical possibility, a space of resistance" from which "counterhegemonic discourse" can emerge.[63] The question then becomes which forms of revolutionary practice, of acting-in-concert and of self-organization, can enact and express rather than repress and conceal *this* logic of the political that moves against and beyond hegemony, thus remaining "counterhegemonic" in the sense of transgressing the constrictions of hegemony, as much as it moves against and beyond the borders of a world divided along state lines.

"Time and the Figure of the Citizen," *International Journal of Politics, Culture, and Society* 33 (2020): 545–59.

[63] bell hooks, "Choosing the Margin as a Space of Radical Openness," *Framework: The Journal of Cinema and Media* 36 (1989): 20, 23.

PART IV

INDIGENOUS DEMOCRACIES

Gitxsan Democracy: On Its Own Terms

Val Napoleon

We live in societies that may be politically democratic but are socially fascist, which is more than ever the ideal regime for global neoliberalism. But this duality creates instability. Will the future be more democratic or, to the contrary, will fascism move from a social to a political regime? It will depend on us. Each generation fights with the weapons it has.[1]

Democracies are dying democratically.[2]

- Boaventura de Sousa Santos

INTRODUCTION

Democracy is generally understood and discussed as operating within a state and applying to those people within the procedural grasp and coercive power of the state.[3] From this view, the democratic determinants are who gets heard both formally (i.e. through votes, representative government, and legal and civic administration) and informally (i.e. media voices and spaces, economic participation and class, and education privileges).[4] How might we conceive of democracy within nonstate societies such as historic Indigenous societies? How would it operate and what would its determinants be?

---

[1] Boaventura de Sousa Santos, "We Live in Politically Democratic but Socially Fascist Societies," *CPAL Social*, November 30, 2016, www.envio.org.ni/articulo/5269.

[2] Boaventura de Sousa Santos, "The Crises of Democracy: Boaventura de Sousa Santos and James Tully" (webinar, *Global Politics in Critical Perspectives – Transatlantic Dialogues*, University of Victoria, Victoria, BC, March 15, 2019), www.youtube.com/watch?v=-i9aFUsTipk.

[3] Michael Blake, Simone Chambers, and Arthur Ripstein, "Talking Philosophy: War and Peace Part 2," May 19, 2015, in *IDEAS*, produced by Greg Kelly and CBC Radio, www.cbc.ca/radio/ideas/talking-philosophy-war-and-peace-part-2-1.3324750.

[4] Ibid.

Within what has been described as the deepest crisis of liberal democracy since the 1930s, I want to take up and explore some of the current challenges to democratic governance from an Indigenous perspective and from within a historic nonstate political ordering of Indigenous societies. How is the global democratic crisis being experienced in Indigenous communities, and how might Indigenous insights and responses, so sorely needed, invigorate larger conversations about liberal democracy? One of my aims here is to examine several worries that I have about what appears to be a general lack of critical analysis and inattention to serious questions concerning Indigenous democracies, governance, and citizenship.

One of my worries is the deficit approach being applied to Indigenous peoples and societies. The assumption driving this impoverished approach is that Indigenous societies were never democratic and, further, that historically and to the present day, Indigenous societies violate human rights[5] through the operations of their political ordering, economies, and legal orders and law. These so-called deficits provide the justification for further impositions of state democratic constructs which create more hammers to force the reshaping of Indigenous democracies and citizenries into acceptable colonial forms. The process and effect of this deficit approach creates what de Sousa Santos has called abyssal thinking, wherein one imaginary operates to exhaust all other possibilities, thereby rendering those other possibilities invisible.[6]

My other related worry is created by the persistent idealization and romanticization of Indigenous practices based on the assumption that there is no need to be critical of either historic or present-day Indigenous politics, law, and economies. In their efforts to be supportive of Indigenous peoples, some Indigenous and non-Indigenous academics take the position that they cannot acknowledge or discuss Indigenous sexism, internal oppressive power dynamics, or other political dysfunctions lest they further undermine Indigenous peoples and perpetuate colonial oppression. The reality is that today there are some Indigenous communities that are dangerous for women and girls because they are absolutely shameless in their sexism,[7] and there are extensive local conflicts within and between communities.[8] When historic

---

[5] I am not taking up the issues and questions concerning definitions and limitations of human rights constructions here.

[6] Boaventura de Sousa Santos, "Beyond Abyssal Thinking: From Global Lines to Ecologies of Knowledges," *Eurozine*, June 29, 2007, www.eurozine.com/beyond-abyssal-thinking/.

[7] See, for example, Val Napoleon, "An Imaginary for Our Sisters," in *Indigenous Spirituality and Religious Freedom*, ed. Jeffery Hewitt and Richard Moon (Toronto: University of Toronto Press, forthcoming); Emily Snyder, Val Napoleon, and John Borrows. "Gender and Violence: Drawing on Indigenous Legal Resources," *UBC Law Review* 48, no. 2 (2015): 593–654.

[8] I have written about the extensive conflicts within and between Indigenous communities elsewhere. See, for example, Val Napoleon, "Demanding More from Ourselves: Indigenous Civility and Incivility," in *Civic Freedom in an Age of Diversity: The Public Philosophy of James Tully*, ed. Dimitri Karmis and Jocelyn Maclure (Montreal: McGill-Queen's University Press, forthcoming).

problems are denied in Indigenous societies, and when present-day problems are blamed entirely on colonialism, the consequence is the erasure of historic Indigenous intellectual resources, resiliencies, and processes that might be drawn upon today.

I have three overarching objectives in this chapter. First, I want to demonstrate how current negotiations between Gitxsan[9] communities and the Canadian (i.e. federal and provincial) governments are a form of abyssal thinking, and as such operate to further undermine Gitxsan democracy and governance. To support this argument, I draw on the work of Boaventura de Sousa Santos and his analysis regarding modern western thinking in the global struggle for social justice.[10] While I am focusing on the Gitxsan to avoid pan-Indigeniety and to allow a deeper analysis, this discussion may be extrapolated more broadly to apply to other Indigenous peoples.

Second, I want to examine one exemplar of Indigenous democracy: that of the historic and present-day Gitxsan society from northwest British Columbia. My basic contention is that, while not perfect, historic Gitxsan democracy is an example of intense democracy, a far more politically inclusive form of governance than the current model of what is perhaps the worst form of representative democracy imposed through colonization with the federal *Indian Act.*[11]

Finally, I want to apply Kirsten Rundle's articulation of Lon Fuller's legalities and relationships to Gitxsan governance in order to expand and develop other ways of thinking about and restating law and governances in Gitxsan society and, by extrapolation, in other Indigenous societies.[12] My intention here is to create another method, and an accompanying grammar, with which to analyze contemporary forms of Indigenous governance and some of the arising issues.

CANADIAN ABYSSAL THINKING

Modern Western thinking is abyssal thinking. It consists of a system of visible and invisible distinction, the invisible ones being the foundation of the visible ones. The invisible distinctions are established through radical lines that divide social reality into two realms, the realm of "this side of the line" and the realm of the "other side of the line". The division is such that "the other side of the line" vanishes . . .

What fundamentally characterizes abyssal thinking is thus the impossibility of the co-presence of the two sides of the line. To the extent that it prevails, this side of

---

[9] The Gitxsan were one of the plaintiff groups in the seminal title court action, *Delgamuukw* v. *British Columbia* [1997] 3 SCR 1010. The other plaintiff group was the Wet'suwet'en.

[10] de Sousa Santos, "Beyond Abyssal Thinking," 1.   [11] *Indian Act*, RSC 1985, c. I-5.

[12] Kirsten Rundle, "Fuller's Relationships," in "The Rule of Law and Democracy," ed. Hirohide Takikawa, special issue, *Archiv für Rechts- und Sozialphilosophie* 161 (2019): 17–37. Also helpful is Kirsten Rundle, *Forms Liberate: Reclaiming the Jurisprudence of Lon L. Fuller* (Oxford: Hart Publishing, 2012).

the line only prevails by exhausting the field of relevant reality. Beyond it, there is only nonexistence, invisibility, non-dialectical absence.[13]

In 2019, a northern Gitxsan group invited me to attend one of their negotiating meetings with federal and provincial negotiators.[14] Rather than taking the usual course of litigating for a declaration of Aboriginal title from a Canadian court, these Gitxsan were instead negotiating for a declaration of their Aboriginal title over their historical lands with the provincial and federal governments.[15] My role was to describe Gitxsan law and political ordering, how it worked, and how it constituted a valid form of democracy. Within this conceptualization of democracy, specifically Gitxsan democracy, "Citizenship is not a status given by the institutions of the modern constitutional state and international law, but negotiated practices in which one becomes a citizen through participation."[16]

This Gitxsan group was comprised of representatives from their own historic political and legal system rather than the band council as set up under the *Indian Act*.[17] Hence, these Gitxsan people were the chiefs, wing chiefs, and members of the historic Gitxsan matrilineal kinship groups, the huwilp,[18] commonly known in English as the House.[19] I will expand further on Gitxsan political and legal ordering, and its operation in what follows.

The problem was that the federal and provincial negotiators were having great difficulty seeing and comprehending Gitxsan democracy as legitimate political and legal forms of ordering. Instead, the federal and provincial negotiators expressed concern about what they perceived as the lack or deficit of Gitxsan democracy because Gitxsan people did not hold elections to vote for their House chiefs or wing chiefs – past or present. What they failed to see was a society that Richard Overstall describes as being formed by threads of kinship

---

[13] Santos, "Beyond Abyssal Thinking," 1.

[14] Over the years, many Indigenous and non-Indigenous scholars have written extensively about Canada's colonial past, so I do not take that up here. For example, see generally, the various and numerous works of John Borrows, Gordon Christie, Kent McNeil, Patricia Monture, Paul Chartrand, Jeff Corntassel, Kiera Ladner, and Shiri Pasternak.

[15] This session took place in Victoria, British Columbia. Over two days, there were about twenty Gitxsan people in attendance, and eight to ten federal and provincial representatives.

[16] James Tully, *Public Philosophy in a New Key*, vol. 2, *Imperialism and Civic Freedom* (Cambridge: Cambridge University Press, 2008), 248.

[17] Indigenous peoples in Canada have always been creative and pragmatic about the *Indian Act* and have pushed for incremental changes as one way to increase local authorities. See, for example, Naiomi Metallic, "Indian Act By-Laws: A Viable Means for First Nations to (Re)Assert Control over Local Matters Now and Not Later," *UNB Law Journal* 67 (2016): 211–34.

[18] Every Gitxsan is born into their mother's House (*wilp*). *Huwilp* is the plural form. Houses are associations of related lineages with the mutually agreed ability to manage property, including resources and territories. See Richard Overstall, "Tsimshian Power Point" [unpublished, archived with the author].

[19] The English term "House" derives from the former long house. Historically, the long houses included House members as well as their spouses, and as the Gitxsan are exogamous, the spouses would have been from a different clan.

and threads of contract which "weave a complex legal and social fabric."[20] Gitxsan law and political ordering constitute and are constituted by these threads, the warp and woof, the fundamental structure of Gitxsan society. Ralph Waldo Emerson has aptly and beautifully commented that the "Old and new make the warp and woof of every moment. There is no thread that is not a twist of these two strands."[21]

According to the federal and provincial negotiators, this absence of elections and voting in Gitxsan society violated the democratic rights of Canadian citizens under the *Canadian Charter of Rights and Freedoms*,[22] specifically the following:

3. Every citizen of Canada has the right to vote in an election of members of the House of Commons or of a legislative assembly and to be qualified for membership therein.
4. (1) No House of Commons and no legislative assembly shall continue for longer than five years from the date fixed for the return of the writs at a general election of its members.

The imperative of the federal and provincial negotiators was simple: Gitxsan people are Canadian citizens so there must be Gitxsan elections so they can vote for their chiefs and wing chiefs in the future. A failure to provide such elections for Gitxsan people would violate their democratic rights as per the *Charter of Rights and Freedoms*. The experience of the Gitxsan in these frustrating negotiations brings to mind the inspiring work of James Tully:

At the end of the day, therefore, what keeps the imperial network going and the structural relationships of domination in their background place, is nothing more (or less) than the activities of powerfully situated actors to resist, contain, roll-back and circumscribe the uncontainable democratizing negotiations and confrontations of civic citizens in a multiplicity of local nodes.[23]

The federal and provincial negotiators also expressed concern about the Gitxsan discriminating against each other and against non-Gitxsan if they did not explicitly recognize and incorporate other rights and freedoms as set out in the *Canadian Charter of Rights and Freedoms*. Additionally, the federal and provincial negotiators expressed their discomfort about potential Gitxsan violations of human rights as per federal and provincial legislation, though they provided no examples except the lack of elections.

---

[20] Overstall, "Tsimshian Power Point."
[21] Ralph Waldo Emerson, *Collected Works of Ralph Waldo Emerson*, vol. 7, *Society and Solitude*, ed. Alfred R. Ferguson, Jean Ferguson Carr, and Douglas Emery Wilson (Charlottesville, VA: InteLex Corporation, 2008), 86.
[22] Part I of the *Constitution Act*, 1982, being Schedule B to the *Canada Act* (UK), 1982, c. 11.
[23] James Tully, *On Global Citizenship: James Tully in Dialogue* (London: Bloomsbury, 2014), 73.

From what mindset was the federal and provincial operating? How might they understand the logics of their role and position as they met with Gitxsan? Lawyer and legal historian Richard Overstall offers this insight:

One of the invisibilities for the federal negotiators is how their adherence to representative democracy is moulded and blinded by path dependence. This concept argues that present options for political, economic and technological acts are constrained by prior decisions and history. ... For representative democracy, as performed in post-colonial Canada, it may be useful to see how its predecessor English institutions came in to being. ... The representative democracy path thus retain its origins of supreme executive and legislative power backed by a compliant bureaucracy and a monopoly of legitimate violence, albeit with the possibility every four years or so of a popular vote between two or three very similar groups of executives and legislators.[24]

These 2019 negotiations were yet another effort on the part of the Gitxsan to address the continual "path dependant"[25] demands of the state. Over the years, when descriptions and explanations of their legal and political ordering fell on deaf ears, this Gitxsan group pragmatically created new structures and instruments intended to somehow meld the Gitxsan matrilineal kinship system with representative Canadian democracy and governance structures. These pragmatic responses have meant that the Gitxsan, and other Indigenous peoples, have their own historic legal and political institutions as well as contemporary legal and political institutions. Despite contradictions between the past and present institutions, both historic and contemporary law and political authorities continue to operate through them. This is a situation that generates ongoing problems and internal conflicts, with the basic result of undermining and delegitimizing Gitxsan governance and law.[26]

So, how might de Sousa Santos' abyssal thinking be helpfully applied to the Gitxsan? Boaventura de Sousa Santos is writing about the Western tension between social regulation and social emancipation, and the visible foundation beneath metropolitan societies and the invisible foundation beneath colonial territories. Again, according to de Sousa Santos, the "intensely visible

[24] Richard Overstall, private correspondence, May 17, 2020. According to Overstall, "If we were to start, for example, in early medieval times, we would see kinship-based, community-centred social and economic networks regulated by legal orders not unlike those in indigenous societies today. Then came marauding Vikings forcing the various petty kingdoms to cooperate in a coordinated defence network. The attendant taxation and military service requirement led to a centralised bureaucracy and a warrior aristocracy with a supreme monarch and war leader. The aristocracy then had the power to coerce appropriate common lands to their private property, abolish, and later criminalise, community access rights (customary law) to pastures and forests, and drive the peasantry from their communities. Over the next few centuries, political power was wrested from the monarch, then the aristocracy, then the property-owners, and then the men. The common law, however, continues to emphasise protection of private property above the common welfare."
[25] Ibid.
[26] I have written about this elsewhere. See, for example, Val Napoleon, "Legal Pluralism and Reconciliation," *Māori Law Journal* (2019): 1–22.

distinctions structuring social reality on this side of the line are grounded in the invisibility of the distinction between this side of the line and the other side."[27] What is visible to the federal and provincial negotiators is the Canadian state complete with its own forms of political, legal, and economic institutions – and all that created these legitimacies and institutions – histories, power, and corresponding narratives. The colonial ideology of this imaginary "exhausts" anything beyond itself because its very definition is a denial of other legitimacies.

In turn, what remains invisible to the federal and provincial negotiators are the Gitxsan political, legal, and economic institutions – and all that created these legitimacies and institutions – histories, power, and corresponding narratives. Through their interactions with the Gitxsan, the federal and provincial negotiators maintain and uphold their visible universe while denying and erasing that which comprises Gitxsan society, past and present, unless it is recognizable and cognizant to state forms. In effect, the federal and provincial negotiators are "policing the boundaries of relevant knowledge," thereby wasting the "immense wealth of cognitive experiences" of the Gitxsan.[28] This colonial policing is strengthened by the abyssal incommensurability strategy, wherein that which is beyond the Canadian state is simply characterized as incommensurable, as well as deficient and inferior.[29]

Boaventura de Sousa Santos argues that the "first condition for post-abyssal thinking is radical co-presence. Radical co-presence means that the practices and agents on both sides of the line are contemporary in equal terms."[30] Creating this condition for the Gitxsan means comprehensively restating and articulating their own society – complete with institutions, law, economies, polities, histories, knowledges, and meaning-holding/creating narratives. Radical copresence means that the federal and provincial representatives expand their abilities to imagine, see, and appreciate other expressions of law, political participation, and inclusion. This simple solution means first understanding one's own limitations and then deliberately developing a shared standard for evidence because, as political philosopher Michael Blake writes, "When there is no shared standard for evidence, then people who disagree with us are not really making claims about a shared world of evidence. They are doing something else entirely; they are declaring their political allegiance or moral worldview [in the absence of shared evidence]."[31]

---

[27] de Sousa Santos, "Beyond Abyssal Thinking," 2.   [28] Ibid., 16.

[29] Ibid. I have argued elsewhere that incommensurability is a colonial story. See Hadley Friedland and Val Napoleon, "Gathering the Threads: Indigenous Legal Methodology," *Lakehead Law Journal* 33, no. 1 (2015): 17–44.

[30] de Sousa Santos, "Beyond Abyssal Thinking," 11.

[31] Michael Blake, "Why Bullshit Hurts Democracy More Than Lies," *The Conversation*, May 14, 2018, http://theconversation.com/why-bullshit-hurts-democracy-more-than-lies-96331.

Arguably, abyssal thinking has become a part of neocolonialism, as is evidenced by the public claims that the "government is failing to defend the democratic rights of First Nations communities to resist their hereditary leaders."[32] Abuses of power and corruption, along with the promise and failure of law, are the stuff of world history and are also recorded in Indigenous oral histories. These are reasonable collective struggles for Indigenous peoples but are only manageable when their legal orders are intact, complete with accountability, political inclusion, fairness, and legitimate processes. However, what unfortunately happens is that the media, the state, and others opportunistically pick up on Indigenous conflicts only to reduce them to their simplest parts, and, further, polarize these into, for example, hereditary leadership versus elected band councils.

These kinds of political dichotomies are a failure of basic civility where collective and legitimate processes of reason are not applied because Indigenous legal orders have been undermined.[33] For change to occur and for radical copresence to be possible, the Gitxsan requires global cognitive justice, enabled by no less than a new kind of post-abyssal thinking.[34]

GITXSAN DEMOCRACY

How are Gitxsan democracy and law invisible to Canada according to de Sousa Santos' abyssal thinking paradigm? In the next section, I explore one historic narrative to begin making visible Gitxsan resources for thinking about citizenship and democracy as the first step to radical copresence.[35] What is important to this narrative exploration is that citizenship and intense democracy are evident and operating within two nonstate societies: the Gitxsan and the Nisga'a.[36] This narrative was told by John Brown (Kwiyaihl) from the Gitxsan village of Kispiox and recorded by early anthropologist Marius Barbeau in 1920.[37] Oral histories are one form of the intellectual property owned by the Gitxsan and are further explained later in the chapter. While reading the narrative, keep in mind that access and the extensive trade system were essential to both the Nisga'a and Gitxsan economies.

---

[32] Robert Jago, "Canada's Hollow Concern for First Nations Democracy," *The Walrus*, July 19, 2019, https://thewalrus.ca/canadas-hollow-concern-for-first-nations-democracy.

[33] For a discussion about the loss of civility and its consequence, see Napoleon, "Indigenous Civility."

[34] de Sousa Santos, "Beyond Abyssal Thinking," 1.

[35] For further information on this methodology, see Friedland and Napoleon, "Gathering"; and Hadley Friedland and Val Napoleon, "An Inside Job: Engaging with Indigenous Legal Traditions through Stories," *McGill Law Journal* 61, no. 4 (2016): 725–54

[36] The Gitxsan and Nisga'a are from the Tsimshian linguistic group located on the north coast of British Columbia.

[37] George F. MacDonald and John J. Cove, *Tsimshian Narratives 2: Trade and Warfare* (Ottawa: Canadian Museum of Civilization, 1987), 164.

A Peace Ceremony Between the Nisga'a and the Kisgegas

The people from the Nisga'a Nass Valley and the people from Gitxsan village of Kisgegas had made friends. This peace agreement was broken when Meluleq, the [Frog][38] chief of Kisgegas killed Tsastawrawn, a Nisga'a. Wiraix [Wolf], also from Kisgegas, murdered another Nisga'a named Guxmawen. In retaliation, a Nisga'a murdered Kwisema. For a long time, the Kisgegas did not go to the Nass Valley.

The Nisga'a sent word to the Kisgegas that they wanted to make friends and [they proposed a Gawaganii (Gitxsan term), or Peace Ceremony].[39] When they arrived, there was a large party of them. The Kisgegas gathered together to meet them. They had invited people from [the Gitxsan villages of] Kispiox and Gitanmaax. The Nisga'a feast party camped just above Kisgegas village.

Meluleq was ready for the ceremonies, and he stripped himself naked to meet his guests. Wiraix did the same. Tsenshoot followed their example, as well as Guxmawen.[40] All this for meeting one another. The flies were very bad at that time of the year, but they did not [show that they minded] them. They did not even brush them away, although they could hardly endure them.

One of the Nisga'a said, "This is the last day for your village!"

Wiraix answered, "You have entered the Wolves' mouths. You won't be alive tomorrow."

Tsenshoot spoke to Meluleq, "You won't see the sun tomorrow. This is the last time you will look at the sun!"

Meluleq answered, "The crows and the animals will eat your flesh. You make me angry now!"

The Kisgegas gathered and built a barricade with big trees in front of their village and they built another barricade in front of the Nisga'a [camp]. They put the barricade across to show that the Nisga'a were not to pass beyond it. If one of the Nisga'a went beyond this barricade, those on the opposite side would kill him. The same with the Kisgegas: if they went beyond their barricade, they would be destroyed. Then the Kisgegas went back to their houses, and the Nisga'a went back to their camp.

The Gitxsan fired off blank cartridges, only powder, without bullets in their guns. The Nisga'a did likewise.

Then the Kisgegas sang songs, and they sang a peace song. The Nisga'a also sang peace songs. The Kisgegas blew white swan-down on the heads of the Nisga'a, and, in turn, the Nisga'a did the same to them. They composed a song

---

[38] Meluleq is erroneously listed as a Wolf Chief in the MacDonald and Cove publication; ibid. Thanks to Richard Overstall for catching this error.

[39] In the McDonald and Cove publication (ibid.,) Gawaganii is incorrectly spelled as Hawaagyan. Again, I am grateful to Richard Overstall's detailed knowledge.

[40] While the former Guxmawen was killed, the name Guxmawen would have been given to the next person in line for it.

about the peace, the words of which were that they were making peace. This was a peace performance.

In the evening, the invited Nisga'a guests arrived at the village and the Kisgegas allowed them to come forward. The Nisga'a gathered on one side of the village. Two people were delegated for the peace performance. Guxmawen did not come in person but he sent his daughter on his behalf; she stood in his stead. The other was Tsemshoot, also Nisga'a.

All the Kisgegas came out of their houses. No one had dangerous weapons, only sticks and their hands. The Nisga'a hit some Kisgegas, and the Kisgegas hit the Nisga'a with their hands and with the sticks. Both Tsemshoot and Guxmawen's daughter had sticks and they kept waving these around until they were both captured. The Kisgegas captors covered Tsemshoot and Guxmawen's daughter with a caribou hides and took them prisoner. Then the mock fighting stopped.

They all sang the song that they had composed during the night about making peace, with the words about how they were to make peace. Then everyone entered the houses. Tsemshoot was taken to Meluleq's house and there were two men to guard him. While Tsemshoot stood, they placed caribou skins all along the house for him to walk on until he got to the back of the house. A very big caribou skin was spread out and they on this they piled many pillows for Tsemshoot to sit on. It was a great seat for him. They piled trade blankets to about four feet high. When he wanted water, the guards brought it to him.

They did the same for Guxmawen's daughter, and she was seated at the back of Wiraix's house. Two men of noble birth stood on each side of her to guard and watch her. The whole village gave a grand feast. The Kisgegas gave many furs to all the Nisga'a: beaver, marten, caribou, and fisher pelts. The Nisga'a went back to their camp with a bundle of various skins given them by different Kisgegas.

In the morning, the Nisga'a gave their dance. Those performing in the Peace Ceremony were not given food. That was the rule. Nobody in the song or dance was allowed to eat for one day. After they fasted for one day, the very best food was prepared and passed around. The bodyguards of Tsenshoot and Guxmanwen's daughter had also fasted, so they were led to the food too, and they ate to their satisfaction.

The dance lasted for four days in one of the largest houses in the village. Then four men led the prisoners to that house. They were seated at the back of that house for the last big dance. The Nisga'a sat on one side, and the Gisgegas on the other. The Nisga'a danced until midday, and they picked out four of the best men and placed them on seats of honor.

Meluleq took a white tail feather of an eagle and dipped it in blood so that one half turned red. He gave this feather to Tsenshoot, placing it in his hand.

Waraix did the same with Guxmawen's daughter. They got the very best white handkerchief from the white man's store and wrapped her hand in it, and on her head, he planted two swan's feathers that he got from the Nass.

The villagers got ready before the Nisga'a could leave them. They gave the Nisga'a a farewell dance, dancing behind them until they were out of sight. The Nisga'a also danced as they were on their way homewards. They sang a song in the Sekani language, advising them that they would enjoy peace with them forever. The Kisgegas gave the Nisga'a a song, and the Nisga'a gave the Kisgegas another song.

Then they went back with them to the Nass. Tsenshoot took one of the swan's feathers and returned it to Meluleq before returning to his own people. This was a sign of deep friendship that was interpreted with the words "I have given you peace and friendship for years to come." Guxmawen's daughter said the same words to Wiraix. The Peace Ceremony was over.

Analysis

As we turn to the analysis of the above narrative, John Borrows provides an important reminder to not idealize Indigenous peoples.

We need such laws *not only* because we are good people with life-affirming values and behaviours. We also require these laws because we are "messed up". Indigenous law must be practiced in the real world with all its complexity. . . . Law does not just flow from what is beautiful in Anishinaabe or Canadian life. Law also springs from conflict. It emerges from our responses to real-life needs, which are often rooted in violence, abuse, exploitation, dishonesty, political corruption, and other self-serving and destructive behaviours.[41]

The Peace Ceremony is a complicated oral history and it would be easy to get lost in its detail and in our own responses to difference – those aspects that are beyond our own terms of reference and experience. Given this, it is important to be specific about the question one is asking of the narratives, stories, or oral histories.[42] To center this analysis on questions of governance and to inform my discussion of Gitxsan democracy, the question I am asking of this narrative is: *How should one respond to a violent rupture of a long-term political relationship with a neighboring people?* And since this analysis is about nonstate democracy, the "who" and "why" of responding to this rupture of arrangement between neighboring peoples are significant.

There are a number of basic elements that are relevant to the question I am asking of the narrative, and I have highlighted these here for ease of reference.

- The Gitxsan and the Nisga'a are neighboring peoples, their lands are adjacent. The two peoples had "made friends," suggesting they had not always enjoyed peace, but their relationship was peaceful at the onset of the narrative.
- This peaceful relationship was disrupted by three murders: (1) Gitxsan Meluleq killed Nisga'a Tsastawrawn, (2) Gitxsan Wiraix killed Nisga'a Guxmawen, and (3) A Nisga'a (unnamed) killed Gitxsan Kwisema.

---

[41] John Borrows, *Law's Indigenous Ethics* (Toronto: University of Toronto Press, 2019), 239.
[42] See Friedland and Napoleon, "Gathering"; and Friedland and Napoleon, "An Inside Job."

- Consequently, the Gitxsan did not travel to the Nass Valley for a long time.
- The Nisga'a requested a return to peace, and they initiated a peace.
- The Nisga'a traveled to Kisgegas, and they made a camp just above Kisgegas village.
- The Kisgegas invited other Gitxsan from the villages of Gitanmaax and Kispiox.
- Meluleq and Wiraix prepared by stripping themselves naked to meet their Nisga'a guests. In turn, Nisga'a Tsenshoot and Guxmawen also stripped in order to meet with the Gitxsan. Without clothing, everyone suffered terribly because of the bad blackfly season, and they "did not show that they minded."
- Both Nisga'a and Gitxsan traded insults, the Gitxsan built two barricades, and both sides fired blanks at the other.
- Both sides sang peace songs, and they blew white swan feathers on each other. A new peace song was composed.
- Two Nisga'a were delegated for the Peace Ceremony: one was Guxmawen's daughter and the other Tsemshoot.
- The Gitxsan and the Nisga'a armed themselves with sticks, and then they hit each other using only their hands and the sticks. Guxmawen's daughter and Tsemshoot also had sticks which they waved around until they were 'captured'.
- Guxmawen's daughter and Tsemshoot were separately taken to different longhouses, they were covered in caribou hides, and more caribou hides were placed on the earth for them to walk on to the back of the longhouse. Additional trade blankets were piled high, many pillows were placed for them to sit on, and guards of noble birth watched them and tended to their needs.
- Kisgegas gave a big feast and different Kisgegas gave many furs of all kinds to the Nisga'a. Those who were part of the Peace Ceremony fasted.
- The next morning, the Nisga'a performed their dance, then those who had fasted were fed.
- The dance lasted four days, then the 'prisoners' were brought to the longhouse for the last dance.
- The Kisgegas were seated on one side, the Nisga'a on the other. Four 'best' Nisga'a were placed in the seats of honor.
- Meluleq took a white tail feather, dipped it in blood so that half of the feather was red. He gave this feather to Tsemshoot. Waraix did the same with Guxmawen's daughter.
- Waraix also wrapped Guxmawen's daughter's hand in a white man's handkerchief, and then he placed two white swan feathers in her hair (the feathers were from the Nass).

- The Kisgegas gave the Nisga'a a farewell dance, and they danced behind the Nisga'a as they left for the Nass Valley. The Nisga'a also danced on their way home.
- The Kisgegas gave the Nisga'a a song, and the Nisga'a gave the Kisgegas a song.
- Tsenshoot gave Meluleq one of the swan feathers back, and pledged peace and friendship for years to come. Guxmawen's daughter did the same with Wiraix.

This is a rich and perhaps deceptively simple narrative. For this analysis, there are two main legal responses to the question I have posed to this narrative: (1) the Nisga'a decided to restore peace by initiating a Peace Ceremony, and (2) the Gitxsan accepted the invitation to restore peace and to host the Peace Ceremony .

For the most part, the reasoning for these two legal responses is implicit rather than explicit. What is at the heart of this narrative is that the relationship between the Nisga'a and Gitxsan was important and had previously been restored and maintained, and this was the continuing primary response. The valuable gifting of a name, songs, and dances are all very precious as well as structural for each people's governing institutions. These gifts also comprise part of the intellectual property for both peoples, and their inclusion for the Peace Ceremony indicates the paramountcy of peace between the two peoples. The relationship between the Gitxsan and Nisga'a enabled trade, territorial access, and travel, all of which were managed through carefully arranged marriages and lineages. Restoring relationships usually requires accepting responsibility for harms and compensation. The Gitxsan acknowledged their responsibility for the events leading to the Peace Ceremony and they paid compensation in the form of the furs and feasting. The Nisga'a accepted their responsibility for reacting to violence with violence by initiating the Peace Ceremony and by gifting the Gitxsan with a name and a song.

However, there is so much more going on in this rich narrative that provides important insights into how people were managing themselves and the conflict. As the first step, both the Nisga'a and the Gitxsan accepted responsibility for the conflict and for its resolve – individually and collectively. Secondly, key individuals from both parties made themselves completely vulnerable (naked) and transparent (no weapons) to the other. Third, both sides exercised exquisite physical, emotional, and mental discipline in the mock battle of fake bullets, sticks, and hands. All the parties would have been extraordinarily careful to not accidentally injure one another in their physical demonstration of war and their implicit acknowledgment of its ultimate possibility.

Fourth, the songs, names, and dances are all legal expressions and ongoing performative requirements for the public feast (the main legal, economic, and political institution for both the Gitxsan and Nisga'a), and continue to be performed by Tsenshoot, Guxmawen, Meluleq, and Wiraix, and others to this day. In this way, for both the Nisga'a and Gitxsan, the Peace Ceremony continues to be inscribed with legal and political meaning, becoming part of an ongoing public memory and part of the precedent record from which to draw from for solving future conflicts.

Finally, both the Gitxsan and Nisga'a had to have had the political and legal authority to act on behalf of their respective Houses to have initiated this major inter-societal event and for it to be recorded in the oral histories and for it to shape the ongoing relationship between the peoples. The songs, dances, and names form the architecture (i.e. the warp and woof) of Gitxsan decentralized governance, and they also hold articulations of law. What is invisible in the narrative, and in the enactment of the respective political and legal authorities, are the discussions, disagreements, and consent that would have taken place prior to the Peace Ceremony. Many, many people, all legal agents to the fullest extent themselves, were necessary to make the Peace Ceremony possible: preparing enormous quantities of food (i.e. gathering, hunting, fishing, etc.), hunting and preparing the hides and furs, enacting the mock battle, creating and performing the songs and dances, and formal witnessing of the entire process for future recall.

The Peace Ceremony narrative stands for many things, including the human potential for violence, and the continuing need for individual and collective agency in rebuilding, maintaining, and protecting relationships between peoples. There are also some elements that raise questions that can generate more discussion and learning. For instance, why did the Nisga'a sing a Sekani song? Likely it would have been a gift from the Sekani, and the narrative captures this detail to emphasize the importance of relationships with other neighboring peoples. Another question is about Guxmawen traveling to Kisgegas, but not participating in the Peace Ceremony. Instead, his daughter[43] participated in the Peace Ceremony on his behalf, and likely this would have been related to a saving-of-face requirement for Guxmawen. The richness is that these and other questions can be explored in future conversations in a way that ensures that law is part of people's everyday lives – in a way that generates questions rather than focuses on answers.

GITXSAN RELATIONSHIPS

[This is] a starting point for a new kind of inquiry into the relational dimensions of contemporary conditions of the rule of law. Three key ideas from Fuller's juris-prudence are reflected ... The first is the centrality of relationships. The second is

---

[43] The Gitxsan and Nisga'a are both matrilineal so Guxmawen's daughter would have been in a different House than her father. This may be why her name was not recorded, but that is unclear from this published version of this narrative. It is also unclear as to whether she was the daughter of the first Guxmawen or the second, but for the purposes of this analysis, nothing turns on that question.

the significance of the form of a relevant legal modality to the shape and fate of those relationships. The third is the possibility that certain legal forms will, for relational reasons, be unsuited to the contexts within which they might come to operate.[44]

With this brief introduction to Gitxsan society, I want to bring the relationships that create Gitxsan society into focus. To begin, the Gitxsan are a nonstate, decentralized society wherein political and legal authorities are distributed and acted on horizontally between matrilineal kinship groups of extended families – the House – within which there are reciprocal legal obligations.[45] This is an exogamous system, so each person's father's House is a part of a different clan with separate responsibilities to each Gitxsan citizen. The Gitxsan legal, political, and economic orders operate through these dense networks of kinship ties. Each individual Gitxsan person is a legal agent within her or his House. Beyond the House, which is relationally autonomous,[46] it is the House that is the collective legal agent in all external interactions with other Houses and with the larger networks of clans and inter-societal alliances.

House chief 'names' are part of the House's governing structure and intellectual property, and are the form through which House territories and other property are held in trust. The authority of a House chief depends on the fulfillment of the House's legal and political obligations through the entire system. Without centralized and hierarchical bureaucracies, Gitxsan society is maintained by a series of stabilizing tensions created by an absolute requirement to cooperate and a deep corresponding ethic of competition and autonomy – from the individual to the larger kinship levels. For example, the authority and ability of the House chief to fulfill her or his larger legal obligations depends on the willing economic contributions and labor of each member. However, since a person's House membership operates as a placeholder rather than locking people in, members can choose to align themselves elsewhere in the system, thereby causing a significant economic loss to the House chief and the House.[47]

Liability in this system is collective. For example, a person is responsible to their House for their actions, but it is the House that is liable for that individual's actions in the larger network. Furthermore, injuries caused by individuals are also collective, so if someone is injured, the entire House is considered injured and there is consequent collective liability and

---

[44] Rundle, "Fuller's Relationships," 24.

[45] I lived and worked in Gitxsan lands with Gitxsan peoples for more than two decades, and my doctoral work was on Gitxsan law and developing a Gitxsan legal theory: Val Napoleon, "Ayook: Gitksan Legal Order, Law, and Legal Theory" (DPhil Law thesis, University of Victoria, 2009), 91 [unpublished, archived with author].

[46] See, generally, Jennifer Nedelsky, *Law's Relations: A Relational Theory of Self, Autonomy, and Law* (Oxford: Oxford University Press, 2011).

[47] An individual may be adopted into a different House, or they may simply align their labor and wealth to another House.

compensation. Admittedly, this is a gross simplification of a complex society, but it nonetheless contains the essence of how the kinship network operates throughout Gitxsan society. It is this complex of legal, economic, and political ordering that is the basis of Gitxsan citizenship and democracy – mutually constituting and fluid with Gitxsan citizens – as individual and collective agents, accountable to and responsible for the maintenance of the larger whole.

To return to Rundle's relationship theory, she argues that relationships and their demands were necessary to and constituted Lon Fuller's legalities, and, further, that a society's institutional forms have carriage for those relationships because they hold the "responsibilities and opportunities for the authority of law itself."[48] According to Rundle, Fuller's jurisprudence applies to all governing relationships, not just to a state's legislative function. This insight frees Rundle's analysis from being state-centric and releases its potential application to nonstate societies such as the Gitxsan.

Rundle's theory advocates the centrality of relationships to a society's legal order and its constituting legalities.[49] Gitxsan society is entirely constructed of individual and collective relationships, kinship networks through which Gitxsan law and governance operate and are collaboratively managed. Each individual legal agent has responsibilities to their kinship network, and they have the ability to exercise choice and accountability in how they align themselves and contribute to the collective.[50] This kind of relational accountability, operating at individual and collective levels, constitutes a form of intense democracy, or what Christine Keating calls "fullest democracy."[51]

The second theme of Rundle's relationship theory concerns the "significance of the form of a relevant legal modality to the shape and fate of those relationships."[52] The paramount political and legal unit within Gitxsan society is the House, which is organized matrilineally, and, at least historically, the size of the House allowed for face-to-face interaction of all House members within each House.[53] These kinship relations are crosscutting, extending beyond the matrilineal families, clans, and villages, and also connecting to other peoples such as the Nisga'a, Haida, Tsimshian, Wet'suwet'en, and beyond. In this way, they are the relational filament weaving the largest

---

[48] Rundle, "Fuller's Relationships," 19.   [49] Napoleon, "Ayook," 24.

[50] Collectively, members can remove names from House chiefs who fail to fulfill their responsibilities. See ibid.

[51] Christine Keating, *Decolonizing Democracy: Transforming the Social Contract in India* (Pennsylvania: Pennsylvania State University Press, 2011), 108.

[52] Rundle, "Fuller's Relationships," 24.

[53] Overstall, "Tsimshian Power Point." Historically, the Houses that did not have enough women and girls would shrink in size, meaning that the unit would have great difficulty upholding its legal, political, and economic obligations to the land, the House, and to other Houses. The options would be to adopt women and girls from other Houses or combine with another House for as long as their numbers were low.

political collectivity – that of the society – but are also building important political, legal, and economic connections to other peoples. Gitxsan democracy, then, captures Gitxsan people within its nonstate procedural grasp and collective coercive power, as demonstrated by the Peace Ceremony.[54]

Finally, Rundle's theory includes the possibility that certain legal forms will, for relational reasons, be unsuited to the contexts within which they might come to operate.[55] As mentioned earlier, colonialism in Canada included the *Indian Act*, which set out the imposed structure and procedures for electing small, representative administrative entities. This colonial process included dividing larger societies of Indigenous peoples into small groups that were geographically pinned on reserves as per the *Indian Act* and the *Constitution Act, 1867*.[56] The consequence of imposing this particular form of representative democracy has been devastating to Gitxsan ordering, where former historic political and legal accountability crossed village boundaries and extended over the entirety of Gitxsan lands. In short, the larger legal order has been fractured into six small reserves, and has undermined the historic political and legal institutions of Gitxsan society. This is the very embodiment of de Sousa Santos' assertion that "Democracies are dying democratically,"[57] but in this case, it is the attempted murder of intense Gitxsan democracy 'democratically' via colonial legislation and by agreement. Nonetheless, the Gitxsan are still the Gitxsan, but now are struggling with conflicts arising from the imposed governing structures and diminishment of the Gitxsan legal order.[58]

CONCLUSION

When Cree legal scholar Darcy Lindberg analogized the universe to law, he wrote that one must learn to see all the stars in the universe because all the stars matter.[59] These other legal orders, institutions, and law are rendered invisible by the Canadian state's grid of intelligibility. Given this, the project of creating radical copresence means adding to the national legal imagination and expanding the Canadian grid of intelligibility. This work, for Indigenous peoples, including the Gitxsan, means substantively and procedurally articulating Gitxsan law and legal institutions to support the practice of

---

[54] Blake, *Talking Philosophy*.   [55] Rundle, "Fuller's Relationships," 24.
[56] *Constitution Act, 1867*, RSC 1985, Appendix II, No. 5.
[57] de Sousa Santos, "The Crises of Democracy."
[58] I have written about this elsewhere. See, for example, Val Napoleon, "Aboriginal Self Determination: Individual Self and Collective Selves," *Atlantis: A Women's Studies Journal* 29, no. 2 (2005): 31–46; and Val Napoleon, "Living Together: Gitksan Legal Reasoning as a Foundation for Consent" in *Between Consenting Peoples: Political Community and the Meaning of Consent*, ed. Jeremy Webber and Colin McLeod (Vancouver: UBC Press, 2010), 45–76.
[59] Darcy Lindberg, "Brain Tanning and Shut Eye Dancing: Recognizing Legal Resources within Cree Ceremonies" (2016) [unpublished, archived with author].

Gitxsan law. All the attendant questions have to be worked out while doing the research and in the actual practice of Gitxsan law.

The image in Figure 11.1 captures Lindberg's analogy and it illustrates the wonder of first seeing those formerly invisible stars.[60] This powerful image also embodies de Sousa Santos' abyssal thinking, wherein the visible is made visible by lifting the curtain of abyssal limitations, and, in doing so, that beyond the curtain can become copresent.

The challenge for the Gitxsan and other Indigenous peoples is to rebuild their legal orders by the hard work of critically and collaboratively rearticulating and restating their historic legal resources. This approach will enable Gitxsan peoples to restore the best practices of their former intense democracies, complete with inclusive and active citizenship, for today's political and legal negotiations, and self-determination and governance demands.

FIGURE 11.1 Cover of *L'atmosphère: Météorologie populaire*

---

[60] This image is the work of an unknown artist, printed in Camille Flammarion, *L'atmosphère: Météorologie populaire* (Paris, 1888), 163. It is on the front cover of Helge Dedek and Shauna Van Praagh, eds., *Stateless Law: Evolving Boundaries of a Discipline* (New York: Routledge, 2015).

In taking on the work of rebuilding and restating Indigenous law, we should not "overlook the concrete possibilities available for creative and effective negotiations and confrontations of civicisation and de-imperialism,"[61] or that "Another world is actual" not just possible: "Despite the devastating trends, another world of legal, political, ecological, and even economic diversity has survived and continues to be the loci of civic activities for millions of people."[62]

---

[61] Tully, *On Global Citizenship*, 73.   [62] Tully, *Public Philosophy*, 301.

Democratic Futures and the Problem of Settler States

An Essay on the Conceptual Demands of Democracy and the Need for Political Histories of Membership

Joshua Nichols

The future of democracy within settler states is, much like its past, radically contested, deeply complicated and ultimately uncertain. This fact is, in one sense, unsurprising. After all, the future of democracy has never been certain. Of the various forms of government possible within the Western world, democracy is the least stable. As a concept it refers simply to the rule of the *demos* (the common people).[1] That much is clear, but how are we to determine the boundaries of a people? Two possible methods spring to mind. We could adopt a territorial definition and thereby define membership by reference to boundaries that are set in relation with neighboring groups (*jus soli*). Alternatively, we could base the definition on a conventional set of rules for determining kinship. In this case membership becomes a function of recognized familial relationships (*jus sanguinis*). It is also possible to develop a mixed approach, but no matter the approach taken the selection is strictly *conventional*. In other words, the question of membership leaves democracy contested at its conceptual foundations – there simply is no a priori definition of *the* people.

This brings us to the next conceptual knot in democracy. If democracy is indeed the rule of the people, then the process for determining who is in and who is out needs to be broadly accepted and understood, as it is part and parcel of the authority structure within that social order. Put differently, in a democracy legal questions of membership are conceptually bound up with the question of both the legal process of determining membership and the justificatory practices that are used to legitimize those determinations. If we attempt to craft a legal process for determining membership without reference to the explanatory requirements

---

[1] I should note here that I am addressing the future of democracy within settler states that fit within the broad tradition of representative democracy. In this tradition there is a higher degree of tension placed on the identity of the *demos* as the authoritative body, and so the procedures and practices of legality and legitimacy must be connected to it.

of legitimacy (which are historically and contextually specific), then the outcome will be *normatively illegible* (viz. it will not be understood as a legitimate move within the constitutional order). If we reverse our approach and instead attempt to determine membership by reference to the explanatory requirements alone, then the outcome will be *legally illegible* (viz. it will not be received as a valid legal move within the constitutional order). If we attempt to see the relationship between legality and legitimacy as an either/or problem, then it seems that democracy is stranded on the horns of a dilemma between the semantics of formal legal rules and the pragmatics that enable one to make sense of actual social practices.

This dilemma is not inevitable, it is simply a product of approaching the relationship as being fundamentally disjunctive in nature. Seen through this lens, democracy is caught up in paradoxes of membership and authority that seem to leave us with little other choice than accepting the notion that legal authority is an act of *pure independence* (viz. commands made by an actor without correlative responsibility).[2] This idea of authority as *pure independence* is as incoherent as the idea of one player in a chess match being able to self-authorize their actions as a legitimate move in the game. This leaves us with little recourse but to appeal to some makeshift conceptual black-box to cover over the paradox of authority (viz. Kant's *thing-in-itself*). We can find our way out of this paradoxical dead end by reconsidering the relationship between legality and legitimacy. For example, the fundamental constitutional convention of "what touches all should be agreed to by all" (quod omnes tangit ab omnibus comprobetur, or q.o.t.) helpfully reminds us that *legality and legitimacy* are inextricably interconnected. This interconnection is also clearly reflected in the notion of freedom that Rousseau develops, which holds that "[o]bedience to a law one has prescribed for oneself is freedom."[3] It is possible to argue that that these examples set a standard of legitimacy that is practically unrealizable and

---

[2] Robert Brandom's discussion of Hegel's critique of Kant via the unhappy concept of Mastery is instructive on this point. See Robert B. Brandom, *A Spirit of Trust: A Reading of Hegel's Phenomenology* (Cambridge, MA: Harvard University Press, 2019), 313–52.

[3] This citation is from book 1, chapter 7 of Rousseau's *On the Social Contract*, and its logical structure is echoed again in Rousseau's definition of law in book 2, chapter 6. See Jean-Jacques Rousseau, "On the Social Contract," in *Basic Political Writings*, trans. Donald A. Cress (Indianapolis: Hackett, 1987), 151, 161. Kant attempted to jump over the question of legal foundations (viz. the actual source of laws) by bracketing the source of semantic content and highlighting the freedom of choosing the law as your own. This leaves him with an ultimately spooky and incoherent notion of the source of authority (viz. the thing-in-itself). Hegel retains the notion of freedom that Kant helpfully developed and moves from Kant's notion of individual autonomy to a social recognitive model. As Robert Brandom clearly explains in his masterful reading of the Phenomenology, "[t]he idea, central to modernity as Hegel conceives it, that normative attitudes are *instituted* by normative statuses, is the idea that statuses are to begin with merely *virtual*, as the *objects of attitudes* of attributing and acknowledging them, become *actual* when those attitudes are suitably situated in such complex constellation." Brandom, *A Spirit of Trust*, 313

so, if we adopt them, then no legal order could be taken as being legitimate. We are thus thrust back into paradox. But, here again we are jumping over the social process of judgment and evaluation and attempting to evaluate the relationship between semantics and pragmatics in the frictionless space of armchair reasoning. It is as if we had decided that the criterion for determining the validity of legal semantics is unquestioning pragmatic acceptance, which is as absurd as looking for a game that is entirely circumscribed by rules. Simply put, if we are to begin to make sense of democratic forms of government, then the relationship between legality and legitimacy cannot simply be ignored.

Two cases draw this point home. First, even if we assume that it is possible to satisfy the ideal foundational conditions set by the convention of q.o.t., the issue of membership must remain open. This is true by virtue of the simple fact that we have to account for the consent of those who are born into membership. If the question is treated as closed, then the foundational logic of the society changes from consent to historical convention by virtue of natural reproduction. There is thus a conceptual change that takes place from the foundational moment when the membership is constituted by their consent and its continuation by future generations whose consent is not relevant. If we rigidly maintain this position, we are immediately adrift in absurdities. It seems that in order to determine whether or not a given society is a democracy or not we would need to have a very clear picture of its founding moment. We would then set off in hunt of a foundational generation, but what kinds of records would we have at our disposal? How are we to interpret these records? Here again we find that our choices bristle with political significance. This problem is further magnified if we consider the fact that the notion of what counts as consent is also necessarily *conventional*. We thus have to consider the political and legal implications of how we determine what consent means. Is the requirement that consent is indicated once and for all in a written contract? Is it to be imputed by appeal to what rational actors would be bound to commit themselves to? Is it subject entirely to the ongoing and active consent of individual members? Each interpretation of consent is a *political decision* that leads us down very different constitutional paths.

Second, if we consider the actual historical foundations of presently existing states, we quickly see that none of them can resolve the problem of membership. The political history of their rules of membership is a motley assortment of legislation and explanatory conventions (viz. they are *representative democracies*). If we omit these histories, then we necessarily view the composition of the state as a mechanical result of the legal conventions that are currently practiced there. This external and descriptive method is akin to determining the number of chess pieces on the board by watching how the players move them. This will provide us with a count of the pieces, but it will tell us next to nothing about the actual rules of chess. H. L. A. Hart clearly and succinctly unpacks the limitations of this kind of external perspective in *The Concept of Law*:

If, however, the observer really keeps austerely to this extreme external point of view and does not give any account of the manner in which members of the group who accept the rules view their own regular behavior, his description of their life cannot be in terms of rules at all, and so not in the terms of rule-dependent notions of obligation or duty. Instead, it will be in terms of observable regularities of conduct, probabilities, and signs. For such an observer, deviations by a member of the group from normal conduct will be a sign that hostile reaction is likely to follow, and nothing more. His view will be like the view of one who, having observed the working of a traffic signal in a busy street for some time, limits himself to saying that when the light turns red there is a high probability that the traffic light will stop. He treats the light merely as a natural *sign that* people will behave in certain ways, as clouds are a *sign that* rain will come.[4]

A political history of membership provides us with the kind of internal perspectives that allow us to make *sense* of membership in actual states. That is, it allows us to go beyond the narrowly defined limits of external descriptions (and their guesswork in the fancy dress of "objectivity") and meaningfully make our way about in the hustle and bustle of everyday politics.

The everyday reality of settler states vividly demonstrates the need for a political history of membership. On the one hand, states such as Canada, New Zealand, Australia and the United States (to select only a few of the current descendants of the British Empire) are, like every other modern state, a conventionally constructed membership. But the conventions that led to Indigenous peoples being included as *minorities within* these states do not fit neatly within the confines of either the jus soli or jus sanguinis. The settler states acquired territories by defining the peoples they encountered as lacking the legal capacities necessary to be recognized as peoples. The territories of these states were thus acquired via a complicated mixture of practices of coercion (viz. racist legal fictions, unilateral assertions, force and fraud) as well as practices of consent (viz. treaty-making and multifarious practices of intersocietal law and governance). Simply put, Indigenous peoples did not contract into the settler states; they were conscripted into them. As a result, settler states have been left with no plausible explanation for this conscription. They have generally opted to respond by claiming that their legal authority is self-authorizing and unquestionable. This sets down a bright line between law and politics and situates the question of legitimacy squarely on the political side. This strategy of nonresponse (or nonjusticiability) has not resolved these conflicts. Rather, it has produced a body of jurisprudence whose doctrines, tests and principles are so painfully confused and convoluted that they simply cannot be understood as being consistent with the rest of constitutional law. In response to the incoherence of the law in this area, jurists in settler states have opted to

---

[4] H. L. A. Hart, *The Concept of Law*, 2nd ed. (Oxford: Oxford University Press, 1994), 89–90.

basically wall the area off by labeling it "sui generis." If this strategy were practically effective, then we would expect these sui generis legal areas to gradually slow down and eventually simply vanish, like some kind of vestigial limb, but the opposite has proven to be the case. In other words, the legalistic approach to the question of authority has failed to make any meaningful progress in resolving the foundational crisis of legitimacy that divides settler states and Indigenous peoples. The sui generis jurisprudence of Aboriginal law has continually expanded, taking us further and further down the rabbit-hole of self-constituting and self-authorizing authority. If we are going to work our way out of this crisis, we will need to start by retracing the steps that led us here.

How did we get to this point? During the long nineteenth century, each of the settler states developed complicated constitutional structures that featured categorically distinct forms of government. We can roughly divide these forms of government into two ideal types of membership, which have a wide variety of local and regional variations. First, there are those who are recognized by the government of the settler state as citizens and thereby governed by a system of rules that they have a say in making (viz. the constitutional structure was *normatively legible* to some of those operating within it). In practice, these representative democracies developed categorical distinctions in membership and these distinctions took their color from their context. Put somewhat differently, the legal pragmatics were subject, at least in part, to the local semantics of authority, but this authority was justified in relation to the modern standard of self-governing citizens. But these categorical unfreedoms are thus normatively legible only to the degree that the citizens find them to be so. Second, there are those who are unilaterally defined as "Indians" and governed by administrative commands backed by force. This form of government was *normatively illegible* to those who were subject to it because it was using formal legal mechanisms to recode their normative framework, or, to use the terminology of the time, to *civilize* the Indians. The first type of government fits within the broad confines of the concept of democracy (albeit its fit is uncomfortable due to the politics of determining the franchise), whereas the second openly contradicts it.

This feature is by no means exclusive to settler states. All states (indeed, all associations) are riven by *political histories* of the exclusion and oppression of so-called "minorities" and "aliens."[5] Where the uniqueness of the settler states first begins to show is in terms of degree. That is, while all states deal with conflicts arising from issues of membership (e.g. secession movements, overlapping claims to territory by neighboring states), within settler states the entirety of their claim to territory rests on the legal exclusion and/or diminishment of Indigenous peoples. As a result of this unique degree of pressure on the question of membership, settler states have developed

---

[5] I qualify the term "minorities" because this concept presumes that there is some account that makes group B necessarily a part of the larger group A.

extensive and complicated legal and political structures to meet this challenge. This difference of degree led them to develop vocabularies of law that were *different in kind*.

The categorical difference between these legal vocabularies is particularly important when we are trying to get a sense of what the futures of democracy could be at this particular moment in history. This means that the political histories of membership in settler states offer us a unique opportunity to gain some insight into the possible futures of democracy in nation-states. Put differently, the intense pressures on the question of membership in settler states have produced something like a core sample of the political climate of Western modernity. In this way, I believe that one of our best chances to find something meaningful to say about the futures of democracy now is to begin the work of writing the political histories of membership in settler states. These histories cannot serve as prediction machines for the future of democracy (this can only ever be the territory of prophets, seers and charlatans), but they can provide us with concrete examples of situations wherein the presuppositions of membership in nation-states are exposed and contradicted by the demands of factual situations.

Among settler states, Canada provides us with a particularly unique sample: its constitutional order has been forced to respond to both the claims of Indigenous peoples and the problem of secession. The principled architecture of the Supreme Court's response to this problem can be found in two cases, namely, *R. v. Sparrow* and the *Reference re Secession of Quebec*. The contrast between these two cases can help us to see the different historical lenses that the Court has used to respond to these two constitutional conflicts. While a fine-grained appreciation of the details of these cases is needed to really draw out this distinction, let us simply say here that the principles of these cases are *not consistent with one another*. Rather, they are rooted in the histories of two categorically distinct *vocabularies of law*. We can label these two as "democratic constitutionalism" (e.g. the combination of mixed constitutionalism and popular sovereignty introduced by the American and French Revolutions) and "administrative governance" (e.g. Colonial Administration). They correspond to two different understandings of the relationship between law and the legitimacy of the political order that stem from the so-called Second Empire of the long nineteenth century. Therefore, by understanding the principled differences between these cases we can understand the relationship between these vocabularies of law and the future of democracy in modern nation-states.

Now that we have a rough sense of the significance of both Canada and these two cases, I will set out an itinerary for the rest of this chapter. I aim for this to be an *essay* in the etymological sense of the term. By that I mean that I am offering a limited case study and not a systematic treatise. This is merely an initial walk across very complicated terrain, and my aim is to pick out some features and draw your attention to them. The more philosophically robust and legally systematic mapping of these features in their wider context will need to come later. That caveat in place, I have divided the chapter into two sections: first, I will elaborate on what I mean by a political history of membership. I will then make use of the concept by using it to provide readings of *Sparrow* and the *Secession Reference* as cases within a political history of membership in Canada.

WHAT IS A POLITICAL HISTORY OF MEMBERSHIP?
A METHODOLOGICAL NOTE ON THE DISTINCTION BETWEEN LAW AND POLITICS

What is a political history of membership? One way of getting at this question is to understand what follows from the fact that the concept of membership cannot be removed from contestation. As I have pointed out, it is possible to remove the question of membership from one vocabulary. For example, the legal system can treat the question of membership as being nonjusticiable, but this does not settle the question; it simply shifts the venues and vocabularies of contestation. This changing of vocabularies can be difficult to see if we approach the problem from the presumption that questions of law are, in some way, categorically distinct from those of politics. While it is simply true the vocabularies of law and politics have distinct institutional practices (viz. the judicial branch of government operates by rules distinct from those found in the executive and legislative branches), we cannot plausibly claim to understand a legal system without offering an account of how the actors within that system make sense of what they are doing. We must appreciate the fact that the vocabularies of law are necessarily historical and that all competent actors need access to this dimension of the legal system to operate within it. Without this kind of account, we must limit ourselves to simply describing what the actors we observe *might be doing*. If we are depending on this kind of descriptive approach to make sense of what is happening in an actual legal system, things can go frightfully awry. In order to be able to claim that we understand what social actors are doing within the legal system we must be able to account for the rules that any current system operates by and how the social actors actually make sense of those rules. If we do not understand the relationship between the rules and how social actors interpret them, we cannot make sense of the daily operations of the legal system.

Let's try and unpack the above point a bit more clearly. If we attempt to get a clear view of the legal system by setting aside its historical development and instead working from an abstract theoretical model like the imperative theory of law, we do indeed manage to articulate a clearer picture of what the law is, but it is by necessity a picture of what the social actors *might* be doing (as H. L. A. Hart clearly shows in response to Austin by exploring the significance of legal rules[6]). It

---

[6] For Hart's response to Austin see *The Concept of Law*, chapters I–IV.

is a *re-presentation* of the meaning of the actual, everyday practices of social actors that are being described. By this I simply mean that the simple imperative theory is built upon a series of presumptions, and these presumptions have significant costs. The presumptions help us by enabling us to construct a manageable view of the multiform complexity of the everyday world, but they also blind us to certain aspects of this complexity. If we presume that we are able to merely *describe* a given object or situation, then we are blind to the normative implications that are necessarily bound up with our use of language. This blindness is what Wilfred Sellers calls "descriptivism" (Robert Brandom uses the term "semantic naiveté" in a similar manner).[7] In order to make our way through this mistake we need to pay more attention to the relationship between description and evaluation. Sellers helpfully draws out this relationship:

Although describing and explaining (predicting, retrodicting, understanding) are *distinguishable*, they are also, in an important sense, *inseparable*. It is only because the expressions in terms of which we describe objects, even such basic expressions as words for perceptible characteristics of molar objects, locate these objects in a space of implications, that they describe at all, rather than merely label. The descriptive and explanatory resources of language advance hand in hand.[8]

Once we see that describing and explaining are inseparable, we can see where we went wrong. So, with this clearly in mind, let's reconsider the presumptions implicit in laying claim to a descriptive account of the concept of law. If we choose to simply set aside the theories of law that were the historical accompaniment of the common law in a given period, we are also choosing to subtract the normative framework that actual legal actors used to make sense of their legal system. We are treating these rival theories as rival descriptions of the law and not as normative frameworks for practically doing things within a legal system. While it is true that setting the other theories to one side and starting again from a different set of presumptions does produce different possibilities for the concept of law, this cannot be understood as merely a *descriptive* account. Any such project is necessarily a *re-evaluation* of the concept of law from a limited perspective.

This theoretical lens (to use a common metaphor) provides us with a set of new explanations and ways of practically making our way about the law. But

---

[7] For Wilfred Sellars' use of "descriptivism" I have in mind his essay "Counterfactuals, Dispositions, and the Causal Modalities," in *Minnesota Studies in the Philosophy of Science*, vol. 2, *Concepts, Theories, and the Mind-Body Problem*, ed. Herbert Feigl, Michael Scriven, and Grover Maxwell (Minneapolis: University of Minnesota Press, 1957), §79; and Robert B. Brandom's discussion of it in chapter 1 of his excellent book *From Empiricism to Expressivism: Brandom Reads Sellars* (Cambridge, MA: Harvard University Press, 2015). For Brandom's concept of "semantic naiveté," see Robert B. Brandom, "Reason, Genealogy, and the Hermeneutics of Magnanimity" (Howison Lecture in Philosophy, University of California, Berkeley, CA, March 13, 2013), https://gradlectures.berkeley.edu/lecture/magnanimity.

[8] Wilfred Sellers, "Counterfactuals, Dispositions, and the Causal Modalities" in *Minnesota Studies*, vol. 2, ed. Feigl, Scriven, and Maxwell, §108.

the lens is also shaping the world that we practically navigate.[9] In this way it is
like a pair of glasses: they enable us to see more clearly, but only within a limited
field of view – as Wittgenstein reminds us, in the case of the eye and the field of
sight, "you do *not* really see the eye."[10] These glasses cannot provide us a direct
and unmediated view of objective reality (Wilfred Seller's attack on the "myth
of the given" comes to mind here).[11] All that these glasses can offer us is
a historical picture of the law. This necessarily means that by picking up the
glasses of contrasting theoretical perspectives (e.g. those of Hobbes and
Harrington or Blackstone and Bentham) we get a clearer view of what
historical actors were doing in their context and what they built into the legal
vocabulary that we have inherited. In other words, these glasses can help us
understand why historical actors made the moves that they did within their
contexts *and* we can begin to notice how versions of these vocabularies continue
to be active in the everyday workings of the legal present.

If we set all of these accumulated glasses aside and chose instead another pair,
then we risk forgetting that they are on our face.[12] In this case, we lose track of

---

[9] Nelson Goodman's classic text *Ways of Worldmaking* (Indianapolis: Hackett, 1978) comes to
mind here.

[10] Ludwig Wittgenstein, *Tractatus Logico-Philosophicus*, trans. Charles Kay Ogden (London:
Routledge, 1922), §5.633.

[11] For Wilfred Sellars' concept of the "myth of the given," see his essay "Empiricism and the
Philosophy of Mind," in *Minnesota Studies in the Philosophy of Science*, vol. 1, *The Foundations
of Science and the Concepts of Psychology and Psycho-Analysis*, eds. Herbert Feigl and
Michael Scriven (Minneapolis, MN: University of Minnesota Press, 1956), 253–329. This
essay was originally presented at the University of London Special Lectures in Philosophy for
1956 as "The Myth of the Given: Three Lectures on Empiricism and the Philosophy of Mind."

[12] Hart's critique of Austin's theory in the first half of *The Concept of Law* is clear, thorough, and
forceful. There is room for nuance in Hart's positivism, but its limitations are nonetheless built into
the presuppositions that accompany its claim to being merely *descriptive*. For example, how
exactly does Hart ground his notion of "primitive law"? While it may be true that what he
means is simple (and not the pejorative notion of "primitive" that resonates so strongly with the
dark legacy of Colonial Imperialism) it is altogether unclear how exactly this determination is
made outside of the confines of armchair thought experiments. How exactly does Hart's descriptive sociologist arrive at the conclusion that the social order s/he is observing lacks a *legal system*?
After all, if a legal system is defined simply as a coupling of primary and secondary rules, how does
one determine if a given society has the "minimum content" required to establish that they do
indeed possess a legal system? Before we jump into a catalog of descriptive methodology, we
should carefully consider if a society composed only of primary rules would even be possible? That
is, is it possible for a society to have no rules about their rules? This idea of a society outside of the
possibility of change (or outside of history) has a long history in the justifications of Colonial
Imperialism. For example, Kant argued that the Tahitians lived in this static space of unreflective
normative life, and on this basis he argued that their lives were no different (or more valuable) than
sheep. Immanuel Kant, *Political Writings*, ed. Hans Reiss, trans. H. B. Nisbet (New York:
Cambridge University Press, 1991), 219–20. Returning to Hart, is it not more plausible that the
descriptive sociologist can only describe the observed behavior in the evaluative and explanatory
context that s/he operates in? And so, there is no way for the descriptive sociologist to say for
certain whether or not a given society lacks rules about rules. Even if the descriptive sociologist is
equipped with the more prescient and circumspect capacities of observation and description, those

the fact that our view is partial, and we lose the ability to make sense of the everyday practical reality of the legal system. At the extreme, this blinkered approach to the law produces a legal system whose reality fits Weber's description of the "iron cage" of the future, which was inhabited by a

mechanized petrifaction, embellished with a sort of convulsive self-importance. For of the last stage of this cultural development, it might truly be said: "Specialists without spirit, sensualists without hearts – this nullity imagines it has attained a level of civilization never before achieved."[13]

The deeply rooted pessimism here is palpable, but it does not close off the horizon of the future. The "iron cage" is *a view* of the future. Weber was cognizant of this. As Skinner helpfully demonstrates, Weber's historical project in *The Protestant Ethic and the Spirit of Capitalism* was to account for how the vocabularies of the Protestant reformation played a central role in *"legitimizing* the rise of capitalism."[14] This kind of history offers us something like *"its own time comprehended in thoughts"* (to borrow Hegel's evocative phrase).[15] In other

descriptions are looking for what they are familiar with. It is caught by the same limits that Hart so clearly stated those observing behavior at a stop sign would have. Thus, the capacities of descriptive sociology for pointing out rules and talking about rules is limited by their evaluative context. This does not mean that Hart's account of the law is somehow unworkable. Rather, it simply indicates a problem that Hart was aware of, but those who have extended his work outside of the context he was working in have stretched his concept of law past its evaluative limitations. We can think through the problem via Quine's notion of radical translation. In his famous though experiment from chapter 2 of *Word and Object*, Quine presents a case in which translation of a natural language must proceed without any prior linguistic knowledge and solely on the basis of the observed behavior of the speakers who sees a rabbit (Willard Van Orman Quine, *Word and Object* [Cambridge, MA: MIT Press, 1960]). The native speaker (who uses the unknown language of Arunta) uses the word "gavagai," which leads the interpreter to believe that the word is equivalent to "rabbit." But there is no way of being certain that this is what the speaker means because the interpreter does not have access to the other speaker's frame of reference or "space of implications" (to borrow Sellers' phrase). This does not lead to strong cultural relativism. This would be like jumping from the indeterminacy of translation to the impossibility of translation. Rather, as Donald Davidson shows us in his account of radical interpretation, understanding is not possible without mutual recognition. If an interpreter begins by doubting whether the beliefs of their interlocutor have an equal claim to holistic coherence and correspondence, only misunderstanding and confusion can result (Davidson's work on these concepts is spread throughout his work, but the obvious starting point is his seminal essay "Radical Interpretation," *Dialectica* 27 (1973): 313–28). This can help them build the kind of tenuous connections that allow for translation between natural languages to make some degree of *sense*. I believe that Hart's notion of law as being composed out of primary and secondary rules is far more helpful when it is paired with the philosophical tools that are needed to escape the dogma of descriptivism (*pace* Quine and Sellers for the oversimplified conjunction).

[13] Max Weber, *The Protestant Ethic and the Spirit of Capitalism*, trans. Talcott Parsons (London: Routledge, 1992), 182.

[14] Quentin Skinner, *Visions of Politics*, vol. 1, *Regarding Method* (Cambridge: Cambridge University Press, 2002), 157.

[15] Georg Wilhelm Friedrich Hegel, *Elements of the Philosophy of Right*, ed. Allen W. Wood, trans. Hugh Barr Nisbet (Cambridge: Cambridge University Press, 1991), 21(original emphasis).

words, it demonstrates that situated historical actors can and do play a role in constructing the normative vocabularies that allow them to act within the legal and political systems of their time. Skinner unpacks the significance of this in relation to Weber:

> the earliest capitalists lacked legitimacy in the moral climate in which they found themselves. They therefore needed, as a condition of flourishing, to find some means of legitimizing their behavior ... one of the means they found was to appropriate the evaluative vocabulary of the Protestant religion – greatly to the horror of the religious, who saw themselves as the victims of a trick ... If it was a trick, however, it certainly worked. The distinctive moral vocabulary of Protestantism not only helped to increase the acceptability of capitalism, but arguably helped to channel its evolution in specific directions, and in particular towards an ethic of industriousness. The relative acceptability of this new pattern of social behavior then helped in turn to ensure that the underlying economic system developed and flourished. *It is for this reason that, even if the early capitalists were never genuinely motivated by the religious principles they professed, it remains essential to refer to those principles if we wish to explain how and why the capitalist system evolved.*[16]

This is precisely what I am calling the "political histories of membership" provide us with. But they are not confined to explaining how and why a given system evolved. Rather, they orient us toward the present moment of a legal system and, in the best case, provide us with the opportunity to intervene and "channel its evolution in specific directions." That is, they provide us with the practical tools necessary to interpret the everyday reality of actual legal systems and open avenues for encouraging principled change in ordinary language.

SPARROW AND THE SECESSION REFERENCE AS CHAPTERS IN THE POLITICAL HISTORY OF MEMBERSHIP

In the introduction I argued that settler states are unique in relation to other states because their claim to territory rests on the legal exclusion and/or diminishment of Indigenous peoples. This is a uniqueness of degree. For example, Spain has contested areas of jurisdiction in the substate nationalities of Catalonia, Galicia and the Basque Country, but these contested regions do not extend over the entirety of Spain. Thus, settler states are unique due to the degree of contested jurisdiction over their territory. This difference meant that in settler states the question of constitutional legitimacy was existential (viz. without a legitimate legal claim these nation-states could not exist) and so they developed vast administrative systems to address the issue, which were constructed with two categorically distinct legal vocabularies. This meant that the settler states of the long nineteenth century had a kind of bicameral constitutional order. There was the normal constitutional order built upon

---

[16] Quentin Skinner, *Visions of Politics*, 157 (emphasis added).

the principles of self-determination and constitutional law, and the Indian administrative system that operates as a state of emergency whose object was the interminable work of civilizing the uncivilized.

These administrative systems were constructed on the basis of a legal vocabulary whose concept of authority is self-constituting, irresponsible to those it governs, and ultimately incoherent. J. S. Mill attempted to legitimize this irresponsible form of government in the following manner:

> Despotism is a legitimate mode of government in dealing with barbarians, provided the end be their improvement, and the means justified by actually effecting that end. Liberty, as a principle, has no application to any state of things anterior to the time when mankind have become capable of being improved by free and equal discussion.[17]

Let's unpack this a little. Mill effectively claims that the criterion for determining the legitimacy of this form of government rests in the capacity of those who claim authority to objectively know the civilizational status of those subject to it (viz. the conflict of interest here is clear). Thus, normative legibility is still the criterion of legitimacy, but (thanks to a claim to the universality of one normative framework) the onus is reversed. In this model of the state, if the basis of authority is not legible to you that is proof that you have not attained the degree of enlightenment that is required for freedom. The Kafkaesque nature of this model of government is obvious: there is no possibility of barbarians attaining liberty, there is only the "iron cage" of the future.

As a consequence of these two vocabularies of law, the theories of sovereignty that the courts have developed in settler states are not consistent with one another. By this I mean that the theory of sovereignty that is used to explain the constitutional order for citizens is distinct from the one that is used to explain the constitutional order for Indians. One of the basic criteria of the former was its *normative legibility* to the citizenry (viz. authority required their recognition and so the pragmatic doings of law had to reflect the semantic context) whereas the latter was *normatively illegible* by design (viz. authority required only their obedience).[18]

This two-chambered constitutional structure was explicit for the nineteenth and much of the twentieth century, but the post-WWII process of decolonization required them to formally abandon the "temporary despotisms" of Indian administration. This has led settler states to use the legal vocabulary of minority rights to address the claims of Indigenous

---

[17] John Stuart Mill, *On Liberty and Considerations on Representative Government*, ed. Ronald Buchanan McCallum (Oxford: Basil Blackwell, 1948), 9.

[18] I have found David Dyzenhaus' work on the form of public law particularly instructive in spelling out the contrast I have in mind and mapping out its possible consequences for the rule of law. In particular, see David Dyzenhaus, "Process and Substance as Aspects of the Public Law Form," *Cambridge Law Journal* 74, no. 2 (2015): 284–306; and David Dyzenhaus, "The Inevitable Social Contract," *Res Publica* 27 (2021): 187–202, https://doi.org/10.1007/s11158-020-09467-z.

peoples. This can make it difficult to appreciate the seriousness of the constitutional problem. On the surface it seems that Indigenous peoples are categorically distinct from substate national groups, but that is only because the settler states have unilaterally categorized the object of these conflicts. They are not seen as conflicts over jurisdiction (like those with subnationalists) but as conflicts over minority rights. The problem here is that the unilateral categorization of one party by the other does not determine the actual object of a conflict between parties. It simply confuses the matter. For the last 150 years, Indigenous peoples in settler states have consistently articulated their claims in the vocabulary of jurisdiction and settler states have unilaterally responded with the vocabulary of rights. They have done so because the vocabulary of rights is downstream of the question of sovereignty (viz. it is a question of finding the right mix of rights to stabilize the sovereign-to-subjects relationship). This has led them down a kind of constitutional rabbit-hole wherein the courts make decisions based on policy and then half-heartedly assemble the legal authorities after the fact. It is a rabbit-hole because the resultant body of jurisprudence would only make sense within the nonsensical confines of a Lewis Carrol novel. The source of this confusion is that these settler states have retained theories of sovereignty that are theoretically unilateral, legally unquestionable and ultimately incoherent.[19] We can see how these two vocabularies persist within Canadian constitutional law by analyzing *Sparrow* and the *Secession Reference*.

Sparrow and Administrative Government

In *Sparrow*, the Court had to provide an interpretive framework for an unusual constitutional provision. The wording of s. 35(1) of the *Constitution Act, 1982* does little more than point to content that is not actually provided (viz. existing Aboriginal and treaty rights). The position of the provision in the scheme of the act provides some insight into its significance, but it also greatly magnifies the problem posed by its vague wording. Section 35 is outside the scope of the

---

[19] Two examples of this will suffice for my purposes here: in 1886 the US Supreme Court issued their decision in *United States* v. *Kagama*, 118 US 375 (1886) and attributed plenary power over Indian tribes to Congress based on an interpretation of the Commerce Clause of the Constitution that has no plausible basis in constitutional law. For more on this, see Robert N. Clinton, "There is No Supremacy Clause for Indian Tribes," *Arizona State Law Journal* 34, no. 1 (2002): 113–260; and Philip P. Frickey, "Domesticating Federal Indian Law," *Minnesota Law Review* 81, no. 1 (1996): 31–95. Similarly, in Canada we could point to the unquestionable presumption that the Crown is in possession of sovereignty, legislative power and underlying title, which extends from the UK Privy Council decision in *St. Catharine's Milling and Lumber Co.* v. *R.* [1888] UKPC 70, 14 App Cas 46, to the foundational case of the post-1982 constitutional order, *R. v. Sparrow* [1990] 1 SCR 1075, [1990] 70 DLR (4th) 385. For more on this, see Kent McNeil, *Flawed Precedent: The St. Catherine's Case and Aboriginal Title* (Vancouver: UBC Press, 2019); and Joshua Nichols, *A Reconciliation without Recollection? An Investigation of the Foundations of Aboriginal Law in Canada* (Toronto: University of Toronto Press, 2020).

Charter and thus it is not subject to the reasonable limitations of s. 1 or the override power of s. 33. This means that the legal quality of s. 35 has more in common with the relationship between ss. 91 and 92 of the *Constitution Act, 1867*. It establishes a jurisdictional line within the division of powers. But this left the Court in a very difficult position. If they interpreted the provision in this manner, they would effectively be declaring any and all legislation that touched on "existing Aboriginal and treaty rights" null and void. This would doubtlessly result in constitutional deadlock and so they set out to find the "appropriate interpretive framework for s. 35(1)" by starting with an examination of its "background."[20] One would naturally presume that the background the Court has in mind would include a consideration of the legislative context of the provision (e.g. the extensive collection of Hansard, committee reports, related litigation, the history of the treaties), but instead they simply stated that "there was from the outset never any doubt that sovereignty and legislative power, and indeed the underlying title, to such lands vested in the Crown."[21] The first authority that they cite for this (curious) proposition is *Johnson v. M'Intosh*, which is the *locus classicus* for the so-called "doctrine of discovery."[22]

The Sparrow framework is built upon the most pernicious legal fictions of the nineteenth century (viz. an unstable amalgam of the doctrine of discovery and the civilization thesis). By failing to address these foundations the Courts have given the Crown's assertion of sovereignty over Indigenous peoples a strange extratextual quality: it simply has what it claims to have and is not required to tether this power to the constitutional order. Instead of securely limiting Crown sovereignty within the constitutional order the Courts have positioned Indigenous peoples as a special minority within Canada that has access to

---

[20] *Sparrow*, 1102. [21] *Sparrow*, 1103.
[22] It should also be noted that the Court does not explain how *Johnson v. M'Intosh*, 21 US (8 Wheat.) 543 (1823) supports their account of Crown sovereignty. First, *Johnson v. M'Intosh* is by no means settled authority within the United States as it is the first case of three that Chief Justice Marshall decided in relation to the Piankeshaw. His decisions in *The Cherokee Nation v. The State of Georgia*, 30 US 1, 5 Pet. 1, 8 L Ed 25 (1831) and *Samuel S. Worcester v. State of Georgia*, 31 US 515, 6 Pet 515, 8 L Ed 483 (1832) considerably modify the legal effect of discovery from something that seemingly enables the discoverer to diminish the legal rights of the other party to the desired level (like some kind of constitutional procrustean bed) to a first in time, first in right negotiating right with Indigenous peoples contra other European powers. Second, it is not clear that *Johnson v. M'Intosh* actually is authority for the strong version of the doctrine of discovery as it is a case that involves a land purchase agreement between a private citizen of the United States and the Piankeshaw. The citizen is trying to enforce the terms of this contrast within the US courts, but the US policy is that its citizens cannot make these kinds of agreements as that is the sole purview of Congress (mirroring the *Royal Proclamation of 1763*). In this case the only legal decision in *Johnson v. M'Intosh* is that the plaintiff is seeking the remedy in the wrong court as his contract is only subject to the law of the Piankeshaw. For this reading of the case, see Philp P. Frickey, "Marshalling Past and Present: Colonialism, Constitutionalism, and Interpretation in Federal Indian Law," *Harvard Law Review* 107 (1993): 381.

a sui generis set of group rights. They did so by basing their interpretation of the background of s. 35(1) on the vocabulary of administrative government, which starts from the presupposition that the Crown has unilateral *power-over* Indigenous peoples (viz. what Brandom – following Hegel – labels as "pure independence"). This vocabulary of law systematically mistakes the distinction between power and authority (viz. it assumes that to have *power* is to have *authority*). This mistake has systematic effects that ultimately render its account of the actual legal order incoherent. As Hart forcefully argues contra Austin, a theory that mistakes the distinction between power and authority purchases "the pleasing uniformity of pattern to which they reduce all laws at too high a price: that of distorting the different social functions which different types of legal rules perform."[23]

By looking to this "background" to determine the meaning of s. 35(1) the Court in *Sparrow* ensured that the Canadian project of reconciliation with Indigenous peoples could never make progress toward its stated purpose. This is because it unilaterally fixes the constitutional framework that the two parties are contesting. That is, the position taken in *Sparrow* presumes that Indigenous peoples are minorities and that the Crown is in possession of (unquestionable) sovereignty, legislative power, and underlying title. This assertion of *power as authority* locks Indigenous peoples into the framework of the Canadian constitutional order as conscripts.

Within the confines of the *Sparrow* framework, the parties cannot resolve their conflict because the legal vocabulary for resolving that kind of conflict has been removed from the board. As a result, the court has forced the parties into a surreal game in which a conflict between foundational partners over the jurisdiction in a federal constitutional order can only take place through the vocabulary of Charter-like rights. This is surreal precisely because the legal vocabulary of rights necessarily presumes that the actual issue of the conflict (viz. the nature of the constitutional relationship between the parties) is settled. This has effectively led to the development of a jurisprudence that can, at best, be described as thin principled and fact bound. Or, to be more direct, it has led to the creation of a legal labyrinth whose shifting walls and doors have rendered the constitutional order normatively illegible.

To repurpose Bentham's phrase, *Sparrow* has left the Canadian constitutional order looking like "non-sense upon stilts."[24] The problem with this kind of "non-sense" is that it is often contagious. The vocabulary of

---

[23] Hart, *The Concept of Law*, 38

[24] This was the phrase that Jeremy Bentham used in 1796 to attack the notion of natural rights in the French *Declaration of the Rights of Man and the Citizen* in his *Anarchical Fallacies*. I am repurposing his polemical metaphor to the opposite effect as I view his collapse of the distinction between the state and the government – which begins with his attack on Blackstone in *Fragment on Government* in 1776 – as making the legal distinction between legal authority and coercive force unintelligible. For more detailed criticism on this move in Bentham's work and its consequences, see David Dyzenhaus, "The Genealogy of Legal Positivism" *Oxford Journal of Legal*

administrative government is not confined to one corner of the constitutional order. It lives in the worrying and multiform expansions of the discretionary powers of the executive. After all, the vocabulary of administrative government includes that key legal tool in the kit of nineteenth-century colonial empire: *martial law*. Legally unresponsible forms of government have been expanding in the twenty-first century, but they have deep roots in the nineteenth century. If we fail to notice how these administrative systems and their legitimating legal vocabulary work together within existing legal systems, then we cannot begin to understand the future of democracy.

The *Secession Reference* and Democratic Constitutionalism

The vocabulary of democratic constitutionalism in the *Secession Reference* has presented the Canadian constitutional order with the possibility of moving past the limitations of the nation-state and toward the deep pluralism of diverse federalism (borrowing Charles Taylor's instructive work on "deep diversity").[25] This gist of the case is rather simple: when a partner of a federal constitutional order voices a desire to leave the federation, all of the partners are obligated to come to the negotiating table and see if they can find a way to meet the underlying concerns of the aggrieved partner. This is how the Court openly mediates between the demands of *legality and legitimacy*.[26] Legality alone would have counseled them to find that any claim to alter the constitutional order without fulfilling its amending formula is simply without legal effect. This would provide a formally correct answer, but it would have the same binding force that the Imperial Crown's formally correct claims to sovereign power had once the Declaration of Independence was issued – namely, very little. The Court clearly pointed to the risks of this narrow interpretive approach when they characterized the constitutional order that would result from it as a "straitjacket."[27] Alternatively, if they had heeded the demands of legitimacy alone, then a unilateral right to secession would be consistent with the principle

Studies 24, no. 1 (2004): 39–67; and Quentin Skinner's analysis in *From Humanism to Hobbes: Studies in Rhetoric and Politics* (Cambridge: Cambridge University Press, 2018), 374–83.

[25] Charles Taylor, *Reconciling the Solitudes: Essays on Canadian Federalism and Nationalism*, ed. Guy Laforest (Montreal: McGill-Queen's Press, 1994), 155.

[26] *Reference re Secession of Quebec* [1998] 2 SCR 217, para. 33. Some legal scholars may object to the use of the term "legitimacy" by claiming that it is a political concept without purchase in legal analysis. In my view this objection trades on a distinction between law and politics that strongly resembles the fact-value distinction in philosophy and suffers from the same kind of metaphysical confusions (i.e. the notion of facts without values or values without facts, which is needed to maintain the bright line version of the distinction). While there are indeed meaningful distinctions between the use of the concept of legitimacy in political and legal vocabularies, the concept of legitimacy itself is not somehow out of bounds in legal analysis. For a more detailed and sophisticated account of this distinction, see David Dyzenhaus' account of legal legitimacy in "Process and Substance," 284–306.

[27] *Reference re Secession of Quebec*, para. 150.

of self-government. This would effectively remove the binding effect of constitutional law *holus bolus*. In such a world, the form and substance of political association is lost, leaving only an endless cycle of fracture and subdivision. By mediating between these two principles the Court successfully avoids both of these risks.

The combination of diverse federalism and democratic constitutionalism that the Court put forward in the *Secession Reference* is built on the presumption that the Canadian state is composed of plural legal orders.[28] This presumption of plurality is of central importance because it leads to the construction of legal vocabulary that acknowledges that legal orders require both formal coherence and normative legibility. By taking a step back from the stifling confines of *Sparrow* and its nineteenth-century conception of absolute sovereignty we see that sovereignty can be the product of negotiations between jurisdictional partners within a federal or confederal relationship. In other words, this vocabulary of law carefully distinguishes between power and authority and thereby has the interpretive resources to show how authority is dependent on processes of mutual recognition. Once we understand the vocabulary that the Court makes use of in the *Secession Reference*, we can apply them to the problem of *Sparrow* and provide a meaningful path forward in reconciliation. This means that tools for modification and adjustment are no longer the exclusive purview of a cadre of legal engineers working on the magical combination of rights that will achieve the formal requirements of reconciliation behind the backs of Indigenous peoples. Rather, the vocabulary of legitimacy is openly set on the table between partners so that they can use them together to renegotiate the shared constitutional framework.

CONCLUSION

Those without a political history of membership are blind to the profound risk posed by the vocabulary of administrative governance, and this vocabulary was used to build part of the constitutional order in the settler states. In these states, sovereignty has been attributed to the executive branch on the basis of its unilateral assertion alone, and this commits these states to systematically mistaking power for authority.[29] This legal fiction is so potent that it has been used to recharacterize treaties as surrender agreements.[30] The concern with the idea of democratic nation-states in the nineteenth century was that they would

[28] See Tully's foundational contribution to constitutional thinking in James Tully, *Strange Multiplicity: Constitutionalism in an Age of Diversity* (Cambridge: Cambridge University Press, 1995); as well as James Tully, "The Unattained Yet Attainable Democracy: Canada and Quebec Face the New Century" (Desjardins Lecture, McGill University, Montreal, QC, March 23, 2000).

[29] Examples of this fact can be seen in *United States* v. *Kagama* and *St. Catharines Milling*.

[30] I address the history of treaty interpretation in the Canadian courts in Joshua Nichols, "A Narrowing Field of View: An Investigation into the Relationship Between the Principles of

be totalizing (Burke, Acton, Tocqueville and others voiced this concern) and so would not leave open the space for rational dissent. The risk was that a loss of the division of powers (so prized by Montesquieu) would concentrate power in a way that compelled obedience without providing any kind of *normative guidance* (viz. law understood – through Bentham and Austin – as the fancy dress of threats backed by force). This concern is by no means theoretical; rather, it is the everyday constitutional reality of Indigenous peoples in settler states. The vocabulary of law that catches them in this "web of meaning" (to repurpose Geertz's phrase[31]) is not confined to that little traveled attic of constitutional law known as Aboriginal law. Philp Frickey provides us with a clear and forceful analysis of the US version of this legal vocabulary:

Kagama was the first case in which the Supreme Court essentially embraced the doctrine that Congress has plenary power over Indian affairs. Its apparent inconsistency with the most fundamental of constitutional principles – the *McCulloch* understanding that Congress ordinarily possesses only that authority delegated to it in the Constitution – is an embarrassment of constitutional theory. Its slipshod method of bootstrapping a congressional plenary power over Indian affairs is an embarrassment of logic. Its holding, which intimates that congressional power over Indian affairs is limitless, is an embarrassment of humanity.[32]

In settler states, the need to mediate between the demands of the nation-state (viz. a single people with sovereign authority over a bounded territory) and the realities of colonial empire presented two paths: the first leaned hard on the formal requirements of the nation-state and set to work civilizing those populations that could not be seamlessly fused into the body politic (the focus on children as the tabula rasa for the uniform citizenry of the future). Those following this perspective jumped over the issue of legitimacy with the thousand-league boots of colonial fictions that simply determined the legal rights of others on the fiction that such work could be done via objective evaluation alone (viz. it is possible to objectively define and identify the uncivilized). This work of constructing a legal vocabulary for the problem of legally acquiring occupied territory and conscripting Indigenous peoples was done in libraries, courtrooms and legislatures far away from those it presumed to diminish. The systematic distortion that accompanies the conflation of power and authority was missed because the legal process was designed to treat this as its unquestionable background presumption. Put otherwise, the cause of these distortions is baked into the rules of the game, and thus those playing the game in the courts are left with the maddening task of making sense of the whirlwind of principles, doctrines and tests that exist in the jurisprudence. But this should

Treaty Interpretation and the Conceptual Framework of Canadian Federalism," *Osgoode Hall Law Journal* 56, no. 2 (2019): 350–95.

[31] Clifford Geertz, *Available Light: Anthropological Reflections on Philosophical Topics* (Princeton, NJ: Princeton University Press, 2000), p. 17.

[32] Philip P. Frickey, "Domesticating Federal Indian Law," 35.

not be taken as grounds for a pessimistic rejection of constitutional law within settler states. We must remember that this was only one of the vocabularies of law that were used to account for the relationship between settler states (and the Imperial families) and Indigenous peoples.

The other vocabulary of law (which I have labeled "democratic constitutionalism") was used in more workaday contexts than its rival. Whereas the vocabulary of administrative governance often dominated the specialized registers of colonial bureaucracy, legislatures and the courts, the vocabulary of democratic constitutionalism was more commonly used on the ground by treaty negotiators.[33] This was by no means a process that can be idealized. It was plagued by fraud and coercion, but nonetheless this was part of the on-the-ground practice of law and politics on the frontier. It could not function with background presumption that power and authority are one and the same as this would make the entire process of treaty-making senseless. How could one conduct negotiations on such terms? The only possible case that comes to mind is a kind of caricature of surrender negotiations following a crushing military defeat, but even in this extreme case, power and authority are not strictly equivalent. Courts have interpreted the treaties with exactly this distorting presumption, but the constitutional risks of this narrow formalism are frighteningly high. As Chief Justice Marshall clearly explained in *Worcestor*, the narrow interpretive approach should be rejected because

[s]uch a construction would be inconsistent with the spirit of this and of all subsequent treaties, especially of those articles which recognise the right of the Cherokees to declare hostilities and to make war. *It would convert a treaty of peace covertly into an act annihilating the political existence of one of the parties.*[34]

The significance of this move to retain the "political existence" of the Cherokee nation is difficult to overstate. It is not simply that the Chief Justice is preoccupied with doing justice to the Cherokee nation. He clearly recognizes that this act of justice is a two-way street. By maintaining that the Cherokee nation is a "distinct community, occupying its own territory" he preserves the legal and normative coherence of the constitutional order.[35] Simply put, this interpretation retains the sense-making capacity of constitutional law by maintaining the distinction between power and authority.

If the Courts of settler states accept such a construction, it would allow the legislative and executive branches to effectively have the ability to remove the sovereign character of another party by unilateral declaration. This could seem

---

[33] For more on this, see Michael Asch, *On Being Here to Stay: Treaties and Aboriginal Rights in Canada* (Toronto: University of Toronto Press, 2014); Aimee Craft, *Breathing Life into the Stone Fort Treaty: An Anishnabe Understanding of Treaty One* (Vancouver: UBC Press, 2013); and Robert A. Williams Jr., *Linking Arms Together: American Indian Treaty Visions of Law and Peace, 1600–1800* (Oxford: Oxford University Press, 1997).

[34] *Worcester v. Georgia*, 31 US 515 (1832), 519 (emphasis added).

[35] *Worcester v. Georgia*, 520.

to be compulsory for the "courts of the conqueror" (viz. the sovereignty of the Crown is understood to be nonjusticiable, and for good reason: if it were treated as a zero-sum proposition then the courts could delegitimate the constitutional order they operate within), but allowing this move introduces a strange loophole within the constitutional order. There are no constitutional norms to connect the declaration of legality to a comprehensible legitimating explanation (e.g. it is not conquest, not a normal surrender). This leaves it as a kind of free-floating – or, perhaps more clearly, "extra-constitutional" – plenary power that cannot be openly expressed as it contradicts the legal and normative principles that render the constitutional order legible to its citizenry.[36] Now, if we continue to attribute legitimacy to the background presumption that settler states have unquestionable power over Indigenous peoples, we also necessarily have attributed absolute sovereign power to the executive. This loss of the distinction between power and authority could be used to eclipse the distinction between the government and the state. In other words, when the courts take this kind of sovereignty as the background presupposition, they have used their judicial discretion to untether the executive from its constitutional bounds. The sole criterion for the legitimacy for such a sovereign is its self-determined power. In this instance the courts have left their constitutional posts and taken up work as the sovereign's valet. If we accept this as a coherent and reliable picture of reality, then it seems that the futures of democracy are rather dim. After all, these spooky bootstrapping sovereigns will only suffer the rights of its citizens so long as it is convenient for them to do so. But we do not need to give into this pessimism. We can reject that vocabulary of law as incoherent. We can remind ourselves that for law to be binding (in more than the crude sense of the power of the gunman) it must be normatively legible; it must make sense to us as a rule. This means that we have to face the fact that legality and legitimacy are necessarily connected and that we cannot jump over this requirement with the pseudo-descriptive categorization of custom versus system. The only viable way forward is to make use of the imperfect tools that have developed within the vocabulary of democratic constitutionalism to construct a constitutional order that is legible to all of those it claims to include. If Western liberal democracies fail to properly understand this history, then they are doomed to suffer a similar fate.

---

[36] Philip Frickey uses the phrase "extra-constitutional" to characterize the so-called doctrine of the plenary power of Congress over Indian Tribes that the US Supreme Court first formulated in *United States* v. *Kagama*. See Philip P. Frickey, "Domesticating Federal Indian Law," 67.

13

Cracking the Settler Colonial Concrete

Theorizing Engagements with Indigenous Resurgence Through the Politics from Below

Stacie Swain

> In the way that we engage rather than disengage, we change what wants to appear unchangeable.
>
> - Dian Million[1]

In August 2018, poet and scholar Rita Wong was sentenced to twenty-eight days in jail for blocking the gates to the Trans Mountain pipeline tank terminal in Burnaby, British Columbia. She did so in solidarity with Protect the Inlet, a movement led by the Coast Salish peoples who built Kwekwecnewtxw, a traditional Watch House, as part of their resurgence and resistance to settler colonialism.[2] More than 200 people were arrested that summer. In a statement that Wong released after her sentencing, she wrote:

I . . . intend to ask the court to respect Coast Salish laws that uphold our responsibilities to care for the land and waters that make life, liberty and peace possible for everyone . . . We can all learn from natural law and Coast Salish law that we have a reciprocal relationship with the land; and that we all have a responsibility to care for the land's health, which is ultimately our health too.[3]

---

[1] Dian Million, "Spirit and Matter: Resurgence as Rising and (Re)Creation as Ethos" (Indigenous Resurgence in an Age of Reconciliation, University of Victoria, March 18, 2017), www.uvic.ca/socialsciences/intd/indigenousnationhood/workshops/irar/index.php.

[2] I tend to use "resistance" and "resurgence" interchangeably throughout this chapter. While they are often differentiated, with the former understood as reactive and state-oriented and the latter proactive and autonomous, I understand each as containing aspects of the other. For a more thorough discussion of the relationship between these terms, see Michael Asch, John Borrows, and James Tully, eds., *Resurgence and Reconciliation: Indigenous-Settler Relations and Earth Teachings* (Toronto: University of Toronto Press, 2018).

[3] Rita Wong and Kimberly Richards, "Acting under Natural Laws," *Canadian Theatre Review* 182 (2020): 26–29, https://doi.org/10.3138/ctr.182.005.

Wong's statement expresses her respect for Coast Salish law, recognizes relationships of interdependence and reciprocity within that law, and acknowledges learning her responsibility to care for the land from these legal principles. While it is not unusual for Indigenous peoples to cite their own laws within Canadian courts, Wong's statement is notable for doing so because she is an (un)settler of Chinese descent. In other words, she is not Indigenous to the territories in question. Despite the consequences of doing so, people like Wong disrupt settler colonialism by engaging with Indigenous resurgence.[4] This process of engagement, and the collectivities that such engagements generate, comprise the subject of this chapter.

For my purposes, settler colonialism can be understood as the attempted elimination or enclosure of Indigenous lands and peoples plus the concomitant production of a new society through colonization and settlement.[5] Settler colonialism can also be characterized by "a predatory economy that is entirely at odds with the deep reciprocity that forms the

---

[4] Two aspects of this chapter that I struggled with include the terminology for those who I discuss in this chapter – settler, non-Indigenous, or those who are not Indigenous to the place in question – and attending to processes of racialization. I recognize that race inflects my terminology and what I am describing, which is how people engage with Indigenous resurgence movements. I am conscious of the debate over whether Black people should be included within the category of the "settler," and how histories of slavery or indentured service and ongoing racialization, for example, differently condition people's positions within settler colonial projects and engagements with Indigenous resurgence. In addition, some of those who engage with Indigenous resurgence in the stories I describe are themselves Indigenous to places other than those under discussion. While Indigenous peoples from different territories may have ancestral connections or shared experiences that shape their engagement with Indigenous resurgence, I was wary of over-narrowing the process I describe by using the term "settler." I also did not want to discount that the process I discuss could resonate for those who *are* Indigenous to the places in question, but were disconnected from their Indigenous homelands and communities. In fact, much of the theory I draw upon – for example, Johnny Mack, "Hoquotist: Reorienting through Storied Practice," in *Storied Communities: Narratives of Contact and Arrival in Constituting Political Community*, ed. Hester Lessard, Rebecca Johnson, and Jeremy H. A. Webber (Vancouver: UBC Press, 2011), 287–307; Million, "Spirit and Matter"; Val Napoleon and Hadley Friedland, "Accessing Tully: Political Philosophy for the Everyday and the Everyone," in *Freedom and Democracy in an Imperial Context: Dialogues with James Tully*, ed. Robert Nichols and Jakeet Singh (New York: Routledge, 2014), 202–19; and Leanne Betasamosake Simpson, *As We Have Always Done: Indigenous Freedom through Radical Resistance* (Minneapolis: University of Minnesota Press, 2017) – continue a literature in which "decolonizing of the mind" is a task for all subjects of colonialism and imperialism, beyond ancestry or phenotype. I see this chapter as fitting within this strand of theory, while recognizing the complexity of the debates noted earlier.

[5] Heidi Kiiwetinepinesiik Stark, "Criminal Empire: The Making of the Savage in a Lawless Land," *Theory & Event* 19, no. 4 (2016), www.ucis.pitt.edu/global/sites/default/files/Downloadables/ProQuestDocuments-2020-07-04%5B8893%5D.pdf; Patrick Wolfe, "Settler Colonialism and the Elimination of the Native," *Journal of Genocide Research* 8, no. 4 (2006): 387–409, https://doi.org/10.1080/14623520601056240.

cultural core of many Indigenous peoples' relationships with land,"[6] such that capital accumulation is valued over supportive relations with each other and sustainable relationships with the earth. These predatory relations have brought settler colonial societies into the coconstitutive social and ecological crises that differentially affect individuals and groups within stratified liberal democracies.[7] As scholars argue, however, settler colonialism is "imperfect" – it is unfinished, or not fully "settled."[8] As such, settler colonial states are always attempting to perfect their dominion over Indigenous lands and peoples.

In other words, settler colonial states attempt to enclose *and* foreclose Indigenous relationships to place and political authority.[9] Although Indigenous peoples continue to point out their relationships to place prior to settler presence, as Dian Million describes, "Still, the concrete is real, a metaphor that readily conveys the institutional essentializing of capitalist forms. It is meant to convey permanence when nothing is permanent, it's all spirit, where there is only ever change."[10] I understand "concretization" as the

[6] Glen S. Coulthard, "For Our Nations to Live, Capitalism Must Die," *Unsettling America* (blog), November 5, 2013, https://unsettlingamerica.wordpress.com/2013/11/05/for-our-nations-to-live-capitalism-must-die.

[7] For a discussion of congruent social and ecological crises, see Umeek E. Richard Atleo, *Principles of Tsawalk: An Indigenous Approach to Global Crisis* (Vancouver: UBC Press, 2011); Arthur Manuel and Ronald M. Derrickson, *The Reconciliation Manifesto: Recovering the Land, Rebuilding the Economy* (Toronto: James Lorimer and Company Ltd., Publishers, 2017); James Tully, "Reconciliation Here on Earth," in *Resurgence and Reconciliation: Indigenous-Settler Relations and Earth Teachings*, ed. Michael Asch, John Borrows, and James Tully (Toronto: University of Toronto Press, 2018), 83–120.

[8] Lisa Ford, *Settler Sovereignty: Jurisdiction and Indigenous People in America and Australia, 1788–1836* (Cambridge, MA: Harvard University Press, 2010); Shiri Pasternak, *Grounded Authority: The Algonquins of Barriere Lake Against the State* (Minneapolis: University of Minnesota Press, 2017).

[9] This sense of enclosure can be understood as operating through material, legal, discursive, and affective registers. In other words, while colonialism works through the enclosure of land, such as in the creation of private property and reserves, these logics of containment also work through legal ideas such as "Indian Status" and discourses on "vanishing," "imaginary," or "authentic" Indians. See Daniel Francis, *The Imaginary Indian: The Image of the Indian in Canadian Culture*, 2nd ed. (Vancouver: Arsenal Pulp Press, 2011); Cole Harris, *Making Native Space: Colonialism, Resistance, and Reserves in British Columbia*, Canadian Studies Series (Vancouver: UBC Press, 2002); Paige Raibmon, *Authentic Indians: Episodes of Encounter from the Late-Nineteenth-Century Northwest Coast* (Durham: Duke University Press, 2005); and Traci Brynne Voyles, *Wastelanding: Legacies of Uranium Mining in Navajo Country* (Minneapolis: University of Minnesota Press, 2015). Million particularly highlights the affective experience of enclosure, such as when Indigenous people come to understand themselves through frameworks of crises and intergenerational trauma, as offered by capitalist management within neoliberal states; Million, "Spirit and Matter."

[10] Million, "Spirit and Matter." My thinking around "settler colonial concrete" is also inspired by Sarah Hunt's consideration of the "colonialscape" as the colonial legal system and related infrastructures that attempt to overlay prior, deeper, Indigenous relationships to place and the legal orders drawn from those relationships. Sarah Hunt, "Witnessing the Colonialscape:

process through which settler colonialism attempts to perfect itself. Concretization instills a sense of permanence or inevitability – a sense in which the predatory and oppressive relations of settler colonialism are *perceived as* inevitable, unchangeable, and the only viable possibility – despite the ongoing presence of Indigenous nations and their legal, social, and political orders. Settler colonial concretization works by incentivizing subjects – Indigenous and otherwise – to understand themselves, the world, and their agency within it through the matrices of empire, capitalism, and colonialism.

As "subjects of empire" within settler colonial contexts, diverse Indigenous peoples come to identify with and understand themselves through asymmetrical and nonreciprocal forms of recognition, and this understanding maintains the political and economic hierarchies of imperial power and colonial domination.[11] In contrast, Indigenous resurgence movements offer conceptual and practical resources to refuse imperial subject positions and hierarchies. Indigenous theorists, such as Glen Coulthard and Leanne Betasamosake Simpson, have theorized Indigenous ways of understanding and living through the concept of "grounded normativity."[12] Grounded normativities are deeply rooted in Indigenous relationships to land and forms of political community, and emphasize political responsibilities to place, people, and other-than-human beings. For those embedded within settler colonial concrete, however, grounded normativity can seem opaque or inaccessible because Indigenous peoples' ontologies and epistemologies have been mystified, or even made to seem "mystical," by Cartesian and Enlightenment-based epistemologies.[13] Yet people who are not embedded in grounded normativity, and who are not Indigenous to the place being protected, still engage with Indigenous resurgence despite the consequences of doing so – for example,

---

Lighting the Intimate Fires of Indigenous Legal Pluralism" (PhD Thesis, Simon Fraser University, 2014), http://summit.sfu.ca/item/14145.

[11] In other words, the spatialities, subjectivities, and (infra)structures of colonialism and capitalism can look and feel as though they are unchangeable or inevitable. This sense of permanence, to echo Coulthard, can have the effect of fixing the relations through which colonialism and capitalism get reproduced. Glen Sean Coulthard, *Red Skin, White Masks: Rejecting the Colonial Politics of Recognition* (Minneapolis: University of Minnesota Press, 2014).

[12] Coulthard, *Red Skin*; Glen Coulthard and Leanne Betasamosake Simpson, "Grounded Normativity / Place-Based Solidarity," *American Quarterly* 68, no. 2 (2016): 249–55, https://doi.org/10.1353/aq.2016.0038; Jessica Hallenbeck et al., "Red Skin, White Masks: Rejecting the Colonial Politics of Recognition," *The AAG Review of Books* 4, no. 2 (2016): 111–20, https://doi.org/10.1080/2325548X.2016.1146013; and Simpson, *As We Have Always Done;*.

[13] This opacity can also be considered a strength: see Simpson, *As We Have Always Done*. For a consideration of Cartesian dualism and Enlightenment-based epistemologies, see Silvia Beatriz Federici, *Caliban and the Witch*, 2nd rev. ed. (New York: Autonomedia, 2014) in relation to the rise of capitalism; or, in relation to Indigenous peoples specifically, Vine Deloria Jr., *Red Earth, White Lies: Native Americans and the Myth of Scientific Fact* (Golden, CO: Fulcrum Pub, 1997); and Linda Tuhiwai Smith, *Decolonizing Methodologies: Research and Indigenous Peoples*, 2nd ed. (London: Zed Books, 2012). For further discussion of the "mystical Indian" trope found in Deloria, see Francis, *The Imaginary Indian*; Raibmon, *Authentic Indians*.

those such as Wong, as a woman of Chinese descent, and other non-Coast Salish people who were arrested at Kwekwecnewtxw. Given the mystification of grounded normativity, how do people come to refuse the incentives of settler colonialism and take up a political practice that furthers Indigenous resurgence, instead of concretizing settler colonial hierarchies of domination?

In this chapter, I suggest that engaging with Indigenous resurgence can engender forms of political subjecthood and agency that complement grounded normativity, and in doing so disrupt the perception that settler colonialism has concretized. I characterize the collectivities generated through engagement with Indigenous resurgence as *relational, practice-based,* and animated by a *place-based ethic of responsibility*. In section one of this chapter, I provide an argument that begins with theories of Indigenous resurgence and grounded normativity. In section two, I offer three stories of engagement with Indigenous resurgence in which to ground my theoretical argument. These stories are drawn from my own experience, for which I am indebted to Kwakwa̲ka̲'wakw, Secwépemc, and Lkwungen and W̱SÁNEĆ places and peoples.[14] In section three, I discuss the stories through the concepts proposed in my theoretical argument. In my understanding, Indigenous resurgence movements disrupt the concretization of settler colonialism by embodying decolonial political relations that are drawn from grounded normativity. As a basis from which to engage with and relate to others, grounded normativity also offers opportunities to connect and collaborate with those who share ethical commitments and a political project. The stories in section two offer examples of such cooperative work, and I deploy political theorist Jakeet Singh's work on the "politics of recognition and self-determination from below" to understand how engagement can complement grounded normativity. Because both grounded normativity and politics from below are premised upon principles of mutual recognition and interdependent self-determination, their conjunction can precipitate ways of understanding oneself and acting in the world that are implicated within and informed by resurgent Indigenous nations' relationships to place, political responsibilities, and practices of reciprocity. To paraphrase Wong, all those who live within Indigenous territories have the potential to learn from natural and Indigenous laws.[15] The relational and practice-based collectivities that do so, I conclude,

---

[14] In these stories, I chose to only identify Indigenous leaders who have been publicly active and whose role in the events discussed is well-known, and a builder with whom I have worked together multiple times and gained permission. I am indebted and grateful to all those who have been involved, and recognize that here, I offer only my own partial and situated perspective on the events I describe.

[15] Due to the constraints of space, I have not addressed "natural law" within this chapter. An earlier draft focused more explicitly on water and wild salmon, which have their own laws that we can also learn from. For human–fish relations and their political implications, see the work of Zoe Todd, such as in "Refracting the State Through Human-Fish Relations: Fishing, Indigenous Legal Orders and Colonialism in North/Western Canada," *Decolonization: Indigeneity,*

also disrupt settler colonial concretization because they constitute a network of democratic movements – ones that recognize Indigenous forms of political authority that settler colonialism attempts to eliminate and foreclose.

THEORY

The events in the stories I provide are contingent upon Indigenous resurgence, which makes it both a necessary and pragmatic starting point. While by no means homogenous, the Indigenous resurgence literature suggests that for Indigenous peoples, the pathway to a sustainable and ethical future lies in reconnecting to traditional practices while being open to and adapting to modern technologies. As Gina Starblanket notes:

The term "resurgence" implies a process of renewal or awakening from a period of dormancy. In Indigenous contexts, it also carries a particular cultural and political connotation, referring to *a form of mobilization and action* that is grounded in the revitalization of our traditional ways. *Practices* of resurgence emerge from a worldview that acknowledges *a living relationship* between past, present, and future, and *makes possible the imagination* of strategies of cultural renewal based on the interplay of pre-colonial pasts and decolonial futures.[16]

As a form of mobilization, action, and practice, Indigenous resurgence movements reactivate the ethical and political commitments within Indigenous social, political, legal, and spiritual orders. These commitments can be understood as legal and political responsibilities, which flow from the historical and ongoing relationships that an Indigenous nation has with place, people, and other-than-human beings. While not being exempt from internal power dynamics,[17] Indigenous resurgence can be understood as a prefigurative political project, which imagines alternatives to settler colonialism's hierarchies of domination.

While Indigenous resurgence can be understood as a prefigurative political project, the frame of reference and means through which Indigenous ethico-political commitments are activated and embodied can be understood as

---

Education & Society 7, no. 1 (2018): 60–75, https://jps.library.utoronto.ca/index.php/des/art-icle/view/30393.

[16] Gina Starblanket, "Being Indigenous Feminists: Resurgences Against Contemporary Patriarchy," in *Making Space for Indigenous Feminism*, ed. Joyce A. Green, 2nd ed. (Blackpoint, NS: Fernwood Publishing, 2017), 25 (emphasis added).

[17] While recognizing the power and promise of Indigenous resurgence movements, I also do not mean to place them outside of power relations and the human capacity for error. For a discussion of problematic dynamics such as sexism, homophobia, and heteropatriarchy within Indigenous resurgence literature and movements, see Simpson, *As We Have Always Done*; Starblanket, "Being Indigenous Feminists"; and Gina Starblanket and Heidi Kiiwetinepinesiik Stark, "Toward a Relational Paradigm – Four Points for Consideration: Knowledge, Gender, Land and Modernity," in *Resurgence and Reconciliation: Indigenous-Settler Relations and Earth Teachings*, ed. Michael Asch, John Borrows, and James Tully (Toronto: University of Toronto Press, 2018), 175–208.

"grounded normativity." As Nishnaabeg scholar and artist Leanne Betasamosake Simpson explains, grounded normativities are the "intelligence systems that hold the potential, the theory as practice, for making ethical, sustainable, Indigenous worlds."[18] Grounded normativity sets out the place-based and nation-specific responsibilities that are drawn out from Indigenous forms of organization and relations with the world; upholding these responsibilities enables Indigenous peoples to live in good relationships with each other, the land, the waters, and other-than-human beings.[19] As the base of Indigenous political systems, economies, and nationhood, grounded normativities also create "process-centered modes of living that generate profoundly different conceptualizations of nationhood and governmentality" from nation to nation.[20] As a concept within Indigenous political theory, grounded normativity therefore offers resources for understanding how the ethical commitments of Indigenous legal and governance orders provide a foundation from which to critique "the imperatives of colonial sovereignty and capitalist accumulation."[21] In practice, grounded normativities provide a perspective or frame of reference from which to understand oneself and the world, and embodied techniques through which to express political agency *against* and *instead of* how settler colonialism interpellates and incentives. As Simpson and Coulthard describe, "Grounded normativity teaches us how to live our lives in relation to other people and nonhuman life forms in a profoundly nonauthoritarian, nondominating, nonexploitive manner."[22] Grounded normativities are how Indigenous resurgence movements embody the decolonial relations that they envision.

As argued, Indigenous resurgence and grounded normativity provide forms of political subjecthood and agency that significantly differ from those offered by empire, capitalism, and settler colonialism. However, it is worth taking a step back to ask what precipitates an understanding of one's practices *as* expressions of political agency within the context of collective movements against oppressive structures. Legal scholars Val Napoleon and Hadley Friedland ask a similar question: how can people in marginalized subject positions, and those who work with them, view their everyday practices as "practices of citizenship" within anti-imperial and decolonizing movements – in light of the sense of powerlessness often felt by such subjects?[23] Their theoretical work is instructive for other contexts in which a sense of

---

[18] Simpson, *As We Have Always Done*.
[19] Also, "Grounded normativity houses and reproduces the practices and procedures, based on deep reciprocity, that are inherently informed by an intimate relationship to place." Simpson and Coulthard, "Grounded Normativity," 254.
[20] Simpson, *As We Have Always Done*, 22.   [21] Coulthard, *Red Skin*, 64.
[22] Simpson and Coulthard, "Grounded Normativity," 254.
[23] Napoleon and Friedland, "Accessing Tully," 202. People in marginalized subject positions, for example, include those experiencing poverty, homelessness, incarceration, and colonial gender violence; Napoleon and Friedland also include frontline workers and institutions who work with people in marginalized positions within their discussion.

powerlessness is inculcated, such as I posited for settler colonialism earlier. Settler colonial society can be understood as one such context because political possibilities are constrained by the concretization of unjust relations of domination; settler colonialism encloses subjecthood and agency, forecloses alternatives, and institutionalizes a sense of permanence or inevitability. Napoleon and Friedland suggest that the shift in perspective from powerlessness within one frame of reference to political agency within another involves three factors: the recognition that one has the "freedom to act otherwise," even within limits; the development of "a broader frame of meaning" through which to understand one's actions; and the connection of one's actions to a larger political project. To build on their work, in the context of settler colonialism individuals must see themselves as more than "subjects of empire." Rather, subjects must understand themselves and their actions through more liberatory frames of reference, such as those offered within the grounded normativities of Indigenous nations. Then, connecting to a collective, political project such as Indigenous resurgence allows for new possibilities and cooperation between those who are engaged in practices of freedom or practices that resist domination and oppression.

Thus far, I have built upon political theorists, primarily Indigenous, to suggest that grounded normativity and Indigenous resurgence offer anti- and decolonial forms of subjecthood and agency for Indigenous peoples. In doing so, they subvert the logics of settler colonialism and disrupt its concretization. While somewhat abstract up to this point, I will ground this theory in sections two and three. In my introduction, however, I pose a question: how do people who are *not* Indigenous to a place in question come to refuse the incentives of settler colonialism and disrupt its concretization by taking up a political praxis that complements Indigenous resurgence?[24] An initial reason to ask this question is because Indigenous resurgence is often conceptualized as a turn inward, away from the settler colonial state – and perhaps society, too. Further, as described earlier, the resurgence literature shows that grounded normativity is place-based and nation-specific: it is embedded in relationships to the lands and waters, stories, songs, dances, ceremonies, subsistence practices, and other such learned perspectives and embodied techniques.[25] Grounded normativities can therefore be inaccessible to those who are not

---

[24] In asking this, I recognize that Indigenous resurgence is primarily *by* and *for* Indigenous peoples. While this chapter does not focus on Indigenous peoples per se, it is informed by Indigenous political theory, organizing, and mobilization. At rallies and events, one often hears "we are doing this for *all* of you," or "for *all* of our children." I am interested in what engagement with Indigenous resurgence looks like for those who are not Indigenous to the place being protected or Indigenous at all, the latter being a category that I include myself within; this is the subject position and relationship that I attempt to theorize in this chapter.

[25] Mack's discussion of story in "*Hoquotist*" might be understood as grounded normativity, used as a basis for engaging with the BC Treaty Process. For Mack, the BC Treaty Process extends "an imperial story of dispossession and assimilation ... aimed at strengthening state control of

embedded within them – not because they are inherently opaque or mystical, but because settler colonialism attempts to erase or capture them within imperial, capitalist, and liberal frames of reference.[26] However, grounded normativities must be able to be engaged with and learned, even if incrementally. I say this for one, because members of diverse Indigenous nations return to grounded normativity despite the displacements and disconnections of settler colonialism. Further, Indigenous scholars turn outward and explain their own nation's grounded normativities as a basis from which to engage with others.[27] The act of turning outward is key here, because I suggest that it creates the opportunity for those who are not Indigenous to a place in question to engage with and learn from Indigenous resurgence within a shared, collective political project.

As Simpson and Coulthard describe, "grounded normativity teaches us how to be in respectful diplomatic relationships with other Indigenous and non-Indigenous nations with whom we might share territorial responsibilities or common political or economic interests."[28] On a more intimate scale than the nation, Simpson conceptualizes networks of consensual and reciprocal relationships through the constellation as drawn from her own nation's grounded normativity. Speaking to the opacity previously mentioned, like the land itself constellations are "visible to everyone all night" but "unreadable theory and imagery to the colonizer or those who aren't embedded in grounded normativity."[29] For Simpson constellations are entry points that function in relationship with others, and thus also offer lessons on connection and cooperation: "Constellations in relationship with other constellations form

---

indigenous lands and domesticating indigenous peoples by liberalizing their modes of political and social order," Mack, "*Hoquotist*," 290–1. Key differences between Mack's example and the stories that I include in this chapter are the parties engaging with each other and whether they *share* a political project. While State–Indigenous relations are important to analyze and critique (i.e. John Borrows, *Recovering Canada: The Resurgence of Indigenous Law* (Toronto: University of Toronto Press, 2002); and Dale A. Turner, *This Is Not a Peace Pipe: Towards a Critical Indigenous Philosophy* (Toronto: University of Toronto Press, 2006)), here I am more interested in interactions between grassroots Indigenous movements and what Gaudry refers to as "the socially-conscious settler community" co-operating within the context of Indigenous-led resistance and resurgence projects: Adam Gaudry, "Researching the Resurgence: Insurgent Research and Community-Engaged Methodologies in 21st-Century Academic Inquiry," in *Research as Resistance: Revisiting Critical, Indigenous, and Anti-Oppressive Approaches*, ed. Leslie Allison Brown and Susan Strega, 2nd ed. (Toronto: Canadian Scholars' Press, 2015), 243–65.

26 As Simpson highlights, this opacity can be understood as a benefit *because of* settler colonialism's attempt to perfect itself through erasure, elimination, and transformation. Simpson, *As We Have Always Done*, 213–17.

27 For example, Simpson, *As We Have Always Done*, especially within the chapters on Nishnaabeg internationalism and land as pedagogy; Umeek, *Tsawalk*, on the Nuu-cha-nulth concept of Tsawalk.

28 Simpson and Coulthard, "Grounded Normativity," 254

29 Simpson, *As We Have Always Done*, above, 213.

flight paths out of settler colonialism into Indigeneity. They become doorways out of the enclosure of settler colonialism and into Indigenous worlds. They can be small collectives of like-minded people working and living together, amplifying the renewal of Indigenous place-based practices."[30] In the stories that follow, I talk about engagements with Indigenous resurgence as examples of such collectives that support the renewal of Indigenous place-based practices. The point that I aim to develop further is the process through which Indigenous resurgence movements open doorways for others to see and step through – not into an absence, nothingness, or lawlessness, but into generative relations that engender forms of subjecthood and agency that complement grounded normativity.[31] Grounded normativity offers ways to relate that refuse the concrete enclosures of settler colonialism, with an emphasis upon practice and collaboration from the ground up.

With an eye toward those who are engaging with grounded normativity instead of those fully embedded within it, I suggest that Singh's "politics of recognition and self-determination from below" can be used as a complementary approach. Singh contrasts politics from below against top-down or statist projects, emphasizing politics from below as a form of "building or practicing alternative cultures of politics from the ground up." These alternative politics tend to be "articulated in the relatively provisional voice of a much less dominant social actor who is participating in an ongoing social struggle and critical dialogue with many other (differently situated) social actors."[32] As I understand it, this aptly describes the situation of Indigenous nations and others within stratified settler societies, sharing in struggles against imperialism, capitalism, and colonialism. The politics of recognition from below requires mutual rather than unidirectional recognition between subjects as relational actors sharing in struggle,[33] wherein power is

[30] Ibid., 217.
[31] Informed by Indigenous scholarship, non-Indigenous theorists also call for more collective and land- or place-approaches. For example, Tully, in "Reconciliation Here on Earth," offers a political philosophy of collective liberation with reconciliation understood as an informal, double process of "reconciliation with" Indigenous peoples *and* the earth, instead of reconciliation as dictated by the state or understood as "reconciliation to" unsustainable and oppressive relations. These processes must be enacted through practices that transform relations, particularly as non-Indigenous people learn from Indigenous peoples' relations with other-than-human beings. Here, I am interested in offering engagements with Indigenous resurgence as a theory for *how* this transformation comes about; admittedly, this is probably not the only way or perhaps even the ideal way. In conversation with Napoleon and Friedland, Tully points out that "the question of how a person moves from being a passive subject of unjust relations to being an active agent of change in and over that relationship is necessarily case specific" – a point that I agree with. Generally, however, "a person becomes an active agent by being drawn into ethical cooperative work," and it is this process that I focus on. Napoleon and Friedland, "Accessing Tully," 215–16.
[32] Jakeet Singh, "Recognition and Self-Determination: Approaches from Above and Below," in *Recognition versus Self-Determination: Dilemmas of Emancipatory Politics*, ed. Avigail Eisenberg et al. (Vancouver: UBC Press, 2015), 48.
[33] Singh, "Recognition and Self-Determination," 53. An additional note: within the dynamics of mutual recognition that are discussed in this chapter, I do not specify a term through which those

understood as cooperative or interactive instead of coercive; coupled to power, freedom can be understood as a form of "situated agency" within power relations.[34] In my reading, this "situated agency" resembles the principles of relationality and reciprocity that often animate Indigenous resurgence movements. Within these movements, grounded normativities propose a dynamic of recognition that is premised upon seeing oneself as situated in relation to *and* interdependent with others (including place and nonhuman others) – instead of through the hierarchical politics of recognition offered by the settler state and society – which affects one's expressions of political agency and instills the responsibility to sustain one another through practices of reciprocity. The politics of recognition and self-determination from below and grounded normativity complement each other in their shared emphasis upon practicing alternatives from the ground up, mutual recognition, and situated or relational agency expressed in pursuit of freedom, which is a mutual benefit.

To summarize my theoretical contribution, I propose that we understand engagements with Indigenous resurgence that occur through a politics from below as generating collectivities that are *relational*, *practice-based*, and animated by a *place-based ethic of responsibility*. As Singh describes, politics from below are "a kind of ethico-political practice" to bring about "alternative ethico-political goods," instead of "a particular institutional telos" within imperial relations.[35] In the context of settler colonialism, those "alternative ethico-political goods" include a more just and sustainable relationship with Indigenous peoples, the earth, and each other more broadly. As Wong alludes to in her statement upon sentencing, these ways to relate are premised upon principles of interdependence, responsibility, and reciprocity learned from resurgent Indigenous nations. Others are drawn into relational and practice-based collectivities through ethical, cooperative work alongside Indigenous resurgence movements. Relational and practice-based collectivities animated by a place-based ethic of responsibility have implications within settler colonial contexts: they offer alternatives to settler colonial relations of domination, in the form of collective cooperation and collaboration with diverse Indigenous nations grounded in their own normativities. By enacting these alternatives, relational and practice-based collectivities generated through engagement with Indigenous resurgence disrupt the concretization of settler colonialism. In the

---

who are not Indigenous to the place in question might be recognized. Possible terms might include ally, accomplice, coconspirator, or, perhaps more ideally, terms drawn from Indigenous languages. Such concepts may be case-specific, and I have chosen to leave this open-ended while recognizing that the question warrants further reflection and discussion.

[34] Singh, "Recognition and Self-Determination," 55.

[35] Ibid., 63; further, "self-determination from below focuses less on appropriating institutional power in the traditional sense than on transforming power relations by disrupting the hegemonic norms that conduct one's conduct (by conducting oneself differently) and/or by working to modify or transform those norms in accordance with alternative ethico-political goods"; ibid., 65.

next two sections, I turn to movements and engagements to illustrate this process.

STORIES

In this section, I narrate three stories of engagement with Indigenous resurgence movements. I aim to ground my theory of relational and practice-based collectivities, animated by a place-based ethic of responsibility, within the movements and places that the theory is drawn from. I relate these stories from my own experience, as a white, cis, able-bodied settler of Ukrainian–British descent, who grew up in Treaty 6 territory south of Amiskwaciwâskahikan/ ᐊᒥᐢᑲᐧᒋᐋᐧᐢᑲᐦᐃᑲᐣ (Edmonton). I moved to Lkwungen and W̱SÁNEĆ territories in August 2017, after which I began to physically engage with Indigenous resurgence movements. I offer these stories from my own perspective because the engagements taught me, and others working alongside me, to see beyond the concrete that calcifies our current, unsustainable social and ecological situation.

My methodological approach is informed by Paulo Freire's conceptualization of praxis. For Freire, praxis requires the identification of a problem, action to address that problem, and reflection, which informs further action.[36] As such, theorizing, acting, and reflecting are coconstitutive elements of any attempt to transform conditions of oppression. In each story presented here, settler colonialism in a range of forms, including the predatory relations identified earlier, can be acknowledged and understood as the problem. This problem spurred me and others to act alongside Indigenous resurgence, and against settler colonialism. For me, writing this chapter is a form of reflection – one form of dialogue alongside other, ongoing conversations. The engagements in the stories herein were not perfect, in part because of my own situated whiteness, but they have also been place-based, generative processes of relationship building, learning responsibilities, and practicing reciprocity. As moments of engagement with Indigenous resurgence through politics from below, I consider them through the framework of "flows, rivers, kinships, [and] knowledges that do not create enclosure, but that create relations, help, support, other ways of thinking and moving concrete."[37]

Story 1

It is February, and the dusting of snow on the trees that line the narrow highway glows gold in the sun. Two friends and I are on our way to Port McNeill, on the northeast side of Vancouver Island. From there, we will take a ferry to Yalis/ Alert Bay, and then a smaller boat to a place called Swanson Island. We are there in answer to a call for supporters put out by hereditary Chief Ernest Alfred of

[36] Paulo Freire, *Pedagogy of the Oppressed* (London: Penguin Books, 2017).
[37] Million, "Spirit and Matter."

the 'Namgis nation, who has been (re)occupying a cabin built by the Norwegian corporation Marine Harvest Seafood (now called Mowi) since September 9, 2017. The cabin, seemingly abandoned along with three others, sits across a small bay from an open-water net pen fish farm. When we arrive off the dock in Alert Bay, we are met by an organizer of the group *Maya'xala Xan's Awinakola*, which translates (if insufficiently) to "respect our land, sea, and sky," because we are part of and depend upon them. The sign-up form on the Maya'xala xan's Awinakola group's website states "You will be provided with Protocol from the 'Namgis and Mamalilikala Tribes. You will be expected to maya'xala – respect and follow and adhere to the ground rules of being at the farm."

We are told to expect a quiet week because the fish farm is currently empty, and are given instructions on what to monitor, how to order food supplies, and what amenities the cabin offers. There is a wood-burning stove to heat the cabin, internet if we turn the generator on at night, and a composting toilet. In addition to monitoring activity on the fish farm, we are welcome to do small improvement projects around the site. I hammer thin strips of wood across the slippery boards up to the composting toilet, one friend patches rotting slats in the walkway, while another builds a wooden frame for the camp stove inside. The mornings begin with a quick and icy splash from the rain barrel, while days are filled by reading and eagle-watching interspersed with walks. Once darkness falls, we stoke the fire, drink tea, eat chocolate, and play cards. We sleep on the floor next to the stove.

Our time on Swanson Island brings a strange mix of feelings. It is often idyllic, alternatively anger- and sadness-inducing, and sometimes exciting. The first evening there, we witness a stunning orange, purple, and deep blue sunset. As the light fades from the sky, the array of pens and floating docks across the bay is hidden within the black silhouette of the land that marks the water's edge. The waters off Swanson Island, like others within the Broughton Archipelago Marine Conservation Area, are host to open-net pen fish farms. The pens are regularly filled with imported Atlantic salmon smolts who spend about two years growing before being collected, canned, and shipped to other countries. While the salmon are in the pens the fish farmers feed them food pellets which, along with their feces, can pass through the nets to litter the seabed. Similarly, small fish can pass through the nets and juvenile wild salmon can get trapped within them. The net-pens are breeding grounds for sea lice, which pass through and pass on piscine ortho-reovirus, a disease that reduces wild salmon's musculature and thus their ability to move quickly, catch prey, and travel upstream to their spawning grounds.

The lands and waterways that belong to the wild salmon also comprise the territories of several nations within the Kwakwaka'wakw, those who speak Kwak'wala. At least five of the local nations – the 'Namgis, Musgamagw Dzawada'enuxw, Mamalilikala, Kwikwasut'inuxw Haxwa'mis, and Gwawaenuk – have been united in their opposition to fish farms for more than thirty years.[38] Elected and traditional leaders issued multiple eviction notices to the fish farms in 2001, 2003, and in August and December of 2017. These eviction notices have also been delivered through oral tradition, such as by Ma'a̱mtagila matriarch Tsastilqualus Umbas in 2019. Swanson Occupation, in addition to occupations and camps near other fish farm sites, is part of the local nations' movement to re-establish presence and assert jurisdiction over the lands and waters that they have never ceded or signed treaties to share. In the December 2017 eviction notice, Musgamagw Dzawada'enu̱x̱w identify open-water pens as "a serious risk to our wild salmon, environment, culture, and way of life."[39]

By coming to Swanson Occupation, my friends and I give Chief Ernest a period of respite with his relatives in town. While there, we watch the fish farm through binoculars and a telescope, listen to a squawking CB radio, and record the names of the boats that come and go and how many people arrive and leave with them. One day a large boat comes, with a long blue tube that we learn is sucking dead fish from within the net. Next comes a barge loaded with nets and white bags, which we are told is probably feed. Contrary to the expectations of the local nations, the Swanson Island fish farm is being prepped to host another shipload of Atlantic salmon smolts. The smolts will be propelled into the pens through a tube like the one that sucked the dead fish up. My friends and I return to the city at the end of our six days, where we begin to learn more about the fish farm industry and Kwakwa̱ka'wakw resistance. Over the next few months we organize a phone bank, which leads to us becoming engaged with a community of others acting in support of Kwakwa̱ka'wakw resistance and resurgence.

Story 2

In August 2018, I helped to organize a bus trip that departed from the Lkwungen and W̱SÁNEĆ territories of Victoria, BC, took a ferry across the Salish Sea, made several stops in Vancouver, and traveled to Secwépemcul'ecw – the territories of the Secwépemc nation, which lie on the eastern side of the Rocky Mountain Range. The bus trip, which had more than twenty people of Indigenous and non-Indigenous heritage on it, began with an invitation extended by the Tiny House Warriors (THW). The THW are a movement, largely made up of Secwépemc women and families, which intends to place ten

---

[38] To these nations, we should add the Ma'a̱mtagila, who were declared legally extinct by the Canadian government when they merged with a neighboring nation, as arranged by an Indian Agent. The legality and permanence of that merger, however, is deeply contested and Ma'a̱mtagila people have been very active in the fight against fish farms, among other unsustainable industries.

[39] Musgamagw Dzawada'enu̱x̱w Cleansing Our Waters. 2017. "Musgamagw Dzawada'enu̱x̱w Eviction Notice." December 1, 2017: www.facebook.com/fishfarmsgetout/photos/a.129800151 3557940.1073741833.128222860513 5231/1781164285241658/?type=3&theater

tiny houses in the path of the Trans Mountain Pipeline Expansion (TMX).[40] The expansion would not only increase the flow of oil through Secwépemcul'ecw, but also bring transient workers for construction and the industrial "man camps" associated with large-scale oil and gas infrastructure.

On the bus trip, our destination was meant to be the THW village at Blue River, then the highest point on the "Canadian" side of the Rocky Mountains: Mount Robson Provincial Park, where Mount Robson overlooks the visitor center.[41] We were going there for an event called "Our Water Gives Life: WUCWMILCETKWE." Before reaching Blue River or Mount Robson, however, our journey was beset with difficulties. First, some people's gear was stolen from the bus in the wee hours of the morning that we were leaving. Then, officers of the Royal Canadian Mounted Police (RCMP) met us in the Vancouver parking lot where we had arranged to pick passengers up, indicating that they were aware of our route and surveilling our movements. Once on our way, the community action bus – a blue school bus converted to biofuel – chugged up the hills of the Coquihalla highway before overheating in the hot August weather. We pulled over once, then again, near the apex of a hill inundated with smoke and a forest fire visible on the far side of the neighboring mountain. While we debated what to do, someone smudged the bus with sage. We opted to continue on, and were pleasantly shocked to see the bus levels stabilize enough to coast into Kamloops that night. Now in Secwépemc lands under the jurisdiction of the women traveling on the bus with us, we cooked dinner and changed to a mini-bus organized by the THW. Late that night, the mini-bus delivered us to a Mount Robson campground where we (re)claimed a group campsite and set up tents for a few hours of sleep.

The next day, the hot afternoon brought another form of heat: the RCMP's Aboriginal police liaisons, who pressured us to leave despite Secwépemc people asserting their right to be on their territory, threatening us with forcible removal and arrest. Then the THW pulled a tiny house onto the visitor center lawn, and we joined them there. The afternoon featured drumming and singing by the Secwépemc and others, music and dancing on the service road, and speakers from Kwekwecnewtxw/Protect the Inlet and other Indigenous land defenders from further afield. We shared barbequed wild salmon that our bus picked up from a reserve downriver, alongside bannock, potatoes, corn on the cob, and a grain salad. When the gathering concluded we camped near the visitor center, and the next morning we ate breakfast, listened to stories, and then moved with the tiny house to blockade a small bridge over the Fraser River. There,

---

[40] The original TMX pipeline was built in 1953 without Secwépemc consent. The expansion project proposes to twin the pipeline. For more on this, see Henderson, Chapter 14, this volume.

[41] I have found Mount Robson referred to as *Yuh-hai-has-kun* or "Mountain of the Spiral Road" in Secwépemctsin, but was not able to verify this through a Secwépemc source. I opted not to include this term within the body of the chapter, but want to signal that "Mount Robson" is the mountain's settler colonial name.

within a stone's throw of a TMX pumping station and with the green water rushing over the rocks below, an elder offered a prayer. While sage burned in an abalone shell on one of the concrete barriers, we tied red ribbons to the bridge in honor of missing and murdered Indigenous women, girls, and two-spirit people up- and downriver. Secwépemc/Ktunaxa woman warrior, birth keeper, and traditional tattoo artist Kanahus Manuel spoke of fulfilling her responsibilities to the river rushing below, the berry bushes fed by it, and to her own nation, but also to those who are connected to the Secwépemc through the river and the infrastructure of TMX. Some of the wild salmon who swim through Kwakwaka'wakw territories migrate as far as Rearguard Falls, a mere ten minute drive away from the Mount Robson visitor center. On our journey back to the Salish Sea, we stop to visit the THW village at Blue River and are shown where to gather and eat some wild blueberries. The newly serviced community action bus is filled with singing as we descend toward the coast and the places we reside. This is not an ending, however: the THW continue their work in Blue River, while others go on to blockade tank terminals at Kwekwecnewtxw, resist RCMP invasion at Gidumt'en, (re) occupy the BC Legislature, and build tiny homes and Little Big Houses for the people and places we relate to.

Story 3

As an early fall morning sleepily dawns some months later, I arrive on the University of Victoria campus with coffee in hand. In the green space next to the Students' Union Building, I take out my keys to unlock the tall, blue, padlocked construction fencing. After I swing open one fence panel to create a gap, I set up an awning, tables, lawn chairs, signage, and tee-shirts that read "water is life" and "protect the sacred." Further inside sits a flatbed trailer with its wheels taken off, leveled on wooden blocks atop a small hillock. On the trailer, a structure is taking shape. The morning sun filters through misty clouds, illuminating the dewdrops that line the grass and piles of tarp-covered tools and lumber. As I work on one side, Catherine pulls her truck up and unlocks another, smaller gap. Catherine is a builder who began building tiny houses as a volunteer with the THW in Neskonlith, and who now lends her time, knowledge, and experience to building projects organized within Lkwungen and W̱SÁNEĆ territories. On the first morning that we met here, W̱SÁNEĆ/ Skx̱wu7mesh plant and language revitalist Tiffany Joseph had welcomed volunteers and shared teachings about the place, the land, and her people, including her family's long-running relationships with members of other Indigenous nations.

Standing in the cool morning air, Catherine and I sip our coffee together. We chat about how many build volunteers have signed up for that day, what tasks they will work on, what's for lunch, and if there's a workshop happening that evening or not. As volunteers start to arrive, the sounds of conversation and construction begin to fill the air. This particular moment is easy for me to evoke from my memories of October 2018 and September 2019. In those times, UVic students and community members (Indigenous and non-Indigenous) came together to provide material infrastructure for Indigenous resurgence movements: first for the THW resisting TMX by returning to their lands, and then for the Ma'amtagila (Kwakwaka'wakw) nation fighting against fish farms and deforestation. The first was one of three tiny houses sent to the THW, while the second was a "Little Big House" for matriarch Tsastilqualus and her kin to move home to Hiladi, "the place to make things right." At Hiladi the Matriarch Camp will rematriate the land and rebuild their nation, like the THW are doing across the Salish Sea and upriver. As the summer arrives they are collecting seeds, starter plants, and tools to support their move home.

DISCUSSION

I offer these stories as examples of engagement with Indigenous resurgence movements. They can be understood as examples in which grounded normativity and politics from below function complementarily to generate relational and practice-based collectivities comprised of those who are Indigenous to a place in question and those who may not be. These collectivities are animated by a place-based ethic of accountability, learned from principles of relationship, interdependence, and reciprocity present within the grounded normativities under discussion. As Million cautions, however, "These are familiar words now, relations, reciprocity, resurgence – but it is also our responsibility to look closely at what we practice to bring these closer into living."[42] In this section, I reflect upon the stories of engagement through the concepts developed earlier. To keep the discussion manageable, I focus on three questions: How do the movements in question enact their grounded normativities within political projects of resurgence to create opportunities for cooperation and collaboration? How does the process through which others engage with these movements represent a politics of recognition and self-determination from below? And how does a place-based ethic of responsibility manifest within and through these engagements?[43] Relational and practice-based collectivities, I argue, constitute networks that are informed by and implicated within Indigenous resurgence. These networks disrupt the concretization of settler colonialism by embodying alternative relations.

A brief consideration of settler colonialism's concretization helps to provide context for what follows. As discussed in my introduction, the enclosures and

---

[42] Million, "Spirit and Matter."
[43] Due to the constraints of space, I look closely at connections within and across the stories and contexts they take place in, potentially at the expense of depth. My own limitations should not be taken to indicate that movements themselves are without deep roots or that engagements with these movements are momentary and shallow.

foreclosures of empire, colonialism, and capitalism can be understood as logics and techniques of concretization. For example, the histories that shaped Kwakwaka'awkw, Secwépemc, Lkwungen, and W̱SÁNEĆ contexts include the enclosure of Indigenous children within residential schools and Indigenous nations within reserves. Although contested by the Indigenous peoples they attempt to contain throughout history and into today, these enclosures limit the mobility of Indigenous peoples while opening up their lands and waters for settler colonial infrastructure such as fish farms, pipelines, cities, and university campuses. In doing so, they also attempt to foreclose the possibility of Indigenous political authority, law, and governance. Disconnected or restricted from land use, life ways, and livelihoods,[44] the Indigenous peoples of these places have been subjected to predatory and oppressive systems: as wage workers in canneries or fish farms, subjects of environmental racism and gender-based sexual violence in communities near industrial projects, and consumers within colonial and capitalist structures that occupy stolen lands, such as universities. Within these sites, those who are embedded within settler colonialism populate and reproduce settler colonial structures, logics, and norms. Concretization occurs when people do so as if there is no other choice – thinking and acting as if settler colonialism is permanent or inevitable.

Despite settler colonialism's attempt to concretize, diverse Indigenous nations have dynamic legal and governance orders that persist and manifest within Indigenous resurgence movements. Practices of resurgence are *not* in idealized, precontact forms; they *are* drawn from grounded normativities, based in tradition but adapted to modern exigencies. Examples include the Watch House at the tank terminal in Coast Salish territories, Secwépemc using tiny homes on trailers to rebuild villages because their "land is home," or members of Kwakwaka̱'wakw nations delivering written and oral eviction notices to fish farms by canoe and speedboat, while wearing once-forbidden regalia. These are members within Indigenous nations exercising sovereignty.[45] As the THW say, "We are committed to upholding our collective and spiritual responsibility and jurisdiction to look after the land, the language and the culture of our people." This

---

[44] See Harris, *Making Native Space*; Hunt, "Witnessing the Colonialscape"; Douglas C. Harris, *Fish, Law, and Colonialism: The Legal Capture of Salmon in British Columbia* (Toronto: University of Toronto Press, 2001), https://doi.org/10.3138/9781442674912; Rauna Kuokkanen, "From Indigenous Economies to Market-Based Self-Governance: A Feminist Political Economy Analysis," *Canadian Journal of Political Science* 44, no. 2 (2011): 275–97, https://doi.org/10.1017/S0008423911000126.

[45] Admittedly, the question of who holds sovereignty within Indigenous nations is a contested one, and one that has been heavily impacted by colonization and the imperialism of western political concepts – including "sovereignty" itself. Conflicts between hereditary and band governance systems are a case in point, as are concepts of sovereignty and jurisdiction that are tied to the reserve versus traditional territories. Here, I tend to understand sovereignty as grounded in title, which is a collective right held by grassroots people and confirmed on the ground (rather than delegated by the Crown), as discussed in Manuel and Derrickson, *Reconciliation Manifesto*, 117–20.

responsibility may arise from the legal principle of *Qwenqwent*, or humility and human dependence upon the land, which is expressed within Secwépemc language and stories.[46] Or, as one of the Musgamagw Dzawada'enux̱w eviction notices reads, "We are here because we feel it is necessary, in order to preserve and protect these lands and waters that have been the home of our people for thousands of years. It is our right and responsibility to be here." As Sarah Hunt contends, Musgamagw Dzawada'enux̱w boarding fish farms were not performing civil disobedience, and I would add that nor were the 'Na̱mgis, and Ma'a̱mtagila alongside them.[47] Rather, they were enacting their responsibilities to wild salmon, to each other, and to the land and waters in accordance with their laws.[48] This can be understood through the framework of *maya'xala xan's awinakola*, which approximately translates to respect our land, sea, and sky, which includes the living beings within these realms. By being on the lands and waters to protect their homelands from colonial and capitalist harm, Secwépemc and Kwakwa̱ka'wakw people represent Indigenous resurgence movements embedded within their respective grounded normativities, upholding their ethical commitments and political responsibilities to place, other-than-humans, and each other.

In taking up their political responsibilities, Secwépemc and Kwakwa̱ka'wakw resurgence movements have also turned outward, inviting others to work alongside and share in their political projects. As the Maya'xala Xans Awinakola website explains, visitors to Swanson Island would be provided with protocol and expected to *maya'xala* – respect, adhere to, and follow the ground rules of being there. The THW "Our Land is Home" project states "The Tiny House Warriors are building something beautiful that models hope, possibility and solutions to the world. We invite anyone and everyone to join us."[49] Further, the trip to Secwépemcul'ecw only came about because of the THW's invitation to "Our Water Gives Life: WUCWMILCETKWE":

We are inviting you to join us on this beautiful day to acknowledge and give thanks to the headwaters of the Fraser River, that form in Secwépemc Territory ... We ask you to gather with us on this day for this family-friendly event of music, sharing food and witnessing the lands and water at risk at the Sacred Headwaters.[50]

---

[46] See Shuswap Nation Tribal Council and Indigenous Law Research Unit, "Secwépemc Lands and Resources Law Analysis Project Summary," June 21, 2016, especially 38–47.

[47] Sarah Hunt, "Justice at the Shoreline: Rethinking Sovereignty through Coastal Wisdom" (Landsdowne Lecture, University of Victoria, Victoria, BC, March 8, 2018).

[48] The operation of multiple and sometimes competing legal systems within the same territory has been similarly addressed by John Borrows in *Freedom and Indigenous Constitutionalism* (Toronto: University of Toronto Press, 2016); Borrows argues that "an act of disobedience may, in another context, be considered obedience to either Indigenous peoples' law or the state's own unenforced or unrealized standards"; 53.

[49] Tiny House Warriors, "Tiny House Warriors," http://tinyhousewarriors.com.

[50] Tiny House Warriors, "Mountain Music Concert: Tiny House Warriors," Facebook, August 16, 2018, www.facebook.com/events/234468630738226 (spelling and grammar adjusted for readability).

By identifying ways to relate to others and to place, these invitations reflect the legal principles, ethical commitments, and political responsibilities contained within their respective nations' grounded normativities. To recall Simpson's constellation metaphor, I understand these invitations as Indigenous nations embedded in grounded normativity opening a doorway and inviting others to approach and step through it. When people do so, it creates an opportunity for collective, ethical, cooperative work based on mutual recognition and self-determination – a politics from below.

To reiterate one aspect of my theoretical argument, I suggest that a praxis based on mutual recognition and self-determination from the bottom-up, where a politics from below complements grounded normativity, has the potential to shift the frame of reference through which participants understand their political subjecthood and agency. In other words, those engaged in relational and practice-based collectivities are not necessarily *embedded* within grounded normativity – though their political subjecthood and agency can be implicated within and informed by grounded normativity to amplify what Simpson refers to as "the renewal of Indigenous place-based practices" – or Indigenous resurgence. Namely, upon entering into relationship with Indigenous places and people through a dynamic of mutual recognition, those who were not Indigenous to the place in question must recognize the ongoing sovereignty and jurisdiction of Kwakwa̱ka'wakw and Secwépemc people. Pursuant to this, and because this dynamic of recognition is reciprocal, those who are engaging with Indigenous resurgence are recognized in turn by members of Indigenous nations who are grounded in their own governance and laws. This recognition interpellates those who are not Indigenous to the place in question not *as* "Indigenous" in any sense of the term nor as members of Indigenous nations, but as relational actors situated within the web of relationships that inhabit and include that place. Expressions of political agency, or practices of self-determination, are conditioned by this recognition and the relationships that follow; in other words, mutual recognition from below informs political conduct or praxis. Put simply, those who recognize Indigenous nationhood must act as such – these relationships shape behavior. For example, fish farm occupiers practice *maya'xala* through the protocols provided, and bus trip participants listen to and follow the lead of Secwépemc people while present within Secwépemcul'ecw.[51] Taking up a political praxis through a politics from below, engaged with Indigenous resurgence, means learning from Indigenous ways of understanding and relating to place, other people, and other-than-human beings.

---

[51] To add: Indigenous legal principles may not be fully known, understood, or perfectly upheld throughout engagement. This is a risk of engagement, but also an aspect of learning. A lack of mastery should be expected within and not understood as an impediment to engagement. Rather, a deeper understanding can only come *through* engagement – cooperation, action, and reflection. On the flipside of this, engagement requires humility and reflexivity. Engagement should not lead others to think of their work as done, but, rather, cultivate an ongoing sensibility and praxis that is informed by local Indigenous laws and relationships to place.

From this learning, a place-based ethic of responsibility extends outward from Indigenous grounded normativities to others relating to that place. In other words, those who are not Indigenous to a place in question come to see their own responsibilities within and to place. As discussed, Kwakwaka'wakw and Secwépemc resurgence movements draw their political practices from place-based grounded normativities, which contain principles of responsibility, interdependence, and reciprocity. In the stories presented here, I and those with me on Swanson Island and within Secwépemcul'ecw bore witness to these principles in practice. To illustrate this, I will draw upon my own experience, as someone who was raised in "oil country" and who now lives on Coast Salish lands. After spending time on Swanson Island to protect the salmon, I learned about how wild salmon travel throughout coastal waters and into the interior, as a keystone species that feeds other animals and the forests, in addition to Indigenous nations. For example, as the invitation to "Our Water Gives Life: WUCWMILCETKWE" describes, "This area is Sacred to Secwépemc and have [sic] nourished thousands of years of Secwépemc and all Indigenous Peoples and Nations downstream that depend on the Fraser River." At the headwaters of the Fraser River in the interior we heard Kanahus Manuel speak upon her responsibility to others connected by the water – not only the wild salmon and those who depend upon them, but also women, girls, and two-spirit people endangered in both directions along the pipeline crossing Secwépemcul'ecw, toward the Alberta tar sands in one direction, with the tank terminal in Burnaby and the supertankers traversing the coastline of Vancouver Island in the other. From a perspective drawn from place, the interdependencies across these places – and the ways in which settler colonial infrastructures attempt to disconnect and sever them – become much more visible, as does one's own implication within them. From this shift in perspective and recognition of interdependence, as learned from Indigenous grounded normativities, flows a place-based ethic of responsibility. This ethic, in turn, can engender a political praxis of reciprocity that creates further opportunities for collaborative work in solidarity with Indigenous resurgence.

Having developed a place-based ethic of responsibility, those who have engaged are motivated to give back to the Indigenous peoples and places they relate to and learn from. To see how a place-based ethic of responsibility can engender a reciprocal praxis, we can most easily look to the Tiny House and Little Big House builds.[52] These build projects were made possible by engagements with Kwawkwaka'wakw and Secwépemc people embodying the

---

[52] Practices of reciprocity can also be small repairs or maintenance at reclamation sites such as Swanson Island. On a larger scale, the first campus Tiny House took place in part because of the trip to Secwépemcul'ecw. The Little Big House might not have come about had the Tiny House builds not broadened a collectivity that shares the project of supporting Indigenous peoples' land-based practices, and was an opportunity for myself and others to reciprocate for the ways we have benefitted and learned from Kwakwaka'wakw stewardship.

grounded normativities of their nations within their own territories. Given where the builds took place and to recognize Indigenous political authority, it is important to recognize that some of these engagements were between W̱SÁNEĆ and Secwépemc people, or W̱SÁNEĆ and Ma'a̱mtagila people. For example, at the first build on campus, Tiffany Joseph spoke of her family's connection to the Secwépemc/Ktunaxa Manuel family through several generations; at the second, Tiffany and Ma'a̱mtagila matriarch Tsastilqualus each spoke of their mutual love and respect. In addition, the builds arose from prior engagements and collaborations between those who are Indigenous to the place(s) in question and others who are not. For instance, the builder involved went to Secwpemcul'ecw to build Tiny Houses and brought this knowledge back to the island, and there was a Tiny House built by community members on W̱SÁNEĆ territories a year or so before the campus build took place.[53] The two build projects I speak of were entirely volunteer-run. This included organizing meetings, fundraising, physically building the houses, holding art and screen-printing workshops, hosting panels and talks, and feeding volunteers throughout. Many volunteers participated in multiple builds, transmitting knowledge, learning new skills, and building relationships. As sites of engagement that provide material support for Indigenous resurgence, the build sites provide opportunities for collective, cooperative work – those who take this work up constitute what I have termed relational and practice-based collectivities. That collaborative work is geared toward amplifying the land-based practices of Indigenous resurgence – those who protect the territories that sustain all of us, and whose invitations into that work make our own interdependence and responsibilities visible. In giving back to Indigenous people protecting the land, we give back to the lands and waters that sustain us. Understood from within a place-based ethic of responsibility, the Tiny House and the Little Big House are material embodiments of reciprocity in practice.

The engagements that I discuss, including the builds, would not have been possible without the Indigenous resurgence movements at the center of them. Through these movements and the networks extending out from them, people learn ways to relate that are drawn from Indigenous normativities; the relational and practice-based collectivities generated through these processes will help sustain Indigenous resistance and resurgence. I feel compelled, however, to address an issue that I see as both a limitation and a possibility within my experience and this discussion. The stories that I share and reflect upon primarily center upon Secwépemc and Kwakwa̱ka̱'wakw resurgence and grounded normativities. However, it is the Lkwungen and W̱SÁNEĆ peoples who have legal and governance orders that respect the land, water, and wild salmon *here* and *now*, where the builds took place and where I write this chapter from. In the

---

[53] There was also another off-campus Tiny House build, highway march, and community feast in the summer between the two I discuss, which was largely organized by people who had participated in the first UVic build. See Henderson, Chapter 14, this volume.

stories, however, I have provided little evidence of engagement with the ways that Indigenous resurgence and grounded normativities are embodied and practiced by members of Lkwungen or W̱SÁNEĆ nations. They too have distinct ways of relating and upholding responsibilities to place, to the water of the Salish Sea and up rivers like the Goldstream, where wild salmon still return to spawn.[54] While my own focus in this chapter doesn't preclude those who were involved from having prior, deeper engagements with the Indigenous peoples of these lands, it does reveal where the build projects and I still need to do more learning, relationship building, and cooperative work. From the theoretical perspective I argue for here, however, this limitation is also where the potential lies. Participation within relational and practice-based collectivities induces others to see themselves as subjects and agents within broader, place-based networks of interdependence, responsibility, and reciprocity. This shift in perspective may also lead one to look more closely at the place one lives, where the concrete of settler colonialism may appear to be more solidified but cracks remain and can be widened.[55] For example, engaging with place and wild salmon alongside Kwakwa̱ka'wakw and Secwépemc people embedded in grounded normativity may precipitate not only recognizing the Goldstream River as SELEKTEⱢ, but also wondering how the stream that runs beneath a road, on the commute to campus instead of within a provincial park, formerly and still sustains life – and how one's everyday actions may impact its ability to do so.[56] Engaging with Indigenous resurgence, even if partially and imperfectly, can serve as a step toward relationships and practices for living more responsibly with *these* lands and waters.

CONCLUSION

The relational networks comprised of resurgent Indigenous nations and those who engage with them can be made visible by looking to place. The collectivities that make up these networks can be understood as democratic movements that recognize the political authority and vitality of resurgent Indigenous

---

[54] For an excellent discussion of W̱SÁNEĆ relationships and laws related to the Goldstream river and salmon that spawn in the waters there, see Robert YEL̵ḰÁTTE Clifford, "W̱SÁNEĆ Legal Theory and the Fuel Spill at SELEKTEⱢ (Goldstream River)," *McGill Law Journal* 16, no. 4 (2016): 755–93.

[55] This shift in perspective must be accompanied with a caution not to oversimplify or homogenize Indigenous nations or their legal orders across different places, or erase Indigenous nations within shared or overlapping territories. For example, Clifford's W̱SÁNEĆ legal theory may differ between groupings within the W̱SÁNEĆ and cannot stand in for Lkwungen laws belonging to the nearby Songhees and Esquimalt nations. Both learning and relating to others, however, are processual; within these processes, complexity offers an opportunity for richness, not an excuse to disengage and perpetuate colonial violence.

[56] Here I do not mean to imply that Indigenous resurgence isn't also happening in cities – it is, at different scales of visibility. Rather, I suspect that it takes more work for others, such as I, to denaturalize the settler colonialism of urban space and recognize cities as Indigenous places.

nationhood in the present, in the places we live and interact with and within. By relating and acting in ways that refuse the incentives of empire, capitalism, and liberalism, these networks of relational and practice-based collectivities threaten the permanence and inevitability of settler colonial structures and institutions.[57] Evidence of this can be seen in the surveillance of Indigenous movements and rights activists by Canadian Security and Intelligence Services (CSIS) and the RCMP, the latter of whom monitored me and others within Secwépemcul'ecw. As Jeffrey Monaghan and Miles Howe show, when it comes to Indigenous movements the Canadian security state's pre-emptive surveillance and policing tactics "translate the potential 'successes'" of Indigenous social movements that challenge injustice "into 'risks' associated with public order," revealing a logic of enmity.[58] Settler colonial surveillance tactics do not emphasize actual violence or lawlessness, but rather various noncriminal criteria that demonstrate an individual or group's potential for "virality": their mobility, appeal to others, and ability to network and "gain popular support" through affiliation and alliance-making.[59] As one surveillance report warns, "the longer a protest continues, the stronger and larger the web of interconnectivity grows and the more difficult it will be to disentangle."[60] This attempt to disentangle – to disconnect, enclose, and foreclose by concretizing colonial and capitalist structures – is a primary logic of settler colonialism.[61] Through engagement, connection, and collaboration with Indigenous resurgence, relational and practice-based collectivities have the potential to subvert settler colonial logics such as this. Because this web of interconnectivity is premised upon ways to relate to place, each other, and other-than-human beings that are drawn from grounded normativities, the web runs deeper than the settler colonial security apparatus is willing to permit – hence the arrests that began this chapter.

Rather than "protests" against a hegemonic order, we can understand relational and practice-based collectivities as generative democratic movements in which people act otherwise than the predatory logics of imperialism, capitalism, and colonialism. These movements recognize Indigenous political authorities within specific places. Like water and wild

---

[57] One could argue that, in reality, the predatory relations of settler colonialism, including the violence of the RCMP, constitute a much more urgent and genuine "threat" than Indigenous resurgence movements acting to support sustainable self-determination.

[58] Miles Howe and Jeffrey Monaghan, "Strategic Incapacitation of Indigenous Dissent: Crowd Theories, Risk Management, and Settler Colonial Policing," *Canadian Journal of Sociology* 43, no. 4 (2018): 327.

[59] Howe and Monaghan, "Strategic Incapacitation of Indigenous Dissent," 338.

[60] As cited in Howe and Monaghan, "Strategic Incapacitation of Indigenous Dissent," 338.

[61] For more on the concept of colonial entanglement, see Brydon Kramer, "Entangled with/in Empire: Indigenous Nations, Settler Preservations, and the Return of Buffalo to Banff National Park" (unpublished MA thesis, University of Victoria, 2020), https://dspace.library.uvic.ca/bitstream/handle/1828/12476/Kramer_Brydon_MA_2020.pdf.

salmon, resurgent Indigenous nations and places have their own logics and laws. Through a political praxis that complements the grounded normativities of Indigenous nations, a politics of recognition and self-determination from below, relational and practice-based collectivities learn how to live more responsibly with both people and place. These networked webs of alliance and affiliation span below, through, and beyond the settler colonial state, flowing with the waters and following the movements of wild salmon and Indigenous resurgence. Further, these relational networks have the potential to be made denser through the extension of place-based ethics of responsibility and practices of reciprocity. This density holds the promise and power to widen cracks and fissures in the settler colonial concrete. By making these webs of relationship and practice visible through the stories I share in this chapter, I am not revealing anything that is not already known and shown through Indigenous political theory and mobilization at a range of sites and scales. What I am trying to show, however, is the process by which others can be drawn into, informed by, and agential within Indigenous ethico-political frameworks – in addition to but, more importantly, *instead of* settler colonial ways of relating to and understanding the world. To paraphrase the epigraph to this chapter, engagements with Indigenous resurgence *can* and *do* change what wants to appear unchangeable – they demystify settler colonialism and show that its predatory relations are *not* permanent nor inevitable. Neither democratic theory nor political praxis should proceed as if they were.

14

Like a Brick Through the Overton Window

Reorienting Our Politics, from the House of Commons to the Tiny House

Phil Henderson

It's difficult to know where to begin telling a story that, fundamentally, is about relationships cultivated and nurtured over millennia. This is especially true when, as that story catches up to present-day realities, the gnashing maw of empire too easily consumes all attention. In this chapter I focus on the struggles around and against the proposed expansion of the Trans Mountain Pipeline (TMX). But the political strife on which these events open a window is built on decades of contestation over the extractive processes and material flows of a globally sprawling fossil fuel industry that is the primary catalyst of a truly epochal reckoning for life as we – those enduring the last days of the Holocene – know it. More to the point, this decades-old battle against fossil capital has been brought to a head by the Canadian state's belligerent and monomaniacal commitment to propping-up a national fossil fuel industry – Canada being itself a contested political project (re)produced, in part, through a centuries-old and ongoing imperialist effort to conquer Indigenous peoples and to dispossess them of their territories.

In both popular and academic discourses, land/water defenders continue to be represented as "protestors."[1] Framing Indigenous-led anti-imperialist struggles in this way is premised on the assumption that the state is *the*

---

[1] In the absence of further specification, I intend for this term to encompass both the Indigenous people(s) who are leading the defense of their nations' territories *and* the non-Indigenous allies who are working in solidarity with them in that struggle. See Adam Barker and Russell Myers Ross, "Reoccupation and Resurgence: Indigenous Protest Camps in Canada," in *Protest Camps in International Context: Spaces, Infrastructures and Media of Resistance*, ed. Gavin Brown et al. (Bristol: Policy Press, 2018); Jeff Brady, "2 Years After Standing Rock Protests, Tensions Remain But Oil Business Booms," *NPR*, November 29, 2018, www.npr.org/2018/11/29/671701019/2-years-after-standing-rock-protests-north-dakota-oil-business-is-booming; Omar Mosleh, "'They Came to Destroy and Create Fear': Indigenous Protester Says Men Attacked Trans Mountain Protest Champ," *The Star*, April 22, 2020; Lisa Polewski, "Protesters Arrested at Residential Development in Caledonia: OPP," *Global News*, August 5, 2020.

constituted and singular political authority. As John Borrows notes, the ascription of 'protestor' or of 'civil disobedience' erases the presence of other sources of law that are being upheld and defended, an erasure that works to solidify the hegemony of state authority.[2] The grassroots land/water defenders who take center stage in the latter portion of this chapter are examples of 'democratic practices of *contestation*' only insofar as one chooses to politicize their actions while accepting the supposed neutrality of imperial institutions and processes. Manu Karuka helpfully displaces imperialism's presumption of neutrality – its effort at disappearance – by naming empire's governing logic as "countersovereignty," making the violence of everyday life lived through empire cognizable.[3] This reframing begins from the observation that empire rests on "*reactive* anxiety, [and] *fragile* modes of power that can take overwhelmingly violent form" in their efforts to deny and displace the existing and persisting political authority of Indigenous nations.[4]

Karuka's formulation is helpful not only for noting that the empire has no clothes, but also for insisting on the central importance of Indigenous modes of social relations that govern in place prior to and endure through the colonial present.[5] The politics central to this chapter emerge from and are driven by a staunch commitment to the defense and integrity of modes of social relations and systems of governance that sustain and enhance life. These politics are not principally about contesting or resisting, even as that language is easiest for discussion; instead, these politics are about upholding Indigenous political authority. In much of what passes for the canon of Euro-American political theory, Indigenous peoples are positioned between two poles of racist misrepresentation. On one side are the false Lockean presumptions about Indigenous peoples' prepolitical, pre-agricultural societies and, on the other, are the equally fictitious Rousseauian narratives about noble, ecologically pure, and therefore vestigal "savage" communities.[6] Other contributors to this volume expertly deconstruct this constitutive exclusion at the heart of Euro-American thought by highlighting the intelligence, the fecundity, and the durability of Indigenous governance systems (see Part IV on "Indigenous Democracies" in this volume; especially Swain (Chapter 13), as there is

[2] John Borrows, *Freedom and Indigenous Constitutionalism* (Toronto: University of Toronto Press, 2016), 52–55; Warren Magnusson, "Decentring the State, Or Looking for Politics," in *Organizing Dissent: Contemporary Social Movements in Theory and Practice*, ed. William Carroll (Toronto: Garamond, 1992), 69–80; Vicky Osterweil, *In Defense of Looting: A Riotous History of Uncivil Action* (New York: Bold Type Books, 2020), 1–20.

[3] Manu Karuka, *Empire's Tracks: Indigenous Nations, Chinese Workers, and the Transcontinental Railroad* (Oakland, CA: University of California Press, 2019), 1–2.

[4] Ibid., xii (emphasis added).

[5] Ibid., 20–37; Soren C. Larsen and Jay T. Johnson, *Being Together in Place: Indigenous Coexistence in a More than Human World* (Minneapolis: University of Minnesota Press, 2017).

[6] James Tully, *Strange Multiplicity: Constitutionalism in an Age of Diversity* (Cambridge: Cambridge University Press, 1995), 71–78, 80.

considerable cross-pollination in our thinking), and a much wider body of Indigenous thought and scholarship exists with which political theorists should familiarize themselves.[7] In my discussion of the struggles against TMX, I take the vitality and the vital importance of Indigenous sovereignties as my political starting place. I do this foremost because Indigenous peoples have a right to govern themselves, their territories, and their relations unencumbered by imperial regimes. But I also suggest that, inasmuch as it necessitates a confrontation with the cannibalistic urges of empire and the increasingly unlivable ecology those drives are producing, the resurgence of Indigenous sovereignties is a struggle in defense of life itself.[8] As James Tully says, in this struggle "[n]o one is offsite or not responsible. The choice is change or self-destruction."[9]

This chapter is structured in three parts. In the first, I provide a history of the struggle against TMX, up to the Canadian federal government's reapproval of the project on June 18, 2019. In the second section I examine the federal government's press conference reapproving TMX in juxtaposition to a press conference held minutes later by a coalition of First Nations and municipal governments opposed to the project. Here, I consider both the logic and the limitations of strategies of hegemony and counterhegemony. The third section moves to the level of grassroots politics, focusing on the week-long project to build a Tiny House and the 20 km march up the Saanich Peninsula to send it on it's way to Secwépemcul'ecw, where the Tiny House Warriors now use the House in the resurgence of Secwépemc governance and in their fight to halt the construction of TMX through their territories. Drawing on my own engagement with the Tiny House project, as well as on local reporting and editorials, I am particularly interested in reflecting on a more expansive view of the political, one in which power and authority are not mediated through logics

---

[7] Umeek E. Richard Atleo, *Tsawalk: A Nuu-chah-nulth Worldview* (Vancouver: UBC Press, 2004); John Borrows, *Drawing Out Law: Spirit's Guide* (Toronto: University of Toronto Press, 2010); Nick Estes, *Our History Is the Future: Standing Rock versus the Dakota Access Pipeline, the Long Tradition of Indigenous Resistance* (London: Verso, 2019); Jerry Fontaine, *Our Hearts Are as One Fire: An Ojibway-Anishinabe Vision for the Future* (Vancouver: UBC Press, 2020); Carwyn Jones, "A Māori Constitutional Tradition," *New Zealand Journal of Public and International Law* 12, no. 1 (2014): 187–203; Robin Wall Kimmerer, *Braiding Sweetgrass: Indigenous Wisdom, Scientific Knowledge, and the Teachings of Plants* (Minneapolis: Milkweed Editions, 2013); and Kayanesenh Paul Williams, *Kayanerenkó:wa: The Great Law of Peace* (Winnipeg: University of Manitoba Press, 2018).

[8] Umeek E. Richard Atleo, *Principles of Tsawalk: An Indigenous Approach to Global Crisis* (Vancouver: UBC Press, 2011); Jack D. Forbes, *Columbus and Other Cannibals: The Wétiko Disease of Exploitation, Imperialism, and Terrorism* (New York: Seven Stories Press, 2008); Winona LaDuke, *To Be a Water Protector: The Rise of the Wiindigoo Slayers* (Halifax: Fernwood Publishing, 2020); and Boyce Richardson, *Strangers Devour the Land* (White River Junction, VT: Chelsea Green Publishing, 1991).

[9] James Tully, "Foreward: A Canadian Tragedy," in Sarah Marie Wiebe, *Everyday Exposure: Indigenous Mobilization and Environmental Justice in Canada's Chemical Valley* (Vancouver: UBC Press, 2016), xiii

of hegemony/counterhegemony. While engaging this ethic of turning away from the state as *the* site of political activity, I also nevertheless want to avoid overly reductive or easy answers by considering the very serious problem that the state continues to pose for anti-imperialist struggles today. Throughout this I am informed by Karuka's problematique for anti-imperialists in the twenty-first century, which has echoes of both Tully and Rosa Luxemburg: that today we face a choice between "[d]ecolonization, or mass extinction."[10] This is the lens through which I consider what the resurgence of Indigenous sovereignties means in an era of ongoing climate catastrophe from my own positionality as a settler – a non-Indigenous person, interpellated as a citizen by an occupying colonial state.

TRANSMOUNTAIN, A HISTORY OF EXPANDING STRUGGLE

In this section I reconstruct the pertinent history of TMX. Unless noted otherwise, in detailing the history of Trans Mountain's engagement with the National Energy Board (NEB) and various stakeholders up until mid-2018, I rely predominantly on Justice Dawson's decision in *Tsleil-Waututh Nation v. Canada* (2018) – the Federal Court of Appeals decision that "quashed" the initial Cabinet approval of TMX. For details subsequent to 2018 or outside of the realm of official record, I rely primarily on news reporting, excepting in circumstances – such as the Protect the Inlet March and Tiny House builds – where I participated in the demonstrations or direct actions.

In December 2013 the Trans Mountain Corporation, which at the time was owned by Kinder Morgan, applied to the NEB for a certificate of public convenience and necessity authorizing the Trans Mountain Expansion Project (TMX). The project primarily entailed: (1) construction of roughly 987 km of new pipeline 'twinned' to the 1,147 km of existing line; (2) construction or modification of pumping stations and tanks, with a doubling of the Burnaby Mountain tank farm from thirteen to twenty-six storage tanks; (3) expansion of the Westridge dock facility; and (4) construction of two wholly new pipelines from the Burnaby storage facility to the Westridge docks. While the language of 'twinning' evokes a sense of parity, upon completion TMX is actually intended to increase the pipeline's transportation capacity nearly threefold: from 300,000 barrels per day to 890,000 per day. Furthermore, as the project is meant primarily to facilitate an export pivot from America to Asian and Pacific Rim states, the so-called 'downstream' impacts of the project on shipping are of an even greater order of magnitude. Filings with the NEB estimate tanker shipping jumping from roughly five tankers per month to thirty-four tankers per month – an increase of nearly 700 percent as a consequence of TMX.

Between December 2013 and November 2016, the NEB pursued a three-phase process to review TMX's social, economic, and ecological impacts in

[10] Karuka, *Empire's Tracks*, 200.

consultation with Indigenous peoples and First Nations. The bulk of meetings occurred between April 2014 and February 2016, during which time, Justice Dawson notes, many Indigenous participants raised serious concerns not only about the project itself but also about how their participation in consultations was confined to relatively narrow post hoc issues of mitigation and revenue sharing. Higher-order questions about sovereignty, jurisdiction, and their right under the United Nations Declaration on the Rights of Indigenous Peoples (UNDRIP) to offer/withhold their free, prior, and informed consent for the project as a whole were not on the table during these consultations. As such, the NEB's recommendation in May 2016 – prior to completing Phase III of consultations – that the Cabinet approve TMX was met with severe consternation from many Indigenous peoples; the assertion that the project is in the "public interest," clarified just how fundamental Canada's exclusion of Indigenous governance is.

Despite the NEB's recommendation, many who opposed TMX remained inordinately hopeful that the project would be cancelled. Their hope was a consequence of their sense that, in spite of the failings of the state's regulatory arms, a major victory seemed to have been secured in the legislative and executive branch of government with the recent election of Justin Trudeau. Moreover, this hope was not based merely on projection. As Martin Lukacs details, Trudeau's 2015 campaign was peppered with rhetoric wholly novel to Canada's partisan landscape. The promise of "nation-to-nation" relationships with Indigenous peoples, and even of "decolonization," that Trudeau offered on the campaign trail seemed to fulfill the vision of UNDRIP.[11] Moreover, cancellation of such hotly contested infrastructure as TMX seemed assured given that one of Trudeau's constant refrains throughout the campaign and beyond was that while governments "may be able to issue permits ... only communities can grant permission" – a sentiment he delivered to the Calgary Petroleum Club as long ago as 2013.[12] Many were therefore dismayed when Trudeau announced his Cabinet's approval of TMX on November 29, 2016, following completion of Phase III of the review process. Without any apparent sense of contradiction, this approval came at the same press conference in which Trudeau cancelled the Northern Gateway and Energy East pipelines, citing both Indigenous objections and climate concerns.

Following the approval of TMX a series of legal challenges were launched, the most successful of which was brought by səl'ilwətaʔɬ (Tsleil-Waututh) and Sḵwx̱wú7mesh Úxwumixw (Squamish) First Nations, endorsed by both Vancouver and Burnaby alongside a number of other interveners. As opposition

[11] Martin Lukacs, *The Trudeau Formula: Seduction and Betrayal in an Age of Discontent* (Montreal: Black Rose Books, 2019), 136.

[12] Justin Trudeau, "Speech to the Calgary Petroleum Club," October 30, 2013, Liberal Party of Canada, transcript, https://liberal.ca/liberal-party-canada-leader-justin-trudeaus-speech-calgary-petroleum-club.

was being partly channeled through state judicial apparatuses, a number of grassroots groups also coalesced around campaigns of both public outreach and direct action. While much of the grassroots organizing against TMX took expected forms (marches, petitions, and other demonstrations of collective opposition), Lukacs details how surprising the opposition to the project was in both its breadth and depth, with thousands of people indicating their preparedness to risk arrest.[13] At the gates of the Burnaby storage tank facility, a soft blockade slowed work on the site. Day after day new people came forward, defying an injunction issued in 2018, standing in front of the facility gate, snarling construction and operations traffic. Hundreds – including prominent local and national figures – have been arrested as a consequence of their dissent.[14]

As alluded to in the introduction, much of this dissent refuses to travel under the title of civil disobedience. Dissidents position themselves instead as *proponents* or *defenders* of the lands and waters under threat, as well as of the Indigenous governance systems that are at the heart of organizing – both materially and conceptually – this resistance.[15] This is perhaps clearest in the *Women's Declaration Against the Trans Mountain Man Camps*, issued from Secwépemcul'ecw in November of 2017.[16] As the Declaration makes clear, Secwépemc sovereignty over "the land, waters, and resources" within their territories remains fully intact. They effectively tie together the threats that TMX poses to their sovereignty as a political body, to their territories, and to their own bodies through the degradation/toxification of land and the threat of gendered and sexualized violence that accompanies heavy industry: "We, as Secwépemc women, declare that we do no [sic] consent! We do not consent to the desecration of our sacred land; we do not consent to the transgressions on our sacred bodies!" However, rather than channeling their dissent toward the courts or appeals to elected officials, this Declaration announces their intention to construct "ten solarized Tiny Houses on our land," an act that they note is just as much about "housing ... Secwépemc families, re-establishing our village sites, and asserting our Secwépemc responsibility to our lands and waters" as it is about blocking TMX. I return to the Tiny House Warriors in the third section of this chapter, but want to note here how radically they shift the terms and location of the struggle over TMX. To call the Declaration a "refusal" of the state and its legal apparatuses seems to imply a degree of priority that those institutions clearly do not command. This Declaration embodies a compelling theory of power, in which the space of the political was never confined within

---

[13] Lukacs, *Trudeau Formula*, 95–101.
[14] Lauren Boothby, "More Than 200 People Arrested at Pipeline Protests in Burnaby," *Burnaby Now*, May 30, 2018.
[15] See Swain, Chapter 13, this volume for a striking example.
[16] "Women's Declaration Against Trans Mountain Man Camps," Secwépemcul'ecw Assembly, Secwépemc Women's Warrior Society and Tiny House Warriors, November 2017, www .secwepemculecw.org/women-s-declaration.

the limestone buildings of state capitals – nor even in opposition directed at those presumed 'centers of power' – but is produced through collectivities and is always already located in and responsible to the living relations of the territories in which those collectivities persist.

One of the broadest demonstrations of grassroots opposition to TMX came on March 10, 2018, when 20,000 people joined the Protect the Inlet March to Burnaby Mountain. Headed by Indigenous leaders from along the proposed pipeline route, but primarily from local nations like səl'ilwətaʔɬ, Sḵwx̱wú7mesh Úxwumixw and xʷməθkʷəy̓əm (Musqueam), the show of immense collective power and solidarity was also the strategically chosen moment in which members of səl'ilwətaʔɬ revealed a project to both assert their governance *and* strengthen their on-the-ground opposition to TMX. As thousands demonstrated their collective power by marching past the gates of the storage tank facility in defiance of the court orders, just a stone's throw from the injunction zone a crew under the leadership of Will George busily constructed Kwekwecnewtxw, or "a place to watch from."[17] Built in the style of Salish watch houses, Kwekwecnewtxw evokes and actualizes Salish jurisdiction. A millennia-long practice of governance meant to ensure community safety, today the threat Kwekwecnewtxw guards against is posed by an infrastructure project that is facilitated through, and itself serves to further facilitate, colonial dispossession.[18] Since March 2018, Kwekwecnewtxw has acted not only as an assertion of Indigenous governance, and as a hub and home for the grassroots resistance to TMX, it has also been an invaluable bridge spanning Indigenous and settler communities. That Kwekwecnewtxw has sustained itself over such a long duration is enormously educative: both in its direct efforts at community engagement, but also as an example of the capacity that grassroots coalitions have to create and sustain frontlines against the imperial nexus of the state and industry.

Faced with an entrenched and expanding resistance, the responses from the state and industry are perhaps not surprising, even though their brashness should never fail to be shocking. As Lukacs details, faced with a popular upswell against this project, the fossil fuel industry leaned heavily on the state, calling upon politicians to impose a "law and order" regime that advances and protects their infrastructure.[19] In 2018 David Dodge, former Governor of the Bank of Canada, told a crowd in Edmonton that as opposition "fanaticism" grew, it made certain that people "are going to die in protesting construction of this pipeline."[20] Though he later walked back his statement, in the days following TMX's approval the then Minister of Natural Resources, Jim Carr, threatened that his government was prepared to advance construction against public dissent

---

[17] "Visit the spiritual resistance to #StopKM at Kwekwecnewtxw," Protect the Inlet, 2019, http://web.archive.org/web/20210124185559/https://protecttheinlet.ca/structure/.

[18] Robert Nichols, *Theft Is Property! Dispossession and Critical Theory* (Durham, NC: Duke University Press, 2020).

[19] Lukacs, *Trudeau Formula*, 95–130.   [20] Ibid., 97.

"through [the Canadian state's] defence forces, through its police forces."[21] In spite of these assurances, however, the confidence that capital had in the project eroded rapidly. In April 2018, barely a month after the Protect the Inlet March, Kinder Morgan announced that it was halting all "non-essential activities and related spending" on TMX in order to consult shareholders, setting May 31 as a deadline by which to determine the viability of the project.[22] Faced with the imminent collapse of their cornerstone infrastructure project, the Trudeau Cabinet announced on May 29 that the federal government was purchasing Trans Mountain from Kinder Morgan for $4.5 billion dollars – a sum that includes only existing infrastructure and not the immense, outstanding construction costs.[23] The government affirmed its commitment to financing the completion of TMX, in the hopes of later finding a private investor to buy the expanded pipeline.

It was likely because of this increasingly apparent integration of the state and fossil fuel industry that many opponents of TMX responded to the federal Court of Appeals' August 30 ruling in *Tsleil-Waututh* v. *Canada* (2018) so jubilantly. In Metulia/Victoria, BC, hundreds poured into the downtown core that evening in an impromptu celebration of the decision to "quash" Cabinet's approval of TMX. The possibility that TMX could be defeated so cleanly, and without the need for an even more protracted or escalated struggle, overawed the fact that the Court's decision was, in fact, quite technical and narrow in scope. Far from a decision to "quash" TMX itself, *Tsleil-Waututh* merely remitted approval of the project back to Cabinet for further consideration on two points: (1) a more thorough assessment of the ecological impact on the Salish Sea caused by marine traffic associated with TMX, and (2) to more adequately "explore possible accommodation of those concerns" raised by Indigenous peoples and First Nations. Indeed, the Court even went so far as to affirm that Canada had "acted in good faith" in its consultations, even if they had come up somewhat short. No doubt the Court's rosy portrayal was due, in part, to the overly constrained scope of the issues under consideration. For instance, the fact that TMX would significantly contribute to accelerating the climate catastrophe, increasing Canada's overall greenhouse gas emissions by as much as 2 percent, was only obliquely noted in the Court's reference to an Environment Canada report, but the consequences of this were never directly considered by the Court.

More directly pertinent to participants in the *Tsleil-Waututh* case itself, however, was the fact that the Court confined the scope of its proceedings to

[21] Ibid., 96; Catharine Tunney, "Jim Carr Says Military Comments Not a Threat to Pipeline Protesters," *CBC News*, December 2, 2016, www.cbc.ca/news/politics/jim-carr-protests-pipeline-military-1.3878258.

[22] Stephanie Ip and Patrick Johnston, "Kinder Morgan Halts Non-Essential Work on Trans Mountain Pipeline and Sets Drop-Dead Deadline," *Vancouver Sun*, April 9, 2018, https://vancouversun.com/news/local-news/kinder-morgan-to-halt-its-spending-on-trans-mountain-pipeline-due-to-b-c-opposition.

[23] "Our History," Trans Mountain, www.transmountain.com/history.

reviewing the process initiated by the NEB in 2013. Drawing on industry-wide trends, Kinder Morgan had deliberately minimized TMX's review process by relying on the logic of "pipe in the ground." The potential impact of the project was minimized because it was portrayed as *merely* expanding *existing* infrastructure, rather than establishing *new* corridors.[24] Not only does this conceal the enormity of TMX's ecological impact, it also serves to fully elide Canada's historic failure to live up to its own – already highly constrained – duty to consult with Indigenous peoples in the initial construction of Trans Mountain. By choosing to start the clock on the duty to consult only in 2013, and thereby ignoring the reality that Trans Mountain was constructed in 1951 as the wave of Canada's apartheid laws was only just beginning to break, the Court's review of TMX legitimates the lack of historic consultations – much less consent – with Indigenous peoples all along the route. Furthermore, as this approach actualized the returns on Kinder Morgan's investment in a "pipe in the ground" strategy, it makes clear how the Canadian state works toward the erasure of Indigenous nations' jurisdictions in a way that "augments and reinforces the intracapitalist coalition supporting and advocating for pipelines and oil infrastructure."[25]

Importantly, TMX is not novel in terms of the Courts' using the existence of private property to retroactively legitimate the dispossession/displacement of Indigenous peoples.[26] Nor is the state's intervention to salvage and complete a floundering infrastructure project – in order to potentiate its sell-off into private hands – wholly unexpected to students of Canadian history. As Reg Whittaker notes, "the basic engine of development in Canada" has been *"private enterprise at public expense."*[27] Pithier commentators have remarked that Canada is simply "three mining companies in a trench coat, wearing a stupid hat and carrying a gun."[28]

HEGEMONY ...

While intense, the excitement about the *Tsleil-Waututh* decision was short-lived, as the government announced almost immediately that it intended to fulfill the Court's skeletal outline of the steps necessary to discharge its

[24] Shiri Pasternak, Katie Mazer, and D. T. Cochrane, "The Financing Problem of Colonialism: How Indigenous Jurisdiction is Valued in Pipeline Politics," in *Standing with Standing Rock: Voices from the #NODAPL Movement*, ed. Nick Estes and Jaskiran Dhillon (Minneapolis: University of Minnesota Press, 2019), 226.

[25] Ibid., 224.

[26] See *Chippewas of Sarnia Band* v. *Attorney General of Canada* [2000] 51 OR (3d) 641; and, for discussion of the case, Deanne Aline Marie LeBlanc, "Identifying the Settler Denizen Within Settler Colonialism" (unpublished MA thesis, University of Victoria, 2014), 24–25.

[27] Reg Whittaker, *A Sovereign Idea: Essays on Canada as a Democratic Community* (Montreal: McGill-Queen's University Press, 1992), 20 (emphasis in original).

[28] Alex V. Green, "Canada Is Fake: What Americans Think of as Their Friendly Neighbor to the North, If They Think of It at All, Is a Scam," *The Outline*, February 19, 2020, https://theoutline.com/post/8686/canada-is-fake.

obligations. It came as little surprise, then, nine and a half months later on June 18, 2019, when the government announced with all the false contrition in the world that it had listened to the Court's calls to "do better" and was now prepared to reapprove TMX.[29] Flanked by Ministers Morneau (Finance), McKenna (Environment), MacAulay (Agriculture), and Sohi (Natural Resources), Trudeau's press conference attempted to execute a major pivot in the conversation around TMX. The strategic reason for the absence of the Ministers of both Crown-Indigenous Relations and Indigenous Services was apparent throughout the press conference in which Trudeau portrayed his critics as mired in false choices between 'the economy' and 'the environment.' Throughout this conference Trudeau strenuously avoided reckoning with the fact that TMX is contested primarily and most stridently on the grounds that it violates the jurisdictions and sovereignties of numerous Indigenous nations.

The promised nation-to-nation relationships with Indigenous peoples – which Trudeau continually says are the country's "most important relationship" – were not mentioned.[30] Instead, Trudeau opened this press conference by asserting that his government was elected in 2015 on paired commitments of "growing the middle class" and to "protect our environment and fight climate change." Implicit in this assertion is the suggestion that he would be seeking re-election only months later in the fall of 2019 on those same priorities. Alleging that his partisan challengers believe these objectives are irreconcilable, Trudeau insisted that they were not only "complementary" to one another but that TMX is preternaturally capable of threading them together. In spite of the apparent ease with which his government appropriated billions of dollars to purchase fossil fuel infrastructure only a year prior, Trudeau repeatedly emphasized that while he viewed it as absolutely vital, a transition away from fossil fuels would be costly. Trudeau estimated that the tax revenue from TMX "could be around $500 million per year" – at which rate the government would recoup the cost of its impulse purchase in a mere decade. He went on to outline that the construction and operation of the pipeline will not only create opportunities for people to "earn a good living," but that all revenue earned from the completed TMX would be earmarked to be "invested in Canada's clean energy transition" –including "any profits from the sale of the pipeline." In one of the few unprompted references to Indigenous peoples in his press conference, Trudeau indicated that his

29 CBC News, "Ministers Answer Questions on Trans Mountain Expansion Approval," streamed live on June 18, 2019, YouTube video, 26:24, https://www.youtube.com/watch?v=nQjdlnxtPzE; CBC News, "Trudeau Cabinet Approves Trans Mountain Pipeline Expansion Project," streamed live on June 18, 2019, YouTube video, 20:17, www.youtube.com/watch?v=MFot-hZRhEk.
30 Susana Mas, "Trudeau Lays Out Plan for New Relationship with Indigenous People," *CBC News*, December 5, 2015, www.cbc.ca/news/politics/justin-trudeau-afn-indigenous-aboriginal-people-1.3354747.

government is encouraging possible Indigenous buyers. Seemingly, the only way Indigenous nations can have a say over fossil fuel infrastructure in their territories is if they are prepared to bankroll it.

Trudeau sought to deepen his case for TMX by further asserting that the project – increasingly treated as a panacea for all woes – would solve a "core economic problem" facing the fossil fuel industry in Canada. Overlooking the mere externality of the climate catastrophe, Trudeau noted that the single biggest crisis facing Canadian fossil fuel exports is that they are beholden to a monopoly buyer. As Trudeau suggested, the fact that nearly all fossil fuels extracted in the territories claimed by Canada are bound for American refineries means that the price of Canadian oil is dictated south of the 49th Parallel. Never mind that fossil fuel exports are sold in private markets – not primarily to states – or that global commodities trading in crude oil was already in sharp decline, Trudeau was effectively stitching together a case for TMX grounded in an overt petronationalism.[31] This was made apparent as Trudeau paired a rather obtuse invocation of Trump and the growing fear Canadians have that "anything can happen with our neighbours to the south" with his strident assertion that "Canadians are our own people, and we make our own choices." Given not only the evident fractures that exist around just TMX but also the well-noted historic failings of the Canadian state-building project to constitute a coherent "people" for itself, Trudeau's struggle to leverage TMX in the cause of maintaining hegemony could hardly be more apparent.[32]

The political left in Canada has its own long and twisting relationship with economic nationalism, typically grounded in anti-Americanism, but which has recently aligned itself with petronationalism.[33] The political and ideological work that Trudeau's press conference did, however, is of a different species than even those troubled projects. It is a near-perfect embodiment of what Lukacs calls "the Trudeau formula," which he distills as a political program advancing the promise of "changeless change."[34] As Trudeau appropriates the rhetoric and affects of more progressive, at times even radical, political movements, his

[31] James M. Griffin, "Petro-Nationalism: The Futile Search for Oil Security," *The Energy Journal* 36, no. 1 (2015): 25–41; Andreas Malm and the Zetkin Collective, *White Skin, Black Fuel: On the Danger of Fossil Fascism* (London: Random House, 2021).

[32] Peter H. Russell, *Canada's Constitutional Odyssey: A Country Based on Incomplete Conquests* (Toronto: University Press, 2017); Peter H. Russell, *Constitutional Odyssey: Can Canadians Become a Sovereign Peoples?* (Toronto: University of Toronto Press, 1992); and Whittaker, *Sovereign Idea*; see also Jacques Rancière, *Staging the People: The Proletarian and His Double* (London: Verso Books, 2011).

[33] Irving Martin Abella, *Nationalism, Communism, and Canadian Labour: The CIO, the Communist Party, and the Canadian Congress of Labour 1935–1956* (Toronto: University of Toronto Press, 1973); Kari Levitt, *Silent Surrender: The Multinational Corporation in Canada* (Montreal: McGill-Queen's University Press, 1970); and Jason Markusoff, "The Rise of Alberta's Unapologetic Petro-Patriots," *Maclean's Magazine*, July 15, 2019, www.macleans.ca /news/canada/the-rise-of-albertas-unapologetic-petro-patriots.

[34] Lukacs, *Trudeau Formula*, 11.

policies make clear that "his goal was not to transform the status quo but to smoothly defend it."[35] What is more, while Trudeau maintains this rhetoric while in office and in flagrant contradiction of the actual consequences of his policies, the Trudeau formula is in fact a striking development in the classic Liberal Party playbook of 'campaigning from the left, governing from the right.'[36]

Despite the vigor of Lukacs' analysis, he underemphasizes the enormity of what the Trudeau formula achieves. Far from being merely a cynical electoral strategy, I want to suggest that by maintaining adherence to a rhetoric of social/economic/environmental justice while pursuing policies directly antagonistic to those goals, Trudeau has stumbled upon a major ideological project that is causing a massive reduction in the horizon of the politically possible – the so-called "Overton window."[37] To suggest that Trudeau is merely appropriating, misusing, and denuding more transformative or radical political discourses is to identify only one half of the ideological work being done. More troublingly, the deeper consequence of the Trudeau formula is that it actually *transmutes* the public understanding of the content and meaning behind the discourses that he appropriates. Put more plainly: for the vast majority of casual observers of national politics, there is no necessary contradiction between Trudeau's appropriation of transformative rhetoric and his status quo politics. Rather, many come, wholly understandably, to associate that otherwise transformative rhetoric with the continuity of the material conditions under which a sizable majority of them continue to struggle. By pairing the rhetoric of transformation with the actual continuity of the status quo, the Trudeau formula makes concrete the Thatcherite declaration that 'there is no alternative.' This is perhaps nowhere more apparent than in the case of Trudeau's pursuit of "reconciliation" with Indigenous peoples – a project whose meaning is so perverted as to be somehow congruent with the invasion of untreatied lands by paramilitary police in order to remove Indigenous land/water defenders from their territories. Such is the toxic vacuity of the Trudeau formula that grassroots leaders such as Freda Huson of the Wet'suwet'en nation and director of the Unist'ot'en Camp declared "reconciliation" to be dead in light of the very real violence that her nation continues to face.[38]

[35] Lukacs, *Trudeau Formula*, 12.
[36] Stephen Clarkson, *The Big Red Machine: How the Liberal Party Dominates Canadian Politics* (Vancouver: UBC Press, 2005).
[37] "A Brief Explanation of the Overton Window," Mackinac Centre for Public Policy, www .mackinac.org/OvertonWindow.
[38] Charlie Smith, "RCMP Arrest Unist'ot'en Matriarchs During Ceremony to Honour Missing and Murdered Indigenous Women and Girls," *The Georgia Straight*, February 10, 2020, www.straight .com/news/1358106/rcmp-arrest-unistoten-matriarchs-during-ceremony-honour-missing-and-murdered-indigenous; tawinikay, "Reconciliation Is Dead: A Strategic Proposal," *It's Going Down* (blog), February 15, 2020, https://itsgoingdown.org/reconciliation-is-dead-a-strategic-proposal.

I should note that part of the Trudeau formula's success is contingent on the contemporary partisan landscape in which Trudeau operates. Briefly stated, this is one in which an increasingly verbose and outwardly reactionary Conservative Party and its surrogates have been only too ready to denigrate Trudeau as some sort of rabid "social justice warrior."[39] This charge serves to reify Trudeau's false claims of pursuing a transformative politics. At the same time, the ostensible parliamentary left, embodied predominantly by the New Democratic Party (NDP), has – by the admission of many of its own supporters – abandoned positions that are even marginally oppositional to such dominant social formations as capitalism, settler colonialism, white supremacism, and cisheteropatriarchy.[40] The Trudeau formula dramatically curtails the horizon of political possibility largely because – on the partisan landscape – it is unchallenged from the left and is perversely validated in its self-presentation from the right. Given this, the emergence of a project of counterhegemony in rebuttal to Trudeau's June 18 reapproval of TMX is all the more remarkable.

. . . AND ANTICOLONIAL STRATEGY

As Trudeau wrapped up in Ottawa, across the continent another press conference hosted at səl'ilwətaʔɬ was beginning.[41] This press conference was remarkable not only in that it modeled a different relationship to place – the abstracted distance of the state-eye view from Ottawa was displaced by systems of governance firmly rooted in the territories threatened by TMX – it also displayed a strikingly more dispersed theory of power and authority.[42] Contrasting the singular authority of the prime minister and his Cabinet, on stage in this second press conference were representatives from səl'ilwətaʔɬ, Sḵwx̱wú7mesh Úxwumixw, and xʷməθkʷəy̓əm, alongside other Indigenous leadership from Sumas First Nation, Tsartlip First Nation, the Neskonlith

[39] Jonathan Kay, "The Rise and (Possible) Fall of Justin Trudeau Show the Perils of Woke Governance," *Quillette*, March 7, 2019, https://quillette.com/2019/03/07/the-rise-and-possible-fall-of-justin-trudeau-show-the-perils-of-woke-governance; Postmedia Editorial, "Trudeau Needs to Leave His Social Justice Warrior Cape at Home," *Toronto Sun*, May 22, 2018, https://torontosun.com/opinion/editorials/editorial-trudeau-needs-to-leave-his-social-justice-warrior-cape-at-home.

[40] Avi Lewis, "Social Democracy and the Left in Canada: Past, Present, and Future," in *Party of Conscience: The CCF, The NDP, and Social Democracy in Canada*, ed. Roberta Lexier et al. (Toronto: Between the Lines, 2018), 197–214; Abdul Malik, "Jack Layton is the NDP's Third Rail," *Canadian Dimension*, September 1, 2020, https://canadiandimension.com/articles/view/jack-layton-is-the-ndps-third-rail; see also Ralph Miliband, *Parliamentary Socialism: A Study in the Politics of Labour* (London: Merlin Press, 1961).

[41] Tsleil-Waututh Nation Sacred Trust, "Live at the Trans Mountain Pipeline Announcement Press Conference," Facebook, June 18, 2019, www.facebook.com/630937800297791/videos/612471812592081.

[42] James C. Scott, *Seeing Like a State: How Certain Schemes to Improve the Human Condition Failed* (New Haven: Yale University Press, 1998).

Indian Band, and Stewart Phillip, the Grand Chief of the Union of BC Indian Chiefs, also on stage were Vancouver Mayor Kennedy Stewart and Councilor Jean Swanson – both of whom had been arrested on Burnaby Mountain. Embodying a commitment to polyvocality and inter-nationalism, this press conference centered on the imminent and very material threat that TMX poses. As Rueben George (səl'ilwətaʔɬ) stated in his introductory comments, those gathered on the stage were there because Trudeau's actions in reapproving TMX "are hurting Canadians." This necessitates the formation of a coalition prepared to "protect what we love" in a way that is grounded in Indigenous governance systems that teach the necessity "to protect all the human being on our lands and waters, that's *our* law." Chief Leah George-Wilson (səl'ilwətaʔɬ) affirmed this sentiment. She asserts that her "obligation is not to oil. Our obligation is to the land, the water, to our people, to the whales" and that none of the prime minister's comments or consultation processes had adequately addressed those concerns or the risks that his Cabinet is imposing on her nation.

Chief Dalton Silver (Sumas First Nation) noted that what this boils down to is a shared responsibility to protect the Salish Sea from harm. This responsibility exists far beyond the shoreline of the Sea itself, Silver continued: it begins hundreds of miles inland from the Sea at the headwaters and flows downstream through the territories of his own nation. Radically distinct from the abstracted, Cartesian thinking of the Cabinet and the NEB – the excesses of which had treated the Salish Sea as somehow separable from the overland route of the pipeline, resulting in the *Tsleil-Waututh* decision forcing a temporary delay of TMX so that the project's impacts on the Salish Sea could be considered – Silver articulates his nation's theory of responsible governance as one that is produced through the actual material relationships of the territories in which it is situated. Sumas is not connected to the nations and communities around the Salish Sea merely as a consequence of the inevitable destruction that TMX represents; they are primarily connected through the life-sustaining relationships embodied in flows of water, runs of salmon, and the political alliances that are embedded within and have enhanced those relationships since time immemorial. This is as concrete a realization of how Trudeau's pursuit of TMX manifests the countersovereignty of imperial regimes as one is likely to find. Grand Chief Phillip made this all the more clear by noting that his sense of déjà vu at the Cabinet's announcement is a consequence of the fact that, for Indigenous peoples, persisting in their governance under direct threat by the colonial state is very much "another day at the office," even as he staunchly asserts that "Indigenous peoples walking ... in solidarity with their friends and neighbours and their allies" is the pathway toward victory over this project.

To at least some degree, this coalition can be helpfully understood as an effort to build and to make visible a *counterhegemonic* formation that challenges the ongoing accomplishment of a petronationalist hegemony forwarded by the Canadian federal government. As William Carroll notes, the "deep transformation" portended by counterhegemonic struggles "gets its start on, and draws much of its vitality from, the immediate field of the conjunctural, in resistance to the agenda of the dominant hegemony."[43] Put more simply, while they often appear as both primarily *responsive* to the actions of the constituted authority and confined to relatively *particular* issues or interests, the deeper undercurrents of counterhegemonic struggles envision a truly radical uprooting of the dominant order. Importantly, the strategic terrain of counterhegemony is also embedded in struggles that are of immediate and material consequence to the communities with/ in whom solidarity and affinity are being built, rather than persisting predominantly in the realm of ideals. Struggling toward this deep transformation, counterhegemonic formations seek to draw "together subaltern social forces around an alternative ethico-political conception of the world, constructing a common interest."[44] The shared threat that TMX represents to these communities has contributed to the stitching together of an alliance between First Nations and municipalities. Moreover, inasmuch as Indigenous-led decolonization struggles are always local in character, requiring alliances or ententes with neighboring communities, and insomuch as TMX is a particular struggle in the much wider battle against climate catastrophe, the coalition stepping forward to challenge Trudeau embodies a transformational critique of the dominant order.

This coalition against TMX is similar to Carroll's account of counterhegemonic struggles in another important way. Carroll writes that, for a counterhegemonic movement to "walk on both legs," it is "elemental" that it engage in a struggle that aims at "reclaiming the state." While Carroll insists that this is a matter of strategic – rather than normative – importance and that the state need not be "privileged" as *the* site of struggle, a concerted effort toward "democratizing state practices" must be "understood as one part of broader transformations."[45] Put plainly, the state's ability to martial both considerable violence but also enormous capacity means that it must be taken seriously as a location of political struggle – a point which is likely all too apparent to those responding to Trudeau's press conference, given the deprivation forced on First Nations by the Indian Act and the strain endured by municipal governments under neoliberalization.

Chief George-Wilson's promise that Tsleil-Waututh will continue the fight against TMX using "all legal tools" should, I think, be read in this vein as being one part of a counterhegemonic struggle. Far from an effort to seek recognition from the colonial government, the strategy that Tsleil-Waututh and its allies are pursuing is one that leverages the internal contradictions of the Canadian state to their own – anticolonial – purposes. Whereas many persist in presenting the state as a unified and homogeneous thing, the strategy being pursued against TMX is premised on the political utility found in the contradictions between the

[43] William K. Carroll, "Hegemony, Counter-Hegemony, Anti-Hegemony," *Journal of the Society for Socialist Studies* 3 (2006): 20.
[44] Ibid., 21.   [45] Ibid.

governing logics of various state apparatuses.[46] The relatively immediate logics that capture the legislative and executive branches, directing their commitment toward a market-logic that necessitates the diminution of Indigenous political authority, run into contradiction when they confront the courts' commitment to stabilizing colonization over the longue durée, a project that can accommodate the relatively capacious conception of Aboriginal rights outlined by the Canadian judiciary. Leveraging the space of contradiction between the multiple logics contained within the state is an effective strategy that, since the *Calder* decision (1973), has used the judicial elements of the state to significantly curtail many of Canada's most egregious colonial excesses.

Importantly, this is *not* pointing to the existence of so-called checks and balances; rather, it reveals the existence within the state of multiple colonial logics that can both articulate, but also contradict, with one another. In spite of the potential that struggles within the judicial sphere have unlocked, the foundational commitment of the judiciary to colonization is widely understood. Long noted by grassroots Indigenous leaders and scholars, the courts themselves freely admit it when they acknowledge that it is beyond the scope of their powers to interrogate the Canadian Crown's assertion of allodial title.[47]

SENDING OUT GRASSROOTS IN AN EXTINCTION EVENT

It is, in part, because the multiple apparatuses constituting the state share a foundational commitment to maintaining colonization that Indigenous peoples have always pursued a variety of anti-imperialist strategies. While strategies of counterhegemony – engaging anti-imperialist struggles within/against the terrain of existing state apparatuses – have yielded crucial victories, many Indigenous leaders and scholars assert that, ultimately, liberation cannot be achieved through state avenues. Rather, they emphasize the importance of Indigenous governance systems' resurgent cultural practices as an embodiment of their nations' jurisdictions throughout their territories.[48]

[46] Emma Battell Lowman and Adam J. Barker, *Settler: Identity and Colonialism in 21st Century Canada* (Halifax: Fernwood Publishing, 2015); Lorenzo Veracini, *Settler Colonialism: A Theoretical Overview* (Springer: New York, 2010); see also Jaskiran Dhillon, *Prairie Rising: Indigenous Youth, Decolonization, and the Politics of Intervention* (Toronto: University of Toronto Press, 2017).

[47] Gordon Christie, *Canadian Law and Indigenous Self-Determination: A Naturalist Analysis* (Toronto: University of Toronto Press, 2019), 342–83; Arthur Manuel, *Unsettling Canada: A National Wake-Up Call* (Toronto: Between the Lines, 2015), 107–24; see also *Delgamuukw v. British Columbia* [1997] 3 SCR 1010; *Reference re Secession of Quebec* [1998] 2 SCR 217.

[48] Glen Sean Coulthard, *Red Skin, White Mask: Rejecting the Colonial Politics of Recognition* (Minneapolis: University of Minnesota Press, 2014); Estes, *Our History*, 2019; Manuel, *Unsettling Canada*, 2015; Audra Simpson, *Mohawk Interruptus: Political Life Across the Borders of Settler States* (Durham: Duke University Press, 2014); Leanne Betasamosake Simpson, *As We Have Always Done: Indigenous Freedom Through Radical Resistance* (Minneapolis: University of Minnesota Press, 2017).

Moreover, as I stated in the introduction, Indigenous governance systems exist both prior to and without any necessary reference to the processes of imperialism through which they persist. Leanne Betasamosake Simpson describes this precisely when she writes that the processes of resurgence are, in many ways, "just Indigenous life as it has always unfolded."[49] This is striking in its resonance with how Chief Silver characterized Sumas First Nation's sovereignty as being about an obligation to defend the land and waters that sustain his nation and all those who live in the territories. As Chief Silver is engaged in a vital counterhegemonic struggle by which to leverage the state's internal contradictions, creating space for those obligations to be pursued without threat of colonial violence, those who are focused on *grassroots* strategies for resurgence pursue those obligations without making them cognizable within colonial structures. By being inattentive to these dynamics, to the primacy of Indigenous sovereignties on the ground, many non-Indigenous commentators continue to miss some of the most transformative anti-imperialist work; the grassroots resistance to TMX is no different.

Before discussing the Tiny House build and the accompanying march, it feels necessary to make a few clear delineations. Given the preceding discussion and some of the literature with which I am engaged, some may equate the following discussion with political movements that scholars such as Carroll (disparagingly) and Richard Day (approvingly) describe as being committed to antihegemonic strategies.[50] "Antihegemonic" does *not*, however, properly describe the relationships I discuss as they are at work on the ground, because the very question of hegemony (and whether it is to be retained, resisted, or rejected) gives undue priority to the state as *the* space of politics. At once fully recognizing the importance of movement and dynamism *within* and *between* Indigenous governance systems – both in terms of actual geographic mobility and in terms of cultural movements – I nevertheless ask that the reader take the sovereignties of Indigenous nations as their lodestar in understanding what I describe as politics at the "grassroots."[51] This framing is, importantly, *not*

---

[49] Simpson, *As We Have Always Done*, 247.

[50] Carroll, "Hegemony," 2006; Richard Day, *Gramsci Is Dead: Anarchist Currents in the Newest Social Movements* (London: Pluto Press, 2005).

[51] On geographic mobility, see Borrows, *Indigenous Constitutionalism*, 19–49; David A. Chang, *The World and All the Things Upon It: Native Hawaiian Geographies of Exploration* (Minneapolis: University of Minnesota, 2016); Susan M. Hill, *The Clay We Are Made Of: Haudenosaunee Land Tenure on the Grand River* (Winnipeg: University of Manitoba Press, 2017). On cultural mobility see Robert Alexander Innes, *Elder Brother and the Law of the People: Contemporary Kinship and Cowessess First Nation* (Winnipeg: University of Manitoba, 2013); Scott Richard Lyons, *X-Marks: Native Signatures of Assent* (Minneapolis: University of Minnesota Press. 2010); Lee Maracle, *Memory Serves: Oratories*, ed. Smaro Kamboureli (Edmonton: NeWest Press, 2015); Paige Raibmon, *Authentic Indians: Episodes of Encounter from the Late-Nineteenth-Century Northwest Coast* (Durham, NC: Duke University Press, 2005); Linda Tuhiwai Smith, *Decolonizing Methodologies: Research and Indigenous Peoples*, 2nd ed. (London: ZED Books, 2012).

my own creation, but rather comes out of the vernacular of the very organizing communities that it describes.

Delineating further, while the image of the "grassroots" seems tailor-made to evoke the notion of a politics "from below," I also want to resist that characterization. While I share many of the political and intellectual commitments that scholars like Jakeet Singh expertly describe as part of their method of seeing the space of politics "from below," its presentation of a hierarchical relationship is inapt for the context in which I am thinking here.[52] This is because, even as it seeks to describe suppressed but still extant agency within actually existing relations of domination and exploitation, the framing of above/below – inadvertently – recapitulates the erasure of Indigenous political authority by subordinating it to the presumed priority of imperial systems.[53] The sovereignties of Indigenous nations are better understood as neither *below*, nor as necessarily vying *against* empire through counter-/antihegemonic strategies, but rather as fully constituted and extant orders of political authority *in their own right*.

As the coalition assembled at səl'ilwəta?ɬ announced their continued commitment to the fight against TMX, across the Salish Sea in the territories of the Lkwungen and WSÁNEĆ peoples, volunteers tidied up a lot just outside of the downtown core of Metulia/Victoria. Over the preceding ten days, this space had been a flurry of activity around construction of a mobile Tiny House in solidarity with the Tiny House Warriors of the Secwépemc nation. As noted, the Tiny House Warriors announced in 2017 that they intended to use a fleet of tiny houses to assert their jurisdiction as Secwépemc women and that, as a consequence, TMX could not pass through Secwépemcul'ecw. This was their fourth Tiny House overall, and the third one built in Metulia/Victoria.

While imperfect and uncertain in the same ways as any political project, the Tiny House build is remarkable for the ways in which it draws upon, thickens, and generates relationships within the various communities that surround the build. Volunteers working on the House are supported by the socially reproductive labor of others as lunches are provided by individuals and affinity-based community groups like Food Not Bombs and the Community Cabbage meal program. Leftovers make their way to community-houses or else are dropped off at nearby food programs. Artists are also pivotal in this build: visual artists donate designs and studios produce screen-printed t-shirts sold on a pay-what-you-can basis to cover build costs; likewise, musicians host

---

[52] Jakeet Singh, "Recognition and Self-Determination: Approaches from Above and Below," in *Recognition Versus Self-Determination: Dilemmas in Emancipatory Politics*, ed. Avigail Eisenberg et al. (Vancouver: UBC Press, 2014), 47–74; see also Peter Linebaugh and Marcus Rediker, *The Many Headed Hydra: The Hidden History of the Revolutionary Atlantic* (London: Verso Books, 2012); Scott Neigh, *Resisting the State: Canadian History through the Stories of Activists* (Halifax: Fernwood Publishing, 2012).

[53] See *St. Catharine's Milling and Lumber Co. v. R.* [1888] UKPC 70, 14 App Cas 46; *The Cherokee Nation v. The State of Georgia*, 30 US 1, 5 Pet. 1, 8 L Ed 25 (1831).

a fundraising dance-party with an accompanying silent auction. Members of the Fearless Collective host a workshop on the build site for Indigenous and racialized community members, out of which comes the creative vision for a mural that accompanies the House to Secwépemcul'ecw, celebrating the Indigenous women, matriarchs, and femmes who are "Protecting What Heals Us" in the face of the threat posed by TMX.

A series of "Tiny House Talks" are held on the build site most nights after construction wraps, with the explicit aim of broadening and deepening the community's intellectual tools. Workshops link the struggle against imperialism in Canada to struggles in the Middle East, the South Pacific, and Latin America; think tactically about the tools of direct action; and interrogate how we carry the logics of empire within our daily, intimate lives. It was out of these Tiny House Talks that a vision for the future work of this community was brought forward by Tsastilqualus Umbas, an Indigenous matriarch; several months later, that vision culminated in the Little Big House build, a crucial step forward in the struggle to evict fish-farming operations from Kwakwaka'wakw waters in the Broughton Archipelago and to rematriate Ma'amtagila territories. Likewise, these relationships became a vital resource months later as the community was mobilized in solidarity with the uprisings that occurred following Canada's re-invasion of Wet'suwet'en territory.

In spite of the vibrancy of the political space created through this flurry of activity, and despite the enormity of the TMX debate at the time, the Tiny House received almost no media attention during construction. The sole exception was a lone cameraperson from local news, who showed up to the build site after being tipped-off that the street-entrenched community may be congregating in order to establish a tent city. Media coverage only turned toward the Tiny House as a consequence of the 20 km march on June 22 that sent the House up the Saanich Peninsula to govern and defend Secwépemcul'ecw. The march itself was truly stunning: as the sun rose over the Salish Sea, hundreds of supporters gathered in Centennial Square, where they were welcomed by local elders. Within the hour a stream of people poured into the streets, led by representatives of the Tiny House Warriors, as well as of Protect the Inlet and of Kwekwecnewtxw, and tailed by the Tiny House itself—adorned with a banner that read "decolonization or mass extinction." The incredible reach of the inter-nationalist grassroots coalition opposed to TMX and the terms of the struggle were in full evidence. Winding through the streets, drum circles and round dances were set up at various intersections and bridges, temporarily reclaiming city infrastructure, declaring an anti-imperialist future. As it moved up the Peninsula, members of local nations came out to greet the march, welcoming their relations to the territories with food, stories, drums, and company. Nearly 12 hours and just over 20kms later, the Tiny House pulled into Island View Park, where a feast was held to celebrate this resurgence of Indigenous governance.

Unsurprisingly, sustained media attention arrived only as a consequence of the march that closed the entirety of the northbound traffic on a major arterial highway for several hours. Despite the entirely predictable nature of this turn of events, it is nevertheless worth analyzing some of the leading commentary, as I consider it a revealing window into how the space of the political is dominantly constructed. Particularly revealing in this vein was a piece authored by the Victoria *Times Colonist*'s editorial board on June 25, originally entitled "Highway March a Plodding Farce" – though the online version was later retitled as "Effective Protests can be Difficult. Just Look at Saturday's Effort."[54] In the editorial, as in Trudeau's press conference, the march and the resistance to TMX that it is a part of were reduced to an environmentalist protest which had made a "mockery" of its own cause – there was no mention about the assertion of Indigenous sovereignties, despite it being core to everything. Primarily, the authors took umbrage at the idea that the march may have inconvenienced motorists – a charge which led them to assert that for every extra ounce of gasoline burned because of traffic delays, the march was an effort "that reeked of hypocrisy."

Setting aside the impossibly zero-sum calculation that this editorial wants to hold environmentalist movements to, I think it is even more striking for the theory of power and political authority that it evidences. The authors write that, confronted by the "life and death" reality of the climate catastrophe, "[w]e need answers and we need solutions." As such, they implore their readers, and especially those who participated in the march, to "become part of the solution" by making an effort to "talk to decision-makers." The editorial continues: "we need to convince those in power, around the world, that something must be done quickly." While this is simply presented as common sense, the authors are in fact reifying a conception of power and authority as necessarily 'power-over': the power to command or direct. They specifically treat that power-over as also being simultaneously power wielded at a distance, to which one must make an appeal, a supplication, or – in the most extreme cases – a protest. Moreover, given the presence of numerous Indigenous leaders, First Nations, and municipal representatives in the march, clearly only *certain* (read: colonial) institutional positions are deemed to have been imbued with power. In short, power here is presumed as the property of those who hold state offices.

Coincidentally, on the very day that the *Colonist* published its editorial, the United Nations (UN) Human Rights Council's Special Rapporteur on Extreme Poverty and Human Rights released a report on "Climate Change and Poverty."[55]

[54] "Effective Protests Can Be Difficult. Just Look at Saturday's Effort," *Times Colonist*, June 25, 2019, www.timescolonist.com/opinion/editorials/editorial-effective-protests-can-be-difficult-just-look-at-saturday-s-effort-1.23866187.

[55] Special Rapporteur on Extreme Poverty and Human Rights, *Climate Change and Poverty: Report of the Special Rapporteur on Extreme Poverty and Human Rights* (Geneva: United Nations, 2019), https://undocs.org/A/HRC/41/39.

In a truly daunting assessment of the ecological crisis, the Special Rapporteur warns of the "climate apartheid" that is emerging globally (12). Those with means are already isolating themselves against the impacts of the climate catastrophe which they are instrumental in causing, while the poor and marginalized are left to fend for themselves. The report warns that "the best-case outcome is widespread death and suffering by the end of this century"; the worst, humanity on "the brink of extinction" (14). Clearly, then, it shares the sense that climate change generally, but also specific projects like TMX that expand fossil fuel extraction and consumption, are matters of life and death. Interestingly, however, whereas the *Colonist* critiqued the Indigenous-led grassroots resistance to TMX as missing an opportunity to engage with "those in power," the Special Rapporteur concludes that because states are power structures that "overwhelmingly stand for the status quo and are thus unlikely to take a strong lead when radical change is needed," the "real driving force for progress can only come from community mobilization" (16). This report lays bare the necessity of coming to grips with the fact that, inasmuch as it is composed of those who are most directly affected by the consequences – especially the ecological consequences – of empire, the space of grassroots politics is *the leading* space of transformative struggle

Most generously, the *Colonist* editorial is read as a form of realpolitik; however, their understanding of power – which is widely shared – as an object of state offices erases the reality of power as produced through processes of collective action. Realizing how tightly the *Colonist* hews to this rigidly statist theory of power reveals the bleak irony of their crescendoing coda that "[w]e need answers and we need solutions. We should not expect to get them from those souls who are easily led." Far from being easily led, I think of those who participated in the Tiny House Build, the march, and who are defending Secwépemcul'ecw and all the territories downstream from TMX as remarkable for the degree to which they understand themselves and their comrades as historically situated, collectively empowered, and therefore responsible actors. Rather than seeking anyone's advice on what constitutes 'effective protest,' these grassroots strategies set aside the logic of offering *protestations* to those 'in power.' Instead, they participate in the (re)assertion of Indigenous governance systems in ways that eschew appeals to the hegemonic order entirely. This collectively produced, grassroots politics does not appeal to or protest those *with* power, because it is a site of power itself. As media responses to the march reveal, most often that power is made legible when it is read as being asserted against the constituted authority of the state and industry through blockades, the withdrawing of labor, or riotous acts. But the true strength of this grassroots politics is not in what it seeks to *abolish* – the actually existing infrastructure and institutions of empire – but in what it *defends* and what it *produces*: That is, the territories that support the flourishing of life itself, and the systems of governance that have learned over millennia how to accommodate themselves to the places in which they have grown.

CONCLUSION

Original construction of the Trans Mountain pipeline in 1951 was motivated, in part, as a response by the imperial core to the globally rising tide of anticolonial struggles. Most acutely, Mohammad Mosaddegh's ascendancy to the premiership of Iran, on a platform of popular reforms including the nationalization of oil resources hitherto dominated by British Petroleum, provided the rhetorical backdrop against which Canadian investors and politicians accelerated the Trans Mountain project. As detailed by Laura Gray, the supposed threat posed to the imperial core by the Iranian people securing for themselves control over natural resources was to be counterposed by Canada's entrenchment of fossil fuel extraction from, and transport through, the territories of numerous unconsenting Indigenous nations for export to global markets.[56] Karuka's observation that empire works through logics of countersovereignty – constantly reshaping itself in response to resistance movements – is made abundantly clear here, as the success of anticolonial struggles elsewhere is used as a perverse justification to further entrench the dispossession of, and environmental threats to, Indigenous peoples within the territories claimed by Canada. Trans Mountain was birthed and is being reborn as a stop-gap in the faltering circuitry of imperial domination. But a world linked through imperial circuits is also a world linked in struggles for liberation.

To focus solely on the circuits of imperialism is to persist in a mode of scholarship that assumes a states-eye view as *the* lens on the political.[57] Rather than continuing in political science's oldest traditions of seeing like a state, in this chapter I have attempted to understand the struggle against TMX as an Indigenous-led project of anti-imperialist internationalism, which has manifestations that orient themselves to the space of politics in ways that are informed by logics of both counterhegemony and grassroots coalition-building. More to the point, in accounting for these struggles I have attempted to show the primacy of Indigenous sovereignties as modes of governing social relations that build on the intergenerational production and transference of knowledges that emerge in and with the places in which they are situated.

To displace the centrality of the state in this account is not to deny its importance; indeed, such displacement is in fact necessary in order to see how these anti-imperialist struggles have and continue to (re)politicize the state in ways that very often outstrip the tools of critique and analysis available to political scientists. As the horizon of political possibilities provided within the confines of liberal democracy continues shrinking or transforming into more authoritarian and reactionary versions of itself, these struggles – linked with countless others – are reminders not only of our collective power to build, unbuild, and rebuild our relations, but also of our fundamental obligation to do so.

[56] Laura Gray, "Trans Mountain 1953: Public Response in Alberta and British Columbia" (unpublished MA thesis, University of Victoria, 2019), 19–21.
[57] Magnusson, "Decentring the State"; Scott, *Like a State*.

15

Governing Ourselves: Reflections on Reinvigorating Democracy Stimulated by Gitxsan Governance

Jeremy Webber

INTRODUCTION

In this chapter, I explore how we can give added precision to – how we can give added life to – the idea that democracy means that the people rule themselves. I especially want to reach towards a vision of democracy in which a political community's citizens see themselves, fundamentally, as custodians of their society's legal and political order. I do so by reflecting upon, and seeking inspiration from, a political order in which members do typically have that sense: the Gitxsan people of northwestern British Columbia.

Democracy has been called, famously, an 'essentially contested concept'.[1] We are in one phase of that contestation and, in reflecting upon how we should go forward, I start from the premise that we should focus upon a core aspiration that typifies a great many understandings of democracy – namely, that *democracy is about the people ruling themselves*. It is about the people participating in the good of self-government. That aspiration does not eliminate democracy's contested character. There remain important and disputed questions about who constitutes the people, about the mechanisms through which the people should exercise their authority, about the dividing line between matters that should be determined collectively and those left to

I thank, in the text, many who shared their knowledge with me, but I should also thank those who generously read and commented upon drafts of this paper. They are Darlene Russell (Gux-gal-galsxw); Katie Ludwig (Gal-sim-giget); Audrey Lundquist (Guu jenn sim Simogit); Audrey's daughter Nicole Jackson, who was the first to welcome me, with great encouragement, at the headstone-placing ceremonies in honour of her grandmother, Lily Jackson (Na gwa); Glen Williams (Malii); Barbara, Gord, and Jamie Sterritt; Val Napoleon; Jim Tully; Amalia Amaya Navarro; Harry Arthurs; John Borrows; Patricia Cochran; Coel Kirkby; Sarah Marsden; Calvin Sandborn; and Rebekah Smith.
[1] Bryce W. Gallie, 'Essentially Contested Concepts', *Proceedings of the Aristotelian Society* 56 (1955–56): 167–98.

individual determination, and doubtless many others. Nevertheless, the focus on self-government does real work. It excludes arguments that justify democracy primarily on grounds that have nothing to do with the distinctive good of self-government, such as what makes governments effective, how one maintains political stability, how one secures a wide informational base for governmental decision-making, or how one limits one's rulers. These considerations may identify additional benefits of democracy or parallel goals but they are not, on their own, sufficient substitutes for the core aspiration. Indeed, I suspect that those who advance them rarely see them as substitutes. Rather, these arguments a) are a way of clinging to a form of government that people value because of the core aspiration but that needs buttressing against critiques of democracy's limited achievement of that aspiration in practice, or b) are calculated to persuade an authoritarian regime to permit a democratic transition.

Focusing on the core aspiration keeps our gaze fixed upon the essential appeal of democracy: the hope that, in some material sense, citizens might understand their government's decisions to be their own decisions – that the citizens themselves might, in a way that they accept, 'own' those decisions. The core aspiration is essentially the same as the idea that government should be based on the consent of the governed (although, in this context, consent is not what one might think, as we will see).[2] The core aspiration is also closely related to popular sovereignty, understood to be 'the grounding of the ultimate authority for law and governance within one's own society, so that political power is, in a very real sense, self-authorized and self-determined – not dependent for its authority on the gift of any outside party.'[3] The core aspiration gives voice to what it means to be a citizen. It expresses the dignity in citizenship.

Arguably, it is precisely this aspiration that is in question in our current juncture. The fundamental challenge in many western democracies is the widespread view that the core aspiration is not being fulfilled – indeed, may not be capable of being realized – in current states and institutional structures. Such an alienation from government is a defining element in populist movements of both right and left.[4] It can be seen in the intergenerational

[2] Jeremy Webber, 'The Meanings of Consent', in *Between Consenting Peoples: Political Community and the Meaning of Consent*, ed. Jeremy Webber and Colin Macleod (Vancouver: UBC Press, 2010), 3–41.

[3] Jeremy Webber, 'Contending Sovereignties', in *The Oxford Handbook of the Canadian Constitution*, ed. Peter Oliver, Patrick Macklem, and Nathalie Des Rosiers (New York: Oxford University Press, 2017), 293.

[4] Margaret Canovan, 'Trust the People! Populism and the Two Faces of Democracy', *Political Studies* 47, no. 1 (1999): 2–16; Pierre Rosanvallon, *Le siècle du populisme: Histoire, théorie, critique* (Paris: Éditions du Seuil, 2020), 72–73; Cas Mudde and Cristóbal Rovira Kaltwasser, 'Exclusionary vs. Inclusionary Populism: Comparing Contemporary Europe and Latin America', *Government and Opposition* 48, no. 2 (2013): 147–74; Cas Mudde and Cristóbal

tensions afflicting many democracies: in the perception that political leadership is ageing, paying insufficient attention to political succession, and neglecting the economic and environmental interests of youth and future generations.[5] It is also, patently, a central theme in today's battles over diversity and inclusion. The challenges themselves are not unprecedented. The drive of people of colour (or women, or sexual minorities, or immigrants ...) for inclusion continues struggles that are long-standing and pervasive. The alienation associated with populism and generational sclerosis has recurred throughout the history of contemporary democracies. Indeed, when it comes to the core aspiration, our reach will always exceed our grasp, not least because democracy seeks to realize collective agency in human communities that are inevitably characterized by disagreement. The very fact that the meaning of democracy is contested means that its realization will be imperfect. That is not, however, an argument for inaction. The value of essentially contested concepts is precisely in the struggle to define and realize them, even if – especially if – those ends are never fully achieved. If one accepts the core aspiration in any form, one must continually strive to do better. And the injustices themselves, on almost any view, are real and demand a response.

How can one do so? How can one develop the relationship of citizens to their governments so that they see those governments, with justification, as an expression of their political agency rather than a power that is opposed to them? The answers to those questions are many and varied. One might say that they include the whole history of democracy. When it comes to practical strategies for achieving the core aspiration, we all have much more to learn from a Stacey Abrams or a Greta Thunberg than you have from me.[6] But it is often the case, in situations like this, that we stumble over the terms in which we conceive of the aspiration. We aim for something we cannot achieve and neglect those things we can. Here, then, I want to contribute to how one might conceive of and take steps toward the core aspiration.

Or, to put this chapter's purpose another way, the thoroughly dominant form of our constitutional discourse presumes a separation between government and people – or, at the very least, a counterposing of the two. Liberal democratic writings speak of government being 'constrained' by law

Rovira Kaltwasser, *Populism: A Very Short Introduction* (New York: Oxford University Press, 2017).

[5] Roberto Stefan Foa, et al., 'Youth and Satisfaction with Democracy: Reversing the Democratic Disconnect?' (Cambridge: Centre for the Future of Democracy, 2020), www.cam.ac.uk/system/files/youth_and_satisfaction_with_democracy.pdf.

[6] Hence the wisdom of James Tully's 'public philosophy' and John Borrows' 'physical philosophy'. See John Borrows, *Freedom and Indigenous Constitutionalism* (Toronto: University of Toronto Press, 2016), 10–13; Patricia Cochran, 'Physical Legal Methodology', in Freya Kodar, ed., 'John Borrows' *Freedom and Indigenous Constitutionalism*: Critical Engagements', *Lakehead Law Journal* 3, no. 2 (2019): 107–10; and James Tully, *Public Philosophy in a New Key*, vol. 1, *Democracy and Civic Freedom* (Cambridge: Cambridge University Press, 2008), 291–316.

and the institutions of electoral democracy. Rights are, above all, conceived as restrictions on government. Constitutions create 'checks and balances.' For its part, progressive politics is about 'speaking truth to power', progressive scholarly critique about recognizing that we are subject to a pervasive governmentality, capillary, inescapable. In contrast, I believe that we need to re-establish, for our age, democracy as a sphere of possibility, a cooperative endeavour to make our world a better place, to achieve goals (action on climate change; better healthcare; more equal distribution of wealth; education for all; equality for women, people of colour, Indigenous peoples, sexual minorities; environmental protection ... the list goes on) that we would be unable to secure as individuals. Of course, you, dear reader, might now be full of objections, for that vision has never disappeared. Checks on state power on the one hand, and attempts to harness that power on the other, march hand in hand in progressive movements. Rosanvallon has chronicled the wide variety of means by which democratic institutions have blended, throughout democracy's history, empowerment and oversight.[7] But is it wrong to think that confidence in the positive vision of democratic action is now at a low ebb? How might we act to reinforce the sense that government can be ours?

This chapter tries to clarify that objective by reflecting on an institutional context in which members do consider themselves to be custodians of their legal and governmental order: the governance structures of the Gitxsan people of northwestern British Columbia. This is the same Indigenous people that is the focus of Val Napoleon's contribution to this volume (Chapter 11). Indeed, I owe a great debt to Professor Napoleon (Gyooksgan) for my understanding of Gitxsan society.[8] My purpose is not to claim to be an expert on Gitxsan governance. Nor is my focus the significant and continuing impact of colonialism on Gitxsan institutions. Rather, I seek to draw inspiration for the governance of societies generally from what has been, for me, an immensely stimulating engagement with Gitxsan institutions.

The organization of Gitxsan society does not take a state-like form.[9] By this I mean that its institutional structure is not arranged in a comprehensive and

---

[7] Pierre Rosanvallon, *La contre-démocratie: La politique à l'âge de la défiance* (Paris: Éditions du Seuil, 2006).

[8] See, especially, Val Napoleon, 'Ayook: Gitksan Legal Order, Law, and Legal Theory' (unpublished DPhil thesis, University of Victoria, 2009); Val Napoleon, 'Did I Break It? Recording Indigenous (Customary) Law', *Potchefstroom Electronic Law Journal* 22 (2019), https://adric.ca/wp-content/uploads/2020/10/Napoleon-Did-I-Break-It-Published-2019-1.pdf; and Val Napoleon, 'Living Together: Gitksan Legal Reasoning as a Foundation for Consent', in *Between Consenting Peoples: Political Community and the Meaning of Consent*, ed. Jeremy Webber and Colin McLeod (Vancouver: UBC Press, 2010), 45–76. However, my debt to Professor Napoleon goes well beyond these works.

[9] The description of Gitxsan society and governance that follows draws on a number of sources, principally discussions with the individuals mentioned in the text accompanying the last paragraph of this chapter's introduction; attendance at the feasts noted there; the works of Val Napoleon cited in note 8; the testimony given in the litigation leading to *Delgamuukw*

highly rationalized architecture, with jurisdictions for creating, interpreting, and enforcing law so arranged that every question is, in principle, subject to a single authoritative answer. Instead, the authority to articulate and interpret the law is widely distributed in society, so that the kinship groups generally called in English 'Houses' (Gitxsan: *wilp* and *huwilp*), the groupings of related Houses known as *wil'naat'ahl*, and various combinations of Houses assembled in feasts all bear their own traditions of Gitxsan law and have authority to interpret and act upon those traditions. Indeed, this is itself a simplification, for especially knowledgeable individuals play important roles in their own right, villages often have distinctive practices and discourses within the broader Gitxsan people, the Gitxsan people as a whole bear a strong sense that they share a common order of law and governance, and there are such close affinities with and connections to the legal orders of the Nisga'a and Tsimshian (neighbouring peoples that speak closely related languages) that one might consider them all variations on a single legal tradition. Moreover, there is an ethic of non-interference and non-imposition among these different instances. Significant disagreements on process and substance can therefore persist indefinitely.

This means that questions about the maintenance of community have a continual presence in Gitxsan society. The task of sustaining community is a matter for conscious effort each time the community assembles to accomplish legal work. Its members are directly responsible for that work, a responsibility that, if it runs into trouble, can lead Houses or groups of Houses to choose to disengage, withdrawing in whole or in part from Gitxsan institutions for varying periods of time. The existence of Gitxsan society is not taken for granted so that the measures necessary to sustain it recede from view. They are not masked by a political identity and institutional frame so dominant that the identity and frame are unimpeachable, as tends to be the case with states.

By reflecting on Gitxsan institutions, then, one can see what it takes to sustain a vibrant society grounded in the active adherence of its members. To

v. *British Columbia* [1997] 3 SCR 1010 (cited in note 10); Margaret Anderson and Marjorie Halpin, eds., *Potlatch at Gitsegukla: William Beynon's 1945 Field Notebooks* (Vancouver: UBC Press, 2000); Richard Daly, *Our Box Was Full: An Ethnography for the Delgamuukw Plaintiffs* (Vancouver, BC: UBC Press, 2005); Wilson Duff, ed., *Histories, Territories, and Law of the Kitwancool* (Victoria, BC: British Columbia Provincial Museum, 1959); Susan Marsden, 'Northwest Coast *Adawx* Study', in *First Nations Cultural Heritage and Law: Case Studies, Voices, and Perspectives*, ed. Catherine Bell and Val Napoleon (Vancouver: UBC Press, 2008), 114–49; Richard Overstall, in consultation with Val Napoleon and Katie Ludwig, 'The Law Is Opened: The Constitutional Role of Tangible and Intangible Property in Gitanyow', in *First Nations Cultural Heritage*, 92–113; Richard Overstall, 'Encountering the Spirit in the Land: "Property" in a Kinship-Based Legal Order', in *Despotic Dominion: Property Rights in British Settler Societies*, ed. John McLaren, A. R. Buck and Nancy E. Wright (Vancouver: UBC Press, 2005), 22–49; Neil J. Sterritt, *Mapping My Way Home: A Gitxsan History* (Smithers BC: Creekstone Press, 2016); and Neil J. Sterritt, et al., *Tribal Boundaries in the Nass Watershed* (Vancouver: UBC Press, 1998).

be clear, I will not be advocating a simple transfer of approaches from Gitxsan society to large and diverse polities. Central features of Gitxsan society – such as the role of kin relations, their grounding in histories of great antiquity, the marriage of people to territory, the sense of kinship with non-human beings, even simple questions of population and scale – are clearly not transferable to contemporary non-Indigenous societies, at least not in so many terms. Nor do I mean to suggest that the themes explored here have no counterparts in non-Indigenous political traditions. Fortunately, they frequently do. Rather, my objective is to seek inspiration, clarification, imaginative stimulus, and reinvigoration from an engagement with the Gitxsan thought and practice of law and governance.

My great thanks to those, infinitely more knowledgeable than I am, who generously shared their knowledge with me at many points, especially Glen Williams (Malii), Katie Ludwig (Gal-sim-giget), Darlene Russell (Gux-gal-galsxw), and Audrey Lundquist (Guu jenn sim Simogit). I am particularly grateful to the late Neil J. Sterritt (Madiigam Gyamk), who shared his knowledge, understanding, and wisdom, answering my many questions. My gratitude too to the people who welcomed me to ceremonies, especially those of Malii and Haxbagwootxw (Vince Jackson). I continue to feel a deep obligation to those, now so many passed away, who gave their testimony in the *Delgamuukw* litigation, and from whom, at this distance, I have learned so much.[10] Any mistakes, of course, are my own.

THE INSTITUTIONS AND ORGANIZATION OF GITXSAN GOVERNANCE

I begin with an overview of Gitxsan governance, drawing, from that description, the principal characteristics of the Gitxsan people's responsibility for law and governance. I will focus on institutions derived from Gitxsan tradition. Those institutions co-exist in sometimes contested relationship with structures introduced by Canada's *Indian Act*, or patterned on non-Indigenous models. I refrain from dealing with the latter not because I doubt their legitimacy – those institutions too have become embedded in many Indigenous societies and, if so, I am not entitled to doubt their place – but because, for this chapter, I seek to reflect upon non-state forms of Gitxsan governance. As we will see, in that governance, the paradigmatic institution for the accomplishment of legal operations is the feast (*yukw*, or *li'liget*). The feast cannot be understood without grasping the kinship relations of Gitxsan society. We therefore begin there.

Those kin relations centre on the House. In Gitxsan society, every individual is a member of a House. Each House owns a particular territory (averaging

---

[10] The *Delgamuukw* transcripts are an invaluable archive. They have been digitized by the University of British Columbia Library and are now available online: https://open .library.ubc.ca/collections/delgamuukw.

approximately 575 square kilometres) that it administers, from which its members are entitled to draw their sustenance and for which the House is responsible. The term 'ownership' fails to capture the full character of that relationship. Ken Muldoe (Delgamuukw) described the relation as a 'marriage of the Chief and the land'.[11] As that metaphor suggests, the relationship to land is more than merely instrumental (although the land's pragmatic value in sustaining those dependent upon it is indeed important). The relationship also involves a metaphysical bond. A House's territory forms part of a set of possessions, of foundational value to the House, that includes the House's distinctive crests, songs, dances, regalia, names, and relationships with non-human beings. The entitlement to all these treasures is held within the histories of the House, the *adaawk*, passed down and supplemented through generations of recounting in the feast hall.

A House generally consists of between 20 and 200 members.[12] One inherits one's House membership from one's mother, so Houses take the form of extended lineages related through the female line. In Gitxsan country (including the semi-autonomous Gitanyow), there are something like sixty-eight Houses. Each of these Houses is represented by a head chief, who has special responsibility for safeguarding the House's relationship to the territory and all their treasured possessions, protecting the reputation of the House, the organization of harvesting upon the land (and thus for the welfare of all members of the House), and leading the decision-making of the House, which tends to occur through consultation among the principal members of the House and related Houses. In a sense, the head chief stands for the House. When an individual becomes head chief of their House, they assume the chiefly name by which the House itself is known and has typically been known for many generations. Thus, the chief bearing the name Delgamuukw is the head chief of the House of Delgamuukw.

Individuals accede to chiefly names substantially through inheritance. The names belong to the House and are in practice controlled (to a significant extent) by extended families associated with those names (again, with the relevant family members always reckoned through the female line, for one must be a member of the House to bear one of its names). Moreover, inheritance of a chiefly name, especially the most important names, is not automatic. Potential chiefs pass through a succession of increasingly significant names held by the House as they are trained and occupy

---

[11] Opening statement of Chief Gisday Wa (Alfred Joseph) and Chief Delgamuukw (Ken Muldoe), *Delgamuukw Trial Transcripts*, May 12, 1987, https://open.library.ubc.ca/collections/delgamuukw/items/1.0018360#po2-3r0f.

[12] Napoleon, 'Ayook', 4; Overstall, in 'Encountering the Spirit', 32, says 50 to 150 members is optimum. An average membership of about 190 is suggested by the population estimates in Gitanyow Hereditary Chiefs Office, 'An Indigenous Approach to Sustainability Assessment: Written Submission on 'The Environmental and Regulatory Reviews Discussion Paper', June 2017', October 13, 2017, 3.

progressively more important roles. When an important name becomes available (generally, in the case of a head chief, because of the death of the previous holder), there are typically more than one potential candidate. The relative fitness of the candidates – their knowledge, their character, their training, their wealth, their relationship to the former chief – is then weighed by the principal members of the House. Ideally, those members ultimately agree on the best candidate. That House then holds a feast at which the name is conferred. Names can also be stripped from a holder who is considered by their House to have failed to fulfil their responsibilities, although this rarely occurs (a removal is also accomplished in a feast). A chiefly name therefore has some of the characteristics of an office. A head chief is acutely aware that they are one in a very long line of individuals who have held that name. They seek to live up to the name and to add to, not detract from, its lustre.[13]

The Houses, then, are the principal property-holding and administrative bodies in Gitxsan society, but they are not self-sufficient. Importantly, Houses are dependent on other Houses for marriage partners. One is forbidden from marrying within one's clan, and because every House exists within one of four clans in Gitxsan society, marrying outside one's clan also means that one always, at least in principle,[14] marries a member of a different House. Each marriage, each household, is therefore a meeting of Houses, of territories, of histories. Since spouses generally live together, every House has on its territories spouses who are members of other Houses. Moreover, the children of the spouses inherit the House membership of the mother; thus, if the couple resides on the lands of the husband's House, the children too are members of a House that is not the owner of the lands. Gitxsan society therefore recognizes the right of a spouse to harvest resources on the lands of their spouse's House, of children to harvest on the lands of their father's House, and indeed, to some extent, of grandchildren to harvest on their grandfather's lands, all subject to them acknowledging and complying with the authority of the House chief over those lands. Moreover, there are other expectations and responsibilities, which I won't describe here, that spouses and fathers have towards Houses to which they are related by marriage. Thus, when one considers that every marriage generates such relations, that the relations extend for the lifetime of the holder, and that marriage partners are typically drawn from a number of Houses (including Nisga'a and Tsimshian Houses), Gitxsan country is crisscrossed by

---

[13] Daly, *Our Box Was Full*, 88–89, 267–68; Duff, *Histories, Territories*, 37, 40; Napoleon, 'Ayook', 6–7, 67–71, 96–107. See also, for the Gitxsan's close relatives, the Tsimshian, Christopher Roth, *Becoming Tsimshian: The Social Life of Names* (Seattle: University of Washington Press, 2008).

[14] Some marriages do occur in violation of these rules. These are treated, by many Gitxsan, as k'aas' – the equivalent of incest. They play havoc with the cross-cutting obligations and responsibilities of membership. Occasionally, one of the partners is adopted into another House to regularize the situation, but many consider such adoptions improper. See Napoleon, 'Ayook', 80–83.

a complex web of entitlements and responsibilities: both the central entitlements of House members, and the more limited entitlements of those connected to the House by marriage or filiation.

This brings us to the feast. The feast is the forum in which the principal work of law and governance is accomplished, such as conferring names (which, as we have seen, also confers a much broader set of rights and responsibilities); effecting marriages, divorces, and adoptions; the settlement of rights and obligations upon death; the recognition and correction of wrongs; the payment of debts; and, historically and perhaps increasingly again today, making or at least communicating the main decisions over the administration of the House's territory and symbolic possessions.

A feast is hosted by the House that wants the work done. Other Houses must be invited to attend, the number of Houses depending on the importance of the work to be performed. In the feast, members sit with their House (thus spouses sit apart from each other), the Houses themselves being seated within the hall in a manner determined by their relationship to the host House. Members of the host House do not dine at the feast; they occupy one end of the hall, welcoming and seating the guests, preparing or overseeing the preparation of the food, serving the food to the attending Houses, conducting the work of law and governance for which the feast was called, and thanking the attending Houses with gifts at the end. The participation of the attending Houses is essential to the accomplishment of the work. The success of that work is a function of the approval by the attending Houses for what the host House has done. In the feast's final act, the Houses are invited to voice that approval – not their approval for the specific choices made, but that the work has been done properly. Indeed, there may be other instances of assent over the course of the feast; when names are conferred, for example, representatives of the recipient's father's side are invited to welcome the recipient by their new name. The witnessing that occurs throughout the feast can itself be taken as a degree of tacit approval. If guests do not accept what is being done at a feast – if the disagreement is sufficiently serious – they can depart or refuse to attend in the first place. If guests do leave, or even state clear objections, the hosts will be deeply embarrassed. The very legitimacy of what they have done will be thrown into question. They will have lost the currency that a feast is designed to provide, namely acceptance that the House conducts its affairs appropriately and that what it has done therefore deserves respect.[15]

For that reason, there is usually extensive consultation within the host House, beyond the House with persons renowned for their knowledge, and with principal members of other Houses prior to the feast to ensure that any difficulties are identified and settled in advance.[16] Thus, much of the practical work of assembling support occurs before the feast. But that should not distract

---

[15] See Daly, *Our Box Was Full*, 57–98; Overstall, 'Encountering the Spirit', 35; Napoleon, 'Ayook', 150–56, 160–64; Napoleon, 'Living Together'.

[16] Napoleon, 'Ayook', 124–28, Napoleon, 'Living Together'.

us from the centrality of the feast itself. The discussions in advance occur so that the feast – the only forum in which certain types of legal work can be accomplished – proceeds smoothly. They are therefore structured and geared to that need. Moreover, there are occasions – rare occasions – when approval is emphatically withheld. Such a result is cataclysmic for the host House.[17] And even if the work of the feast is approved, the speeches by guest Houses at the last act of the feast are an occasion not only for ratifying what has been accomplished but for correcting, expressing approval in guarded terms, or supplementing what the host House (or other guests) have asserted. For those reasons, the feast will be the predominant focus in the discussion that follows.

WHAT THE FEAST TELLS US ABOUT POLITICAL COMMUNITY

What features, then, can we see in the feast that might inform our understanding about the kind of belonging, responsibilities, and entitlements that are inherent in collective self-government?

To begin, note that the lines of authority – judgement and approval – are exercised laterally, not top-down.[18] The legitimacy of work accomplished at a feast depends upon the accumulated approval of the other Houses. The more the Houses approve the work, the more successful the legal operations will have been – and the voicing of approval is relative: a House's approval can be expressed with greater or lesser enthusiasm, with or without subtle corrections. Moreover, each House judges the work according to its own understanding of the tradition. Of course, there is a sense of participating in a common normative order. One hears participants say that 'We are all Temlahan people' (referring to the ancient village that is a common point of origin among the great majority of Gitxsan Houses). That assumption of commonality serves a regulatory function in the legal order: it underpins the authority attributed to the approbation of other Houses; it is why Houses seek the opinions of and listen attentively to knowledgeable Gitxsan generally. Nevertheless, House members cherish deeply – indeed, have a responsibility to cherish – the stories and teachings carried by their own House's *adaawk*. They do not have an obligation to surrender their position in deference to contrasting views, even a consensus view. Certainly, there is a firm ethic against Houses commenting directly on other Houses' *adaawk*. The custody of the normative order lies with the Houses. Authority is distributed.

This means that it is not strictly accurate to say that norms are adjudicated in the feast. Disagreements are not subject to determination and can endure for generations. Nevertheless, there is a weighing of assertions, a counterposing of interpretations, through which assertions are often adjusted and a predominant

---

[17] See the example recounted in Daly, *Our Box Was Full*, 290–95.

[18] Napoleon, 'Ayook', 150–56, refers to this as a system of 'reciprocal accountability' and shows how it extends well beyond the feast.

position, a gravitational centre in the discussion, emerges. Uncompromising statements of what Gitxsan law requires can co-exist with an ethic of non-imposition. It is a question of jurisdiction, not a lack of concern with truth. What then regulates disagreement? What keeps the society from flying apart? To some extent, it is the process of reasoning, articulation and response, and emergent coalescence, but that process can only go so far. Ultimately, on some matters, one reaches a point where unresolvable disagreement remains and the Houses are faced with a choice: do they push the disagreement to the breaking point, or do they acquiesce in what appears to be the predominant outcome? Sometimes they do break and withdraw altogether or from certain forms of cooperation. But note the cost. The Houses may lose, to some degree, the benefits of cooperation, such as the peaceable resolution of disputes, the cross-cutting access to territories (which often have different attributes), the ability to engage in communal activities such as certain fisheries, the ability to obtain the affirmation and legitimacy conferred by a feast, and access to marriage partners. The desire to continue these benefits of community can lead – and generally does lead – to acquiescence, although even then the resolution often involves a measure of agreeing to disagree. Those acquiescing are entitled to continue to affirm that their position is right. And, indeed, sometimes the outcome makes concessions, through process or substance, to that position.[19]

Note the characteristics, then, of this political community. The society is not held together by coercion; it is held together by the desire to continue to live in community, with the myriad benefits that entails, by what we might call 'conviviality'. Nor is it held together by consent to a set of substantive propositions, even those provisions that represent predominant opinion within Gitxsan society. Continued community is compatible with persistent agreement to disagree.

This vision of community is tolerant of different modes of belonging. This is true in the sense that different Houses or groupings of Houses can have different degrees of integration into the collaborative networks of Gitxsan society. In a significant sense, Gitxsan society is federal, with members being attached to and participating in webs of interaction at different levels: family, House, village, *wil'naat'ahl*, and feasts that bring together larger or smaller numbers of Houses. That engagement can be asymmetrical. The Gitanyow Houses, for example, generally decline to participate in political initiatives at the level of the Gitxsan as a whole, although they intermarry with other Gitxsan Houses and participate fully in the Gitxsan system of feasting.[20] Gitxsan society also accepts, at the individual level, different reasons for belonging, even different

---

[19] See the example discussed at length in Napoleon, 'Living Together'.

[20] Consider this example: although Gitanyow generally guards its political independence, it is one of four bands participating in the Gitksan Government Commission, which provides technical and advisory services regarding a number of areas of band administration. Gitsegukla and Gitwangak do not participate in that body.

visions of the purpose and value of living in society. This is typical of Indigenous societies. To take an example from the Cowichan Tribes in southern Vancouver Island, I remember being struck, at a conference organized jointly with the Cowichan and conducted according to Cowichan protocols, by the words of one community member who, when speaking of Cowichan law and governance, talked of the satisfactions he obtained from fishing.[21] Those satisfactions would not be what a political philosopher (including a Cowichan political philosopher) would tend to think of first, but the diversity of discourse nevertheless has an important human reality, one that we ignore at our peril (the peril of becoming learned fools). Any community is bound together by multiple forms of attachment. Participants in Gitxsan ceremonies, like those of other Indigenous peoples, are a broad spectrum of their community; their contributions and forms of attachment are similarly broad in content and register.

Such a vision of community welcomes diversity in another way. The lack of a single, canonical, compulsory mode of belonging means that participants of different origins can, at least potentially, find a place within Gitxsan society. I spoke of the different histories, different *adaawk*, of different Houses. Those *adaawk* disclose the Houses' distinctive origins and movements into and through the region, including at times their different ethnic origins. Not only do they record intermarriage with non-Gitxsan neighbours (or non-human beings), but the origin of certain Houses lies outside the Gitxsan orbit. Some Houses of the Frog clan in Gitanyow appear to be descended from the Gitxsan's neighbours to the north, an Athapaskan-speaking people (a different linguistic family from the Tsimshianic family to which the Gitxsan language belongs) called the Tsetsaut.[22] One northern House not associated with Gitanyow is currently seeking recognition as a separate nation from the rest of the Gitxsan Houses; it too claims connection to the Tsetsaut.[23] The Wet'suwet'en people, the Gitxsan's neighbours to the southeast, also speak an Athapaskan language, yet they have adopted the Gitxsan system of Houses, feast and intermarry with Gitxsan, have an important village on Gitxsan territory, and brought major Aboriginal title litigation in concert with the Gitxsan.[24] At the individual level too, non-Gitxsan individuals are from time to time adopted into Gitxsan Houses, assuming a place within the system of kinship by which Gitxsan

[21] Personal observation, Conference on Indigenous Law in Coast Salish Traditions, organized jointly by Cowichan Tribes, Research Group on Indigenous Peoples and Governance, Pierre Elliott Trudeau Foundation, University of Victoria Faculty of Law, and the Consortium for Democratic Constitutionalism (Demcon), 14–16 October 2010.

[22] Sterritt et al., *Tribal Boundaries*, 19, 21.

[23] This is the Tsetsaut/Skii km Lax Ha Nation. For one element of litigation tied to this assertion of independence which speaks to some of the background, see *Malii v. British Columbia (Attorney-General)* (2019) BCSC 2060.

[24] For the foundation of this relationship, see Sterritt, *Mapping My Way*, 65–69. The Gitxsan and the Wet'suwet'en jointly brought the litigation that resulted in *Delgamuukw*.

society is regulated (although adoptees may lack certain capacities, such as the capacity to bear the principal names).[25]

Of course, as a result of their long history of living together, the Gitxsan have developed a commonality that goes well beyond the simple choice to work together. It includes interconnected modes of life, a common language, related forms of law, governance, relationships to land, and the histories, songs, stories, and bodies of commentary and reflection that have been borne by that language (and which now are transmitted in English as well). That commonality is grounded in centuries of interaction, intermarriage, collaboration, conflict, and inter-feasting and now constitutes a variegated, interlocked body of discourse, not least chronicling and sustaining the very practices of law and governance we have seen in this chapter. That discourse is dynamic, continually extended, added to, deepened through the wisdom of its members, influenced by encounters with other peoples' traditions, and applied and adjusted to new situations. This tradition itself constitutes a basis for commitment to the Gitxsan as a whole – for being Gitxsan, for considering themselves 'Temlahan people.' It constitutes the body of story and practice through which they have defined their place in history and on the land, which continues to frame their action in society, and through which they voice their disagreements. Consent as the basis of political community has often been conceived not as a conscious exercise of the will, a choice at a moment in time, or a subscription to a common set of propositions, but rather as a continuing adherence to one's society, the maintaining of a degree of concord between one's inherited traditions and one's actions in society.[26] Gitxsan certainly are attached to their people in this latter way. Their actions in the feast hall are understood to be their actions as Gitxsan, actions that they own, even when they disagree with the specific measure adopted.

Their social identity is, in other words, grounded in the very fact of conducting their legal and governance functions together, through forms that they understand and to which they are attached. The ground of their belonging is not, as in a contract, their agreement to a finite set of principles but their continued participation in institutions in which they may frequently disagree but where they grow to understand each other, where they have the opportunity to build cooperative projects (or to dismantle them), and through which they acquire, when they work at it, an understanding of and fluency in evoking some of the reasons for attachment to the land and to their societies. Belonging to community consists in doing community.

To build community, then, one must draw members into the work of community. Gitxsan society does that, from children's and young people's initiation to the land and the community's relations to it, to the structured succession of names and roles as one accedes to increasingly more challenging leadership roles, to participation in the work of the Houses and, especially, in

---

[25] Napoleon, 'Ayook', 131–36.   [26] Webber, 'Meanings of Consent', 17–20.

feasts. Within feasts, members' responsibility for sustaining community is manifest. It is inherent in the act of witnessing the work performed at the feast,[27] the value of which is emphasized by the approval sought of the attending Houses, by the gifts given to them by the host House in appreciation of their role, and by the ethic that if one attends a feast one attends it to the end. For me, though, the most striking example is the *tsek*: the contribution bowl. Feasts are long. Today, they commonly begin at about 5:30 or 6:00 pm and last until 1:00 or 2:00 am (and that is in addition to other collective work that is frequently accomplished earlier on the same day such as, for a feast for the placing of a headstone, the formal receiving of delegations from other Houses, each of whom comes dressed in their regalia, sing their principal mourning song, and express their condolences; the washing of the headstone; and its placing on the grave). A substantial part of the duration of a feast – often something like one to two hours – is devoted to the contribution of funds by House members and by those closely connected to the House to the work of the feast. Those contributing form a line, and as they contribute their names and the amount of their contribution are publicly announced. Those amounts are then tallied, the obligations relating to the feast are tallied too, and the payment of those obligations is then made within the feast itself, with the recipient's name, the service, and the amount of the payment also announced. Any balance is used for charitable donations (also announced) or distributed to guests as part of the gratitude to them for attending. I confess that having been raised in a Christian tradition, with an acute awareness of the duty to separate God and mammon, this intrusion of the material on the spiritual was startling for me, but I was grateful for it. It makes abundantly clear that community requires commitment and work and money and that it is up to members to sustain that community. Political community is not done for us. It is done by us.[28]

In this account, I have sought to explore the essential groundwork of Gitxsan political community. Although I have found Gitxsan governance profoundly thought-provoking and inspiring, I don't want to leave the impression that Gitxsan society is idealized and conflict-free – a society, in other words, unlike any other human society, in which nothing really needs to be decided or done.[29] That would be to ignore one of the lessons of the practicality of the *tsek*. And

[27] Napoleon, 'Ayook', 160–64. See also the exploration of witnessing in the proceedings of the Stó:lo people of southwestern British Columbia in Andrée Boisselle, 'Law's Hidden Canvas: Teasing Out the Threads of Coast Salish Legal Sensibility' (unpublished PhD thesis, University of Victoria, 2017), 201–77.

[28] For the *tsek*, see Daly, *Our Box Was Full*, 85–91. A similar realism is manifest in the use of territories. There too, the acknowledgement of the head chief's authority over resource use takes the form, in part, of a contribution of some of the product to the chief. Gitxsan will often use an analogy to taxation to explain that contribution.

[29] Val Napoleon has urged us forcefully to reject such an idealization, not least in her contribution to this volume (Chapter 11).

lest the lateral character of authority in the feast lead one to think that Gitxsan society is radically egalitarian, note that the institution of the feast developed in Gitxsan society when that society was built around a pronounced distinction between chiefly families, commoners, and slaves. Indeed, there was a time when only members of chiefly families participated in the feast.[30] Gitxsan society has now moved in substantially egalitarian directions, with slavery long gone, with women very often holding principal chiefly names and speaking for their Houses in feasts,[31] and with broad consultation and participation in feasts (although the principal chiefly names still tend to be passed down within chiefly families). Like any human society, Gitxsan society is dynamic, typified by disagreements and change and capable of dealing with such processes. But that does not nullify the fact that the lateral forms of authority and approval typical of Gitxsan society hold particular insights for popular sovereignty and democracy. We now turn to those lessons – to the sharpened focus that can be drawn from Gitxsan practice.

LESSONS FOR DEMOCRATIC REFORM

An engagement with Gitxsan governance can help us to clarify the sense in which people understand that a government is theirs. Self-government does not – it cannot – require agreement to the substance of everything government does. That is an impossible standard in human communities, wherein citizens inevitably disagree. Disagreement applies to the substantive norms that govern the society. It also applies to the processes by which the community establishes or interprets norms.[32] Indeed, theories that claim to be based on consent are typically one great fudge: they focus not on what citizens *do* consent to but what the theorist presumes they *would* or *should* consent to. The citizens' reasoning is ascribed to them, stipulated and applied by the theorist.[33] Moreover, this attributed consent – the theorist's stipulation of the citizens' consent – is then used to justify the binding character of the constitution. It thereby constrains, not enables, citizens' agency. A non-consenting citizen cannot, by dissenting, liberate themselves from the government's control. The theorist's stipulated 'consent' nullifies citizens' actual dissent.

So, if not agreement, then what binds human societies together? The Gitxsan experience suggests that the commitment to live in community is grounded simply in one's realization of the value of living in community and the cost of abandoning that support and cooperation. Such a realization stems from a wide

---

[30] See Daly, *Our Box Was Full*, 194–210; Duff, *Histories, Territories*, 38, 40; Napoleon, 'Ayook', 148–50.
[31] Indeed, some women have always held chiefly names in Gitxsan society, although the number and prominence of women chiefs appears to have increased.
[32] Jeremy Waldron, *Law and Disagreement* (New York: Oxford University Press, 1999).
[33] Webber, 'Meanings of Consent', 9–12.

range of phenomena: the practical reality of interdependence with others (including one's reliance on others for one's upbringing or the need to cooperate in activities beyond the capacity of a single individual); the benefits one obtains from being able to draw upon what one's predecessors have achieved; access to resources controlled by others; the value of participating in a common linguistic community and in the storehouse of knowledge carried by that community; a sense of deep connection to the territory and to its spirits; or one's familiarity with and mastery of the common institutions of the people. Indeed, there are as many reasons sustaining members' connection as there are members (probably more). They alone justify a member acquiescing in a decision or in institutions with which they may not wholly agree. That is why 'conviviality' rather than 'consent' is such a useful term: it captures the commitment to live together without over-stipulating what the commitment must be based on. This primordial commitment is multiform. It may end up being conditional – one may, in an extreme situation, feel compelled to abandon one's community – but that involves the severing of many strands of belonging.

In Gitxsan society, that belonging is conceived predominantly in terms of kinship. The use of kinship to determine political membership is not as archaic as one might think. Consider how citizens of today's nation-states acquire their citizenship. Very often, one inherits one's citizenship from one's parents (the jus sanguinis). Even when citizenship is obtained by being born on a state's territory (the jus soli), that principle often co-exists with the jus sanguinis and, in any case, one's place of birth is almost always a consequence of the decisions of one's parents. *Choosing* to become a citizen is the exception, not the rule. It is a common exception, one that deserves great respect in an era of migration. I exercised such a choice when I became an Australian citizen, combining that allegiance with the Canadian citizenship I had acquired at my birth. Nevertheless, the choice to become a citizen, while significant, is just one step in the process of aligning oneself with a community and finding a place within that community, which engages both one's own subjectivity and the community's openness to relationship. It was that complexity of attachment that allowed me to torment my spouse's Uncle Bill, a gruff (and much-loved) Australian patriot, by saying: 'I'm more Australian than you are, Uncle Bill. I'm Australian by choice. You are just Australian by the accident of birth.'

Moreover, one should not fall into the error of assuming that kinship in Indigenous societies is a matter of partiality towards one's immediate family (although Gitxsan people, being human, do feel the tug of that kind of partiality). Think of the extensive web of relations created by Gitxsan kinship: not just the membership one has in one's House (which itself can involve connections that are distant in degree), but the multiple relations that the system of kinship creates to other Houses. Remember that one *must* marry outside one's House, and that, as a result of those marriages, spouses and descendants acquire both responsibilities and rights to share in the resources of each House's territories. Michael Asch speaks of such out-marriage rules, common in Indigenous societies, as suggesting that one's being is incomplete until it is joined with another's, and sees that notion as lying at the foundation of treaties.[34] Each marriage extends the web of kinship. Think too of the Gitxsan's intermarriage with neighbouring peoples (noted by Val Napoleon, Chapter 11), including the welcoming of new Houses into the Gitxsan fold. In a foundational story of the people of Gitanyow, the House of Gwass-łam invites the House of Mah-ley (Malii) to join with them and form a new society on Gwass-łam's territory.[35] And, of course, individuals too are deliberately brought into Houses through adoption.

Kinship in Gitxsan society is, in short, a way of coming into relationship with others, of building an interlocking society of relationships, that is not reducible to agreement with a set of canonical principles. It clearly understands that community exists prior to one's articulation of principles – that one is born into relationship. Moreover, the Gitxsan web of relations extends to non-human beings and to the land itself. Compare the Cree concept of *wahkohtowin* (interrelatedness). As Jobin, Friedland, Beausoleil, and Kappo say, 'A core aspect of *wahkohtowin* is family relationships; *wahkohtowin* also extends outward in different ways to other Indigenous peoples, to non-Indigenous people, and to relations with non-human beings.' Moreover, '*wahkohtowin* and 'the obligation to extend *wahkohtowin*' continue to exist as such beyond any given struggle – and, importantly, even if we disagree.'[36] As this suggests, the web of relationship extends far. To be clear, it would be a mistake to treat kin relations as being purely metaphorical in Indigenous societies; familial connection, by descent, marriage, or adoption, does operate at the conception's core. But it then results in a vision of a community connected through webs of alliance and cooperation. It defines a sphere in which relations of interdependence are sufficiently strong to sustain institutional forms. I am not suggesting that non-Indigenous societies adopt kinship as their organizing principle – though *fraternité* certainly was tried at an important point in liberalism's development! But shouldn't we think of society as being defined by conviviality, by interdependence, more than by consent? Wouldn't that be more faithful to the multi-stranded nature of our attachments?

Of course, one may then seek to build agreement as to what one will do together, as indeed the Gitxsan do. But note that that search for agreement comes *after* one's recognition of community and that it is rarely if ever perfectly achieved. It is not foundational. It becomes the continual, never finished, always essential work of community. Indeed, participation in that work is precisely what it means to be a responsible member. It is through working together that,

---

[34] Michael Asch, *On Being Here to Stay: Treaties and Aboriginal Rights in Canada* (Toronto: University of Toronto Press, 2014), 127–31, especially 127n7.

[35] Duff, *Histories, Territories*, 26–27.

[36] Shalene Jobin, et al., 'Wahkohtowin ◁ᴵᵈᴵᴵᔕᐁᐳ: Principles, Process, and Pedagogy', *Canadian Legal Education Annual Review* (forthcoming): 27, 12.

ideally, one consolidates one's sense of membership and builds one's grasp of the society's procedures, historical knowledge, rhetorical strategies, economies, lands, people, and beings – a mastery of how to work together that is itself a reason for continued adherence. Participation in this work is, as Jim Tully has said, what it means to become a citizen.[37] Thus, if we want to build belonging, we should seek to foster participation. Participation is not just an attribute of citizenship. It is how one consolidates and deepens one's citizenship.

The Gitxsan see this work as a responsibility, not simply an entitlement. Potential chiefs are trained in the skills that leadership requires and then named on their ability to shoulder such responsibilities. Witnessing and approving the results of a feast emphasize that feast-work can only be accomplished with the active attention and judgement of other Houses; indeed, in Gitxsan society, it is that recognition that gives the work the only force it possesses. The *tsek* renders manifest members' obligation to sustain materially the society's institutions – a support essential to the political identity and agency of the Gitxsan people.

One can see analogues for each of the previous paragraphs' affirmations in the operations of state law and governance, but the analogues are often masked by the apparent solidity, the apparent givenness, the heavy institutionalization, of the state. Can we reinforce a comparable responsibility by rendering it visible? One example might be the Australian requirement of compulsory voting. It emphasizes that there is a quid pro quo engaged by the right of citizenship: one must participate in the act of deciding the overall orientation of one's government. A citizen may spoil their ballot, but they need to grasp that ballot and decide what to do with it. It is worth thinking of other ways of rendering visible the interdependence of rights and responsibilities. Might governments' create specially designated funds inspired by the transparency of the *tsek*: a solidarity fund, for example, replenished each year by a progressively graduated proportion of one's tax bill, for achieving the work of economic redistribution? As it stands now, government-administered pensions, employment insurance, and medical insurance build public support for government not just because they address compelling human needs (which they do) but because they crystallize interdependence and mutual responsibility in practical form.

For participation to succeed in forming attachment, opportunities for participation have to be accessible and they have to matter. One reason why Gitxsan society engages its members is that the Gitxsan people is a composite of political communities: families, Houses, in some cases *wil'naat'ahl*, feasting among Houses. These polities each have their own membership, their own ways of doing things, their own stories; some have their own property. They can decline to go along with others' decisions, adhere in part to them, or harmonize their actions with others in ways of their own choosing. They are not held within a mandatory, uniform, centrally determined and enforced

[37] James Tully, *Public Philosophy in a New Key*, vol. 2, *Imperialism and Civic Freedom* (Cambridge: Cambridge University Press, 2008), 99–100.

structure of law. Each one is a context for collective self-determination in its own right. This allows for the graduated opportunities for political participation that de Tocqueville famously ascribed to voluntary associations, together with different intensities and levels of prominence of roles. Note, however, that in Gitxsan society these polities have a sphere of autonomy and a role in general governance that most states now deny to voluntary associations. Moreover, Gitxsan polities are voluntary only in the sense that an individual can exit Gitxsan political society altogether. Your House membership is regulated by the system of kinship and by the Houses themselves, and, within that system, you are expected to fulfil your responsibilities to the extent you are able.

The Gitxsan structure of polities can be seen, then, as essentially federal, but with an array of polities that is more extensive than the more familiar federalism of states. The Gitxsan structure is not encased within a uniform framework. The ability to dis-adhere is real, albeit costly in terms of the ability to cooperate into the future. The Gitxsan approach tolerates asymmetry so that the patterns of inter-Gitxsan cooperation tend to be quite various – more akin, in some ways, to the diverse patterns of collaboration and autonomy that exist among states in the international realm rather than that between units of a federation. This diversity is a function of the Houses' ability to make their own decisions.

Can we build, within states, a similar structure of graduated and efficacious polities? Many elements of such a structure that once existed have since been undermined. Unions no longer have the presence or power they once had. Forums for political dialogue that brought citizens into interaction with those with whom they disagreed have increasingly been replaced by echo chambers. Finding ways to restore such engagement should be a crucial objective of our time. Some suggestions: First, to be effective, these forums have to be more than voluntary. They have to be treated, to a degree, as analogous to local government, able to make decisions of public consequence (as indeed the Gitxsan's institutions are).[38] One reason for the decline of unions is that many jurisdictions have come to treat them as voluntary associations, not as institutions representing their diverse workforce for the purpose of workplace governance. Second, it helps if they have power over resources. Indeed, the ability to participate in the allocation of resources draws members into governance, making participation consequential, rendering the institutions more representative, and training participants in the stewardship and deployment of resources. Third, it may be necessary to meet political community where it resides, empowering forums where people already convene – environmental groups, religious denominations, unions, student

---

[38] See Archon Fung and Eric Olin Wright, 'Deepening Democracy: Innovations in Empowered Participatory Governance', *Politics & Society* 29, no. 1 (2001): 21, 23–24; and Patrick Heller, 'Moving the State: The Politics of Democratic Decentralization in Kerala, South Africa, and Porto Alegre', *Politics & Society* 29, no. 1 (2001): 158.

organizations, arts councils, parents' forums, renters' associations, sports clubs, and many others – and using those as the building blocks for more broadly based organization.[39]

The inclusion of religious organizations in this list may set off alarm bells in some readers' minds. It is true that recognizing existing communities may be in tension with one's wish to create forums that are themselves diverse (though the uniformity even of religious organizations should not be overstated). The extent to which constituent organizations are democratically controlled should also count in this process. But generally, our shorthand conceptions of equality frequently suggest that citizens should be treated identically. Devolved decision-making necessarily produces differential treatment. How do we ensure those differences are okay? These are serious questions. There is a strong case for some mandatory constraints. Such constraints are compatible with the spirit of devolution. After all, the devolved units together create a composite political community, and component units may well require the observance of certain principles as a condition for that cooperation (gender and racial equality, among others). But, if one genuinely wants to deepen democratic participation, those constraints need to be kept as minimal as possible. It is important to remember that the very visibility of devolved decision-making imports a level of accountability – one that takes a form analogous to the lateral constraints in Gitxsan society.

Consider this example. In 2004, an Islamic organization in Ontario stated its intention to use arbitration under that province's *Arbitration Act, 1991* SO 1991, c 17, to deal with the consequences of family separation using Muslim personal law (some Christian and Jewish groups were already engaging in arbitration based on their religious traditions). This generated furore and the government of the day appointed former Attorney-General Marion Boyd to review the situation. She recommended that arbitration based on religious law be permitted subject to a list of requirements, including that arbitrators in such matters prepare and distribute a statement of the principles they would be observing, that the arbitrations only occur if procedural requirements specified in the report were observed, and that the arbitrations be made subject to judicial review on specified grounds.[40] This report was criticized because it would still permit the rights resulting from family break-up to be adjudicated on the basis of religious law. But note what happens in the absence of such adjudication. The vast majority of marital disputes are settled by agreement of the parties. If this were not the case, the courts would be

---

[39] See, generally, Saul Alinsky, *Reveille for Radicals* (Chicago: University of Chicago Press, 1946), 99–111 and, regarding religious entities as a foundation for broad-based organizing, Jeffrey Stout, *Blessed Are the Organized: Grassroots Democracy in America* (Princeton: Princeton University Press, 2010), 4–5, for example.

[40] Marion Boyd, *Dispute Resolution in Family Law: Protecting Choice, Promoting Inclusion*, Report Prepared for the Ministry of the Attorney General of Ontario (December 2004).

incapable of handling the burden. Those private settlements are subject to very little oversight and are concluded on the basis of who knows what principles. In contrast, the Boyd recommendations would have opened those standards to transparency, public commentary, deliberation, procedural protections, and an enhanced measure of judicial review. Note the harnessing of the lateral processes of publicity and commentary. Our current processes tend to draw a bright line between public decision-making, which aspires to be transparent and uniform, and private decision-making, which is invisible and largely uncontrolled. We should instead embrace a gradation of publics together with a gradation of publicness.

Another way to put this argument is that we ought to come to terms with the facticity of political community. All political communities, including states, have a non-neutral, non-universal composition, one that is reflected in their decision-making. Consider this example: In the 1970s and 1980s in the southern United States, litigation challenged the position of historically Black colleges and universities (HBCUs) on the basis that their states' university systems were, in effect, still segregated. Why? Because the HBCUs still attracted disproportionate numbers of African-American students because of the composition of their governing boards, their larger numbers of African-American faculty, and their programmes directed towards African-American students. But how, then, does one desegregate them? By giving them white-majority boards, hiring more white faculty, and changing their programming? One solution strongly pressed but ultimately defeated was to merge the HBCUs with historically white institutions, so that the HBCUs' distinctive character would be eliminated.[41] The fact is that state institutions have a particular character that is a product of their citizenry refracted through their institutions. They are nevertheless empowered to make real decisions. I am proposing that we extend that ability to political communities within the state. If we do so, not only will there be increased opportunities for political participation, our institutions can also escape, to some degree, the impersonality, limited responsiveness, and exclusively top-down character of conventional bureaucratic administration.[42]

This prescription is not anti-state. Indeed, I suspect that greater participation in such forums will lead to greater participation at the level of the state as well, that the state will be more representative, that its variegations will be more visible, and that in consequence the state will have greater legitimacy to pursue vigorous policies, as indeed it must if we are to address the great challenges of our time. For this strategy to work there does need to be a range of agencies,

---

[41] See the cases discussed in Wendy Brown-Scott, 'Race Consciousness in Higher Education: Does "Sound Educational Policy" Support the Continued Existence of Historically Black Colleges?', *Emory Law Journal* 43, no. 1 (1994): 50–53.

[42] See, for example, Anna Yeatman et al., *Individualization and the Delivery of Welfare Services: Contestation and Complexity* (Basingstoke: Palgrave Macmillan, 2009).

sufficient to allow for very broad participation, and there has to be a ladder of opportunities for participation extending to the society as a whole, as there effectively is in Gitxsan society. This has been the experience in the Scandinavian countries. There, social services are frequently delivered by agencies identified with segments of society. Yet the coverage of those agencies is extensive, and the engagement possible within them feeds into the institutions of the state as a whole, broadening and empowering them.[43]

One last lesson from Gitxsan society: Note that Gitxsan political participation is intimately wedded to ceremony and ritual. A feast is marked by set-pieces having symbolic significance: the seating of each guest with their House; the encounter between the host House's *nax nok* (a troublesome and unpredictable spirit) and the guest Houses' invocation of their own *nax nok*; the distribution of goods as an expression of gratitude to the attending Houses; the host House's songs and dances as the work of the feast begins; the order of contributions to the *tsek* by relationship to the House, ending with those of the spouses of House members; the House representatives' commentary on the work of the feast. Indeed, Indigenous peoples often refer to their political processes as 'ceremonies'. In Gitxsan society, it is often the case that the feast itself is primarily ceremonial, with the substantive deliberations, the negotiations, conducted prior to the feast. And yet the ceremonial elements clearly do real work. One obvious example is the response at the end of the feast by each attending House. That event, at the very least, expresses the principle that the most important actions of each House are subject to the approval of other Houses – indeed, derive their force from being seen by the other Houses to be done in the right way. Moreover, that final act of the feast impels and regulates the discussions that occur before the feast, during which the host House strives to ensure that the work will be approved. The preparations for the feast are under the structured, symbolic control of the feast's final event.

This is a reminder of the work that ceremony does in non-Indigenous political life too. Voting is the method by which representatives are chosen, but it is also a powerful affirmation of citizens' absolute equality. The achievement of equality in practice may remain elusive, but each election emphasizes that it is a foundational principle and reaffirms it as a standard for critical evaluation. To take another example, I argued above for compulsory voting not as a way of getting more representative outcomes (though one might make that case) but because of the message it sends about citizens' responsibility. And, as a third example, if administration of some governmental services is devolved to grassroots organizations, perhaps we should require that each organization provide a report of their activities to a meeting of their counterparts, in which

[43] Lars Skov Henriksen, Kristen Strømsnes, and Lars Svedberg, 'Understanding Civic Engagement in the Scandinavian Context', in *Civic Engagement in Scandinavia: Volunteering, Informal Help and Giving in Denmark, Norway and Sweden*, ed. Lars Skov Henriksen, Kristen Strømsnes, and Lars Svedberg (Cham: Springer, 2019), 1–31.

each organization would assess and comment upon each other's activities. Think what would be learned but also, more importantly, what such a step would communicate about the direction of authority, responsibility, and accountability. Finally, note that the symbols embedded in such practices have the merit of stimulating participation and engagement. Not only do they require parties to act for their very operation, but their implications are open, demanding continued interpretation.

CONCLUSION

The panoply of approaches discussed herein would broaden the foundation of democratic engagement and, I hope, justify citizens in perceiving government to be truly theirs. They are founded on the affirmations that we need to live together in society, that societies are not defined by our substantive agreements, but that we can nevertheless aspire to govern ourselves collectively through practices of participatory decision-making. The greater the engagement, and the more extensive the mechanisms for accountability to each other, the more democratic our institutions will be.

Self-government does not repose upon a firm foundation outside of human endeavour. There is no such terra firma. Rather, it reposes on the quality of our structured interaction, on our ability to speak, on our readiness to hear, on the engaged responsibility of the citizens themselves, and on the institutional structures that allow us to contribute to, test, and assess that engagement. As citizens, we ultimately hold the health of our democratic orders in our hands.

PART V

INTERNATIONAL/GLOBAL DEMOCRACIES

16

The Overlapping Crises of Democracy, Globalization, and Global Governance

David Held

The crisis of contemporary democracy has become a major subject of political commentary. But the symptoms of this crisis – the votes for Brexit and Trump, among other things – were not foreseen. Nor were the underlying causes of this new constellation of politics. Focusing on the internal development of national polities does not alone help us unlock the deep drivers of change. It is only at the intersection of the national and international, of the nation-state and the global, that the real reasons can be found for the retreat to nationalism and authoritarianism, and the emergence of multifaceted threats to globalization.

In order to grasp the reasons why we are at a crossroads in global politics, it is important to understand 'gridlock' and the way it threatens the hold and reach of the post-Second World War settlement and, alongside it, the principles of the democratic project and global cooperation.[1]

The post-war institutions, put in place to create a peaceful and prosperous world order, established conditions under which a plethora of other social and economic processes, associated with globalization, could thrive. This allowed interdependence to deepen as new countries joined the global economy, companies expanded multinationally, and once distant people and places found themselves increasingly intertwined.

But the virtuous circle between deepening interdependence and expanding global governance could not last because it set in motion trends that ultimately undermined its effectiveness. Why? There are four reasons for this, or four pathways to gridlock: rising multipolarity, harder problems, institutional inertia, and institutional fragmentation. Each pathway can be thought of as a growing trend that embodies a specific mix of causal mechanisms.

First, reaching agreement in international negotiations is made more complicated by the rise of new powers such as India, China and Brazil, because a more diverse array of interests have to be hammered into agreement

---

[1] Thomas Hale, David Held, and Kevin Young, *Gridlock: Why Global Cooperation Is Failing When We Need It Most* (Cambridge: Polity Press, 2013).

for any global deal to be made. On the one hand, multipolarity is a positive sign of development; on the other hand, it can bring both more voices and more interests to the table that are hard to weave into coherent outcomes.

Second, the problems we are facing on a global scale have grown more complex, penetrating deep into domestic policies, and are often extremely difficult to resolve. Multipolarity collides with complexity, making negotiations tougher and harder.

Third, the core multilateral institutions created seventy years ago – for example, the UN Security Council – have proven difficult to change as established interests cling to outmoded decision-making rules that fail to reflect current conditions.

Fourth, in many areas, transnational institutions have proliferated with overlapping and contradictory mandates, creating a confusing fragmentation of authority.

To manage the global economy, reign in global finance, or confront other global challenges, we must cooperate. But many of our tools for global policy-making are breaking down or inadequate – chiefly, state-to-state negotiations over treaties and international institutions – at a time when our fates are acutely interwoven. The result is a dangerous drift in global politics punctuated by surges of violence and the desperate movement of peoples looking for stability and security.

Today, however, gridlock has set in motion a self-reinforcing element, which contributes to the crises of our time in new and distinct ways.[2] There are four stages to this process (see Figure 16.1).

FIGURE 16.1 The vicious cycle of self-reinforcing gridlock

---

[2] Thomas Hale and David Held, *Beyond Gridlock* (Cambridge: Polity Press, 2017), 252–57.

First, as noted, we face a multilateral system that is less and less able to manage global challenges, even as growing interdependence increases our need for such management.

Second, this has led to real and, in many cases, serious harm to major sectors of the global population, often creating complex and disruptive knock-on effects. Perhaps the most spectacular recent example was the 2008–9 global financial crisis, which wrought havoc on the world economy in general, and on many countries in particular.

Third, these developments have been a major impetus to significant political destabilization. Rising economic inequality, a long-term trend in many economies, has been made more salient by the financial crisis, reinforcing a stark political cleavage between those who have benefited from the globalization, digitization, and automation of the economy, and those who feel left behind, including many working-class voters in industrialized countries. This division is particularly acute in spatial terms, in the cleavage between global cities and their hinterlands.

The financial crisis is only one area where gridlock has undercut the management of global challenges. Other examples include the failure to create a sustainable peace in large parts of the Middle East following the post-9/11 wars. This has had a particularly destructive impact on the global governance of migration. With millions of refugees fleeing their homelands, many recipient countries have experienced a potent political backlash from right-wing national groups and disgruntled populations, which further reduces the ability of countries to generate effective solutions to problems at the regional and global levels. The resulting erosion of global cooperation is the fourth and final element of self-reinforcing gridlock, starting the whole cycle anew.

Modern democracy was supported by the post-Second World War institutional breakthroughs that provided the momentum for decades of geopolitical stability, economic growth, and the intensification of globalization, even though there were, of course, proxy wars fought out in the global South. However, what works then does not work now, as gridlock freezes problem-solving capacity in global politics, engendering a crisis of democracy, as the politics of compromise and accommodation gives way to populism and authoritarianism.

The 1930s saw the rise of xenophobia and nationalism in the context of prolonged and protracted economic strife, the lingering impact of World War I, weak international institutions, and a desperate search for scapegoats. The 2010s has notable parallels: the protracted fallout of the financial crisis, the clamour for protectionism, ineffective regional and international institutions, and a growing xenophobic discourse that places virtually all blame for every problem on some form of Other. In the 1930s, the politics of accommodation gave way to the politics of dehumanization, war, and slaughter. In the 2010s, we are taking steps down a dangerously similar path. The question remains: will knowing this help us choose a different route?

17

The Contested Freedom of the Moderns

Conceiving Norm Contestation as the "Glue"
for Reordering the Globalized World

Antje Wiener

Fundamental norms such as democracy, sovereignty, citizenship, and the rule of law are both foundational and deeply contested concepts at the same time. Their foundational role has been extensively discussed with reference to modern nation-states, and constitutional orders in national, regional and global contexts, respectively. Today, fundamental norms, and their contestations, bear the potential for fleshing out the future of democracies within a global order. While these norms' contested quality has been conceptually acknowledged in Philosophy and Political Theory, it has only come to the fore as a topical issue in current debates of international politics and international law through contestation in practice. These contestations have questioned heretofore well-established political and legal orders. The role of fundamental norms has thus moved, one could claim, from taking a *rear-seat* in Political Theory toward making *headlines* in everyday politics of global governance. Tasked with the project of flagging issues that mark the potential 'future of democracies',[1] this contribution takes this move into the political limelight as an opportunity. It argues that, despite their purposes of warranting freedom and justice within and through modern constitutional frames, due to their value-based and practice-based roots the contestedness of fundamental norms does not come as a surprise. Instead, it is to be expected, for all norms are in principle contested. This implies that in order to counter potentially disruptive effects of norm contestation in light of the multitude of those affected by the norms of governance, norms have been 'bound' by constitutional means. The trajectory of emergent forms of modern constitutionalism has demonstrated this process in detail.

Yet, modern constitutionalism faces a dual challenge that raises a number of conceptual and political questions with regard to the future of democracies.

[1] See Tully, Introduction, this volume.

This dual challenge is enhanced by the increasingly globalized nature of politics and policy-making. The first challenge emanates from its 'locally bound' organization within modern nation-states. As the canon of contributions to this volume demonstrates, this local boundedness of constitutional norms is challenged by processes of societal alienation, regional dis-/integration, and political fragmentation. As the limits of constitutional rule are perforated, the taming power of modern constitutions has been weakened. Globally, the political effects of this change range from regression into nationalism to progression into novel forms of multilateralism.[2] The second challenge emanates from modern constitutionalism's 'globally unbound' organization beyond the state. As International Relations (IR) and International Law (IL) scholarship on global governance and global constitutionalism has shown, especially with reference to the "power" of norms, this political and legal weight of fundamental norms of governance in the global realm has been weakened. The crisis of the rule of law and the role of law are the expressions of a weakening liberal order.[3]

This chapter addresses both challenges as related. The argument builds on norms research in IR, especially the strand which represents a wider societal and political approach (compare, by contrast, the narrower policy-focused approach). Accordingly, norm contestation is developed as the constitutive 'glue' of societies and orders, quite in the Polanyian sense, rather than a 'means' to implement governance rules. The remainder of this chapter develops the argument in four sections. The first section highlights the research gap between state-negotiated norms of global governance on the one hand, and societal contestations of norms on the other. It argues that the gap has been created by the separate development of two literatures, namely the IR literature on global governance and the literature on democratic theory, in conceptual isolation. To demonstrate the point, section two recalls James Tully's claim about the "Unfreedom of the Moderns,"[4] which I summarize as the notorious absence of "elucidating dialogue" among affected agents of

---

[2] Gráinne de Búrca, Robert O. Keohane, and Charles F. Sabel, "New Modes of Pluralist Global Governance," *New York University Journal of International Law & Politics* 45 (2013): 723–86. Julia C. Morse and Robert O. Keohane, "Contested Multilateralism," *Review of International Organizations* 9 (2014): 385–412.

[3] Tanja Börzel and Michael Zürn, "Contestations of the Liberal International Order: From Liberal Multilateralism to Postnational Liberalism," *International Organization* 75, no. 2 (2021): 282–305; Heike Krieger and Andrea Liese, "A Metamorphosis of International Law?: Value Changes in the International Legal Order from the Perspectives of Legal and Political Science," *KFG Working Paper Series 'The International Rule of Law – Rise or Decline?'* (2016), 27; Georg Nolte and Heike Krieger, "The International Rule of Law – Rise or Decline? Points of Departure" (KFG Working Paper Series, KFG International Law – Rise or Decline?, Freie Universität Berlin, Berlin, 2016), 1; and Thomas Risse, Stephen C. Ropp, and Kathryn Sikkink, *The Persistent Power of Human Rights: From Commitment to Compliance* (Cambridge: Cambridge University Press 2013).

[4] James Tully, "The Unfreedom of the Moderns in Comparison to Their Ideals of Constitutional Democracy," *The Modern Law Review* 65 (2002): 204–28.

governance. The third section follows up from this normative context and summarizes the core assumptions about norm contestation as a condition for "sustainable normativity" in a society.[5] It details contestation as a twofold practice which distinguishes access to reactive and proactive engagement with norm(ative) change, thereby shedding light on societal interactions vis-à-vis order-building. Section four flags implications for framing a practice-based, bottom-up perspective on the future of democracies.

ENGAGING SOCIETAL INTERACTION: THE DUAL QUALITY OF NORMS AND SOCIETAL MULTIPLICITY

This section identifies a conceptual gap between state-negotiated norms of global governance and societal contestations of norms (i.e. a lacking focus on the ontology of societal multiplicity).

This dual challenge bears the danger of the fall of the global liberal order which has come to be represented by the United Nations' role in global politics for seventy-five years now, in light of the rise of authoritarian rule in a growing number of national states. Yet, this picture frames context in which democratic development stands to be addressed in a state-centered view, leaving the role of societal actors and their potential for advancing and shaping the future of democracies largely to one side. For example, society-based research on global change has addressed the rise of social movements addressing a wide range of grievances both within and across national boundaries. Is there, then, potential for countering the challenges of modern constitutional arrangements in a globalized world from a societal perspective? This chapter suggests that there is. Not all is lost.

The following elaborates on this claim. I argue that there are potential opportunities for shaping future democracies as options for a more inclusive and just form of governance. The argument is developed against two literatures. These are highlighted by, first, critical public philosophy's claim about the "unfreedom of the moderns"[6] that results from negating the constructive potential of society's "strange multiplicity" within modern constitutional settings,[7] and, second, by the notion of "contested compliance"[8] and the definition of norms as having a "dual quality"[9] in global governance settings.

---

[5] Antje Wiener, *Contestation and Constitution of Norms in Global International Relations* (Cambridge: Cambridge University Press, 2018).

[6] Tully, "Unfreedom," 204.

[7] James Tully, *Strange Multiplicity: Constitutionalism in an Age of Diversity* (Cambridge: Cambridge University Press, 1995).

[8] Michael Byers, "Policing the High Seas: The Proliferation Security Initiative," *The American Journal of International Law* 98 (2004): 526–45; Antje Wiener, "Contested Compliance: Interventions on the Normative Structure of World Politics," *European Journal of International Relations* 10 (2004): 189–234.

[9] Antje Wiener, "The Dual Quality of Norms and Governance Beyond the State: Sociological and Normative Approaches to Interaction," *Critical Review of International Social and Political*

Together, these claims point to a problematique with regard to the future of democracies in a globalized world, in light of a liberal global order which has been established on the foundation of modern freedoms (i.e. the foundational norms of constitutionalism) which have become globalized through the transfer of norms from local (national) into global (regional, transnational, international) contexts. Notably, this transfer – albeit mediated by heads and representatives of states – has bracketed the possibility of societal engagement during the process. This bracketing has caused a double alienation from the value-based quality of these fundamental norms. The first consists in the exclusion of local cultural knowledge from norm generation in the national constitutional context. This is enhanced by the second step of transferring a selection of fundamental norms into international organizations with no warranties to remove them on behalf of those who are directly affected. Against this background, *contestations* of fundamental norms in IR are understood as questioning the (proclaimed) freedom of the moderns, which, as Tully has demonstrated convincingly, must actually be conceived as 'unfreedoms' given their bracketing of cultural values. This bracketing of societally devised cultural values precludes the value-based dimension of fundamental norms.

A brief example helps to illustrate the point. From a global governance perspective, the transfer of norms from national constitutional contexts into the global context of international organizations could be dubbed as 'uploading'. Conversely, following international negotiations, agreements, and treaties, the implementation of these norms by norm-followers around the world could be dubbed 'downloading'. Most of the compliance literature has sought to enforce the latter through shaming, sanctioning, or coercion of states that were unwilling to comply. The point of this illustration is the reification of a norm's formal validity whilst neglecting its substantive content, and, therefore, its potential for change. A number of studies highlighted the role of transnational litigation networks, crisscrossing global orders, and norm contestation, and have generated novel research that highlighted the societal dimension. The concept of the 'dual quality' of norms sought to debracket normative quality by identifying norms as both socially constructed and structuring. Yet, addressing the socially constructed quality has proved a challenge to state-based norms research. Here, practice-based norms research has offered promising new perspectives on the societal input of norms, and their impact on political ordering. And Rosenberg's proposed shift toward "societal multiplicity," which takes account of the consequences of inter- and inner-societal relations,[10] offers a welcome counterpoint to state-centered perspectives norms.

Philosophy 10 (2007): 47–69; Carla Winston, "The Nature of Norms and the Evolution of Transitional Justice" (PhD thesis, University of British Columbia, 2016).

[10] Justin Rosenberg, "International Relations in the Prison of Political Science," *International Relations* 30 (2016): 127–53; Justin Rosenberg, "Internationale Beziehungen und die Konsequenzen der Multiplizität," *Zeitschrift für internationale Beziehungen* 26 (2019): 107–22.

To shed light on norm contestedness as an opportunity insofar as it facilitates research on the potential substantive change of norms that emerges through inner- and inter-societal interaction, therefore, this contribution begins from the contestation of fundamental norms (aka the freedom of the moderns) at different sites in global society. While the contestedness of fundamental norms is common knowledge, it is nonetheless notable that there is little systematic research which analyzes how this contestedness plays out. Second, this contestedness has implications for how we relate to norms in everyday practice and how we conceptualize norms in theory.[11] The questions are, therefore, what are the effects for politics and policy-making (i.e. democracy in practice), on the one hand, and for conceptualizations of democracy as a foundational norm of (modern) constitutionalism (i.e. democracy in theory), on the other? This contribution takes these as guiding questions in order to explore the future of democracies in a globalized world, and specifically with regard to global society against the background of the literature on norm contestation in IR theory. Accordingly, 'democracy' is defined as a value-based "fundamental norm" with little specification with regard to its implementation, yet with wide-ranging claims about its universal reach.[12]

This tension between the norm's substantively elusive frame and claims about its normative universal validity, would per se generate contestation with regard to implementation in policy and politics. The tension has been demonstrated by empirical research that locates contestation at multiple local sites in world society.[13] In Political Theory, such tensions have been identified as conflicts that emerge between the wider "civic" and the narrower "civil" spaces of society,[14] or between everyday "ordinary" and "universal virtues,"[15] respectively. In the context of nation-states, the tensions are kept at bay by constitutions that set the rules of engagement which regulate political disagreement or conflict. While specific normative opportunity structures vary, liberal democracies share a core of foundational norms. In these national contexts, norm-following is regulated by politics and sanctionable by law. By contrast, in global society, where no such matching constitutional settings exist, the tensions pose a different challenge. And, if and when they are not addressed in time, contestations may potentially spark wider global conflict, including diplomatic rows, weaponized conflict, and institutional decline. To counter these tensions, international relations are routinely

---

[11] Owen, Chapter 2, this volume.
[12] Compare the norm-typology in Wiener, *Contestation and Constitution*, 58–63.
[13] Amitav Acharya, "How Ideas Spread: Whose Norms Matter? Norm Localization and Institutional Change in Asian Regionalism," *International Organization* 58 (2004): 239–75; Wiener, *Contestation and Constitution*; and Lisbeth Zimmermann, *Global Norms with a Local Face: Rule-of-Law Promotion and Norm Translation* (Cambridge: Cambridge University Press, 2017).
[14] Owen, Chapter 2, this volume.
[15] Michael Ignatieff, "Human Rights, Global Ethics, and the Ordinary Virtues," *Ethics & International Affairs* 31(2016): 3–16.

confronted with establishing and/or improving the means to facilitate norm implementation. With regard to the normatively most far-reaching fundamental norms, this process is backed with resort to adjacent or sustaining norms and policies, such as, for example, "organizing principles" that identify procedures and means in the context of selected policy areas, and "standards and regulations" that define their specific rules of implementation.[16]

IR scholarship has addressed the point that fundamental norms are deeply contested in conversations with the neighboring disciplines of European integration, international organization, international law, and migration studies. The contestation of norms is regularly presented as a problem (i.e. of norm-following), which must be dealt with in order to develop effective means toward achieving compliance.[17] At the same time, however, others have argued that norm contestation is an integral part of the process of legitimation in IR.[18] This argument builds on "agonism" as Tully's third of "six features of constitutional democracy."[19] In doing so, it frames norm conflicts in today's globalized world as 'contested freedoms of the moderns'. The point is demonstrated against Tully's 'unfreedom of the moderns'. Empirically, it suggests turning toward local sites where 'modern' freedoms (i.e. fundamental norms of governance) are contested by affected stakeholders, in order to reveal the work of these unfreedoms, and relatedly, to flag ways of countering them. Conceptually, the aim is to explore opportunities for mutually elucidating dialogue among a plurality of unequal global stakeholders to bring the diversity of sociocultural experiences to bear on their expectations toward democracy on a global scale. The next section addresses this point.

THE UNFREEDOM OF THE MODERNS, AGONISM, AND THE PROMISE OF ELUCIDATING DIALOGUE

This section recalls Tully's claim about the "Unfreedom of the Moderns" and the central role of agonism (contestation) for the purpose of including the multitude of affected stakeholders in establishing norms of governance.

Tully situates his seminal claim about the 'unfreedom of the moderns' against a conceptual debate between Jürgen Habermas and John Rawls. As he argues, in essence this debate established that "two critical and abstract principles have been singled out as *guiding norms* for the critical discussion of the conditions of legitimacy of contemporary forms of political association. These are the principle of *constitutionalism (or the rule of law)* and the principle of *democracy*

---

[16] Antje Wiener, *A Theory of Contestation* (Berlin: Springer, 2014). Compare also Hart's primary and secondary rules of international law: H. L. A. Hart, *The Concept of Law* (Clarendon Press/ Oxford University Press, 1994).

[17] Abram Chayes and Antonia Handler Chayes, *The New Sovereignty: Compliance with International Regulatory Agreements* (Cambridge, MA: Harvard University Press, 1995).

[18] Wiener, *A Theory of Contestation.* [19] Tully, "Unfreedom," 205.

(*or popular sovereignty*)."[20] Against this backdrop, Tully's claim about the "unfreedom of the moderns" is guided by six specific features, and it is illustrated by engaging a mutually "elucidating dialogue" between two distinct constitutional orders – in this case, Europe and North America. A project that seeks to address the considerably larger variety of constitutional orders within a global context faces two additional challenges: the first consists in taking account of a quantitative "plurality" of sites and agents;[21] the second consists in accounting for the "diversity" of qualitatively distinct experiences and expectations. Both are relevant for reordering governance in a globalized world. The challenges are addressed by Tully's third feature, which he identifies as

the *'agonistic' dimension* of constitutional democracy because it entails that *no rule of law, procedure or agreement is permanently insulated from disputation in practice in an open society*. The *democratic practices of disputation and contestation* that were previously assumed to rest on permanent constitutional arrangements, to which the people were supposed to have agreed once and for all, are now seen to apply to those arrangements as well, and thus *'agonism' (the Greek word for contest) is seen to be a defining feature of democratic constitutionalism*, one which partly explains and also reinforces the co-equal status of the two principles.[22]

This chapter dwells on this feature. Following from the conception of contestation, as a 'defining feature of democratic constitutionalism' it conceives the practice of contestation as the 'glue' for democratic governance in a globalized context.[23] It further argues that more systematic research on norm contestation would therefore offer an important means toward filling the gap between the formal validity of global governance norms, on the one hand, and their cultural and social validations in the global multitude of everyday experience, on the other. Framing contestation in this way thus offers an analytical angle on the crucial – and often bracketed – relation between fact-based and value-based dynamics of norms.[24] As will be demonstrated in the following section, the angle is taken up and more systematically framed by contestation research in IR theory.

Before turning to that analytical frame, the following elaborates on the rationale that by presenting the two principles of modern constitutionalism as fundamentally

---

[20] Tully, "Unfreedom, " 205 (emphasis added).
[21] Amitav Acharya, "After Liberal Hegemony: The Advent of a Multiplex World Order," *Ethics and International Affairs* 31 (2017): 271–85; and Amitav Acharya, "Global International Relations (IR) and Regional Worlds: A New Agenda for International Studies," *International Studies Quarterly* 58 (2014): 647–59.
[22] Tully, "Unfreedom," 208 (emphasis added).
[23] Karl Polanyi, *The Great Transformation: The Political and Economic Origins of Our Time* (Boston: Beacon Press, 1957).
[24] Jonathan Havercroft, "Social Constructivism and International Ethics," in *Routledge Handbook on Ethics and International Relations*, ed. Brent Steele and Eric Heinze (London: Routledge, 2018), 116–29; Jason Ralph, "On Norms and Practice: Crypto-Normativity" (paper, International Studies Association Annual Conference, International Studies Association, March 24, 2020).

contested, Tully offers an invaluable conceptual angle toward this analytical framing from IR theory. By shedding light on practices of norm- and value-construction that are "prior to" and/or "outside of" a modern conceptual frame, Tully shows that adopting a modern standpoint therefore bears the danger of overlooking the underlying set of customary norms and values. This angle offers a mediated lack of societal reflection that undermines these two principles' universal validity, for their perception of 'freedom' rests on false assumptions. Thus, the conception of the 'unfreedom of the moderns' sheds light on the mediated effect of bracketing sociocultural practices and background experience in the constitutive process of fundamental constitutional norms. It follows that any attempt to resolve, enhance, or expand democratic legitimacy, and that begins from a 'modern' standpoint, is likely to bracket cultural diversity. This implies two types of exclusion from the process of constitutional ordering in a globalized world (i.e. quantitative exclusion with regard to a plurality of affected stakeholders from the democratic process in national societies, as well as qualitative exclusion with regard to the diversity of sociocultural background knowledge and its impact on normative substance), from which will be addressed in detail here. The only way to overcome the dilemma of the 'unfreedom of the moderns' therefore consists in taking modern freedoms themselves as profoundly contested. Enabling those affected by the norms of governance to contest them would be the way forward, for it is through this practice of contestation on and from the ground that norm(ative) change becomes possible.

The litmus test of the lasting effect of enhanced access to contestation in a globalized world consists in the question of how the effects of these contestatory practices work within societal boundaries and across them in IR. From international norms research we know that norms do not travel well, and individual agents tend to carry their normative baggage across borders, only to run into conflicts on the other side, as it were,[25] as individuals carry distinct "normative baggage" across manifold boundaries.[26] It is here where an ontological shift toward "societal multiplicity" matters,[27] for it highlights the consequences of inter-societal and inner-societal interactions, with reference to both quantitative and qualitative drivers of multiplicity.[28]

In a nutshell, then, Tully's take on fundamental norms and their role in generating and maintaining the legitimacy of political associations reveals two

---

[25] Thomas Risse, "Transnational Actors and World Politics," in *Corporate Ethics and Corporate Governance*, ed. Walter Zimmerli, Markus Holzinger, and Klaus Richter (Berlin, Heidelberg: Springer, 2007), 251–86.

[26] Uwe Puetter and Antje Wiener, "The Quality of Norms is What Actors Make of It: Critical Constructivist Research on Norms," *Journal of International Law and International Relations* 5 (2009): 1–16.

[27] Rosenberg, "Internationale Beziehungen," 107–22.

[28] Antje Wiener, "Norm(ative) Change in International Relations: A Conceptual Framework" (KFG Working Paper Series, KFG International Law – Rise or Decline?, Freie Universität Berlin, Berlin, 2020), 44.

important insights. Both matter for this chapter's task of assessing the future of democracies in a globalized world. First, constitutionalism and democracy are perceived as *guiding norms* of modern constitutionalism and, as such, they are, secondly, devised *from* given constitutional orders. As Tully shows, following a research logic that extends from the order to the norm actually implies a twofold mechanism with the effect of maintaining, sustaining, and – with a view toward global governance – extending the 'unfreedom of the moderns'. This effect implies that the inability to engage with the wealth of cultural diversity is prolonged rather than challenged.

Given that cultural diversity is constructed through everyday social practices which generate knowledge that is represented individually as background knowledge,[29] benefiting from that knowledge requires the means to represent its effect for normative reordering within a globalized world. This is achieved neither through inclusion of culturally diverse groups within a given order, nor by establishing enhanced participation of individuals according to the given norms of current orders, for both prevent the possibility to critique, change, and rethink, through learning from this 'strange multiplicity'.[30] To activate that learning potential therefore calls for more systematic and reflexive engagement with cultural diversity as an enabling condition for rethinking the future of democracies in a globalized world. The cycle-grid model which is presented below targets this challenge based on the interlinked practices of contestation and validation.[31]

To that end, a more consistent and rigorous research focus on cultural diversity and its effect on transformative change (and hence the normative structure of meaning-in-use that sustains any political order) therefore takes the reverse direction and conceptualizes constitutional reordering *from norms toward order*.[32] As Tully has demonstrated with reference to the repertoire of distinct Canadian constitutional traditions, this bottom-up approach is the condition for devising the parameters of 'contemporary constitutionalism'.[33] A practice-based logic of inquiry then would contribute to re-establishing the freedom *for* the moderns, enabling them to learn from experience and change their concepts of (liberal) order accordingly. This remains hypothetical, to be

[29] Emanuel Adler, *World Ordering: A Social Theory of Cognitive Evolution* (Cambridge: Cambridge University Press, 2019); and Etienne Wenger, *Communities of Practice: Learning, Meaning, and Identity* (Cambridge: Cambridge University Press, 1998).

[30] Research on global knowledge generation offers one promising research focus. Compare, for example, studies that address the social construction of "global space" and the role of the "global" in IR theory. See Karin M. Fierke and Vivienne Jabri, "Global Conversations: Relationality, Embodiment and Power in the Move Towards a Global IR," *Global Constitutionalism* 8, no. 3 (2019): 506–35.

[31] Compare Figure 17.1.

[32] Antje Wiener et al., "Global Constitutionalism as Agora: Interdisciplinary Encounters, Cultural Recognition and Global Diversity," *Global Constitutionalism* 8 (2019): 1–11.

[33] James Tully, *Strange Multiplicity*.

sure, for it pre-empts a scenario in which the 'moderns' actually wish to be freed from the blurred vision that is implied by the top-down order-to-norm perspective. And it is here, where the contestations of norms that we observe in everyday politics, come onto the – research – stage, for these contestations essentially take issue with the 'freedom of the moderns' by contesting fundamental norms. To provide an example, let us return to contemporary IR theory, and especially the field of norms studies, where two opposing research logics contribute to the reification of these norms, and, vice-versa, the reconstitution of these norms. Both logics are applied by distinct standpoints, and both are currently at work. The first – *reifying* – standpoint holds that contestation affects norm robustness. Accordingly, it is considered as a 'danger' which potentially undermines the liberal order. The second – *rethinking* – standpoint contends that norm contestation is a precondition for the democratic legitimacy of norms in global society. Accordingly, it is considered as an opportunity with a view to making the global order more inclusive and more just.

The reifying standpoint applies a logic of inquiry that centers on national interest in security[34] that depends on the stability of a given international order. The rethinking standpoint applies a logic of inquiry that centers on the challenge of access to contestation for those affected by the norms that govern them, applying the *quad omnes tangit principle* (i.e. what touches all must be approved for all)[35] as a minimal condition for legitimacy in global society.[36] As norms studies in IR theory have highlighted, it is not altogether obvious whether the goal of this discussion about the potential benefits of cultural diversity for democratic legitimacy on a global scale consists in re-establishing freedom *for* the moderns (wearing a veil of innocence about the promises of cultural diversity) or whether, in fact, it brings with it the challenge of establishing freedom *from* the moderns (as representatives of dominant Western political thought). The former typically focuses on policy, the latter on politics. The following section details a model toward more systematic studies of norm contestation and their effect in a globalized world.

---

[34] J. Ann Tickner, "The Disciplining of International Studies," in Brett Ashley Leeds et al., "Forum: Power and Rules in the Profession of International Studies," *International Studies Review* 21 (2019): 193–96.

[35] Compare Landau: "When Bartholomé de Las Casas dealt with the question of legitimizing the Spanish rule over American Indians in his book De Thesauris in Peru around 1545, he considered submission of the Indians to Spanish rule by force would be a servitude contrary as well to natural law as to human reason. According to Las Casas 'a free people or community accepting a burden had to give their free consent; all whom the matter touched should be called.' Las Casas combined the legal maxim 'Quod omnes tangit' with the idea of a natural right of liberty shared by the Indians." See Peter Landau, "The Origin of the Regula iuris 'Quod omnes tangit' in the Anglo-Norman School of Canon Law during the Twelfth Century," *Bulletin of Medieval Canon Law* 32 (2015): 19.

[36] David Owen and James Tully, "Redistribution and Recognition: Two Approaches," in *Multiculturalism and Political Theory*, ed. Anthony Simon Laden and David Owen (Cambridge: Cambridge University Press, 2007), 265–91.

THE DUAL QUALITY OF NORMS AND SUSTAINABLE NORMATIVITY

This section presents the *cycle-grid model* to frame democracy from below. It details practices of contestation (i.e. reactive and proactive) and validation (formal, societal, cultural) to address the gap between societal interactions and global order-building.

As this chapter's argument about closing the gap posits, freedom from the moderns requires a better concept of transformative change through politics. The point is substantiated by a practice-based approach to norms which facilitates a fresh view on the culturally diverse roots of contemporary order. Approached from this agonistic standpoint, a contemporary order is always to a certain extent in-the-making, driven by contestation. Through this process, norm change and transformative change will be perceived as coconstitutive practices that work at difference scales of global society, thereby connecting localized normative opportunity structures representing norms as tangible features of political order, on the one hand, and global normative structures of meaning-in-use representing knowledge constellations as the more intangible cultural features, on the other.

The making of order thus remains ongoing and in-progress, and its legitimacy depends on the degree to which it is capable of responding to everyday challenges and crises. Against this background, it follows that what is often called the 'recognition problem' or the 'diversity dilemma' – that is, the challenge of acknowledging cultural diversity in a constitutional frame – may become less of a dilemma and more of a virtue.[37] For scholars coming to the discussion about cultural diversity from IR theory, this observation about cultural diversity as vice vs. virtue allows for critical scrutiny regarding the effect of research logics that engage in *uploading* guiding norms of Western liberal order(s) to the 'global level' (i.e. constituting the modern global liberal order) to then engage in *downloading* the same norms to any domestic political order (i.e. diffusing the norms of the global liberal order). The process leaves the 'rest' to comply with the guiding norms of the West. It reflects the unfreedom of the moderns that rests on two grounds. According to Tully, this exclusion takes two forms.

The first and "most outstanding form of exclusion remains the one Dewey identified as paramount: the exclusion of those subject to national and transnational corporations from *having a democratic say* over them";[38]

The second form of unfreedom is brought about by *relations of assimilation*. Subjects are permitted and often encouraged to participate in democratic practices of deliberation yet are constrained to deliberate in a particular way, in a particular type of institution and over a particular range of issues so their agreements and disagreements serve to reinforce rather than challenge the status quo.[39]

---

[37] Hannes Hansen-Magnusson, Antje Vetterlein, and Antje Wiener, "The Problem of Non-Compliance: Knowledge Gaps and Moments of Contestation in Global Governance," *Journal of International Relations and Development* 23 (2018): 636–56.

[38] Tully, "Unfreedom," 202.   [39] Tully, "Unfreedom," 116 (emphasis added).

A growing literature on globalized conditions of unequal access to democratic participation and representation questions the universal validity of these fundamental norms. Given that norms are by definition not only structuring but also socially constructed through interaction at local sites, this literature argues that norms are always in principle contested. It thus calls for more research on the emergence of norms through practice. With regard to the contested validity of norms, therefore, all norms are treated as coming from 'somewhere', including 'liberal norms'. The legitimacy of norms is thus not enhanced by claiming the validity of liberal norms of the moderns for actors 'everywhere', but by first, unveiling the freedoms promoted by the moderns through global governance; second, contesting them; and third, re-constructing normative validity through these local practices. This point is sustained by norms research in IR, which has demonstrated that contestation and its effects must be understood 'all the way down' and 'all the way up'[40] in order to take full account of these conditions of diversity and plurality. It is sustained by the claim that norms are social facts. That is, even though they are regularly framed in constitutional, political, and/or legal institutional terms which aspire to bear universal claims, their implementation always requires a sociocultural fit. As Finnemore and Toope have emphasized in their reply to modernist neo-institutionalist claims about compliance,[41] successful norm implementation depends on the social environment in which they are expected to 'work'.[42] As further studies have demonstrated, this is well documented by cases in IR where norms were contested, despite their constitution in treaties and other kinds of international agreements.[43]

International relations and global governance institutions derive their democratic legitimation from their appropriation of fundamental modern norms as their constitutional foundation. These are the warrantors of the 'freedom of the moderns.' The contestedness of norms has developed in tandem with this 'modern' background at the organized, macro-scale of global order. To address what democracy might become, therefore, does not begin from considering contestation a problem ('danger') and aiming to counter contestedness in order for the foundational norms of this order to 'function'

---

[40] Holger Niemann and Henrik Schillinger, "Contestation 'All the Way Down'? The Grammar of Contestation in Norm Research," *Review of International Studies* 43 (2017): 29–49.

[41] Kenneth W. Abbott et al., "The Concept of Legalization," *International Organization* 54, 3 (2000): 401–19.

[42] Martha Finnemore and Stephen J. Toope, "Alternatives to 'Legalization': Richer Views of Law and Politics," *International Organization* 55 (2001): 743–58.

[43] Jutta Brunnée and Stephen J. Toope, "Constructivism and International Law," in *Interdisciplinary Perspectives on International Law and International Relations: The State of the Art*, ed. Jeffrey L. Dunoff and Mark A. Pollack (Cambridge: Cambridge University Press, 2012), 121–25; Byers, "Policing the High Seas," 526–45; Jennifer M. Welsh, "Norm Contestation and the Responsibility to Protect," *Global Responsibility to Protect* 5 (2013): 365–96; Wiener, *A Theory of Contestation*, 69; and Wiener, "Contested Compliance," 189–234.

more smoothly (i.e. using the political tools of sanctioning, shaming, or coercion). Instead, it begins from the opposite assumption and conceives contestation as an opportunity for achieving democratic legitimacy in the global realm. This is achieved with reference to the concept of "sustainable normativity."[44] Rather than improving ways of implementing fundamental norms of global governance, the goal is to generate the link between societal practices and these removed norms of global governance. In order to identify these links (i.e. fill the gap), Tully's central proposition to engage the potential of cultures of diversity more assertively in current social science theory is applied as the guiding standard. It rests on the proposition that "different practices of reasoning-with-others are grounded in *distinctive customary local knowledges*, repertoires of practical skills, genres of argumentation and tacit ways of relating to one another. These culturally and historically diverse genres of practical know-how or savoir-faire (*metis* in Greek) are the *intersubjective bases of culturally diverse practices of deliberation.*"[45]

Against this background, the chapter now turns to a frame that enables more systematic empirical research on norm contestation and its effect on rethinking and reordering political organization in a globalized world. To that end, it identifies the concept of contestation as a twofold practice which has been developed by the literature on norms research in IR theory and illustrates how this practice-based approach may be applied to counter the unfreedom of the moderns in global society. It aims seeks to account for norm validation as a principled practice that originates from 'somewhere'. To that end, it 'places' contestations of fundamental norms in the context at local 'sites'. By doing so, it aims to arrive at a more 'contemporary' understanding of democratic legitimacy that reflects the conditions of 'diversity' and 'multiplicity'[46]. The model has been developed against Tully's critique. Accordingly, it offers a frame for critical practice-based research with the aim to counter the perpetuation of the 'unfreedom of the moderns' and its diffusion from and by liberal orders. It brings to bear the critique of Western roots of the global liberal order and centers on that order's lacking capability to include 'all affected' by its norms[47] – that is, the modern setting in which stakeholders' access to the constitution of guiding norms of global order has long-remained restricted. Due to the underlying principles (i.e. the two guiding norms of the rule of law and democracy) of this liberal global order, the only mechanisms of change include inclusion and participation according to the given norms of that order, for, in today's contested liberal global order, these norms still represent the modern constitutive prototypes of the constitutional

---

[44] Wiener, *A Theory of Contestation*, 69.   [45] Tully, "Unfreedom," 223.
[46] Acharya, "Global International Relations," 647–59; Rosenberg, "International Relations," 127–53; and Tully, *Strange Multiplicity*.
[47] Acharya, "After Liberal Hegemony," 271–85; Owen and Tully, "Redistribution and Recognition," 265–91.

frame that defines normative opportunity structures and the rules of political engagement *on site.*

To counter this logic therefore involves rethinking these rules of engagement with a view to enabling access to norm contestation "all the way"[48] in order to achieve "sustainable normativity" in a re-ordered globalized world.

By developing the concept of "sustainable normativity" against the background of T. H. Marshall's "Citizenship and Social Class,"[49] Wiener has drawn attention to the central question of "access" to citizenship rights and, subsequently, "access" to proactive norm contestation.[50] To address unequal access conditions that shape the possibilities and constraints for political participation of the multitude of affected stakeholders in global society, she proposes drawing on the *quod omnes tangit* principle (what touches all must be approved by all) for framing central normative questions for norms research, such as "whose practices count?" (observation) and "whose practices ought to count?" (evaluation).[51] Following this frame, empirical research begins from observing global norm contestations and traces them to local sites in order to evaluate affected stakeholders' access to norm contestation. Following Marshall, this access is conditioned by the normative opportunity structure on site. Its qualitatively distinct realization is identified by two distinctions. First, access to contestation is qualified with reference to political effects as (a) reactive contestation (i.e. objection), and (b) the politically far more effective proactive contestation (i.e. critical engagement with these norms' substance). Second, and accounting for knowledge as value-based, three types of norm validation, to which diverse and multiple stakeholders have access, are to be distinguished: formal validation (in a position of political/legal power), social validation (in a position of a solid social group/community), and cultural validation (individually generated cultural knowledge, aka normative baggage). The types of validation therefore provide a key to societally qualified access to the two practices of contestation in light of the normative opportunity structures that set the conditions for norm(ative) change locally. Both help to map distinct degrees of sustainable normativity on site. To counter unequal access – which is the given condition in global society – it then engages selected stakeholder groups' respective discursive interventions in a global multilogue to identify norm(ative) change. Here, more systematic research on societal multiplicity would facilitate helpful and more detailed insights.

A starting point which takes account of inter- and inner-societal relations has been offered by norms research that seeks to "reverse this bracketing of

---

[48] Niemann and Schillinger, "Contestation 'All the Way Down'?," 29–49.
[49] Thomas H. Marshall, *Citizenship and Social Class* (London: Cambridge University Press, 1950).
[50] Antje Wiener, "The Embedded *Acquis Communautaire*: Transmission Belt and Prism of New Governance," *European Law Journal* 4 (1998): 294–315; Wiener, *Contestation and Constitution*, 71–72.
[51] Wiener, *Contestation and Constitution*, 1.

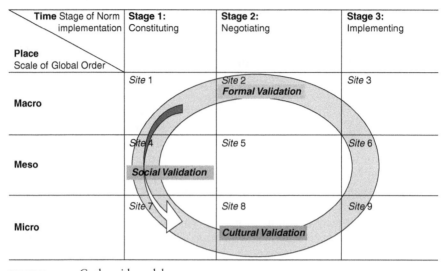

FIGURE 17.1 Cycle-grid model
Source: Antje Wiener, *Contestation and Constitution of Norms in Global International Relations* (Cambridge: Cambridge University Press, 2018), p. 44.

a value-based perspective on norms, and to sketch a conceptual framework that centers on practice-based norm(ative) change."[52] To that end, practices of contestation are distinguished according to their normative effect. This research builds on the theories of contestation and interactive international law. It argues that a turn toward practices of contestation and validation enables us to assess degrees of "sustainable normativity"[53] that reflect the state of legitimacy in the global order. These degrees are read off empirical research on reactive and proactive contestation on locally defined sites. As long as both practices of contestation are in balance, the conditions of sustainable normativity are satisfied. As soon as either reactive or proactive contestation develops the strong-hand, sustainable normativity is challenged – that is, an imbalance in favor of reactive contestation is expected to lead to political conflict (which may trickle across societal boundaries, igniting conflicts elsewhere), and an imbalance in favor of proactive contestation may imply a decline in opportunities for political protest. The following summarizes a possible way of framing political practices of contestation as interactions with reference to the "cycle-grid model."[54]

The model consists of a graph which comprises a three-by-three grid to indicate local sites of interaction (in relation to norm development and global order), and an overlay of a spinning cycle which entails distinct modes of validation (in relation to political power). The model allows for applying the ethnographic

[52] Ibid.   [53] Ibid., chap. 3.   [54] Ibid., 23–24, 61.

method of "following the conflict" based on sensitizing reading of news, reports, documents, and then subsequently "zooming in" on local sites. In detail, the model frames the task of mapping local practices on distinct "sites" (Who are the agents? Where are they engaging? What are their demands?). Each of these sites is conditioned by a "normative opportunity structure" that entails the "rules of engagement" and sets enabling and constraining conditions for stakeholders' "access to contestation." The sites are grouped along the two dimensions of global order, which are distinguished according to scope as part of the micro-, meso-, and macro-scales along the vertical dimension, and the process of norm development, including constitution, negotiation, and implementation, along the horizontal line of the grid. The cycle indicates the potential for access to validation, which depends on an individual agent's position in society and which are therefore distinguished as formal, social, and cultural practices of validation on the cycle.[55]

To summarize, the characteristic interplay between the quantitative and qualitative dimensions of the multitude of affected stakeholders who take part in the practice is demonstrated thus: While reactive contestation can be observed quantitatively with regard to agents, sites, and times where norm compliance or norm violation is objected, in turn proactive contestation needs to be evaluated qualitatively according to the conditions that facilitate access to critical engagement with norms and their meaning-in-use. The practices of contestation nicely pinpoint Rosenberg's point about consequences of multiplicity that potentially consist in either 'danger' or 'opportunity'. For, if reactive contestation – expressed by the spectrum of political activities including the spectrum of contentious politics (social movements, protest, and so on) to the more silent neglection of norms[56] – is not met by favorable conditions of access to proactive contestation, the necessary balance between both practices becomes lopsided. The likely result is conflict, which may represent a danger to societal stability, security, and so on. In turn, if reactive contestation is met by favorable conditions of access to proactive contestation, the diversity of voices is able to engage in deliberations to negotiate a compromise. The latter entails the potential of an opportunity, in so far as the political opportunity structure may be changed, for example, by offering access to previously neglected groups of stakeholders, establishing new pathways to participation for societal groups, or revising normative substance. Taken together, therefore, both practices reflect the quantitative–qualitative challenge raised by a multiplicity-ontology. Reactive contestation highlights affected agents' objection vis-à-vis a given order and/or its rules of engagement (i.e. the local normative opportunity structure). In turn, proactive contestation allows for shaping conditions for qualitative change of that order (i.e. reflecting the global normative structure of meaning-in-use). It is

[55] Compare Wiener, *Contestation and Constitution*, 23–24, 61.
[56] Charles Tilly, "Social Movements as Historically Specific Clusters of Political Performances," *Berkeley Journal of Sociology* 38 (1993): 1–30; Anette Stimmer and Lea Wisken, "The Dynamics of Dissent: When Actions Are Louder than Words," *International Affairs* 95 (2019): 515–33.

argued that reactive and proactive practices of contestation provide a helpful vantage point for framing the interplay between quantitative and qualitative multiplicity and its impact on international ordering.

To summarize, the norm-typology distinguishes three types of norms, and the cycle-grid model distinguishes two kinds of practices. The wider societal approach to norms centers on the dictum that in order to achieve sustainable normativity, access to contestation is a sine qua non. And, the possibility of achieving and maintaining sustainable normativity depends on the (re) constitution of globally recognized norms at local sites. They need to be read off these practices. To assess these practices' effects, these are distinguished as reactive and proactive contestation in order to facilitate the empirical study of *mapping contestations* with the normative evaluation of distinct *practices of validation*. Both practices play a distinct role with regard to understanding and engaging with affected stakeholders' access to participation in shaping order in global society. The first enables us to account for stakeholder (or citizen) engagement through empirical observation by desk- and/or field-study; the second offers standards for normative evaluation of access to engagement according to the all-affected principle.

FREEDOM FROM THE MODERNS: CONTESTATION AS A VIRTUE

This section provides an outlook on the future of democracies in a globalized world.

The argument advanced by this chapter began from this volume's preceding discussions at the Victoria workshop and the three leading questions about problems of contemporary democracies, their connections, and ways to counter them, respectively. It began from Tully's warning to perpetuate the two unfreedoms of the moderns by including previously excluded stakeholders and then assimilating their distinct democratic practices. The argument centered on the problem that follows from these unfreedoms, namely the deeply undermined civic freedoms of affected stakeholders and their perpetual exclusion as a problem which cannot be solved by enhancing inclusion and democratic participation, but which must be addressed by a logic of inquiry that aims at means *other than* inclusion. These other means, it was suggested, consist in bringing cultural knowledge to bear in its own right where diversity becomes a "virtue rather than a vice."[57]

It was argued that, notwithstanding the modern canon of constitutional norms and its representation in a plurality of national constitutional orders and global governance institutions, it is important to note that the contestedness of a norm depends on contingent local practice. In a global context, it follows that it is not only highlighted through *practice* on the ground, but it increases in relation to the plurality of sites that we wish to account for. Following this contribution's

[57] Hansen-Magnusson et al., "The Problem of Non-Compliance," 636–56.

particular focus on addressing *democracy within a global frame*, this implies accounting for *multiple futures* of democracy. To explore this focus and flag conceptual challenges and how to address them analytically, the chapter centered on the *practice* of norm contestation at a multiplicity of *sites*. Following leading concepts in the field of norms research in IR theory, then, the constructive dynamic is one that evolves from practice to a norm's meaning-in-use. The argument was developed against the *quod omnes tangit* principle, which allows for the most far-reaching questions to that end: namely, "Whose practices count?" and, relatedly, "Whose practices ought to count?"[58] The practice-based dynamic of this driver (i.e. practices of contestation) is pitched against the conception of democracy as a foundational norm of modern constitutionalism.

To bring cultural background knowledge as the experience of a 'strange multiplicity' that requires renegotiation through inter-societal and inner-societal dialogue, the chapter highlighted the added value of practice-based research on norm contestation. The conceptual proposal distinguishes between the two standpoints of reifying and rethinking the 'unfreedom of the moderns' (i.e. either locating norms in a given order or identifying norms through observed practices). And it proposed a more systematic empirical and normative frame to explore the project of rethinking and reordering constitutional settings in a globalized world with reference to the cycle-grid model and a general norm-typology that allow for zooming in on distinct sites of contestation. Accordingly, the effect of contestedness on the future of democracies (note the plural) stands to be assessed from these sites up. Two related steps illustrated this claim. The first sketched a practice-based approach toward exploring the meaningful use of norms from IR theory for research on democracy in the wider social sciences. The second framed the application of this approach with a view to exploring democracy as a fundamental norm, rather than focusing on democracy as a type of political system or regime. In addition to this contribution to democracy studies, this contribution proposed that this approach has an additional benefit for IR, for it speaks to a long-standing conceptual gap in IR. This gap was identified by extant IR theories' conceptualization of the global political order as an order of global governance that was established by inter-state negotiations. These negotiations at the top have been constitutive for a modern regulatory order with a lacking societal foundation.

In Tully's words, the structure of modern national constitutions was forged through regulatory practices. Leaving customary practices largely to one side in the process, the fundamental constitutional norms that expressed the basic agreement of social contracts were extracted from these societies. The first form of unfreedom has been incorporated into international law, for example, based on contract law and the principle of consent.[59] While the degree will

---

[58] Wiener, *Contestation and Constitution*, 1.
[59] Friedrich Kratochwil, "The Limits of Contract," *European Journal of International Law* 5 (1994): 465–91.

differ pending on a given context, having new members comply with a set of given norms that establish the order of an international organization will invariably involve the subordination and suppression of cultural diversity.[60] The procedure has been perpetuated through countless contracts on membership in international organizations of the UN system, as well as regional organizations such as the quasi-constitutional nonstate polity of the European Union (EU), for example. While critical voices have pointed to the importance of taking "contested compliance" more seriously as "interventions in the normative structure of world politics" that matter for long-term assessments of normative sustainability in contexts of regional and global,[61] cultural recognition is predominantly approached as a problem rather than an opportunity for transformative change[62]. To reverse this process of progressive elimination of diversity, stakeholders require access to engage with the norms that govern them. Its success depends on stakeholders' access to the two practices of contestation and norm validation, respectively. Here, the distinction between reactive and proactive contestation – where reactive contestation restricts affected stakeholders to the practice of mere objection, whereas proactive contestation would allow affected stakeholders to critically engage with the norms that constitute the order – comes in helpful.

The second form of unfreedom may even be more damaging with regard to its effects. This is the case because it leads to the perpetual hollowing out of cultural background knowledge that is part of the top-down order-to-norm logic. It follows that, unless they are subjected to critical scrutiny, logics of inquiry that take the liberal order's universal hegemony for granted will invariably contribute to more exclusion despite the claim of, for example, seeking to enhance the 'diffusion' of and 'compliance' with 'democratic norms'. Here Wiener refers to three types of norm validation: formal validation, social recognition, and cultural validation, respectively. At best, each affected stakeholder has access to all three. However, in most concrete situations, stakeholders will have either access to social and cultural validation, or only to the latter. The *scalar model* allows for evaluating practice-based transformative change of normative orders in global society, and how to counter forms of exclusion with reference to the practices of contestation and validation.

To summarize, contestation practices indicate the quality of the direct relation between stakeholders and norms. By distinguishing between either reactive

---

[60] Sundhya Pahuja and Anne Saunders, "Rival Worlds and the Place of the Corporation in International Law," in *The Battle for International Law: South-North Perspectives on the Decolonization Era*, ed. Philipp Dann and Jochen von Bernstorff (Oxford: Oxford University Press, 2018), 141–74.

[61] Antje Wiener, "Contested Compliance," 189–234; Jean L. Cohen, *Globalization and Sovereignty: Rethinking Legality, Legitimacy, and Constitutionalism* (Cambridge: Cambridge University Press, 2012).

[62] Christian Reus-Smit, "Cultural Diversity and International Order," *International Organization* 71 (2017): 851–85.

contestation (i.e. objection to norms or their violation) or proactive contestation (i.e. critical engagement with norms and their interpretations), research is able to identify the 'sites' where norm conflicts occur, the involved stakeholders, and the normative opportunity structure that condition stakeholders' access to participation. In turn, validation practices are distinguished with reference to meta-theoretical considerations about the dimension of knowledge a stakeholder is enabled to apply when practicing norm contestation. Against the background of IR theory, three dimensions matter in this regard: formal validation, social recognition, and cultural validation. Formal validation – also called 'legal' validation[63] – follows the international law literature. Social recognition follows the social constructivist literature on norms. which holds that processes of reiterated interaction in social groups will generate shared norms, which are habitually acknowledged as appropriate.[64] Finally, cultural validation has been conceptualized against the background of the post-structural and critical constructivist literature on discursive practice in IR.[65]

While the order-to-norm approach perceives cultural validation as the least powerful of the three practices of norm validation, the opposite is the case with the bottom-up norm-to-order logic of inquiry. Against the latter and applied to the comparative study of the unfreedom of the moderns, cultural validation turns out to be the most important practice. In fact, its ability to counter the unfreedom of the moderns makes it a warden with regard to chances of developing genuinely 'contemporary' conditions for democracy.[66] The key role of cultural validation lies in its capability to mobilize individually held cultural background knowledge to bear in the constitution and change of norms. It thus turns into a sine qua non condition for preserving background experience as a common cultural heritage. The proposal therefore is to consider cultural diversity a global good (rather than a global problem). Finding the means to safeguard this cultural diversity based on strengthened representation in societal orders is thus central to establishing the future of democracies that respect the culturally diverse sources of global society and enable the plurality of agents.

---

[63] Jutta Brunnée and Stephen J. Toope, *Legitimacy and Legality in International Law: An International Account* (Cambridge: Cambridge University Press, 2010).

[64] James G. March and Johan P. Olsen, *Rediscovering Institutions: The Organizational Basis of Politics* (New York: Free Press, 1989); James G. March and Johan P. Olsen, "The Institutional Dynamics of International Political Orders," *International Organization* 52 (1998): 943–69; Martha Finnemore and Kathryn Sikkink, "International Norm Dynamics and Political Change," *International Organization* 52 (1998): 887–917.

[65] Jennifer Milliken, "The Study of Discourse in International Relations: A Critique of Research and Methods," *European Journal of International Relations* 5 (1999): 225–54; Wenger, *Communities of Practice*; Emanuel Adler, "Seizing the Middle Ground: Constructivism in World Politics," *European Journal of International Relations* 3, no. 3 (1997): 319–63.

[66] James Tully, *Strange Multiplicity*.

18

Conditional Authority and Democratic Legitimacy in Pluralist Space

Keith Cherry

> Legal pluralism is the key concept in a postmodern view of law. Not the legal pluralism of traditional legal anthropology in which the different legal orders are conceived as separate entities coexisting in the same political space, but rather the conception of different legal spaces superimposed, interpenetrated, and mixed in our minds as much as in our actions ... We live in a time of porous legality.
>
> - Boaventura de Sousa Santos[1]

This chapter takes up the theme of "democratic multiplicity" not by attending closely to any one democratic tradition, but rather by attempting to engage seriously with some of the ways in which various traditions intra-act and shape one another. As Santos points out, it is not as if one person is a subject of an Indigenous democracy, while another is a citizen of the state, and another a subject of international law – rather, each of these sites of authority co-exists, layered on top of one another, shaping one another in complex and asymmetrical intra-action. The democratic character of our lives therefore depends not only on multiple sites of governance, but also on the relationships between them.

I am a cis, straight, white, Settler male from L'nu (Mi'Kmaq) territories, subject to the Peace and Friendship Treaties of 1726, 1749, 1752, 1760, 1778, and 1779. I currently write and live on Lekwungen and W̱SÁNEĆ territories, subject to the Doulas Treaties of 1850 and 1852 respectively.

  This chapter has benefited greatly from comments from and conversations with Jim Tully, Josh Nichols, Pablo Ouziel, and especially Avigail Eisenberg. I am grateful for their help, and all errors remain my own. I would also like to acknowledge the generous finical support of the Killam Foundation, the Center for Global Studies at the University of Victoria, and the Center for Constitutional Studies at the University of Alberta.
[1] Boaventura de Sousa Santos, "Law: A Map of Misreading. Toward a Postmodern Conception of Law," *Journal of Law and Society* 14, no. 3 (1987): 298–302.

Yann Allard Tremblay helpfully lays out two broad approaches to these relationships.[2] The modernist view recognizes a plurality of authorities but subordinates them to the state. For modernists, it is the state that determines the authority of all other actors by extending or withholding recognition according to its own logics. Modernist scholarship therefore focuses on the reasons why a state should or should not accommodate various claims. Conversely, the pluralist view – the view embraced in this chapter – sees the state as merely one authority among many. Under this view, the state enjoys no particular claim to manage the overall environment or determine the boundaries of other authorities. As a result, pluralist scholarship focuses on the dynamics of negotiation and contestation between authorities.

From a pluralist perspective, practices of recognition and interaction form an integral part of our legal and political systems.[3] Accordingly, Roughan argues that in order to be legitimate, an authority must not only make justified appeals to its own subjects, but also interact in justified ways with other sources of authority.[4] Likewise, Young argues that legitimate authorities must pursue nondomination both toward their own subjects and in their relations with other authorities.[5] In other words, the question of democracy must be addressed at two levels. We must ask how each tradition enacts democracy internally, but also how it relates to and intra-acts with other sites of collective decision-making. This chapter takes up the second question and focuses on the practices various orders, state and nonstate alike, use to manage, negotiate, and contest the boundaries of their respective claims.

Sometimes, overlapping authorities choose to recognize and accommodate one another's claims by dividing jurisdictions between them either geographically or by subject matter, as in federal arrangements. This allows each authority to act unilaterally in its own domains, thereby minimizing the need for coordination and maximizing the autonomy of each party. Where both parties assert a claim to the same spaces or subjects, overlapping authorities have sometimes embraced practices of co-decision, where representatives of each wield power jointly and seek collaborative consent.[6] This is the case in Northern Ireland, where Irish and Northern Irish authorities share power

---

[2] Yann Allard-Tremblay, "The Modern and the Political Pluralist Perspectives on Political Authorities," *The Review of Politics* 80, no. 4 (2018): 675–700.

[3] Ralf Michaels, "Law and Recognition – Towards a Relational Concept of Law," in *In Pursuit of Pluralist Jurisprudence*, ed. Nicole Roughan and Andrew Halpin (Cambridge: Cambridge University Press, 2017), 90–115.

[4] Nicole Roughan, *Authorities: Conflicts, Cooperation, and Transnational Legal Theory* (Oxford: Oxford University Press, 2013).

[5] Iris Marion Young, "Two Concepts of Self-Determination," in *Ethnicity, Nationalism, and Minority Rights*, ed. Stephen May, Tariq Madood, and Judith Squires (Cambridge: Cambridge University Press, 2004), 176–96.

[6] Merrell-Ann Phare et al., *Collaborative Consent and Water in British Columbia: Towards Watershed Co-Governance* (Victoria: POLIS Water Sustainability Project and the Centre for Indigenous Environmental Resources, 2017).

through consociational arrangements,[7] on Haida Gwaii, where land use decisions are made by a joint council of Haida and Settlers,[8] and in many arrangements between the Maori and New Zealand.[9] While such arrangements lack the autonomy of federal alternatives, they ensure that both parties' views are represented at all times. In other cases, however, multiple authorities continue to wield authority over the same spaces or subjects independently, but in a coordinated fashion. Like federalism, this allows each actor to carry itself differently, rather than committing to a shared compromise, but, like co-decision, it eschews unilateralism. This chapter focuses on the later set of practices, taking up some of the ways overlapping authorities have found to coordinate decision-making without either dividing jurisdiction between them or wielding power jointly though co-decision.

In particular, I focus on practices of conditional authority – sites where an actor accepts competing authority claims, but also subjects those claims to certain conditions. In order to have its claim recognized, an actor must meet standards of their peers. I explore this practice as it appears in two sites: the Northwest coast of Turtle Island,[10] and in the Europe integration project. In both cases, I argue that conditional forms of authority can be a tool of hegemonic rule, but can also be a means of challenging power asymmetries. Most interestingly, practices of conditional authority can offer forms of mutual influence that make the social order responsive to multiple independent standards of democracy at once. In so doing, I contend that they represent one way authorities can attend to the external dimensions of democratic legitimacy.

I begin by discussing a range of conditional practices present in the European integration project, and then explore some practices present in parts of Turtle Island. Building on these observations, I present a preliminary typology of conditional practices, and conclude by reflecting on how the observed

---

[7] For discussion, see John McGarry and Brendan O'Leary, "Consociational Theory, Northern Ireland's Conflict, and Its Agreement. Part 1: What Consociationalists Can Learn from Northern Ireland," *Government and Opposition* 41, no. 1 (2006): 43–63.

[8] Haida Nation and Her Majesty the Queen in Right of the Province of British Columbia, "Kunst'aa Guu–Kunst'aayah Reconciliation Protocol," December 11, 2009, www.llbc.leg.bc.ca/public/pub-docs/bcdocs2010/462194/haida_reconciliation_protocol.pdf. For discussion, see Jeremy Webber, "We Are Still in the Age of Encounter: Section 35 and a Canada Beyond Sovereignty," in *From Recognition to Reconciliation: Essays on the Constitutional Entrenchment of Aboriginal and Treaty Rights*, ed. Patrick Macklem and Douglas Sanderson (Toronto: University of Toronto Press, 2016), 63–99.

[9] For discussion see Roughan, *Authorities*, chap. 13.

[10] The term "Turtle Island" is drawn from the occurrence of the turtle in many Indigenous creation stories, including the Anishinaabe and Haudenosaunee. The term is commonly used to refer to North America while implicitly calling into question the European prerogative to name, govern, and exploit lands which were already occupied, governed, and named when they arrived. Gary Snyder, "The Rediscovery of Turtle Island," in *Deep Ecology for the 21st Century*, ed. George Sessions (Boulder: Shambhala, 1995), 454–62.

practices of conditional authority can help us to pursue democratic legitimacy in pluralist spaces.

CONDITIONAL AUTHORITY IN EUROPE

Forms of conditional authority are common in Europe. For example, the Union operates through subsidiarity – the principle that action ought to be taken at the European level only when it cannot be effectively taken at the national or regional levels.[11] National governments police the principle and can request control over any matter in which they feel competent.[12] Thus, the Union can make valid authority claims only where lower orders of government have abstained from competing claims. The Union's claim to implement policy is therefore valid only when certain conditions are met to the satisfaction of other authorities. In this way, the principle of subsidiarity uses conditional authority structures as means to keep a potentially overbearing partner from dominating its peers.

Similar practices have also emerged from the bottom up. Consider the relationship between the radically participatory, grassroots, and anti-institutional 15 M movement and a range of would-be electoral partners, mostly notably Podemos.[13] The 15 M activists govern themselves through participatory public assembles in a deliberate rejection of representative structures. Yet 15 M assemblies also sometimes support candidates in local, regional, national, and European elections. In this sense, 15 M and parties like Podemos are 'joining hands' across different conceptions of democracy.[14] This relationship has been fractious, but some in 15 M are experimenting with new ways to make the authority of elected representatives contingent upon the ongoing support of parallel, directly democratic institutions. For example, some activists have proposed that politicians partner with their constituents through public assemblies or online consultative tools where legislation can be drafted, major decisions considered, and proposals developed.[15] Representatives would be required to vote accordingly in the legislature, and could lose 15 M support at any time for failing to satisfy this condition. Thus, politicians can leverage 15 M's considerable grassroots clout, but only if they meet standards of conduct set by

---

[11] For discussion see Paul Craig and Gráinne de Búrca, *EU Law: Text, Cases, and Materials*, 5th ed. (Oxford: Oxford University Press, 2011), 100–5.

[12] Craig and De Burca, *EU Law*, 94–100.

[13] For extended discussions of 15 M and its relationship to Podemos, see Pablo Ouziel, "'*Vamos Lentos Porque Vamos Lejos*': Towards a Dialogical Understanding of Spain's 15Ms" (unpublished PhD thesis, University of Victoria, 2015); Pablo Ouziel, *Democracy Here and Now: The Exemplary Case of Spain* (Toronto: University of Toronto Press, 2022).

[14] Ouziel, "*Vamos Lentos*"; and Ouziel, *Democracy Here and Now*.

[15] See, for example, Jairo Vargas, "Partido X: '*Empecemos por lo más fácil: echémosles de ahí*'," *Público*, October 8, 2013, www.publico.es/actualidad/partido-x-empecemos-mas-facil.html; Aitor Riveiro, "El Movimiento por la democracia dresenta su hoja de ruta para un proceso constituyente," *El Diario*, March 12, 2014, www.eldiario.es/politica/movimiento-democracia-presenta-proceso-constituyente_1_4986189.html.

the assemblies themselves. Once again, the use of conditional authority works as a means to prevent relations of domination – indeed, to upset the prevailing power imbalance between representatives and constituents in an effort to forge relationships which can be understood as democratic from both participatory and representative perspectives.[16] In both these cases, conditional authority mechanisms work from the bottom up, as a check on actual or potential relationships of domination between the parties.

In other cases, conditions are imposed from the top down and function as means for powerful actors to secure compliance with their preferred norms. For example, Eurozone states are subject to the European Stability and Growth Pact (SGP) and the European Fiscal Compact (EFC), which oblige member states to maintain budget deficits of less than 3 percent of GDP and overall national debt levels under 60 percent of GDP.[17] The European Commission monitors these conditions and countries that violate them risk substantial economic sanctions.[18] In this sense, national spending authority is conditioned upon meeting certain externally determined, substantive macroeconomic outcomes.

Loans to indebted countries are another prominent mechanism of conditionality, as transnational credit is often dependent on a package of policy reforms. During the 2008 financial crisis, for example, Greek voters chose a left-wing government committed to kick-starting economic growth through taxation and government spending. The European Central Bank, European Commission, and IMF, however, refused to offer loans unless the government committed to austerity instead.[19] The government put the matter to referendum and voters overwhelmingly rejected the lenders' plan. Nevertheless, the Greek government could not afford the costs of governance without the loan and thus faced the prospect of having to leave the Eurozone or even the EU in order to pursue its preferred policies.[20] Its continuing participation in the EU is thus conditioned upon meeting certain substantive policy outcomes.[21] To the extent that these outcomes are in question, so too is Greece's membership in the bloc.

Though the power dynamics permeating these examples are meaningfully different, all of these cases share a unidirectional structure in that one party is a condition-setter and the other a condition-receiver.

---

[16] Ouziel, "*Vamos Lentos*," 245, 249.

[17] "The Stability and Growth Pact," European Commission, EU Economic Governance, http://ec .europa.eu/economy_finance/economic_governance/sgp/index_en.htm.

[18] "Six-Pack? Two-Pack? Fiscal Compact? A Short Guide to the New EU Fiscal Governance," European Commission, https://fotavgeia.blogspot.com/2016/04/six-pack-two-pack-fiscal-compact-short.html. McGiffen describes these developments as a "quantum leap of economic surveillance"; Steve McGiffen, Bloodless Coup d'Etat: The European Union's Response to the Eurozone Crisis," Socialism and Democracy 25, no. 2 (2011): 38; See also John Erik Fossum and Augustín José Menéndez, eds., *The European Union in Crises or the European Union as Crises? ARENA Report No 2* (Oslo: ARENA Centre for European Studies, 2014).

[19] For discussion of the Greek bailout generally, see Yanis Varoufakis, *And the Weak Suffer What They Must?* (New York: Nation Books, 2016).

[20] Ibid., 151.   [21] McGiffen, "Bloodless Coup d'Etat," 41.

Constitutional Pluralism

Perhaps the most interesting practices of conditional authority in Europe come from the interaction between EU and National courts, where each actor is both condition-setter and condition-receiver at the same time. The European Court of Justice (hereafter ECJ) has moved to place conditions on national law-making by proclaiming the supremacy of EU law over conflicting national legislation,[22] and even over national constitutions.[23] As a result, national legislators are constrained to exercise their discretion within the parameters of EU law, as interpreted by the ECJ. National courts, however, have contested the ECJ's claims of supremacy.[24] In a now famous pair of cases, the *Solange* decisions, the German Constitutional Court first ruled that because the EU did not provide human rights protections, it was incumbent upon German courts to review EU laws for compatibility with the German constitution.[25] In this way, EU supremacy was subjected to certain limits – Union measures which violated basic rights would not be applied. This represented a clear challenge to the authority of the ECJ. Rather than confront the German court directly, the ECJ busily developed a human rights jurisprudence based on the constitutions of its member states and the European Convention on Human Rights, to which Germany was a signatory. In *Solange 2*, the German Constitutional Court responded to this development, finding that the EU system now provided internal protections essentially equivalent to those in German Law.[26] As a result, German courts would no longer review EU laws on human rights grounds unless evidence could be presented that the EU system as a whole no longer provides equivalent human rights protection. These decisions have been euphemistically referred to as the *So-long-as* decisions: so long as the EU does not systematically violate the German constitution, it will be considered supreme.[27] So-long-as German legislators act within EU law, their acts will be upheld by the ECJ. In short, each actor receives the support of the other in exchange for satisfying certain conditions.

The so-long-as approach has since spread to other courts around the continent, most of whom now place conditions of some sort on EU supremacy in exchange for their acceptance of ECJ supremacy. This ad-hoc arrangement is significant because it effectively makes conditionality

---

[22] Case 6/64, *Costa v. ENEL* [1964] ECR 585.

[23] Case 11/70, *Internationale Handelsgesellschaft mbH* v. *Einfuhr- und Vorratsstelle für Getreide und Futtermittel* [1970] ECR 1125.

[24] For discussion, see Paul Craig, "The ECJ, National Courts and the Supremacy of Community Law" in *The European Constitution in the Making*, ed. Ingolf Pernice and Roberto Miccu (Baden-Baden: Nomos, 2004), 35–52; Miguel Poiares Maduro, "Contrapunctual Law" in *Sovereignty in Transition*, ed. Neil Walker (Portland: Hart Publishing, 2003).

[25] *Solange I*, BVerfGE Case 37/271, [1974] 14 CMLR 540 (German Constitutional Court).

[26] *Solange II*, BVerfGE Case 73/339, [1987] 3 CMLR 225 (German Constitutional Court).

[27] For discussion, see Mattias Kumm, "The Jurisprudence of Constitutional Conflict: Constitutional Supremacy in Europe Before and After the Constitutional Treaty," *European Law Journal* 11, no. 3 (2005): 262–307.

multilateral: both the ECJ and its national interlocutors are condition-setters, but also condition-receivers. Each actor polices the other, such that each actor must satisfy multiple standards at once.

In fact, in *Celmer*, the ECJ made this system of conditional acceptance and mutual policing horizontal, as well as vertical, ruling that Ireland does not have to honor extradition requests made by another member state if that state's justice system is systematically deficient.[28] Thus, the acceptance of extradition requests between states is conditional: it turns on the extraditing party's assessment of the requesting party's legal system. This creates a system of peer-review between national courts, with each monitoring the others and cooperating only on a conditional basis. In essence, each court has to accommodate the concerns of the others in order to have its own claims accommodated in turn. Importantly, each actor retains the ability to contest the system unilaterally, limited only by its need for the cooperation of others.

The overall legal environment in Europe is thus shaped not only by the copresence of EU and national law, but also by their interaction. The claims of each are shaped by interaction with the other, such that European legality can only be understood as an inter-legality – a hybrid made of components which are themselves hybrid. Maduro describes the resulting system as "constitutional pluralism," while Sabel and Gerstenberg call it "coordinate constitutionalism." These authors stress that each court's legitimacy and authority is constituted at least in part on the recognition of other courts.[29] This creates a system of autonomous but closely coordinated action, as each court maneuvers to make claims that are true to its own internal interests and ideologies, while also acceptable to its peers. In comparison to other forms of conditional authority, then, the relationship between European courts is reciprocal, with each actor constrained by the claims of the other.

CONDITIONAL AUTHORITY ON THE NORTHWEST COAST OF TURTLE ISLAND

As in Europe, practices of conditional authority are common on the parts of Turtle Island sometimes called Canada. Treaties signed in the most recent phase of treaty-making, the so-called Modern treaties, for example, often feature equivalence provisions, allowing First Nations to legislate freely, but only provided that they meet or exceed federal and provincial standards.[30] Paramountcy provisions are

---

[28] Case 216/18, *Minister for Justice and Equality* v. *LM* [2018] ECLI:EU:C:2018:586.

[29] Maduro, "Contrapunctual Law," 520–522 especially. Charles F. Sabel and Oliver Gerstenberg, "Constitutionalising an Overlapping Consensus: The ECJ and the Emergence of a Coordinate Constitutional Order," *European Law Journal* 16, no. 5 (2010), 545, 550 especially.

[30] The following references take the Tsawwassen agreement as an illustrative example, but the same is true of the modern treaty process generally. See, for example, Tsawwassen First Nation, Government of British Columbia, Government of Canada, "Tsawwassen Final Agreement," December 6, 2007, chap. 1, sections 23, 24, 25.

also common – First Nations' jurisdiction is valid, unless it conflicts with federal or provincial law.[31] Even in areas where First Nations' jurisdiction is paramount, it must operate within the confines of the Canadian Charter.[32] In all these ways, the authority that modern treaties grant is premised on certain conditions. Where those conditions are not met, Settler courts will withhold their recognition and support.

Section 35 of the Canadian constitution also creates conditional forms of authority. For example, Aboriginal rights are constitutionally protected – but only if they are compatible with crown sovereignty.[33] Aboriginal title allows a group to "choose the uses to which land is put,"[34] but title land cannot be used for purposes incompatible with Settler courts' understanding of Aboriginal connection to the land, and it cannot be alienated except to the crown.[35] As a result, First Nations rights are only recognized when they meet certain conditions.[36] In all these cases, dominant Settler authorities use practices of conditional authority to impose their standards on subaltern nations, such that conditions act as a form of neocolonialism.[37]

In other cases, conditional practices have emerged from the bottom up, as a means to prevent or disrupt relations of domination. For example, when Coastal Gas Link (hereafter CGL) began construction of a pipeline on Wet'suwet'en territory in Northern BC, the Unist'ot'en House group, whose traditional territory the pipeline crosses, asserted their title by establishing a healing camp in the path of the pipeline and preventing access to the territory by pipeline workers. As the Unist'ot'en camp cultivated relationships with extensive networks of supporters, they laid down broad protocols for their allies – conditions which solidarity actions must meet.[38] In this sense, supporters can take autonomous action in the name of the Wet'suwet'en, but only subject to certain conditions. Allies accept these constraints as a deliberate means to upset prevailing power imbalances between Settler and Indigenous communities. Swain and Henderson's chapters in this volume (13 and 14), each in their own way, shed further light on this dynamic.

---

[31] Ibid., chap. 1, section 19.   [32] Ibid., chap. 2, section 9,

[33] *Mitchell* v. *M.N.R.* [2001] 1 SCR 911.

[34] *Tsilhqot'in Nation* v. *British Columbia* [2014] 2 SCR 256.   [35] Ibid., 74.

[36] The Crown is also subject to conditions under this regime – it cannot infringe Aboriginal rights or title without passing a self-imposed justificatory test. R. v. *Sparrow* [1990] 1 SCR 1075, [1990] 70 DLR (4th) 385. However, this test constitutes an auto-limitation, rather than an interaction between systems.

[37] For extended discussion see Kwame Nkrumah, *Neo-Colonialism: The Last Stage of Imperialism* (London: Thomas Nelson & Sons, 1965).

[38] See, for example, the "fundraising protocols" and the protocols contained in the "supporter toolkit," as well as the process to seek approval for proposed solidarity actions. "Fundraising Protocols," Unist'ot'en Camp, http://unistoten.camp/fundraiserprotocols; "Supporter Toolkit," Unist'ot'en Camp, http://unistoten.camp/supportertoolkit2020.

As in Europe, unidirectional forms of condition setting can function either to entrench or to disrupt prevailing power relationships.

The Potlache System

As in Europe, there are also some examples where conditions operate multilaterally, such that each actor is at once a condition-giver and a condition-receiver. One particularly advanced example comes from the Northwest coast Potlache system, one version of which is discussed thoughtfully by Webber in Chapter 15 of this volume. According to Trosper, Indigenous governance on the Northwest coast is generally conducted through linked groups of Houses.[39] Each house selects its own leadership, but leadership claims have to be validated through Potlaches: in order to claim a title, the contender must host a ritual feast, inviting the title holders of neighbouring houses.[40] Once assembled, neighbouring dignitaries observe rites designed to demonstrate that the claimant is qualified. They also receive gifts, which serve both as a recognition of their titles and as proof that the claimant is able to manage the claimed territory well and produce wealth from it. If they are satisfied, they affirm the claimant's title. If they refuse or express only qualified support, the claimant's authority is to that degree undermined. In this sense, one's claim to authority is contingent on the support of other title holders. Where neighbouring title holders refuse to validate a claim or course of action, members of the House have to consider whether to hold their course and sacrifice the cooperation of their neighbours, change course, or even select a new title holder in order to maintain the benefits of conviviality.[41]

Once installed, both authority and title to land remain contingent on several duties, notably a duty to take care of the claimed land and preserve its productive capacity for future generations, and a duty to redistribute a portion of wealth generated within the territory to other Houses.[42] Once again, these duties are monitored through regular Potlaches. Because hosting a Potlache involves distributing significant wealth, it requires efforts on behalf of the entire House. As a result, the ability to Potlache serves as proof that a) the territory is still productive, b) the members of a house are satisfied and willing to contribute materially to seeing the current title holder maintain their position, and c) the title holder recognizes and respects the authority claims of other Houses by extending invitations to them.[43]

If, at any point, neighbouring title holders feel that a given official is not taking care of their responsibilities, they can refuse to validate their authority claim and withhold invitations to their own Potlaches. Likewise, members of a given house could refuse to contribute to a Potlache, thereby throwing their

[39] Ronald Trosper, *Resilience, Reciprocity and Ecological Economics* (London: Routledge, 2011).
[40] Ibid., 22.   [41] See Webber, Chapter 15, this volume.
[42] Trosper, *Resilience*, especially chap. 5.   [43] Ibid., 22, 67.

title holders' position into question. Each title holder therefore had an incentive to cultivate the active support of their own House, and of neighbouring Houses as well. Trosper calls this system "contingent proprietorship" because valid title claims are contingent upon meeting certain external and internal conditions. In this system, multidirectional conditions make each House a condition-setter and a condition-receiver, making the overall relationship an object of dialogue and negotiation over time.[44]

A PRELIMINARY TYPOLOGY OF CONDITIONAL AUTHORITY

Both on Turtle Island and in Europe, practices of conditional authority provide a window into one way that different traditions of collective decision-making are braided together in practice, co-structuring the political.

As we have seen, unidirectional forms of condition setting often arise in contexts of profound power asymmetry, where dominant actors impose conditions on subaltern actors unilaterally. We might call these instances 'imperial condition setting'. The IMF, for example, offers conditional loans to structurally impoverished countries who have little choice but to accept them. As a result, the IMF's conditions are often experienced as an undemocratic imposition. In these contexts, conditions work as a form of indirect rule which allows one party to control the other without taking on the administrative, political, and military costs of colonizing them directly. The current Greek government, for example, exercises authority within the conditions laid down by its lenders. Likewise, the modern treaty process in BC offers First Nations forms of autonomous authority within the parameters laid out by the federal and provincial governments. These relationships are inherently asymmetrical. The condition-setter has robust autonomy, and also enjoys the power to impose conditions. The condition-receiver enjoys only a constrained form of autonomy, and often has little ability to influence the condition-setter.[45]

---

[44] The multilateral relationship between hereditary house leaders also takes place in a context where elected band councils, created by the Canadian government, make competing claims to authority. Relations between elected councils and house-based governance systems are fraught and complex, and at least some members feel that hereditary chiefs do not consult widely enough to claim broad democratic mandates in the manner Trosper describes. Assessing the democratic quality of Wet'suwet'en house governance is, however, both beyond the scope of this chapter and inappropriate for me as a Settler with a deeply limited understanding of traditional governance systems and local political conditions. It is, however, noteworthy that elected and traditional governments each adjust their claims in light of one another, as they move toward their own conceptions of inter-political space. For an oral discussion, see John Borrows, "The Great Way of Decision Making: Constituting Indigenous Law with John Borrows," April 21, 2020, in *RAVEN (De)Briefs*, produced by Susan Smitten and RAVEN Trust, podcast.

[45] For an illuminating study of this dynamic as it relates to debt, see Maurizio Lazzarato, *The Making of the Indebted Man: An Essay on the Neoliberal Condition* (Los Angeles: Semiotext(e), 2012), 33, 72 especially.

However, unidirectional condition setting can also be used to deliberately upset power imbalances. The Unist'ot'en Camp's use of "supporter protocols", for example, allows subaltern actors to exert influence over their socially privileged supporters. Likewise, the structure of 15 M/Podemos connections seek to make ordinarily privileged officials subject to constraints from normally marginal citizens. In both cases, unidirectional condition setting functions as a form of tactical asymmetry to prevent or contest relations of domination. In these ways, unidirectional condition setting practices can be 'counter-imperial' as well, working to destabilize, rather than entrench, existing power dynamics.

Perhaps the most interesting forms of conditional authority, however, are those where conditions are mutual, such that each actor is both a condition-receiver and a condition-setter at the same time. We might call these instances 'reciprocal condition setting'. In the Potlache system, or the relationship between European courts, for example, every actor is, to some extent, dependent on the support of its peers. This makes each tradition of collective decision-making responsive to several different standards of legitimacy simultaneously: their own standards, and those of other actors. In this way, each actor is both constrained by and able to exercise agency though its relationship with every other actor.

The resulting relationships are capable of holding complex tensions. Relations are both cooperative, in that actors rely on one another's support, and also competitive, in that each is seeking to shape the environment according to its own needs and interests.[46] As with the imperial and counter-imperial types above, power dynamics remain central. Yet, where counter-imperial conditions work as a tactical corrective that presumes a broader set of hegemon–subaltern relations, reciprocal condition setting is non-imperial, in that it can proceed absent relations of domination. In fact, in an argument that resonates with Young's account of legitimacy in pluralist settings,[47] Angelbeck posits that reciprocal condition setting is part of a complex set of practices on the Northwest Coast which work together to prevent the emergence of any dominant political actor.[48] Their goal is not therefore to unsettle an existing imperialism, but rather to prevent a state of imperialism from coming into being. Put differently, their goal is to build and maintain a state of relational nondomination. In this way, practices of reciprocal condition setting in particular may represent an important means to pursue legitimate relations between overlapping authorities, thus attending to the relational aspects of democratic legitimacy.

[46] Donna Haraway, *Staying with the Trouble: Making Kin in the Chthulucene* (Durham, NC: Duke University Press, 2016), 60, 62.

[47] Young, "Self-Determination."

[48] William O. Angelbeck, "'They Recognize No Superior Chief': Power, Practice, Anarchism and Warfare in the Coast Salish Past" (unpublished PhD thesis, University of British Columbia, 2009); see also Brian Thom, "The Anathema of Aggregation: Towards 21st Century Self-Government in the Coast Salish World," *Anthropologica* 52, no. 1 (2010): 33–48.

THEORIZING DEMOCRATIC LEGITIMACY IN PLURALIST SPACE

Having explored a range of practices of conditional authority being enacted in two diverse settings, it is now worth reflecting on what these practices mean for democratic theory and, in particular, how they can help us think about democratic legitimacy.

In her account of 'relative authority', Roughan argues that legitimate authorities must not only make justified appeals to their own subjects, but also interact in justified ways with other sources of authority. To assess this second feature, Roughan introduces the 'relative authority test':

(i) The relationship between the authorities must improve or at least not diminish the prospects of conformity to reason[49] for [the subjects of each authority] ...

(ii) The relationship must be consistent with the values protected by the procedures conferring standing upon each authority ...

(iii) There must be no overriding undefeated reasons against having that relationship.[50]

Without endorsing it as the only or even the best way to assess democratic legitimacy in pluralist contexts, I nevertheless contend that such a test allows us to explore the extent to which practices of reciprocal condition setting might allow overlapping authorities to attend to the relational or pluralist dimensions of their legitimacy.

First, because each authority retains distinct decision-making processes, each is able to freely follow the internal logic or 'reason' of their tradition. The need to meet the conditions of other authorities does compromise the ability to freely follow the logic of one's own tradition to some extent, in that this logic is no longer the only factor weighing upon a decision. Rather, actors are bound to take

---

[49] While Roughan's emphasis on "reason" might be taken to imply a universal standard of conduct, Roughan seems to accept that each community will have its own version of reason, according to its own ontological and epistemological foundations. I therefore take her to mean not that pluralist arrangements must facilitate universal reason, but rather than they must facilitate each group living according to its own distinct conception of reason. In other words, the criteria require that pluralist arrangements be comprehensible and justifiable within the logic of each participating tradition. To avoid any confusion with universal concepts of reason, I have generally used "logic" rather than reason in this chapter. See Roughan, *Authorities*, chap. 8.

[50] Roughan, *Authorities*, 237. In chapter 8, Roughan offers another formulation of the test, whereby a legitimate interaction is one that:

"(a) improves or at least does not diminish the prospects of conformity to reason for subjects of either authority; (b) is consistent with the values protected by the justified procedures that confer standing upon either authority; (c) is consistent with the balance of governance reasons applying in the circumstances; and (d) is consistent with side-effect reasons generated by the overlap or interaction."

This version breaks the "no undefeated reasons against the relationship" criteria in two, considering governance and side-effect factors separately. For reasons of space, simplicity, and clarity of argument, I have chosen to engage with the less detailed formulation.

into account one another's logics as well. However, the decision of *how* to respond to the conditions of others remains subject to the logic of each tradition. Moreover, any loss of reasoning autonomy is compensated for by the fact that other authorities must also take your logics into account, thereby preventing their decisions from seriously impeding your ability to live according to that logic. Thus, authorities trade some degree of decision-making autonomy for some degree of influence over their peers. While internal decisions are somewhat less strictly dictated by an authority's internal logic, the decisions of others are made responsive to this logic. Whether this trade-off increases or decreases the overall ability of the subjects of any given authority to live according to their own logics will therefore depend on how seriously subjects of that authority are impacted by the decisions of other authorities. In cases where these impacts are significant, reciprocal condition setting will likely improve the overall ability for subjects to live in accordance with their own logics.

Regarding the second criteria, condition setting is not necessarily equal, as we have seen. Conditions can be unilateral, or some parties might set more extensive or more stringent conditions than others. Thus, where subjects confer equal standings on each of the authorities in question – for example, where both claim an exclusive right to governance, or where both claim the right to negotiate with other authorities – both parties can set conditions equally (reciprocally) and be acting in accordance with the level of authority conferred on each by its subjects. Where the authority conferred on one party by its subjects is lesser than the authority conferred by another by its subjects – for example, where one party claims comprehensive governance rights and the other claims only minor forms of self-determination – condition-setting practices can provide ways to recognize this asymmetry. Thus, reciprocal condition setting can often be compatible with the authority conferred upon each party by its subjects, whether these are equal or not.

Finally, there must be no overriding reasons against the relationship. Roughan mentions necessity in particular: where "necessary" actions would be prevented or impaired, reciprocal condition setting may not be appropriate.[51] However, both the remarkable success of judicial dialogue in the EU and the millennia-long success of Potlache systems suggest that practices of reciprocal condition setting are capable of successfully managing relationships over time without preventing either actor from taking necessary actions. Indeed, the capacity of each actor to take such steps as it deems necessary is a defining feature of the reciprocal condition setting dynamic – should either party feel that truly necessary goals are being frustrated, they would simply act autonomously and sacrifice the cooperation of the other party.[52]

[51] Roughan, *Authorities*, 340–41.
[52] For example, Maduro argues that the fact that either level of court has the capacity to take actions not approved by the others is actually essential to Europe's system of Constitutional

Thus, under certain conditions, reciprocal condition setting provides one way for each party to engage with its peers in ways that can be plausibly justified, thereby attending to the pluralist dimensions of democratic legitimacy. Even if Roughan's test is not definitive, the primae facie case for the utility of conditional authority is strong. In fact, compared to federal arrangements or co-decision mechanisms, reciprocal condition setting offers a distinct way of seeking pluralist or relative legitimacy.

In federal contexts, each authority rules unilaterally within its jurisdictions and is powerless beyond them. Thus, we might say that the authority of each party is deep, but not broad. This allows each party to act according to its own logics and its logics alone – within its jurisdictions. However, it also means that actions outside of its jurisdiction are unlikely to reflect its logics at all. Such arrangements therefore involve a trade-off. Where each party prioritizes control over different aspects of governance, this trade-off may allow each party to relate in ways that maximize their ability to act according to their own logics, at least where those logics matter most.

Conversely, co-decision mechanisms allow each party to share decision-making on a potentially expansive set of shared concerns. This guarantees that every issue of concern to either party will be responsive to that party's logics – but only alongside and in conversation with the logics of others. In comparison with federalism, such arrangements offer each party a form of authority that is broad, but not deep. Once again, a trade-off is involved. Where comprehensive input is more important to the parties than particular areas of autonomy, co-decision may allow each party to inter-relate in ways that further their ability to live according to their own logics.

Reciprocal condition-setting practices offer a distinct set of trade-offs. Here, each party retains its own distinct institutions operating according to their own logics, thus offering a deeper form of autonomy than co-decision mechanisms. However, each party is also able to exert influence on a broad range of topics, offering a broader sort of authority than federal arrangements. We might say that the authority of a party is as broad as it needs to be in order to protect its interests, and as deep as it can be without adversely affecting other interests. Where the concerns of the parties overlap too much to divide jurisdictions in a federal manner, yet the parties value maintaining distinct institutions without collapsing them into a shared, compromise body, reciprocal condition setting may represent a preferable way for overlapping authorities to legitimize their interactions.

In comparison to federal and co-decision structures, practices of conditional authority are also distinct in that they need not be fully articulated or structured in advance. Instead, conditions can be articulated gradually over time, in response to real problems and in dialogue with other authorities. Indeed, the

pluralism. Maduro, "Contrapunctual Law." Webber makes a similar point in his exploration of the Gitxsan feast system.

German Constitutional Court continues to elaborate, clarify, and adjust the conditions it places on EU authority even now, sixty years after those standards were originally imagined. Rather than relying on a priori standards capable of meeting any hypothetical concern, the court is able to articulate concrete standards in relation to particular concerns as they arise, and to modify those standards as the EU adjusts its conduct. Likewise, as Webber shows, the Gitxsan have been adjusting the substance and form of their relations since time immemorial. This makes practices of reciprocal condition setting flexible and responsive, and also allows them to proceed in cases where agreeing on the shape of federal or co-decision structures would be challenging or impossible.

In an almost functionalist manner, practices of reciprocal condition setting and the dialogues they create can also facilitate the gradual emergence of imperfectly shared inter-societal norms.[53] As each party articulates its logics in conversation with others, a shared body of transnational precedent begins to emerge, allowing parties to deepen their mutual understanding and cooperation over time. In this way, the dialogues created through reciprocal condition setting can be especially appropriate where trust and mutual understanding cannot be taken for granted but, rather, need to be cultivated over time.

Last, because condition setting is driven by real concerns, the dialogue it creates does not take place in the abstract, but is instead constitutively situated in lived experiences and the unequal power relations that structure them.[54] Thus, reciprocal condition setting provides a means to call existing power imbalances and the de-democratizing practices[55] that sustain them into question over time.

Practices of conditional authority, and of reciprocal condition setting in particular, therefore constitute a useful set of tools that overlapping authorities can bring to bear in attempts to legitimize their pluralist relations. In the context of complex relationships, actors may even choose to draw on several approaches in concert. In the EU, for example, some powers rest at the national level and others at the European level, as in federal structures. In most matters of EU jurisdiction, the European Parliament (representing the people of Europe as a demos of its own) and the Council of Ministers (representing each state as a distinct demos) engage in legislative co-decision. European courts, however, engage in practices of reciprocal condition setting. Europe therefore strives toward relative or pluralist legitimacy by operationalizing a number of practices of interrelation at once. As Lord and Magnette argue, the EU has iteratively developed "political systems that are not configured for the

[53] For an account how transnational norms develop in contexts of persisting asymmetry and contestation, see, for example, Jeremy Webber, "Relations of Force and Relations of Justice: The Emergence of Normative Community between Colonists and Aboriginal Peoples," *Osgoode Hall Law Journal* 33, no.4 (1995): 624–55.
[54] For an excellent discussion, see Monika Kirloskar-Steinbach, ed., *Dialogue and Decolonization* (Bloomington, IN: Indiana University Press, forthcoming).
[55] See Nelems, Chapter 9, this volume.

articulation of any one view of legitimacy but for the mediation of relationships between several."[56]

Likewise, on Turtle Island, early-contact treaty practices often divided jurisdiction either territorially or personally, but also established a norm of co-decision for subjects of shared concern.[57] Treaty terms can also be seen as laying out a series of conditions that Settlers must meet in order to exercise legitimate authority on Indigenous lands: for example, providing certain medical or educational services, setting aside certain lands, or guaranteeing certain rights. In this way, treaty-diplomacy could involve aspects of federal, co-decision, and conditional authority practices all used in concert to pursue pluralist or relative legitimacy. Indeed, oral accounts of treaty-making from both Settler and Indigenous histories stress that treaty-making was as much about sharing authority as it was about securing mutual independence.[58]

More recently, patterns of interaction between Settler and Indigenous authorities have, of course, become dramatically lopsided and unjust. As discussed, the division of jurisdiction through modern treaties has been paired with paramountcy and equivalence provisions which leave Settler authorities autonomous in their own jurisdictions while subjecting Indigenous authorities to imposed conditions, thereby skewing the relationship in favor of Settler authorities. Likewise, most practices of co-decision have become relationships of co-management instead, wherein shared bodies play advisory roles subordinated to dominant Settler institutions.[59] Similarly, condition-setting practices have become predominantly unilateral, especially through insistence that the Canadian *Charter of Rights* applies to First Nations governments.[60]

---

[56] Christopher Lord and Paul Magnette, "E Pluribus Unum? Creative Disagreement about Legitimacy in the EU," *Journal of Common Market Studies* 42, no. 1 (2004), 184 especially.

[57] For discussion, see Keith Cherry, *Practices of Pluralism: A Comparative Analysis of Trans-Systemic Relationships in Europe and on Turtle Island* (unpublished PhD thesis, University of Victoria, 2020), 30–32, 67–70 especially.

[58] See, for example, Michael Asch, *On Being Here to Stay: Treaties and Aboriginal Rights in Canada* (Toronto: University of Toronto Press, 2014), chap. 7 especially. See also Michael Asch, "Confederation Treaties and Reconciliation: Stepping Back into the Future," in *Resurgence and Reconciliation: Indigenous-Settler Relations and Earth Teachings*, ed. James Tully, Michael Asch, and John Borrows (Toronto: University of Toronto Press, 2018), 35–39; Neil Vallance, "Sharing the Land: The Formation of the Vancouver Island (or 'Douglas') Treaties of 1850–1854 in Historical, Legal and Comparative Context" (unpublished PhD thesis, University of Victoria, 2015); Harold Cardinal and Walter Hildebrandt, *Treaty Elders of Saskatchewan: Our Dream Is That Our Peoples Will One Day Be Clearly Recognized as Nations* (Calgary: University of Calgary Press, 2013), generally and especially at 14–16.

[59] For discussion see Phare et al., *Collaborative Consent*, 15.

[60] For discussion, see Bill Rafoss, *The Application of the Canadian Charter of Rights and Freedoms to First Nation's Jurisdiction: An Analysis of the Debate* (unpublished MA thesis, University of Saskatchewan, 2005).

While the literature on treaty federalism[61] focuses on realigning the relationship between Settler and Indigenous authorities by adjusting jurisdictional boundaries and (re)creating co-decision forums, making condition-setting practices reciprocal could complement this approach. For example, future treaties could not only subject First Nations to the *Charter* as interpreted by Canadian courts, but also subject federal and provincial governments to standards set by each Nation and articulated, policed, and adjusted by independent Indigenous legal institutions. Federal, provincial, and Indigenous bodies would all be able to govern within their negotiated jurisdictions, but each would have to respect the fundamental standards of the others. Each would have its own institutional voice and, thus, an iterative dialogue between Indigenous and Canadian law could begin.

In all these ways, practices of reciprocal condition setting may have something to offer to overlapping authorities that are interested in democratizing their relationships and thereby attending to the relative dimensions of their legitimacy.

CONCLUSIONS

In sum, conditional forms of authority require the condition-receiver to meet multiple standards of legitimacy at once in order to receive the support of its peers. As we have seen, this practice can be unilateral, either as a way for dominant powers to enforce standards on subaltern counterparts, or as a way to tactically upset prevailing power imbalances, creating space for subaltern voices in relations of persisting asymmetry. When practices of conditionality are reciprocal, however, both partners are constrained not only by their own internal standards of legitimacy, but also by those of their interlocutors. This allows actors to co-articulate social regulation in a way that can be justified to all participants without requiring them to either divide jurisdictions between them or converge around a shared decision-making structure. Thus, reciprocal condition setting represents a novel way that overlapping authorities can attend to the relational components of their legitimacy. In so doing, these practices furnish one way pursue democratic legitimacy in pluralist space.

---

[61] For discussion, see James Youngblood Henderson, "Empowering Treaty Federalism," *Saskatchewan Law Review* 58, no. 1 (1994): 241–329; Joshua Nichols and Amy Swiffen, eds., "Special issue on Treaty Federalism," *The Review* 24, no. 1 (2019).

PART VI

JOINING HANDS: ECO-DEMOCRATIC INTEGRATION

19

On Gaia Democracies

James Tully

THE SUSTAINABILITY CRISES AND TWO GAIA DEMOCRATIC RESPONSES

The Crises

We humans are aware that we are caught up in serious problems or crises of democratic, social and ecological sustainability and well-being. Over the last 500 years the West has developed a complex global social system that is socially and ecologically unsustainable in the long run, and ultimately self-destructive. It exploits, undermines and destroys the informal, biodiverse social and ecological conditions that sustain life on earth for Homo sapiens and many other species and ecosystems. This exceptionally complex social system – or, rather, assemblage of interlocking systems of production, consumption, regulation and warfare – has been spread around the world in the language of civilization, modernization, globalization, peace and representative democratization. It has always been met with various forms of resistance and counter-responses, and thus should be characterized, as Edward Said argued, as a 'contrapuntal ensemble'.[1] It is a modernizing assemblage of 'vicious' social systems in the technical sense that the regular feedback loops within these social systems reproduce and intensify the destructive effects of the systems on the informal, everyday social spheres, ecosphere, biosphere and abiotic sphere on which they depend and which they exploit.[2]

---

[1] Edward Said, *Culture and Imperialism* (New York: Vintage, 1994). See Jeanne Morefield, Chapter 7, this volume.

[2] This chapter draws on James Tully, 'Reconciliation Here on Earth,' in *Resurgence and Reconciliation: Indigenous-Settler Relations and Earth Teachings*, ed. Michael Asch, John Borrows and James Tully (Toronto: University of Toronto Press, 2018), 83–132; James Tully, 'Life Sustains Life 1: Value, Social and Ecological,' in *Nature and Value*, ed. Akeel Bilgrami (New York: Columbia University Press, 2020), 163–80; and James Tully, 'Life

The well-known effects are global warming, climate change, escalating pollution and the diseases it causes; the melting of polar icecaps and glaciers, and the release of even more lethal greenhouse gases this produces; the acidification of oceans and the vicious cycles this generates; the depletion of non-renewable resources; and the use of renewable resources more quickly than they can renew themselves. The economic scramble over what is left is increasingly damaging to the environment. It has cascading effects on weather and global human and species suffering. These lead to more destructive wars and war preparation to protect these unsustainable social systems; rapid increases in climate refugees and war refugees; and starvation, poverty, racism, and inequalities in life chances.

We have known that this global ensemble is unsustainable socially and ecologically since the first meetings on the sustainability crisis in the 1950s and 1960s at the United Nations. These warnings were followed by Rachel Carson, Barry Commoner, the first Earth Day in 1970, The Club of Rome, *The Limits to Growth*, the Brundtland Report in the 1980s and the emergence of the concept of sustainability and well-being as a meta-norm in national and international relations. Thousands of scientists have reaffirmed and extended these findings and summarized them in the reports of the Intergovernmental Panel on Climate Change (IPCC). Yet the crisis continues despite efforts to address, govern and regulate it by state-based representative democracies and their global institutions. As David Held summarizes in Chapter 16, these institutions are in a 'gridlock' that sustains the trajectory of the vicious systems. We are already into the sixth mass extinction of biological diversity, and biological diversity is a necessary condition of sustainable life on earth. If these trends continue, much of the earth will be less habitable or uninhabitable by the turn of the century. This is referred to as the Medea hypothesis.[3]

Thus, the great question today is: What have we learned over the last seventy years and how can we address the crises most effectively today? The regeneration of Gaia *philia* and Gaia democracies is my response to this question.

Four Phases of Life Systems

The first thing we have learned from the study of complex social and ecological systems is that it is not unusual for them to become vicious and unsustainable in the way ours have. They develop in such a way that they use up the conditions that sustain them, degrading or destroying the interdependent life forms on

Sustains Life 2: The Ways of Regeneration with the Living Earth,' in *Nature and Value*, ed. Bilgrami, 181–204. These chapters contain more detailed arguments and references.
[3] Mark Lynas, *One Final Warning: Six Degrees of Climate Emergency* (London: 4th Estate, 2020); David Wallace-Wells, *The Uninhabitable Earth: Life After Warming* (New York: Tim Duggan Books, 2019); Peter Ward, *The Medea Hypothesis* (Princeton: Princeton University Press, 2009).

which they depend, and, thus, ultimately, destroying themselves. There are many examples of this in the history of life systems, both human and non-human, as the academic literature on civilizational collapse and super-predation shows. Moreover, and more importantly, there are also many examples of members of both social and ecological vicious systems changing their unsustainable behaviour and transforming their systems into virtuous and sustainable systems before collapse, and other examples of recovering from collapse and regenerating 'virtuous' or self-sustaining systems.

Accordingly, the complex life-systems sciences hypothesize that there are four phases of life systems. The first, virtuous or sustainable phase consists of cooperation, contestation and conciliation cycles. That is, the individual and collective members of these systems sustain themselves in lifeways that co-sustain the well-being of all the interdependent members, relationships and systems on whom they inter- and co-depend that comprise the complex webs of life and their strong coupling with abiotic earth systems. When some members engage in unsustainable ways of life, the systems evolve ways of conciliating these members back into sustainable life patterns. That is, life sustains life. This phase is thus 'homeotelic'. The orientation of and to cooperation is predominant.[4]

The second, transitional or degenerative phase occurs when a system is unable to conciliate unsustainable behaviour. The unsustainable behaviour continues to develop by means of positive feedback loops that reinforce and increase the behaviour further and further from dynamic equilibrium. Common examples of this transitory phase are the transitions from a homeotelic predator–prey system towards a super-predatory system and the escalating violence and counter-violence dialectic or 'security dilemma' of the global arms race. The third phase occurs when the unsustainable behaviour increases to a tipping point that transforms the system as a whole into a predominantly vicious, unsustainable and, eventually, self-destructive system. Our current global assemblage of vicious social systems and the sixth mass extinction they are causing during the 'great acceleration' since World War II are in this third phase. It is 'heterotelic': oriented to ruthless competition or struggles for existence rather than cooperation.[5]

Fortunately for life on earth, there is a fourth phase. This 'regeneration' phase occurs when the members of unsustainable systems find ways to practice and regenerate sustainable ways of living. Regeneration of co-sustainable forms of life grows by means of negative feedback loops and reconnecting with the power of neighbouring life systems. They gradually displace or transform the unsustainable systems, either before they collapse or

---

[4] Edward Goldsmith, *The Way: An Ecological World-View* (Athens: University of Georgia Press, 1998), 239–45. The four cycles that Nelems mentions in Chapter 9 constitute an example of a system in the homeotelic phase.

[5] Goldsmith, *The Way*, 261–67.

afterwards. These processes are referred to as ecological succession or reconnecting with *anima mundi*: the power or animacy that runs through and sustains all life on earth.[6] For example, twenty-one human civilizations have come and gone. Life has recovered from five previous mass extinctions. Overall, life has sustained and complexified life through multiple examples of these four types of phases for 3.8 billion years or we would not be here. However, over the last seventy years the extinction of species and ecosystems (biodiversity) has occurred at a rate that far exceeds the historical norm. Although Life will survive the sixth mass extinction, whether or how many Homo sapiens will survive is unknown.[7]

Thus, the fourth phase of complex systems – of regeneration and transformation of vicious systems – is of immense importance for us. We can learn from these examples and think of how to apply them to our own situation. The vicious social systems that cause the sustainability crises are not automatons, as the doomsayers claim. They are very complex local and global social systems to which we are subject and on which most of us depend for our livelihood. Our daily, habitual ways of thinking and acting within them reproduces them. However, we are not so enslaved to them that we cannot think or act otherwise. We are free to reflect on them and to ask the questions we are asking: namely, how can we act and live differently in order to regenerate sustainable systems and transform our unsustainable ones. Moreover, we are free to act on how we answer these questions.

I will discuss two complementary traditions in which people are responding to the sustainability crises in this way. They are examples of Gaia democracies. There are also several examples in the chapters of this volume.

The Problem to Which Gaia Democracies Are Responses

At the core of Gaia democracies responses is the hunch that the reason we have difficulty responding effectively to the sustainability and well-being crisis as a whole is that we misperceive its nature. The reason we misperceive the nature of crisis is that we view it from within the ways of thinking and acting that sustain the vicious social systems that are causing it. It is our socialization and self-formation as conscripts within the vicious social systems that discloses the world around us and our relationships with the environment in a way that overlooks or distorts how they degrade the conditions that sustain life. Thus, even when we can no longer ignore or discount the damage we are doing, we

---

[6] This is the central themes of Stephen Harding, *Animate Earth: Science, Intuition and Gaia*, 2nd ed. (Cambridge: Green Books, 2013); see also Fritjof Capra and Pier Luigi Luisi, *The Systems View of Life: A Unifying Vision* (Cambridge: Cambridge University Press, 2015). For ecological succession, see subsection 'The Animacy of Symbiosis'.

[7] Harding, *Animate Earth*, 208–49.

respond in the standard problem-solving ways of the vicious systems, thereby reproducing rather than changing them.

Accordingly, the problem is not simply one of misperception, but also of being caught up in an unsustainable way of life that generates this way of perceiving the world. One of the first earth scientists to point this out was Barry Commoner in 1970:[8]

To survive on earth, human beings require the stable, continuing existence of a suitable environment. Yet the evidence is overwhelming that the way in which we now live on earth is driving its thin, life-supporting skin, and ourselves with it, to destruction. To understand this calamity, we need to begin with a close look at the nature of the environment itself. Most of us find this a difficult thing to do, for there is a kind of ambiguity in our relation to the environment. Biologically, human beings *participate in* the environmental system as subsidiary parts of the whole. Yet, human society is designed *to exploit* the environment as a whole, to produce wealth. The paradoxical role we play in the natural environment – at once participant and exploiter – distorts our perception of it.

[That is,] all of modern technology leads us to believe that we have made our own environment and no longer depend on the one provided by nature. We have become enticed into a nearly *fatal illusion*: that through our machines we have at last escaped from dependence on the natural environment. [Yet,] every human activity depends on the integrity and proper functioning of the ecosphere. [my italics]

I will discuss how our exploitive social systems generate this ambiguity and illusion of externality and independence later in the chapter. I would like to begin with the following question: How do we free ourselves from the unsustainable way of life that generates this illusion and misperception and move around to seeing ourselves as interdependent participants within and with the living earth to which we belong? This is the way of becoming democratic citizens of Gaia democracies. Because our perception of the world is partly shaped by our mode of being in the world, we cannot see clearly the way forward unless we begin to change our way of being in the world to a more sustainable way. As in ecological succession, we have to begin to be the change we wish to bring about in order to see more clearly the nature of that change.[9]

One of the first, non-Indigenous people to see this clearly was Aldo Leopold in *Sand County Almanac* (1949). He argued that if we are to live in ways that sustain the conditions of life on earth for us and future generations, then we have to move from seeing ourselves as the all-knowing conquerors and controllers of nature to seeing ourselves as plain members and citizens of the biotic communities in which we live and on which we depend for every breathe and step we take. We need to take this engaged turn in order to observe and learn by trial and error how to participate in these life cycles in mutually

---

[8] Barry Commoner, *The Closing Circle: Nature, Man and Technology* (New York: Alfred A. Knopf Inc., 1971), 14–15.
[9] Harding, *Animate Earth*, 250–56.

sustaining ways. In Gaia democracies humans treat all lifeforms as fellow citizens, and the interdependent relationships and responsibilities among them as co-learning and co-governance relationships. Leopold called this evolutionary transformation the 'land ethic'. I refer to it as Gaia ethics:

All ethics so far evolved rest upon a single premise: that the individual is a member of a community of interdependent parts . . . The land ethic simply enlarges the boundaries of the community to include soils, waters, plants, and animals, or collectively: the land.
    In short, a land ethic changes the role of *Homo sapiens* from conqueror of the land-community to plain member and citizen of it. It implies respect for his fellow-members, and also respect for the community as such.

The reason this transformation is necessary is that the conqueror and controller of nature role is 'self-defeating'. It is based on the presumption that the conqueror-controller 'knows, *ex cathedra*, just what makes the community clock tick, and just what and who is valuable, and what and who is worthless, in community life. It always turns out that he knows neither, and this is why his conquests eventually defeat themselves'.[10]

Two Traditions of Gaia Democracies in Response to a Shared Problem

The first of two traditions of Gaia democracies is the family of ecosocial democracies that many Indigenous peoples have been practicing for thousands of years. It is embodied in the traditional ecological knowledge and wisdom (TEKW) and practices they have acquired over centuries of learning by trial and error how to participate as evolving apprentices in mutually sustainable ways with 'mother earth'. These are referred to as earth teachings learned from studying earthways.[11] The second tradition is much more recent. It comprises the communities of practice of ecosocial democracies that have developed in practice and in dialogue with the ecological and life sciences, and sometimes in dialogue with Indigenous peoples.

    The remarkable feature of these two very different traditions is that they share a commitment to participatory democracy. For both, in different languages and ways, the power of self-government consists in people becoming a 'people' (*demos*) and 'citizens' in the course of exercising powers of self-government (*kratos*) by, with and for each other in observing, learning, discussing, interacting, contesting and resolving disputes together – of governing and being governed together – without anyone ruling over them (*arche*). That is, democratic self-government (*demos+kratos*) is engaged *power and knowledge with and for each other*. This

[10] Aldo Leopold, 'The Land Ethic', in *A Sand County Almanac: With Essays on Conservation from Round River* (New York: Ballantine Books, 1966), 239–40.
[11] John Borrows, 'Earth-Bound: Indigenous Resurgence and Environmental Reconciliation', in *Resurgence and Reconciliation*, ed. Asch, Borrows and Tully, 49–82; Aaron Mills, 'Rooted Constitutionalism: Growing Political Community', *Resurgence and Reconciliation*, ed. Asch, Borrows and Tully, 133–74.

is the classic Athenian conception of democracy.[12] In contrast, all non-democratic forms of government employ different forms of *power and knowledge over the governed* in ruler–ruled or master–subject hierarchical relationships (*arche*).[13] These two Gaia democracy traditions extend the classic Athenian conception of democracy from the polis to Gaia.

THE LIVING EARTH TRADITION OF GAIA DEMOCRACIES

Gaia Hypothesis

In the 1960s Sir James Lovelock, an earth systems scientist, discovered the Gaia Hypothesis. Despite the vast changes in the solar energy coming to earth over the last 3.8 billion years, and despite the vast changes in the forms of life on earth over the same long period, and despite all the changes in earth, ocean and atmospheric conditions over the same period, the atmospheric conditions and temperature of earth have somehow remained in the range that sustains life on earth. The hypothesis is that the biosphere, and all the systems of life that compose it, somehow regulate the atmosphere and temperature to sustain life. That is, the biotic and abiotic sphere as a whole is self-governing: self-organizing (sympoiesis) and self-sustaining (symbiosis and symbiogenesis).

The Gaia hypothesis has survived a number of tests and it is now considered a theory. A majority of the scientists on the IPCC have endorsed it, in slightly different ways.

This has led to attempts to explain how the systems that compose the ecosphere actually regulate the content and temperature of the atmosphere within a broad range of cycles that sustain most forms of life over vast stretches of time. This research has grown hand-in-hand with life and earth systems theory and complexity theory.[14]

The Animacy of Symbiosis: Life Sustains Life

For the purposes of those of us who wish to know how we should live within this complex system in mutually sustaining ways, the important insight came

---

[12] Josiah Ober, 'The Original Meaning of 'Democracy': Capacity to Do Things, Not Majority Rule,' (Princeton/Stanford Working Papers in Classics, Stanford University, Stanford, CA, 2007), http://dx .doi.org/10.2139/ssrn.1024775. Protagoras, the great defender of Athenian democracy, understood democracy as the way in which humans participate in the co-evolution of all forms of life: Plato, *Protagoras*, ed. Gregory Vlastos (Indianapolis: The Bobbs-Merrill Company, 1956).

[13] For an introduction to power-with (*kratos*) and power-over (*arche*), see James Tully, 'Integral Nonviolence: On the Significance of Gandhi Today,' *Politika*, 2019, www.politika.io/en/notice/ the-power-of-integral-nonviolence-on-the-significance-of-gandhi-today.

[14] James Lovelock, *The Vanishing Face of Gaia: A Final Warning* (London: Penguin Books, 2009); Harding, *Animate Earth*; John Gribbin and Mary Gribbin, *He Knew He Was Right: The Irrepressible Life of James Lovelock* (London: Penguin Books, 2009).

from Lovelock's colleague, the life scientist Lyn Margulis. She argued that the Gaia hypothesis is not based on the assumption that the system of systems that compose the ecosphere is itself a purposeful living being that regulates the climate and temperature to sustain life. Rather, given the holistic, regulative role that feedback loops of the system play, the self-sustaining quality of Gaia is an emergent property of the ways that the life systems that compose Gaia coordinate their interactions. In her famous words, 'the Gaia hypothesis is just symbiosis and symbiogenesis on a planetary scale'.[15] Life systems and their members sustain themselves in ways that also co-sustain the interdependent life systems and members on which they interdepend.

Stephen Harding describes the Gaia hypothesis or theory in the following way:[16]

The key insight of the theory is wonderfully holistic and non-hierarchical: it suggests that it is the *Gaian system as a whole* that does the regulating, that the sum of all the complex feedbacks between, life, atmosphere, rocks and water give rise to Gaia, the evolving, self-regulating planetary entity that has maintained habitable conditions on the surface of our planet over vast stretches of geological time.

The emergence of new properties in the course of the complex interaction of life systems is the way that life itself has developed in increasingly complex ways: that is, through life systems living-with each other in complex interdependent ways (symbiosis) and giving rise to new life systems (symbiogenesis). Spatially, symbiosis refers to the immensely complex webs or networks that link all forms of life in relationships of reciprocal interdependence. Temporally, these networks are cyclical. They form cycles in which another member uses the waste of one interdependent member in some sustaining way, so nothing is wasted, and at a temporality that enables species and ecosystem renewal. Photosynthesis is the paradigm of this spatio-temporal quality of reciprocal interdependency and cyclical renewability. Indeed, it is the basis of life sustaining life.[17]

Homo sapiens, as one minor species among millions, are members and citizens just like all others, with ecosocial democratic responsibilities to participate in ways that reciprocally co-sustain the networks that sustain us: that is, in virtuous ways.

Life systems are not automatically harmonious. They are often far from equilibrium, patchy, full of cheaters or free riders, and subject to perturbations that can cause virtuous systems, and their co-dependent systems, to tip into vicious states, as we have seen. Yet, despite that indeterminacy, their remarkable qualities of resilience enable them to sustain themselves over vast stretches of time. If vicious systems were the major factor

---

[15] Lyn Margulis, *Symbiotic Planet: A New Look at Evolution* (New York: Basic Books, 1998), 120.
[16] Harding, *Animate Earth*, 70.
[17] For the emergence of photosynthesis, see Commoner, *The Closing Circle*.

in evolution, then life on earth would have ceased long ago. The opposite is the case. Life has become more complex: symbiosis and symbiogenesis have prevailed most of the time, even recovering from mass extinctions.

Vicious systems are also not automatons. They too are far from equilibrium and subject to tipping points. The resilient powers of generation of life (sympoiesis) have the capacity to regenerate symbiotic networks within and around vicious systems, or on and around the ruins of them. This is the fourth, regeneration and transformation phase of life systems. They do this not by viciously counter-attacking a vicious system, but by means of cultivating symbiotic and symbiogenetic counter-communities of practice all around it and gradually transforming or replacing it. This is ecological succession.

Ecological succession works as the means of systemic transformation because life systems are *autotelic*: the means employed to generate and cultivate them determine the end. This internal relationship between means and ends is one of the great discoveries or rediscoveries of the ecological and human sciences in the twentieth century.[18] In Mahatma Gandhi's phrase, just as the type of seed prefigures the plant, so, too, humans have to be the change they wish to bring about – for example, peace by peaceful means, democracy by democratic means, and sustainable life systems by sustainable means. Here is an illustrative example provided by geographer Michael Simpson of an old-growth forest recovering from decades of clear cutting:[19]

Living systems do not only reproduce themselves. Their very life processes nourish their habitat and strengthen the conditions of life around them. They thereby create an organism that is larger than themselves or their individual species. When a forest is growing back from a disturbance, herbaceous (non-woody) plants are the first to move in. These plants exude sugars that attract bacteria around their roots. The bacteria in turn exude an alkaline 'bioslime' that creates a favorable habitat for themselves as well as for the pioneer plant species. The alkaline condition of the bioslime also allows the bacteria to break down ammonia in the soil into nitrates that are taken up by plants, allowing them to grow vegetatively. This cycle of life creating the conditions for more life continues as the forest gradually grows into a rich, biodiverse ecosystem (ecological succession). Living systems are not only self-regulating but they are relational in so far as they build the conditions of life around them.

Symbiosis and Symbiogenesis in Ecosocial Systems: A New Synthesis

The human sciences have entered into a dialogue with these life and earth sciences in the following ways. First, the concepts 'symbiosis' and 'symbiogenesis' have a long history in the human sciences. They refer to how diverse individual human beings and communities have lived together in

[18] See, for example, Aldous Huxley, *Ends and Means* (Oxford: Oxford University Press, 1946).
[19] Professor Michael Simpson, Department of Geography, Glasgow University, personal correspondence, April 11, 2013.

interdependent relationships of peace and mutual support. Moreover, communities of practice researchers argue that informal symbiotic social relationships of mutual aid exist within and across every social system – even within the most vicious and damaging social systems. Accordingly, the vicious social systems that are embedded within and damaging the ecosystems that sustain life are also embedded within and damaging *informal* symbiotic social systems that sustain the communities in which we live. As early as 1902, Peter Kropotkin, in *Mutual Aid*, argued that ecological and social relationships of mutual aid have been the major factor in human evolution, outweighing vicious struggles for existence.[20]

Second, there is widespread awareness that there are not two parallel paths of symbiotic evolution, one for non-human life and the other for human life. Rather, non-human symbiotic ecosystems and human symbiotic social systems are now perceived as evolving interdependently and reciprocally. They are studied as interdependent, coupled or co-evolving. Homo sapiens are studied as co-evolving and co-sustaining apprentices within their ecosocial systems.[21] This is a revolution relative to the dominant view that humans and their social systems are separate from and independent controllers of the natural world. The consequence is the realization that 'we can no longer understand the dynamics of either the natural system or the human subsystem in isolation without understanding the dynamics of the other component'.[22] Accordingly, all social systems are ecosocial systems.

Third, the human sciences are now focusing on designing all kinds of social systems so they interact symbiotically, rather than destructively, with the ecosystems in which they are embedded. The way to do this is to design them so they interact with their surrounding ecosystems in relationships of reciprocal interdependency and cycles in which the resources we use and the ecosystems we effect always have time to renew themselves. As Fritjof Capra explains:[23]

The key to an operational definition of ecological sustainability is the realization that we do not need to invent sustainable human communities from scratch but can model them after nature's ecosystems, which are sustainable communities of plants, animals and micro-organisms. Since the outstanding characteristic of the Earth household is its inherent ability to sustain life, a sustainable human community is one designed in such a manner that its ways of life, businesses, economies, federations, physical structures, and technologies do not interfere with nature's inherent ability to sustain life. Sustainable

[20] Peter Kropotkin, *Mutual Aid: A Factor of Evolution* (Mineola, NY: Dover Publications, 2006).

[21] Kim Sterelny, *The Evolving Apprentice: How Evolution Made Humans Unique* (Cambridge, MA: MIT Press, 2012).

[22] William E. Rees, 'Thinking Resilience,' in *The Post-Carbon Reader: Managing the 21st Century's Sustainability Crises*, ed. Richard Heinberg and Daniel Lerch (Healsburg, CA: Watershed Media, 2010), 32.

[23] Fritjof Capra, *The Hidden Connections: A Science for Sustainable Living* (New York: Anchor, 2002), 230–31.

communities and networks evolve their patterns of living over time in continual inter-action with other living systems, both human and non-human.

Moreover, a key feature is that sustainable human communities are designed so the unused by-products of any enterprise are usable by other enterprises. There is thus zero waste. These circular, sustainable systems of production, use and consumption are 'cradle to cradle' systems, in contrast to the current 'waste' or 'cradle to grave' systems that dominate contemporary economies. They are designed on the 'biomimicry' of circular ecosystems such as old-growth forests.[24]

INDIGENOUS GAIA DEMOCRACY TRADITIONS

The Gift–Gratitude–Reciprocity Worldview

I will now try to describe some of the main features of Indigenous traditions of earth democracy that I have learned from Nuu Chah Nulth scholar Richard Atleo Senior (Umeek) and Anishinaabe scholars John Borrows and Aaron Mills. According to Umeek, the central idea is expressed in the Nuu Chah Nulth concept 'Tsawalk'.[25] It expresses the insight that every living being is connected and sustained through relationships of reciprocal interdependence. These are fundamentally cyclical kinship relationships of gift–gratitude–reciprocity. They are the ground of our being. Although humans often take selfish advantage of these sustaining relationships and take without either taking care of a gift or reciprocating by giving to others (ingratitude), and so initiate vicious cycles, Tsawalk usually outweighs and outlasts these violations. Humans learn how to live together in reciprocally sustaining ways by learning from mother earth and their more-than-human relatives, who also make mistakes.

Humans begin to learn ecoliteracy through participatory self-formation and self-understanding as participants engaging reciprocally with ecosocial webs of life. By apprenticeship in the practices passed on by their ancestors, they come to acquire ways of perceiving and orienting oneself in the world that discloses it as a living system and humans as one species among an extended family of more-than-human relatives. This is a participatory, kincentric and cyclical way of life. The flora and fauna, sun and moon, creeks and oceans, are our kin – interdependent relatives or relations. They grow up to realize they have responsibilities to co-sustain the ecosocial relationships on which we depend. They are participatory democratic agents in the life systems as a whole, just like

[24] William McDonough and Michael Braungart, *Cradle to Cradle: Remaking the Way We Make Things* (New York: Farrar, Strauss and Giroux, 2002).

[25] Umeek E. Richard Atleo, *Tsawalk: A Nuu-chah-nulth Worldview* (Vancouver: UBC Press, 2004); and Umeek E. Richard Atleo, *Principles of Tsawalk: An Indigenous Approach to Global Crisis* (Vancouver: UBC Press, 2011).

other earthlings. Mother Earth takes care of us and we take care of her in gratitude and reciprocity. Moreover, humans learn from these basic life cycles to be grateful for the gifts and to reciprocate in turn, thereby bringing into being cyclical human relationships of mutual aid.[26]

Potawatomi Environment and Forest biologist Robin Lee Kimmerer explains the richness of the gift-reciprocity view by showing its similarity to Western systems view of life:[27]

Reciprocity – returning the gift – is not just good manners; it is how the biophysical world works. Balance in ecological systems arises from negative feedback loops, from cycles of giving and taking. Reciprocity among parts of the living earth produces [dynamic] equilibrium, in which life as we know it can flourish.

The Cedar Trees Institute that hosted the Workshop for this volume is founded on this gift–gratitude–reciprocity worldview, as far as we understand it, and in respect and reciprocity for being accepted as guests on the traditional territories of the WSÁNEĆ (Saanich), Songhees (Lkwungen), and Wyomilth (Esquimalt) First Nations.

The role of clans, masks, dancing, storytelling and giving thanks to mother earth is to help us learn these earth ways and lifeways. We learn by putting ourselves in the shoes of other relatives and learning how they sustain themselves, and thus how we can reciprocally relate to them in co-sustaining ways. We also train to enter into perceptual dialogical relationships with the animate earth through all our senses (synaesthesia). Through participation, apprentices begin to experience the animacy of the living earth: the power of gift-reciprocity relationships. It animates all life and is by far the greatest power on earth. By participating in its relationships and cycles in good ways we experience being animated by and belonging to mother earth.

Having learned these lessons from Mother Earth and her earth ways, Indigenous people apply them in their lifeways. They design their social systems on the life-sustaining, gift-reciprocity earth systems. The Indigenous word for governance among the northwest coast nations is 'potlatche'. It is translated as the English word 'gift'. However, unlike the English word 'gift', potlatche refers to the mutual exchange of gifts that always derive from and give rise to relations of reciprocity. They exist in and sustain life cycles. They reunite life-sustaining circles that either have been breached or simply need to be recollected and re-animated. This is Indigenous democratic, reconciliatory governance.

[26] John Borrows, 'Earth-Bound,' 49–82. For a comprehensive account of Anishinaabe Gaia democracy, see Aaron Mills, 'Miinigowiziwin: All That Has Been Given for Living Well Together: One Vision of Anishinaabe Constitutionalism' (PhD thesis, University of Victoria, 2019).
[27] Robin Wall Kimmerer, 'Reciprocity – Returning the Gift,' *Minding Nature* 7, no. 2 (2014): 18–24, www.humansandnature.org/returning-the-gift.

Four Phases of Gift–Gratitude–Reciprocity Systems

Indigenous gift-reciprocity relationships also go through virtuous, degenerative, vicious and regenerative phases. Indigenous ecosocial knowledge is pragmatic knowledge learned by trial and error. Once we see ourselves as plain members and citizens within Mother Earth this is the only way we can learn. The Raven Cycle Stories shared among the Indigenous peoples of the Northwest coast are full of learning stories of this kind. The most common Raven story is of some people failing to reciprocate for the gifts given to them by mother earth, their fellow flora and fauna or from fellow human beings. They become selfish, independent aggressive, greedy, avaricious and ungrateful. They take without reciprocating. When this happens, Raven comes along and tells stories that illustrate the mistakes they make and point in the general direction of how to correct them by reconnecting and regenerating good gift-reciprocity relationships. He always does this in puzzling, paradoxical, self-contradictory and hilarious ways that show he too is far from omniscient. This technique is in itself an important lesson in epistemic humility.

Robert Davidson, a great contemporary Haida artist, gives an example. When people become vicious, Raven points out this misperception and self-centredness by taking away one eye of the persons involved. In so doing, Raven enables them, paradoxically, to see the damage they are doing to mother earth and to future generations by not reciprocating. They lack the depth of vision to see the gift-reciprocity relations they are damaging. The next step, then, is to return to the earth teachings, reconnect with the broader gift-reciprocity systems, and regenerate healthy relationships with mother earth and each other. According to Davidson, this kind of reconnective and regenerative Gaia citizenship is what the Haida are doing on Haida Gwaii today in response to four generations of vicious settler resource extraction and the participation of some Haida in it.[28]

Many Indigenous peoples have similar stories. The Anishinaabe call vicious actors 'Windigo' and the Cree call them 'Wetiko'. On the Northwest coast, the Kwakwaka'wakw people have a famous Atla'gimma ('Spirits of the Forests') dance in which the virtuous citizens overpower the vicious members by surrounding them with gift–gratitude–reciprocity activities and offers of joining hands until the vicious members see the benefits of cooperation.[29] It

---

[28] Robert Davidson, 'Untitled Document,' in Robert Davidson et al., *Robert Davidson Exhibition: A Voice from Inside* (Vancouver: Derek Simpson Gallery, 1992), 3. For the movement of transformative reconnection on Haida Gwaii to which Davidson refers, see Louise Takeda, *Islands' Spirits Rising: Reclaiming the Forests of Haida Gwaii* (Vancouver: UBC Press, 2015).

[29] See Douglas Deur (Moxmowisa), Kim Recalama-Clutsei (Oqwilawagwa), and William White (Kasalid/Xelimulh), 'The Teachings of Chief Kwaxsistalla Adam Dick and the Atla'gimma ('Spirit of the Forest') Dance,' in *Plants, Peoples, and Places: The Roles of Ethnobotany and Ethnoecology in Indigenous Peoples' Land Rights in Canada and Beyond*, ed. Nancy J. Turner (Montreal: McGill-Queens University Press, 2020), xvii–xxiv; and James Tully, 'On Resurgence and Transformative Reconciliation,' in *Plants, Peoples, and Places*, ed. Turner, 402–18. For

362 *James Tully*

enacts the spirit of ecological succession that Mike Simpson describes in the botanical terminology noted earlier.

Transition to the Vicious Systems

In summary, I am suggesting there is a convergence or kinship between the Gaia democracies of Indigenous peoples and of the contemporary non-Indigenous ecosocial communities of practice influenced by recent western life and earth sciences. They appear to converge on the characterization of virtuous, degenerative and vicious ecosocial systems, and on the symbiotic way to transition from a vicious to a virtuous system. If this conjecture is at least partially correct, then it provides some common ground on which to discuss joining hands and working together in mutually respectful, democratic ways in response to the shared crises. However, before I turn to examples, I will describe briefly the main features of the global social systems that are causing the crises. These are the vicious systems that Gaia citizens need to understand and change.

MAIN FEATURES OF VICIOUS SOCIAL SYSTEMS THAT CAUSE THE CRISES

The Great Transformation and Acceleration

Rather than building social systems that participate in and co-sustain the social and ecological relationships of reciprocal interdependence on which they depend, the West built social systems that commodify, exploit and degrade them, and spread them around the world by imperial processes of colonization, modernization, globalization and representative democratization. These violent processes are presented as the universal and necessary linear stages of development and progress to modernization, democracy and world peace. Most of the major modern Western political traditions from the Enlightenment to the present share this generic worldview, while differing over specifics on the left, centre and right. In the 1940s, Karl Polanyi argued that these modernizing processes disembed humans from life-sustaining ecosocial systems and re-embed them in abstract, global vicious social systems that overlook, exploit and destroy the underlying virtuous ecosocial systems on which they depend. He called these processes the 'great transformation'. The more recent social science on the 'great acceleration' since World War II builds on this base. Polanyi also predicted that if humans did not transform these systems they would destroy sustainable social systems and the environment. His analysis continues to be updated and applied to the 'great acceleration' after

Cree and Anishinaabe stories of vicious and virtuous cycles, see Hadley Friedland, *The Wetiko (Windigo) Legal Principles: Cree and Anishinabek Responses to Violence and Victimization* (Toronto: University of Toronto Press, 2018).

World War II. Nevertheless, the dire warnings are met with both inaction and gridlock or, at best, mitigation within the shared worldview and its constitutive institutions.[30]

One of the main reasons that moderns have difficulty in seeing clearly the ways these modernizing systems cause the sustainability crises is that, as subjects of them, they are deeply socialized into its legitimating worldview and the competing interpretations within it. Consequently, they misperceive through this modernist lens the destructive relationships between the processes and the background, informal social and ecological systems they exploit yet also depend upon, as Barry Commoner argued. I will now describe these processes briefly so we can see how they operate and then how the dominant form of modern government – representative democracy – is subject to them.[31]

The first process was the enclosure of common lands in Europe, and the second enclosure through the dispossession of the embedded lifeways of indigenous peoples throughout the world by means of colonization. These processes involved genocide, slavery, displacement, reservations, residential schools and the discrediting of their embedded ways of knowing and being as 'primitive' and at the lowest possible level of cognitive and historical development.

The second set of processes consisted in the conversion of most of the earth into the private property of corporations by the global spread of Western corporate and property law and its violent enforcement by colonial authorities and, after decolonization, neocolonial military-political complexes. These processes reconceive the living earth as a limitless storehouse of commodifiable 'natural resources' disembedded from their interdependent participation in the fragile symbiotic networks and renewability cycles that sustain life for billions of years. These resources are re-embedded in the abstract, competitive relations of the global market system. The competition among corporations, driven by profit-seeking and exploitive technological development, is exhausting non-renewable resources and using up renewables more rapidly than they renew themselves naturally.[32] The destruction that this system causes to the earth systems throughout the chains of dispossession, extraction, finance, commodification,

---

[30] Karl Polanyi, *Great Transformation: The Political and Economic Origins of Our Time*, 2nd ed. (Boston: Beacon Press, 2001); For an introduction to the vast, recent literature on Polanyi's hypothesis, see Charles Dilworth, *Too Smart for Our Own Good: The Ecological Predicament of Humankind* (Cambridge: Cambridge University Press, 2012); 'The Great Acceleration,' International Geosphere-Biosphere Programme, www.igbp.net/globalchange/greatacceleration .4.1b8ae20512db692f2a680001630.html.

[31] See James Tully, *Public Philosophy in a New Key*, vol. 2, *Imperialism and Civic Freedom* (Cambridge: Cambridge University Press, 2008); James Tully, 'Rediscovering the World of Franz Boas: Anthropology, Equality/Diversity, and World Peace,' in *Indigenous Visions: Rediscovering the World of Franz Boas*, ed. Ned Blackhawk and Isaiah Lorado Wilner (New Haven: Yale University Press, 2018), 111–46.

[32] Michael T. Klare, *The Race for What's Left: The Global Scramble for the World's Last Resources* (New York: Picador, 2012).

production, consumption and waste disposal is treated as an externality for which the corporations are not responsible. They tend to resist regulation unless the costs are subsidized.

The third set of modernizing processes effect a similar transformation of human productive capacities. They disembed humans and their capacities to produce and consume from the informal, intersubjective, symbiotic, informal social relationships that sustain them, their families and their communities (social capital). They re-embed individual productive capacities into the abstract, competitive, and unequal relationships of the global labour market as commodities for sale to private or public corporations for a wage or salary. The corporations govern their employees non-democratically. Individuals and unions are constrained to compete for jobs with other workers near and far, as well as with automation, the unemployed and the precarious informal global economies of the poor. The degradation and destruction that these processes cause to the cultivation of cooperative, democratic working and socializing ethics and relationships of mutual aid that sustain human communities and their well-being are treated as another externality of modernization. Corporations are seldom held responsible for these effects, yet they function perversely to drive wages further down.[33]

The fourth and more recent process is the emergence of the global age of surveillance capitalism with the Internet. Every aspect of the behaviour of individual users of the Internet is mined by large internet corporations, sold to other corporations, processed through algorithms and then employed to subtlety influence and govern the future behaviour of users in almost every area of their lives in a post-truth age. As a result, users are disembedded from their ecosocial lifeworld and freely subject themselves to the world of cyberspace. Simultaneously, the political and military institutions of modern states also engage in the surveillance of their own citizens and the citizens and governments of other states. The damage that these algorithmic modes of governance, meme interpolation and alienation from the ecosocial lifeworld do to ecosocial, democratic self-formation through tough, critical, truth-seeking and accountable dialogues with differently situated fellow citizens here and now is unacknowledged or treated as another externality.[34]

In short, the modern assemblage of systemic processes are extractive and exploitive rather than regenerative, linear rather than cyclical, externalizing rather than internalizing, and thus vicious and life-destroying rather than

---

[33] Joel Bakan, *The New Corporation: How 'Good' Corporations Are Bad for Democracy* (Toronto: Penguin Canada, 2020); Mike Davis, *Old Gods New Enigmas: Marx's Lost Theory* (London: Verso, 2020).

[34] Shosana Zuboff, *The Age of Surveillance Capitalism: The Fight for a Human Future at the New Frontier of Power* (London: Profile Books, 2019); Edward Snowden, *Permanent Record* (New York: Metropolitan Books, 2019).

virtuous and sustainable. As Kimmerer, Joanna Macy, and others argue, it is a monstrous vicious system; a Windigo that super-preys on life's gift–gratitude–reciprocity relationships.[35] In these respects, it is the antithesis of cyclical, ecosocial economics and politics.[36]

Modern Representative Government: The Great Democratic Disconnection and Deficit

> As I would not be a slave, so I would not be a master. This expresses my idea of democracy. Whatever differs from this, to the extent of the difference, is no democracy.
>
> Abraham Lincoln, 'Fragment on Democracy', August, 1858

The fifth systemic process of modernization is the spread of representative government around the world of modern states and international institutions as the mode of governance of this assemblage of systems. This process of 'democratization', as it is called, began in eighteenth-century Western Europe, spread to the non-Western world through colonization and decolonization, the Mandate System of the League of Nations, and is continued today under the auspices of the United Nations Constitutional Assistance Programs. Like the other processes, it is imposed on non-Western societies by violent means on the widely shared premise of modern political thought that authoritarian means are necessary and they lead 'less-developed' peoples up through stages of development to representative democracy, the rule of law, free markets, international institutions and perpetual peace.[37]

The best 'democratic' argument for elected representative government to replace monarchy in the eighteenth century was presented by William Paine in *The Rights of Man* (1792):[38]

Simple democracy was society governing itself without the aid of secondary means. By *ingrafting representation upon democracy* [italics added] we arrive at a system of government capable of embracing and confederating all the various interests and every extent of territory and population . . . It is on this system that the American government is

---

[35] Robin Wall Kimmerer, *Braiding Sweetgrass: Indigenous Wisdom, Scientific Knowledge, and the Teaching of Plants* (Minneapolis: Milkweed Editions, 2013), 303–80.

[36] Herman B. Daly and John B. Cobb Jr., *For the Common Good: Redirecting the Economy Toward Community, the Environment and a Sustainable Future* (Boston: Beacon Press, 1994); Lester R. Brown, *World on the Edge: How to Prevent Environmental and Economic Collapse* (New York: Norton, 2011). Brown argues that if the costs of repairing the social and ecological damage were internalized, the economic system as a whole would be unprofitable and collapse.

[37] Tully, *Public Philosophy*, vol. 2. For critical discussions of this interpretation, see Robert Nichols and Jakeet Singh, eds., *Freedom and Democracy in an Imperial Context* (London: Routledge, 2014).

[38] William Paine, *The Rights of Man*, ed. Gregory Claeys (Indianapolis: Hackett Publishing Company, 1992), 142–43.

founded. It is *representation ingrafted upon democracy* [italics added] ... What Athens
was in miniature, America will be in magnitude. The one was the wonder of the ancient
world; the other is becoming the admiration and model of the present.

On this hopeful democratic view, representative governments would grow out of
and extend thriving local democracies, just as a grafted branch extends an already
living tree and its permaculture. It would thus solve the scale problem of size and
population of governments in modern states without abandoning democracy.
Unfortunately, as John Stuart Mill, Karl Marx and Peter Kropotkin pointed out
fifty years later, this is not what happened. Instead of the people governing
themselves, competing political parties campaigned and governed over the
people, yet always in the name of the people. The proper name for ruler/ruled
form of government should be demoarchy (rule over (arche) and in the name of the
people by the elected party), not democracy (the self-government of the people
themselves). Mill and Marx argued that it tends to be rule by the class that controls
public opinion. Since the claim that the party which gains a majority or plurality of
votes is governing for the people can be used to justify just about any legislation,
Mill presented the classic liberal response that has become the global norm of
legitimacy. The government has to be constrained by a constitution that places
certain fundamental rights beyond democratic negotiation: that is, 'constitutional
democracy' (or, more accurately, constitutional representative demoarchy).[39]

This has had two consequences. The first is that the modern legal systems
constitutionalized, or constitutionally protected, the constitutive features of the
four vicious and unsustainable systemic processes of the previous section,
thereby placing them beyond democratic negotiation. Second, the democratic
participation of citizens is legalized as the 'civil' rights to participate within the
institutions of the representative system: voting, campaigning, expressing
opinions and deliberating within the official public spheres in hopes of
influencing public policy and elected officials, and the right to civil
disobedience if it is exercised with the objective of promoting constitutional
democracy. In these two main ways, constitutional representative demoarchy is
disconnected from, rather than 'ingrafted upon', participatory democracy.

In this respect, the establishment and eventual globalization of representative
constitutional demoarchy as the primary meaning of 'democracy' and
'democratization' serves to legitimate the triumph of the elite republican
model that the propertied authors of *The Federalist Papers* advanced *against*
democracy, yet cleverly disguised under the name of democracy. They wrote:[40]

'[A] pure democracy', by which I mean a society consisting of a small number of citizens,
who assemble and administer the government in person, can admit of no cure for the

[39] John Stuart Mill, 'On Liberty', in *On Liberty and Other Essays*, ed. John Gray (Oxford: Oxford
University Press, 1991), 6–10; Karl Marx and Friedrich Engels, *The Communist Manifesto*
(Oxford: Oxford University Press, 1998), 4–5.
[40] Alexander Hamilton, James Madison, and John Jay, *The Federalist Papers* (New York: Penguin
Books, 1961), 81, 82, 84.

mischiefs of faction … Hence it is that such democracies have ever been spectacles of turbulence and contention; have ever been found incompatible with personal security or the rights of property; and have in general been as short in their lives as they have been violent in their deaths … A republic, by which I mean a government in which the scheme of representation takes place, opens a different prospect and promises the cure for which we are seeking … Let us examine the points in which it varies from pure democracy, and we shall comprehend both the nature of the cure and the efficacy which it must derive from the Union … [In conclusion, a] rage for paper money, for an abolition of debts, for an equal division of property, or for any other improper or wicked project, will be less apt to pervade the whole body of the Union than a particular member of it [by means of representation and federation].

As the young Marx pointed out, and as we will see in the following section, participatory democracy did not disappear. Humans exercising powers of self-government with and for each other informally in everyday relationships and systems is the basis of all sustainable social life, as our increasingly divisive and anti-social age reminds us. These informal relations continue under any form of government. Constitutional representative demoarchy, like other forms of ruler/ruled constitutions, depends on and colonizes this unacknowledged democratic lifeworld, and, as noted, concentrates official political power in representative institutions, thereby weakening and disempowering local self-government.[41] The reconceptualization of this form of government as 'democracy' and 'democratization' is one of the great conceptual transformations that accompanied and continues to legitimate modernization.[42] Participatory democracy was renamed 'radical democracy', cooperativism, community-based organization and, by Kropotkin, 'anarchy' (that is, self-government without the division of the people into rulers and ruled).[43]

The justification of representative demoarchy as 'democratic' is not participation, but, rather, the consent of the governed for the party that wins the majority or plurality of votes in elections, whether or not the individual votes for the winning party; or simply by the tacit consent of going along with the outcome without voting. The people are said to 'delegate' or 'alienate' their powers of self-government to the ruling party in elections. Yet, this too is a conceptual innovation. Voters do not delegate or alienate their powers of self-government to elected representatives. Rather, as Rousseau noted, they abnegate their exercise of them. They delegate or alienate to elected representatives the right to exercise political power-over them by means of legislation and enforcement through the rule of law.

[41] Karl Marx, 'Critique of Hegel's Doctrine of the State,' in *Karl Marx: Early Writings*, trans. Rodney Livingstone and Gregor Benton (London: Penguin Books, 1975), 86–90.
[42] For the detailed history of this conceptual transformation, see Francis Dupuis-Déri, *Démocratie. Histoire politique d'un mot: Aux États-Unis et en France* (Québec: Lux Éditeur, 2013).
[43] See David Held, 'Direct Democracy and the End of Politics,' in *Models of Democracy*, 3rd ed. (Cambridge: Polity Press, 2006), 96–123.

Representatives rarely exercise the democratic powers with each other as free and equal co-governors by working 'across the aisle' with members of other parties. Rather, they legislate by means of majority votes over minority party members. Even within governing parties, power-over is concentrated further in presidencies, prime ministers, cabinets, whipping party members and various hierarchical offices. These are classic forms of power-over, not democratic power-with, which facilitate rather than foreclose the iron law of oligarchy.[44] Moreover, non-democratic, bureaucratic ministries, hierarchical public and private institutions and military-industrial-research-expertise complexes surround representative institutions. Furthermore, representatives are dependent on private corporations for campaign funding, jobs in their ridings and taxes, and subject to continual lobbying. They are thus constrained to act in accord with the linear economic development model or face defeat in the next election. Despite these manifestly non-democratic systems, these modern states are routinely called 'democratic societies'. Finally, since World War II, representative governments and corporations have constructed a system of institutions of global governance and international law that can override domestic governments that attempt to change the unsustainable status quo.[45] As David Held concludes, 'Representative democracy, accordingly, is democracy 'made safe' for the modern world and, particularly, for the modern capitalist economy'.[46]

For these reasons, as David Held and his co-authors have shown, it is not surprising that state-centred representative governments and international institutions generate vicious, systemic gridlock or minor changes when actors attempt to address the sustainability crises through these channels.[47] It is the gridlock of systemic processes of democratic disconnection and deficit.[48]

The fatal flaw of these demoarchic, power-over forms of government is that the governing parties do not have to listen to and work with the opposition parties or citizens who voted against them. They can simply impose their will, often with a patina of 'consultation' to give it the appearance of democratic legitimacy. This power-over position invariably comes with the presumption that they also have knowledge-over what is best for the demos. Modern political theory reinforces this presumption. Yet, the only way governors can learn what

---

[44] That is, the elite theorists of representative democracies and the radical critics of them over the last century are both correct.

[45] James Tully et al., 'Introducing Global Integral Constitutionalism,' *Global Constitutionalism: Human Rights, Democracy, Law* 5, no. 1 (2016): 1–15.

[46] David Held, *Democracy and the Global Order* (San Francisco: Stanford University Press, 1995), 70.

[47] Thomas Hale, David Held, and Kevin Young, *Gridlock: Why Global Cooperation Is Failing When We Need It Most* (Cambridge: Polity Press, 2013); Thomas Hale and David Held, *Beyond Gridlock* (Cambridge: Polity Press, 2017). Compare Jeanne Morefield, Chapter 7, this volume.

[48] For an exemplary analysis of disconnection and deficit, see Oliver Schmidtke, Chapter 4, this volume.

counts as ill-being, repair and sustainable well-being of the diverse, interdependent members and situations of the people is to enter into dialogues of mutual education and enlightenment with them as equals. They can then work up sustainable ways of cooperating, putting them into practice, reviewing and contesting them, and beginning the learning cycle again. This is the pragmatic public reasoning-with and exercising power-with of equal citizens and governors that participatory democracy enables and enacts in conjunction with responsive representative democracy.[49]

Aristotle was among the first to articulate the unique, epistemic superiority of democracy in comparison with ruler/ruled forms of government:[50]

For the many, of whom each individual is not a good man, when they meet together may be better than the few good, if regarded not individually but collectively, just as a feast to which many contribute is better than a dinner provided out of a single purse. For each individual among the many has a share of excellence and practical wisdom, and when they meet together, just as they become in a manner one man, who has many feet, and hands, and senses, so too with their character and thought. Hence, the many are better judges than a single man.

Leopold also pointed out the power-over flaw of presumptive knowledge, not only over the demos but also over the natural world. It is 'eventually self-defeating'. In addition, Davidson argued that power-over leads the holders to be 'one-eyed', voracious and self-destructive, rather than listening to, learning from and cooperating with their fellow citizens, human and more-than-human. Accordingly, the task today is to extend linguistic dialogues of mutual learning among 'all affected' humans to perceptual dialogues among humans and more-than-human lifeforms so we can learn their sustainability conditions. These dialogues are taking place among Indigenous knowledge holders, ecological and social scientists, stakeholders, government officials and many other participants.[51] These are examples of democratic Gaian 'joining hands' – of public reasoning and acting together. It is to these practices of regeneration that we now turn.

RECONNECTING AND ANIMATING GAIA DEMOCRACIES BY BEING THE CHANGE

The major obstacle to change is that, as subjects of this assemblage of vicious systems, we are socialized into thinking and acting in accord with its

---

[49] James Tully, *Public Philosophy in a New Key*, vol. 1, *Democracy and Civic Freedom* (Cambridge: Cambridge University Press, 2008), 291–316.

[50] Aristotle, *The Politics and the Constitution of Athens*, ed. Stephen Everson (Cambridge: Cambridge University Press, 1996), 76, 1281a40–b7.

[51] For the practice of a human-nature perceptual dialogue, see David Abram, *The Spell of the Sensuous* (New York: Vintage, 1996); Harding, *Animate Earth*; Turner, ed., *Plants, Peoples, and Places*; Borrows, 'Earth-Bound', 49–82; Eduardo Kohn, *How Trees Think: Towards an Anthropology Beyond the Human* (Berkeley: University of California Press, 2013).

modernizing worldview and corresponding technical languages of veridiction. Yet, these languages misdescribe, and so cause us to misperceive, its undemocratic and unsustainable relationships. There have been three types of attempts to transform the systems from within. The first was violent revolution during decolonization.[52] The second comprises attempts to gain institutional political power by various progressive parties and impose reforms from above. This approach is moderately successful in some cases, yet also subject to roll-back when it threatens the status quo.[53] The third consists of attempts to democratize representative democracies by exercising the institutional civil rights of participation within them and advancing ecosocial agendas. This way has been the most successful, yet it too runs up against limits of various kinds. But as long as we remain within these vicious systems, we will tend to either deny or discount the crises, or, if we recognize them and try to respond from within, our reforms are limited to the problem-solving techniques within the systems.

Gaia democracy offers another way. It is the way of being the change, as in ecological succession. We have seen examples in the two Gaia democracies in the previous sections. It rests on the premise that the means themselves must be ecosocial and democratic with all citizens-governors of the unjust relationships humans inhabit if they are to bring about a sustainable ecosocial, democratic future. As Laden, Owen and Thomasson illustrate in their chapters (1, 2, and 3, respectively), the democratic 'way' is crafted to listen to and co-sustain all affected. The autotelic character of means also explains why non-democratic means reproduce, rather than transform, the vicious status quo.

As Gaia citizens begin to be the change here and now by practicing ecosocial democracy in their daily lives, they, *eo ipso*, begin to free themselves and their perceptions from the vicious systems. They begin to perceive the larger, interdependent living ecosocial ecological world in which we live, breath and have our being. Harding describes examples of this kind of self-transformation by famous ecologists.[54] Macy and Stephanie Kaza show us how we can begin to do this in our own lives.[55] One of the best guidebooks is *Our Ecological Footprint* by Mathias Wackernagel and William Rees, first published in 1995.[56] It shows readers how to calculate the effect of every footstep they

---

[52] Adom Getachew, *Worldmaking After Empire: The Rise and Fall of Self-Determination* (Princeton: Princeton University Press, 2019).

[53] Tarik Kochi, 'The End of Global Constitutionalism and Rise of Anti-Democratic Politics,' *Global Society* 34, no. 4 (2020): 487–507, http://doi.org/10.1080/13600826.2020.1749037.

[54] Harding, *Animate Earth*, 46–67.

[55] Joanna Macy and Chris Johnstone, *Active Hope: How to Face the Mess We're in Without Going Crazy* (Novato, CA: New World Library, 2012); Stephanie Kaza, *Mindfully Green: A Personal and Spiritual Guide to Whole Earth Thinking* (Boston: Shambhala, 2008).

[56] Mathis Wackernagel, *Our Ecological Footprint: Reducing Human Impact on the Earth* (Gabriola Island, BC: New Society Press, 1996).

take in and on the environment and how to change it to reduce their impact on the living earth to a sustainable level. To be transformative, these ecological practices have to be updated to include and integrate our ecosocial and democratic footsteps with and for all interdependent partners.[57] In this careful way, citizens can repair the damage that the vicious systems cause as they go along – the regeneration of a local and global Gaia democracies permaculture by Gaia democratic means.

Millions of people are engaged apprentices in these kinds of practices and learning by trial and error. A central feature of this way of regeneration is that there is no privileged position or actor. It is a way of being in communities of practice whenever and wherever we find ourselves, in every step, here and now. Whether one is involved in producing, consuming, trading, lawmaking, government, teaching, healthcare, protesting, boycotting, volunteering, Indigenous-settler partnerships, 'democratize work', and so on, there is the possibility of everyday Gaian democratization.[58] To be genuinely democratizing, these practices treat all differently situated and affected members of the interdependent ecosocial relationships at issue as free and equal co-citizens and co-governors, as a matter of democratic justice. That is, democratizing practices are, *eo ipso*, decolonizing practices. They bring to light, contest and decolonize the power-over relationships of race, Indigeneity, class, gender, sexual orientation, ableism and global north and south inequality as they decolonize power-over relationships to the living earth.[59] This volume provides many examples.

The first step is to cultivate ecosocial democratic ethics in communities of practice of various kinds. Gandhians call these 'constructive programs', Indigenous peoples 'land-based resurgence', African-Americans 'beloved communities', engaged Buddhists 'sanghas', farmers 'food sovereignty', and other community-based Gaia democracies. They involve ecosocial democratic economics, technologies, citizen-governance and participatory modes of representation and networking. As citizens engage in these activities around the world, they withdraw from and non-cooperate with the unsustainable systems that these replace or transform. They cultivate a cyclical and sustainable countermodernity.[60]

These ways of ecosocial transition build on the informal, democratic social relationships of mutual aid among humans that continue to exist even in the

---

[57] See, for example, Timothy Morton, *Being Ecological* (New York: MIT Press, 2018); Kelly Anne Patricia Aguirre Turner, 'Re-Storying Political Theory: Indigenous Resurgence, Idle No More, and Colonial Apprehension' (unpublished PhD thesis, University of Victoria, 2019).

[58] See, for example, 'Work, Democratize, Decommodify, Remediate,' Democratizing Work, https://democratizingwork.org.

[59] See Monika Kirloskar-Steinbach, ed., *Dialogue and Decolonization* (Bloomington, IN: Indiana University Press, forthcoming).

[60] See, for example, David Hardiman, *Gandhi in His Times and Ours: The Global Legacy of His Ideas* (New York: Columbia University Press, 2003); Forman, Chapter 8 and Nelems, Chapter 9, this volume. For other examples, see note 2, this chapter.

most ruthlessly competitive institutions and vicious situations of natural disasters, famine, migration and war.[61] They are the basis of sociality. As Nelems explains in her chapter, we do not always perceive these informal social relationships from within the competitive and divisive social systems we inhabit. Yet, when a crisis arises, such as the COVID 19 pandemic, they appear and enable humans to survive.

Another necessary step is for participatory democrats to join hands and work democratically with citizens who are trying to democratize the institutions of representative government along Gaian lines from within, yet without subordination of the former to the latter. This is crucial because, in homage to Paine, Kimmerer and Abraham Lincoln in the previous section, their unique kinds of joining hands can 'graft' and 'braid' together participatory and representative democracies, making both more democratic in Lincoln's sense. Sustainable modes of participatory democracy are the permaculture of healthy representative democracy. They ensure that representative governments 'represent' democratic peoples (demoi). Their interdependent braids mutually empower and enhance both partners.[62] In his concluding and integrative chapter, Ouziel provides a survey of the ways of joining hands illustrated in all the chapters of this volume. These ecosocial democratic connections and networks among all five families of democracy are also conduits of mutual education in democratic diversity, as Webber illustrates in Chapter 15.

As these communities of practice grow, they become the democratic basis of and for practices of nonviolent civic contestation, negotiation, conflict resolution and reconciliation (*Satyagraha*). The chapters by Swain (13) and Henderson (14) on Indigenous-settler joining hands, Forman on 'unwalling citizenship' (8), Celikates on 'democratizing revolution' (10), and Wiener on 'norm contestation' (17) are examples of this distinctive mode of speaking truth to power on the one hand and offering to join hands and negotiate on the other, as Barbara Deming famously described it.[63] These democratic contestations, negotiations and reconciliations can lead, step by step, to multiple tipping points and the gradual replacement or transformation of vicious social systems by or into virtuous and sustainable systems.[64]

---

[61] Rebeca Solnit, *A Paradise Built in Hell: The Extraordinary Communities that Arise in Disaster* (New York: Penguin, 2009).

[62] Forman, Chapter 8, this volume; Pablo Ouziel, *Democracy Here and Now: The Exemplary Case of Spain* (Toronto: University of Toronto Press, 2022); James Tully, *On Global Citizenship: James Tully in Dialogue* (London: Bloomsbury, 2014), 84–100.

[63] Barbara Deming, 'On Revolution and Equilibrium', in *Revolution and Equilibrium* (New York: Grossman Publishers, 1971), 194–221.

[64] For nonviolent civil resistance in response to the sustainability crises, see Daniel Hunter, *Climate Resistance Handbook* (Boston: Daniel Hunter and 350.org, 2019), https://trainings.350.org /climate-resistance-handbook. For contestation at the international level, see Wiener, Chapter 17 in this volume.

The local/global integration of all these Gaian democratic practices not only reconnects them democratically with each other and overcomes the democratic deficit. It also reconnects them with the animacy of the Gaian lifeworld, *anima mundi*, the greatest power on earth. Gaia animates them in reciprocity and they co-regenerate together.[65]

---

[65] Richard Bartlett Gregg, *The Power of Nonviolence*, ed. James Tully (Cambridge: Cambridge University Press, 2018), was one of the first researcher-practitioners to present this whole argument in a comprehensive form. Gregg published the first edition in 1934, after living and working with Gandhi, and then published revised versions in 1944 and 1959. The pragmatic philosophy of ecosocial succession as the replacement for top-down reform, violent revolution, and war was introduced in new chapters in the 1944 edition, in the course of six years of correspondence with Gandhi.

Democracies Joining Hands in the Here and Now

Pablo Ouziel

In the Introduction, James Tully foregrounds the horrendous inequalities of life chances that lie at the basis of the multiple crises humanity is facing. As the volume has progressed, the project of "democratizing democracy" that brought all of the contributors together has emerged as a response. It has become clear that the volume is not defining one family of democracy in contrast and competition with other forms of democracy.[1] Rather, it is a book about the "eco-social-democratic footprint of every step one takes alone or with others."[2] In this sense, it attempts to describe how different types of democracy – state, Indigenous, international, grassroots, and Gaia democracies – are in practice woven together in healthy and virtuous ways that provide paths past the ecosocial crises we face.

In the spirit of the Cedar Trees Institute (CTI) gift–gratitude–reciprocity worldview, I aim to further amplify the voices that participated in both the conference and the edited volume, in order to reveal the numerous ways in which, in practice, different forms of democracy are woven together in democratizing ways.[3] Through their chapters, the contributors crystalize the myriad of ways in which citizens of representative democracies across the globe have become witnesses to and participants in the democratic dying of their liberal democracies.[4] Although this is without a doubt a point of deep concern amongst the contributors, through their exchanges we get a clear idea of how ever more citizens are also contesting nondemocratically constructed relationships with their

[1] See Tully, Introduction.
[2] James Tully, email correspondence with author, November 10, 2020.
[3] The Cedar Trees Institute (CTI) is home to pioneering engaged research and citizenship at the nexus of the local and the global, of practice and theory. The Institute is rooted in a nonviolent integral ethics that guides all aspects of research, education and public engagement.
[4] "Democracies are dying democratically" is an expression used by Boaventura de Sousa Santos to explain phenomena like the presidency of Donald Trump in the United States and Jair Bolsonaro's presidency of Brazil. See Val Napoleon, Chapter 11, this volume and Boaventura's own chapter (5) in this volume for a more in-depth understanding of what is meant by this idea.

governors. We can see how citizens across the planet are gaining awareness of their contributions to and responsibilities toward dedemocratization processes. At the same time, growing numbers of people are colearning to weave different democratic traditions together in ways that move away from power-over, governor–governed relationships and experiment with new, power-with, citizen-to-citizen relations as they democratize their democracies from below. It is perhaps because of this that we might be reaching a tipping point regarding the way in which citizens understand their position vis-à-vis each other and those that govern different aspects of their lives. We see this shift as the common thread uniting various attempts to democratize democratic practice, and we see this volume as a contribution in that general direction.

This volume is therefore a response to the ways ideology, dogma and disciplining thwart aspectival seeing and thinking, trapping us in familiar ideas and making untangling ourselves from the vicious processes that are facilitating the current conjuncture an arduous and challenging task. Instead, the fellows and friends of the CTI respond by trying to use the power of dialogue to open up new ways of seeing and acting democratically. In so doing, they model an answer to one of the most important questions of our time: How do we relate with each other and with all other living beings democratically? Through dialogue, the authors in this volume are themselves enacting democratizing processes and thereby exploring new possibilities for democracy moving forward. The volume begins a conversation about how types of democracy join hands or fail to do so, opening up a new integrated field of study of democratic theory and practice that includes diverse types of democracy and ways of studying these types and their interconnections locally and globally. This is the primary motivation for this volume and the workshop and conference that preceded it.

A reading of the chapters in the volume as a multilogue among types of democracy reveals how, although liberal representative democracy is in crisis, many types of democracies are alive, even experiencing a resurgence. Their experiences, practices and possibilities are becoming more accessible to growing numbers of people. This multilogue between democratic traditions also reveals that many of the problems of liberal representative democracy that plague and limit our imaginaries of what it means to be democratic stem from the tendency to limit discussions of democracy to its representative liberal form. In fact, as the volume argues, the crisis of democracy is partly caused by not seeing the field of democracy in the broadened and (potentially) integrated way in which the volume presents it. Unless we are able to understand the field of democracy in an integrated manner, we will fail to act democratically within it in integrated ways.

At present, most theorists, scientists and citizens focus on their own type of democracy. Most often, their focus ignores, isolates or opposes other types of democracies and their interconnections. In contrast, we from the CTI aim to use dialogue to generate transformative cycles of democratic succession, transition and transformation. We refer to this as 'democracy here and now' and 'democratic democratization'. It is through deep listening and dialogues of reciprocal learning between and across types of democracies that we can better understand how to coordinate and democratize our struggles for democracy through democratic means.

LOOKING BACK

Back in March of 2019, when we held our workshop and conference in Victoria, the world was experiencing a multiplicity of crises that already seemed to be reaching their respective tipping points. Income inequality, ecological crisis and political repression had already triggered unprecedented mass mobilizations around the world. One year later, the Covid-19 pandemic led governments across the globe to make unprecedented transformations in the way we organize and interact, using the crisis to reinforce governor–governed relations through a serious planetary reduction or suspension of civil rights; a growing tendency toward expert-led, top-down, governance; and a renewed suppression and demonization of popular democratic contestation. At a time like this, it is more important than ever to remain vigilant, critical and dialogical. We must avoid falling into the trap of letting 'institutional experts' determine our fate without us having a say. We must hold firm in our faith that complex problems can be solved and crises managed in genuinely democratic ways. Failing to do so could lead to even weaker formal democratic institutions of representation, an ever-increasing pauperization of most humans and an accelerated depletion of all life on earth.

Our workshop, and the volume it birthed, is a testament to our faith in our ability to tackle these complex and critically important topics in democratic ways. In the workshop we tried to imagine, at least in our person-to-person conversations, that we were equal democrats exploring how we could work well together without subordination, assimilation or recolonization. Our dialogue circles therefore engaged with a double movement, both engaging in a genealogical visualization of Western imperialism while also asking ourselves how we can now study and learn from the people and peoples who are marginalized by this tradition.

To have a multilogue of this kind is very difficult for everybody involved; it requires getting the tone right as the conversation moves around from one perspective to another. Sometimes, a participant's epistemology is to look away as much as possible from Western concepts.[5] Often there is no shared

---

[5] Here I am thinking of Peyman Vahabzadeh, who, in the context of our dialogue circle, presented the figure of the refugee as a theoretical construct that can help the mental rethinking of democracy. According to Vahabzadeh, looking from the angle of such a radically heterogeneous inassimilable figure can help us rethink radically our present condition and go beyond it. Adding a metaphor from his hiking experiences at night, he explains how hiking in the dark one learns that sometimes the best way to actually find your path is not to look at the path but to look away: "If you look at the tree the path shines on the corner of your eye. Following from this, my epistemology is looking as much as I can away from Western concepts although my training has been in the Western tradition." Democracy and its Futures workshop and conference, University of Victoria, Victoria, BC March 21–22, 2019.

diagnosis of what the issues are: "What are the symptoms and what are the causes?"[6] At times, people are wondering who the patient is.[7] Nevertheless, in the process of reciprocal learning we expand the field of what counts as democracy. By deparochializing democracy, representative institutions appear as one amongst many modalities of democracy. At the same time, such a move also helps us to think about the planet as being full of types of democratic activities and practices, networks and so on that may give us more avenues of research or/and more spaces of hope where we engage with people who are regenerating democratic relations amongst themselves.

In a certain sense, our multilogue has been an experiment in joining hands.[8] A space in which lateral relationships count more than hierarchical ones. As a consequence, an underlying thread in our conversation has been a discussion regarding horizontality and verticality in politics and other social relationships. For Fonna Forman, such a language helps with the critique of institutions that should not be behaving as vertically as they do.[9] Robin Celikates points out that some of the institutions that need to be transformed struggle to change direction; they seem to have a gravitational pull toward verticality built into them.[10] Christina Gray suggests that we think of vertical and horizontal alignments symbolically as a concentric circle with no beginning and no end and in which you can be in a different position at different times.[11] For Heidi Stark, the problem might not necessarily be with whether some things are vertical or horizontal, but the way in which the verticality is being constructed.[12]

As David Owen highlights, there are plenty of examples in the world in which we live where functions are sent up a level without authority being sent up a level.[13]

---

[6] David Owen during our first dialogue circle at the Workshop.

[7] Anoush Terjanan during our first dialogue circle at the Workshop. Terjanan participated in our conference but could not contribute a chapter to this volume.

[8] During the workshop's first dialogue circle, Jeanne Morefield referred to joining hands as "the James Tully practice" and described it as the pincer move that deconstructs and reconstructs at the same time.

[9] Fonna Forman during our second dialogue circle with graduate students at the Workshop. Forman points to the number of universities that are relating to communities that are struggling and are doing so vertically instead of horizontally.

[10] Robin Celikates during our second dialogue circle with graduate students at the workshop. Celikates highlights the importance of being aware of the limits of trying to make vertical institutions more horizontal. As he puts it, "one of the things about the institution is that in the end it is almost always stronger than the individuals that try to change it."

[11] Christina Gray during our second dialogue circle with graduate students at the Workshop.

[12] Heidi Kiiwetinepinesiik Stark during our second dialogue circle with graduate students at the Workshop. Stark describes vertical relationships in which someone might be transferring up particular responsibilities or obligations but not necessarily have to carry them out or exercise them in coercive ways. Stark participated in our conference but could not contribute a chapter to this volume.

[13] David Owen during our second dialogue circle with graduate students at the Workshop. Owen points to most global regimes and diverse federalism as examples where horizontality shifts into verticality while the authority remains at the horizontal level. He also refers to Arendt's sparse

Chantal Mouffe sees the tendency among certain horizontal movements to refuse any form of leadership – because of the fact that they understand verticality as necessarily authoritarian – as problematic.[14] Jeanne Morefield, although inclined toward horizontal modes of organizing, questions how its slow temporality can grow in the context of urgency.[15] In response to this challenge regarding the efficiency of horizontality in times of big decisions and great perils, Keith Cherry reflects on the climate crisis and how much of the argument against horizontality in that context emphasizes that the problem is so large that only the state is large enough to take the dramatic action needed. According to Cherry, those who follow this line of argument are hypnotized by the abstract but seldom actual potential capacity of states to tackle climate change, when in fact the actual bulk of the action is happening in more horizontal citizen-led spaces.[16]

What crystalizes through my deep engagement with the horizontal 15M movement of 2011 in Spain is that those engaging with each other horizontally to deal with urgent crises are making a clear distinction between having a sense of urgency and being in a rush.[17] The move to verticality they see as rushed, whereas their horizontality is understood as a democratic response to the urgency. As Cherry points out, it is not verticality per se that they are critiquing, but the fact that in the rush of crisis leadership is not distributed randomly but instead reveals a consistent elite with a vested interest in maintaining and deepening both verticality and the crises that sustain it.[18]

Although verticality and horizontality were ever-present during our conference conversations, other themes acquired prominence as the multilogue advanced. John Borrows emphasized the importance of listening and learning to listen more and more deeply.[19] Heidi Stark pointed to Indigenous communities as a learning ground from which to better understand how different nations live together.[20] Stark asked us to broaden our imagining of a real recognition of

speculations on the council system and the early days of the Russian Revolution and the Soviets as examples where authority is mediated at various levels but always based at the bottom.

[14] Chantal Mouffe during our second dialogue circle with graduate students at the Workshop. For Mouffe, a leader can be the symbol of common affects and, in that sense, she thinks it plays an important role in political struggles.

[15] Jeanne Morefield during our second dialogue circle with graduate students at the Workshop.

[16] Keith Cherry during our second dialogue circle with graduate students at the Workshop. As Cherry puts it, when having to choose between an enormous but potential capacity (the state) or a very small but actual capacity (social movements), he sides with the small but actual. For him the presumption that vertical organizations are necessarily more efficacious shows a lack of actual engagement with horizontality.

[17] See Pablo Ouziel, *Democracy Here and Now: The Exemplary Case of Spain* (Toronto: University of Toronto Press, 2022).

[18] Keith Cherry during our second dialogue circle with graduate students at the Workshop.

[19] John Borrows at the public discussion of the Workshop. As Borrows puts it: "How do I listen more in quiet, when political life and activism and the things that I am concerned about seem to point all in other directions."

[20] Heidi Kiiwetinepinesiik Stark at the public discussion of the workshop.

Indigenous nationhood and governance that need not be a threat to the state but reconfigures it in innovative ways.

For Johnny Mack, the deep kind of pluralism experienced during the workshop and conference is not of the kind that presumes the rigid structures that we associate with liberal democratic institutions. Instead as he describes it, it presumes an agency that humans have to act outside of such rigidity.[21] As Mack puts it, the workshop's dialogical gift–gratitude–reciprocity approach to democracy resonates with how many Indigenous peoples on Turtle Island turn to multiple spaces that have to do with the kinds of relationships that communities form with the land and the lifeways they find on it. As Mack emphasizes, when relating with their kin, Indigenous peoples do not talk about democracies but talk instead about families and relationships through that register.[22] These kinds of kincentric relations inspire what we refer to as "joining hands," and both the conference and this volume are learning-from and learning-with such kinship relationships.

JOINING HANDS HERE AND NOW

One important theme of this volume is that if we have a better grasp of 'the entangled, crisscrossing and overlapping relationships' that exist today amongst various forms of democracy, we will have better chances for coordination and cooperation amongst them as the multiplicity of crises humanity is generating, contributing to and facing intensify.[23] When these relationships are democratic from the point of view of all participants, we can think of them as a way of "joining hands" across democratic traditions: each participant stands in their own concepts of democracy, yet together they form linkages which allow for shared struggles and endeavors without homogenizing or hierarchicalizing. If we take joining hands seriously, its processes of cooperation and contestation by means of critical democratic dialogue reveal to us the actuality of a 'participatory democratic countermodernity' in the 'here and now'. Joining hands relationships are the actual living expression in the here and now of Peter Kropotkin's mutual aid. As Kropotkin pointed out, it is these relationships that have kept human communities from extinction against all

---

[21] Johnny Mack at the public discussion of the Workshop.

[22] Ibid. In contrast to the dialogical and horizontal nature of the workshop, Mack contrasts the current postpolitical conjuncture as one in which Indigenous Peoples in Canada have no space where they have "the authority to make law where there isn't already law." As he puts it, the question is whether it is provincial or federal, so what ends up happening is that lawyers do not look to the people to decide what is lawful and meaningful relative to the land, but instead look to federal and provincial regulatory regimes and work to draft laws in a way that harmonizes with them so as to not trigger a conflict. His concern is that the different treaties and the regulatory regimes they put in place, together with the way of understanding law and regulation relating to territory that they represent, will come to displace the other, deeper democratic foundation that Indigenous peoples inherit from their ancestors.

[23] Tully, Introduction.

odds as they have struggled over the centuries (and continue to struggle) to
overcome dominant vicious power-over systems of subordination and control.[24]

In my work with the 15M movement in Spain, I disclose six distinct types of
joining hands relationships between civil citizens (those seeking to reform and
improve existing institutions within their democracies) and civic citizens (those
seeking to broaden their traditions by exercising democratic cogovernance in
new ways, beyond existing institutions).[25] I see these six distinct types of joining
hands relationships that I witnessed working within 15M also operating within
the chapters of this volume. Table 20.1 presents the six joining hands
relationships as I have learned-with them in discussions with both 15M and
the contributors to this volume.

These six ways of joining hands and the different ways in which they are
exemplified by the previous chapters present us with a Banyan tree of
"democratizing demoarchies," or efforts to reform low-intensity democratic
institutions, while serving to excavate long-standing modes of direct democracy
that are often overlooked in mainstream political imaginaries.[26]

What the chapters in the volume are showing is not a joining of hands of the
middle-class population with their middle-class legislators. If, for example, one
considers what Forman explains in Chapter 8, what one sees are exemplary cases
of the precariat self-organizing and joining hands across diverse forms of

TABLE 20.1 *Six distinct types of joining hands relationships*[27]

JH1	civic citizens joining hands with each other
JH2	civil citizens joining hands with each other
JH3	civic and civil citizens joining hands
JH4	civic citizens work with representative governments
JH5	civil citizens work with representative governments
JH6	civic-civil citizens are joining hands with each other in order to influence governments

[24] Peter Kropotkin, *Mutual Aid: A Factor of Evolution* (Mineola, NY: Dover Publications, 2006).
[25] When thinking of "joining hands," I have in mind a dynamic process rather than a steady state
through which communities of practice relate with supporters and potential supporters outside
of their particular communities of practice.
[26] I am thinking of the Banyan tree, with its innumerable interrelated branches, in the manner that
Mahatma Gandhi thought about it – that is, with joining hands relationships as "the parent
trunk from which innumerable branches shoot out." See James Tully, "Integral Nonviolence," in
Richard B. Gregg, *The Power of Nonviolence*, ed. James Tully (Cambridge: Cambridge
University Press, 2018), xxix. 15M is a classic case of this integral approach at joining hands,
therefore it is not surprising that the six distinct types of joining hands relationships were thought
about in dialogue with those being 15M in Spain.
[27] The table is borrowed from Ouziel, *Democracy Here and Now*.

precarious existence. It is true that often when the precariat try to join hands with established parties, they are rapidly sidelined by middle-class left parties worldwide, or are used instrumentally, as we have seen in the case of the United States with the Democratic Party or in Spain with party-movement Podemos. Nevertheless, as the 15M mantra says, *vamos lentos porque vamos lejos* (we go ever so slowly because we are going on forever). Following from this, with patience and through ever-growing concentric circles of critical democratic dialogue, democratic families can continue their ongoing processes of democratizing democracy.

If we look at Anthony Laden's chapter, he describes democratic politics as an ongoing activity with no ending as long as "people remain committed to continue working out together how to live together."[28] In this manner, the chapter mostly presents the basic features of civic-to-civic joining hands relationships (JH1) oriented around sustainability conditions. Although addressed to civil citizens, it encourages them to think about democratic participation in the civic sense while thinking about the sustainability crisis (JH3).

Owen's chapter reminds us of the importance of democratic agency – 'freedoms of and in participation, and with fellow citizens'.[29] At the same time, it also highlights the importance of seeing democratic struggles as bifocal – that is, as consisting of both a focus on defending, securing and extending rights (JH2, JH5), and on the prefigurative civic enactment of alternative civil orders (JH1, JH3, JH4, JH6).[30] Throughout the chapter, Owen clearly contrasts civil and civic modes of citizenship. Nevertheless, as the chapter progresses he argues for civic modes of engagement as the better way to join hands with nonmembers of the civil order, such as immigrants and refugees (JH1). What he reveals is how civic citizens can offer this kind of joining hands relationship to refugees, and thus enable them to present their demands and be listened to.

Lasse Thomassen's chapter invites us to think about democracy as a question to be pressed. He sees democracy as both solution and experiment and reminds us that when thinking about what democracy is, since there is no ultimate answer we are inevitably left with a plurality of answers.[31] Thomassen is describing a feature of all forms of democratic citizenship – provisionality. Nevertheless, this feature of democracy is clearly a civic property in the sense of deparochializing one's own viewpoint, being open to the views of others and acknowledging the nonfinality of any agreement. The provisionality is what makes possible all six joining hands relationships mentioned above (JH1, JH2, JH3, JH4, JH5, JH6).

Oliver Schmidtke's chapter emphasizes how community and civic engagement nurture each other and are dependent on each other in order to be sustainable. His main concern is that unless channels for citizens to have a say remain open and effective, the simplistic message of right populist movements and parties will continue to gain ground as political struggles intensify.

---

[28] Laden, Chapter 1.   [29] Owen, Chapter 2.   [30] Ibid.   [31] Thomassen, Chapter 3.

In essence, what Schmidtke is writing about are the failures of civil-oriented political demoarchic parties that are losing touch with civic communities of participatory democracy. Rightly, he is blaming these parties for the present crisis for failing to join hands in respectful ways. In this piece, Schmidtke revives an old German tradition called "associationalism" that began in the 1830s (JH4, JH5, JH6).

In his chapter, Boaventura de Sousa Santos is mainly concerned with the fact that civil demoarchy is in essence open to capture by authoritarian movements.[32] He is adamant that demoarchy is currently moving in such a direction. It is true that he does not write much about alternatives in this text, except by highlighting mass civil-oriented movements on the left. Nevertheless, in his other writings de Sousa Santos is emphatic about the importance of civic Gaia participatory democracy on the ground and coordinating through platforms such as the World Social Forum 2.0 at a planetary level to promote alter-glocal change (JH1, JH3, JH4, JH6).

In Chapter 6, Mouffe speaks about the current conjuncture in Western Europe, inscribing herself in it and trying to understand it in order to intervene. She acknowledges there is much to learn from our discussions in Victoria on civic and civil citizens, horizontality and verticality and joining hands, and that much can be learned from the struggles of Indigenous peoples in Turtle Island. Nevertheless, from her viewpoint, what is most important in the here and now is to intervene in order to impede the development of more oppressive and authoritarian regimes across the globe.[33] Ultimately, Mouffe is asking all sorts of participatory civic democrats to join hands with party-civil citizens in order to gain political power in representative governments. That is,

[32] We know that the term "democracy" is made up of the two Greek terms: *demos*, meaning the people who come together and govern themselves; and *kratos*, meaning power. This means that democracy is a form of self-government in which the people themselves exercise power. That is, they reason together, they exercise power together and they agree and/or disagree together. Democracy is not, therefore, a representative system. As Tully points out, democracy was a special form of government even in Athens, and Athenian theorists of democracy contrasted it with other forms of government where some segment of the population ruled over the other, such as, for example, mon*archy* or olig*archy* (using the term *archy*, which means rule). These are forms of rule where one segment of the population rules over others, whether it is a minority or a majority or a system like the one we have in representative democracies today. These forms of rule are not democratic in the original sense of the term. In representative democracies today, it is not "we the people" who exercise power, but through elections we pass it on to our representatives who then rule over us. What we have is a system that is really, from the original meaning of the term democracy, antidemocratic. Following from this, and in alignment with Tully, I find the term "demoarchy" more accurate when speaking about what is commonly referred to as representative democracy today. Instead of people exercising power together (democracy), what we have is people who come together and allow the differentiation of society into those who are ruled and those who rule (demoarchy). James Tully, "What Are the Biggest Challenges Democracy Is Facing Today?" (lecture, Constitutionalism in the Age of Populism, University of Victoria, Victoria, BC, March 6–8, 2020), www.youtube.com/watch?v=WvG-oQDduFw.

[33] Chantal Mouffe during our first dialogue circle at the Workshop.

she enjoins civic citizens to join hands with civil citizens in parties and movements (JH3, JH6). She encourages civic citizens to remain civic in their own activities (JH1), but encourages them to help their civil fellows capture and transform the institutions of the state.

Morefield approaches both political problems and dialogue with humility and openness. Without a doubt, she is angry at the closures that she sees and wants to bust them open. Yet, she quickly reminds herself about the need for generosity in her analysis. As she puts it, the liberal societies that are settler colonial states and imperial states need to stop the "constant preening in the mirror without looking in the mirror."[34] According to Morefield, this unseeing allows for exclusion, domination and dispossession to continue while citizens still imagine themselves to be living in liberal democracies.[35] Morefield is promoting a reflection that does not look away but looks at the past in order to reconceive a different kind of democratic practice in the future. What Morefield is doing is to describe the hegemony of imperial political relationships and top-down politics of liberalism and authoritarianism, and she is calling for civic, participatory democracy from below, around solidarity and compassion. She encourages civic citizens to join hands with each other (JH1).

Celikates argues that democracies that are now in crisis have actually been structurally in an enduring crisis for many excluded population groups. These include groups that have been colonized, marginalized, assimilated and/or subjected to forms of genocide, cultural or physical, by those states whose crises of democracy we today lament.[36] As Celikates puts it, "the good old days that some seem to be longing for when diagnosing the crisis of democracy have not been so good for quite a lot of people and peoples."[37] Following from this, and learning with Hannah Arendt, Celikates presents a substantive argument for reconceiving revolution in a tighter relationship to actual existing practices of democracy. Endorsing Arendt's conception of revolution as "begin something new," he addresses self-reflexive and self-limiting notions of revolution while embracing a logic of the political that moves "beyond and against hegemony" while also moving "beyond and against the borders of a world divided along state lines." He seeks to construct a new concept of revolution that does not subordinate 'here and now democracy' to some future project, but, rather, grounds revolution in democracy here and now (JH1, JH2, JH3, JH6).[38]

In both the conference and in her chapter, Forman's emphasis is on learning to do better as academics by listening better. For Forman, researchers can contribute to addressing specific crises by learning horizontal practices of

---

[34] Jeanne Morefield during our second dialogue circle with graduate students at the Workshop.
[35] Ibid.
[36] Robin Celikates during our second dialogue circle with graduate students at the Workshop.
[37] Ibid.   [38] Celikates, Chapter 10.

engagement with members of affected communities. What she advocates for is the cocreation of spaces in which community members and researchers assemble as partners to share knowledges and learn-with one another how to coproduce new knowledge together.[39] Practicing a 'political theory in solidarity with border communities', Forman gives us an astonishing account of civic, democratic, Gaia citizenship among local, poor, oppressed US and Mexican citizens who organize into *demoi* both to improve their own lives and neighborhoods, and to contest the power-over structures of the dominant societies.[40] What is particularly interesting about her work is that it demonstrates the *glocal* element of the struggle as local communities scale-up globally their contestation and constructive programs (JH1, JH2, JH3, JH4, JH5, JH6).

Rebeccah Nelems' 'radical copresence' and her 'canopies of understanding' lay the foundation for a deeper understanding of how coexisting yet distinct worldviews 'intra-actively' relate to one another through inter-beingness.[41] In her pluriverse of democratizing practices one experiences the unsettling of Western thought. What the chapter is doing is contrasting Gaia and demoarchic citizenship and then showing how Gaia citizens are able to join hands with demoarchic citizens. Through this interaction, she sees Gaia citizens as able to show demoarchic citizens the limitations and destructiveness of their own form of citizenship. The chapter is an invitation for demoarchic citizens to join hands with a larger and more pluralistic Gaia citizenship and its way of seeing the world we are in as plain members and citizens of Gaia (JH3, JH6).

Val Napoleon's contribution, both during the conference and in her chapter, points to what different kinds of democracies and different kinds of citizenship look like when there are no hierarchical state organizations maintaining systems of law and their respective institutions of enforcement. What she highlights is that, when this is the case, how one understands oneself and one's obligations in that legal order is very different.[42] Therefore, what we must do as scholars is to learn by asking critical questions about such systems without treating them as cultural artifacts. Following from this, she describes Gitxsan democracy as an example of intense democracy, and explains how colonial legislation is attempting to murder it 'democratically'.[43] As an alternative to learn from and with, Napoleon discusses how two Indigenous peoples are joining hands across deep differences and resolving conflicts. I am hesitant to use my own language of description to explain what it is that these Indigenous communities are doing, because Napoleon's emphasis is always on keeping descriptions of what is going on in "their own terms." While I see many connections to the diverse ways of joining hands I am describing, I also honor that translating

---

[39] Ibid.   [40] Forman, Chapter 8.   [41] Nelems, Chapter 9.
[42] Val Napoleon during our second dialogue circle with graduate students at the Workshop.
[43] Napoleon, Chapter 11.

Gitxsan practices into my own language would act along the lines of the colonial logic she is trying to challenge in her writing.

Josh Nichols, in his usual style, throws cold water on any democratic claims made by the Canadian state in regards to its relationship to Indigenous peoples. For Nichols, it is clear that in Canada Indigenous peoples "have been subjected to sovereign power without any claim to actual representative accountability."[44] What he seeks to do is to explain two types of membership in different *demoi*: Indigenous and Settler. He shows how historically these types of membership have failed to join hands, and suggests that in order to resolve this we need to study the history of these two conflicting forms of citizenship so that new ways of joining hands between them as equals can take place (JH1, JH2, JH3, JH4, JH5, JH6).

Stacie Swain successfully draws on a lot of complex recent theory to compose her own appropriate language of description of what is going on in the three stories she tells in Chapter 13. She argues that non-Indigenous allies can become democratic citizens of shared *demoi* by engaging with Indigenous democratic organizations that are themselves grounded in a normativity of gift–gratitude–reciprocity ecosocial relationships. This is how non-Indigenous subjects become active ethical responsible agents. This is what the Laurier Memorial calls being a 'good guest'.[45] Her chapter is a beautiful example of participatory democratic civic and Gaia citizens forming a *demos* among themselves and then joining hands with, and under the authority of, the First Nation with whom they are cogenerating relations of solidarity (JH1, JH4).

Phil Henderson's chapter points to how those of us living through the last days of the Holocene can struggle against the "cannibalistic urges of empire."[46] Learning from and with grassroots political movements, he advocates for an expanded and expansive view of the political "in which power and authority are not mediated through logics of hegemony/counter-hegemony."[47] He highlights that this type of grassroots politics draws its strength from what it is defending and producing rather than from what it seeks to abolish. Henderson's chapter compliments Swain's chapter closely, focusing on the Canadian state's blockage of Swain's types of joining hands relationships (JH1, JH4, JH6).

Jeremy Webber's chapter explores the diverse practices that generate and sustain democratic community by putting Gitxsan and Canadian practices of citizenship and self-determination in dialogue. He carefully describes how the institutions and practices of Gitxsan governance allow participants to join hands with others across difference and over time. Webber then shows how

---

[44] Nichols, Chapter 12.
[45] Memorial to Sir Wilfred Laurier, Premier of the Dominion of Canada from the Chiefs of the Shuswap, Okanagan and Couteau Tribes of British Columbia presented at Kamloops, BC, August 25, 1910, www.skeetchestn.ca/files/documents/Governance/memorialtosirwilfredlaurier1910.pdf.
[46] Henderson, Chapter 14.   [47] Ibid.

these processes actively create and sustain the foundations of communal self-determination. Turning to the present crises in liberal practices of citizenship and community, he shows what non-Indigenous citizens of representative democracies can learn from Gitxsan governance about sustainable, engaged democratic praxis. In so doing, Webber shows how the engaged, contested and never-finished process of joining hands is not merely something that different democratic traditions can choose to do; rather, it represents the very process through which democracy is constituted and maintained, both between traditions and within them (**JH2, JH3, JH5, JH6**).

In his chapter David Held asks us to look at the intersection of the national and international in order to identify what is causing the retreat to nationalism and authoritarianism.[48] According to Held, it is also in this space that one sees what is generating the multiple threats to globalization that our modern societies are experiencing. His chapter shows how the failure of these power-over systems to join hands is causing the global gridlock we are enduring. As he argues, the inability of national and international institutions to enact power-with forms of joining hands and only knowing how to practice power-over/under forms of joining hands has spiraled our societies into the reproduction of vicious cycles which are deepening the multifaceted crises. Held does think that there is a solution to be found in the reform of these institutions, yet, at the same time, his chapter leaves open the possibility that a deeper transformation is necessary (**JH4, JH5, JH6**).

Antje Wiener invites us to be less shy about broadening our imaginary in regards to the type of institutional change that is possible. As she points out, often the crises our societies face are responded to by filling the institutions that are already there with new meaning.[49] Yet, as she puts it, sometimes we need different institutions. We need to think more boldly and rethink institutions such as the United Nations and the European Union. Inviting us and all affected and/or responsible governance institutions to enter into much needed dialogues of reciprocal learning, she is advocating for an 'ontology of societal multiplicity'.[50] The chapter describes international democratic practices of both civic and civil citizens while inviting us to seek joining hands with the powers-that-be so that changes to the status quo can be negotiated (**JH1, JH2, JH3, JH4, JH5, JH6**).

Keith Cherry's chapter addresses different ways of joining hands. Alongside common federal and co-decision practices, Cherry introduces what he calls "conditional authority" as a means of democratizing relationships between democratic traditions. He makes distinctions between what he describes as the "mutual" and "asymmetrical" varieties of such authority. The chapter relates nicely to a number of the other chapters. In particular, it helps to

[48] Held, Chapter 16.
[49] Antje Wiener during our second dialogue circle with graduate students at the Workshop.
[50] Wiener, Chapter 17.

connect western legal pluralism chapters with Indigenous pluralism and Indigenous-Western pluralism chapters, showing how both settings have embraced diverse practices of conditional authority. Cherry's is a complex account of joining hands across different types of governments and, within them, their different types of citizenship (civic, civil, Indigenous). The result of these attempts at joining hands (legal pluralism) generates a new, more democratic form of citizenship among the participants that is cogenerated as a result of their participation and the change it induces in their understanding of self and other (JH1, JH2, JH3, JH4, JH5, JH6).

Tully in his usual mode, acknowledges the vicious social systems that we inhabit and are reproducing, but reminds us of the fact that we are able to think and 'act otherwise'.[51] He explains how demoarchy and capitalism are destroying the planet and causing the democratic crisis we are facing. Then, he tries to persuade demoarchic citizens to reorient themselves, learn-with, and join hands with Gaia democratic citizens. According to Tully, Gaia democratic citizens can inspire demoarchy citizens through exemplarity in their constructive programs (countermodernities) and through their negotiation and reconciliation dialogues (Satyagraha contestation). That is, dialogues that are always open to revision and starting anew in a circular way. For Tully, this is the only way forward because of the relation between means and ends: democratization must be carried out by democratic means – something that Satyagraha does by always treating the demoarchic opponent as already a democratic citizen and member of the "we" (never as an "other").

MOVING FORWARD IN THE HERE AND NOW

All of these modes of being democratic, and their joining hands intra-actions, constitute the 'democratic permaculture' of the present and the ground of a sustainable future. Learning-with the five families of democracies outlined in the Introduction and disclosed throughout the chapters, the democratic dying of democracy can be avoided. The current conjunctures that democracies across the planet need to respond to call for an extraordinary effort by all affected. We all need to look beyond our own family of democracy and embrace a 'radical copresence' with other democratic families. We need a democratic ethos that sustains all democracies. Such an ethos requires the kind of virtues, capabilities and skill sets presented by the contributors. We hope, therefore, that it adds to the regeneration of democracy as we collectively begin the process of reversing its hollowing out. We have not presented an abstract, theoretical and future-oriented account of some utopian 'democracy-to-come', but have focused instead on disclosing the actual and living pluriverse of democracies interbeing in the here and now.

---

[51] Tully, Chapter 19.

As the volume comes to an end, still in the midst of a global pandemic, we are beginning to see how a post-Trump world is far from being a virtuous one. Much work is still needed, and we hope this volume can help orient and set the tone by offering a multiplicity of ways in which we can relate to ourselves and others. Enacting democratic relationships with one another requires practices of care of the self to sustain us in our ability to continue to do so. By inviting all readers into this pluriverse of democracy we are welcoming you into a space of cocaring, colearning and cotransformation.

Bibliography

Abbott, Kenneth W., Robert O. Keohane, Andrew Moravcsik, Anne-Marie Slaughter, and Duncan Snidal. "The Concept of Legalization." *International Organization* 54, 3 (2000): 401–19.

Abella, Irving Martin. *Nationalism, Communism, and Canadian Labour: The CIO, the Communist Party, and the Canadian Congress of Labour 1935–1956.* Toronto: University of Toronto Press, 1973.

Abensour, Miguel. *Democracy Against the State.* Cambridge: Polity, 2011.

Abourahme, Nasser. "Revolution after Revolution: The Commune as Line of Flight in Palestinian Anticolonialism." *Critical Times* 4, no. 3 (2021): 445–75. https://doi.org/10.1215/26410478-9355217.

Abram, David. *The Spell of the Sensuous.* New York: Vintage, 1996.

Abts, Koen and Stefan Rummens. "Populism versus Democracy." *Political Studies* 55, no. 2 (2007): 405–24.

Acharya, Amitav. "After Liberal Hegemony: The Advent of a Multiplex World Order." *Ethics and International Affairs* 31 (2017): 271–85.

Acharya, Amitav. "Global International Relations (IR) and Regional Worlds: A New Agenda for International Studies." *International Studies Quarterly* 58 (2014): 647–59.

Acharya, Amitav. "How Ideas Spread: Whose Norms Matter? Norm Localization and Institutional Change in Asian Regionalism." *International Organization* 58 (2004): 239–75.

Adamczak, Bini. *Beziehungsweise Revolution: 1917, 1968 und kommende.* Berlin: Suhrkamp, 2017.

Adler, Emanuel. "Seizing the Middle Ground: Constructivism in World Politics." *European Journal of International Relations* 3, no. 3 (1997): 319–63.

Adler, Emanuel. *World Ordering: A Social Theory of Cognitive Evolution.* Cambridge: Cambridge University Press, 2019.

Aguirre Turner, Kelly Anne Patricia. "Re-Storying Political Theory: Indigenous Resurgence, Idle No More, and Colonial Apprehension." Unpublished PhD thesis, University of Victoria, 2019.

Akbar, Amna A. "The Left Is Remaking Politics." *The New York Times,* July 12, 2020. www.nytimes.com/2020/07/11/opinion/sunday/defund-police-cancel-rent.html.

Akomolafe, Bayo. "Through the imprisoned archetypal figure of Baldur, I continue to find a useful way to think and talk about 'whiteness'." Facebook, August 6, 2020. www.facebook.com/permalink.php?story_fbid=615959105699366&id=130394687589146.

Akomolafe, Bayo. "Without prejudice to my American brothers and sisters, who have been, and are, fighting with every drop of their blood to topple the alarmingly pro-fascist villainy of Donald Trump." Facebook, August 30, 2020. www.facebook.com/permalink.php?story_fbid=635532823741994&id=130394687589146.

Albertazzi, Daniele, Arianna Giovannini, and Antonella Seddone. "'No Regionalism Please, We Are Leghisti!' The Transformation of the Italian Lega Nord under the Leadership of Matteo Salvini." *Regional & Federal Studies* 28, no. 5 (2018): 645–71.

Albertazzi, Daniele and Duncan McDonnell. "Conclusion: Populism and Twenty-First Century Western European Democracy." In *Twenty-First Century Populism*, edited by Daniele Albertazzi and Duncan McDonnell, 217–23. Basingstoke: Palgrave Macmillan, 2008.

Alinsky, Saul. *Reveille for Radicals*. Chicago, IL: University of Chicago Press, 1946.

Allard-Tremblay, Yann. "The Modern and the Political Pluralist Perspectives on Political Authorities." *The Review of Politics* 80, no. 4 (2018): 675–700.

Allen, Amy. *The End of Progress: Decolonizing the Normative Foundations of Critical Theory*. New York: Columbia University Press, 2016.

Anderson, Elijah. *The Cosmopolitan Canopy: Race and Civility in Everyday Life*. New York: W. W. Norton & Company, 2011.

Anderson, Margaret and Marjorie Halpin, eds. *Potlatch at Gitsegukla: William Beynon's 1945 Field Notebooks*. Vancouver: UBC Press, 2000.

Angelbeck, William O. "'They Recognize No Superior Chief': Power, Practice, Anarchism and Warfare in the Coast Salish Past." Unpublished PhD thesis, University of British Columbia, 2009.

Appleyard, Donald and Kevin Lynch. *Temporary Paradise? A Look at the Special Landscape of the San Diego Region: A Report to the City of San Diego*. Cambridge, MA: Massachusetts Institute of Technology, 1974.

Archibugi, Daniele, David Held, and Martin Köhler. *Re-Imagining Political Community: Studies in Cosmopolitan Democracy*. Cambridge: Polity Press, 1998.

Arendt, Hannah. "Civil Disobedience." In *Crises of the Republic*, 51–102. New York: Harcourt Brace & Company, 1972.

Arendt, Hannah. "Freedom and Politics: A Lecture." *Chicago Review* 14, no. 1 (1960): 28–46.

Arendt, Hannah. "Freiheit und Politik." In *Zwischen Vergangenheit und Zukunft: Übungen im politischen Denken I*, 201–26. München: Piper, 2000.

Arendt, Hannah. *On Revolution*. London: Penguin, 1990.

Arendt, Hannah. *On Violence*. New York: Harcourt, Brace, Jovanovich, 1970.

Arendt, Hannah. "Totalitarian Imperialism: Reflections on the Hungarian Revolution." *The Journal of Politics* 20, no. 1 (1958): 5–43.

Arendt, Hannah. *Über die Revolution*. München: Piper, 1994.

Aristotle. *The Politics and the Constitution of Athens*. edited by Stephen Everson. Cambridge: Cambridge University Press, 1996.

Armitage, David. *Foundations of Modern International Thought*. Cambridge: Cambridge University Press, 2013.

Asch, Michael. "Confederation Treaties and Reconciliation: Stepping Back into the Future." In *Resurgence and Reconciliation*, edited by Michael Asch, John Borrows, and James Tully, 29–48. Toronto/Buffalo: University of Toronto Press, 2018.

Asch, Michael. *On Being Here to Stay: Treaties and Aboriginal Rights in Canada.* Toronto: University of Toronto Press, 2014.

Asch, Michael, John Borrows, and James Tully, eds. *Resurgence and Reconciliation: Indigenous-Settler Relations and Earth Teachings.* Toronto/Buffalo: University of Toronto Press, 2018.

Atleo, Umeek E. Richard. *Principles of Tsawalk: An Indigenous Approach to Global Crisis.* Vancouver: UBC Press, 2011.

Azoulay, Ariella. "Revolution." *Political Concepts* 2 (2013). www.politicalconcepts.org /revolution-ariella-azoulay.

Babic, Milan. "Let's Talk About the Interregnum: Gramsci and the Crisis of the Liberal International Order." *International Affairs* 96, no. 3 (2020): 767–86.

Bakan, Joel. *The New Corporation: How "Good" Corporations Are Bad for Democracy.* Toronto: Penguin Canada, 2020.

Balibar, Etienne. *Citizenship.* Cambridge: Polity, 2015.

Balibar, Etienne. *Equaliberty: Political Essays.* Durham, NC: Duke University Press, 2014.

Balibar, Etienne. "The Idea of Revolution: Yesterday, Today and Tomorrow." *ΑΡΙΑΔΝΗ* 22 (2015–16): 228–44.

Balibar, Etienne. "Reflections on Gewalt." *Historical Materialism: Research in Critical Marxist Theory* 17 (2009): 99–125.

Balibar, Etienne. *Violence and Civility.* New York: Columbia University Press, 2015.

Barad, Karen. *Meeting the Universe Halfway.* Durham, NC: Duke University Press, 2007.

Barker, Adam and Russell Myers Ross. "Reoccupation and Resurgence: Indigenous Protest Camps in Canada." In *Protest Camps in International Context: Spaces, Infrastructures and Media of Resistance*, edited by Gavin Brown, Anna Feigenbaum, Fabian Frenzel, and Patrick McCurdy, 199–219. Bristol: Policy Press, 2018.

Barr, Robert R. "Populists, Outsiders and Anti-Establishment Politics." *Party Politics* 15 (2009): 29–48.

Battell Lowman, Emma and Adam J. Barker. *Settler: Identity and Colonialism in 21st Century Canada.* Halifax: Fernwood Publishing, 2015.

Bauböck, Rainer. *Democratic Inclusion: Rainer Bauböck in Dialogue.* Manchester: Manchester University Press, 2018.

Bayat, Asef. *Revolution without Revolutionaries: Making Sense of the Arab Spring.* Palo Alto, CA: Stanford University Press, 2017.

Bell, Catherine and Val Napoleon, eds. *First Nations Cultural Heritage and Law: Case Studies, Voices, and Perspectives.* Vancouver: UBC Press, 2008.

Bell, Duncan. "Political Realism and International Relations." *Philosophy Compass* 12 (2017): 12: e12403.

Bellamy, Richard and Dario Castiglione. "Three Models of Democracy, Political Community and Representation in the EU." *Journal of European Public Policy* 20, no. 2 (2013): 206–23.

Benjamin, Walter. *Illuminations.* New York: Shocken, 1969.

Berger, Peter and Thomas Luckmann. *The Social Construction of Reality.* Random House: New York, 1967.

Berman, Sheri. "Populism Is a Symptom Rather Than a Cause: Democratic Disconnect, the Decline of the Center-Left, and the Rise of Populism in Western Europe." *Polity* 51 (2019): 654–67.

Berman, Sheri and Maria Snegovaya. "Populism and the Decline of Social Democracy." *Journal of Democracy* 30, no. 3 (2019): 5–19.

Bhambra, Gurminder. "Whither Europe? Postcolonial versus Neocolonial Cosmopolitanism." *Interventions: International Journal of Postcolonial Studies* 18, no.2 (2016): 187–202.

Bhambra, Gurminder and John Holmwood. "Colonialism, Postcolonialism and the Liberal Welfare State." *New Political Economy* 23, no. 5 (2018): 574–87.

Bilgrami, Akeel, ed. *Nature and Value*. New York: Columbia University Press, 2020.

Blake, Michael. "Why Bullshit Hurts Democracy More Than Lies." *The Conversation*, May 14, 2018. http://theconversation.com/why-bullshit-hurts-democracy-more-than-lies-96331.

Blake, Michael, Simone Chambers, and Arthur Ripstein. "Talking Philosophy: War and Peace Part 2." May 19, 2015, in *IDEAS*. Produced by Greg Kelly and CBC Radio. www.cbc.ca/radio/ideas/talking-philosophy-war-and-peace-part-2-1.3326225.

Boel, Niels, Carsten Jensen, and André Sonnichsen. "Populism and the Claim to a Moral Monopoly: An Interview with Jan-Werner Müller." *Politik* 20, no. 4 (2017): 71–85.

Boisselle, Andrée. "Law's Hidden Canvas: Teasing Out the Threads of Coast Salish Legal Sensibility." Unpublished PhD thesis, University of Victoria, 2017.

Bondurant, Joan V. *Conquest of Violence: The Gandhian Philosophy of Conflict*. Revised ed. Princeton: Princeton University Press, 1988.

Bonikowski, Bart. "Ethno-Nationalist Populism and the Mobilization of Collective Resentment." *The British Journal of Sociology* 68 (2017): 181–213.

Bonikowski, Bart, Daphne Halikiopoulou, Eric Kaufmann, and Matthijs Rooduijn. "Populism and Nationalism in a Comparative Perspective: A Scholarly Exchange." *Nations and Nationalism* 25, no. 1 (2019): 58–81.

Boothby, Lauren. "More Than 200 People Arrested at Pipeline Protests in Burnaby." *Burnaby Now*, May 30, 2018.

Borradori, Giovanna and Jacques Derrida. "Autoimmunity: Real and Symbolic Suicides." In *Philosophy in a Time of Terror: Dialogues with Jürgen Habermas and Jacques Derrida*, 85–136. Chicago: University of Chicago Press, 2003.

Borrows, John. *Drawing Out Law: Spirit's Guide*. Toronto: University of Toronto Press, 2010.

Borrows, John. "Earth-Bound: Indigenous Resurgence and Environmental Reconciliation." In *Resurgence and Reconciliation*, edited by Michael Asch, John Borrows, and James Tully, 49–82. Toronto/Buffalo: University of Toronto Press, 2018.

Borrows, John. *Freedom and Indigenous Constitutionalism*. Toronto: University of Toronto Press, 2016.

Borrows, John. "The Great Way of Decision Making: Constituting Indigenous Law with John Borrows." April 21, 2020, in *RAVEN (De)Briefs*, produced by Susan Smitten and RAVEN Trust, podcast.

Borrows, John. *Law's Indigenous Ethics*. Toronto: University of Toronto Press, 2019.

Borrows, John. *Recovering Canada: The Resurgence of Indigenous Law*. Toronto/Buffalo: University of Toronto Press, 2002.

Börzel, Tanja and Michael Zürn. "Contestations of the Liberal International Order: From Liberal Multilateralism to Postnational Liberalism." *International Organization* 75, no. 2 (2021): 282–305.

Boyd, Marion. *Dispute Resolution in Family Law: Protecting Choice, Promoting Inclusion.* Report Prepared for the Ministry of the Attorney General of Ontario. December 2004.

Bradley, Quintin. "Bringing Democracy Back Home: Community Localism and the Domestication of Political Space." *Environment and Planning D: Society and Space* 32, no. 4 (2014): 642–57.

Brady, Jeff. "2 Years After Standing Rock Protests, Tensions Remain but Oil Business Booms." *NPR*, November 29, 2018. www.npr.org/2018/11/29/671701019/2-years-after-standing-rock-protests-north-dakota-oil-business-is-booming.

Brandom, Robert B. *From Empiricism to Expressivism: Brandom Reads Sellars.* Cambridge, MA: Harvard University Press, 2015.

Brandom, Robert B. "Reason, Genealogy, and the Hermeneutics of Magnanimity." Howison Lecture in Philosophy, University of California, Berkeley, CA, March 13, 2013. https://gradlectures.berkeley.edu/lecture/magnanimity.

Brandom, Robert B. *A Spirit of Trust: A Reading of Hegel's Phenomenology.* Cambridge, MA: Harvard University Press, 2019.

Briggs, John. "Reembodying, Human Consciousness in the Earth." *Consciousness: Ideas for the Twenty-First Century* 2, no. 2 (2016): 1–23.

Brown, Lester R. *World on the Edge: How to Prevent Environmental and Economic Collapse.* New York: Norton, 2011.

Brown, Wendy. *Edgework.* Princeton, NJ: Princeton, 2005.

Brown, Wendy. *In the Ruins of Neoliberalism: The Rise of Antidemocratic Politics in the West.* New York: Columbia University Press, 2019.

Brown, Wendy. *Undoing the Demos: Neoliberalism's Stealth Revolution.* New York: Zone Books, 2015.

Brown, Wendy. *Walled States, Waning Sovereignty.* Princeton, NJ: Princeton University Press, 2010.

Brown-Scott, Wendy. "Race Consciousness in Higher Education: Does 'Sound Educational Policy' Support the Continued Existence of Historically Black Colleges?" *Emory Law Journal* 43, no. 1 (1994): 1–81.

Brubaker, Rogers. "Populism and Nationalism." *Nations and Nationalism* 26, no. 1 (2020): 44–66.

Brunnée, Jutta and Stephen J. Toope. "Constructivism and International Law." In *Interdisciplinary Perspectives on International Law and International Relations: The State of the Art*, edited by Jeffrey L. Dunoff and Mark A. Pollack, 119–45. Cambridge: Cambridge University Press, 2012.

Brunnée, Jutta and Stephen J. Toope. *Legitimacy and Legality in International Law: An International Account.* Cambridge: Cambridge University Press, 2010.

Burke, Edmund. *Reflections on the Revolution in France.* New Haven: Yale University Press, 2003.

Butler, Judith. *The Force of Nonviolence.* London: Verso, 2020.

Butler, Judith. *Notes Toward a Performative Theory of Assembly.* Cambridge, MA: Harvard University Press, 2015.

Byers, Michael. "Policing the High Seas: The Proliferation Security Initiative." *The American Journal of International Law* 98 (2004): 526–45.

Byrd, Jodi A., Alyosha Goldstein, Jodi Melamed, and Chandan Reddy. "Predatory Value: Economies of Dispossession and Disturbed Relationalities." *Social Text* 36, no. 2 (2018): 1–18.

Caiani, Manuela and Patricia Kroll. "Nationalism and Populism in Radical Right Discourses in Italy and Germany." *Javnost: The Public* 24 (2017): 336–54.

Canovan, Margaret. "Taking Politics to the People: Populism as the Ideology of Democracy." In *Democracies and the Populist Challenge*, edited by Yves Mény and Yves Surel, 25–44. London: Palgrave Macmillan, 2002.

Canovan, Margaret. "Trust the People! Populism and the Two Faces of Democracy." *Political Studies* 47, no. 1 (1999): 2–16.

Capra, Fritjof. *The Hidden Connections: A Science for Sustainable Living*. New York: Anchor, 2002.

Capra, Fritjof and Pier Luigi Luisi. *The Systems View of Life: A Unifying Vision*. Cambridge: Cambridge University Press, 2015.

Cardinal, Harold and Walter Hildebrandt. *Treaty Elders of Saskatchewan: Our Dream Is That Our Peoples Will One Day Be Clearly Recognized as Nations*. Calgary: University of Calgary Press, 2013.

Carroll, William K. "Hegemony, Counter-Hegemony, Anti-Hegemony." *Journal of the Society for Socialist Studies* 3 (2006): 9–43.

Case 11/70, *Internationale Handelsgesellschaft mbH v. Einfuhr- und Vorratsstelle für Getreide und Futtermittel* [1970] ECR 1125.

Case 216/18, *Minister for Justice and Equality v. LM* [2018] ECLI:EU:C:2018: 586.

Case 6/64, *Costa v. ENEL* [1964] ECR 585.

Castoriadis, Cornelius. "Does the Idea of Revolution Still Make Sense?" *Thesis Eleven* 26 (1990): 123–38.

Castoriadis, Cornelius. "Power, Politics, Autonomy." In *Philosophy, Politics, Autonomy*, 143–74. New York: Oxford University Press, 1991.

Castoriadis, Cornelius. "The Proletarian Revolution Against the Bureaucracy." In *Political and Social Writings*, vol. 2, *1955–1960*, edited and translated by David Ames Curtis, 57–89. Minneapolis: University of Minnesota Press, 1988.

Castoriadis, Cornelius. "The Revolutionary Exigency," in *Political and Social Writings*, vol. 3, *1961–1979*, edited and translated by David Ames Curtis, 227–49. Minneapolis: University of Minnesota Press, 1993.

CBC News. "Ministers Answer Questions on Trans Mountain Expansion Approval." Streamed live on June 18, 2019. YouTube video, 26: 24. https://www.youtube.com /watch?v=nQjdlnxtPzE.

CBC News. "Trudeau Cabinet Approves Trans Mountain Pipeline Expansion Project." Streamed live on June 18, 2019. YouTube video, 20: 17. www.youtube.com/watch? v=MFot-hZRhEk.

Celikates, Robin. "Constituent Power Beyond Exceptionalism: Irregular Migration, Disobedience, and (Re-)Constitution." *Journal of International Political Theory* 15, no. 1 (2019): 67–81.

Celikates, Robin. "Die Negativität der Revolution: Selbstreflexivität und Selbstbegrenzung jenseits des Liberalismus." In *Negativität: Kunst, Recht, Politik*, edited by Thomas Khurana, Dirk Quadflieg, Francesca Raimondi, Juliane Rebentisch, and Dirk Setton, 329–40. Berlin: Suhrkamp, 2018.

Celikates, Robin. "Learning from the Streets: Civil Disobedience in Theory and Practice." In *Global Activism: Art and Conflict in the 21st Century*, edited by Peter Weibel, 65–72. Cambridge, MA: MIT Press, 2015.

Celikates, Robin. "Radical Democratic Disobedience." In *Cambridge Companion to Civil Disobedience*, edited by William Scheuerman, 128–52. Cambridge: Cambridge University Press, 2021.

Césaire, Aimé. *Discourse on Colonialism*. New York; Monthly Review Press, 2000.

Chang, David A. *The World and All the Things Upon It: Native Hawaiian Geographies of Exploration*. Minneapolis: University of Minnesota, 2016.

Chayes, Abram and Antonia Handler Chayes. *The New Sovereignty: Compliance with International Regulatory Agreements*. Cambridge, MA: Harvard University Press, 1995.

Cherry, Keith. "Practices of Pluralism: A Comparative Analysis of Trans-Systemic Relationships in Europe and on Turtle Island." Unpublished PhD thesis, University of Victoria, 2020.

Chippewas of Sarnia Band v. Attorney General of Canada [2000] 51 OR (3d) 641.

Chowdhry, Geeta. "Edward Said and Contrapuntal Reading: Implications for Critical Interventions in International Relations." *Millennium* 36, no. 1 (2007): 101–16.

Christie, Gordon. *Canadian Law and Indigenous Self-Determination: A Naturalist Analysis*. Toronto: University of Toronto Press, 2019.

Cissé, Madjiguène. *Parole de sans-papiers*. Paris: La Dispute, 1999.

Clarkson, Stephen. *The Big Red Machine: How the Liberal Party Dominates Canadian Politics*. Vancouver: UBC Press, 2005.

Clifford, Robert YELKÁTTE. "W̱SÁNEĆ Legal Theory and the Fuel Spill at SELEKTEȽ (Goldstream River)." *McGill Law Journal* 16, no. 4 (2016): 755–93.

Clinton, Robert N. "There Is No Supremacy Clause for Indian Tribes." *Arizona State Law Journal* 34, no. 1 (2002): 113–260.

Cochran, Patricia. "Physical Legal Methodology." In "John Borrows' *Freedom and Indigenous Constitutionalism*: Critical Engagements," edited by Freya Kodar. *Lakehead Law Journal* 3, no. 2 (2019): 107–10.

Cocks, Joan. "A New Cosmopolitanism? V. S. Naipaul and Edward Said." *Constellations* 7, no. 1 (2000): 46–63.

Cohen, Jean L. *Globalization and Sovereignty: Rethinking Legality, Legitimacy, and Constitutionalism*. Cambridge: Cambridge University Press, 2012.

Cohen, Jean L., and Andrew Arato. *Civil Society and Political Theory*. Cambridge, MA: MIT Press, 1992.

Commoner, Barry. *The Closing Circle: Nature, Man, and Technology*. New York: Knopf, 1971.

Conference on Indigenous Law in Coast Salish Traditions, organized jointly by Cowichan Tribes, Research Group on Indigenous Peoples and Governance, Pierre Elliott Trudeau Foundation, University of Victoria Faculty of Law, and the Consortium for Democratic Constitutionalism (Demcon). October 14–16, 2010.

Connolly, William. *Aspirational Fascism: The Struggle for Multifaceted Democracy Under Trumpism*. Minneapolis, MN: University of Minnesota, 2017.

Constitution Act, 1867, RSC 1985, Appendix II, No. 5.

Conway, Janet and Jakeet Singh. "Radical Democracy in Global Perspective: Notes from the Pluriverse." *Third World Quarterly* 32, no. 4 (2011): 689–706.

Coulthard, Glen S. "For Our Nations to Live, Capitalism Must Die." *Unsettling America* (blog), November 5, 2013. https://unsettlingamerica.wordpress.com/2013/11/05/for-our-nations-to-live-capitalism-must-die.

Coulthard, Glen Sean. *Red Skin, White Masks: Rejecting the Colonial Politics of Recognition.* Minneapolis: University of Minnesota Press, 2014.

Coulthard, Glen Sean. "Response." *Historical Materialism: Research in Critical Marxist Theory* 24, no. 3 (2016): 92–103.

Coulthard, Glen and Leanne Betasamosake Simpson. "Grounded Normativity / Place-Based Solidarity." *American Quarterly* 68, no. 2 (2016): 249–55. https://doi.org/10.1353/aq.2016.0038.

Craft, Aimee. *Breathing Life into the Stone Fort Treaty: An Anishnabe Understanding of Treaty One.* Vancouver: UBC Press, 2013.

Craig, Paul. "The ECJ, National Courts and the Supremacy of Community Law." In *The European Constitution in the Making*, edited by Ingolf Pernice and Roberto Miccu, 35–52. Bade-Baden: Nomos, 2004.

Craig, Paul and Gráinne de Búrca. *EU Law: Text, Cases, and Materials.* 5th ed. Oxford: Oxford University Press, 2011.

Crum, Ben and John Erik Fossum. "The Multilevel Parliamentary Field: A Framework for Theorizing Representative Democracy in the EU." *European Political Science Review* 1, no. 2 (2009): 249–71.

Çubukçu, Ayça. "Of Rebels and Disobedients: Reflections on Arendt, Race, Lawbreaking." *Law and Critique* 32 (2021): 33–50.

Dallmayr, Frederick. "The Politics of Nonidentity: Adorno, Postmodernism – And Edward Said." *Political Theory* 25, no. 1 (1997): 33–56.

Dalton, Dennis. *Mahatma Gandhi: Nonviolent Power in Action.* New York: Columbia University Press, 2012.

Daly, Herman B. and John B. Cobb Jr. *For the Common Good: Redirecting the Economy Toward Community, the Environment and a Sustainable Future.* Boston: Beacon Press, 1994.

Daly, Richard. *Our Box Was Full: An Ethnography for the Delgamuukw Plaintiffs.* Vancouver: UBC Press, 2005.

Dardot, Pierre and Christian Laval. *L'ombre d'octobre: La révolution russe et le spectre des soviets.* Montreal: Lux, 2017.

Davidson, Donald. "Radical Interpretation." *Dialectica* 27 (1973): 313–28.

Davidson, Robert. "Untitled Document." In Robert Davidson, Peter L. Macnair, and Derek Simpkins Gallery of Tribal Art. *Robert Davidson Exhibition: A Voice from Inside*, 1–3. Vancouver: Derek Simpson Gallery of Tribal Art, 1992.

Davis, Mike. *Old Gods New Enigmas: Marx's Lost Theory.* London: Verso, 2020.

Day, Richard. *Gramsci Is Dead: Anarchist Currents in the Newest Social Movements.* London: Pluto Press, 2005.

Dean, Jodi. *Crowds and Party.* London: Verso, 2016.

de Búrca, Gráinne, Robert O. Keohane, and Charles F. Sabel. "New Modes of Pluralist Global Governance." *New York University Journal of International Law & Politics* 45 (2013): 723–86.

De Cleen, Benjamin. "Populism and Nationalism." in *The Oxford Handbook of Populism*, edited by Cristóbal Rovira Kaltwasser, Paul A. Taggart, Paulina Ochoa Espejo, and Pierre Ostiguy, 342–62. Oxford: Oxford University Press, 2017.

De Cleen, Benjamin and Yannis Stavrakakis. "Distinctions and Articulations: A Discourse Theoretical Framework for the Study of Populism and Nationalism." *Javnost: The Public* 24, no. 4 (2017): 301–19.

Dedek, Helge and Shauna Van Praagh, eds. *Stateless Law: Evolving Boundaries of a Discipline.* New York: Routledge, 2015.

de Genova, Nicholas. "Rebordering 'The People': Notes on Theorizing Populism." *South Atlantic Quarterly* 117, no. 2 (2018): 357–74.

Delgamuukw transcripts. https://open.library.ubc.ca/collections/delgamuukw.

Delgamuukw v. British Columbia [1997] 3 SCR 1010.

della Porta, Donatella. *Can Democracy Be Saved? Participation, Deliberation and Social Movements.* Malden, MA: Polity Press, 2013.

della Porta, Donatella and Gianni Piazza. "Local Contention, Global Framing: The Protest Campaigns Against the TAV in Val di Susa and the Bridge on the Messina Straits." *Environmental Politics* 16, no. 5 (2007): 864–82.

Deloria, Vine, Jr. *Red Earth, White Lies: Native Americans and the Myth of Scientific Fact.* Golden, CO: Fulcrum Pub, 1997.

Deming, Barbara. "On Revolution and Equilibrium." In *Revolution and Equilibrium*, 194–221. New York: Grossman Publishers, 1971.

Democratizing Work. "Work, Democratize, Decommodify, Remediate." *Global Forum on Democratizing Work*, October 5–7, 2021. https://democratizingwork.org.

Derrida, Jacques. *The Animal That Therefore I Am (More to Follow).* New York: Fordham University Press, 2008.

Derrida, Jacques. *Aporias.* Stanford: Stanford University Press, 1993.

Derrida, Jacques. *Rogues: Two Essays on Reason* Stanford: Stanford University Press, 2005.

Derrida, Jacques. *Specters of Marx: The State of the Debt, the Work of Mourning and the New International.* New York: Routledge, 1993.

Deur (Moxmowisa), Douglas, Kim Recalama-Clutsei (Oqwilawagwa), and William White (Kasalid/Xelimulh). "The Teachings of Chief Kwaxsistalla Adam Dick and the Atla'gimma ('Spirit of the Forest') Dance." In *Plants, Peoples, and Places: The Roles of Ethnobotany and Ethnoecology in Indigenous Peoples' Land Rights in Canada and Beyond*, xvii–xxiv, edited by Nancy J. Turner. Montreal: McGill-Queens University Press, 2020.

Dhillon, Jaskiran. *Prairie Rising: Indigenous Youth, Decolonization, and the Politics of Intervention.* Toronto: University of Toronto Press, 2017.

Dilworth, Charles. *Too Smart for Our Own Good: The Ecological Predicament of Humankind.* Cambridge: Cambridge University Press, 2012.

Disch, Lisa, Mathijs van de Sande, and Nadia Urbinati. *The Constructivist Turn in Political Representation.* Edinburgh: Edinburgh University Press, 2019.

Donahue, Thomas J., and Paulina Ochoa Espejo. "The Analytical-Continental Divide: Styles of Dealing with Problems." *European Journal of Political Theory* 15, no. 2 (2016): 138–54.

Duff, Wilson, ed. *Histories, Territories, and Law of the Kitwancool.* Victoria: British Columbia Provincial Museum, 1959.

Dunn, Adam, and David Owen. "Instituting Citizenship." In *On Global Citizenship: James Tully in Dialogue*, edited by James Tully. London: Bloomsbury, 2014, 247–65.

Duprey, John. *New York Daily News*, April 1959.

Dupuis-Déri, Francis. *Démocratie. Histoire politique d'un mot: Aux États-Unis et en France*. Québec: Lux Éditeur, 2013.

Duvall, Raymond and Latha Varadarajan. "Travelling in Paradox: Edward Said and Critical International Relations." *Millennium* 36, no. 1 (2007): 83–99.

Dyzenhaus, David. "The Genealogy of Legal Positivism." *Oxford Journal of Legal Studies* 24, no. 1 (2004): 39–67.

Dyzenhaus, David. "The Inevitable Social Contract." *Res Publica* 27 (2021): 187–202. https://doi.org/10.1007/s11158-020-09467-z.

Dyzenhaus, David. "Process and Substance as Aspects of the Public Law Form." *Cambridge Law Journal* 74, no. 2 (2015): 284–306.

Eatwell, Roger and Matthew Goodwin. *National Populism: The Revolt Against Liberal Democracy*. London: Penguin UK, 2018.

Eisenstein, Charles. *The More Beautiful World Our Hearts Know Is Possible*. California: North Atlantic Books, 2013.

Emerson, Ralph Waldo. *Collected Works of Ralph Waldo Emerson, vol. 7, Society and Solitude*, edited by Alfred R. Ferguson, Jean Ferguson Carr, and Douglas Emery Wilson. Charlottesville, VA: InteLex Corporation, 2008.

Engels, Friedrich. "On Authority." In *The Marx-Engels Reader*, edited by Robert C. Tucker, 730–3. New York: Norton, 1978.

Engler, Mark and Paul Engler. *This Is an Uprising: How Nonviolent Revolt Is Shaping the Twenty-First Century*. New York: Nation Books, 2016.

Estes, Nick. *Our History Is the Future: Standing Rock versus the Dakota Access Pipeline, the Long Tradition of Indigenous Resistance*. London: Verso, 2019.

Estes, Nick and Jaskiran Dhillon, eds. *Standing with Standing Rock: Voices from the #NoDAPL Movement*. Minneapolis: University of Minnesota Press, 2019.

EUCAnet. www.eucanet.org.

European Commission. "Six-Pack? Two-Pack? Fiscal Compact? A Short Guide to the New EU Fiscal Governance." https://fotavgeia.blogspot.com/2016/04/six-pack-two-pack-fiscal-compact-short.html.

European Commission. "The Stability and Growth Pact." EU Economic Governance. http://ec.europa.eu/economy_finance/economic_governance/sgp/index_en.htm.

Fassin, Didier. "From Right to Favor: The Refugee Question as Moral Crisis." *The Nation*, April 5, 2016. www.thenation.com/article/archive/from-right-to-favor/.

Federici, Silvia Beatriz. *Caliban and the Witch*. 2nd revised ed. New York: Autonomedia, 2014.

Ferreras, Isabelle, Julie Battilana, Dominique Méda, and 3,000 others. "Democratizing Work." *Il Manifesto*, May 15, 2020. https://global.ilmanifesto.it/democratizing-work.

Fierke, Karin M. and Vivienne Jabri. "Global Conversations: Relationality, Embodiment and Power in the Move Towards a Global IR." *Global Constitutionalism* 8, no. 3 (2019): 506–35.

Finnemore, Martha and Kathryn Sikkink. "International Norm Dynamics and Political Change." *International Organization* 52 (1998): 887–917.

Finnemore, Martha and Stephen J. Toope, "Alternatives to 'Legalization': Richer Views of Law and Politics." *International Organization* 55 (2001): 743–58.

Fish, Stanley. "Boutique Multiculturalism, or Why Liberals Are Incapable of Thinking about Hate Speech." *Critical Inquiry* 23, no. 2 (1997): 378–95.

Fitzi, Gregor Juergen Mackert, and Bryan S. Turner, eds. *Populism and the Crisis of Democracy, vol. 3, Migration, Gender and Religion*. New York: Routledge, 2018.

Flammarion, Camille. *L'atmosphère: Météorologie populaire*. Paris, 1888.

Foa, Roberto Stefan, Andrew Klassen, Daniella Wenger, Alex Rand, and Michael Slade. "Youth and Satisfaction with Democracy: Reversing the Democratic Disconnect?" Cambridge, UK: Centre for the Future of Democracy, 2020. www.cam.ac.uk/system/files/youth_and_satisfaction_with_democracy.pdf.

Fontaine, Jerry. *Our Hearts Are as One Fire: An Ojibway-Anishinabe Vision for the Future*. Vancouver: UBC Press, 2020.

Forbes, Jack D. *Columbus and Other Cannibals: The Wétiko Disease of Exploitation, Imperialism, and Terrorism*. New York: Seven Stories Press, 2008.

Ford, Lisa. *Settler Sovereignty: Jurisdiction and Indigenous People in America and Australia, 1788–1836*. Cambridge, MA: Harvard University Press, 2010.

Forman, Fonna. *Adam Smith and the Circles of Sympathy: Cosmopolitanism and Moral Theory*. Cambridge: Cambridge University Press, 2010.

Forman, Fonna. "Social Norms and the Cross-Border Citizen: From Adam Smith to Antanas Mockus." In *Cultural Agents Reloaded: The Legacy of Antanas Mockus*, edited by Carlo Tognato, 333–56. Cambridge, MA: Harvard University Press, 2018.

Forman, Fonna and Teddy Cruz. "Access All Areas: The Porosity of a Hostile Border." *Architectural Review*, May 27, 2019. www.architectural-review.com/essays/access-all-areas-the-porosity-of-a-hostile-border.

Forman, Fonna and Teddy Cruz. "Changing Practice: Engaging Informal Public Demands." In *Informal Markets Worlds – Reader: The Architecture of Economic Pressure*, edited by Helge Mooshammer, Peter Mörtenböck, Teddy Cruz, and Fonna Forman, 203–23. Rotterdam: naio10 Publishers, 2015.

Forman, Fonna and Teddy Cruz. "Citizenship Culture and the Transnational Environmental Commons." In *Nature's Nation: American Art and Environment*, edited by Karl Kusserow and Alan Braddock, 416–27. New Haven: Yale University Press, 2018.

Forman, Fonna and Teddy Cruz. "Critical Proximities at the Border: Redistributing Knowledges Across Walls." In *Spatial Practices: Modes of Action and Engagement in the City*, edited by Melanie Dodd, 189–201. London: Routledge, 2020.

Forman, Fonna and Teddy Cruz. "Global Justice at the Municipal Scale: The Case of Medellín, Colombia." In *Institutional Cosmopolitanism*, edited by Luis Cabrera, 189–215. New York: Oxford University Press, 2018.

Forman, Fonna and Teddy Cruz. "Interdependence as a Political Tool: Three Building Blocks for Gaza." In *Open Gaza: Architectures of Hope*, edited by Michael Sorkin and Deen Sharp, 302–25. New York: American University in Cairo Press, 2020.

Forman, Fonna and Teddy Cruz. "Latin America and a New Political Leadership: Experimental Acts of Co-Existence." In *Public Servants: Art and the Crisis of the Common Good*, edited by Johanna Burton, Shannon Jackson, and Dominic Wilsdon, 71–90. Boston: MIT Press, 2016.

Forman, Fonna and Teddy Cruz. *Unwalling Citizenship: The Political Equator*. London: Verso, forthcoming.

Forman, Fonna and Teddy Cruz. "The Wall: The San Diego–Tijuana Border." *Artforum* 54, no. 10 (2016): 370–5.

Forman, Fonna and Veerabhadran Ramanathan. "Climate Change and Mass Migration: A Probabilistic Case for Urgent Action." In *Humanitarianism and Mass Migration: Confronting the World Crisis*, edited by Marcelo M. Suárez-Orozco, 239–50. Berkeley: University of California Press, 2019.

Fossum, John Erik and Augustín José Menéndez, eds. *The European Union in Crises or the European Union as Crises? ARENA Report No 2.* Oslo: ARENA Centre for European Studies, 2014.

Foucault, Michel. *Hermeneutics of the Subject.* New York: Palgrave MacMillan, 2001.

Francis, Daniel. *The Imaginary Indian: The Image of the Indian in Canadian Culture.* 2nd ed. Vancouver: Arsenal Pulp Press, 2011.

Fraser, Nancy. "A New Form of Capitalism? A Reply to Boltanski and Esquerre." *New Left Review* 106 (2017): 57–65.

Fraser, Nancy. "Recognition without Ethics?" *Theory, Culture & Society* 18, nos. 2–3 (2001): 21–42.

Freire, Paulo. *Pedagogy of the Oppressed.* London: Penguin Books, 2017.

Frickey, Philip P. "Domesticating Federal Indian Law." *Minnesota Law Review* 81, no. 1 (1996): 31–95.

Frickey, Philp P. "Marshalling Past and Present: Colonialism, Constitutionalism, and Interpretation in Federal Indian Law." *Harvard Law Review* 107 (1993): 381–440.

Friedland, Hadley. *The Wetiko (Windigo) Legal Principles: Cree and Anishinabek Responses to Violence and Victimization.* Toronto: University of Toronto Press, 2018.

Friedland, Hadley and Val Napoleon. "Gathering the Threads: Indigenous Legal Methodology." *Lakehead Law Journal* 33, no. 1 (2015): 17–44.

Friedland, Hadley and Val Napoleon. "An Inside Job: Engaging with Indigenous Legal Traditions through Stories." *McGill Law Journal* 61, no. 4 (2016): 725–54.

Friedland, Lewis A. "Communication, Community, and Democracy: Toward a Theory of the Communicatively-Integrated Community." *Communication Research* 28, no. 4 (2001): 358–91.

Fromm, Eric. *The Anatomy of Human Destructiveness.* New York: Henry Holt and Company, 1973.

Fung, Archon and Eric Olin Wright. "Deepening Democracy: Innovations in Empowered Participatory Governance." *Politics & Society* 29, no. 1 (2001): 5–41.

Gago, Verónica. *Feminist International: How to Change Everything.* London: Verso, 2020.

Gallie, Bryce W. "Essentially Contested Concepts." *Proceedings of the Aristotelian Society* 56 (1955–56): 167–98.

Gane, Nicholas. "The Governmentalities of Neoliberalism: Panopticism, Post-Panopticism, and Beyond." *The Sociological Review* 60 (2012): 611–34.

Gaudry, Adam. "Researching the Resurgence: Insurgent Research and Community-Engaged Methodologies in 21st-Century Academic Inquiry." In *Research as Resistance: Revisiting Critical, Indigenous, and Anti-Oppressive Approaches,* edited by Leslie Allison Brown and Susan Strega, 243–65. 2nd ed. Toronto: Canadian Scholars' Press, 2015.

Geddes, Patrick. *Cities in Evolution: An Introduction to the Town Planning Movement and to the Study of Civics.* London: Williams, 1915.

Getachew, Adom. *Worldmaking After Empire: The Rise and Fall of Self-Determination.* Princeton, NJ: Princeton University Press, 2019.

Gitanyow Hereditary Chiefs Office. "An Indigenous Approach to Sustainability Assessment: Written Submission on 'The Environmental and Regulatory Reviews Discussion Paper, June 2017'." October 13, 2017. https://letstalkimpactassessment.ca/8869/widgets/34212/documents/16910.

Goldsmith, Edward. *The Way: An Ecological World-View*. Athens: University of Georgia Press, 1998.

Goldsmith, Jack. "Liberal Democracy and Cosmopolitan Duty." *Stanford Law Review* 55, no. 5 (2003): 1667–96.

Goodin, Robert. "Enfranchising All Affected Interests, and Its Alternatives." *Philosophy and Public Affairs* 35 (2007): 40–68.

Goodman, Nelson. *Ways of Worldmaking*. Indianapolis: Hackett, 1978.

Gray, Laura. "Trans Mountain 1953: Public Response in Alberta and British Columbia." Unpublished MA thesis, University of Victoria, 2019.

Green, Alex V. "Canada is Fake: What Americans Think of as Their Friendly Neighbor to the North, If They Think of It at All, Is a Scam." *The Outline*, February 19, 2020. https://theoutline.com/post/8686/canada-is-fake.

Gregg, Richard Bartlett. *The Power of Nonviolence*. Edited by James Tully. Cambridge: Cambridge University Press, 2018.

Gribbin, John and Mary Gribbin, *He Knew He Was Right: The Irrepressible Life of James Lovelock*. London: Penguin Books, 2009.

Griffin, James M. "Petro-Nationalism: The Futile Search for Oil Security." *The Energy Journal* 36, no. 1 (2015): 25–41.

Haida Nation and Her Majesty the Queen in Right of the Province of British Columbia. "Kunst'aa Guu–Kunst'aayah Reconciliation Protocol." December 11, 2009. www .llbc.leg.bc.ca/public/pubdocs/bcdocs2010/462194/haida_reconciliation_protocol.pdf .

Hale, Thomas and David Held. *Beyond Gridlock*. Cambridge: Polity Press, 2017.

Hale, Thomas, David Held, and Kevin Young. *Gridlock: Why Global Cooperation Is Failing When We Need It Most*. Cambridge: Polity Press, 2013.

Hall, Stuart. "The Great Moving Right Show." *Marxism Today*, January 1979, 14–20.

Hall, Stuart. "Signification, Representation, Ideology: Althusser and the Post-Structuralist Debates." *Critical Studies in Mass Communication* 2 (1985): 91–114.

Hallenbeck, Jessica, Mike Krebs, Sarah Hunt, et al. "Red Skin, White Masks: Rejecting the Colonial Politics of Recognition." *The AAG Review of Books* 4, no. 2 (2016): 111–20. https://doi.org/10.1080/2325548X.2016.1146013.

Hamilton, Alexander, James Madison, and John Jay. *The Federalist Papers*. New York: Penguin Books, 1961.

Hansen-Magnusson, Hannes, Antje Vetterlein, and Antje Wiener. "The Problem of Non-Compliance: Knowledge Gaps and Moments of Contestation in Global Governance." *Journal of International Relations and Development* 23 (2018): 636–56.

Haraway, Donna. *Staying with the Trouble: Making Kin in the Chthulucene*. Durham, NC: Duke University Press, 2016.

Hardiman, David. *Gandhi in His Times and Ours: The Global Legacy of His Ideas*. New York: Columbia University Press, 2003.

Harding, Stephen. *Animate Earth: Science, Intuition and Gaia*. 2nd ed. Cambridge: Green Books, 2013.

Hardt, Michael and Sandro Mezzadra, eds. "October! The Soviet Centenary." Special issue, *South Atlantic Quarterly* 116, no. 4 (2017).

Harris, Cole. *Making Native Space: Colonialism, Resistance, and Reserves in British Columbia*. Canadian Studies Series. Vancouver: UBC Press, 2002.

Harris, Douglas C. *Fish, Law, and Colonialism: The Legal Capture of Salmon in British Columbia.* Toronto: University of Toronto Press, 2001. https://doi.org/10.3138/9781442674912.

Hart, H. L. A. *The Concept of Law.* 2nd ed. Oxford: Oxford University Press, 1994.

Havercroft, Jonathan. "Social Constructivism and International Ethics." In *Routledge Handbook on Ethics and International Relations*, edited by Brent Steele and Eric Heinze, 116–29. London: Routledge, 2018.

Hayden, Patrick. *Cosmopolitan Global Politics.* London: Routledge, 2017.

Hegel, Georg Wilhelm Friedrich. *Elements of the Philosophy of Right*, edited by Allen W. Wood, translated by H. B. Nisbet. Cambridge: Cambridge University Press, 1991.

Held, David. "The Changing Contours of Political Community: Rethinking Democracy in the Context of Globalisation." *Theoria: A Journal of Social and Political Theory* 94 (1999): 30–47.

Held, David. *Democracy and the Global Order.* San Francisco, CA: Stanford University Press, 1995.

Held, David. "Direct Democracy and the End of Politics." In *Models of Democracy.* 3rd ed. Cambridge: Polity Press, 2006, 96–123.

Held, David. *Models of Democracy.* 3rd ed. Cambridge: Polity Press, 2006.

Heller, Patrick. "Moving the State: The Politics of Democratic Decentralization in Kerala, South Africa, and Porto Alegre." *Politics & Society* 29, no. 1 (2001): 131–63.

Henderson, James Youngblood. "Empowering Treaty Federalism." *Saskatchewan Law Review* 58, no. 1 (1994): 241–329.

Henriksen, Lars Skov, Kristen Strømsnes, and Lars Svedberg. "Understanding Civic Engagement in the Scandinavian Context." In *Civic Engagement in Scandinavia: Volunteering, Informal Help and Giving in Denmark, Norway and Sweden Models of Democracy*, edited by Lars Skov Henrikson, Kristen Strømsnes, and Lars Svedberg, 1–31. Cham: Springer, 2019.

Hill, Susan M. *The Clay We Are Made Of: Haudenosaunee Land Tenure on the Grand River.* Winnipeg: University of Manitoba Press, 2017.

Hirschman, Albert. *Crossing Boundaries: Selected Writings.* New York: Zone Books, 1998.

Hirschman, Albert. *Getting Ahead Collectively: Grassroots Experiences in Latin America.* Oxford: Pergamon, 1984.

Hirschman, Albert O. *The Rhetoric of Reaction: Perversity, Futility, Jeopardy.* Cambridge, MA: Harvard University Press, 1991.

hooks, bell. "Choosing the Margin as a Space of Radical Openness." *Framework: The Journal of Cinema and Media* 36 (1989): 15–23.

Howe, Miles and Jeffrey Monaghan. "Strategic Incapacitation of Indigenous Dissent: Crowd Theories, Risk Management, and Settler Colonial Policing." *Canadian Journal of Sociology* 43, no. 4 (2018): 325–48.

Hunt, Sarah. "Justice at the Shoreline: Rethinking Sovereignty through Coastal Wisdom." Landsdowne Lecture, University of Victoria, Victoria, BC, March 8, 2018.

Hunt, Sarah. "Witnessing the Colonialscape: Lighting the Intimate Fires of Indigenous Legal Pluralism." Unpublished PhD Thesis, Simon Fraser University, 2014. http://summit.sfu.ca/item/14145.

Hunter, Daniel. *Climate Resistance Handbook.* Boston: Daniel Hunter and 350.org, 2019. https://trainings.350.org/climate-resistance-handbook.

Huxley, Aldous. *Ends and Means.* Oxford: Oxford University Press, 1946.

Ignatieff, Michael. "Human Rights, Global Ethics, and the Ordinary Virtues." *Ethics & International Affairs* 31(2016): 3–16.

Ikenberry, John. "The Next Liberal Order: The Age of Contagion Demands More Internationalism, Not Less." *Foreign Affairs* 99, no. 4 (2020): 133–43.

Ikenberry, John. "The Plot Against American Foreign Policy." *Foreign Affairs* 96, no. 3 (2017): 2–9.

Indian Act, RSC 1985, c. I-5.

Innes, Robert Alexander. *Elder Brother and the Law of the People: Contemporary Kinship and Cowessess First Nation*. Winnipeg: University of Manitoba, 2013.

International Geosphere-Biosphere Programme. "The Great Acceleration." www.igbp.net/globalchange/greatacceleration.4.1b8ae20512db692f2a680001630.html.

Ip, Stephanie and Patrick Johnston. "Kinder Morgan Halts Non-Essential Work on Trans Mountain Pipeline and Sets Drop-Dead Deadline." *Vancouver Sun*, April 9, 2018. https://vancouversun.com/news/local-news/kinder-morgan-to-halt-its-spending-on-trans-mountain-pipeline-due-to-b-c-opposition.

Isaac, Jeffrey. "It's Happening Here and Now: Thoughts on the Recent Immigration Detentions and William E. Connolly's 'Aspirational Fascism'." *Public Seminar*, June 25, 2018. www.publicseminar.org/2018/06/its-happening-here-and-now.

Jago, Robert. "Canada's Hollow Concern for First Nations Democracy." *The Walrus*, July 19, 2019. https://thewalrus.ca/canadas-hollow-concern-for-first-nations-democracy.

Jobin, Shalene, Hadley Friedland, Renee Beausoleil, and Tara Kappo. "Wahkohtowin ◁ꞈᗡᐞᑊᗡ: Principles, Process, and Pedagogy." *Canadian Legal Education Annual Review* 9 (2021): 75.

Johnson v. M'Intosh, 21 US (8 Wheat.) 543 (1823).

Jones, Carwyn. "A Māori Constitutional Tradition." *New Zealand Journal of Public and International Law* 12, no. 1 (2014): 187–203.

Kant, Immanuel. *Political Writings*, edited by Hans Reiss, translated by H. B. Nisbet. New York: Cambridge University Press, 1991.

Kapoor, Ilan. "Deliberative Democracy or Agonistic Pluralism? The Relevance of the Habermas-Mouffe Debate for Third World Politics." *Alternatives* 27, no.4 (2002): 459–87.

Karakayalı, Serhat and Özge Yaka. "The Spirit of Gezi: The Recomposition of Political Subjectivities in Turkey." *New Formations* 83 (2014): 117–38.

Karmis, Dimitri and Jocelyn Maclure, eds. *Civic Freedom in an Age of Diversity: The Public Philosophy of James Tully*. Montreal: McGill-Queen's University Press, forthcoming.

Karuka, Manu. *Empire's Tracks: Indigenous Nations, Chinese Workers, and the Transcontinental Railroad*. Oakland: University of California Press, 2019.

Kasparek, Bernd and Marc Speer. "Of Hope: Hungary and the Long Summer of Migration," translated by Elena Buck. *bordermonitoring.eu*, September 9, 2015. http://bordermonitoring.eu/ungarn/2015/09/of-hope-en.

Kay, Jonathan. "The Rise and (Possible) Fall of Justin Trudeau Show the Perils of Woke Governance." *Quillette*, March 7, 2019. https://quillette.com/2019/03/07/the-rise-and-possible-fall-of-justin-trudeau-show-the-perils-of-woke-governance.

Kaza, Stephanie. *Mindfully Green: A Personal and Spiritual Guide to Whole Earth Thinking*. Boston: Shambhala, 2008.

Keane, John. *The New Despotism*. Cambridge, MA: Harvard University Press, 2020.

Keating, Christine. *Decolonizing Democracy: Transforming the Social Contract in India*. University Park: Pennsylvania State University Press, 2011.

Keenan, Alan. *Democracy in Question: Democratic Openness in a Time of Political Closure*. Stanford: Stanford University Press, 2003.

Kimmerer, Robin Wall. *Braiding Sweetgrass: Indigenous Wisdom, Scientific Knowledge, and the Teachings of Plants*. Minneapolis: Milkweed Editions, 2013.

Kimmerer, Robin Wall. "Reciprocity – Returning the Gift." *Minding Nature* 7, no. 2 (2014): 18–24. www.humansandnature.org/returning-the-gift.

King, Martin Luther, Jr. *Stride Toward Freedom: The Montgomery Story*. Revised edition. Boston, MA: Beacon Press, 2010.

King, Martin Luther, Jr. *Where Do We Go from Here: Chaos or Community?* Boston, MA: Beacon Press, 2010.

Kirloskar-Steinbach, Monika, ed. *Dialogue and Decolonization*. Bloomington: Indiana University Press, forthcoming.

Klare, Michael T. *The Race for What's Left: The Global Scramble for the World's Last Resources*. New York: Picador, 2012.

Klinenberg, Eric. *Palaces for the People: How Social Infrastructure Can Help Fight Inequality, Polarization, and the Decline of Civic Life*. New York: Broadway Books, 2018.

Kochi, Tarik. "The End of Global Constitutionalism and Rise of Antidemocratic Politics." *Global Society* 34, no. 4 (2020): 487–507. https://doi.org/10.1080 /13600826.2020.1749037.

Kohn, Eduardo. *How Trees Think: Towards an Anthropology Beyond the Human*. Berkeley: University of California Press, 2013.

Koppetsch, Cornelia. *Die Gesellschaft des Zorns: Rechtspopulismus im Globalen Zeitalter*. Bielefeld: Transcript Verlag, 2019.

Koselleck, Reinhart. "Begriffsgeschichte und Sozialgeschichte." In *Vergangene Zukunft: Zur Semantik geschichtlicher Zeiten*, 107–29. Frankfurt: Suhrkamp 1995.

Kramer, Brydon. "Entangled with/in Empire: Indigenous Nations, Settler Preservations, and the Return of Buffalo to Banff National Park." MA thesis, University of Victoria, 2020. https://dspace.library.uvic.ca/bitstream/handle/1828/12476/Kramer_Brydon_MA_2020 .pdf.

Kratochwil, Friedrich. "The Limits of Contract." *European Journal of International Law* 5 (1994): 465–91.

Krieger, Heike and Andrea Liese. "A Metamorphosis of International Law?: Value Changes in the International Legal Order From the Perspectives of Legal and Political Science." *KFG Working Paper Series 'The International Rule of Law–Rise or Decline?'* (2016).

Kropotkin, Peter. *Mutual Aid: A Factor of Evolution*. Mineola, NY: Dover Publications, 2006.

Kumm, Mattias. "The Jurisprudence of Constitutional Conflict: Constitutional Supremacy in Europe Before and After the Constitutional Treaty." *European Law Journal* 11, no. 3 (2005): 262–307.

Kuokkanen, Rauna. "From Indigenous Economies to Market-Based Self-Governance: A Feminist Political Economy Analysis." *Canadian Journal of Political Science* 44, no. 2 (2011): 275–97. https://doi.org/10.1017/S0008423911000126.

Kymlicka, Will. "Citizenship in an Era of Globalization." In *The Cosmopolitan Reader Vergangene Zukunft: Zur Semantik geschichtlicher Zeiten*, edited by Garret Brown and David Held, 435–43. Cambridge: Polity, 2010.

LaCapra, Dominick. *Writing History, Writing Trauma.* 2nd ed. Baltimore, MD: Johns Hopkins University Press, 2014.

Laclau, Ernesto. "Beyond Emancipation." In *Emancipation(s)*, 1–19. London: Verso, 1996.

Laclau, Ernesto. *On Populist Reason.* London: Verso, 2005.

Laden, Anthony Simon. *Reasoning: A Social Picture.* Oxford: Oxford University Press, 2012.

LaDuke, Winona. *To Be a Water Protector: The Rise of the Wiindigoo Slayers.* Halifax: Fernwood Publishing, 2020.

Lamour, Christian and Renáta Varga. "The Border as a Resource in Right-Wing Populist Discourse: Viktor Orbán and the Diasporas in a Multi-Scalar Europe." *Journal of Borderlands Studies* 35, no. 3 (2020): 335–50.

Landau, Peter. "The Origin of the Regula iuris 'Quod omnes tangit' in the Anglo-Norman School of Canon Law during the Twelfth Century." *Bulletin of Medieval Canon Law* 32 (2015): 19–35.

Larsen, Soren C. and Jay T. Johnson. *Being Together in Place: Indigenous Coexistence in a More than Human World.* Minneapolis: University of Minnesota Press, 2017.

Lavenex, Sandra. "Globalization and the Vertical Challenge to Democracy." In *Democracy in the Age of Globalization and Mediatization*, edited by Hanspeter Kriesi, Daniel Bochsler, Jrg Matthes, et al., 105–34. London: Palgrave Macmillan, 2013.

Lazzarato, Maurizio. *The Making of the Indebted Man: An Essay on the Neoliberal Condition.* Los Angeles, CA: Semiotext(e), 2012.

LeBlanc, Deanne Aline Marie. "Identifying the Settler Denizen Within Settler Colonialism." Unpublished MA thesis, University of Victoria, 2014.

Leopold, Aldo. "The Land Ethic." In *A Sand County Almanac: With Essays on Conservation from Round River*, 237–64. Oxford: Oxford University Press, 1966.

Levine, Peter A. *Waking the Tiger.* Berkeley, CA: North Atlantic Books, 1997.

Levitt, Kari. *Silent Surrender: The Multinational Corporation in Canada.* Montreal: McGill-Queen's University Press, 1970.

Levitsky, Steven and Daniel Ziblatt. *How Democracies Die.* New York: Crown, 2018.

Lewis, Avi. "Social Democracy and the Left in Canada: Past, Present, and Future." In *Party of Conscience: The CCF, The NDP, and Social Democracy in Canada*, edited by Roberta Lexier, Stephanie Bangarth, and Jonathan Weier, 197–214. Toronto: Between the Lines, 2018.

Lindahl, Hans. *Fault-Lines of Globalization.* Oxford: Oxford University Press, 2013.

Linebaugh, Peter and Marcus Rediker. *The Many Headed Hydra: The Hidden History of the Revolutionary Atlantic.* London: Verso Books, 2012.

Little, Adrian. "Community and Radical Democracy." *Journal of Political Ideologies* 7, no.3 (2002): 369–82.

Loick, Daniel. "21 Theses on the Politics of Forms of Life." *Theory & Event* 20, no. 3 (2017): 788–803.

Lord, Christopher and Paul Magnette. "E Pluribus Unum? Creative Disagreement about Legitimacy in the EU." *Journal of Common Market Studies* 42, no. 1 (2004): 183–202.

Lovelock, James. *The Vanishing Face of Gaia: A Final Warning.* London: Penguin Books, 2009.

Lukacs, Martin. *The Trudeau Formula: Seduction and Betrayal in an Age of Discontent.* Montreal: Black Rose Books, 2019.

Lynas, Mark. *One Final Warning: Six Degrees of Climate Emergency.* London: 4th Estate, 2020.

Lyons, Scott Richard. *X-Marks: Native Signatures of Assent.* Minneapolis: University of Minnesota Press. 2010.

MacDonald, George F. and John J. Cove. *Tsimshian Narratives 2: Trade and Warfare.* Ottawa: Canadian Museum of Civilization, 1987.

MacIntyre, Alasdair. *After Virtue: A Study in Moral Theory.* Notre Dame, IN: University of Notre Dame Press, 2007.

Mack, Johnny. "Hoquotist: Reorienting through Storied Practice." In *Storied Communities: Narratives of Contact and Arrival in Constituting Political Community*, edited by Hester Lessard, Rebecca Johnson, and Jeremy H. A. Webber, 287–307. Vancouver: UBC Press, 2011.

Mackinac Centre for Public Policy. "A Brief Explanation of The Overton Window." www.mackinac.org/OvertonWindow.

Macy, Joanna and Chris Johnstone. *How to Face the Mess We're in Without Going Crazy.* Novato, CA: New World Library, 2012.

Maduro, Miguel Poiares. "Contrapunctual Law." In *Sovereignty in Transition*, edited by Neil Walker, 501–37. Portland, OR: Hart Publishing, 2003.

Magnusson, Warren. "Decentring the State, Or Looking for Politics." In *Organizing Dissent: Contemporary Social Movements in Theory and Practice*, edited by William Carroll, 69–80. Toronto: Garamond, 1992.

Magnusson, Warren. "The Symbiosis of the Urban and the Political." *International Journal of Urban and Regional Research* 38, no. 5 (2014): 1561–75.

Malii v. British Columbia (Attorney-General) (2019) BCSC 2060.

Malik, Abdul. "Jack Layton is the NDP's Third Rail." *Canadian Dimension*, September 1, 2020. https://canadiandimension.com/articles/view/jack-layton-is-the-ndps-third-rail.

Malm, Andreas and the Zetkin Collective. *White Skin, Black Fuel: On the Danger of Fossil Fascism.* London: Random House, 2021.

Manuel, Arthur. *Unsettling Canada: A National Wake-Up Call.* Toronto: Between the Lines, 2015.

Manuel, Arthur and Ronald M. Derrickson. *The Reconciliation Manifesto: Recovering the Land, Rebuilding the Economy.* Toronto: James Lorimer and Company Ltd., Publishers, 2017.

Maracle, Lee. *Memory Serves: Oratories*, edited by Smaro Kamboureli. Edmonton: NeWest Press, 2015.

March, James G. and Johan P. Olsen. "The Institutional Dynamics of International Political Orders." *International Organization* 52 (1998): 943–69.

March, James G. and Johan P. Olsen. *Rediscovering Institutions: The Organizational Basis of Politics.* New York: Free Press, 1989.

March, Luke and Cas Mudde. "What's Left of the Radical Left? The European Radical Left After 1989: Decline *and* Mutation." *Comparative European Politics* 3, no. 1 (2006): 23–49.

Marchart, Oliver. *Neu Beginnen: Hannah Arendt, die Revolution und die Globalisierung.* Vienna: Turia + Kant, 2005.

Marchart, Oliver. *Post-Foundational Political Thought: Political Difference in Nancy, Lefort, Badiou and Laclau.* Edinburgh: Edinburgh University Press, 2007.

Marcuse, Herbert. "Ethics and Revolution." In *Ethics and Society: Original Essays on Contemporary Moral Problems*, edited by R.T. de George, 133–48. Garden City, NY: Anchor, 1966.

Margulis, Lyn. *Symbiotic Planet: A New Look at Evolution*. New York: Basic Books, 1998.

Markusoff, Jason. "The Rise of Alberta's Unapologetic Petro-Patriots." *Maclean's Magazine*, July 15, 2019. www.macleans.ca/news/canada/the-rise-of-albertas-unapologetic-petro-patriots.

Marsden, Susan. "Northwest Coast Adawx Study." In *First Nations Cultural Heritage and Law: Case Studies, Voices, and Perspectives*, 114–49, edited by Catherine Bell and Val Napoleon. Vancouver: UBC Press, 2008.

Marshall, Thomas H. *Citizenship and Social Class*. London: Cambridge University Press, 1950.

Marwell, Nicole P. and Michael McQuarrie. "People, Place, and System: Organizations and the Renewal of Urban Social Theory." *The ANNALS of the American Academy of Political and Social Science* 647, no. 1 (2013): 126–43.

Marx, Karl. "Contribution to the Critique of Hegel's Philosophy of Right." In *The Marx-Engels Reader*, edited by Robert C. Tucker. New York: Norton, 1978, 16–25.

Marx, Karl. "Contribution to the Critique of Hegel's Philosophy of Right: Introduction." In *The Marx-Engels Reader*, edited by Robert C. Tucker. New York: Norton, 1978, 53–65.

Marx, Karl. "Critique of Hegel's Doctrine of the State." In *Karl Marx: Early Writings*, translated by Rodney Livingstone and Gregor Benton, 86–90. London: Penguin Books, 1975.

Marx, Karl. "The Eighteenth Brumaire of Louis Bonaparte." In *The Marx-Engels Reader*, edited by Robert C. Tucker. New York: Norton, 1978, 594–617.

Marx, Karl and Friedrich Engels. *The Communist Manifesto*. Oxford: Oxford University Press, 1998.

Mas, Susana. "Trudeau Lays Out Plan for New Relationship with Indigenous People." *CBC News*, December 5, 2015. www.cbc.ca/news/politics/justin-trudeau-afn-indigenous-aboriginal-people-1.3354747.

McCaffrie, Brendan and Sadiya Akram. "Crisis of Democracy?: Recognizing the Democratic Potential of Alternative Forms of Political Participation." *Democratic Theory* 1, no. 2 (2014): 47–55.

McCandless, Keith and Henri Lipmanowicz. *The Surprising Power of Liberating Structures*. Seattle: Liberating Structures Press, 2013.

McDonough, William and Michael Braungart. *Cradle to Cradle: Remaking the Way We Make Things*. New York: Farrar, Strauss and Giroux, 2002.

McGarry, John and Brendan O'Leary. "Consociational Theory, Northern Ireland's Conflict, and Its Agreement. Part 1: What Consociationalists Can Learn from Northern Ireland." *Government and Opposition* 41, no. 1 (2006): 43–63.

McGiffen, Steve. "Bloodless Coup d'Etat: The European Union's Response to the Eurozone Crisis." *Socialism and Democracy* 25, no. 2 (2011): 25–43.

McLachlin, Beverley. "Canadian Constitutionalism and the Ethic of Inclusion and Accommodation." *Western Journal of Legal Studies* 6, no. 3 (2016): 1–12.

McNeil, Kent. *Flawed Precedent: The St. Catherine's Case and Aboriginal Title*. Vancouver: UBC Press, 2019.

McNevin, Anne. *Contesting Citizenship: Irregular Migrants and New Frontiers of the Political*. New York: Columbia University Press, 2011.

McNevin, Anne. "Time and the Figure of the Citizen." *International Journal of Politics, Culture, and Society* 33 (2020): 545–59.

McQuarrie, Michael. "The Revolt of the Rust Belt: Place and Politics in the Age of Anger." *The British Journal of Sociology* 68 (2017): 120–52.

Memorial to Sir Wilfred Laurier, Premier of the Dominion of Canada from the Chiefs of the Shuswap, Okanagan and Couteau Tribes of British Columbia presented at Kamloops, BC, August 25, 1910. www.skeetchestn.ca/files/documents/Governance/memorialtosirwilfredlaurier1910.pdf.

Menke, Christoph. *Critique of Rights*. Cambridge: Polity, 2019.

Menke, Christoph. "The Possibility of Revolution." *Crisis and Critique* 4, no. 2 (2017): 312–22.

Menke, Christoph. *Reflections of Equality*. Palo Alto, CA: Stanford University Press, 2006.

Menke, Christoph. "Two Kinds of Practice: On the Relation Between Social Discipline and the Aesthetics of Existence." *Constellations* 10 (2003): 199–210.

Metallic, Naiomi. "Indian Act By-Laws: A Viable Means for First Nations to (Re)Assert Control over Local Matters Now and Not Later." *UNB Law Journal* 67 (2016): 211–34.

Mezzadra, Sandro. "Abolitionist Vistas of the Human: Border Struggles, Migration and Freedom of Movement." *Citizenship Studies* 24, no. 4 (2020): 424–40.

Mezzadra, Sandro. *Diritto di fuga*. Verona: Ombre Corte, 2006.

Michaels, Ralf. "Law and Recognition – Towards a Relational Concept of Law." In *In Pursuit of Pluralist Jurisprudence*, edited by Nicole Roughan and Andrew Halpin, 90–115. Cambridge: Cambridge University Press, 2017.

Miliband, Ralph. *Parliamentary Socialism: A Study in the Politics of Labour*. London: Merlin Press, 1961.

Mill, John Stuart. "On Liberty." In *On Liberty and Other Essays*. Edited by John Gray, 5–130. Oxford: Oxford University Press, 1991.

Mill, John Stuart. *On Liberty and Considerations on Representative Government*. Edited by Ronald Buchanan McCallum. Oxford: Basil Blackwell, 1948.

Milliken, Jennifer. "The Study of Discourse in International Relations: A Critique of Research and Methods." *European Journal of International Relations* 5 (1999): 225–54.

Million, Dian. Symposium: "Spirit and Matter: Resurgence as Rising and (Re)Creation as Ethos." Indigenous Resurgence in an Age of Reconciliation, University of Victoria, March 18, 2017. www.uvic.ca/socialsciences/intd/indigenousnationhood/workshops/irar/index.php.

Mills, Aaron. "Miinigowiziwin: All That Has Been Given for Living Well Together: One Vision of Anishinaabe Constitutionalism." Unpublished PhD thesis, University of Victoria, 2019.

Mills, Aaron. "Rooted Constitutionalism: Growing Political Community." In *Resurgence and Reconciliation*, edited by Michael Asch, John Borrows, and James Tully, 133–74. Toronto/Buffalo: University of Toronto Press, 2018.

Mockus, Antanas. "Building 'Citizenship Culture' in Bogotá." *Journal of International Affairs* 65, no. 2 (2012): 143–6.

Moffitt, Benjamin and Simon Tormey. "Rethinking Populism: Politics, Mediatisation and Political Style." *Political Studies* 62, no. 2 (2014): 381–97.

Morgenthau, Hans. *Politics Among Nations.* 7th ed. New York: McGraw Hill, 2005.

Morse, Julia C. and Robert O. Keohane. "Contested Multilateralism." *Review of International Organizations* 9 (2014): 385–412.

Morton, Timothy. *Being Ecological.* New York: MIT Press, 2018.

Mosleh, Omar. "'They Came to Destroy and Create Fear': Indigenous Protester Says Men Attacked Trans Mountain Protest Champ." *The Star*, April 22, 2020.

Mouffe, Chantal. "Carl Schmitt and the Paradox of Liberal Democracy." *Canadian Journal of Law & Jurisprudence* 10, no. 1 (1999): 21–33.

Mouffe, Chantal. *The Democratic Paradox.* London: Verso, 2000.

Mouffe, Chantal. *For a Left Populism.* London: Verso, 2018.

Mouffe, Chantal. *On the Political.* London: Routledge, 2005.

Mudde, Cas. *Populist Radical Right Parties in Europe.* Cambridge: Cambridge University Press, 2007.

Mudde, Cas. "Populist Radical Right Parties in Europe Today." In *Transformations of Populism in Europe and the Americas: History and Recent Trends*, edited by John Abromeit, Gary Marotta, Bridget María Chesterton, and York Norman, 295–307. London: Bloomsbury, 2016.

Mudde, Cas and Cristóbal Rovira Kaltwasser. *Populism: A Very Short Introduction.* New York: Oxford University Press, 2017.

Mudde, Cas and Cristóbal Rovira Kaltwasser. "Populism: Corrective and Threat to Democracy." In *Populism in Europe and the Americas: Threat or Corrective for Democracy?*, edited by Cas Mudde and Cristóbal Rovira Kaltwasser, 205–22. Cambridge: Cambridge University Press, 2012.

Mudde, Cas and Cristóbal Rovira Kaltwasser. "Exclusionary vs. Inclusionary Populism: Comparing Contemporary Europe and Latin America." *Government and Opposition* 48, no. 2 (2013): 147–74.

Müller, Jan-Werner. *Contesting Democracy: Political Ideas in Twentieth Century Europe.* New Haven, CT: Yale University Press, 2011.

Müller, Jan-Werner. *What Is Populism?* London: Penguin, 2017.

Musso, Juliet and Christopher Weare. "Social Capital and Community Representation: How Multiform Networks Promote Local Democracy in Los Angeles." *Urban Studies* 54, no. 11 (2017): 2521–39.

Mustafa, Sana. "Nothing About Us Without Us: Why Refugee Inclusion Is Long Overdue." *Refugees Deeply*, June 20, 2018. www.newsdeeply.com/refugees/community/2018/06/20/nothing-about-us-without-us-why-refugee-inclusion-is-long-overdue.

Napoleon, Val. "Aboriginal Self Determination: Individual Self and Collective Selves." *Atlantis: A Women's Studies Journal* 29, no. 2 (2005): 31–46.

Napoleon, Val. "An Imaginary for Our Sisters." In *Indigenous Spirituality and Religious Freedom*, edited by Jeffery Hewitt and Richard Moon. Toronto: University of Toronto Press, forthcoming.

Napoleon, Val. "Ayook: Gitksan Legal Order, Law, and Legal Theory." Unpublished DPhil Law thesis, University of Victoria, 2009.

Napoleon, Val. "Demanding More from Ourselves: Indigenous Civility and Incivility." In *Civic Freedom in an Age of Diversity: The Public Philosophy of James Tully*, edited by Dimitri Karmis and Jocelyn Maclure, chapter 11. Montreal: McGill-Queen's University Press, forthcoming.

Napoleon, Val. "Did I Break It? Recording Indigenous (Customary) Law." *Potchefstroom Electronic Law Journal* 22 (2019). https://adric.ca/wp-content/uploads/2020/10/Napoleon-Did-I-Break-It-Published-2019-1.pdf.

Napoleon, Val. "Legal Pluralism and Reconciliation." *Māori Law Journal* (2019): 1–22.

Napoleon, Val. "Living Together: Gitksan Legal Reasoning as a Foundation for Consent." In *Between Consenting Peoples: Political Community and the Meaning of Consent*, edited by Jeremy Webber, and Colin McLeod. Vancouver: UBC Press, 2010, 45–76.

Napoleon, Val and Hadley Friedland. "Accessing Tully: Political Philosophy for the Everyday and the Everyone." In *Freedom and Democracy in an Imperial Context*, edited by Robert Nichols and Jakeet Singh. London: Routledge, 2014, 202–19.

Nedelsky, Jennifer. *Law's Relations: A Relational Theory of Self, Autonomy, and Law.* Oxford: Oxford University Press, 2011.

Neigh, Scott. *Resisting the State: Canadian History through the Stories of Activists.* Halifax: Fernwood Publishing, 2012.

Newman, Janet and John Clarke. *Publics, Politics and Power: Remaking the Public in Public Services.* London: Sage, 2009.

Nhat Hanh, Thich. *The Heart of Understanding.* Berkeley: Parallax Press, 2009.

Nichols, Joshua. "A Narrowing Field of View: An Investigation into the Relationship Between the Principles of Treaty Interpretation and the Conceptual Framework of Canadian Federalism." *Osgoode Hall Law Journal* 56, no. 2 (2019): 350–95.

Nichols, Joshua. *A Reconciliation without Recollection? An Investigation of the Foundations of Aboriginal Law in Canada.* Toronto: University of Toronto Press, 2020.

Nichols, Joshua and Amy Swiffen, eds. "Special issue on Treaty Federalism." *The Review* 24, no. 1 (2019).

Nichols, Robert. *Theft is Property! Dispossession and Critical Theory.* Durham, NC: Duke University Press, 2020.

Nichols, Robert and Jakeet Singh, eds. *Freedom and Democracy in an Imperial Context.* London: Routledge, 2014.

Niemann, Holger and Henrik Schillinger. "Contestation 'All the Way Down'? The Grammar of Contestation in Norm Research." *Review of International Studies* 43 (2017): 29–49.

Nkrumah, Kwame. *Neo-Colonialism: The Last Stage of Imperialism.* London: Thomas Nelson & Sons, 1965.

Nolte, Georg and Heike Krieger. "The International Rule of Law – Rise or Decline? Points of Departure." KFG Working Paper Series, KFG International Law – Rise or Decline?, Freie Universität Berlin, Berlin, 2016.

Nussbaum, Martha. "Kant and Stoic Cosmopolitanism." *The Journal of Political Philosophy* 5, no. 1 (1997): 1–25.

O'Neil, Cathy. *Weapons of Math Destruction: How Big Data Increases Inequality and Threatens Democracy.* New York: Penguin Random House, 2016.

Ober, Josiah. *Athenian Legacies: Essays on the Politics of Going on Together.* Princeton, NJ: Princeton University Press, 2018.

Ober, Josiah. "The Original Meaning of 'Democracy': Capacity to Do Things, Not Majority Rule." Princeton/Stanford Working Papers in Classics, Stanford University, Stanford, CA, 2007. http://dx.doi.org/10.2139/ssrn.1024775.

Ogden, Curtis. *Strengthening the Network Within*. Boston, MA: Interaction Institute for Social Change, 2016.

Osterweil, Vicky. *In Defense of Looting: A Riotous History of Uncivil Action*. New York: Bold Type Books, 2020.

Ouziel, Pablo. *Democracy Here and Now: The Exemplary Case of Spain*. Toronto: University of Toronto Press, 2022.

Ouziel, Pablo. "'*Vamos Lentos Porque Vamos Lejos*': Towards a Dialogical Understanding of Spain's 15 Ms." Unpublished PhD thesis, University of Victoria, 2015.

Overstall, Richard. "Encountering the Spirit in the Land: 'Property' in a Kinship-Based Legal Order." In *Despotic Dominion: Property Rights in British Settler Societies*, edited by John McLaren, A.R. Buck and Nancy E. Wright, 22–49. Vancouver: UBC Press, 2005.

Overstall, Richard, in consultation with Val Napoleon and Katie Ludwig. "The Law Is Opened: The Constitutional Role of Tangible and Intangible Property in Gitanyow." In *First Nations Cultural Heritage*, edited by Catherine Bell and Val Napoleon, 92–113. Vancouver: UBC Press, 2008.

Owen, David. "Constituting the Demos, Constituting the Polity." *Ethics & Global Politics* 5 (2012): 129–52.

Owen, David. "Exemplarity and Public Philosophy." In *Civic Freedom in an Age of Diversity: The Public Philosophy of James Tully*, edited by Dimitri Karmis and Jocelyn Maclure, chapter 16. Montreal: McGill-Queen's University Press, forthcoming.

Owen, David. "Hans Lindahl's *Fault Lines of Globalization*: Identity, Individuation and Legal Order." *Contemporary Political Theory* 16 (2017): 248–68.

Owen, David and James Tully. "Redistribution and Recognition: Two Approaches." In *Multiculturalism and Political Theory*, edited by Anthony Simon Laden and David Owen, 265–91. Cambridge: Cambridge University Press, 2007.

Pahuja, Sundhya and Anne Saunders. "Rival Worlds and the Place of the Corporation in International Law." In *The Battle for International Law: South-North Perspectives on the Decolonization Era*, edited by Philipp Dann and Jochen von Bernstorff, 141–74. Oxford: Oxford University Press, 2018.

Paine, William. *The Rights of Man*, edited by Gregory Claeys. Indianapolis: Hackett Publishing Company, 1992.

Parker, Joe. *Democracy Beyond the Nation State*. New York and London: Routledge, 2017.

Part I of the *Constitution Act*, 1982, being Schedule B to the *Canada Act* (UK), 1982, c. 11.

Pasternak, Shiri. *Grounded Authority: The Algonquins of Barriere Lake Against the State*. Minneapolis: University of Minnesota Press, 2017.

Pasternak, Shiri, Katie Mazer, and D. T. Cochrane. "The Financing Problem of Colonialism: How Indigenous Jurisdiction Is Valued in Pipeline Politics." In *Standing with Standing Rock: Voices from the #NoDAPL Movement*, edited by Nick Estes and Jaskiran Dhillon, 222–34. Minneapolis: University of Minnesota Press, 2019.

Patsias, Caroline, Anne Latendresse, and Laurence Bherer. "Participatory Democracy, Decentralization and Local Governance: The Montreal Participatory Budget in the Light of 'Empowered Participatory Governance'." *International Journal of Urban and Regional Research* 37, no. 6 (2013): 2214–30.

Phare, Merrell-Ann, Rosie Simms, Oliver M. Brandes, and Michael Miltenberger. *Collaborative Consent and Water in British Columbia: Towards Watershed Co-Governance*. Victoria: POLIS Water Sustainability Project and the Centre for Indigenous Environmental Resources, 2017.

Phillips, Leigh. "EU Ushers in 'Silent Revolution' in control of national economic policies." *EU Observer*, March 16, 2011. https://euobserver.com/institutional/31993.

Pitts, Jennifer. "Political Theory of Empire and Imperialism." *Annual Review of Political Science* 13 (2010): 211–35.

Plato. *Protagoras*, edited by Gregory Vlastos. Indianapolis, IN: The Bobbs-Merrill Company, 1956.

Polanyi, Karl. *The Great Transformation: The Political and Economic Origins of Our Time*. Boston, MA: Beacon Press, 1957.

Polanyi, Karl. *Great Transformation: The Political and Economic Origins of Our Time*. 2nd ed. Boston, MA: Beacon Press, 2001.

Polewski, Lisa. "Protesters Arrested at Residential Development in Caledonia: OPP." *Global News*, August 5, 2020. https://globalnews.ca/news/7253109/protesters-arrested-caledonia-opp/.

Postmedia Editorial, "Trudeau Needs to Leave His Social Justice Warrior Cape at Home." *Toronto Sun*, May 22, 2018. https://torontosun.com/opinion/editorials/editorial-trudeau-needs-to-leave-his-social-justice-warrior-cape-at-home.

Protect the Inlet. "Visit the spiritual resistance to #StopKM at Kwekwecnewtxw." 2019. http://web.archive.org/web/20210124185559/https://protecttheinlet.ca/structure/.

Puetter, Uwe and Antje Wiener. "The Quality of Norms is What Actors Make of It: Critical Constructivist Research on Norms." *Journal of International Law and International Relations* 5 (2009): 1–16.

Quine, Willard Van Orman. *Word and Object*. Cambridge, MA: MIT Press, 1960.

R. v. Sparrow [1990] 1 SCR 1075, [1990] 70 DLR (4th) 385.

Raekstad, Paul. "Revolutionary Practice and Prefigurative Politics: A Clarification and Defense." *Constellations* 25, no. 3 (2018): 359–72.

Rafoss, Bill. *The Application of the Canadian Charter of Rights and Freedoms to First Nation's Jurisdiction: An Analysis of the Debate*. Unpublished MA thesis, University of Saskatchewan, 2005.

Raibmon, Paige. *Authentic Indians: Episodes of Encounter from the Late-Nineteenth-Century Northwest Coast*. Durham, NC: Duke University Press, 2005.

Ralph, Jason. "On Norms and Practice: Crypto-Normativity." Paper, International Studies Association Annual Conference, International Studies Association, March 24, 2020.

Rancière, Jacques. *Staging the People: The Proletarian and His Double*. London: Verso Books, 2011.

Rawls, John. *Justice as Fairness: A Restatement*. Cambridge, MA: Harvard University Press, 2001.

Rees, William E. "Thinking Resilience." In *The Post-Carbon Reader: Managing the 21st Century's Sustainability Crises*, edited by Richard Heinberg and Daniel Lerch, 25–42. Healsburg, CA: Watershed Media, 2010.

Reference re Secession of Quebec [1998] 2 SCR 217.

Rensmann, Lars. "Radical Right-Wing Populists in Parliament: Examining the Alternative for Germany in European Context." *German Politics and Society* 36, no. 3 (2018): 41–73.

Restakis, John. *Humanizing the Economy: Co-Operatives in the Age of Capital.* Gabriola Island: New Society, 2010.

Reus-Smit, Christian. "Cultural Diversity and International Order." *International Organization* 71 (2017): 851–85.

Richardson, Boyce. *Strangers Devour the Land.* White River Junction, VT: Chelsea Green Publishing, 1991.

Risse, Mathias. "What We Owe to the Global Poor." *Journal of Ethics* 9, no. 1 (2005): 81–117.

Risse, Thomas. *A Community of Europeans?: Transnational Identities and Public Spheres.* Ithaca, NY: Cornell University Press, 2015.

Risse, Thomas. "Transnational Actors and World Politics." In *Corporate Ethics and Corporate Governance*, edited by Walter Zimmerli, Markus Holzinger, and Klaus Richter, 251–86. Berlin, Heidelberg: Springer, 2007.

Risse, Thomas, Stephen C. Ropp, and Kathryn Sikkink. *The Persistent Power of Human Rights: From Commitment to Compliance.* Cambridge: Cambridge University Press 2013.

Riveiro, Aitor. "El Movimiento por la democracia dresenta su hoja de ruta para un proceso constituyente." *El Diario*, March 12, 2014. www.eldiario.es/politica/movimiento-democracia-presenta-proceso-constituyente_1_4986189.html.

Rogers, Kara. "Biophilia Hypothesis." In *Encyclopaedia Britannica.* www.britannica.com/science/biophilia-hypothesis.

Rosanvallon, Pierre. *La contre-démocratie: La politique à l'âge de la défiance.* Paris: Éditions du Seuil, 2006.

Rosanvallon, Pierre. *Le siècle du populisme: Histoire, théorie, critique.* Paris: Éditions du Seuil, 2020.

Rosen, Michael. *Dignity: Its History and Meaning.* Cambridge, MA: Harvard University Press 2018.

Rosenberg, Justin. "International Relations in the Prison of Political Science." *International Relations* 30 (2016): 127–53.

Rosenberg, Justin. "Internationale Beziehungen und die Konsequenzen der Multiplizität." *Zeitschrift für internationale Beziehungen* 26 (2019): 107–22.

Roth, Christopher. *Becoming Tsimshian: The Social Life of Names.* Seattle: University of Washington Press, 2008.

Roughan, Nicole. *Authorities: Conflicts, Cooperation, and Transnational Legal Theory.* Oxford: Oxford Universsity Press, 2013.

Rousseau, Jean-Jacques. "On the Social Contract." In *Basic Political Writings*, translated by Donald A. Cress, 141–227. Indianapolis: Hackett, 1987.

Rovira Kaltwasser, Cristóbal. "The Responses of Populism to Dahl's Democratic Dilemmas." *Political Studies* 62, no. 3 (2014): 470–87.

Royal Proclamation of 1763. https://indigenousfoundations.arts.ubc.ca/royal_proclamation_1763/.

Rubin, Bob. "A Rare Prouvé Armchair Sold to Benefit Urgent Housing Initiatives in Tijuana." *Sotheby's 20th Century Design*, November 26, 2019. www.sothebys.com/en/articles/a-rare-prouve-armchair-sold-to-benefit-urgent-housing-initiatives-in-tijuana.

Rundle, Kristen. *Forms Liberate: Reclaiming the Jurisprudence of Lon L. Fuller.* Oxford: Hart Publishing, 2012.

Rundle, Kristen. "Fuller's Relationships." In "The Rule of Law and Democracy," edited by Hirohide Takikawa. Special issue, *Archiv für Rechts- und Sozialphilosophie* 161 (2019): 17–37.

Russell, Peter H. *Canada's Constitutional Odyssey: A Country Based on Incomplete Conquests.* Toronto: University Press, 2017.

Russell, Peter H. *Constitutional Odyssey: Can Canadians Become a Sovereign Peoples?* Toronto: University of Toronto Press, 1992.

Sabel, Charles F. and Oliver Gerstenberg. "Constitutionalising an Overlapping Consensus: The ECJ and the Emergence of a Coordinate Constitutional Order." *European Law Journal* 16, no. 5 (2010): 511–50.

Said, Edward. "Criticism, Culture, and Performance." In *Power, Politics, and Culture: Interviews with Edward Said*, edited by Gauri Viswanathan, 94–117. New York: Vintage, 2002.

Said, Edward. *Culture and Imperialism.* New York: Vintage, 1994.

Said, Edward. *Humanism and Democratic Criticism.* New York: Columbia University Press, 2003.

Said, Edward. "A Method for Thinking About Just Peace." In *What Is a Just Peace?*, edited by Pierre Allan and Alexis Keller, 176–94. Oxford: Oxford University Press, 2006.

Said, Edward. "A Method for Thinking About Just Peace." In *What is a Just Peace?*, edited by Pierre Allan and Alexis Keller. Oxford: Oxford Scholarship Online, 2006. 176–94. https://doi.org/10.1093/0199275351.001.0001.

Said, Edward. "Narrative, Geography, and Interpretation." *New Left Review* 180, no. 1 (1990): 84–97.

Said, Edward. *Out of Place.* New York: Random House, 1999.

Said, Edward. *Reflections on Exile and Other Essays.* Cambridge, MA; Harvard University Press, 2000.

Said, Edward. *Representations of the Intellectual.* New York: Vintage Books, 1994.

Said, Edward. "Representing the Colonized: Anthropology's Interlocutors." *Critical Inquiry* 15, no. 2 (1989): 205–25.

Said, Edward. *The World, The Text, and the Critic.* Cambridge, MA: Harvard University Press, 1984.

Salmela, Mikko and Christian von Scheve. "Emotional Roots of Right-Wing Political Populism." *Social Science Information* 56, no. 4 (2017): 567–95.

Samuel S. Worcester v. *State of Georgia*, 31 US 515, 6 Pet 515, 8 L Ed 483 (1832).

Sandel, Michael J. *The Tyranny of Merit: What's Become of the Common Good?* New York: MacMillan, 2020.

Santos, Boaventura de Sousa. "As democracias também morrem democraticamente." *Jornal de Letras, Artes e Ideias*, October 24, 2018, 29–30.

Santos, Boaventura de Sousa. "Beyond Abyssal Thinking: From Global Lines to Ecologies of Knowledges." *Eurozine*, June 29, 2007. www.eurozine.com/beyond-abyssal-thinking/.

Santos, Boaventura de Sousa. "The Crises of Democracy: Boaventura de Sousa Santos and James Tully." Webinar, *Global Politics in Critical Perspectives – Transatlantic Dialogues*. University of Victoria, Victoria, BC, March 15, 2019. www.youtube.com /watch?v=-i9aFUsTipk.

Santos, Boaventura de Sousa. "Law: A Map of Misreading. Toward a Postmodern Conception of Law." *Journal of Law and Society* 14, no. 3 (1987): 279–302.

Santos, Boaventura de Sousa. *Toward a New Common Sense: Law, Science and Politics in the Paradigmatic Transition.* New York: Routledge, 1995.

Santos, Boaventura de Sousa. *Toward a New Legal Common Sense: Law, Globalization, and Emancipation.* 3rd ed. Cambridge: Cambridge University Press, 2020.

Santos, Boaventura de Sousa. "We Live in Politically Democratic but Socially Fascist Societies." *CPAL Social,* November 30, 2016. www.envio.org.ni/articulo/5269.

Santos, Boaventura de Sousa, and Cesar A. Rodriguez-Garavito, eds. *Law and Globalization from Below: Towards a Cosmopolitan Legality.* Cambridge: Cambridge University Press, 2005.

Santos, Boaventura de Sousa, Maria Manuel Leitão Marques, João Pedroso, and Pedro Lopes Ferreira. *Os Tribunais nas Sociedades Contemporâneas: O Caso Português.* Porto: Afrontamento, 1996.

Sartre, Jean-Paul. *Critique de la raison dialectique, vol. 1, Théorie des ensembles pratiques, précédé de Questions de méthode.* Paris: Gallimard, 1960.

Scharmer, Otto. "Impacting Climate Change by Operating from a Place of Awareness-Based Collective Action." Webinar, *TEDxGAIAjourney: Impacting Climate Change by Operating from a Place of Awareness-Based Collective Action.* Presencing Institute, Cambridge, MA, October 15, 2020. www.presencing.org/programs/live-sessions/tedxgaiajourney.

Scharpf, Fritz W. "After the Crash: A Perspective on Multilevel European Democracy." *European Law Journal* 21, no. 3 (2015): 384–405.

Schmidt, Vivien. "Democracy and Legitimacy in the European Union Revisited: Input, Output and Throughput." *Political Studies* 61, no. 1 (2013): 2–22.

Schmidtke, Oliver. "Politicizing Social Inequality: Competing Narratives from the Alternative for Germany and Left-Wing Movement Stand Up." *Frontiers in Sociology* 5 (2020): 1–11.

Schock, Kurt. *Civil Resistance Today.* Cambridge: Polity Press, 2015.

Scholte, Jan Aart. "Reinventing Global Democracy." *European Journal of International Relations* 20, no. 1 (2014): 3–28.

Scott, James C. *Seeing Like a State: How Certain Schemes to Improve the Human Condition Failed.* New Haven, CT: Yale University Press, 1998.

Scruggs, Gregory. "New San Diego-Tijuana Survey Holds Mirror Up to Border Cities." *Next City,* February 25, 2015. http://nextcity.org/daily/entry/binational-survey-san-diego-tijuana-border-antanas-mockus.

Secwepemcul'ecw Assembly, Secwepemc Women's Warrior Society and Tiny House Warriors. "Women's Declaration Against Trans Mountain Man Camps." November 2017. www.secwepemculecw.org/women-s-declaration.

Sellars, Wilfred. "Counterfactuals, Dispositions, and the Causal Modalities." In *Minnesota Studies in the Philosophy of Science, vol. 2, Concepts, Theories, and the Mind-Body Problem,* edited by Herbert Feigl, Michael Scriven, and Grover Maxwell, 225–308. Minneapolis: University of Minnesota Press, 1957.

Sellars, Wilfred. "Empiricism and the Philosophy of Mind." In *Minnesota Studies in the Philosophy of Science, vol. 1, The Foundations of Science and the Concepts of Psychology and Psycho-Analysis,* edited by Herbert Feigl and Michael Scriven, 253–329. Minneapolis, MN: University of Minnesota Press, 1956.

Shuswap Nation Tribal Council and Indigenous Law Research Unit. "Secwepemc Lands and Resources Law Analysis Project Summary." June 21, 2016. www.skeetchestn.ca/files/documents/Governance/secwepemc-lands-and-resources-law-analysis-summary.pdf.

Simpson, Audra. *Mohawk Interruptus: Political Life Across the Borders of Settler States.* Durham, NC: Duke University Press, 2014.

Simpson, Leanne Betasamosake. *As We Have Always Done: Indigenous Freedom Through Radical Resistance.* Minneapolis: University of Minnesota Press, 2017.

Simpson, Michael. "For a Prefigurative Pandemic Politics: Disrupting the Racial Colonial Quarantine." *Political Geography* 84 (2021): 1–3.

Singh, Jakeet. "Recognition and Self-Determination: Approaches from Above and Below." In *Recognition versus Self-Determination: Dilemmas of Emancipatory Politics*, edited by Avigail Eisenberg, Jeremy Webber, Andrée Boisselle, and Glen Coulthard, 19–98. Vancouver: UBC Press, 2015.

Skinner, Quentin. *From Humanism to Hobbes: Studies in Rhetoric and Politics.* Cambridge: Cambridge University Press, 2018.

Skinner, Quentin. *Visions of Politics*, vol. 1, *Regarding Method.* Cambridge: Cambridge University Press, 2002.

Smith, Charlie. "RCMP Arrest Unist'ot'en Matriarchs During Ceremony to Honour Missing and Murdered Indigenous Women and Girls." *The Georgia Straight*, February 10, 2020. www.straight.com/news/1358106/rcmp-arrest-unistoten-matriarchs-during-ceremony-honour-missing-and-murdered-indigenous.

Smith, Linda Tuhiwai. *Decolonizing Methodologies: Research and Indigenous Peoples.* 2nd ed. London: Zed Books, 2012.

Smith, Rogers M. *That Is Not Who We Are! Populism and Peoplehood.* New Haven, CT: Yale University Press, 2020.

Snowden, Edward. *Permanent Record.* New York: Metropolitan Books, 2019.

Snyder, Emily, Val Napoleon, and John Borrows. "Gender and Violence: Drawing on Indigenous Legal Resources." *UBC Law Review* 48, no. 2 (2015): 593–654.

Snyder, Gary. "The Rediscovery of Turtle Island." In *Deep Ecology for the 21st Century*, edited by George Sessions. Boulder: Shambhala, 1995, 454–62.

Solange I, BVerfGE Case 37/271, [1974] 14 CMLR 540 (German Constitutional Court).

Solange II, BVerfGE Case 73/339, [1987] 3 CMLR 225 (German Constitutional Court).

Solnit, Rebeca. *A Paradise Built in Hell: The Extraordinary Communities that Arise in Disaster.* New York: Penguin, 2009.

Spang, Rebecca L. "How Revolutions Happen." *The Atlantic*, July 4, 2020. www.theatlantic.com/ideas/archive/2020/07/revolution-doesnt-look-like-revolution/613801.

Special Rapporteur on Extreme Poverty and Human Rights. *Climate change and poverty: report of the Special Rapporteur on Extreme Poverty and Human Rights.* Geneva: United Nations, 2019. https://undocs.org/A/HRC/41/39.

Sripati, Vijayashri. *Constitution-Making under UN Auspices: Fostering Dependency in Sovereign Lands.* Oxford: Oxford University Press, 2020.

St. Catharine's Milling and Lumber Co. v. R. [1888] UKPC 70, 14 App Cas 46.

Stanley, Ben. "The Thin Ideology of Populism." *Journal of Political Ideologies* 13, no. 1 (2008): 95–110.

Starblanket, Gina. "Being Indigenous Feminists: Resurgences Against Contemporary Patriarchy." In *Making Space for Indigenous Feminism*, edited by Joyce A. Green, 21–41. 2nd ed. Blackpoint, NS: Fernwood Publishing, 2017.

Starblanket, Gina and Heidi Kiiwetinepinesiik Stark. "Towards a Relational Paradigm – Four Points for Consideration: Knowledge, Gender, Land, and Modernity." In *Resurgence and Reconciliation*, edited by Michael Asch, John Borrows, and James Tully, 175–208. Toronto/Buffalo: University of Toronto Press, 2018.

Stark, Heidi Kiiwetinepinesiik. "Criminal Empire: The Making of the Savage in a Lawless Land." *Theory & Event* 19, no. 4 (2016). www.ucis.pitt.edu/global/sites/default/files/Downloadables/ProQuestDocuments-2020-07-04%5B8893%5D.pdf.

Sterelny, Kim. *The Evolving Apprentice: How Evolution Made Humans Unique.* Cambridge, MA: MIT Press, 2012.

Sterritt, Neil J. *Mapping My Way Home: A Gitxsan History.* Smithers, BC: Creekstone Press, 2016.

Sterritt, Neil J., Susan Marsden, Robert Galois, Peter R. Grant, and Richard Overstall. *Tribal Boundaries in the Nass Watershed.* Vancouver: UBC Press, 1998.

Stierl, Maurice. *Migrant Resistance in Contemporary Europe.* London: Routledge, 2019.

Stimmer, Anette and Lea Wisken. "The Dynamics of Dissent: When Actions Are Louder than Words." *International Affairs* 95 (2019): 515–33.

Stout, Jeffrey. *Blessed Are the Organized: Grassroots Democracy in America.* Princeton, NJ: Princeton University Press, 2010.

Tabuchi, Hiroki, Michael Corkery, and Carlos Mureithi. "Big Oil Is in Trouble. Its Plan: Flood Africa with Plastic." *New York Times*, August 30, 2020. www.nytimes.com/2020/08/30/climate/oil-kenya-africa-plastics-trade.html.

Takeda, Louise. *Islands' Spirits Rising: Reclaiming the Forests of Haida Gwaii.* Vancouver: UBC Press, 2015.

Tardáguila, Cristina, Fabrício Benevenuto, and Pablo Ortellado. "Fake News Is Poisoning Brazilian Politics. WhatsApp Can Stop It." *New York Times*, October 17, 2018. www.nytimes.com/2018/10/17/opinion/brazil-election-fake-news-whatsapp.html.

Tarrow, Sidney and Doug McAdam. "Scale Shift in Transnational Contention." in *Transnational Protest and Global Activism*, edited by Donatella della Porta and Sidney Tarrow, 121–50. Lanham, MD: Rowman & Littlefield, 2005.

tawinikay. "Reconciliation is Dead: A Strategic Proposal." *It's Going Down* (blog). February 15, 2020. https://itsgoingdown.org/reconciliation-is-dead-a-strategic-proposal.

Taylor, Charles. *Reconciling the Solitudes: Essays on Canadian Federalism and Nationalism*, edited by Guy Laforest. Montreal: McGill-Queen's Press, 1994.

Taylor, Charles. *A Secular Age.* Cambridge, MA: Harvard University Press, 2007.

Taylor, Keeanga-Yamahtta. *From #BlackLivesMatter to Black Liberation.* Chicago: Haymarket Books, 2016.

The Cherokee Nation v. *The State of Georgia*, 30 US 1, 5 Pet. 1, 8 L Ed 25 (1831).

Thom, Brian. "The Anathema of Aggregation: Towards 21st Century Self-Government in the Coast Salish World." *Anthropologica* 52, no. 1 (2010): 33–48.

Thomassen, Lasse. "Deliberative Democracy and Provisionality." *Contemporary Political Theory* 10, no. 4 (2011): 423–43. https://doi.org/10.1057/cpt.2010.39.

Thomassen, Lasse. "Political Theory in a Provisional Mode." *Critical Review of Social and Political Philosophy* 13, no. 4 (2010): 453–73.

Thomassen, Lasse. "Representing the People: Laclau as a Theorist of Representation." *New Political Science* 41, no. 2 (2019): 329–44.

Tickner, J. Ann. "The Disciplining of International Studies." In Leeds, Brett Ashle, J. Ann Tickner, Colin Wight, and Jessica De Alba Ulloa. "Forum: Power and Rules in the Profession of International Studies." *International Studies Review* 21 (2019): 193–6.

Tilly, Charles. "Social Movements as Historically Specific Clusters of Political Performances." *Berkeley Journal of Sociology* 38 (1993): 1–30.

Times Colonist. "Effective Protests Can Be Difficult. Just Look at Saturday's Effort."
   June 25, 2019. www.timescolonist.com/opinion/editorials/editorial-effective-protests
   -can-be-difficult-just-look-at-saturday-s-effort-1.23866187.
Tiny House Warriors. "Mountain Music Concert: Tiny House Warriors." Facebook,
   August 16, 2018. www.facebook.com/events/234468630738226.
Tiny House Warriors. "Tiny House Warriors." http://tinyhousewarriors.com.
Todd, Zoe. "Refracting the State Through Human-Fish Relations: Fishing, Indigenous
   Legal Orders and Colonialism in North/Western Canada." *Decolonization:
   Indigeneity, Education & Society* 7, no. 1 (2018): 60–79. https://jps.library.utoronto.ca
   /index.php/des/article/view/30393.
Tomba, Massimiliano. *Insurgent Universality: An Alternative Legacy of Modernity.*
   Oxford: Oxford University Press, 2019.
Trans Mountain. "Our History." www.transmountain.com/history.
Traverso, Enzo. *Left-Wing Melancholia: Marxism, History, and Memory.* New York:
   Columbia University Press, 2017.
Trosper, Ronald. *Resilience, Reciprocity and Ecological Economics.* London:
   Routledge, 2011.
Trudeau, Justin. "Speech to the Calgary Petroleum Club." October 30, 2013. Liberal
   Party of Canada, transcript. https://liberal.ca/liberal-party-canada-leader-justin-
   trudeaus-speech-calgary-petroleum-club.
Tsawwassen First Nation, Government of British Columbia, Government of Canada.
   "Tsawwassen Final Agreement." December 6, 2007. http://tsawwassenfirstnation.com
   /wp-content/uploads/2019/07/1_Tsawwassen_First_Nation_Final_Agreement.pdf.
Tsilhqot'in Nation v. *British Columbia* [2014] 2 SCR 256.
Tsleil-Waututh Nation Sacred Trust. "Live at the Trans Mountain Pipeline
   Announcement Press Conference." Facebook, June 18, 2019. www.facebook.com
   /630937800297791/videos/612471812592081.
Tucker, Robert C., ed. *The Marx-Engels Reader.* New York: Norton, 1978.
Tully, James. "Deparochializing Political Theory and Beyond: A Dialogue Approach to
   Comparative Political Thought." *Journal of World Philosophies* 1, no. 5 (2016):
   51–74.
Tully, James. "Dialogue and Decolonization." In Monika Kirloskar-Steinbach, ed.
   Dialogue and Decolonization. Bloomington: Indiana University Press, forthcoming.
Tully, James. "Foreward: A Canadian Tragedy." In Sarah Marie Wiebe. *Everyday
   Exposure: Indigenous Mobilization and Environmental Justice in Canada's
   Chemical Valley*, xi–xiii. Vancouver: UBC Press, 2016.
Tully, James. "Integral Nonviolence." In Richard Bartlett Gregg, ed., *The Power of
   Nonviolence*, xxi–lxi. Cambridge: Cambridge University Press, 2018.
Tully, James. "Integral Nonviolence: On the Significance of Gandhi Today." *Politika*, 2019.
   www.politika.io/en/notice/the-power-of-integral-nonviolence-on-the-significance-of-gan
   dhi-today.
Tully, James. "Life Sustains Life 1: Value, Social and Ecological." In Akeel Bilgrami, ed.,
   Nature and Value, 163–80. New York: Columbia University Press, 2020.
Tully, James. "Life Sustains Life 2: The Ways of Regeneration with the Living Earth." In
   Akeel Bilgrami, ed. *Nature and Value*, 181–204. New York: Columbia University
   Press, 2020.
Tully, James. *On Global Citizenship: James Tully in Dialogue.* London: Bloomsbury,
   2014.

Tully, James. "On Resurgence and Transformative Reconciliation." In *Plants, Peoples, and Places: The Roles of Ethnobotany and Ethnoecology in Indigenous Peoples' Land Rights in Canada and Beyond*, edited by Nancy J. Turner. Montreal: McGill-Queens University Press, 2020, 402–18.

Tully, James. "Political Philosophy as a Critical Activity." *Political Theory* 30, no. 4 (2002): 533–55.

Tully, James. *Public Philosophy in a New Key, vol. 1, Democracy and Civic Freedom*. Cambridge: Cambridge University Press, 2008.

Tully, James. *Public Philosophy in a New Key, vol. 2, Imperialism and Civic Freedom*. Cambridge: Cambridge University Press, 2008.

Tully, James. "Reconciliation Here on Earth." In *Resurgence and Reconciliation*, edited edited by Michael Asch, John Borrows, and James Tully, 83–132. Toronto/Buffalo: University of Toronto Press, 2018.

Tully, James. "Rediscovering the World of Franz Boas: Anthropology, Equality/ Diversity, and World Peace." In *Indigenous Visions: Rediscovering the World of Franz Boas*, edited by Ned Blackhawk and Isaiah Lorado Wilner, 111–46. New Haven: Yale University Press, 2018.

Tully, James. *Strange Multiplicity: Constitutionalism in an Age of Diversity*. Cambridge: Cambridge University Press, 1995.

Tully, James. "The Unattained Yet Attainable Democracy: Canada and Quebec Face the New Century." Desjardins Lecture, McGill University, Montreal, QC, March 23, 2000.

Tully, James. "The Unfreedom of the Moderns in Comparison to Their Ideals of Constitutional Democracy." *The Modern Law Review* 65 (2002): 204–28.

Tully, James. "What Are the Biggest Challenges Democracy Is Facing Today?" Lecture, Constitutionalism in the Age of Populism. University of Victoria, Victoria, BC, March 6–8, 2020. www.youtube.com/watch?v=WvG-oQDduFw.

Tully, James, Jeffrey L. Dunoff, Anthony F. Lang, Mattias Kumm, and Antje Wiener. "Introducing Global Integral Constitutionalism." *Global Constitutionalism: Human Rights, Democracy, Law* 5, no. 1 (2016): 1–15.

Tunney, Catharine. "Jim Carr Says Military Comments Not a Threat to Pipeline Protesters." *CBC News*, December 2, 2016. www.cbc.ca/news/politics/jim-carr-protests-pipeline-military-1.3878258.

Turner, Dale A. *This Is Not a Peace Pipe: Towards a Critical Indigenous Philosophy*. Toronto: University of Toronto Press, 2006.

Turner, Nancy J., ed. *Plants, Peoples, and Places: The Roles of Ethnobotany and Ethnoecology in Indigenous Peoples' Land Rights in Canada and Beyond*. Montreal: McGill-Queens University Press, 2020.

UNHCR. "*Figures at a Glance.*" www.unhcr.org/figures-at-a-glance.html.

UNHCR. "*Statelessness Around the World.*" www.unhcr.org/statelessness-around-the-world.html.

Unist'ot'en Camp. "Fundraising Protocols." http://unistoten.camp/fundraiserprotocols.

Unist'ot'en Camp. "Supporter Toolkit." http://unistoten.camp/supportertoolkit2020.

United States v. *Kagama*, 118 US 375 (1886).

Urbinati, Nadia. *Me the People: How Populism Transforms Democracy*. Cambridge, MA: Harvard University Press, 2019.

Vahabzadeh, Peyman. *Articulated Experiences*. Albany: State University of New York, 2003.

Valdez, Ines. *Transnational Cosmopolitanism: Kant, Du Bois, and Justice as a Political Craft*. Cambridge: Cambridge University Press, 2019.

Vallance, Neil. "Sharing the Land: The Formation of the Vancouver Island (or 'Douglas') Treaties of 1850–1854 in Historical, Legal and Comparative Context." Unpublished PhD thesis, University of Victoria, 2015.

van de Sande, Mathijs. "Fighting with Tools: Prefiguration and Radical Politics in the Twenty-First Century." *Rethinking Marxism* 27 (2015): 177–94.

Vargas, Jairo. "Partido X: 'Empecemos por lo más fácil: echémosles de ahí'." *Público*, October 8, 2013. www.publico.es/actualidad/partido-x-empecemos-mas-facil.html.

Varoufakis, Yanis. *And the Weak Suffer What They Must?* New York: Nation Books, 2016.

Veracini, Lorenzo. *Settler Colonialism: A Theoretical Overview*. Springer: New York, 2010.

Viewpoint Magazine. "The Border Crossing Us." November 7, 2018. www.viewpointmag.com/2018/11/07/from-what-shore-does-socialism-arrive.

Voyles, Traci Brynne. *Wastelanding: Legacies of Uranium Mining in Navajo Country*. Minneapolis: University of Minnesota Press, 2015.

Wackernagel, Mathis. *Our Ecological Footprint: Reducing Human Impact on the Earth*. Gabriola Island, BC: New Society Press, 1996.

Waldron, Jeremy. *Law and Disagreement*. New York: Oxford University Press, 1999.

Wallace-Wells, David. *The Uninhabitable Earth: Life After Warming*. New York: Tim Duggan Books, 2019.

Walzer, Michael. "What It Means to Be a Liberal." *Dissent*, Spring 2020. www.dissentmagazine.org/article/what-it-means-to-be-liberal.

War Resister's International. *Handbook for Nonviolent Campaigns*. 2nd ed. 2014. http://wri-irg.org/pubs/NonviolenceHandbook.

Ward, Peter. *The Medea Hypothesis*. Princeton: Princeton University Press, 2009.

Webber, Jeremy. "Contending Sovereignties." In *The Oxford Handbook of the Canadian Constitution*, edited by Peter Oliver, Patrick Macklem, and Nathalie Des Rosiers, 281–302. New York: Oxford University Press, 2017.

Webber, Jeremy. "The Meanings of Consent." In Jeremy Webber and Colin McLeod, *Between Consenting Peoples: Political Community and the Meaning of Consent*, edited by Jeremy Webber, and Colin McLeod, 3–41. Vancouver: UBC Press, 2010.

Webber, Jeremy. "Relations of Force and Relations of Justice: The Emergence of Normative Community between Colonists and Aboriginal Peoples." *Osgoode Hall Law Journal* 33, no.4 (1995): 623–60.

Webber, Jeremy. "We Are Still in the Age of Encounter: Section 35 and a Canada Beyond Sovereignty." In *From Recognition to Reconciliation: Essays on the Constitutional Entrenchment of Aboriginal and Treaty Rights*, edited by Patrick Macklem and Douglas Sanderson, 63–99. Toronto: University of Toronto Press, 2016.

Webber, Jeremy and Colin McLeod, eds. *In Between Consenting Peoples: Political Community and the Meaning of Consent*. Vancouver: UBC Press, 2010.

Weber, Max. *The Protestant Ethic and the Spirit of Capitalism*, translated by Talcott Parsons. London: Routledge, 1992.

Welsh, Jennifer M. "Norm Contestation and the Responsibility to Protect." *Global Responsibility to Protect* 5 (2013): 365–96.

Wenger, Etienne. *Communities of Practice: Learning, Meaning, and Identity*. Cambridge: Cambridge University Press, 1998.

Whelan, Frederick G. "Democratic Theory and the Boundary Problem." *Nomos* 25 (1983): 13–47.

White, Nancy. "Moving Online in Pandemic: Ecocycle to Attend to What Is Shifting." *Full Circle Associates*. https://fullcirc.com/2020/03/08/moving-online-in-pandemic-ecocycle-to-attend-to-what-is-shifting.

Whittaker, Reg. *A Sovereign Idea: Essays on Canada as a Democratic Community.* Montreal: McGill-Queen's University Press, 1992.

Whittington, Keith E. "Rogers M. Smith: The Stories We Tell Ourselves." *PS: Political Science & Politics.* 51 no.4 (2018): 895–9.

Wiener, Antje. *Contestation and Constitution of Norms in Global International Relations.* Cambridge: Cambridge University Press, 2018.

Wiener, Antje. "Contested Compliance: Interventions on the Normative Structure of World Politics." *European Journal of International Relations* 10 (2004): 189–234.

Wiener, Antje. "The Dual Quality of Norms and Governance Beyond the State: Sociological and Normative Approaches to Interaction." *Critical Review of International Social and Political Philosophy* 10 (2007): 47–69.

Wiener, Antje. "The Embedded *Acquis Communautaire*: Transmission Belt and Prism of New Governance." *European Law Journal* 4 (1998): 294–315.

Wiener, Antje. "Norm(ative) Change in International Relations: A Conceptual Framework." KFG Working Paper Series, KFG International Law–Rise or Decline? Freie Universität Berlin, Berlin, 2020.

Wiener, Antje. *A Theory of Contestation.* Berlin: Springer, 2014.

Wiener, Antje, Jeffrey L. Dunoff, Jonathan Havercroft, Mattias Kumm, and Kriszta Kovács. "Global Constitutionalism as Agora: Interdisciplinary Encounters, Cultural Recognition and Global Diversity." *Global Constitutionalism* 8 (2019): 1–11.

Williams, Kayanesenh Paul. *Kayanerenkó:wa:The Great Law of Peace.* Winnipeg: University of Manitoba Press, 2018.

Williams, Robert A., Jr. *Linking Arms Together: American Indian Treaty Visions of Law and Peace 1600–1800.* New York: Oxford University Press, 1997.

Williamson, Thad, David Imbroscio, and Gar Alperovitz. *Making a Place for Community: Local Democracy in a Global Era.* New York: Routledge, 2003.

Wilson, Shawn. *Research is Ceremony.* Black Point: Fernwood Publishing, 2008.

Winston, Carla. "The Nature of Norms and the Evolution of Transitional Justice." Unpublished PhD thesis, University of British Columbia, 2016.

WIRED. "Using Live Oak Trees as a Blueprint for Surviving Hurricanes." August 26, 2015. YouTube video, 1: 31, https://ed.ted.com/best_of_web/dKKIiKsz.

Wittgenstein, Ludwig. *Tractatus Logico-Philosophicus.* Translated by Charles Kay Ogden. London: Routledge, 1922.

Wolfe, Patrick. "Settler Colonialism and the Elimination of the Native." *Journal of Genocide Research* 8, no. 4 (2006): 387–409. https://doi.org/10.1080/14623520601056240.

Wong, Rita and Kimberly Richards. "Acting under Natural Laws." *Canadian Theatre Review* 182 (2020): 26–9. https://doi.org/10.3138/ctr.182.005.

Worcester v. *Georgia*, 31 US 515 (1832).

Yan, Miu Chung. "Bridging the Fragmented Community: Revitalizing Settlement Houses in the Global Era." *Journal of Community Practice* 12, nos. 1–2 (2004): 51–69.

Yan, Miu Chung and Sean Lauer, eds. *Neighbourhood Houses: Building Community in Vancouver.* Vancouver: UBC Press, 2021.

Yeatman, Anna, G.W. Dowsett, Michael D. Fine, and Di Gursansky. *Individualization and the Delivery of Welfare Services: Contestation and Complexity*. Basingstoke: Palgrave Macmillan, 2009.

Young, Iris Marion. "Activist Challenges to Deliberative Democracy." *Political Theory* 29, no. 5 (2001): 670–90.

Young, Iris Marion. *Inclusion and Democracy*. Oxford: Oxford University Press, 2002.

Young, Iris Marion. "Two Concepts of Self-Determination." In *Ethnicity, Nationalism, and Minority Rights*, edited by Stephen May, Tariq Madood, and Judith Squires, 176–96. Cambridge: Cambridge University Press, 2004.

Your Neighbourood House, www.yournh.ca.

Zimmermann, Lisbeth. *Global Norms with a Local Face: Rule-of-Law Promotion and Norm Translation*. Cambridge: Cambridge University Press, 2017.

Zuboff, Shosana. *The Age of Surveillance Capitalism: The Fight for a Human Future at the New Frontier of Power*. London: Profile Books, 2019.

Author Index

Subject Index